MW01505303

YALE LAW LIBRARY SERIES IN
LEGAL HISTORY AND REFERENCE

MARITAL PRIVILEGE

Marriage, Inequality, and the Transformation of American Law

SERENA MAYERI

Yale

UNIVERSITY PRESS

New Haven and London

Published with support from the Lillian Goldman Law Library, Yale Law School.

Published with assistance from the income of the Frederick John Kingsbury Memorial Fund and with assistance from the foundation established in memory of Calvin Chapin of the Class of 1788, Yale College.

Yale University Press books may be purchased in quantity for educational, business, or promotional use. For information, please e-mail sales.press@yale.edu (U.S. office) or sales@yaleup.co.uk (U.K. office).

Set in Janson type by IDS Infotech Ltd.
Printed in the United States of America.

Library of Congress Control Number: 2024947879
ISBN 978-0-300-27944-3 (hardcover : alk. paper)

A catalogue record for this book is available from the British Library.

Authorized Representative in the EU: Easy Access System Europe, Mustamäe tee 50, 10621 Tallinn, Estonia, gpsr.requests@easproject.com.

10 9 8 7 6 5 4 3 2 1

For Jason Klenoff

Contents

Introduction

ON A LATE NOVEMBER evening in 2022, Kelley Robinson and her wife sat in the Senate gallery with their one-year-old son as lawmakers voted 61–36 to pass the Respect for Marriage Act (RMA). Five months earlier, the U.S. Supreme Court had called into question constitutional protections for contraception, same-sex marriage, and even interracial unions when it extinguished the constitutional right to abortion in *Dobbs v. Jackson Women's Health Organization*.[1] "Too many of our rights are just one Supreme Court decision away from being lost," Robinson, the first Black woman to lead the Human Rights Campaign (HRC), told National Public Radio. She "worried that at some point, the court would invalidate" her own marriage to Becky George, a gun violence prevention advocate. Robinson expressed the relief of many when she applauded congressional "action to ensure that our marriages are valid, our love will be respected."[2]

After *Dobbs*, Democrats in Congress introduced legislation to codify protections for abortion and contraception as well as marriage equality. Progressives also tried to extend the pandemic-era child tax credit, a monthly allowance that had reduced child poverty by half. Only the RMA, designed to shield marriages from attack if a future Court allows states to restrict who can marry on the basis of sex, race, ethnicity, or national origin, became law.[3] The fact that protection for marriage prevailed—but not a right to sexual and reproductive freedom, or support for needy families—testifies to the enduring status of marriage in American law and political life.

Marriage equality held powerful historical resonance for Robinson, a descendant of enslaved people who migrated from Mississippi to become the first free Black family in Muscatine, Iowa. Robinson grew up in a politically active, church-going Catholic household in Chicago. Her experiences with racism caused her to leave the University of Missouri to work as a waitress and martial-arts instructor. She found her way back to college and politics through Barack Obama's 2008 presidential campaign and her work as an organizer for Planned Parenthood. "For me to be able to sit next to my wife, a first-generation woman of Indian descent; to look at our son—our life was unimaginable a generation before," Robinson reflected.[4]

The practical and legal advantages of marriage loomed at least as large as the symbolic. "Marriage isn't just about the ceremony," as Robinson said. "It's about the 1100 federal benefits that come with marriage," from "being safe and secure in your retirement to building the family of your dreams to being able to see your loved one when they're sick."[5] Robinson and George married in 2020, at the height of the COVID-19 pandemic, in part to ensure they could visit each other in the hospital if one became ill.[6] They understood that recognition of a marriage by the government, employers, and service providers unlocks countless legal privileges, from Social Security to family leave to health insurance coverage.

Within families, too, marital status carries weighty legal consequences. Marriage turns partners into spouses bound by a web of obligations: duties of mutual care and financial support that survive the death of a spouse or dissolution of a relationship. Marital status affects the ease with which adults become recognized as parents and children receive entitlements to support and care. Marriage cemented not only Robinson and George's legal relationship as partners but also their parental status. In 2021, Robinson gave birth to Izaiah, who was conceived through in vitro fertilization (IVF) using George's ova.[7] His mothers' marriage helped Izaiah enjoy rights equal to those of children raised by different-sex biological parents.

The United States is unusual among western nations in the degree to which the state channels benefits through marriage. Wealthy democracies often confer social welfare benefits and entitlements on individuals by virtue of their membership in the polity. Some governments provide health care and social insurance benefits directly to all rather than through employment or marriage to an eligible employee. Others support families through universal allowances granted to children regardless of who is caring for them and directly provide or heavily subsidize childcare. Elsewhere, marital status often matters less in determining partners' obligations to one another: Canada, for instance, assumes that couples who have lived together for a requisite period are common law partners even if they have not formally married.[8]

In the United States, by contrast, marriage remains a key dividing line that determines both legal rights and duties *within* a relationship and entitlement to benefits *from* employers and the government. Marriage's privileged status casts a long shadow over the unmarried. The law not only excludes unmarried persons from benefits but also penalizes sex, pregnancy, childbearing, and parenthood outside of marriage.

Marriage so saturates U.S. law and policy that many who live under its umbrella take its elevated status for granted. The legal primacy of marriage has not gone unchallenged, however. Sylvester Smith, a short-order cook in Selma, Alabama, claimed a right to enjoy a relationship with a man to whom she was not married without losing public assistance to feed her family. Anna Flores protested her discharge from the Navy for "immorality" after she became pregnant outside of marriage. Rosalyn Carr resisted a Connecticut law that required her to appear in court to answer invasive questions about her intimate life or face fines and incarceration for failing to cooperate with the state's attempt to establish her children's paternity. Margaret Gonzales questioned why the federal government denied survivor benefits to her family just because she never married her children's father. Lois Fernandez insisted on the dignity and nobility of single motherhood and the injustice of Pennsylvania laws that discriminated against "illegitimate" children. Ramon Fiallo-Sone claimed U.S. citizenship that would have been his by right had he married his son's mother. Barbara Cox of Madison, Wisconsin, fought for legal recognition and protection for gay and lesbian parents and partners, grandparents, siblings, and other chosen or extended family.

Marital Privilege is a history of how these Americans and many others contested the legal primacy of marriage in the last four decades of the twentieth century. The book recovers battles over legal and constitutional protections for sexual and reproductive autonomy regardless of marital status and for the freedom to live outside the marital nuclear family. It chronicles struggles against laws that punished nonmarital cohabitation and childbearing or made marriage a prerequisite for legal and social benefits.

Marriage's challengers won some victories and suffered many defeats. This book tells their stories: why and how some challenges succeeded, and others did not. It seeks to explain the resilience of marriage as a privileged legal status and its enduring consequences for American law and life.

In 1960, marriage seemed secure: both a pervasive social expectation that most Americans fulfilled and a foundation of public policy. Seventy-two percent of U.S. adults eighteen and over, including 65 percent of women, were married; only 17 percent of women had never married.[9] Marriage rates had declined sharply in the early years of the Great Depression, and World War II ushered unprecedented numbers of married women and Black workers into traditionally white and male-dominated jobs. But a postwar baby boom combined with policies that prioritized opportunities for returning soldiers and Cold War cultural imperatives to revivify conventional gender roles.[10] Between 1946 and the early 1960s, Americans married younger and had more babies than at any other time in the twentieth century.[11]

The mid-century legal regime, what I will call "marital supremacy," bolstered white and male dominance.[12] By making marriage a gateway to public benefits such as Social Security, the government created strong incentives for men and women to marry. Law and public policy rewarded households led by male breadwinners who supported dependent female homemakers and caregivers.[13] But most Black Americans were left out of marriage's benefits by earlier New Deal legislation that excluded agricultural and domestic workers. A two-tier social insurance system reserved earned entitlements for married wage-earning men and relegated families headed by single mothers to the need-based Aid to Dependent Children (ADC), known as "welfare." Once associated with deserving white widows and abandoned wives, ADC in the postwar period increasingly was linked in the public imagination with Black single mothers, fostering anti-welfare sentiment.[14]

The laws of marriage and divorce reinforced husbands' physical and economic power over wives. Earlier reforms such as the Married Women's Property Acts eroded but did not fully displace coverture, the common law doctrine that subsumed a wife's identity beneath her husband's.[15] In exchange for economic support, a wife was legally obliged to accept her husband's choice of domicile and to provide him with family care, sexual access, and household labor.[16] Spouses could not sue each other for injuries, which restricted wives' recourse against violent husbands.[17] Marriage provided a defense to rape: the law presumed that in consenting to marry, women agreed to be sexually available to their husbands in perpetuity.[18] Divorce laws required one spouse to prove the other's fault and their own blamelessness, trapping many women in abusive or unhappy marriages. In most states, husbands controlled family property during marriage and after a divorce.[19]

Marital status affected everything from the lawfulness of sexual intimacy and childbearing to eligibility for public assistance to the custody of children. Depending on the circumstances, marital status could be a bar to employment or a prerequisite to keeping one's job. State laws prohibited fornication (sex outside of marriage), cohabitation (living together unmarried), and sodomy, often with harsher penalties for interracial sex.[20] Nearly half the states still prohibited interracial marriage. Individuals who could not or would not conceal their homosexuality risked unemployment, social ostracism, and jail.[21] Penalties for childbearing outside marriage—disparaged with degrading terms like "bastardy" or "illegitimacy"—targeted families living in poverty, especially women of color and their children. In the nineteenth century, common law marriage had conferred legitimacy on couples who lived as husband and wife without formally marrying, but by 1960 only one-third of states recognized informal unions.[22]

Cracks soon began to appear in the edifice of marital supremacy. Married women's rising workforce participation and the availability of oral contraceptives in the 1960s opened new opportunities. Growing awareness of and discontent with economic and racial inequality fed waves of activism. Civil libertarians rebelled against repressive sexual morality imposed by government fiat.[23] Feminist movements sought equal political, economic, and legal rights for women.[24] Advocates for racial justice fought for more than an end to de jure segregation.[25] Welfare rights leaders argued for a constitutional right to subsistence.[26] Reformers battled criminalization and discrimination based on sexual orientation.[27]

By the early 1970s, critics hoped and defenders feared that marriage as they knew it was under threat.[28] Radical feminists, gay liberationists, and countercultural activists denounced marriage and the nuclear family. Even mainstream legal reformers questioned why marital status continued to shape citizenship. Seismic changes transformed family life during these years, and those that followed. Divorce became widespread, fewer Americans married, and many more lived with nonmarital partners.[29]

U.S. births outside of marriage increased from 5 percent in 1960 to 11 percent in 1970 and 33 percent by 2000.[30]

A widening "marriage gap" separated Americans by race, class, and educational attainment. In 1940, roughly 60 percent of adults, irrespective of race, were married. By 2000, that number declined to 50 percent among whites and 30 percent among Black Americans. In 1960, women with a college education were significantly less likely to be married than those with a high school education. By century's end, these associations reversed: women with a college degree had the highest marriage rates of any demographic group. Marriage rates among female high school graduates fell from 75 percent in 1960 to barely over half; only 35 percent of women without a high school diploma were married in 2000.[31]

Yet marriage proved remarkably resilient: it survived, in part, by changing shape.[32] This book details how marital *supremacy* gave way to marital *privilege*—a different and more durable structure. In 1960, marriage stood as a largely unquestioned bulwark of American public policy, a moral and religious imperative imprinted in stark, formal terms on the face of the law. By 2003, the sharp edges of marital status law had softened. Principles of equality, privacy, and due process cleansed the law of the most overt discrimination against women, people of color, and children born outside of marriage. Penalties for nonmarital sex became more subtle, but they did not disappear. Criminal prohibitions receded unevenly, and legal disadvantages for nonmarital couples and parents took less visible but still damaging forms. Marriage continued to bestow public and private benefits unavailable to the unmarried. The new shape of marriage obscured inequities that still flowed from the law. As marital status correlated more than ever with race, class, and education, the advantages of marital privilege accrued mostly to those who needed them least.

Marriage is everywhere in American law. Boundaries between marriage and nonmarriage are key sites for the regulation of sex, reproduction, and family life as well as social and economic citizenship. This book considers the laws of marriage, cohabitation, divorce, nonconjugal relationships, reproduction, child custody, and parental rights. Equally important, it examines government benefits, zoning, housing, health law, inheritance, criminal law, torts, contracts, social welfare policy, employment law, immigration and nationality, taxation, and military service as they relate to marriage.[33]

Together, these wide-ranging legal categories contain a body of *marital status law*. Considering this body of law together exposes previously hidden patterns and connections. Marital status law operates at all levels of government and throughout the private sector. It suffuses workplaces, homes, and businesses. It is debated everywhere from the halls of Congress to administrative agencies, human resources offices, school board and city council meetings, classrooms, dinner tables, and water coolers. Its benefits and exclusions affect every American, and through immigration law it touches even those who are not, but may wish to become, U.S. citizens or legal residents.

The pervasiveness and stature of marriage may explain why no single social movement attacked it head-on. Unlike the painstaking, incremental litigation that gradually unwound the legal regime of racial segregation, no overarching, concerted campaign set out methodically to change marital law. Changes to the position of marriage in American law came from many directions.[34] Some actors set out to undermine the centrality of marital status. But many saw that outcome more as a collateral consequence of their advocacy for other causes.

This book spotlights lawyers, advocates, and scholars, some well-known, most obscure. It excavates previously hidden stories of those who found themselves ensnared by law and fought back. Many Americans pushed marital boundaries because they had something precious to gain or lose: parental rights to a child they loved, a hard-won career as an educator, or the freedom to make decisions about their bodies and families. Some found in their own plight a larger cause worth fighting for. Others faded from the historical record. By rescuing their stories, we can see change as a bottom-up as well as a top-down process. The innovations of ordinary people often outpaced the attorneys who represented them in court and the judges who decided their cases.

People of color—from influential lawyers and national figures to community activists and litigants—often pioneered claims for equality and justice regardless of family status. Challenges to marriage's legal primacy advanced what Black feminists later named reproductive justice: the right to bodily autonomy, to have children or not, and to raise families in thriving homes and communities with government support rather than surveillance.[35] By recognizing marital status law as a principal terrain on which these battles were fought, the book traces radical visions that laid crucial groundwork for feminist, anti-poverty, and civil libertarian campaigns. Gay and lesbian advocates and litigants also led, sometimes in unexpected ways: they debuted constitutional arguments that others—for instance, workers who lived together unmarried or became pregnant outside of marriage—used to challenge discrimination and exclusion.

Advocates and plaintiffs who challenged marital supremacy made creative and ambitious constitutional claims. They argued for a right to sexual privacy and reproductive autonomy outside of marriage. They exposed how penalties for nonmarital sex and childbearing fell most heavily on poor people of color, especially women; and they identified that disparate impact as a constitutional violation regardless of whether government officials intended to discriminate. They claimed rights to free expression and freedom of association—to live with nonmarital partners and children, and with chosen and extended family, undisturbed by the government. They fought for a right to subsistence for all, regardless of family status. They defended the integrity of their families against attempts to control reproduction and separate children from parents. They demanded that lenders and landlords, employers and schools, bureaucrats and business owners, cease discrimination based on marital and birth status, sexual orientation, and family size. They sought recognition and protection for relationships beyond the traditional legal categories of "blood, marriage, and adoption."

These capacious claims prompted courts, legislators, and administrators to modernize marital status law.[36] But the law took up challengers' critiques only selectively. When we consider marital status law's modernization over time, striking patterns become visible. Courts and lawmakers sympathized with the plight of blameless children born outside of marriage, who unjustly were made to suffer for their parents' sins. In contrast, adults' claims to sexual liberty outside of marriage and freedom from discrimination based on marital status largely failed. Although many states decriminalized nonmarital sex, authorities found other ways to privilege and promote marriage over nonmarriage and to penalize adults who resisted heterosexual marital norms.[37] Arguments for formal sex and racial equality often triumphed. But judges denied claims about the disparate impact of marital status laws based on race, sex, and poverty.

Feminist advocacy eliminated most overt distinctions between the legal rights and duties of husbands and wives. When unmarried women but not men, or Black but not white, teachers lost jobs because of nonmarital pregnancies, courts upheld their employment discrimination claims. The federal government prohibited housing discrimination based on race, sex, and the presence of children in a family. But few proposals to ban discrimination against unmarried and gay cohabiting couples succeeded. Unmarried parents fell short in their quest for equality in social insurance benefits and parental rights. Advocates' efforts to expand the definition of family to include extended family and kinship ties, chosen family, and groups engaged in communal living arrangements usually met with defeat.

The modernization of marital status law followed twin imperatives: compliance with emerging constitutional norms of nondiscrimination and due process, and privatization of economic support within the nuclear family. The selective shift from formal to functional definitions and standards is a case in point. When advocates eliminated overt discrimination or exclusion—for example, categorical bans on unmarried pregnant schoolteachers, on mothers of nonmarital children in public housing, or on gay parents as custodians of children—legal standards based on function often replaced them. Now officials had to show that nonmarital sexual conduct harmed children or impaired an individual's ability to perform their job or to be a good neighbor or tenant. But functional standards often smuggled biases back in under the guise of neutrality. Instead of moral or religious objections, authorities invoked children's welfare or fiscal constraints to justify discrimination based on marital or birth status.

Similarly, functional definitions of family proved double-edged. They expanded the range of household arrangements afforded recognition and benefits to persons who acted like family but were not legally bound by marriage or biological connection or formal adoption. But functional categories often required relationships that resembled marital or nuclear family ties to qualify as legitimate. And the law embraced functional approaches selectively, especially when doing so would ensure that relatives, not the government, would support needy family members. Marital status mattered less, for instance, when legal recognition for a functional parent secured a private source of child support.

Challengers to the legal primacy of marriage faced rising political headwinds. In the early 1960s, constitutional law held out tantalizing promise as a weapon against racial and economic injustice. But with conservatives ascendant in the 1970s expansive theories of sexual freedom, privacy, and equality faltered. By the early 1980s, federal constitutional challenges had run their course. A permissive federal constitutional regime gave all levels of government great latitude to privilege marriage. In the years that followed, some states and localities enacted more progressive

laws while others retrenched. By the end of the twentieth century, a
federal regime of marital privilege with play in the joints for subnational
experimentation was well-established.

Marital Privilege proceeds in four parts. Part I traces early challenges to
marital supremacy, between 1960 and the early 1970s. The first chapter
provides a snapshot of marriage at mid-century and explores advocates'
varied challenges to marital status law. Chapter 2 chronicles early trans-
lations of these critiques into litigation and law reform efforts related to
welfare and birth status. Part II examines the modernization of marital
status law during the long 1970s. Chapter 3 focuses on couples' relationships and their dissolution; chapter 4 considers government benefits,
zoning, and housing; and chapter 5 tackles public employment.

The chapters in Part II each focus on a particular set of legal questions as they affected various historical actors. Part III zeroes in on the
legal treatment of one group, single parents, across a range of contexts.
Chapter 6 compares unmarried mothers' efforts to redefine responsible
citizenship in arenas including work, welfare, military service, and parentage. Chapter 7 covers nonmarital fathers' quests for parental recognition
and rights.

By the early 1980s, the New Right had coalesced and federal constitutional change stalled. Part IV traces the crystallization of marital privilege in the final decades of the twentieth century. Chapter 8 explores how
advocates in the 1980s and 1990s promoted broad definitions of family at
the state and local levels. Chapter 9 describes how federal legislation intensified existing inequalities as advocates struggled with the legacy of
courts' earlier failure to embrace capacious constitutional rights. By century's end, as proponents of equal marriage rights for gay and lesbian
Americans spotlighted the institution's myriad benefits, efforts to displace
marriage as a gateway to the privileges of citizenship seemed ever more
unlikely to succeed.

What accounts for the limited success of challenges to marital primacy? Challengers who sought to unsettle the broader political economy
of marriage met with entrenched opposition. The rise of conservative social and legal movements in the 1970s—just as arguments for sexual freedom, reproductive autonomy, and equality became more powerful and
sophisticated—stymied advocates. Disagreements on the center-left
about gender roles, family structure, and the proper place of government
also shaped marital status law's modernization.[38] Even lawyers and activ-

ists who welcomed a greater role for the state in aiding impoverished households advanced disparate visions and law reform agendas. Many liberals who resisted the conservative ascendancy in other ways nevertheless defended the legal primacy of marriage.

These disagreements underscore the difficulty of unsettling marriage as a pillar of American life. Structurally, marriage has performed powerful functions for the state and for capitalism.[39] Husbands' responsibility to provide for wives and children and wives' provision of caregiving labor in the home excused the state—and employers—from these support obligations.[40] As fewer Americans married, the legal treatment of nonmarriage became less directly punitive. But the state blurred boundaries between marriage and nonmarriage more to ensure private sources of support regardless of marital status than to liberate the unmarried. The marital household's foundational role in social and economic ordering proved difficult to dislodge.[41] And its powerful cultural and religious meanings strengthened Americans' investment in marriage even, or perhaps especially, as fewer achieved the marital ideal.[42] Stripped of its most offensive elements—the overt subordination of women and the cruel persecution of nonmarital children—marriage seemed to many like an invitation, not a barrier, to greater equality.

The resilience of marriage also reflects broader trends in American society and politics. The journey from marital supremacy to marital privilege echoed and abetted contemporaneous developments—the shift from de jure to de facto racial segregation, deepening income and wealth inequality, and the rise of a political economy that prized privatization, personal responsibility, and a minimalist welfare state. The preservation of marital privilege fed on the convergence of interest between neoliberal economics and ascendant social conservatism: both sought to locate primary responsibility for care and social reproduction within the family.[43] Marital privilege, freed by selective legal reforms from overt links to white and male supremacy, enabled that common imperative.

A Note on Terminology

A book about marital status law requires engagement with outdated and often offensive and dehumanizing rhetoric and terminology. When writing in my own voice, I try where possible to use terms such as "marital" and "nonmarital," though these terms are themselves imperfect. But in some instances, "legitimate" and "illegitimate" convey a distinctive legal meaning that otherwise is difficult to capture. For example, a child born outside of marriage may be "legitimated" through various legal processes, so that referring to a "nonmarital child" would convey little about that individual's legal status. In the interest of readability, I have used scare quotes more sparingly when discussing legal and political categories as opposed to individual human beings.

The usage and political valence of terms that refer to what we now call sexual orientation and gender identity have changed—and continue to evolve—over time. I have tried to balance accuracy, self-identification, and the avoidance of anachronism with respectful contemporary usage in the use of terms such as "gay," "lesbian," "LGBT," "LGBTQ+," "queer," "transgender," "same-sex" and "different-sex" marriage, and "marriage equality."

PART I

CHAPTER ONE

Challenging Marital Supremacy

IN 1960, LOUISIANA IGNITED an international firestorm when it purged more than twenty-three thousand "illegitimate" Black children and their mothers from the welfare rolls. The move was part of a "segregation package" passed by the state legislature in retaliation for the court-ordered desegregation of New Orleans schools.[1] Outrage and protests erupted around the nation. Black mothers flooded the local Urban League office to demand action.[2] The American Civil Liberties Union (ACLU) called on the federal Department of Health, Education, and Welfare to intervene. A dozen female city council members from Newcastle-upon-Tyne, England, airlifted food to New Orleans under the banner "Operation Save the Children."[3]

Public attention focused mostly on the injustice to children suddenly without sustenance, but Louisiana's actions went further. The 1960 legislation required Black men to "disclose any children they had fathered outside of marriage" and "barred any woman from voting if she had given birth while unmarried or had ever been in a common-law marriage." Governor Jimmie Davis tried unsuccessfully to make it unlawful for Black women to give birth in public hospitals, and he tried to prescribe up to one year's imprisonment for conceiving a child outside of marriage.[4]

The Louisiana laws reflected a larger phenomenon: morals regulation targeting nonmarital sex, childbearing, and family formation became an important tool in resisting demands for racial justice.[5] In the 1950s and 1960s, Black freedom movements challenged segregation and discrimination in every sphere, from education and employment to voting and public accommodations. As civil rights advocacy produced results in federal courts, Congress, and beyond, opposition took legal as well as extralegal forms. Officials used "suitable home" requirements to deny welfare benefits to families with nonmarital children and mothers suspected of engaging in sex outside of marriage.[6] "Moral character" provisions excluded nonmarital children from white classrooms and their parents from voter rolls.[7] Officials increased regulation of marriage licenses and birth certificates in order to reduce formal and informal marriage and inflate nonmarital childbearing rates among Black residents, which fed pernicious stereotypes that justified continued segregation and exclusion.[8] Other proposals, even more draconian, prescribed the sterilization or incarceration of women who bore nonmarital children.[9]

Debates about "illegitimacy" were inextricably bound up with race and anti-welfare sentiment. They also reflected a broader sense of unease about births outside of marriage. "Storm of Controversy Develops as Illegitimacy Hits New High," blared a typical headline from 1959.[10] In the early 1960s, cities and states convened commissions to address the scourge, which observers attributed variously to the decline of religious morality, the spread of pornography, lax parenting, working mothers, father absence, welfare largesse, poverty, and ignorance.[11] Racist assumptions and animus infused much of the commentary, but even many champions of Black civil rights generally found the rise in nonmarital births troubling.[12]

Policies like Louisiana's cast a harsh light on the dark side of marital status law. They revealed in stark terms how penalties for sex and childbirth outside of marriage buttressed white supremacy. The uproar over punitive anti-illegitimacy policies also reflected a growing consciousness that marital status laws of various kinds played a central role in sustaining inequality and injustice. But just as they disagreed about the causes of and solutions for childbearing outside of marriage, advocates and law reformers differed widely in their assessment of which marital status laws were problematic, why, and what should be done.

The dominant consensus at mid-century held out the marital nuclear family, headed by a male breadwinner and a female homemaker, as the normative ideal. Deviations from this model, especially single-mother households and nonmarital childbearing, were cause for alarm. Many law- and policymakers across the political spectrum took the primacy of marriage and a gendered division of family labor for granted even if they differed on whether and how to address racial and economic inequality.

Advocates for women, in contrast, challenged male domination within marriage and limitations on women's citizenship because of assumptions about their primary role as wives and mothers. They resisted attempts to impose a patriarchal ideal on poor Black families and instead demanded equal opportunities for women regardless of marital status.

A different set of actors, largely disconnected from conversations about equality between men and women, began to study and question the law of nonmarriage in the early to mid-1960s. Members of the expanding network of welfare and civil rights advocates took varied approaches to the relationship of family structure, poverty, and government policy. Some critics, such as the legal scholar and disability activist Jacobus tenBroek, questioned the privatization of financial support and care of children, the poor, and the disabled within the family. Others, such as Harry Krause, an expert on birth status law, believed instead that securing private sources of financial support for nonmarital children by identifying and holding fathers to account should be the primary goal. Justine Wise Polier, a family court judge and reformer, defended unmarried mothers, bucking the conventional wisdom that nonmarital children should be placed for adoption and their maternal history erased. Though each posed a challenge to marital supremacy, these approaches differed in ways that presaged lasting divisions on the center-left.

Civil libertarians and civil rights advocates also cast a critical eye on marital status law. They attacked sexual regulation, including remnants of the nineteenth-century Comstock laws that criminalized contraception, state laws that restricted abortion, and legal penalties for interracial sex and marriage. Though many advocates believed that birth control should be available to the married and unmarried alike, in court they strategically invoked marriage's sanctity and centrality. Those who challenged interracial sex and marriage prohibitions focused on how they bolstered white supremacy and allowed for discriminatory prosecution. Litigation produced breakthroughs in the Supreme Court: in the mid-1960s, doctrines of privacy, equal protection, and due process emerged that advocates would use to resist marital supremacy in the years to come.

Feminism, Marriage, and the Moynihan Report

For some feminists, the chief problem with marital status laws was how they constrained and subordinated women. Women's rights advocates had long chafed against the traditional marital bargain, in which wives

traded housekeeping, family care, and sexual services for economic maintenance. The lawyer Blanche Crozier observed in 1935 that a wife's ostensible legal right to support obscured the reality that married women
enjoyed financial security only at their husbands' pleasure. "In no other
department of life," she wrote, "has anyone had such an ownership of the
time and labor of another person since the abolition of slavery."[13]

Almost two decades later, popular representations of marriage lagged
behind Crozier's critique. Interviews with more than eighteen hundred
women in 1962 led George Gallup to conclude that "few people are as
happy as a housewife." American wives, he said, believed "a man must be
the leader" of his household. Gallup's *Saturday Evening Post* cover spread
featured Eleanor Courter as typical in her conviction that mothers
should not work outside the home and that a wife must "put her husband
first" because "marriages don't work on a 50–50 basis." Gallup quoted a
former "competent career woman" turned mother of three who opined
that a "woman needs a master-slave relationship whether it's husband
and wife, or boss-secretary" in order to feel "needed and useful."[14]

Law reinforced these gender roles. One treatise-writer noted in the
mid-1960s that "many cases still read as though the married woman's
sole function is to be housewife and mother."[15] In an illustrative case, a
court refused to enforce an opera singer's agreement to pay her husband
an allowance if he quit his job to travel with her. A husband had "a duty
to support and live with his wife and the wife must contribute her services and society to the husband and follow him in his choice of domicile." A private agreement could not "change the essential obligations of
the marriage contract."[16]

Marital duties also underwrote women's second-class citizenship.
The Supreme Court held in *Hoyt v. Florida* (1961) that women's position
at "the center of home and family life" justified their exemption from
jury service.[17] Several states altogether forbade women from serving on
juries on similar grounds. In 1966, the Mississippi Supreme Court held
that "the legislature has the right to exclude women so they may continue their service as mothers, wives, and homemakers, and also to protect them (in some areas, they are still upon a pedestal) from the filth,
obscenity, and noxious atmosphere that so often pervades a courtroom
during a jury trial."[18] Combined with the de facto exclusion of Black
men, such "protective" laws meant that all-white, all-male juries routinely acquitted white perpetrators of violence against Black victims and
deprived Black and female defendants of a jury of their peers.[19]

Law and public policy rewarded a gendered division of labor within marriage and cemented husbands' superior economic position. The New Deal welfare state presupposed a male-breadwinner/female-homemaker model in allocating public benefits.[20] Marriage remained the primary path to financial security for women, who became eligible for social insurance through their husbands' earnings and faced widespread employment discrimination.[21] The exceptional woman might pursue an advanced education and professional career, but most who did so expected to sacrifice—or avoid—marriage and motherhood.[22] Married women with children increasingly worked for pay, but their status as wage-earners remained secondary to that of husbands and fathers in theory and practice.[23]

Making heterosexual marriage the gateway to social and economic rights magnified the effects of racial inequality. Black and other non-white women lacked access to the most generous public benefits because they were unlikely to be partnered with men who held the jobs that conferred them.[24] The exclusion of domestic and agricultural workers from the Social Security Act of 1935, along with discrimination and segregation in housing, employment, education, mortgage lending, and health care, made marriage to a breadwinning man both less attainable and less economically valuable to women of color.[25] Black women had long worked outside their homes in larger numbers than white women; by 1960 they were also significantly more likely to be supporting families alone.[26]

When the President's Commission on the Status of Women (PCSW) convened in 1962, prominent officials, lawyers, and advocates for women addressed some but not all of these inequities. The PCSW's report *American Women*, published in 1963, reflected the commission's "ambivalence toward women's roles."[27] Married women's status, throughout, was mediated by their relationship to men. The commission accepted the Social Security Act's foundational assumption: that women's eligibility for benefits would depend largely on their husbands' earnings rather than their own. Nor did the PCSW question that "mothers' insurance benefits" were available only to widows, not widowers. Its report did not seriously contemplate that husbands and fathers might share the burden of household labor and family care.[28]

The PCSW did tackle some of the sex discrimination that women's rights advocates had long opposed. Marriage, the report asserted, should be considered a partnership "in which each spouse makes a different but equally important contribution."[29] Commissioners recommended equal contractual and property rights for married women and men, as well as wives' right to control their own earnings during marriage. But the commission punted on alimony, child support, and property settlements at divorce, calling for further research. Betty Friedan's best-selling book *The Feminine Mystique*, published the same year, went further: she called for reforms to allow women to combine marriage and career and to defy wives' scripted role as dependent homemakers.[30]

Strikingly, neither *The Feminine Mystique* nor *American Women* had much to say about single mothers, low-income women, or Aid to Families with Dependent Children (AFDC), despite AFDC's status as the only social insurance program primarily serving women and children.[31] Welfare organizations lacked representation on the commission and only two pages of the PCSW's report referred to poverty and poor women. Nowhere was AFDC mentioned by name.[32] And commission leaders were loath to endorse the view that mothers with young children—single or not—should be in the workforce. Some worried that doing so would validate lawmakers who extolled the virtues of homemaking and childrearing for white women but pushed Black mothers into low-wage labor.[33]

Daniel Patrick Moynihan's *The Negro Family: The Case for National Action* (1965) instead shaped the national conversation about poverty, race, and family structure. The "Moynihan Report" identified a "tangle of pathology" that threatened poor, urban Black communities: a "matriarchal" family structure characterized by "illegitimate" births, welfare dependency, and juvenile delinquency. Until Black men reclaimed their proper place as breadwinning heads of households, Moynihan warned, poverty, violence, and dysfunction would deepen the chasm between Black and white Americans.[34]

Moynihan's outlook reflected his childhood descent from the middle class: his father, a journalist and alcoholic, abandoned the family when Pat was young, plunging them into poverty. Moynihan shined shoes, worked the docks, graduated from an East Harlem high school, and went to college on the GI Bill. He eventually became a government official, Harvard professor, and later a long-serving senator from New York. But he never forgot the toll his father's absence had taken, especially on his mother, who opened a bar in Hell's Kitchen to make ends meet.[35] In rising rates of single motherhood, Moynihan heard troubling echoes of his own experience.

Many liberal commentators and civil rights leaders excoriated the Moynihan Report for its unflattering portrayal of Black family life. Some interpreted the report—unfairly, in its defenders' view—as a rejection of structural explanations for poverty and racial inequality. But Moynihan's concerns about the growing number of "female-headed households" and "emasculation" of Black men reflected a broad establishment consensus that a male-breadwinner/female-homemaker model of household political economy was integral to racial progress. The solution, many liberals now believed, was to emulate a white, middle-class ideal: Black women should marry, limit their waged work, care for children without relying on public assistance, and give up their supposedly superior educational and job prospects.[36]

The Moynihan Report fueled growing activism among advocates for women, who swiftly criticized its diagnosis and prescriptions and called for renewed efforts to combat sex discrimination. Pauli Murray, turned away from the University of North Carolina's graduate school in 1938 because of race and from Harvard Law School in 1944 because of sex, had long struggled against gender norms. Now a Howard- and Yale-educated civil rights lawyer and feminist strategist, Murray condemned the report's "great disservice to the thousands of Negro women" who had "struggled to prepare themselves for employment" despite "severely restricted economic opportunities."[37] The year before, Murray had reframed the inclusion of sex in Title VII of the landmark 1964 Civil Rights Act—which prohibited discrimination in employment because of race, color, religion, and national origin—as essential to Black advancement. Without the sex amendment, Title VII "would . . . offer genuine equality of opportunity to only half the potential Negro work force," Murray warned.[38]

Like Moynihan's, Murray's prescription for employment law and policy emphasized Black family structure. But Murray drew very different conclusions from women's role as the sole support for one-fifth of nonwhite families. The average Black woman, Murray wrote, had "trouble finding a mate, remains single longer and in higher incidence, bears more children, is in the labor market longer, has less education, earns less, is widowed earlier and carries a heavier economic burden as a family head than her white counterpart." She could not "assume with any degree of confidence that her economic support will come through marriage" and "must be prepared to support herself and others for a considerable period of her life."[39] To Murray, Moynihan's recommendation to establish a patriarchal family structure in poor Black families mistook the symptoms of poverty for its causes and pitted Black men and women against one another in a labor market that subordinated both.

Other prominent advocates soon joined Murray in criticizing Moynihan's analysis. In 1966, the civil rights leader Dorothy Height and the historian Caroline Ware named "lack of income" and "discrimination" as key to Black women's plight and urged robust enforcement of Title VII's race *and* sex discrimination provisions. Rather than degrading poor women with "man in the house" rules, the government should provide adequate income and housing, childcare, and training for remunerative jobs with decent working conditions.[40] Like Murray, Height and Ware saw a principle of nondiscrimination in employment and beyond as crucial to women's survival—especially Black women's—in a world where marriage to a male breadwinner often remained out of reach.[41]

The PCSW's recommendations gingerly questioned sex discrimination within marriage but left the legal regimes of heterosexuality and marital primacy largely unscathed. The more assertive feminist response to Moynihan initially focused on defending Black women's economic advancement as critical rather than antithetical to racial progress. For now, reforms to the legal status of nonmarital families would fall to others.

Poverty, Welfare, and Family Status

The landscape of welfare politics shifted in the early 1960s, as a "new breed" of poverty lawyers began to use constitutional law as a weapon against abusive state policies like Louisiana's suitable home law.[42] At the same time, the civil rights movement's success in challenging racial discrimination and segregation opened new legal and constitutional pathways to attacking discrimination based on birth or family status. Advocates who worked at the intersection of poverty, welfare, and family law took widely varied approaches to reform and to the state's obligations to the poor.

Known for his work on behalf of fellow blind Americans and the physically disabled, Jacobus tenBroek influenced a generation of welfare advocates through his legal scholarship and advocacy.[43] TenBroek wrote pathbreaking articles in the 1940s and 1950s arguing that the constitution should forbid discrimination based on economic status as well as race.[44] The targets of his critique included residency requirements for public assistance that restricted poor people's freedom of movement from state to state.[45] Moreover, tenBroek argued that government aid should be available as a matter of right, to enable individuals not only to survive but to escape poverty altogether.[46]

In a three-part article published in 1964–65, tenBroek criticized what he called a "dual system of family law" in his home state of California. For middle- and upper-class families, he wrote, a private family law regime distributed property rights and entitlements between spouses and among parents and children. Courts adjudicated disputes about who owed what to whom, largely within families or vis-à-vis third-party creditors.[47] In other words, the law assumed marital privacy and autonomy for reasonably affluent families like tenBroek's, whose own marriage was a professional as well as a personal partnership. Hazel, his wife, worked tirelessly by his side: she helped to run the National Federation for the Blind and read to her husband at warp speed, all while maintaining a bustling home and raising three children.[48]

In sharp contrast to how the law treated families like tenBroek's, a legislatively created public law regulated the family lives of the poor. Family unity for poor families minimized public expenditures by using what would otherwise be the separate property of one partner to support the other.[49] For the nonpoor, courts deemed parental rights "paramount" and presumed a parent to be fit until proven otherwise if a nonparent contended for custody. But if neither parent could provide, the state conditioned public support upon intrusive intervention by social workers and state officials, diluting parental rights.[50] Support was extracted wherever it could be found or imposed—from a mother or father, regardless of whether he or she lived with or cared for the child. Additionally, California applied exclusively to the poor a "distinctive type" of informal marriage that imposed support obligations on any "adult male assuming the role of spouse," which made any man living with the mother of AFDC-eligible children a "common-law stepfather."[51] When the state granted aid to a child "deserted or abandoned by a parent," federal and state laws authorized district attorneys to bring suit to recover funds from the missing parent.[52]

TenBroek challenged directly the bedrock assumption of Anglo-American family law: private family responsibility for the financial support of needy relatives. In 1949, tenBroek and Joseph Tussman had speculated hopefully in their classic essay "The Equal Protection of the Laws" that poverty, like race, might be a suspect classification subject to strict judicial scrutiny, a legal standard that required a tight fit between any discriminatory law and a "compelling" governmental interest or objective.[53] Fifteen years later, tenBroek argued that "the social and economic causes of dependency"—that is, "rising unemployment," "racial prejudice and discrimination," "shifting industrial demands," and "obsolescence of traditional skills" rather than individual fault or immoral personal behavior—meant that the relief of economic distress should be the government's obligation.[54]

For tenBroek, public responsibility could alleviate the basic injustice of a dual system that disproportionately burdened and blamed poor families. In his view, the real problem was that legal categories remained subservient to the protection of public coffers. Whether married or unmarried, of legitimate or illegitimate birth, poor Americans faced an entirely different legal system from their wealthier counterparts: legal boundaries between marriage and nonmarriage had a way of disappearing when recognition of a nonmarital relationship would alleviate demands on public resources. TenBroek implicitly suggested that poverty often made formal marital status largely irrelevant when it came to support obligations.

The man who rapidly became the go-to legal expert on "illegitimacy" took a very different approach. Born in Berlin in 1932, Harry Krause emigrated to the United States after World War II to attend college and returned to Germany as a U.S. Army draftee in the 1950s. There he met his future wife, Eva, whom he married in 1958 after graduating third in his class from the University of Michigan Law School and securing a job at an elite Washington, D.C., law firm.[55] Following a brief stint at Ford International, Krause became a law professor at the University of Illinois; his early publications focused on international business, trade, and product liability, but he soon turned to family law.

Unlike tenBroek, Krause believed that legal distinctions based on birth status remained deeply relevant: in his view, they were the chief obstacle to solving the tragedy of father absence and mitigating unnecessary poverty. Nineteenth- and early-twentieth-century reforms had softened the common law doctrine that rendered illegitimate children *filius nullius* (child/son of no one), unable to inherit and powerless to alter their status.[56] But children born outside of marriage continued to face legal disadvantages. Krause focused on laws that deprived nonmarital children of an untapped source of private support, financial and otherwise: their fathers. In the first of several articles published in the mid- to late-1960s, Krause attacked laws that excluded many nonmarital children from paternal support, inheritance, workers' compensation, Social Security benefits, and wrongful death recovery.[57] "It is time that the matter be considered from the standpoint of the child!" Krause declared.[58]

In 1966, Krause drafted a proposed "Uniform Legitimacy Act" (a precursor to the Uniform Parentage Act) to rationalize and standardize the confusing patchwork of state laws on birth status and parentage. States varied greatly in the ease with which they permitted fathers to ac- knowledge or "legitimate" their children; very few allowed mothers to do so unilaterally, and some required marriage.[59] Krause's proposal allowed for the voluntary legitimation of children by fathers with the consent of the child's custodian or a court.

The legal consequences of legitimation, too, varied by state. The uni- form act would establish a "legitimated" nonmarital child's right to support and to inherit equally with marital children, with their father's consent. A child entitled to support would be eligible for workers' compensation ben- efits and wrongful death recovery. The proposed law would allow mothers, children, grandparents—and, significantly, public authorities—to bring pa- ternity actions to impose a legal father-child relationship.[60]

Krause also sought to expand nonmarital children's eligibility for federal government benefits, building on congressional efforts. For in- stance, before 1965, the Social Security Act's definition of "child" for purposes of receiving disability or survivor benefits based on a parent's earnings included only children who could inherit from that parent under state intestacy laws.[61] Most states allowed illegitimate children to inherit from their mothers, but many placed obstacles in the way of pa- ternal inheritance. Theoretically, these children could receive benefits through their mothers, but often a mother's wages were too paltry to qualify for benefits, or her lower earnings meant that a father's benefit would provide significantly more funds.[62]

The 1965 Amendments to the Social Security Act partly eased this problem by substituting a functional definition of fatherhood for the for- mal exclusion of nonmarital children. The amendments extended benefits to nonmarital children whose paternity had been established by a court or was voluntarily acknowledged, and to those who could show that their fa- thers lived with them or contributed significantly to their support.[63] The Senate Finance Committee worried about benefit denials in cases where "a child is living with his mother and father in a normal family relationship and where neither the child nor his friends and neighbors have any reason to think that the parents were never married."[64] Lawmakers estimated that this change would render an additional twenty thousand children immedi- ately eligible for disability and survivor benefits.[65]

After the 1965 amendments some significant discriminations re- mained. Nonmarital children who lacked a father's care or support re- mained ineligible. "It is this group of deserted children," one welfare advocate pointed out, "who are most likely to be receiving public assistance, generally in the form of [AFDC]." The denial of disability and survivor benefits subjected children and their mothers to the "indignities of the public assistance system" and placed families at the mercy of capricious state authorities.[66] Further, mothers of illegitimate children remained ineligible for "mothers' insurance" benefits based on the earnings of their children's fathers. In other words, if no man functioned as a provider the state would not step in to assist mother and child.

In 1967, Congress amended the Social Security Act once again, this time mostly to shore up marital primacy. Now illegitimate children would receive only residual benefits—those left over after a worker's widow and legitimate children had collected their entitlements.[67] Lawmakers expressed grave "concern that such a large number of families have not achieved independence and self-support," resulting in "rapidly increasing costs to the taxpayers." And so the 1967 amendments strengthened incentives for poor parents, including single mothers, to work for wages; required all states to "establish programs to combat illegitimacy"; and withheld additional payments from states whose welfare expenditures increased due to nonmarital births, divorce, or desertion.[68]

This approach reflected congressmembers' antipathy toward recipients who bore children outside of marriage. Lawmakers said that "some children now receiving AFDC would be better off in foster homes or institutions than they are in their own homes," citing "the poor home environment for child upbringing in homes with low standards, including multiple instances of illegitimacy."[69] A desire to keep "employable Negro mothers" available for low-wage seasonal or domestic jobs also motivated reforms.[70] Congress devoted public funds to day care to enable poor mothers to enter the workforce, disregarding recommendations from advocates for women to subsidize universal childcare programs that would serve families of all classes.[71] Lawmakers called for a "closer relationship" between "welfare agencies" and law enforcement in order to recover support from "deserting" parents and reimburse state authorities for their public assistance outlays.[72]

The Social Security Act amendments in 1965 and 1967 advanced some of Krause's goals but few of tenBroek's. Allowing some nonmarital children to receive survivors' and disability benefits through their fathers furthered Krause's mission by enabling more children to benefit from a legal paternal tie. The expanded definition of "child" could promote some families from the second-tier, stigmatized AFDC program to the more respectable wage-based entitlement programs. The changes did not address tenBroek's critique of the dual system that relegated poor families to a separate, inferior, and intrusive legal regime, however. And Krause's proposed reforms—designed primarily to increase fathers' support responsibilities—implicitly reinforced that divide by accepting the very premise tenBroek rejected: that family members should, if possible, be responsible for bearing the costs of dependency.

Yet despite their different emphases, tenBroek and Krause both saw promise in constitutional equal protection law. TenBroek believed that the dual system of family law itself should not pass constitutional muster because poverty was the only basis for these starkly different legal regimes. "Should not poverty as a classifying trait be declared inherently discriminatory and outlawed ... and 'the mere fact of being without funds' be held 'constitutionally an irrelevance like race, creed or color'?" tenBroek demanded. Here he alluded to recent Supreme Court decisions affording rights to indigent criminal defendants.[73] TenBroek analogized the states' systemic and disparate treatment of the poor and nonpoor to racial discrimination and applied a capacious equal protection theory to both.

Precedents attacking discrimination based on race and poverty served a different purpose for Krause than they did for tenBroek. Krause compared "the psychological effects of the stigma of bastardy upon its victim" to those of racial discrimination, "successfully exploited in the battle over school segregation."[74] He cited a medical expert who called nonmarital birth a "psychic catastrophe" for children.[75] And Krause believed it "beyond question that a child's right to a familial relationship with his father is more akin to a 'fundamental right and liberty' or a 'basic civil right of man' than to a mere economic interest" immune from constitutional attack.[76] For Krause, civil rights and civil liberties cases provided a parallel that could justify subjecting birth status classifications to greater judicial scrutiny when they caused harm to children, whose parents' marital status—like their race—lay beyond their control.

Whereas Krause focused on the father-child relationship, New York family court judge Justine Wise Polier had long advocated more humane legal treatment of nonmarital children and their mothers. Polier's father, Rabbi Stephen Wise, helped to found both the American Jewish Congress and the NAACP. Her mother, Louise Waterman Wise, an artist and social worker, established a New York adoption agency that eventually bore her name. Justine spent her young adulthood studying economics at three prestigious women's colleges and posing as a mill worker in Passaic, New Jersey, to uncover abusive labor practices in the industry. At Yale Law School, her activism rankled the university's president and almost cost her admission to the bar. After graduation she became the first female referee for New York's Workman's Compensation Division and later the assistant corporation counsel for New York mayor Fiorello LaGuardia.

In the meantime, Justine Wise married Leo Tulin, a young criminal law professor, and gave birth to a son, Stephen. In 1932, Tulin died of leukemia, leaving her bereft but determined to continue her work and care for her four-year-old son with the help of family and friends. She was a thirty-two-year-old single mother when LaGuardia asked her to serve on the city's Domestic Relations court. Disturbed by the case of an unmarried couple who lost custody of their children, she consented to serve just long enough to study "abuses in the court system" and recommend reforms.[77] She stayed for nearly four decades, battling injustices in the juvenile court system and in poverty law generally. Wise remarried in 1937; her husband, Shad Polier, a Jewish attorney from South Carolina who assisted in the Scottsboro Boys' defense and served on the board of the NAACP Legal Defense Fund, adopted Stephen, and together the Poliers championed civil rights and family welfare causes.[78]

Some of Judge Polier's long-standing concerns about the law of illegitimacy resembled Krause's. In 1947, Polier called on all states to adopt Arizona's position that "every child is the legitimate child of its natural parents," to "correct those archaic laws and customs that have humiliated, separated and stigmatized" children born outside of marriage.[79] In the following decades Polier, long a vocal opponent of racial discrimination, increasingly noted the disparate impact of birth status laws on families of color. In 1966, just as Krause began his own scholarly forays, Polier wrote about "laws and practices affecting the child born out of wedlock."[80] She worked to end the "segregation of support cases" and to develop services comparable to those available to marital children.[81]

Polier parted ways with Krause, however, in her view of the relationship between mothers', fathers', and children's interests and the state's role in social welfare provision. Since the 1940s, Polier had urged "communities [to] provide such adequate and humane care for unmarried mothers before and after the birth of their children" to enable them to keep their children "whenever they are able and willing."[82] Polier's efforts defied mid-century conventional wisdom. A young, white middle-class woman who became pregnant while unmarried often was expected either to marry the child's father or relinquish her baby for adoption after spending her pregnancy sequestered in a home for unwed mothers where her family could keep the shameful event a secret.[83] One appreciative reader wrote to Polier: "I am so glad and grateful that you . . . do not advocate the arbitrary separation of mothers and babies. So many alleged liberals . . . have no especial sympathy for unmarried mothers and their rights." Mothers received assistance "conditioned upon surrendering custody of their babies for adoption," which often caused lasting trauma.[84]

In the 1960s, Polier denounced the dearth of protections provided to children judged delinquent in understaffed juvenile courts; the lack of adequate state support for single mothers; and the abandonment of abused and neglected children to languish in orphanages, foster homes, jails, and reformatories.[85] She decried as "myth" the belief in "a vast increase in illegitimacy" resulting from young Black women's welfare receipt. In fact, Polier wrote in 1966, few Black women could obtain public assistance in southern states, and most who did also worked outside the home in backbreaking jobs for meager wages. Young middle- and upper-class white women now had access to contraception and even abortion. They could, if they wished, "start life anew" after a nonmarital pregnancy. Women of color could not.[86] Most maternity homes and adoption agencies did not serve Black women, who often kept their babies but suffered stigma and charges of cultural pathology.[87]

He did not mention her by name, but Krause may have had advocates like Polier in mind when he called for a shift in focus from "unwed mothers" to nonmarital children and their missing fathers.[88] Polier objected to Krause's "judgmental attitudes" and questioned whether children always benefited from identification of a biological father or whether paternity tests were "more beneficial to the tax-payer than the child."[89]

Polier's diagnosis found expression in a growing movement.[90] Calls grew louder for legally enforceable rights for poor parents and children in need of aid, regardless of marital or birth status. Polier's close friend and collaborator Elizabeth Wickenden urged advocates to turn to the courts in a widely circulated 1963 memo detailing how welfare recipients might make claims under the constitution.[91] Polier and her husband recruited her son's childhood friend, the law professor Charles Reich, to author two articles that laid the intellectual foundation for a new poverty law and welfare rights agenda.[92]

In the coming years, the ideas and legal strategies advanced by Polier, tenBroek, and Krause would be tested in court, as plaintiffs—mostly single mothers of color and their children—used emerging constitutional principles of equality, due process, and privacy to challenge the legal supremacy of marriage. Those constitutional principles, ironically, stemmed partly from decisions that exalted marriage even as they laid groundwork for its transformation.

Civil Rights, Civil Liberties, and the New Constitutional Law of the Family

By 1960, federal constitutional litigation seemed the obvious path to attacking state laws that infringed on liberty and equality. After landmark civil rights victories like *Brown v. Board of Education* (1954), advocates saw the U.S. Supreme Court as a sympathetic audience. Between 1953 and 1969—the tenure of Chief Justice Earl Warren—the Court issued pivotal rulings on racial discrimination, civil liberties, and the rights of criminal defendants.

But the Warren Court, even in its heyday, was far less friendly to claims of equality between men and women and to growing calls for sexual liberation outside as well as within marriage. When the Court upheld Gwendolyn Hoyt's conviction by an all-male jury for her husband's murder in 1961, Justice John Marshall Harlan II's opinion justifying women's exemption from jury service because of their family responsibilities garnered unanimous support from his (all white, all male) colleagues.[93] And the justices avoided confronting the constitutionality of interracial sex and marriage in the years following *Brown*, aware of their incendiary potential.[94] The Court's landmark judicial opinions and the litigation strategies that produced them valorized and privileged marriage in ways that enabled transformations in the law of sex and the family but also threatened to limit their reach.

Challenges to birth control bans in the early 1960s embodied this productive tension between expanding sexual freedoms and reverence for marriage. Oral contraceptives first became widely available in 1960, a social earthquake that transformed Americans' reproductive lives.[95] But birth control supporters already had waged a decades-long campaign against laws limiting or criminalizing contraception.[96] Many of these

laws originated in the late nineteenth century when the anti-vice crusader Anthony Comstock led a campaign against obscenity and sex for
purposes other than procreation within marriage.[97] Birth control bans
survived into the mid-twentieth century in states such as Massachusetts
and Connecticut, where repeal efforts faltered amid steadfast opposition
from the Catholic Church. In practice, married couples of means obtained contraceptives through private physicians, but clinics that served
poor patients could not lawfully distribute them.[98]

Proponents supported contraception for diverse reasons, including a
belief that control over their reproductive lives was essential to women's
autonomy and freedom of conscience; concern about unchecked population growth; a desire to combat poverty; and alarm over rising nonmarital birth rates. Civil libertarians favored access to contraceptives for the
married and unmarried alike. As a young lawyer, Mel Wulf was, by his
own description, "a single man, living in the Village, and sexually active if
not promiscuous," when he became the national ACLU's assistant legal
director in 1958. Wulf, therefore, "had a personal commitment to birth
control" that only deepened after his marriage to Deidre Howard, a fellow birth control activist, in 1962.[99] Harriet Pilpel, a married mother and
a leading lawyer for Planned Parenthood, had begun advocating for birth
control access in the 1930s, inspired in part by her maternal grandmother, who had borne sixteen children.[100]

Even the proposition that married couples should have a right to use
contraception was controversial, however. The Catholic Church opposed
birth control as contrary to the essential purpose of marital sexual relations: procreation, not pleasure. Sex outside of marriage remained unlawful, and the availability of effective contraception removed its most
potent deterrent, unintended pregnancy. Whatever their personal views,
for strategic reasons advocates who challenged contraceptive bans in
court carefully positioned themselves as defenders of marriage.

This approach was not only politic but also grounded in time-
honored legal traditions. The doctrine of marital privacy, with deep roots
in Anglo-American family law, shielded the home from government intrusion and justified courts' reluctance to intervene in an intact marriage.
Alongside the principle of marital unity—expressed by the nineteenth-
century English authority William Blackstone as "the husband and wife
are one person in law"—judges used marital privacy as a reason to look
the other way when husbands abused their wives or failed to support
them.[101] The idea of a man's home as his castle bolstered the case against

restricting married couples' access to contraceptives. And a focus on marriage blunted the criticism that birth control advocates promoted moral depravity. States routinely touted restrictions as safeguards against immorality, promiscuity, and illegitimacy, so advocates could argue that birth control bans swept too broadly if their true purpose was to deter illicit, as opposed to marital, sex.

Marriage provided an alibi for the advancement of sexual freedom in the campaign to overturn Connecticut's birth control ban. Early plaintiffs, in *Poe v. Ullman*, which was argued before the state supreme court in 1959, were married couples who had suffered medical tragedies: repeated miscarriages and stillbirths or devastating pregnancy complications, including the paralysis and death of mothers and infants. Advocates emphasized that, for these families, contraception was literally a matter of life and death. Attorney Catherine Roraback argued that if "rights to life and liberty have meaning," the government could not compel married couples to choose between mortally dangerous pregnancy and sexual abstinence. "Sexual intercourse is not a mere adjunct of marriage," wrote Roraback, a 1948 graduate of Yale Law School who co-founded the Connecticut Civil Liberties Union and never married. "It is part of the basic fabric of the whole marital relation."[102] The amicus brief Mel Wulf co-authored with Ruth Emerson, a 1950 graduate of Yale Law School married to Yale law professor Tom Emerson, "stressed marital and family values to the utmost."[103]

A right to contraception within marriage had its own radical potential: it could allow women to combine marriage and career without risking early pregnancy and motherhood. The married Yale law students Louise Trubek and David Trubek joined the Connecticut lawsuit so that plaintiffs could argue that all married couples, known dire health risks or not, enjoyed a constitutional right to use birth control. As newlyweds, the Trubeks desired "an opportunity to adjust themselves, mentally, spiritually, and physically to each other, so as to establish a secure and permanent marriage" before having children. Moreover, Louise "believed women should have access to birth control so that they could have both a career and a family," and she hoped to avoid "disruption of [her] professional education."[104] Louise was "no sexual radical." A "'good girl' uninterested in sexual freedom," she desired that marriage not derail her ambitions.[105]

Marital privacy arguments found a receptive audience when the challenge to Connecticut's contraceptive ban first reached the U.S. Supreme

Court in 1961. Justice John Marshall Harlan shared his clerk Charles Fried's indignation at the statute's intrusion on "the most intimate details of the marital relation." The *marital* nature of the relationship was determinative, in Harlan's view. No "absolute" right to privacy inhered in sexual relationships. Harlan remained unwilling to say that "adultery, homosexuality, fornication and incest are immune from criminal enquiry, however privately practiced." It was "the intimacy of husband and wife" that the state "always and in every age . . . has fostered and protected."[106] When the Court dismissed *Poe* because of skepticism that Connecticut would enforce its birth control ban, Harlan dissented.[107]

The Connecticut activist Estelle Griswold then set out to provoke a punitive response from the state and rekindle the constitutional challenge. Griswold advertised her intent to follow Planned Parenthood's policy that "no unmarried woman will knowingly be accepted as a patient," except for premarital visits authorized by a clergyman, when she opened her New Haven birth control clinic in November 1961.[108] Many young women "claimed to be engaged" or "borrowed wedding rings" in order to circumvent these rules.[109] One married Yale graduate student, Rosemary Stevens, gave a statement to friendly New Haven detectives after visiting Griswold's clinic and obtaining a diaphragm and contraceptive jelly, explaining her desire not to become pregnant before completing her education. She said that "this opportunity should be made available to all women in this state"; the detective replied, "Don't you mean *married* women, Mrs. Stevens?" Stevens reluctantly assented, to her lasting regret.[110]

Marriage and marital privacy remained integral to the plaintiffs' articulation of the constitutional rights at stake in *Griswold v. Connecticut*, decided by the U.S. Supreme Court in 1965. Tom Emerson argued that the right to privacy "plainly . . . extends to unwarranted government invasion of (1) the sanctity of the home, and (2) the intimacies of the sexual relationship in marriage." At oral argument, he reiterated that the plaintiffs' challenge "goes only to the [ban's] application to married women."[111] Despite dissension among the justices about the birth control ban's constitutionality, none of the *Griswold* opinions suggested directly that the right to privacy extended beyond the marital family.

Justice William O. Douglas's opinion for the Court in *Griswold* struck down Connecticut's contraceptive ban and articulated for the first time a right to privacy, located in the "penumbras and emanations" of several amendments in the Bill of Rights. Freedoms secured by earlier

Court decisions—to educate and bring up children; to form political associations; to think, teach, and inquire; to practice one's religion— created a "zone of privacy" the government could not enter, he wrote.[112]

Griswold protected a right to *marital* privacy: Douglas's brief opinion included an homage to marriage as a "coming together, for better or worse, hopefully enduring, and intimate to the degree of being sacred."[113] The final version omitted an even lengthier paean from Douglas's first draft, which described marriage as "the essence of one form of the ex- pression of love, admiration, and loyalty."[114] Douglas asked: "Would we allow the police to search the sacred precincts of the marital bedroom for telltale signs of the use of contraceptives? The very idea is repulsive to the notions of privacy surrounding the marital relationship."[115] In his concurring opinion Justice Arthur Goldberg, joined by Harlan, was care- ful to reaffirm the government's prerogative to regulate "sexual promis- cuity or misconduct."[116]

Douglas's flowery language about the companionate joys of marriage belied his own checkered marital history. A thirty-year union that pro- duced two children ended in divorce after Douglas's affair with the woman who would become his second wife. His infidelity ended that marriage in 1963, and at age sixty-four Douglas wed a twenty-three- year-old college student. Douglas's children and first three spouses de- scribed him as, at best, hostile and absent, and, at worst, abusive and cruel.[117] Douglas met his fourth wife, then a twenty-two-year-old wait- ress, in the summer of 1965; they married the following year and re- mained together until his death in 1980. Douglas's personal conduct and controversial opinions led to talk of impeachment: Representative Rob- ert Dole (R-KS) quipped that the justice exercised "bad judgment from a matrimonial standpoint, but also in a number of 5–4 decisions by the Supreme Court."[118]

Larger changes rumbled beneath *Griswold*'s pious proclamations about marriage and endorsement of the "proper regulation of sexual pro- miscuity or misconduct."[119] Few doubted that Connecticut's stringent law was an anachronism destined for eventual repeal, regardless of the Court's ruling.[120] A growing gap separated the lofty rhetoric of judicial opinions from the social reality that by 1965 most Americans, regardless of marital status or religious affiliation, expected to have sexual inter- course without procreative consequence.

Griswold also reflected a wider reconsideration of laws that criminal- ized consensual adult sexual conduct. Advocates like Harriet Pilpel had

long argued that criminal prohibitions on sex, even when rarely enforced, enabled selective, discriminatory prosecution.[121] Emerson and
Roraback's brief in *Griswold* invoked a "concept of limited government"
that prevented "intrusions into the personal and intimate life of the citizen."[122] These views were gaining ground. In 1962, the American Law
Institute (ALI) proposed a Model Penal Code that recommended the repeal of criminal penalties for adultery, fornication, and contraceptive use
and supported the liberalization of abortion laws. Influenced by Alfred
Kinsey's findings regarding the prevalence of nonmarital sex, homosexuality, and other "deviant" conduct and by Britain's Wolfenden Report, the
ALI also proposed that sodomy be criminalized only when it involved
public sex or the use of force.[123] Douglas's opinion gestured only
obliquely to this larger criminal law reform movement, but *Griswold*'s
recognition of a privacy right cracked open a door.

Further, although the Court had yet to recognize sex discrimination as
a constitutional violation, advocates drew explicit connections between reproductive freedom and women's equal rights.[124] The ACLU's *Griswold*
brief argued that birth control bans violated equal protection because "the
ability to regulate child-bearing has been a significant factor in the emancipation of married women." Indeed, "effective means of contraception rank
equally with the Nineteenth Amendment [establishing woman suffrage] in
enhancing the opportunity of women who wish to work in industry, business, the arts, and the professions."[125] The *Griswold* opinions nowhere mentioned equality for women.[126] Still, Olive Byrne Richard praised *Griswold* as
vindicating her aunt Margaret Sanger's "50 years of dedication to the liberation of women from enslavement born of bigotry."[127]

Griswold was a partial albeit crucial victory for the unmarried and for
those who would challenge the legal primacy of marriage. A California
lawyer, Larry Livingston, wrote to Mel Wulf in the spring of 1964, predicting success in *Griswold*. "The thing that bothers me," he wrote, "is that the
law may be held unconstitutional as to married couples and, by inference,
constitutional as to everybody else. To me this is nonsense, although I have
been married to the same woman for 48 years."[128] Its focus on *marital* privacy meant that *Griswold* "barely touched other state anti-contraceptive
laws," Planned Parenthood leaders told the *New York Times*.[129]

Griswold did contain kernels of a broader conception of sexual and
reproductive freedom that advocates could seize upon. The decision's ca-
veats about the state's authority to regulate who could marry and to punish sexual conduct outside of marriage left open the question of whether

unmarried persons, interracial couples, and others who transgressed marital norms would reap the benefits of the Court's newfound willingness to limit the state's intervention in Americans' intimate lives.

McLaughlin v. Florida (1964) provided cryptic clues. In 1962, Miami Beach authorities charged Dewey McLaughlin, a Honduran immigrant identified as "colored," and Connie Hoffman, a white woman, with violating Florida's prohibition on an individual sleeping in the same room with a person of a different sex and race. Hoffman's white landlady had encountered McLaughlin emerging from the shower in Hoffman's tiny apartment and alerted police.[130]

Laws applying harsher penalties to interracial than to intraracial sex and cohabitation lingered in nearly half of U.S. states—mostly but not exclusively states that also prohibited interracial marriage. Notably, laws against marital and nonmarital relationships operated synergistically: a state that prevented interracial couples from marrying made any intimate relations illicit and subject to prosecution under general fornication and adultery laws.[131]

Civil rights organizations had long divided over the wisdom of challenging laws that punished interracial intimacy. Well into the twentieth century, allegations of interracial sex provided the pretext for lynching Black men and women who violated social boundaries or challenged white political and economic power. Mid-century segregationist screeds warned that integration of schools and public accommodations would lead inevitably to "miscegenation" or "race-mixing," which stirred violent opposition to movements for racial justice.[132] Civil rights groups such as the NAACP and its Legal Defense Fund (LDF) declined to prioritize decriminalization of interracial sex and marriage for fear of validating white supremacist propaganda.[133] The Supreme Court also dodged cases involving interracial intimacy, sometimes engaging in improbable procedural gymnastics to avoid decisions on the merits.[134]

But by 1963, civil rights leaders, emboldened by courtroom victories in education, voting rights, and public accommodations, launched a direct assault on prohibitions of interracial sex and marriage. Commentators now framed these laws as remnants of a Jim Crow past best relegated to the dustbin of history.[135] Instead of evading the marriage question, LDF lawyers encouraged the justices to tackle it head-on.[136]

In *McLaughlin*, the Court again avoided the marriage issue, but for somewhat different reasons than in the past. Justice Hugo Black thought it "a bad case to reach the issue" since the parties *were* married, but to other people.[137] Instead, Justice Byron White's majority opinion called the Florida law an impermissible racial classification. For some, the Court's recent equal protection decisions made *McLaughlin* an easy case: a Douglas clerk deemed the Florida law "the nearest thing to apartheid in America today."[138] In the end, *McLaughlin* overruled an 1883 decision that upheld a similar law, declaring that its "narrow view of the Equal Protection Clause" had long since been "swept away."[139]

By extending equal protection to interracial intimacy, *McLaughlin* broke new ground. But as in the contraception cases, no one suggested that a state could not prohibit illicit sex, discourage promiscuity, or otherwise regulate nonmarital relationships.[140] Neither the parties' briefs nor the Court's opinions questioned Florida's stated purpose: "to prevent breaches of the basic concepts of sexual decency" by punishing "illicit extramarital and premarital promiscuity."[141] Contemporaneous and retrospective accounts depicted *McLaughlin* as "a waystation on the road to [interracial] marriage": a decision about racial discrimination, not sexual freedom.[142]

Three years later, in *Loving v. Virginia*, a unanimous Court finally struck down prohibitions of interracial marriage. *Loving* powerfully combined equal protection and due process to repudiate "measures designed to maintain White Supremacy," an unusually direct reference to systemic racial subordination. Chief Justice Warren's opinion echoed *Griswold*'s soaring rhetoric affirming the exalted status of marriage. "The freedom to marry," wrote Warren, "has long been recognized as one of the vital personal rights essential to the orderly pursuit of happiness by free men." He continued: "To deny this fundamental freedom on so unsupportable a basis as the racial classifications embodied in these statutes, statutes so directly subversive of the principle of equality at the heart of the Fourteenth Amendment, is surely to deprive all the State's citizens of liberty without due process of law."[143]

More radically, *Loving* signaled that states' long-standing prerogative to regulate marriage no longer shielded family law from federal constitutional scrutiny. Robert F. Drinan, a progressive Jesuit priest and law professor, saw in *Loving* the promise of a family law revolution.[144] From the Court's declaration of the "freedom to marry" Drinan inferred that laws designed to "induce" marriage could also be constitutionally vulnerable.

Drinan boldly speculated that *Loving* jeopardized all legal discrimination against nonmarital children, since adults might be pressured to marry to ensure their offsprings' legitimacy. By criminalizing nonmarital sex, penalties for fornication and "bastardy" too could coerce marriage. Laws punishing adultery subjected men to blackmail and might force them to divorce and remarry; wives who had extramarital affairs often lost custody of children. Even paternity statutes could push men into marriage to avoid support obligations.[145] In Drinan's optimistic view, *Loving*'s freedom to marry included the freedom *not* to marry and threatened all laws that penalized sex and childbearing outside of marriage.

By 1967, the Court had woven into the tapestry of constitutional law the threads of continuity and change. *Griswold* and *Loving* bolstered marriage's primacy even as they contained the seeds of its destruction. If Americans possessed fundamental rights to sexual privacy and to marriage, if states could not regulate marriage with impunity, if laws could not advance white supremacy, if the constitution shielded the family from state intrusion, then key pillars of marriage's legal preeminence might fall even as the Court extolled the institution itself. These decisions opened promising avenues for challenging injustices that social movements would expose and attack in the coming years.

CHAPTER TWO

Hapless and Innocent Children
Birth Status and Welfare

I N APRIL 1967, BARBARA JEAN CAGER applied for Aid to Families with Dependent Children on behalf of her one-year-old and newborn daughters, Tracy and Bridgett. At nineteen, she had already lost her own father, her second baby, Patricia, and Patricia's father. Barbara Jean lived with her mother, four siblings, and three children in "substandard housing" with no plumbing and a pot-bellied stove for heat. Mrs. Cager supported her family through work as a hospital maid, supplemented by old age insurance benefits (OASDI).[1] Barbara Jean had given birth to Bridgett in April and "hope[d] to return to her [unspecified] former job in July." In the meantime, to receive public assistance, she was required by Maryland law to supply the name of Bridgett's father so that the state could bring a paternity action against him. There was little hope of recovering child support: the whereabouts of Tracy's father were unknown and Bridgett's father was incarcerated.

However, the form Ms. Cager completed had another purpose. The local state's attorney, Arthur A. Marshall, Jr., had launched a campaign against illegitimacy and conscripted reluctant welfare officials to apprehend mothers who gave birth to more than one child outside of marriage. When Barbara Jean Cager gave the paternity declaration to Assistant State's Attorney Vincent Femia, he advised her of her rights, charged her with criminal neglect, and booked and jailed her. "Miss

39

C[ager] was frightened and there was no legal counsel available even though it was requested." Eventually, she was released on her own recognizance and told that her children could remain at home pending a court hearing.[2]

The crackdown also ensnared Patty Wilson (a pseudonym), a twenty-three-year-old unmarried part-time barmaid and "hard-working waitress" with three children. Wilson had lived for three years with her children's father, an auto mechanic. Weary of the man's promises to "marry her as soon as he divorced his wife," she moved in with her mother, who provided childcare while Wilson worked. Wilson applied for AFDC after she gave birth in April 1967. Like Ms. Cager, she found herself arrested, charged, and threatened with the loss of her children. The *Washington Post* reported, "Patty admits to being bewildered by her arrest, saying: 'They used big words and said something about neglect.'"[3]

Marshall's initiative was only the latest measure to punish unmarried mothers proposed by Maryland officials. In 1960, months before the Louisiana crisis that opened chapter 1, the Maryland state senator John L. Sanford, Jr. (D-Worcester), had introduced a bill that mandated the "sterilization of any woman convicted of bastardy for the second time" and authorized penalties including incarceration of up to three and a half years, a $1,000 fine, and loss of custody of all of her children.[4] The rising share of public aid recipients who were Black and "illegitimate" drove Maryland's punitive approach.[5]

Editorials condemned the sterilization proposals as "barbarous" and "sadistic." The *Washington Post* compared the policies to Nazi measures and noted that they were aimed at "Negroes."[6] Welfare officials, too, generally opposed sterilization mandates, but individual physicians were among the bill's most vocal supporters.

Few disputed, however, that "illegitimacy" was a growing social problem. Moderate policymakers favored proactive prevention. The Maryland legislature tabled Sanford's sterilization measure but convened a commission whose 1961 report compared "illegitimacy" to public health crises such as tuberculosis and venereal disease. The legislature embraced the report's recommendations to tighten child support enforcement; the commission also urged that nonmarital births be immediately reported to state welfare officials, who would remove children if "child care plans" were not "suitable."[7] Maryland lawmakers then redefined "neglect" to include a parent's failure to provide a "stable moral environment," with multiple births outside of marriage as a criterion.

In 1961, state welfare officials questioned this policy less on grounds of cruelty or legality than of practicality. The director of Maryland's welfare department, Thomas Waxter, declared child removal "highly desirable" but warned that it "would cost a horrendous amount of money." The shortage of adoptive and foster homes meant that children could be left with "senile grandparents, teenage relatives, irresponsible caretakers or their own immature mothers." He depicted young mothers as "culturally and socially retarded"—more pathetic than morally culpable.[8]

By 1967, the arrests of Barbara Jean Cager and other young mothers alarmed advocates for racial justice, welfare rights, and civil liberties and presented ideal facts for a "test case." Other states continued to exclude the (Black) children of single mothers from AFDC by declaring their homes unsuitable. Findings of neglect shunted many families from the welfare office into dependency court, which initiated the removal of Black children from their families into a burgeoning foster care system.[9] The drama of arrest, criminal charges, and publicity distinguished the Maryland policy and provided an opportunity for constitutional challenge.

In the second half of the 1960s, challenges to marital supremacy took many forms, from legislation to court actions to grassroots mobilization. Constitutional litigation attacking laws that penalized nonmarital families, especially Black single mothers and their children, implicated several key social movement struggles: for racial and economic justice, for reproductive freedom and sexual privacy, and for women's liberation from dependence either on men or on stingy and stigmatized public assistance.

Advocates' various approaches to laws and policies that penalized nonmarital childbearing or birth status translated into diverse constitutional arguments and litigation strategies. Some advanced innovative constitutional claims, and others argued by analogy to established precedents. Some challenged marital supremacy directly, while others acknowledged nonmarital childbearing as a social problem but favored remedial rather than punitive solutions. Some attacked what Jacobus tenBroek named the "dual system" of family and welfare law and called on the state to support needy families; others, following Harry Krause, stressed how birth status discrimination undermined the search for private sources of support and exacerbated fatherlessness. Some emphasized the burden placed on blameless children; others advanced capacious visions of *parents'*—especially unmarried mothers'—rights to liberty, privacy, and equality. Impoverished Black women fought for welfare rights:

government support in caring for children on their own, without submitting to state intrusion into their intimate lives.

In contrast to advocates' varied views and motivations, the judicial response proved remarkably consistent. Even before the political winds shifted decisively, the Supreme Court ignored arguments about sexual privacy and equality for adults. Instead, the justices protected "hapless, innocent children," who should not be punished for their parents' "sins." The government retained its prerogative to discourage what it viewed as sexual immorality and to promote formal marriage or legitimation.

By the early 1970s, just as a feminist welfare rights vision began to take shape, the Court shifted to the right. Claims that a law's disparate impact based on race or poverty violated the constitution ran aground, and arguments for a right to basic economic subsistence failed. The justices made clear that without an outright admission of racially discriminatory intent by government officials, states could decide how to allocate meager funds to public assistance programs and impose onerous conditions to qualify for that support.

For the Calvert County circuit judge Perry Gray Bowen, Jr., a former military lawyer and a thirty-nine-year-old father of four, the question presented in Barbara Jean Cager's case was simple: whether the Maryland neglect statute could combat "the problem of illegitimacy, its mounting costs to the taxpayers, and its mounting costs in human misery and suffering."[10] To Bowen, the answer was clearly yes. Nonmarital birth strained public funds and fed intergenerational poverty.[11] Children's "best interests," Bowen opined, "may be . . . better served by taking them out . . . of their mother's orbit and placing them in homes where they will receive minimum standards of moral and ethical training."[12]

Prosecutor Marshall rescinded his threat of criminal charges: he was interested "solely in the welfare of the children and not putting women in jail."[13] But Judge Bowen required that mothers "study and understand methods of birth control and . . . practice them at the risk of losing their children if they do not."[14] Courts, Bowen declared, "would begin to use the neglect law as a 'stronger dose of medicine than just please don't'" to curb mothers "who insist on following their biological bent without regard to their social obligations or their community welfare."[15]

Welfare officials decried Bowen's decision. The U.S. Department of Health, Education, and Welfare (HEW) promised an investigation but hedged that any withdrawal of federal funds would take time.[16] Maryland's welfare director, Raleigh C. Hobson, warned that Bowen's ruling could "wreck" the state's AFDC program.[17] Advocates now cited cruelty as well as cost. Harriet P. Trader of the National Association of Social Workers "called the ruling punitive and not in the best interests of either the child or the taxpayer."[18] State welfare officials cautioned mothers of nonmarital children applying for aid that they might face court action.[19]

Lawmakers searched for other ways to deter nonmarital childbearing, such as mandating birth control instruction for mothers of nonmarital children who received aid and threatening loss of custody, fines, and imprisonment for those who did not work for wages.[20] The *Washington Post*'s editorial board denounced these measures, but some readers endorsed brutal policies in chilling terms.[21] Judith M. Waby of Washington, D.C., called Bowen's decision "long overdue" and declared it "time that the respectable, law abiding, tax paying citizens get a break."[22] Virginia Phillips of Silver Spring suggested mandatory sterilization to deter "out-of-wedlock" births.[23] Willa Pierce of Washington, D.C., cheered efforts to "push 'mothers' out into the working world . . . and not being a parasite on society," believing that by "repeatedly contribut[ing] to the breakdown of the moral fiber of civilization" a woman "forfeits any so-called rights."[24] Such views were not outliers: in 1965 a Gallup poll found that one in five Americans recommended sterilization for women on welfare who had additional children outside of marriage and half favored cutting off assistance.[25]

Advocates launched a fusillade of constitutional and statutory attacks on Judge Bowen's rulings and predicted that *Cager* would ultimately reach the Supreme Court.[26] A team of ACLU and LDF lawyers and scholars met with welfare and legal aid experts at Howard University's law school in October 1967 to strategize.[27] The resulting brief, echoing Jacobus tenBroek, condemned the "dual system of justice" that punished poor women but spared a "wealthy mother rearing a child in an unstable moral environment."[28] Advocates cited due process precedents holding that the state could not terminate custody or parental rights of married or divorced parents without providing notice and a hearing.[29]

The Maryland neglect statute was unconstitutionally vague, advocates argued. "Whose standard of morality is to be applied?" What did "unstable" mean? They imagined homes in which a parent had married and divorced multiple times or in which children were fed a steady diet of pornography or were "consistently" taught "that violence is an acceptable way of life." The mothers' lawyers said that due process "does not tolerate state intervention in a constitutionally protected 'zone of privacy' under the auspices of such imprecision."[30]

Moreover, advocates argued, the parental rights at stake were enormous and could only be compromised with "a showing of real and serious harm." The state ignored how families functioned: the extent of attachment between mother and child, the conditions and quality of the home and care provided, and modern psychology, which taught that the separation of children from their parents caused severe emotional damage. Black children were most likely to suffer moves between many foster placements. Indeed, the county's policy violated the purpose of aid to dependent children: to allow children to receive proper care in their own homes.[31] Bowen's ruling endangered children's well-being in the name of protecting it.[32]

Advocates acknowledged a possible state interest in "preventing promiscuous sexual activity and the resulting production of illegitimate children." But family separation should trigger the "exacting scrutiny" required when state action "directly infring[ed] upon a precious personal liberty." They echoed Krause in saying that even if child removal did deter promiscuity, the state could not "penaliz[e] innocent children for the alleged immorality of their mothers." They argued, again channeling tenBroek, that by subjecting only the poor to family separation as a condition of public assistance, the county violated equal protection. The exorbitant cost of placing children in foster care belied any genuine state interest in saving public funds and exposed the policy's discriminatory and punitive purpose. And Marshall's policy, they said, violated the Eighth Amendment's prohibition on cruel and unusual punishment.[33]

Advocates also advanced arguments about reproductive freedom and autonomy.[34] Howard Murphy, a Black newspaperman and a member of Maryland's Board of Public Welfare, argued that, above all, mothers needed birth control and other services.[35] In 1964, Murphy felt like "the only one saying this," but the 1965 decision in *Griswold v. Connecticut* provided constitutional support for his view.[36] Planned Parenthood insisted that the right to reproductive freedom "may not be diminished *either* by governmental prohibition *or* by governmental coercion."[37] In other words, "All Americans should have the right to obtain *or reject* family planning services." Just as *Griswold* abhorred invasion of the "sacred precincts of the marital bedroom," Bowen's rulings would have a "'maximum destructive impact' upon the right of privacy."[38]

Cager presented a tantalizing opportunity to extend *Griswold* to unmarried individuals and to underscore the government's discriminatory treatment of poor women. It was "unthinkable," wrote Harriet Pilpel, that nonmarriage "rendered individual citizens vulnerable to invasion of personal privacy to which those who are married may not constitutionally be subjected." Maryland imposed "state control over . . . sexual relations" only on the poor. "The constitutional rights of privacy and freedom from arbitrary action are not for the affluent alone."[39]

Despite advocates' hopes, *Cager* never made it to the Supreme Court. The Maryland Court of Appeals took up none of their invitations to rewrite constitutional law. Instead, the court ruled that Maryland's neglect statute did not allow for the removal of children *solely* because a mother had given birth outside of marriage. The best interests of children must be "the ultimate consideration," and here the county had "use[d] the children as pawns in a plan to punish their mothers for their past promiscuity and to discourage them and other females of like weaknesses and inclinations from future productivity."[40]

The predominant voices in the *Cager* litigation were those of civil liberties, civil rights, and birth control advocates: mostly white, mostly male, and mostly lawyers, public officials, and well-heeled community leaders. Court documents and press accounts portrayed the young women in *Cager* as vulnerable victims of a cruel and inhumane policy, not as proactive authors of their own destiny. We know little about their own aspirations and self-conception, thrust involuntarily as they were into the public spotlight by sudden legal jeopardy. Soon, low-income women of color would voice wishes and demands in their own words.

Public Housing and "Illegitimacy"

In Philadelphia, Pennsylvania, Mai Greene moved her family from "one 'unfit' home to another" between 1963 and 1968; after three unsuccessful applications for public housing the specter of homelessness forced her to place her five young children in the custody of the Society to Protect Children. The home Edna Baker shared with six children was "unfit for habitation." Lois Boone lived with four children in a one-bedroom apartment that violated so many housing code provisions that it could have been declared uninhabitable two times over. After struggling for two years to find a decent home left Zenobia Smith hospitalized for a breakdown, her three young children joined her sister and two other children in a one-bedroom dwelling.[41]

These women were among thirteen mothers who sued the Housing Authority of Philadelphia in 1968, challenging an unwritten policy that excluded families with two or more nonmarital children from public housing.[42] Represented by Community Legal Services, they joined the many local chapters of the NAACP, Congress of Racial Equality (CORE), ACLU, and legal aid organizations that lobbied local officials, lodged protests, and filed lawsuits nationwide. Challenges to exclusions from public housing based on family status came from smaller cities such as Chester and Bethlehem, Pennsylvania, and large metropolitan areas such as Chicago, Philadelphia, and New York; western communities like Oakland, California, and southern cities, including Richmond, Louisville, Little Rock, and Atlanta.

Local debates over public housing in the 1960s featured advocacy by and on behalf of women of color and their families, motivated by the growing urgency of providing shelter to families isolated in "slums" or displaced by the migration, unemployment, and demolitions impelled by urban renewal programs. As rates of nonmarital childbearing rose and pressure grew to desegregate public housing projects, many local housing authorities rejected or evicted mothers with nonmarital children or partners. In some locales, exclusion and eviction occurred automatically if applicants or residents could not prove the legitimacy of their children or the legal validity of a common law marriage. In others, officials considered illegitimacy as one criterion for housing eligibility; still others admitted unmarried mothers if they had only a few—or older—nonmarital children or on the condition that they would have no more.

These rules sometimes appeared suddenly when Black families tried to enter previously all-white projects. In Camden, New Jersey, for instance, civil rights leaders filed a complaint after authorities turned away a Black woman with a twelve-year-old nonmarital child when she applied to reside at McGuire Gardens, a project that housed 382 white tenants but only six Black families. Critics attributed the denial to race, since other single mothers lived undisturbed in the project with their children.[43] In New Bern, North Carolina, lawyers charged that the housing authority "operated its public housing on a segregated basis" and was "unlawfully barring, evicting, or threatening to evict seven Negro women on the grounds that they have children out of wedlock."[44] The Wilmington, Delaware, housing authority began a "crackdown on illegitimacy" in 1962 that culminated in the eviction of six Black families the following year.[45]

Housing authorities denied any racially discriminatory intent. Officials could not excuse practices such as nonmarital sex, childbearing, adultery, and cohabitation and at the same time maintain the legitimacy of politically unpopular housing aid, they argued. Some officials staked the future of public housing on the authorities' ability to control who could live in subsidized low-rent projects.[46] Walter Rogers, an attorney for the housing authority in Richmond, Virginia, expressed the view of many when he said in 1969 that decent housing included "standards of conduct as well as physical surroundings."[47]

Public housing residents themselves demanded rules excluding nonmarital families, defenders claimed. The public housing chief in Louisville, Kentucky, told critics in 1967 that the city's policy originated in the early 1950s after residents' objections.[48] The "entire purpose of public housing," "to help low-income families to obtain a better standard of living," would be thwarted by "bringing up their children in a beehive of rampant adultery," wrote the *Delaware County Times* in 1963.[49] Elmira, New York, excluded unmarried mothers to "show normal home moral standards to the older children residing in the project."[50]

Civil rights and anti-poverty advocates attacked housing exclusions from many angles. Some clergymen and community leaders, loath to defend nonmarital sex, implored officials to "hate the sin, not the sinner"[51] and called for more social services. Willard G. Howard of the Bethlehem, Pennsylvania, NAACP called the evictions "despotic and devoid of human feeling." He suggested "a second chance, and a third if necessary, along with plenty of personal help in the form of nurses and resident social workers."[52] As one NAACP leader put it, "If you let [an unmarried mother] stay in the housing project, we can work with her to do her some good, but if she is thrown out, what chance will the children have?"[53] Advocates also explained that welfare policy encouraged unemployed fathers to reside elsewhere so the mother and children might be eligible for AFDC benefits.

Community leaders often emphasized the injustice of excluding blameless children who were already languishing in poverty.[54] The Reverend Maurice Moyer, president of the Wilmington NAACP, maintained, "It is wrong to place innocent children out on the street because of their parents' undesirable conduct."[55] Moreover, such irrational and invidious discrimination violated equal protection, argued local civil rights groups.[56] Since many families with nonmarital children led stable, upstanding lives, exclusion based on birth status alone was unreasonable and unlawful.⁵⁷ In 1963, the NAACP and ACLU challenged evictions by the Chester, Pennsylvania, housing authority because they encroached upon "personal privacy" and "worked a discriminatory hardship upon the poor" by "penaliz[ing] their moral offenses while allowing the well-to-do the privilege of the same behavior."⁵⁸

Activists lodged procedural and substantive complaints. They demanded that housing officials cite specific reasons for exclusion or eviction; promulgate and follow clear written policies; give tenants notice and an opportunity to be heard; and publicize the right to be free from racial discrimination in housing. In Louisville, advocates argued innovatively that the authority's exclusion of women with more than one nonmarital child discriminated based on sex. As the legal aid attorney John O'Mara observed, "Men who have fathered illegitimate children are not excluded from public housing."⁵⁹

State and local courts had mixed reactions to plaintiffs' claims. In Kentucky, Judge Charles M. Allen agreed with Louisville authorities in 1968 that "decent" living conditions mandated by statute encompassed tenants' conduct as well as the apartments' physical attributes. Officials could enact "reasonable" "moral standards," especially since Kentucky criminalized nonmarital childbearing. Allen called O'Mara's sex discrimination argument "ingenious," but he observed that "from a practical standpoint it would be very difficult to determine whether a man had sired illegitimate children."⁶⁰ Similarly, Judge A. Christian Compton upheld the evictions of six unmarried mothers from a Richmond, Virginia, project. The housing authority "cannot allow the very conditions of moral degeneracy to develop ... which the legislature has sought to eradicate." There was "no constitutional right to low-income housing," Compton emphasized.⁶¹

Advocates hoped that federal courts would prove more receptive. Alma Jean Thomas and Estella Watson, Black women in their midtwenties, filed a federal class action lawsuit in 1966 after the Housing Authority of Little Rock, Arkansas, rejected their applications because they had nonmarital children. Lawyers from the NAACP Legal Defense Fund and the Center on Social Welfare Policy and Law argued that the policy was designed to punish poor people, discriminated against "predominantly non-white" low-income families already consigned to racially segregated projects, and violated due process and equal protection. Citing *Griswold*, they said the policy intruded upon a woman's "right to privacy and freedom from inquiry into her personal life."⁶²

Judge Jesse Smith Henley ruled in plaintiffs' favor. Henley did not sanction an "absolute" "prohibition" that drew "no distinction between the unwed mother with one illegitimate child and ... ten of such children" and disregarded other mitigating circumstances.[63] A mother might have "reformed," or "if placed in better surroundings she may lead a more conventional life." An "indiscriminate denial of access" withheld housing from "many of the very people who need it most—the poorest and most ignorant of the poor."[64]

Henley carefully qualified the reach of his ruling, however. Housing authorities could exclude tenants who might replicate in public housing the "the slum environment from which they came."[65] The housing authority could force Ms. Thomas and Ms. Watson, each of whom gave birth to three nonmarital children in three years, to show that they would be acceptable tenants notwithstanding their pasts.[66]

Functional inquiries gradually replaced total bans on families with nonmarital children. After three years of protests by tenants and representatives from churches, social services, and some public officials, Wilmington, Delaware, rescinded its housing exclusion in 1966.[67] Community pressure prompted Lancaster County, Pennsylvania, officials to agree that local organizations could "sponsor" worthy nonmarital families as tenants, with the aim of "drastically reduc[ing] rejections."[68] Other localities, such as Camden, New Jersey, adopted the case-by-case approach directed by a circular published by the U.S. Department of Housing and Urban Development (HUD) in 1968, which provided that marital or birth status could not be the sole criterion for rejecting applicants or evicting tenants.[69] As of 1971, Bethlehem still adjudicated "moral" questions, "such as how many illegitimate children an unmarried woman should be allowed to have before she was asked to give up a housing unit."[70] A bitter dispute in Elmira, New York, ended in 1968 when community groups and tenants reached an agreement with the housing authority that "irregular families" would be handled case by case.[71] In Louisville, litigation dragged on until 1972, when a federal judge approved a settlement stipulating that the city "could no longer deny admittance ... *solely* because a family has illegitimate children."[72]

In Philadelphia, the local chapter of the National Welfare Rights Organization (NWRO), founded in 1967 to fight for low-income single mothers and their children, led the charge against the housing authority's exclusionary policy. In May 1968, two weeks after attorneys filed a complaint in federal district court, Judge Alfred Luongo approved the parties' settlement, which required that officials immediately process the thirteen plaintiffs' applications for public housing "without regard to the existence of children born out of wedlock." The settlement pleased welfare rights groups, but the struggle against discriminatory policies and practices was far from over.[73] Even if they could not categorically exclude residents based on family status alone, authorities often retained discretion to apply more functional criteria in determining who was a worthy tenant. A case-by-case approach licensed intrusive inquiries into mothers' personal lives and sexual conduct, and it enabled officials to impose conditions on access to public housing just as they did other forms of public assistance.

Welfare Rights and Sexual Privacy

In the late 1960s and early 1970s, poor women of color struggled in increasingly vocal and visible ways against laws and policies that aggravated desperate living conditions for poor nonmarital families. For these mothers, marital status law became a key site for making claims to what Black feminists would, decades later, call reproductive justice: sexual freedom and bodily autonomy; the right to have children or not have children and to parent one's children without submitting to punitive state surveillance and intrusion.

Black single mothers who became welfare rights activists during this period articulated distinctive visions of political economy and sexual citizenship. They organized locally and nationally to challenge liberal policymakers and male welfare advocates who harbored paternalistic views of appropriate gender roles. Activists fought for the right to be mothers or not, to marry or cohabit or eschew romantic attachments. They demanded autonomy to make choices about birth control, abortion, and sterilization free from state interference. They opposed work requirements but supported women's right to decent employment and fair working conditions. They protested welfare rules that intruded upon their intimate relationships and dictated their personal lives. Their demands emerged from the daily indignities of trying to make ends meet in the hostile world of poverty, low-wage work, inferior access to medical care and education, and intrusive, demeaning public welfare bureaucracy.[74]

Johnnie Tillmon became one of the most visible and influential of these leaders. The daughter of Arkansas sharecroppers who had worked since childhood in backbreaking low-wage jobs, Tillmon moved to California from Little Rock with her six children after her marriage ended in 1960. She hoped that Los Angeles would provide greater opportunity, but Tillmon found only domestic and laundry work available to "unskilled" Black women. A commercial laundry worker and union steward, she also assisted fellow public housing residents to improve living conditions and mediate disputes. Severe arthritis forced Tillmon to quit her job as a shirt-line operator in 1963, and a long hospital stay compelled her to depend on public assistance to feed, clothe, and house her children.

Aghast at her sudden loss of "all dignity, privacy, and sympathy" in her new role as a public assistance recipient, Tillmon began organizing "welfare mothers" in her community. Together, they demanded adequate grants, childcare, and job training. They registered to vote, launched public education campaigns, even ran for public office.[75] By the mid-1960s, Tillmon had developed "a new model for poor women's mobilization," one that "encouraged alliances with educated middle-class people, but insisted that leadership remain in the hands of poor women."[76]

Poor women's leadership upended many of the assumptions of these educated middle-class people. Many liberals saw low marriage rates and a high incidence of divorce, desertion, and nonmarital childbearing as products of the vicious circle of poverty, curable only through the revitalization of Black men's breadwinning capacity. Female welfare rights leaders took a dimmer view of traditional marriage and male household headship. A reporter observed in 1968 that welfare activists saw marriage's "fixed rules and obligations" as a "means for domination rather than as a means for expressing love."[77] They preferred a relationship model that honored "love, . . . responsibility toward other persons, and freedom to whatever extent that responsibility allows."[78]

In opposing suitable home laws, "man in the house" rules, and midnight raids—all of which denied public assistance to mothers with nonmarital partners—AFDC recipients in the NWRO proclaimed women's freedom of self-determination in matters of family, work, sex, and reproduction. Challenges to marital supremacy therefore played an essential role in welfare rights feminists' novel brand of anti-poverty activism.

Mrs. Sylvester Smith, a thirty-four-year-old mother of four and grand-mother of one who worked full-time as a cook and waitress in Selma, Alabama, did not belong to the organized movement, but her lawsuit came closest to presenting a kindred vision of welfare rights to the

Supreme Court. Like many states, Alabama considered a man to be the "substitute father" for all the children of an AFDC recipient mother if the couple cohabited, whether or not he was the children's biological or functional father.[79] Enforcement reached deep into the intimate lives of women and men, conditioning families' receipt of aid on mothers' chastity (or the appearance thereof).[80] Store proprietors, neighbors, even clergy became targets of social workers' invasive inquiries.

Mrs. Smith's white caseworker, Jacquelyn Stancil, was a stickler for rules, according to Smith's attorney Martin Garbus, co-director of Columbia University's Center on Social Welfare Policy and Law.[81] But with Smith, Stancil met her match. Smith wrote a letter to President Lyndon Johnson in September 1966 protesting her eldest daughter Ida's loss of aid after Ida gave birth to a nonmarital child. Soon thereafter, Stancil, informed by a third party that a man was visiting Mrs. Smith on weekends, warned that she would lose AFDC benefits if she continued to see Willie Williams, a married family friend.[82]

Mrs. Smith refused to confirm or deny anything beyond a friendship with Mr. Williams. "I told [Stancil] it wasn't none of her business," Smith recalled, adding that she had every intention of "going with" whomever she wished so long as she was young enough to enjoy the company of men.[83] Smith wondered aloud why welfare officials should care about her intimate life. "As long as I'm not having no more kids for you to support, why should you bother me?"[84] Williams, who with his wife had nine children, could give Mrs. Smith no more than a few dollars per month.[85] Smith stood her ground during a deposition, citing her right against self-incrimination under the state laws that made sex outside of marriage a crime.[86]

Mrs. Smith's family could not lightly forgo even the stingy AFDC benefit of less than $30 a month. Smith had received aid intermittently since she was widowed at age twenty-three with three young children in her care. After she moved with her daughters to Selma, Smith's two youngest children stayed with their grandparents in the country while Smith worked daily shifts from 3:30 a.m. to noon for $16–20 a week.[87] Asked whether she would continue to work (doing arduous shifts for low wages, away from her family) if she received aid, Smith testified that she would rather be home with her children.[88]

Smith echoed the organized welfare rights movement, claiming the value of her work as a mother.[89] She resisted the system that forced Black women to accept little or no remuneration for their labor inside or outside the home.[90] Working for a "Negro café" may have insulated Mrs. Smith from the full force of repercussions, but stores refused her credit in retaliation for her activism and "there were many days when her children had nothing to eat."[91]

Smith's declaration of sexual independence and insistence that her personal life was nobody's business did not translate neatly or easily into legal or constitutional claims. Her lawyers argued that to condition welfare benefits upon a mother's disclosure of "her most intimate relationships" violated her rights to privacy, due process, equal protection, and freedom of association.[92] Because officials forced mothers to disprove an intimate connection with corroborating testimony, she would "have to open her relationships to neighbors, law enforcement officials, even 'grocers,' all free to spread her story throughout the community."[93] Substitute father regulations posed an impossible—and, advocates argued, unconstitutional—choice: forgo all contact with men, platonic or otherwise; expose oneself to gossip, ridicule, and indignity; or subject one's children to starvation.

In *King v. Smith*, Garbus and his allies also pointed to a growing body of commentary that "called into serious question" the "right (or the duty) of the state to prohibit 'immoral' conduct which damages no other ascertainable public interest."[94] Civil libertarians hoped to constitutionalize the principle that had impelled drafters of the American Law Institute's Model Penal Code to recommend in 1962 that "all sexual practices not involving force, adult corruption of minors, or public offense" be exempt from criminal prosecution since they had no secular purpose.[95]

By 1968 skepticism about moralistic or religious justifications for regulation impelled Alabama to rely instead on rationales such as fairness and fiscal responsibility. The state said the substitute father rule promoted parity for marital families: husbands automatically assumed legal responsibility for supporting children. Moreover, they argued, (white) taxpayers would withdraw their support from AFDC if it promoted "illegitimacy." Alabama's brief insisted the state was "not urging a morality crusade": "Just because cohabitation out of wedlock may also carry with it a theological connotation of 'sin' and by law be 'illegal,'" the state should not be "accused of making moral judgments."[96]

Recent constitutional decisions supported civil libertarians' efforts to banish moralistic justifications. Garbus's brief quoted scholars who found in *Griswold* an emerging privacy right begging for elaboration and read *Loving* to require "a freedom to begin relationships that may lead to marriage."[97] The welfare rights strategist Ed Sparer included the "right to choose one's own standards of morality" alongside the "right to privacy" in his "tentative bill of rights for welfare recipients," published in 1965.[98] The law professor Norman Dorsen and his protégé David Rudovsky wrote in 1967 that *Griswold* could support "a broad challenge to regulations of sexual conduct, including all prohibitions on private sexual activity between consenting adults."[99] However, apart from Mrs. Smith's case, litigation strategies rarely incorporated this bolder ambition to remake marital status law in the image of sexual freedom.

Race, Poverty, and Birth Status Discrimination

A more cautious approach—taken by lawyers for Louise Levy and Minnie Brade Glona in two cases that reached the Supreme Court around the same time as *King v. Smith*—ultimately would prevail. The Levy litigation began in 1964 when a local attorney, Adolph Levy (no relation to the plaintiffs), filed a complaint in Louisiana state court seeking damages on behalf of Louise Levy's five children for their mother's wrongful death from hypertensive uremia in a New Orleans hospital. Levy argued that the statute's exclusion of illegitimate children from recovery violated their rights to equal protection and due process.[100]

Adolph Levy depicted Ms. Levy as a model mother with a fierce work ethic who attended Catholic mass regularly and inculcated moral values in her children.[101] A domestic worker who scraped together enough money to send her children to parochial school, Ms. Levy did not rely on public assistance or even on public education. Levy emphasized that her children's inability to sue would burden government coffers: "The tortfeasor need reimburse no one. The State must support the tragic victims."[102]

Ms. Levy led a conventionally respectable life despite her poverty and unmarried status—she functioned no differently from a "legitimate" mother, lawyers insisted. Unlike Mrs. Smith, she asserted no right to sexual liberty or privacy and made no claims upon public funds. The case did not concern "whether parents who may be morally blameful may recover." Rather, "the sins of the parents are being visited upon the children who had absolutely nothing to do with their status," Attorney Levy wrote.[103] Such biblical allusions were an age-old refrain: they echoed the treatise-writer Timothy Walker, who had written in 1833: "How cruel and unreasonable the law, which would visit the sins of the parents upon the unoffending offspring of their unlawful intercourse."[104]

Recognizing that his clients' case would benefit from greater expertise in constitutional law, Levy requested assistance from the ACLU. Norman Dorsen and his team from New York University's law school took over the case before the U.S. Supreme Court, and Harry Krause wrote an amicus brief for the NAACP Legal Defense Fund.

Dorsen and Krause came to the *Levy* litigation from different vantage points. Dorsen had worked on the Army-McCarthy hearings on allegations of Communist infiltration in the federal government and the military, a "formative" experience that "sensitized [him] to issues of fairness in hearings and other proceedings and the drastic harm that the government can do to free expression."[105] Dorsen went on to clerk for the Supreme Court justice John Marshall Harlan II and became director of the Hays Program in Civil Liberties at New York University (NYU) in 1961. He had in common with Krause a rewarding family life: Dorsen met Harriette Koffler in September 1965 and they were married by Thanksgiving; Harriette was active in liberal political causes and, after a stint raising their three young daughters, she eventually became managing partner at a law firm.[106]

Dorsen immersed himself in battles for constitutional rights and against public aid to parochial schools and racial segregation in housing and education.[107] His writing placed Dorsen on the cutting edge of sexual privacy and liberty, and the welfare expert Elizabeth Wickenden included him in a series of meetings that formulated the welfare rights movement's legal strategy.[108] In 1966 Dorsen observed that indigent Americans suffered civil liberties deprivations that would be "regarded as outrageous" in other circumstances.[109]

Dorsen challenged state requirements that conditioned welfare benefits on adults' relinquishment of privacy and sexual freedom, whereas Krause (as noted in chapter 1) drew attention to "the standpoint of the child" and prized the establishment of paternity to provide private sources of support. Nevertheless, Dorsen and Krause shared similar instincts about how to approach the *Levy* litigation. The law's racially disparate impact troubled both men and recalled Louisiana's infamous 1960 purge from the welfare rolls of Black families with nonmarital children. The ACLU attorney Mel Wulf had written then what he believed was the "first memorandum on the unconstitutionality of differential treatment of children born out of wedlock," which anticipated the *Levy* plaintiffs' arguments.[110] Everyone understood Louisiana's welfare purge as "a punitive step to deter … Negro citizens from pursuing their goal of equality."[111] Even where legislators did not advertise their intent, however, racially discriminatory purpose could be "inferred" from a statute's effects.[112]

Leroy Clark—a Black civil rights lawyer concerned with the intersection of racial and economic justice and the LDF's lead in Barbara Jean Cager's case—asked Krause to write an amicus brief about birth status discrimination's "profound impact on the Negro community."[113] Higher rates of nonmarital childbearing and disparities in the availability of adoption meant that more than 95 percent of children excluded from wrongful death recovery in Louisiana were Black, so the exclusion served as "a euphemism for discrimination against Negroes."[114] These arguments echoed those made in contemporaneous school segregation, housing discrimination, and voting rights cases, where advocates challenged supposedly neutral policies as proxies for discrimination based on race.

Racial discrimination provided an analog as well as an independent basis for finding birth status distinctions unconstitutional. Drawing a parallel to *Brown v. Board of Education*, Wulf argued in his 1960 memo that "any differential treatment to which out-of-wedlock children are subjected is invidious and likely unconstitutional."[115] Both equal protection and due process required that the relationship between a law's objective and the means employed to achieve it must at least be reasonable.

Notably, Wulf's memorandum did not deny that withholding public assistance might possibly deter promiscuity. Nonetheless, it was "unreasonable to attempt to improve a home's moral climate by starving its occupants to death."[116] Need, not status, was the appropriate criterion by which to determine welfare eligibility.

Powerful arguments about sexual freedom and privacy surfaced in *Cager*, animated Garbus's brief in *King v. Smith*, and suffused Dorsen and Rudovsky's other writings. Hardly a trace of these claims appeared in the *Levy* litigation.[117] Instead, plaintiffs spotlighted the punishment of innocent children for their parents' wrongful conduct "on the basis of a condition of birth and a status over which [children] had no control and are powerless to correct."[118] Legal disadvantages compounded the "psychic catastrophe" of illegitimacy that Krause cannily compared to the dignitary and material injuries suffered by Black children in segregated schools and recognized by the Court in *Brown*.[119]

The Levys' allies rejected the notion that the denial of wrongful death recovery to children would deter nonmarital childbearing. But with caution characteristic of the civil rights litigators who chose sympathetic plaintiffs and avoided risky arguments, they did not challenge the state interest in promoting marriage or discouraging illicit sex. Sylvia Law, then a law student and later a leading feminist legal scholar, summed up the strategy: "We have not questioned the value of family (legitimate) system. We have shown that the discrimination here is *wholly ineffectual* in deterring illegitimacy or securing legitimate families."[120]

The Levys' attorneys carefully distinguished their case from another, brought by Minnie Brade Glona, which challenged *mothers'* inability to recover for the wrongful death of their illegitimate children under state law. Glona's teenage son, Billy, had died in an automobile accident in Louisiana in 1964. Ms. Glona enjoyed nothing comparable to the Levy children's amicus support from prominent civil rights organizations, nor did she receive counsel from elite attorneys and scholars, and a federal appeals court had decided against her in a dismissive ruling.[121]

State officials denied that they sought to punish Black or nonmarital children or even to discriminate against immoral sexual behavior. In *Levy*, Louisiana rationalized the wrongful death statute's "withholding of prestige and honor" from nonmarital families as necessary to preserve "marriage and the family" and deter nonmarital childbearing.[122] In *Smith*, the head of the Alabama welfare department, Ruben King, declared, "If a man wants to play then let him pay, and if he has the pleasures of a husband, then he ought to have the responsibilities of a husband. . . . [T]he mother has a choice in this situation to give up her pleasures or to act like a woman ought to act and continue to receive aid."[123] What about the children? asked Garbus. To that King had no answer.

Advocates presented their clients' claims differently, as these cases show, but the response from courts in the birth status cases was largely consistent. Nowhere did judges mention advocates' arguments about race, sexual privacy, or freedom of association, nor did they suggest that states could not rightfully promote marriage and formal family relationships. In *Levy* and *Glona*, Justice William O. Douglas wrote short opinions criticized for their enigmatic treatment of the constitutional issues at stake. In *Levy*, Douglas questioned why "tortfeasors go free merely because the child is illegitimate" and suggested that the "intimate familial relationship between a child and his own mother" implicated a "basic civil right."[124]

Douglas concluded:

Legitimacy or illegitimacy of birth has no relation to the nature of the wrong allegedly inflicted on the mother. These children, though illegitimate, were dependent upon her; she cared for them and nurtured them; they were indeed hers in the biological and in the spiritual sense; in her death they suffered wrong in the sense that any dependent would.[125]

Douglas quoted more Shakespeare than precedent in *Levy* and his opinion did little to clarify how courts should evaluate laws that distinguished between children based on birth status.

Douglas's opinion in Minnie Brade Glona's case was less florid but equally cryptic. *Glona* differed from *Levy*, "where by mere accident of birth the innocent, although illegitimate child was made a 'nonperson.'" As his clerk Charles H. Wilson, Jr., told Chief Justice Warren, if the state wanted to deter illicit sex, then it made more sense to exclude the parent from recovery. Wilson nevertheless found this rationale "unpersuasive," as did a majority of the Court. Douglas wrote that "it would, indeed, be farfetched to assume that women have illegitimate children so that they can be compensated in damages for their death."[126] This sentence questioning the statute's rationality—the relationship between means and ends—became the most-cited part of *Glona*. The absence of doctrinal analysis prompted even sympathetic commentators to accuse Douglas of using "brute force" to achieve the result.[127]

In *King v. Smith*, neither the district court nor the Supreme Court addressed Mrs. Smith's arguments about sexual privacy, equality, and freedom of association. A three-judge panel that included Frank M. Johnson, Jr., and Virgil Pittman, both friends of civil rights, acknowledged the Alabama law's discriminatory purpose and effect in a footnote but did not base its constitutional equal protection ruling on race.[128] Nor did the court question the state's prerogative to discourage illicit sex. Pittman privately thought "unrestricted aid [did] create a climate favorable to promiscuousness."[129] The court found the substitute father rule "irrational" and "unreasonable" because "the punishment . . . is against *needy children*" rather than the adults engaging in immoral conduct. Alabama could instead call nonmarital fathers to account through state paternity, support, and desertion statutes.[130]

The Supreme Court adopted a similarly child-focused, race-blind approach in the case but dodged the constitutional questions. Warren wrote for a unanimous Court that Congress had "determined that immorality and illegitimacy should be dealt with through rehabilitative measures rather than measures that punish dependent children, and that protection of such children is the paramount goal of AFDC."[131] Warren underscored that Alabama remained free to restrain "illicit sexual behavior and illegitimacy . . . by other means, subject to constitutional limitations" that he did not specify.[132] A victory for welfare rights advocates, *King v. Smith* was hardly a ringing endorsement of Mrs. Smith's right to sexual and economic autonomy, and it established no constitutional rights.[133]

Justice Douglas's concurring opinion in *Smith* came closer to questioning whether punishing or deterring adults' sexual relationships was a proper aim of government. He found Alabama's regulation punishing children for their mothers' "sin" constitutionally infirm, and he placed "sin" in quotation marks throughout his opinion. For Douglas, "the immorality of the mother has no rational connection with the needs of her children."[134]

Critics of the majority's rulings in *Levy* and *Glona* perceived them as a direct threat to states' traditional prerogative to regulate family relationships and promote marriage. Justice Harlan's vehement dissent maintained that to privilege claimants based on marital status was perfectly constitutional.[135] An attorney in Louisiana, Donald E. Walter, wrote to Douglas that *Levy* and *Glona* had "shaken my faith in constitutional government as no other such decision has." Walter, who later became a federal judge, warned of the downfall of American civilization, evoking "some future generation . . . enter[ing] the crumbled remains (possibly charred and gutted)" of the Supreme Court to find the proverbial writing on the wall.[136]

Not all reactions from conservatives were negative. The anti-abortion activist and law professor Robert Byrn saw promise in *Levy*.[137] Douglas "started from the premise that illegitimate children are not 'nonpersons.' They are humans, live and have their being." To Byrn, "unborn children too" were " 'persons' within the meaning of the Equal Protection Clause," "possessed of a right to life which is not only sacred and inalienable, but also superior to his parents' rights to practice their religion and to be free of emotional and financial hardship."[138]

Civil libertarians found the decisions hopeful and inspiring. David Rudovsky and John "Chip" Gray, Dorsen's collaborators, interpreted *Levy* as applying strict scrutiny to birth status classifications and read *Glona* to mean that discrimination against unmarried parents, too, should be constitutionally suspect. Freed from the constraints of litigation, Gray and Rudovsky directly challenged the legal primacy of marriage. The state interest in deterring "illegitimacy," they wrote, boiled down to an interest in "formal marriages as such" that should be reexamined "in light of developing concepts of individual freedom and morality." But many, including Harry Krause, continued to question the civil libertarians' argument that the "immoral conduct" of nonmarital childbearing "damage[d] no other public interest."[139] In 1969 it remained to be seen who would prevail in struggles for constitutional rights to basic subsistence and to nonmarital sexual and family relationships.

The Dual System of Welfare Law

Expansive interpretations of sexual privacy and liberty informed *King v. Smith*, and Krause's concern for innocent children animated *Levy*. *Jefferson v. Hackney* perhaps best translated Jacobus tenBroek's critique of the "dual system" of social welfare provision into litigation strategy. In 1969, with the help of legal aid lawyers in Dallas and San Antonio, AFDC recipients filed suit opposing Texas's limitation of welfare grants to only 50 percent of what the state believed was required to meet recipients' needs. By contrast, Texas provided recipients of other forms of public assistance—aid to the aged, blind, and disabled—with nearly 100 percent of the state's standard of need (albeit only a fraction of what the federal government estimated was necessary to sustain a family).[140] The state justified the discrepancy by saying that AFDC recipients, unlike elderly and disabled beneficiaries, could rely on support from relatives or find employment themselves.[141]

Welfare rights strategists considered *Jefferson* their strongest case for arguing that inadequate AFDC provision discriminated against people of color.[142] In Texas, nearly 90 percent of AFDC beneficiaries were Black or Mexican American, and most were young mothers and nonmarital children. In contrast, other public assistance programs served predominantly white, Anglo, elderly citizens.[143]

The Dallas plaintiffs included the community organizer and welfare rights activist Ruth Jefferson, a divorced mother of five, and Emma Gipson, a single mother of three, both of whom were Black. The Texas suit also included Mexican American plaintiffs such as Jose Apolinar Vasquez, a migrant farmworker and father of eight disabled by an automobile accident, whose wife's medical condition prevented her from earning enough for the family's survival. In San Antonio, lawyers selected Maria Davila, "a pretty and sweet but determined" mother of three, over the local welfare rights leader Jo Ann Gutierrez as their first named plaintiff.[144]

Testimony at trial emphasized that "this group of recipients exerts little political power and is extremely unpopular vis-à-vis the other categories of recipients." The *Jefferson* plaintiffs highlighted family status discrimination against AFDC recipients who do "not conform to society's mores," in contrast to elderly white recipients perceived to have "earned" their benefits. They called Texas a "prime and vigorous perpetrator" of racially motivated attempts to punish nonmarital births through criminalization, denial of benefits, suitable home laws, and substitute father regulations.[145]

The plaintiffs' statutory claims enjoyed partial success in the lower courts but by the time the case reached the Supreme Court their path was strewn with legal obstacles.[146] States continued to rein in welfare spending amid a political backlash. In *Dandridge v. Williams* (1970), welfare rights advocates attacked Maryland's "family maximum," which capped benefits per household regardless of how many children lived there.[147] *Dandridge* rejected once and for all the centerpiece of welfare rights litigation, a constitutional right to subsistence. States could allocate scarce resources as they saw fit, the Court said.[148] Nevertheless, a footnote in *Dandridge* left the door open a crack—to challenge a regulation "infected with a racially discriminatory purpose or effect such as to make it inherently suspect."[149]

Subsequent cases emphasized the racially disparate impact of policies that discriminated based on family status. In *New Jersey Welfare Rights Organization v. Cahill*, plaintiffs challenged a New Jersey law that reserved benefits under the state's Aid to Families of the Working Poor (AFWP) program for households composed of "ceremonially married parents living with their natural or adopted children." The AFWP program replaced two programs that assisted "working poor" families regardless of marital status and was part of a package of welfare cuts enacted in 1971.

Several strands of constitutional advocacy converged in *Cahill*. Welfare rights lawyers argued that excluding nonmarital families denied equal protection to illegitimate children in violation of *Levy* and to "unwed parents" in violation of *Glona*. Like the *Jefferson* plaintiffs they highlighted race-based disparate impact.[150] At trial, several witnesses testified that Black couples were more likely to live together, unmarried, with their children. Leontine Young, a social worker, the director of Newark's Child Service Association, and author of the influential book *Out of Wedlock* (1954), opined that "ongoing family life" was "more important than . . . the ceremonial legality of the marriage itself."[151] Admittedly, she said, it was not clear "how often you find one without the other," but there was "no question" that in poor, "disorganized" families, "legal marriage . . . becomes no insurance of stability or continuity."[152] The presence of two parents, more than formal marital status, accurately predicted a household's well-being, Young said.[153]

As Young's ambivalent testimony suggests, the *Cahill* plaintiffs mounted only a limited challenge to marital supremacy. They did not question the AFWP's requirement that two parents be living in the household to qualify. And their lawyers did not argue that sexual privacy or liberty demanded that unmarried cohabitants be treated like married couples. Nor did the plaintiffs themselves assert a right to cohabit.[154] *Cahill* focused on barriers to achieving the ideal: a stable, married, two-parent household headed by a breadwinning husband/father.[155] Cutting aid to the "working poor" would only make staying together economically irrational, since a single mother living with her children and no partner could receive more aid under AFDC.[156] The *Cahill* plaintiffs' position echoed Krause's emphasis on the importance of father-child relationships and the irrelevance of formal marital status more than the systemic critiques of tenBroek or the civil libertarian analyses of Garbus and Dorsen. *Jefferson* and *Cahill* reached a Supreme Court transformed by Nixon appointees—a Court that was closing, not opening, doors to expansive constitutional claims.

Innocent Children

By 1972, a constitutional jurisprudence of "illegitimacy" had crystallized. Where plaintiffs prevailed, they did so on the ground that birth status discrimination burdened innocent children for their parents' transgressions. The Court rejected or ignored arguments about disparate impact based on race and poverty.[157] States retained the prerogative to discourage illicit sex and to promote marriage among adults. Now that the law forbade the punishment of blameless children, the state often invaded parents' privacy in the name of protecting children's well-being as well as public resources.

The Supreme Court's decision in *Weber v. Aetna Casualty* (1972) illustrates this consolidation. Like the Court's previous birth status cases, *Weber* involved a Black family in Louisiana. Willie Mae Weber lived with Henry Clyde Stokes for three years. She bore two of Stokes's children and often cared for his four "legitimate" children while he was on the road as a truck driver.[158] After Stokes died in a job-related accident, his legitimate children reached a workers' compensation settlement that left nothing for his illegitimate children, Letha Marie and Joseph. Ms. Weber's appeal challenged their exclusion from the statutory definition of "child." The Louisiana Supreme Court denied her claims.[159]

Weber reached the U.S. Supreme Court at a time of uncertainty for opponents of birth status discrimination. The year before, in *Labine v. Vincent*, a 5–4 majority had confirmed states' prerogative to privilege marriage in inheritance laws. The majority analogized nonmarital children to "concubines" and distinguished marital relationships ("socially sanctioned, legally recognized") from nonmarital relationships ("illicit and beyond the recognition of the law").[160] In dissent, an indignant Justice Brennan assailed "the untenable and discredited moral prejudice of bygone centuries which vindictively punished not only the illegitimate's parents, but also the hapless, and innocent, children."[161]

The Court also had dodged advocates' arguments that laws burdening the poor violated equal protection. Justice Douglas thought that the equal protection clause prevented Connecticut from denying a divorce to Gladys Boddie because she could not afford the $50 filing fee. But the Court's 1971 decision in Ms. Boddie's favor rested on narrower grounds: the state's "monopolization" of legal dissolution, given "the basic position of the marriage relationship in this society's hierarchy of values," made the fee an affront to due process. *Boddie* disclaimed any implications for indigent parties' access to the courts more generally. And it announced no fundamental right to divorce—or not to marry in the first place.[162]

Then the Court's composition shifted. Nixon appointees Lewis F. Powell, Jr., a conservative Democrat from Virginia, and William H. Rehnquist, a conservative Republican from Arizona, replaced Black and Harlan. Powell, a soft-spoken and gentlemanly corporate lawyer, had authored a confidential memorandum in 1971 for the U.S. Chamber of Commerce that historians later called a neoliberal "call to arms" and a blueprint for the business wing of the conservative legal movement.[163] Powell soon became known for his position at the heart of a Court moving steadily to the right.

Weber, one of Powell's first opinions, solidified the child-focused account of birth status discrimination's harm.[164] Powell assigned the case to his clerk J. Harvie Wilkinson III, the son of close family friends. Powell trimmed some of Wilkinson's most florid prose from his initial draft but retained much of its substance.[165] *Weber*'s closing paragraphs would be quoted time and again:

The status of illegitimacy has expressed through the ages society's condemnation of irresponsible liaisons beyond the bonds of marriage. But visiting this condemnation on the head of an infant is illogical and unjust. Moreover, imposing disabilities on the illegitimate child is contrary to the basic concept of our system that legal burdens should bear some relationship to individual responsibility or wrongdoing. Obviously, no child is responsible for his birth and penalizing the illegitimate child is an ineffectual—as well as an unjust—way of deterring the parent. Courts are powerless to prevent the social opprobrium suffered by these hapless children, but the Equal Protection Clause does enable us to strike down discriminatory laws relating to status of birth where—as in this case—the classification is justified by no legitimate state interest, compelling or otherwise.[166]

Ironically, race virtually disappeared from the first birth status case to be argued by a Black attorney, not by his choice. Vanue Lacour, one of a handful of Black lawyers practicing in Louisiana and an experienced civil rights litigator, requested from the ACLU an amicus brief that would emphasize racial discrimination. But the group rejected Lacour's suggested angle.[167] Arguments about innocent children unjustly punished had worked in *Levy* and in *King v. Smith*, whereas disparate impact claims had yet to land.

Powell's reaction to race-based arguments in *Jefferson*, argued the same week, suggests he would not have been receptive. Clerk Hamilton P. Fox III felt sympathy for the plaintiffs but viewed disparate impact as a slippery slope toward requiring state officials to "take into account racial balance in every situation." Racial impact mattered, Fox believed, only to "show motivation and purpose," and he saw no evidence of intent. Discrepancies between AFDC and other public assistance grants had a rational basis: unlike the aged and disabled, AFDC recipients might work and reduce their "dependency" on public funds. Fox found this logic neither "intelligent" nor "humane," but he "reluctant[ly]" rejected plaintiffs' constitutional claims. Powell agreed.[168]

Justice Rehnquist's majority opinion in *Jefferson* dismissed the plaintiffs' evidence as nothing more than a "naked statistical argument" devoid of any showing of "racial or ethnic prejudice."[169] In dissent, Justice Thurgood Marshall focused mainly on the plaintiffs' statutory claims but protested the majority's finding that "the fact that AFDC is politically unpopular" and "AFDC recipients are disfavored by the State and its citizens, have nothing whatsoever to do with the racial makeup of the program."[170]

Following other defeats, the Court's 5–4 decision in *Jefferson* effectively ended poverty lawyers' attempt to constitutionalize welfare rights. A more conservative Court now saw racial and economic impact as insufficient evidence of an equal protection violation.

After *Jefferson*, plaintiffs had to prove *intentional* racial discrimination by state officials to prevail. Frank P. Samford III thought he just might be able to find that intent in Alabama. Samford, the scion of a prominent white Birmingham family, seemed an unlikely crusader for racial justice. Samford's grandfather, Frank, Sr., who was himself the grandson of a former Alabama governor, presided over Alabama's largest insurance company, strenuously opposed the New Deal, and helped "form the vanguard of Dixiecrat revolt against the national Democratic Party's racial and economic liberalism."[171] Frank III followed his father to Yale College but pursued a different path. After receiving a law degree from the University of Alabama he ran a legal aid clinic there and earned a master's degree at Harvard.[172]

In 1971 Samford and his legal aid colleagues filed a federal lawsuit on behalf of Annie Lee Whitfield and other welfare recipients, challenging the inadequacy of benefits.[173] Whitfield's lawyers relied mostly on statutory arguments and, like the Texas plaintiffs in *Jefferson*, presented (only) statistical evidence of racially disparate impact. However, after the Supreme Court "conclusively shot down" those claims in *Jefferson*, Samford saw proof of discriminatory intent as the only path forward for his clients.

Samford understood the tough battle ahead but two circumstances gave him hope. The first was the notorious racism of his adversary Ruben King, an ally of the segregationist governor George Wallace and head of Alabama's welfare department, who had instituted the substitute father rule challenged in *King v. Smith* (1968). Second, having Judge Frank M. Johnson, Jr., champion of civil rights and Wallace's nemesis, on the panel assured Samford of one relatively sympathetic ear.[174] In August 1973, the district court dismissed the *Whitfield* plaintiffs' statutory and due process claims but granted their request to present evidence of racially discriminatory purpose.[175]

Samford's ambitious strategy in *Whitfield* relied heavily on Alabama's history of racial oppression. He underscored the close correlation between the climb in nonmarital Black families' receipt of AFDC and the transfer of revenue, at AFDC's expense, to the majority-white old age assistance program. Of course, this was the kind of evidence the Court had found insufficient in *Jefferson*. As the ACLU legal director Mel Wulf noted in 1973, to prove "conscious racial discrimination" without relying on "inferen[ces] from statistics" would not be easy. "We surely are not going to get confessions from the Alabama officials that their purpose in reducing ADC was to screw black mothers and kids." Wulf vetoed Samford's request for financial assistance from the ACLU. "In better days, when we had a Supreme Court we could trust . . . I would not hesitate a minute," he wrote.[176]

The state's welfare chief, Ruben King, provided Samford with the direct evidence of intent he needed. Since the 1950s, Alabama legislators had tried to bar mothers of nonmarital children from aid to dependent children, making "clear that it was not illicit sexual activity in general that bothered them but Negro illegitimacy." Stymied by opposition from HEW, state officials turned to the "substitute parent" rule in 1964, in a transparent façade of racial neutrality that "could scarcely have [been] more calculated to affect black people."[177] King's testimony revealed that he had commissioned twice-yearly reports on the racial composition of AFDC, ostensibly to dispel the public impression that welfare recipients were almost entirely Black nonmarital families.[178] Increasing AFDC payments was politically impossible, King said, especially at the expense of old age insurance.[179]

Samford's strategy succeeded at first. The three-judge panel agreed that the stark disparities between AFDC and old age assistance were "racially discriminatory in both purpose and effect" and gave the state sixty days to eliminate the disparities or present a detailed plan to do so.[180] State officials insisted that changes in how the federal government funded Social Security—with more federal dollars funding old age benefits—immunized Alabama against charges of racial discrimination. Samford objected that large disparities remained. The new head of Alabama's Department of Pensions and Security, Julia Oliver, might harbor no racial prejudice at all, but "the effects of racial discrimination have been carried over into the present."[181]

Johnson's chambers considered seriously a ruling for the plaintiffs, but the panel ultimately decided in Alabama's favor. "In dollars," the judges acknowledged, "the state treats the OA beneficiary much better than the AFDC beneficiary." But the Supreme Court had held in *Jefferson* that such a disparity "is not by itself unconstitutional."[182] Determined, Samford appealed to the Supreme Court. Clerk Richard Meserve wrote to Justice Blackmun that even though the racial discrepancies remained "suspicious" he saw "little purpose in the Court wading through the facts."[183] The Court had only shifted further rightward since *Jefferson*, and its summary affirmance in *Whitfield* confirmed that a lingering history of racial discrimination could not taint a state's present-day decisions.[184]

The plaintiffs in *New Jersey Welfare Rights Organization v. Cahill* fared better, but their reception in the courts only affirmed the triumph of a colorblind constitutional interpretation of birth status discrimination as a harm perpetrated against blameless children. The federal district court rejected even the plaintiffs' limited critique of marital supremacy. None of the Supreme Court's precedents questioned states' interests in "preventing illegitimacy," "protecting legitimate family relationships," and "preserv[ing] and strengthen[ing] traditional family life." And the plaintiffs had failed to prove that the policy change hurt Black families more than white.[185]

On appeal to the Supreme Court, *Cahill* landed on the desk of Carol Bruch, clerk to Justice Douglas and the Court's "first single parent."[186] The granddaughter of a Nobel laureate and the daughter of scientists, Bruch had graduated from college at eighteen and married her boyfriend six days later. They had two children together; when the younger child started kindergarten, Bruch enrolled in law school at the University of California, Berkeley. Shortly after she graduated first in her class in 1972, Bruch and her husband divorced. Months later, she became the fourth woman ever to clerk for the Court.[187]

With the race discrimination claim cast aside, all that remained for the Court to decide was whether the AFWP's marriage requirement "discriminat[ed] against the illegitimate children in these families and their unmarried parents."[188] Skeptical of the plaintiff John Wilson's claim that he could not locate his wife to obtain a divorce, Bruch nevertheless recommended that the Court hear the case. In the end, the justices felt no need to call for briefs or oral arguments. A short per curiam opinion in *Cahill* confirmed that the constitutional problem with birth status discrimination concerned neither infringements of adults' freedom nor disparate racial impact, but merely the "illogical and unjust" punishment of innocent children.[189]

This interpretation of illegitimacy's harm to blameless children allowed an evolving and often divided Court to unite around a humanitarian rationale that preserved considerable latitude for states to regulate sex and family life. It obviated any need to consider the constitutional implications of laws that disproportionately affected racial minorities or the poor or to entertain seriously adults' claims of racial and economic justice or sexual freedom. Scrutiny of the relationship between means and ends rather than the government's objectives enabled courts to avoid questioning state prerogatives to encourage formal marriage and deter illicit sex or nonmarital childbearing.

The Court's approach appeared to align with public opinion. A survey conducted by Harry Krause in 1970 found respondents overwhelmingly favored the removal of legal disadvantages that burdened children. In contrast, nearly 70 percent of interviewees in another poll taken in 1974 disagreed with the statement that "it should be legal for adults to have children without getting married," and more than 60 percent disapproved of single women having children.[190]

This child-centered theory of illegitimacy penalties' harm vanquished some discriminatory laws. In so doing, it severed the most obvious links between birth status law and overt white supremacy—first, by removing some of the most egregious birth status discriminations in the name of blameless Black children; and second, by insisting that laws targeting single parents and nonmarital children were race-neutral unless advocates could provide smoking-gun evidence of racially discriminatory intent. Such evidence was increasingly difficult to come by as undisguised racial animus became less acceptable.

The emphasis on rooting out harm to innocent children also underwrote decisions that sanctioned state intrusions into the homes of poor women of color that middle-class marital families would never suffer.[191] In *Wyman v. James*, for instance, Barbara James, a welfare rights activist and the mother of a two-year-old son, Maurice, brought a class action lawsuit against New York's welfare department on behalf of parents compelled to submit to "home visits." Mrs. James and several other Black single mothers described how caseworkers knocked on their doors, often unannounced; asked "personal questions" in front of their children or guests; and caused them acute "embarrass[ment] and resent[ment]," not to mention "fear" of losing benefits.[192] Mrs. James's attorneys said these visits violated parents' constitutional rights to privacy and freedom from unreasonable searches and seizures. Receipt of public assistance, they contended, should not force poor parents to endure intrusions into the "sanctity of the home" guaranteed to the nonindigent.[193]

In addition to loss of aid, the stakes of home visits included children's possible removal from parental custody.[194] Unlike Barbara Jean Cager and her compatriots in Maryland, officials had not arrested Mrs. James or threatened her with incarceration. But in cases involving nonpoor, marital families, the Supreme Court had recognized that "forfeiture of one's own child," while not a "criminal proceeding," was "quasi-punitive" and therefore required due process protections.[195] Accordingly, a majority of the three-judge district court agreed that a warrantless entry by caseworkers violated the Fourth Amendment. The court acknowledged a state interest in preventing child abuse or neglect but concluded that "all families should ... be treated alike."[196] As Lois Sheinfeld wrote in an amicus brief, if all families received regular, "warrantless invasions" from government officials to "dictate the conditions of private life" on pain of losing their children, the "public outcry ... would surely reach the ears of the Gods."[197]

The Supreme Court, however, found no constitutional violation. Home visits merely were "a gentle means" of ensuring that publicly funded assistance reached only its "intended and proper objects." Parents need not consent to a visit; if they turned a caseworker away, "aid then never begins, or merely ceases." And Justice Blackmun cited children's welfare as well as the state's and taxpayers' fiscal interests. He wrote that "what the mother claims as her rights" should not supersede the "paramount needs of the dependent child." Even if a parent felt pressure to acquiesce to home inspection, she sacrificed her privacy to a noble cause: "There is no more worthy object of the public's concern." Blackmun borrowed the state's characterization of Mrs. James as "belligerent" and "evasive," and he noted that "all was not always well with infant Maurice (skull fracture, a dent in the head, a possible rat bite)."

Nowhere did Blackmun—or dissenting Justice Douglas—directly acknowledge child removal as a potential consequence of a home visit. "The caseworker is not a sleuth," wrote Blackmun, "but rather, we trust, is a friend to one in need."[198] Many mothers who found state financial assistance conditioned upon government inspection of their homes and intimate relationships begged to differ. States no longer could punish children for their parents' conduct, but officials often used children's welfare as a justification for laws and policies that invaded mothers' privacy and threatened their families' integrity.

Officials less often enforced criminal laws against nonmarital childbearing, but they remained free to compel mothers' cooperation in pursuing biological fathers for child support and to investigate poor mothers for parental unfitness as well as misuse of public funds.[199] Indeed, in 1974 the Child Support Enforcement Act and the Child Abuse Prevention and Treatment Act created federal mandates for both policies. The shift in child welfare was dramatic: in 1967, when Maryland authorities arrested Barbara Jean Cager, around 10,000 cases of child abuse and neglect were reported to authorities nationwide. By 1975, the number had climbed to 300,000, and federal law now required that each report trigger an investigation that could result in a child's removal.[200]

By 1973, the child-focused argument against birth status discrimination had prevailed in the Supreme Court, softening the most overtly hostile and stigmatizing laws that penalized blameless children while leaving intact the legal primacy of marriage. The constitutional law of the late 1960s and early 1970s vindicated Harry Krause and largely rejected the more ambitious theories offered by Jacobus tenBroek, Johnnie Tillmon, and Barbara James. The Supreme Court's failure to recognize a constitutional right to subsistence left poor Americans dependent on the whims of legislators, who increasingly chose stingier provision in the name of fiscal prudence and personal responsibility.

The Court's cramped interpretation of welfare rights—the product of conservative judicial appointments and a growing political backlash against the Warren Court and Great Society—came as activists deepened their critique of the welfare system. Tillmon translated the experience of Mrs. Smith and thousands like her through an evocative metaphor: "Welfare is like a super-sexist marriage," Tillmon wrote in a *Ms.* article in 1972. "You trade in a man for The Man. But you can't divorce him if he treats you bad." The Man could "cut you off anytime he wants" but "in that case, he keeps the kids." "In an ordinary marriage," Tillmon wrote, "sex is supposed to be for your husband. On A.F.D.C., you're not supposed to have any sex at all. You give up control of your own body" in exchange for a meager welfare check.

Tillmon's critique exposed a *non*marital bargain: just as marriage featured an exchange of a husband's financial support for a wife's services, an unmarried mother had to endure state surveillance and forgo sexual intimacy to receive assistance. Tillmon called instead for a guaranteed minimum income for all, with "no 'categories'—men, women, children, single, married, kids, no kids—just poor people who need aid."[201] Marital status law itself, Tillmon suggested, should be abolished.

But Tillmon's feminist vision of welfare rights activism broke through just as the national movement waned, hobbled by defeats in an increasingly conservative legal and political climate. Opposition from both the left and the right killed proposals for a guaranteed minimum income premised on a breadwinner/homemaker model.[202] Feminist arguments about how sexual liberation and sex equality should transform marital status law would have to move to legal domains beyond poverty and welfare.

PART II

CHAPTER THREE

Making Marriage Safe for Equality
Coupling and Dissolution

N EARLY ALL FEMINISTS IN the late 1960s and early 1970s
agreed that sex roles within marriage—women's confine-
ment to homemaking and motherhood while men monop-
olized paid employment and politics—were a defining
feature of inequality between men and women. The marital status quo
socialized children to adopt gendered roles that disempowered women
by rendering them economically dependent upon men, feminists believed. They differed, however, on whether marriage could be saved.

Radical feminists decried marriage as a male conspiracy to dominate
women, an irredeemable institution that could never shed its oppressive
essence. Marriage, they said, must be abolished for women to achieve
true liberation. As Ti-Grace Atkinson, a dissident member of the National
Organization for Women (NOW), wrote to the feminist lawyer Mary
Eastwood in 1968, "The issue is open and shut: Marriage is incompatible
with freedom for women."[1] Atkinson's breakaway organization, The Feminists, distributed ink stamps and buttons with the slogan "Fuck Marriage,
Not Men."[2] Marriage abolitionists believed that the marital family let
government off the hook for addressing human need, drained energy
from collective action, burdened women with full responsibility for childbearing and childrearing, and fabricated demand for unnecessary consumer products: in short, marriage ensured the reproduction of capitalist
patriarchy.

Setting aside their provocative rhetoric, some of the radicals' goals for legal change resembled those of more moderate feminist organizations—for example, pensions for homemakers and compensation for wives' household labor. But mainstream feminist legal advocates generally sought reform rather than abolition. They believed that "the problem was not marriage, but, rather, '*the male supremacy and sex roles within marriage*,'" in Pat Mainardi's words.[3] Mainardi criticized the "left-lesbian" impulse to jettison marriage: "Women—and men—," she maintained, "would like love, security, companionship, respect and a long-term commitment to each other. Women rarely get much of this, in marriage or out, but we *want* it."[4]

Many feminist professionals remained ambivalent about marriage as an institution, even as they strove for happy marriages themselves. Others questioned whether marriage could ever be compatible with true equality for women. But even those who sympathized with more radical critiques often thought that "the first order of business" should be "to upgrade the wife's marriage," as the sociologist Jessie Bernard wrote in 1972.[5] The most influential feminist lawyers and legal scholars therefore sought to turn husbands and wives into spouses, and mothers and fathers into parents through law reform—not to disrupt the nuclear family as a basic unit of society. Feminist divorce reform efforts, too, focused largely on equalizing the consequences of dissolution for men and women.

Less visibly, some reformers also took aim at the exalted place of marriage in the law. By the early 1970s, constitutional developments opened new opportunities to question distinctions based on marital status. Unmarried mothers argued that they, like married mothers—and thanks to feminist efforts, married fathers—should be eligible for Social Security survivor benefits when their partners died. Unmarried women dissolving long-term cohabiting relationships sought the same equitable distribution of assets to which divorcing women laid claim. And gay and lesbian partners, unable to marry one another, pursued creative approaches to legal recognition. Some sought the legal imprimatur of marriage on their own terms, and others questioned marriage's primacy; many did both simultaneously.

The increasingly conservative political and legal environment of the 1970s limited what reformers could accomplish. Economic recession, deindustrialization, and increasing pressures on middle-class households to draw upon wives' earnings exacerbated cultural anxiety about the decline of the male-headed nuclear family.[6] Ascendant conservatives responded to the uncertainties of postindustrial life by insisting that not only countercultural permissiveness but also liberal economic policies threatened the social order.[7] Once overt white supremacy became less politically acceptable, anti-feminism and opposition to gay rights rose in its stead.[8]

Against this backdrop, advocates achieved the greatest success with reforms that replaced sex-based distinctions between spouses with sex-neutral functional standards. Less fruitful were attempts to overcome structural inequalities between men and women in and outside of marriage and after the dissolution of relationships; to blur the lines between marriage and nonmarriage; or to question the nature of marriage as a heterosexual union. Eliminating formal legal differentiations between husband and wife—the most overt symbols of male marital domination—made marriage a more appealing option for otherwise well-off women, who were best positioned to benefit from marriage. Like the reforms to birth status laws discussed in chapter 2, changes to the law of marriage blunted the severest critiques of marital status law without disturbing the fundamental fact of marriage's legal primacy.

The Quest for Equality Within Marriage

Radical movements for women's and gay liberation in the late 1960s and 1970s renounced patriarchy, heterosexuality, monogamy, and even conjugality. Some legal scholars and advocates embraced this freethinking approach as a welcome provocation, or at least a dramatic foil to make their own aspirations seem modest by comparison. But most feminist law reformers saw their mission as transformative, not destructive. Often aspiring to egalitarian partnerships in their own lives, they sought to eliminate inequalities *within* marriage.

Early sex discrimination casebooks captured this ethos. One of the first, authored by professors Herma Hill Kay, Ruth Bader Ginsburg, and Kenneth Davidson and published in 1974, reprinted parts of Sheila Cronan's polemic comparing marriage to enslavement. Kay's chapters on family law also excerpted essays such as Mainardi's "The Politics of Housework" and Judy Syfers's "I Want a Wife" on unequal divisions of domestic labor.[9] Kay described the obstacles encountered by the "unwed family" but as one reviewer put it, she seemed "most comfortable with a restructuring of traditional marriage so that it can accommodate egalitarian relationships."[10] The other leading sex discrimination casebook of the period, by Barbara Babcock, Eleanor Holmes Norton, Ann Freedman, and Susan Deller Ross, critiqued marriage and divorce law from a gender-egalitarian perspective, apparently assuming "either the desirability or the durability of the traditional nuclear family."[11]

Jessie Bernard encapsulated the modern feminist diagnosis of marriage underpinning law reform efforts.[12] In *The Future of Marriage* (1972), Bernard argued that there were "two marriages in every marital union, his and hers. And his . . . is better than hers." For husbands, there was "no better guarantor of long life, health, and happiness" than "a wife well socialized to perform the 'duties of a wife,' willing to devote her life to taking care of him." By contrast, housewives suffered from "status denigration," anxiety, depression, isolation, and deprivation of personhood. Bernard sympathized with marriage abolitionists but instead prescribed greater "role-sharing" within marriage to improve women's lot.[13]

Marriage and divorce law offered plenty of low-hanging fruit for reformers who agreed. A state-by-state analysis of marriage and divorce law spearheaded by Catherine East revealed pervasive discrimination against wives.[14] State laws mandated that husbands provide support and wives care for families. Husbands had the right to establish the family's domicile; laws forced wives to change their surnames and allowed girls to marry at a younger age than boys.[15] Federal law and policy from the tax code to social insurance programs to military benefit schemes differentiated between husbands and wives (or widows and widowers) and rewarded households containing a primary earner and a dependent homemaker.[16]

Feminist reformers embraced married women's growing labor force participation and argued that law should catch up with facts on the ground. The writer Norman Mailer's infamous remark, oft-quoted by feminists, that he would only be willing to do the dishes if his wife's work were "as valuable" as his, captured two distinct but related problems.[17] First, women faced barriers to entry and advancement in employment, especially the intellectually rewarding and financially remunerative kind. Second, the "women's work" they did perform, in and outside the home, was systematically devalued. Leading feminist family law scholars like Herma Hill Kay hoped to denaturalize "sex roles" and make women independent economic actors. The law, they said, should encourage men to do more caregiving and housework and women to pursue gainful employment and political power.[18] NOW called in 1966 for "a true partnership between the sexes" with "an equitable sharing of the responsibilities of home and children and of the economic burdens of their support."[19]

Prominent Black feminists placed themselves on the vanguard of egalitarian partnerships with men, a living rejoinder to the notion—

popularized by the Moynihan Report—that racial progress depended upon the restoration of men to their "proper" place as heads of households.[20] These women promoted a vision of marriage in which both spouses pursued careers and respected one another as equals.[21] Rejecting the male-breadwinner/female-homemaker ideal, they argued that white couples could learn from their Black counterparts.[22] Black women's high rates of labor-force participation and assertive leadership, they said, exemplified the very gender equality the women's movement now sought. Pauli Murray had long maintained, "People who blame our troubles on 'Negro matriarchy' are ignoring a source of strength in Negro women that ought to be available to white women, too."[23] Patricia Roberts Harris, a former Howard Law School dean and future Cabinet official, declared in 1971, "Black women have a life experience of equality with men to protect, and it is one to be proud of."[24]

Eleanor Holmes Norton and her husband, Edward Norton, a lawyer and government official, deliberately modeled gender-egalitarian marriage. Norton often extolled her husband's feminist attitudes (though "like millions of other Americans, [he] eschew[ed] the label . . . while observing the tenets").[25] She told the *New York Times* in 1970, "The black woman already has a rough equality which came into existence out of necessity and is now ingrained in the black lifestyle. . . . [T]hat gives the black family very much of a head start on egalitarian family life."[26] Norton urged Black couples to "pioneer in establishing new male-female relationships around two careers."[27]

This egalitarian marriage ideal occluded a more complicated reality, even for its champions. Pauli Murray, whose close family and intimate relationships were with women—by the 1960s Murray shared a life, though not a home, with Renee Barlow—had wrestled with sexuality and gender identity. Murray's firsthand experience with marriage was brief and traumatic; in 1947 Murray's article "Why Negro Girls Stay Single" described how men's "emotional immaturity" and "economic insecurity" left many college-educated Black women without suitable mates.[28]

It never was easy for married women to juggle family and work or to achieve genuine equality in tasks and roles, even for those who enjoyed advantages of salary, education, and support from relatives. Norton was pregnant with the first of two children and experiencing severe nausea when she was tapped to lead the New York City Human Rights Commission at age thirty-two. Her daughter Katherine had a developmental disability and required special care and attention. Norton's mother-in-law proved indispensable, as did the ability to hire domestic help when necessary.[29]

The law professor and ACLU lawyer Ruth Bader Ginsburg translated the egalitarian marriage ideal into a series of lawsuits that spanned the 1970s.[30] Ginsburg's own marriage seemed a paragon of equality and harmony, aided by a rare degree of economic privilege. Ginsburg's husband, Marty, a respected tax attorney, supported her career ambitions and shared in the care of household and children.[31] For couples married in 1954, as the Ginsburgs were, an equal partnership between two individuals at the top of their profession was almost unheard of. But times were changing. Wives with young children increasingly worked outside the home and the number of women pursuing careers in male-dominated occupations climbed as feminists fought to pass and enforce anti-discrimination laws in education and employment.[32]

The law of marriage loomed large when feminists catalogued legal discriminations against women at the dawn of the 1970s. Ginsburg's "grandmother brief" in *Reed v. Reed* (1971) laid the groundwork for challenging policies that favored a traditional division of marital labor. In that case, Sally Reed successfully attacked an Idaho statute that included a preference for male estate administrators, which discriminated against all women.[33] Three of the four categories of discrimination identified in the *Reed* brief implicated marriage more directly: men as "heads of households," the "role of motherhood," and employment.[34]

Ginsburg's strategy as head of the ACLU Women's Rights Project owed many debts to Pauli Murray's earlier work. In 1962, Murray recommended that advocates for women pursue litigation under the equal protection clause of the Fourteenth Amendment, an approach modeled on the NAACP Legal Defense Fund's successful campaign against racial segregation. Murray strove to assuage fears among advocates for working-class women that the proposed Equal Rights Amendment (ERA), which declared that the government could not deny "equality of rights . . . on account of sex," would eliminate hard-won protective labor laws for women. Murray therefore distinguished between "social policies which are genuinely protective of the family" and those that "unjustly discriminat[ed] against women as individuals."[35]

For Murray, "function" was the key: laws and policies should target "functional attributes," such as homemaking, parenthood, or other caregiving responsibilities, rather than sex per se. Women, Murray wrote, "seek freedom of choice: to develop their maternal and family functions primarily, or to develop all other individual capacities as fully as the male, or to develop different capacities at different stages of life." Sex-based laws that limited women's education, employment, and civic participation treated all women as primarily mothers and wives: they "disregarded individuality and relegated [all women] to an inferior status."[36]

Ginsburg's litigation realized Murray's ambition to replace sex as a category of legal classification with an individual's functional role. The law, both advocates believed, should address spouses, parents, and workers in a sex-neutral manner, based on what they did rather than who they were. Murray's analysis and advocacy in the 1960s had focused primarily on questions of economic and political participation such as employment and jury service. By the 1970s, influenced by Swedish ideas about gender equality, marriage became a key site not only for opposing male domination but also for promoting Murray's functional approach.[37]

In *Frontiero v. Richardson*, an Air Force lieutenant, Sharron Frontiero, successfully challenged a statute that automatically provided housing and other benefits to the families of military servicemen but denied them to servicewomen like Sharron because her husband, Joseph, did not depend on her for more than half his income. Ginsburg faulted the law for "penaliz[ing] married women who do not conform to the assumed general pattern" in which husbands earned more than wives and were expected to support their dependents.[38] The couple's role reversal meant that Sharron's "labor, by congressional mandate, is worth less than the labor of a similarly situated man in terms of the benefits it brings to the family unit," enforcing wives' "subordination."[39] Frontiero's Supreme Court victory in 1973 was a high-water mark: a plurality of the justices embraced strict scrutiny for sex-based classifications, and all but Rehnquist agreed that the government could not enforce traditional gender roles by providing spousal benefits for wives and not husbands.[40]

Ginsburg then challenged the denial of "mother's insurance benefits" to widowers. Paula Polatschek Wiesenfeld, a schoolteacher who earned more than her husband, died in childbirth in 1972. After her death, Stephen Wiesenfeld sought survivor benefits from the Social Security Administration, intending to reduce his work hours to care for their son, Jason. But officials told him that only women could receive the funds. Ginsburg argued the case on behalf of the Wiesenfelds as a family.[41] She emphasized Paula's role as a breadwinner whose wages earned fewer benefits for her family simply because of her sex, as well as Stephen's wish to nurture their son. By denying benefits to surviving fathers,

Ginsburg said, the government devalued women's breadwinning and men's caregiving, and it deprived children of parental care.[42]

Ginsburg anticipated that the government would defend mothers' benefits as remedial: because women earned less than men, they should receive greater protection when widowed. But far from promoting working women, Congress had fashioned the benefit under the reflexive assumption that "breadwinner was synonymous with father, child tender with mother." In 1971, an advisory committee recommended against extending the "mothers' benefit" to fathers, noting that men rarely took on "the dual role of worker and homemaker." True, many fathers would not choose to stay home with their children, Ginsburg conceded. But Congress could not use "a gender stereotype in lieu of *functional description*."[43] This substitution of "function" for sex echoed Murray's memo for the President's Commission on the Status of Women in 1962.

At the Supreme Court, *Wiesenfeld* landed on the desks of law clerks who came of age in the late 1960s. Justice Blackmun's clerk Richard Blumenthal had worked for Daniel Patrick Moynihan in the Nixon White House before law school. Blumenthal called *Wiesenfeld* "a comparatively easy case," noting that "women are more likely to be needy, even in this increasingly liberated age."[44] Blackmun, too, initially was inclined to uphold the statute.

Justice Brennan's clerk took a different view. Marsha Siegel had graduated from Radcliffe in 1967 and moved to California, where she worked as a journalist and community organizer before earning her law degree from the University of California, Berkeley. By the time she graduated in 1973, Siegel had married Stephen Berzon, and the two had an infant son. In 1975, the Berzons appeared in a *Mademoiselle* article, "Working Mothers: How They Juggle Their Lives." "You get the best of both worlds," the article's subtitle declared, "but not enough of either."[45]

More than fifteen years after Ginsburg found law firms and judges reluctant to hire "a woman, a mother, and a Jew," Berzon, who was all three, almost lost her chance to work for Justice Brennan because he refused to hire female clerks. Brennan's former clerk Stephen Barnett urged the justice to reconsider his "not only sexist . . . [but] literally unconstitutional" aversion, already discordant with his judicial opinions, and Brennan relented.[46] Berzon clerked the same year that Brennan's recently divorced daughter, Nancy, and granddaughter Connie came to live with him, so during the 1974 term the justice and his clerk often left chambers at the same time to pick up children from day care.[47]

Assigned to *Wiesenfeld*, Berzon probed the statute's legislative history, following a lead from Ginsburg's brief.[48] She discovered that the "mothers' insurance" benefits were designed primarily to aid children, not widows. Justice Brennan's opinion, drafted by Berzon, embraced both Ginsburg's sex equality and child-centered arguments. More men than women provided "primary support" to their families. "But such a gender-based generalization," Brennan wrote, "cannot suffice to justify the denigration of the efforts of women who do work and whose earnings contribute significantly to their families' support."[49] And even where a father left childrearing duties to his wife while she was alive, he might nevertheless wish to assume them after her death. "It is no less important for a child to be cared for by its sole surviving parent when that parent is male rather than female," Brennan echoed.[50]

Justice Lewis Powell was ambivalent. Like Brennan, he had just hired his first female clerk, Julia "Penny" Clark.[51] Powell agreed that the statute discriminated against female wage-earners, but privately he recoiled at the idea that fathers might forgo breadwinning to nurture children. Clark speculated that stay-at-home fathers were "a small class, no doubt"; Powell replied, "I would hope so—though the ever-increasing welfare rolls even in prosperous times suggest a high level of indolence."[52]

The statute's child-centered rationale may explain the Court's unusual unanimity in *Wiesenfeld*. "Rehnquist," Ginsburg speculated years later, "was caught by the baby."[53] Ginsburg's vision triumphed by the end of the decade. In *Califano v. Goldfarb*, a majority of the Court agreed that to provide survivor benefits to all widows of all eligible workers— but not to widowers unless they could prove they had been economically dependent on their wives—unconstitutionally reinforced traditional gendered divisions of labor.[54] Ginsburg's litigation campaign removed distinctions between husbands and wives from the law of government benefits—affirming, as a matter of formal law, the feminist model of egalitarian marriage.

The Quest for Equality Without Marriage

Less visibly, unmarried women attacked discriminatory classifications in government benefits law. Unlike Ginsburg's litigation, which was supported by the ACLU Women's Rights Project with funding from the Ford Foundation, these efforts were not part of an organized campaign. Instead, cases arose organically, often when individuals and families appeared on the doorstep of legal aid societies seeking help. Some of the lawyers who challenged family status discrimination held feminist convictions, but rarely did advocates or courts frame litigation against marital and birth status discrimination as part of a larger feminist enterprise.[55] In contrast to Ginsburg's victories, these cases mostly fizzled, and they faded into relative obscurity. But their potential impact on women and families—especially those of color—was at least as significant, and the challenge they posed to *marital*, as opposed to male, supremacy was much more profound.

Legal and constitutional developments in the early 1970s looked promising for challenges to marital status discrimination. In *Stanley v. Illinois* (1972), the Court recognized due process rights for unmarried fathers.[56] The same year, in *Eisenstadt v. Baird*, the Court struck down a Massachusetts law that prohibited the use and dissemination of contraceptives to *unmarried* individuals, extending the right to marital privacy announced in *Griswold v. Connecticut* (1965). Justice Brennan wrote: "If the right of privacy means anything, it is the right of the individual, married or single, to be free from unwarranted governmental intrusion into matters so fundamentally affecting a person as the decision whether to bear or beget a child." The contraceptive ban violated equal protection "by providing dissimilar treatment for married and unmarried persons who are similarly situated."[57] The following year, in *Roe v. Wade* (1973), the Court did not distinguish between the married and unmarried when it legalized abortion.[58]

To traditionalists, these decisions were "wrong in subverting the privileged status of marriage," in the words of the Catholic legal scholar John Noonan. Noonan, whose recommendation that the Church relax its ban on contraception had been overruled by Pope Paul VI, acknowledged the injustice of discriminating against nonmarital children. But he did not countenance equal treatment for unmarried *adults*. "To say that legal immunities and legal benefits may not depend upon marriage" was to risk losing "the most precious of social goods," Noonan warned in 1973.[59]

By then, as discussed in chapter 2, nonmarital children had won eligibility for certain federal benefits, but consequential discriminations persisted. For example, "legitimate" children took priority over "illegitimate" children in the receipt of survivor benefits following a wage-earning parent's death.[60] A Maryland case illustrated the injustice: James T. Hall died in 1969, having earned for his survivors a family payment of almost

$300 per month. Just ten months earlier, James had married Bernice, who had four children from prior relationships. James and Bernice lived together for only a few weeks after the marriage, but her children (his stepchildren) were entitled to share in the Social Security benefits. In contrast, Barbara Griffin, James's nine-year-old nonmarital child, whom he was legally obligated to support—and *did* support until his death—received no benefits because James's stepchildren exhausted the family limit.[61]

The government's rationale for preferring James's stepchildren over his daughter seemed thin. A federal district court invalidated the provision and the Supreme Court summarily affirmed.[62] The Court also overturned discrimination in the provision of disability benefits against illegitimate children born after, as opposed to before, a parent became disabled. Ramon Jimenez had lived with Elizabeth Hernandez in Chicago with their three children until Hernandez left the family in 1968, leaving Jimenez to care for five-year-old Magdalena, three-year-old Alicia, and Eugenio, an infant. Disabled since 1963, Jimenez claimed Social Security benefits for his legal wife, Filomena, and their five children, who lived in Puerto Rico. But when he applied for benefits for his nonmarital children, only the eldest, Magdalena, was eligible. This exclusion struck the legal aid attorney Jane Greengold Stevens as "blatantly unfair." The Supreme Court agreed in a 1974 decision that drew upon its earlier child-focused rulings.[63]

Two significant discriminations remained, and both looked constitutionally vulnerable. The first required illegitimate children whose paternity had not been formally established to prove financial dependence upon their father to receive benefits, although the law assumed the dependence of all formally acknowledged and marital children even if they never lived with their father or received paternal support. The second denied unmarried parents the "mothers' insurance" benefits to which Stephen Wiesenfeld won access.

Both provisions disturbed Herbert Semmel of the Center for Law and Social Policy (CLASP) in Washington. Semmel worked in the poverty law and welfare rights tradition of Jacobus tenBroek rather than that of Harry Krause, Semmel's sometime colleague at the University of Illinois. Krause saw "paternal child abandonment and illegitimacy" as the "crucial problem" driving up welfare costs, and he argued for aggressive child support enforcement measures. Semmel resisted these measures as self-defeating, given that poor families often relied on extended kin networks and most fathers of AFDC recipients could not provide adequate financial support.[64] However, both men saw discrimination against non-marital children in public benefits as a social and constitutional problem that burdened the poorest and most vulnerable.[65]

Gregory Norton, Jr., was one poignant example. Gregory's parents were unmarried high school students when he was born in 1964. Lauri Marie Brown, age fourteen, and Gregory Norton, Sr., age sixteen, lived separately with their respective parents, with Lauri's mother caring for Gregory Jr. "Being so young, and unemployed," Gregory Norton, Sr., could not afford to contribute more than a few dollars and some clothing for the newborn. He joined the military when his son was one year old and was killed in Vietnam fifteen months later at age nineteen, before he completed military benefits paperwork for his son. Gregory Jr.'s grandmother filed an application for Social Security survivor benefits on her grandson's behalf in 1969, to no avail: Gregory Jr. could not prove that he depended upon his father for financial support.[66]

Instead of the Norton case, the Court decided a companion challenge that more obviously implicated unmarried mothers. Belmira Lucas had lived in Providence with Robert Cuffee for almost twenty years, and they had two children together, Darin and Ruby. Unable to divorce her legal spouse because of his disabilities, Lucas could not prove that her relationship with Cuffee was a common law marriage under Rhode Island law.[67] Robert supported Darin and Ruby while they lived together, and they called him "Daddy." But when Belmira's legal husband, Raymond, died in 1965, Belmira did not marry Robert—perhaps out of embarrassment at having lived together unmarried, as she told the court, or perhaps because of Robert's drinking and violent behavior, which soon ended their relationship. Robert went to live with his mother in 1966, visited the children two or three times a week, and gave Ruby money from his mother and aunt when he was not working. Belmira provided most of her family's support, working for the local electric company. Darin and Ruby were ineligible for survivor benefits when Robert died in 1968 because they could not prove dependence on Robert at the time of his death.

In short, Belmira and her children lost out because she had shouldered primary breadwinning responsibility; Robert had not functioned as a father in the eyes of the law.[68] Her case should have recalled the sex discrimination in *Wiesenfeld*, where the Court ruled unconstitutional a law that deprived a child and his surviving parent of benefits because his mother rather than his father was the household's primary earner. Instead, the Court interrupted a string of plaintiff victories in birth status discrimination cases.[69] Three justices dissented, calling the law "the product of a tradition of thinking of illegitimates as less deserving persons than legitimates."[70] But neither they nor the litigants in *Lucas* acknowledged how limitations on the benefits available to nonmarital children disproportionately harmed Black women like Belmira Lucas.

Margaret Gonzales's challenge to the exclusion of unmarried mothers from survivor benefits also appeared destined for success but met with defeat. Gonzales, a cafeteria worker, had lived with Norman W. Boles in Georgetown, Texas, between 1963 and 1966. Their son, Norman J. Boles, was born in 1964. Gonzales and Boles never married, and in 1967 Norman Sr. returned to Tennessee and married a woman who bore him two sons. All three of the Boles children received children's survivor benefits when Norman Sr. died in 1971, but the Social Security Administration denied Gonzales's application for mothers' benefits, ruling that only Nancy Boles, Norman's legal widow, was eligible. With the help of legal aid and the Center for Law and Social Policy, Gonzales and her son filed a class action lawsuit in 1974 on behalf of unmarried mothers and their children.[71]

Herbert Semmel believed that the Supreme Court's decision in *Glona v. American Guarantee Co.* (1968) to invalidate Louisiana's exclusion of mothers from recovery for the wrongful death of their illegitimate children could be read to prohibit birth status distinctions in mothers' benefits.[72] Stephen Wiesenfeld's Supreme Court victory in 1975 provided additional support: if the government could not "[discriminate] among surviving children solely on the basis of the sex of the surviving parent," then how could the state deny a child benefits solely because of her parents' marital status?

Litigants and judges all agreed that the outcome in Margaret Gonzales's case hinged on who the program's primary intended beneficiaries were. If the provision targeted children, then excluding mothers because they never married the wage-earning father seemed like unconstitutional discrimination based on birth status. The federal district court judge Jack Roberts embraced this child-focused interpretation: he called the exclusion "the classic case of visiting the sins of the parents on the child."[73] If mothers' benefits truly were children's benefits by another name, then *Boles* was an easy case.

However, if the benefits targeted mothers—or, after *Wiesenfeld*, parents—then the question was more complicated. The government argued that Congress had merely used marriage as a proxy for economic dependence: if legislators meant the benefit to replace support lost after a wage-earner's death, it was reasonable to assume that married mothers were more likely to have relied upon husbands than unmarried mothers were to have relied on their children's biological fathers. "The theory behind mothers' benefits is that a wife with an entitled child in her care should have the same option that she had before her husband's death. That is, either to stay home, supported by her husband to take care of the children, or else to work and help to support the family," Assistant Solicitor General Harriet Shapiro told the Court.[74] Most never-married mothers had no such choice.

The government's argument exploited the widening gulf between courts' treatment of nonmarital children on one hand and their parents on the other. An "illegitimate" *child* could not be denied benefits automatically on the assumption that she did not depend upon her parent for support; at the very least, the child must be given an opportunity to prove dependence in fact. But the Court still saw marriage as a proxy for economic dependence between *adults*. In 1976, the Court unanimously upheld the exclusion of divorced women under the age of sixty-two from certain Social Security benefits available to similarly situated married women, finding it reasonable to assume that ex-spouses did not rely financially upon one another the way that still-married couples did.[75] The following year, the justices, again unanimously, ruled that the government could terminate disability benefits to John Jobst, a man with cerebral palsy who married Sandra Lee, who also lived with cerebral palsy but did not receive benefits. Congress, the Court ruled, was free to presume that a married person could depend on his or her spouse for support.[76] Noonan's fear that the Court would wholly abolish marital status distinctions had not come true.

The gender-egalitarian, functional principle Ginsburg and her allies championed thus did not extend to unmarried women and men. In cases such as Belmira Lucas's, mothers' very self-sufficiency compromised their nonmarital children's eligibility for state support. Already less likely to be partnered with men whose wages would yield generous Social Security entitlements, unmarried mothers like Margaret Gonzales—disproportionately low-income and of color—could not benefit even from formal equality of access to government benefits. The equation of marriage with dependence—and nonmarriage with mothers' and children's economic independence from fathers—underwrote marital families' privilege at the expense of nonmarital parents and their children.[77] To receive government support, single mothers would still need to rely on AFDC, conditioned upon intrusive state intervention. Otherwise, without marriage or a man who functioned as a father-provider, single mothers could only depend on themselves.

Gay Marriage and Equality

Neither did the equality principle reach gay and lesbian couples, though not for lack of trying. Lesbians and gay men had long used the language of marriage to describe committed partnerships; homophile advocates in the 1950s and 1960s debated the utility of marriage as a framework for gay intimate life.[78] Some prized the label "marriage" as a sign of social and romantic "adjustment," in the psychological lexicon of the day, but most guarded their privacy closely in the era of criminalization and did not seek legal recognition as spouses.[79] In the late 1960s and early 1970s, movements for gay rights and liberation burst into the public consciousness.

Battles against women's subordination and legal repression of homosexuality were more tightly connected than ever. Newly militant gay organizations and radical feminists challenged liberal women's groups and united under the banner of sexual liberation. Kate Millett's *Sexual Politics* (1969) explained the relationship: "A sexual revolution" would end "traditional sexual inhibitions and taboos" that "threaten[ed] patriarchal monogamous marriage: homosexuality, 'illegitimacy,' adolescent, pre- and extra-marital sexuality." Millett wrote that the "goal ... would be a permissive standard of sexual freedom" and abolition of "the ideology of male supremacy."[80]

Some prominent women's rights leaders distanced feminism from lesbian rights and freedoms. But at NOW's national convention in 1971, leaders debated and passed a resolution in support of lesbian rights, forging an uneasy but important alliance between women's and gay liberation. A significant share of NOW's early leaders had (often hidden) intimate partnerships with women, and some local chapters engaged with lesbian feminist and gay rights causes.[81]

Gay and lesbian Americans, like their straight counterparts, harbored diverse views about marriage.[82] Some joined marriage abolitionists, who counted prominent lesbian feminists in their ranks. The activist Carl Wittman spoke for many: "Marriage is a prime example of a straight institution fraught with role playing. Liberation for gay people is defining for ourselves how and with whom we live, instead of measuring our relationships in comparison to straight ones."[83] Even milder critiques often celebrated alternatives to marriage and the nuclear family. "Gay life is not dominated in the way straight life is by institutionalized coupling," observed Jeffrey Escoffier, editor of *The Gay Alternative*, in 1975. Escoffier touted the "value of friendship circles" as "one of the most important discoveries of gay culture" and an "important alternative to the family."[84]

Others longed to assimilate into the "normal" life of family, work, church, and community. Gay men and lesbians who lived otherwise conventional lives sometimes objected to the way "militants" depicted same-sex intimacy. In 1973 Lotti B. Benker reacted negatively to an article that portrayed a "Gay Liberation Front" image of gay life in Rochester: "The majority of gay people I know dress like anybody else walking along Main Street—with modern long hair styles and attractive feminine clothes." They held "financially sound positions ranging from accountants, secretaries, or brokers to retail merchants or advertising experts." Most were homeowners and established in their communities.[85]

To some, respectability remained a promising strategy. Evan Mills wrote in 1967 that gay couples should endeavor "by our example of good citizenship, and rapport with the mainstream of society, government, and the church" to prove worthy of marriage rights.[86] The Reverend Frank Scott of the Metropolitan Community Church in Pittsburgh reassured skeptics that couples celebrating church weddings are "people who are trying to lead good, stable lives filled with love."[87] They reprised earlier homophile and lesbian organizers who valued outward conformity as a path to legitimacy and acceptance.

Many fell somewhere in the middle. Marriage appealed as a source of public and private benefits, legitimacy and recognition, and freedom from the shame and existential danger imposed by the stigma of "sexual deviance." Practical and dignitary benefits often commingled in a couple's accounting of the value of legal marriage.[88] For some white gay male couples especially, combining households could expand available resources and bolster economic status.[89]

Ambivalence about marriage as an institution frequently accompanied a desire to see gay marriage legalized. D. J. Munro, who had several intimate relationships with other women after her marriage to a man ended in the early 1970s, thought legal marriage would give her words to describe "the significant person" in her life without the "sexual connotations" of "lover." But when asked if she would marry her live-in partner of two years, Munro hesitated: "Even the romantic part of me can't quite handle the idea of marriage, because in this society there is no such thing as a marriage of equals."[90]

Others hoped marriage might evolve if it expanded to include gay relationships. Some women viewed same-sex unions as part of a larger feminist project to redefine marriage. As one writer described in *Echo of Sappho* in 1972, "Many women, straight as well as gay, are beginning to feel we shouldn't pattern ourselves after the law in marriage; but we should have the same benefits [such] as [joint] tax return[s] and social security. . . . We should be able to draw up our own contract for marriage, and the law recognize it."[91] Gay couples might have something to teach straight people about marriage, Phil Mullen suggested, if only because they were "more free to think again" about the ingredients of loving partnership given the absence of an unrealistic romantic "ideal" and its institutional trappings.[92]

Don Borbe, a pastor who celebrated "Holy Unions" of gay and lesbian couples at the Metropolitan Community Church in Philadelphia, embraced the values of love and commitment as integral to marriage but eschewed ceremonial vows that promised fidelity "'til death do us part." He emphasized that intimate partnerships should always be negotiable and that "lasting love agreements" were not a moral or religious imperative but rather should be freely undertaken by couples who found a marriage-like union spiritually fulfilling.[93] Sandy and June, a lesbian couple who celebrated their wedding in 1972, wished that "straight" churches would sanction same-sex unions. The lack of legal recognition made a religious bond even stronger, in their view.[94]

Many couples who demanded marriage licenses and litigated marriage equality claims in the early 1970s pursued radical aims through creative methods.[95] Early plaintiffs included gay liberationists whose tactics garnered greater support from marriage abolitionists and radical lesbian feminists than from the more cautious denizens of the homophile/gay rights establishment.[96] Couples diverse along every dimension—race, class, religion, ideology, and region—populated the ranks of early gay and lesbian would-be spouses.[97]

Attempts to obtain marriage licenses—publicized, and sometimes sensationalized—coexisted with antipathy toward monogamy, gender conventions, consumerism, and other elements of the nuclear family. One early plaintiff, John Singer, "called marriage 'wrong' and 'oppressive' from the standpoint of . . . revolutionary morality" and declared that he and his "occasional lover" Paul Barwick "would just as soon abolish marriage."[98] Jack Baker and Mike McConnell rejected "male-female role-playing," as well as the "perfect fidelity" of "straight idealism," and called for a "socio-sexual revolution." They kept their finances separate and championed "equality between marriage partners," arguing that "a husband and wife should handle their finances the way we do."[99]

Some couples sought ancillary legal benefits, highlighting how many were unavailable to same-sex partners. Baker and McConnell, for instance, filed suit under a local anti-discrimination ordinance after three private adoption agencies rejected their applications.[100] Baker, who served in the Air Force for four years, applied for "dependent spouse" benefits on McConnell's behalf but was denied by the Veterans Administration.[101] Relying on a marriage license obtained in Mankato, Minnesota, the couple also filed joint income tax returns. The Minnesota tax department rejected their state return in 1972, ruling that only "husband and wife" could file jointly. Baker and McConnell persisted, calling it "intuitively obvious that both the terms 'husband' and 'wife' are chauvinistic euphemisms for 'spouse.'" After being "laughed at" in several appearances before state legislators, they turned to the federal Internal Revenue Service.[102] A years-long legal battle saw the government deny their joint return but then issue a tax refund to Baker and McConnell, only to rescind the check later, sparking another lawsuit.[103]

Some marriage activists risked liberty as well as livelihoods when they engaged in direct action protests. The *Lesbian Tide* reported in 1976 that a Chicago judge sentenced Toby Schneiter and Nancy Davis to a year in prison after a jury convicted the women of criminal trespass for refusing to leave the county clerk's office without a marriage license.[104] Davis and Schneiter related how working-class women in Cook County Jail cheered their arrival and expressed interest in marrying female partners.[105]

The couple's action provoked heated internal controversy: "male-oriented gay groups" and the lesbian task force at the Chicago chapter of NOW worried about the fate of pending anti-discrimination legislation before the city council. Feminists in Chicago Lesbian Liberation viewed NOW's opposition as a "bid for 'respectability,'" a call to "beg nice for our civil rights on bended knee and maybe we can live next door or work with some straights but never could we publicly acknowledge our love."[106]

Reforms that made marriage law formally sex-neutral helped to inspire efforts to legalize gay marriage. Some feminists still shied away from associating gay liberation with sex equality, however.[107] During congressional hearings on the Equal Rights Amendment in 1971–72, proponents refuted warnings from the scholar Paul Freund and Senator Sam Ervin that "equality of rights . . . on account of sex" would extend to one's choice of spouse.[108] Still, a 1973 *Yale Law Journal* article argued that the ERA would provide a right to marry irrespective of sex, just as *Loving v. Virginia* guaranteed the right regardless of race.[109]

A rising conservative movement seized upon the politically explosive association of gay marriage with sex equality.[110] Phyllis Schlafly used opposition to the ERA to unite conservative Catholics and white evangelical Protestants around a New Right agenda that transformed the Republican Party and realigned American politics.[111] A mother of six who ran for Congress three times and earned a law degree when she was fifty-four, Schlafly built a formidable movement of conservative women to defend "traditional family values," gender roles chief among them. Schlafly made the specter of "homosexual marriage" a rallying cry for STOP ERA.[112] She contended that the ERA not only would eliminate a husband's legal obligation of support and force unwilling wives and mothers into the labor market but also would unleash "radical and lesbian forces" to "wage war on the American family."[113]

The ERA's foes "tapped into an effective strategy of fusing moral ruin with fiscal doom," in the words of the historian Alison Lefkovitz. Same-sex marriage, they warned, would allow gay couples to adopt and corrupt children. And it would strain public coffers by giving the benefits of marriage to the deviant and undeserving.[114]

Such assertions led some ERA proponents to fortify the firewall between the amendment and gay marriage.[115] But others owned the amendment's potentially radical implications: "Many, many supporters of the ERA hope that its real effect will be to help change sex roles, help change society . . . help to make America a society where every person is as free as the next to determine what s/he wants to do and be."[116] Even those who were skeptical of marriage as an institution understood that the extension of sex equality to gay and lesbian Americans would confer important legal protections in areas such as employment and housing and fuel the fight against sex-based discrimination of all kinds.

Courts uniformly repelled advocates' invitation to extend the sex-equality principle to gay marriage, however.[117] The Minnesota Supreme Court disposed of McConnell and Baker's case in a short opinion that reeked of disdain. The U.S. Supreme Court dismissed *Baker v. Nelson* in

1972 for "want of a substantial federal question," signaling that a sex-based equal protection claim had no traction.[118] The Washington state courts took Singer and Barwick's sex discrimination claim more seriously but still denied the state ERA's applicability in a 1974 decision.[119] In court, the sex discrimination argument—along with other arguments for recognizing gay marriage—then lay mostly dormant for two decades. In 1975, a rare legislative effort to redefine marriage as a union between any two persons briefly prospered in Washington, D.C., before succumbing to stiff opposition from conservative clergy.[120]

A selective, and limited, principle of sex equality thus prevailed in marriage law. The most glaring remnants of coverture—the assumption that the husband was household head, that he had unilateral control over property during marriage and the prerogative to determine the family domicile—receded.[121] In *Orr v. Orr* (1979), the Supreme Court ruled that states could not restrict alimony to wives but must instead award support based on sex-neutral functional criteria.[122] Functional roles also replaced sex as a basis for allocating government benefits: the state could no longer assume that husbands and wives followed the male-breadwinner/female-homemaker model but must instead treat them as primary and secondary wage-earners irrespective of sex.

But the fundamental structure of government benefits remained unchanged: the state still channeled social insurance through employment and marriage. Alimony remained discretionary and rare.[123] Mothers' disproportionate responsibility to support and care for nonmarital children went unrewarded: formal sex neutrality in marriage benefits did not help the unmarried. Some mothers with partners who functioned as father-providers or who "legitimated" their children could receive limited benefits, but the rest were left to struggle on their own or relegated to an invasive welfare system. Nor did legal recognition of sex-neutral roles in marriage extend to gay and lesbian relationships.

Formal sex equality also could have the perverse consequence of immunizing laws that perpetuated wives' oppression from constitutional challenge. When feminists attacked laws that protected husbands from prosecution for raping their wives, the extension of exemptions to wives who assaulted husbands often meant that advocates could not point to a sex-based classification that triggered heightened judicial scrutiny. Feminists did manage to eliminate or temper marital rape exemptions in some jurisdictions in the 1970s and 1980s. But many states still imposed lesser penalties and more stringent evidentiary rules for assault within marriage: artifacts of male supremacy survived the demise of coverture in a different, ostensibly neutral guise.[124]

Equality and Dissolution

Even for married women, the move toward sex-neutral marital roles brought limited returns. The hallmarks of egalitarian marriage—shared breadwinning, homemaking, and parenting—presupposed an intact family headed by two upper-middle-class professionals with remunerative jobs who could rely on family members or paid childcare providers. Even these rare couples faced headwinds, including social pressure to conform to traditional roles and persistent discrimination in employment. Tax laws, too, created "a strong pattern of work disincentive for married women" and penalized couples with more equal earnings.[125]

For many American women in the 1970s, equal spousal roles seemed a distant dream. In most families, husbands still outearned their wives and women shouldered caregiving responsibilities. If women and men continued to function differently and the law still devalued caregiving work, sex-neutral laws would just obscure how marriage continued to reproduce gender as a matter of social reality.[126]

Divorce—on the rise in the 1970s and 1980s—presented a yet more daunting challenge, but also an opportunity. Courts refused to intervene in ongoing marital relationships, citing marital privacy, unity, and harmony; most of the law's leverage materialized only when a couple separated or divorced.[127] And even when the unusual (relatively) equal marriage ended, the burdens of supporting two households strained most middle-class families. For dissolving families with fewer resources or more conventionally gendered divisions of labor, divorce threatened to leave women and children destitute.

The traditional marital bargain feminists struggled against short-changed homemakers as well as women who resisted conventional gender roles. Creating a new divorce regime that encouraged egalitarian arrangements in the future and remedied inequalities in the present was a difficult task in itself. Feminists also faced an anti-ERA movement that exploited fears about the demise of gender norms; men's rights advocates who resisted post-divorce responsibilities for women and children; lawmakers' reluctance to extend the public benefits of marriage to divorced and unmarried partners; and a dearth of state support for caregiving.[128]

Unilateral no-fault divorce exposed the hazards for women of easy marital dissolution when property distribution and support laws favored men. Feminists championed creative social insurance programs, tax policy innovations, and the expansion of public assistance, as well as reforms to marital property, alimony, and child support laws.

For the growing number of Americans who lived together without marrying, dissolution posed thorny questions about the rights and obligations of nonmarital partners. Couples who lived as husband and wife without formalizing their relationships had once relied on the doctrine of common law marriage, which absolved families of the stigma of nonmarital sex and childbearing and relieved the public of support obligations when relationships ended in death or desertion.[129] The abolition of common law marriage in most states by the mid-twentieth century left unmarried women who sought property rights or ongoing financial support without remedy. Moreover, cohabitants could not access social insurance, employer-provided health insurance, tax incentives, preferential immigration status, derivative workers' compensation benefits, tenancy rights, and other elements of economic citizenship that formally married couples enjoyed.[130]

Without these public benefits, the private law of inter se obligations (duties owed to one partner by the other) provided unmarried partners their only potential legal recourse. For different-sex cohabitants, the decision not to marry might be one of principle, preference, legal impediment, or simple inaction; for gay and lesbian couples, living outside of marriage was the only option.[131] The absence of a legal structure in which to dissolve a relationship invited the invention of new pathways, pathways that sometimes softened and other times sharpened the boundaries between marriage and nonmarriage.

Schlafly's STOP ERA movement harangued feminists for ignoring or disparaging homemakers who had devoted their lives to traditional wifely and maternal roles only to be cast aside by a women's liberation movement that compared their chosen vocation to enslavement. As Schlafly interpreted the ERA and no-fault reforms, feminists sought to eliminate the legal protections that kept husbands from abdicating their proper roles as providers and to force married women into the workforce.[132]

Schlafly was not wrong in characterizing the feminist ideal of egalitarian marriage as antithetical to her vision of sharply gender-differentiated family roles, with wives happily submitting to their husbands' household leadership and to economic dependence on men. But in fact feminists did not unanimously welcome no-fault divorce. Nor did many enjoy elite education, professional careers, and the promise of financial independence. A significant number had experienced the penury of divorce firsthand. Reformers considered "displaced homemakers" a primary constituency and believed that equality demanded a revaluation of household labor and caregiving work.[133] Without a radical overhaul of the legal treatment of divorced women, no-fault divorce was a potential disaster for women.

Developments in public law reinforced the centrality of marriage to eligibility for state support. Feminists fought a long, uphill battle in the 1970s and 1980s to expand federal government benefits for divorced women, as the historian Suzanne Kahn has documented. Their most ambitious proposals—a health insurance system that did not channel benefits through employment and marriage, a social insurance regime that compensated homemakers directly—foundered. Instead, more incremental, selective reforms "entrenched the public welfare regime's use of marital status."[134]

Social Security reform is a case in point. Some feminists proposed benefits that homemakers would earn for their domestic labor, based on the median income of all workers. This plan held out a modest redistributive promise within and across marriages: tying wives' remuneration to market labor rather than to husbands' income could increase the valuation of domestic work and detach homemakers' compensation from spousal economic status. Another proposal included a "constant attendant allowance" for individuals caring for a person with a disability who was not their spouse, but it gained little traction.[135]

"Earnings sharing," in which spouses—employed or not, male or female—would each receive individual credits based on half of their combined income, attracted more attention. Earnings sharing reflected a "marriage as economic partnership model," which effectively valued women's work in proportion to their husbands' earnings. Conservatives—and the Carter administration—offered counterproposals that would "level social benefits down instead of up," such as requiring both men and women to prove dependency in order to receive benefits. Ultimately, Congress passed modest reforms such as lowering the qualifying duration of marriage from twenty to ten years and allowing divorced spouses to remarry without losing benefits.[136]

Reformers, predominantly white middle-class women operating in an era of welfare retrenchment, increasingly argued that divorced women deserved preferential legal treatment as compared with never-married women, coded as Black and undeserving.[137] Even when they did not say this quiet part aloud, shifting policy priorities, such as a turn to private and employer-sponsored retirement benefits, rendered proposed divorce reforms less useful to low-income women and women of color.[138]

As we saw earlier in this chapter, in the 1970s feminists succeeded in establishing formal equality for married couples and for widows and widowers in the provision of Social Security benefits, whereas unmarried mothers' parallel efforts failed. The contemporaneous campaign to expand divorced women's access to government benefits fell somewhere in the middle and thus cemented both the importance of marriage to public provision of social insurance benefits and the gap between economic haves and have-nots.[139]

The public law of government benefits favored the wives of men with eligible and remunerative jobs. Similarly, the private law of divorce held out much more promise to women with economic privilege than those without. Only formerly married women stood to benefit from reforms that sought to redistribute wealth *between* husband and wives. Such changes would also favor women who could afford to be homemakers, those who had husbands with significant assets who earned substantially more than they from jobs with good benefits.

Feminists in NOW worked for "responsible divorce" reforms that would value homemakers' contributions to household wealth; provide adequate support for women and children after dissolution; and facilitate displaced homemakers' return to the workforce. In the late 1960s, Betty Blaisdell Berry's NOW task force on marriage, divorce, and family demanded paid maternity leave, the right to return to work with seniority and full benefits after childbirth, tax deductions for domestic work and childcare expenses, and government-sponsored childcare centers. Berry called upon the government to guarantee health and accident insurance to the homemaking spouse if a marriage dissolved and to sponsor "retraining for re-entry into the job market."[140] She and her allies explored the possibility that private insurance companies might issue divorce insurance, eventually conceived as a "form of term insurance to be paid to the economically dependent spouse in the form of a pension."[141]

NOW's first decade also produced a sweeping reform agenda for private law as no-fault divorce rapidly gained ground.[142] In 1969, California passed the nation's first "pure" no-fault law. In 1970, the proposed Uniform Marriage and Divorce Act (UMDA) recommended that divorces be granted based on "irreconcilable differences." NOW members worried that lawmakers would liberalize the grounds for divorce but jettison recommendations for more equitable financial allocations.[143] The UMDA, for example, favored limited, short-term "rehabilitative" alimony, which assumed that divorced women could quickly become self-sufficient.[144]

NOW activists had no great love for the old fault-only regime; fault, after all, was a weapon husbands could wield at least as easily as wives. A "guilty" wife usually relinquished alimony rights and, in community property states, an equal share of assets. But "traditional laws prohibiting divorce except for cause gave some dependent partners leverage through genteel blackmail," as one NOW document put it.[145] Until wives obtained equity in the economic consequences of divorce, they reasoned, women could ill afford to give up the veto power that helped them negotiate better settlements.

Berry's task force supported a mutual consent requirement for couples seeking a no-fault divorce: they hoped to retain wives' bargaining leverage without forcing couples to assume an acrimonious, adversarial posture or collude to manufacture fault. And they insisted that property division and spousal support rules reflect wives' homemaking contributions and limited job prospects after years out of the workforce.[146]

Learning about marriage and divorce law became a form of consciousness-raising.[147] Feminists sought to expose the law's hidden marriage "contract": the assumptions about women's economic dependency and sole responsibility for unremunerated homemaking and caregiving; the unenforceability of husbands' support obligations; husbands' right to manage and control property acquired during marriage; wives' inability, in some states, to retain their surnames; husbands' prerogative to choose the couple's domicile over wives' objections; spouses' inability to sue each other in tort; and husbands' unconditional sexual access. If women understood what marriage and divorce entailed, perhaps they could better protect themselves from the emotional and financial consequences. Better yet, they could mobilize to change or at least circumvent the law.

Contracting Around Marriage and Divorce Law

Feminists who sought to reform marriage and divorce law understood that transformation would not come easily. In the meantime, some turned to private relationship contracts.[148] The allure of contracting stemmed in part from feminist outrage about male supremacy in marriage and divorce law. Relationship contracts also appealed to those who eschewed marriage or lacked access to it, such as gay and lesbian couples. As family forms diversified in the wake of the sexual revolution, contract partisans touted individual freedom and cultural pluralism. If some couples wished to conform to traditional gender roles, but others sought egalitarian partnerships, why should both be subject to the same marital regime? As a private agreement between individuals, a contract required little or no government buy-in: lawmakers need not approve of a relationship's terms nor—crucially—expend public resources.

Relationship contracting did potentially upend traditional legal categories and undermine marital primacy. Many contracting proponents intentionally blurred the line between marriage and nonmarriage—and between same-sex and different-sex couples—by suggesting that regardless of marital status or eligibility, partners could create their own bespoke arrangements. Marriage required that (different-sex) couples opt into an indivisible bundle of rights and obligations. In contrast, contracting could allow partners of any sex to choose from an a la carte menu or create their own marital recipe. However, this freedom had limits: couples could not contract around laws that exempted rape within marriage from criminal sanction or that deprived unmarried persons of myriad government and employer benefits available to the married, for example.

Relationship contracts circulated in popular media and among lawyers, social scientists, and marriage counselors. The famous essay "A Marriage Agreement" (1970) described Alix Kates Shulman's frustration and disillusionment when the arrival of children dashed her hopes of an egalitarian division of household labor that would enable her to combine a writing career with motherhood. She drafted a detailed agreement, enumerating each childcare and domestic task, from waking, bathing, dressing, feeding, transporting, entertaining, and helping with homework to shopping, cooking, cleaning, doing laundry, arranging for paid childcare, and staying home with a sick child.[149]

Shulman later revealed that her "agreement" (not, she insisted, a "contract," with the implied legalistic baggage) was a last-ditch, unsuccessful bid to stave off divorce.[150] Others called such documents contracts and encouraged couples to deliberate over their terms. In 1972, the matrimonial lawyer Norman Sheresky and the "thrice-married" writer Marya Mannes asked: "What if we obliged potential marriage partners to explore together *in advance* ... the extent of their intended commitments with regard to children, property sharing, and future alimony should the marriage fail?"[151] Frank discussions of expectations (and finances) might scuttle some marriages, proponents acknowledged, but would strengthen unions that were meant to be.

Some proponents of contracting were highly critical of marriage per se; others claimed a desire to save marriage by making it, in the words of NOW's Nan Wood, "more viable." Some, like Berry, worried most about the economic insecurity of displaced homemakers. Others, among them Eliza Paschall and Bill Morrison of Atlanta NOW, saw private agreements as a challenge to state laws restricting sexual freedom: they sought to eliminate penalties for extramarital sexual exploration and to allow couples to live together without becoming economically interdependent.[152]

Many couples who drew up agreements in the early to mid-1970s did so for feminist reasons.[153] Some contracts provided for romantic fidelity, while others endorsed open marriage. Some made contraception and reproductive decision-making a joint venture; others vested control in the female partner. Some kept property separate; others made all property marital. Some minutely detailed division of household labor and childcare; others opted for general statements of egalitarian principle. Some embraced gender roles but insisted upon an equitable division of property and robust support obligations at dissolution. Others refused to prioritize one spouse's career and provided decision-making protocols when partners' employment conflicted.

NOW's marriage and divorce task force explored relationship contracts in the early 1970s and soon connected with Lenore Weitzman, a protégé (and later spouse) of the family sociologist William J. Goode.[154] Weitzman began considering contracts during a postdoctoral fellowship at Yale Law School. She then moved to California, ground zero for no-fault divorce reform, where she joined NOW's San Francisco chapter and spent the next two decades teaching sociology and writing about family law.

Weitzman suggested that couples—and larger groups—draft "contracts in lieu of marriage" for whatever arrangement suited their needs and desires.[155] Her early writing reflected Weitzman's belief that "many men are burdened by excessive alimony and support payments to first wives which severely limits their ability to support a new family." Often, she wrote, "the first wife could return to work and become more self-supporting," but "the present system provides little incentive for her to do so."[156] Weitzman hoped that giving women "independent control over property, domicile, and sexual relationships" and encouraging "more direct responsibility for children by fathers" would "lead to more egalitarian arrangements."[157]

By the time Weitzman published her first article about contracting in 1974, her attitude toward alimony had shifted: she now concluded (much more accurately) that "for over 90 percent of the divorced women in the United States, alimony is just ... a myth."[158] Weitzman emphasized that the traditional marital bargain—financial support in exchange for domestic services—was unenforceable. It "assume[d] a white, middle-class family," sidelining multigenerational, single-parent, and other family forms common among racial minorities, immigrants, and the poor. Contracts could establish support obligations beyond the nuclear family, allocate "domestic and child-care responsibilities along generational rather than sex-linked lines," and accommodate "communes, group marriages, and other family-like units of more than two adults."[159]

Weitzman's sample contracts included a traditional marriage involving a woman who planned to give up her own career to support her husband's education and medical practice, make a home, and raise children; a dual-career professional couple who wished to evenly divide breadwinning and household responsibilities; an "alternative lifestyle/homosexual couple" with artistic aspirations who planned to alternate wage-earning and housekeeping duties; and a working-class couple's second marriage in which the woman would be "paid for household and child-care services."[160]

Traditionally, courts had been reluctant to enforce contracts that were based on an illicit sexual relationship (in the case of nonmarital cohabitation) or that contemplated divorce (in the case of premarital or marital contracts). Judges also balked at allowing husbands and wives to contract around their gender-specific duties, although some made exceptions for agreements involving property. Some proponents of contracting distinguished between the financial and the personal, predicting that courts would remain reluctant to enforce agreements about day-to-day domestic duties, sexual relations, childcare, and birth control.[161] Others doubted courts should or would intervene to adjudicate disputes, with skeptics raising constitutional concerns about courts invading couples' privacy or curtailing their freedom to make sexual and reproductive decisions.

Enforceability could also be a double-edged sword for feminists, given the bargains women and men might make under conditions of social inequality. The *New Women's Times* warned in 1977 of the pitfalls of "Pre-Marital Contracts Within the Patriarchy," including a "false sense of complacency."[162] Premarital agreements had long been used to keep property separate, often in second marriages where one spouse wished to protect children of a previous relationship. What was to prevent wealthy

men from pressuring eager brides (or paramours) into giving up property and support to which they might otherwise be entitled, further en-
trenching power imbalances and economic inequities? Should additional
safeguards beyond those applicable to ordinary commercial contracts
apply to agreements between intimate partners?

Many contracting proponents thought not. The model of business
partnerships appealed to Weitzman, who proposed a "standard regime"
in which "each partner is to share equally in profits and contribute
equally toward losses."[163] A Uniform *Conjugal* Partnership Act would
translate principles and instruments of business law into a family context
often assumed to be inimical to the arms-length bargaining of the commercial world. By the early 1980s, the law of commercial and intimate
contracts appeared to converge on a middle ground between holding
parties to their bargain as rational actors on equal footing and protecting
parties with less knowledge and fewer resources.[164]

Weitzman acknowledged the potential for exploitation in her book
The Marriage Contract (1981). Men might use their economic power to
"impose a contract that is even more unfavorable than traditional legal
marriage." She believed, however, that "equalization is more likely than
exploitation" when men who were committed enough to egalitarian ideals to contract around patriarchy in the first place had to "'put it in writing.'"[165] Weitzman doubted that women would make agreements that
left them significantly worse off than the traditional marital bargain.

But by the early 1980s, a changed social and legal context diluted the
egalitarian potential of intimate contracts. Easier access to divorce meant
marriage itself had become more like a contract terminable at will. Courts
were beginning to reconsider their hostility to prenuptial agreements, and
the American Law Institute's Uniform Premarital Agreement Act (UPAA)
endorsed this trend. Features of the traditional marriage contract that
feminists had exposed and condemned were "already passé"—at least on
paper if not in social reality.[166] Due in part to feminist activism, equitable
distribution had replaced title-based property division rules in most common law states. Constitutional equal protection rulings extended alimony
to husbands and extinguished laws that gave husbands sole control of
family assets during marriage.[167] Maternal preferences gave way to the
formally gender-neutral best-interests-of-the-child standard.

Contracts to circumvent these more equitable laws arguably helped
men escape ongoing financial responsibility more than they gave women
a fairer division of assets.[168] If feminists wanted to revise the traditional

marriage contract they should do so for all women by establishing egalitarian default rules, argued the law professor Marsha Garrison. Further, Garrison observed that "women who convince their partners to participate in drafting an agreement" would "include disproportionate numbers of affluent, well-educated women whose status is least in need of improvement."[169] In any case, relationship contracts of the sort proposed by Weitzman never became widespread, at least for different-sex couples. Separation agreements reached at dissolution, which received only minimal review from courts, dominated the field of divorce by the 1980s.

As sociologists began to study the economic consequences of divorce for women and children their findings confirmed the fears of feminists like Betty Berry. Weitzman herself decried the devastating impact of the "Divorce Revolution" in an influential book published in 1985. By then, it was clear that divorce left women and children demonstrably worse off than than it left men—although the magnitude of this disparity was hotly debated—and thrust middle-class mothers and their families into economic precarity, even poverty.[170] Backlash from men's rights activists who resisted alimony and child support obligations accounts for some of this retrenchment.[171]

Feminists persevered in advocating for federal divorce reforms. They enjoyed some success in the 1980s, but at a price, as Suzanne Kahn explains: rather than treating marriage as an equal partnership, reforms continued to privilege divorced women based on how long they had been wed and on their (husbands') ability to pay for private insurance. These partial victories, such as shortening the duration of marriage required to receive Social Security benefits post-divorce from twenty to ten years, left out less affluent and never-married women. Never-married or briefly married mothers served as a foil for middle-class and wealthy divorced women who claimed access to military benefits, private pensions, and health care coverage based on their former marital status and their ex-husbands' earnings.[172]

Equality and Nonmarital Cohabitation

Because they could not access public benefits reserved for the married and formerly married, *unmarried* women whose relationships ended could only hope to draw upon private sources of support unless their children qualified for (ungenerous) AFDC benefits. In the 1970s, women who lived with men outside of marriage explored various avenues for holding their former partners to account.

As courts grew more willing to enforce certain express written co-habitation contracts, legal-advice literature increasingly encouraged them.[173] *The Living Together Kit*, published by the attorneys Toni Ihara and Ralph Warner in 1978, advised readers to "put it in writing" "when you are feeling so mellow that no agreement seems necessary."[174] The *Kit* provided several brief sample contracts for sharing property, keeping property separate, purchasing property jointly, and planning joint ventures. Ihara and Warner also included templates for "agreements covering homemaker services" and contracts "covering household expenses and personal idiosyncrasies."[175]

Given how few cohabiting couples entered into written agreements, however, contracts could not solve the problem of penury when long-term, nonmarital relationships dissolved. Reformers therefore experimented with an ascriptive approach that used functional criteria to determine whether to recognize a nonmarital relationship for certain purposes, such as the distribution of property. Critically, whereas common law marriage made partners eligible for government benefits, these new ascriptive approaches pertained only to private obligations between partners.

One variant of ascription simply applied reformed divorce laws to relationships that functionally resembled marriage. As marital property regimes became more egalitarian, equal division rules could extend to couples in marriage-like relationships, as a California appellate court ruled in 1973. Paul Cary and Janet Forbes had adhered to traditional gender roles during their eight-year partnership: they had four children together, shared a surname, purchased a home, pooled their financial resources, and "otherwise conducted all business as husband and wife" despite never formally marrying.[176] The court reasoned that once divorce law no longer considered fault, the formalities of ceremonial marriage mattered little.[177]

Simply blurring the lines between marriage and nonmarriage by substituting functional for formal criteria did not necessarily produce progressive results, however. Reformers who hoped the law would recognize a diverse array of family forms thought *Cary* reaffirmed marriage's privileged status. Herma Hill Kay and Carol Amyx criticized its "reliance on the traditional roles of husband and wife."[178] Functional family definitions could as easily reinscribe as transform the values underpinning formal legal categories.

Some reformers therefore drew upon *Cary*'s functional approach but sought recognition of a broader and looser category of relationships. In

Oregon, H. Jay Folberg and William P. Buren proposed in 1976 the recognition of "domestic partners" who cohabited and accepted "a mutual assumption of rights, duties, and obligations toward one another." Evidence
of joint bank accounts, investments, and mutual assumptions of debts
would demonstrate the requisite financial interdependence, while "do-
mestically, some division of labor . . . which evidences a common pooling
of efforts," especially the joint rearing of children, would suffice.[179]

Several obstacles loomed. Judges often avoided financial settlements
for nonmarital partners that might appear to replicate the discarded doctrine of common law marriage. Some jurists worried that allowing
women to share in the fruits of a "meretricious" relationship would further erode marriage by reducing couples' incentive to formalize their
unions; they invalidated any agreement between nonmarital sexual partners to share in property accumulated during the relationship.

Bucking this tradition, Carol Bruch—now a family law scholar and
advocate—proposed an array of mechanisms to recognize property
rights for "de facto spouses." "Implied-in-fact contracts" arose from "one
party's request that another perform specified services," such as homemaking or working in the family business. Bruch customized the legal
concept of "unjust enrichment" to argue that one partner should not
walk away with the profits from a joint enterprise simply because he held
title to the resulting property. She emphasized the importance of case-
by-case, fact-specific analysis.[180] The availability of various legal and equitable remedies for different factual circumstances could allow many
types of relationships to flourish.

Courts experimented with both contract and partnership theories of
nonmarital relationships. For instance, the Washington Supreme Court
in 1972 used a business partnership theory to compensate a woman for
her labor in connection with a cattle-raising venture pursued during cohabitation.[181] In 1976, the California Supreme Court decided *Marvin v.
Marvin*, which allowed for the enforcement of "implied" contracts where
the parties' conduct reflected an intention to become economically interdependent. Michelle Triola and the actor Lee Marvin lived together for
six years; in 1970 Marvin married his high school sweetheart and insisted
Triola vacate their Malibu home. She sued him, seeking an equal share of
his income and movie royalties during their partnership. Triola's lawyer
persuaded the state's highest court to allow couples to share in some of
the fruits of economic partnership outside of marriage, though Michelle
lost her own case.[182]

Some states, most famously Illinois, rejected all property rights for cohabitants. Women like Victoria Hewitt, whose husband had falsely represented to her that their relationship was the legal equivalent of marriage, lost everything after a seventeen-year union that produced two children.[183] But even states that recognized the possibility of cohabitants sharing resources post-dissolution did not apply *Marvin* to the benefit of economically dependent partners, and *Marvin* proved a weak weapon for female cohabitants. In practice, the default rule of no rights and responsibilities for unmarried cohabitants changed relatively little. Most cohabitants did not enter into written agreements, egalitarian or otherwise, and oral understandings remained difficult to prove.[184]

As the shortcomings of contracts became clearer, feminists disagreed about whether recognizing legal obligations for nonmarital partners who had not agreed to them enhanced or curtailed individual autonomy. Some believed that couples should be free to avoid financial entanglements. Kay and Amyx wrote in 1977 that the law should not treat a couple who intentionally avoided marriage in favor of a nontraditional partnership the same as parties who replicated a traditional marriage in all but formality.[185] As one scholar wrote in 1981: "The choice of cohabitation is, after all, a choice not to marry and it would seem incongruous to attach to it identical consequences."[186] Others worried that such freedom unfairly aided men who might claim to be flouting convention but in fact wanted the traditional privileges of marriage—sexual and homemaking services—without the responsibilities of a husband.[187]

For straight couples, the legal baseline—rights and obligations conferred by marriage—shifted between the late 1960s and the early 1980s, making marriage and divorce at least somewhat more formally sex-neutral. For gay and lesbian couples, the default rule remained, definitively, non-recognition. The political valence of same-sex relationship contracts—not unlike same-sex marriage—could be radical, conventional, or both at once.[188]

Contracting numbered among the legal tools gay and lesbian couples could adapt to set the terms of their partnerships and protect property and decision-making authority from outside interference. Eunice Brown and Arlene Smith lost custody of their eight children to foster homes in 1971; reunited with their children two years later after a legal battle, the women expressed their desire to marry and lamented their inability to find anyone in Flint, Michigan, "willing to perform the ceremony."

Nevertheless, the couple changed their surnames to Willoughby, Ms. Smith's maiden name, and asked their lawyer to "draw up a marriage contract" to "make Eunice feel more secure."[189]

Sympathetic lawyers advised same-sex couples that careful legal planning, including contracts, could guard against hardship in the event of a partner's illness or death. R. James Kellogg wrote (hyperbolically) to "Dear Abby" that "a gay couple can, with the help of a sensitive attorney, legally duplicate marital arrangements in every state."[190] Hayden Curry and Denis Clifford, authors of *A Legal Guide for Lesbian and Gay Couples*, strongly recommended that cohabiting same-sex couples memorialize agreements in writing. "Often our clients are older," Curry explained; "they have a house and money. . . . We hit them on the head with the realization that should they split up, they may end up in court battling over property." Lesbian couples faced a special set of legal problems since they were more likely to bring children into their relationships, and women's earnings barely exceeded half of men's on average.[191] The Lesbian Law Section Collective warned in 1978 of relatives who might swoop in to make medical decisions, claim property, or seek guardianship and child custody. The government, another "source of external interference and discrimination," withheld tax advantages and inheritance privileges.[192]

The California Supreme Court's decision in *Marvin* remained silent on the subject, but advocates hoped that property rights for widowed and separating same-sex partners might follow. B. J. Beckwith, legal director of the Society for Individual Rights, told the *San Francisco Examiner* in 1976 that the gay male couples who dominated his clientele seldom sought court intervention when their relationships dissolved. Beckwith would advise them, "Let's see if we can't divide up this property as if you were businessmen going out of business." Occasionally, couples' acrimony necessitated that lawyers negotiate settlements on clients' behalf. And if courts failed to apply *Marvin* to gay couples, then Beckwith promised a test case.[193]

Scattered reports of judges awarding property to gay partners followed *Marvin*.[194] Sherry "Dimples" Richardson, age twenty-three, won court-ordered compensation for household services from Denease Conley, age twenty-one, in 1978 after their brief relationship ended. Like Michelle Marvin, Richardson had relinquished her job (as a cosmetologist in New York) to provide homemaking and companionship in exchange for sharing in the fruits of her "lesbian husband's" labor (as an airplane mechanic at a California naval base). Unlike the Marvins, Richardson and Conley celebrated their marriage with a ceremony, at Metro-politan Community Church in San Diego. Moreover, they committed to writing their intention to live as "man" and "wife," with Richardson tak-ing responsibility for chores such as cooking and cleaning; in exchange, Conley's income, including military retirement benefits, would be shared property and, eventually, Conley would subsidize Richardson's modeling school education.[195]

Richardson—like many "housewives," one journalist quipped—quickly became disillusioned with her isolated life of household drudg-ery. "I wasn't a wife," Richardson complained; "I was a slave."[196] Her lawsuit sought an award of community property and $6,400 in compen-sation for services rendered.[197] The Superior Court judge Byron F. Lind-sley approved a settlement in which Conley agreed to pay Richardson $100 per month in alimony *pendente lite* (during legal proceedings). Judge Lindsley called the case an ordinary breach of contract action in which "the fact that [the parties] were of the same sex is of no legal con-sequence"; it thus provided no precedent for couples without an express agreement.[198] But by the end of the 1970s, a few courts awarded property to separating same-sex partners through theories such as constructive trust, designed to remedy the unjust enrichment of the breadwinning partner.[199] Anecdotal evidence suggests that gay and lesbian couples were more likely to make express relationship agreements and less likely to turn to the courts to enforce implied contracts.

Legal-advice literature for heterosexual cohabiters counseled gay read-ers that for written property agreements the same templates should suffice, at least in jurisdictions that did not criminalize sodomy. Curry and Clif-ford's *Legal Guide* (1980) advised gay couples that "contract provisions hav-ing to do with the personal conduct of the couples are not enforceable," although including them could be "fun" and could serve as "expressions of intention." The *Legal Guide* related a playful example of a couple who in-cluded in their living-together agreement a clause stating that "Adrian, ad-mittedly being the messier one, will hire a cleaner to do his share of the house-cleaning, and is not required to feel guilty—or to work—if Ken wants to putter and straighten up all night long." Another part provided that "both agree to keep their foolishnesses and private joys confidential."[200]

Because divorce remained unavailable, lesbians should proactively create "a structure of uncoupling," the Lesbian Law Section Collective advised. Lesbians were "not bound by the customs and traditions of het-erosexuals." Some would "adapt [the current system] to serve the real

needs of loving lesbian partners, and others may strike out in new directions."[201] This legal vacuum had salutary aspects: "Lesbians are in the en-
viable position of custom-designing a method that really meets their felt
needs," "a freedom that is not so available to nongay couples."

The Collective recommended negotiating when partners "are loving
and want to be fair," not when crisis engulfed the relationship.[202] Partners
should avoid "sharing everything," a tempting approach "in the first blush
of love." Joint ownership of property often turned into "a mess." Couples
should instead make a "pre-coming together inventory" of all possessions
and keep property separate save a joint checking account for household
expenses. Agreements should provide for partners in case of death, lay out
"a rational method for potential dissolution," and describe "a working
structure for daily living." The Collective also advised partners to make a
will, purchase life insurance, and establish power of attorney.

The Collective paid special attention to process. Lawyers advised
same-sex partners to keep their property disputes out of court in order to
avoid prejudiced judges, government or community harassment, employment repercussions, or family estrangement. The Collective promoted
arbitration or other alternative dispute resolution clauses. More ambi-
tiously, they outlined an "alternative legal structure" in which the community would select a "Lesbian Fairbody" to resolve disputes, ideally with
guidance from written agreements based on model contracts.[203] Avoiding
state involvement shielded those whose encounters with the law often augured oppression rather than liberation. Of course, the inability to call
upon the state also deprived couples of access to institutions that provided benefits during marriage and a structure, however imperfect, for
navigating death of a partner or dissolution of a relationship.

In the late 1960s, traditional marriage looked antiquated and oppressive
to feminists, the opposite of sexual autonomy and gender equality. The
freedom to forge new forms of partnership through agreements tailored
to couples' needs and desires appealed to those seeking unconventional
lifestyles. Reformers hoped that blurring the lines between marriage and
nonmarriage would render both versions of coupling freer and more
equal.

By the early 1980s, however, feminist-inspired legal reform and reaction from conservatives and men's rights groups led to unexpected
changes.[204] Marriage law had long been a key site of the gender subordination and inequality that feminists fought. Now, reforms had gradually

and unevenly vanquished the most rankling remnants of coverture. Progress toward formal equality between husbands and wives came most dramatically in the constitutional law of government benefits, where the state could no longer assume or encourage traditional gender roles. Unmarried mothers, in contrast, did not win the right to receive benefits derived from their male partners' wage-earning, and this setback magnified economic inequalities across as well as within families. The egalitarian marriage movement's limited gains did not reach the growing number of women, particularly women of color and low-income women, who supported households without the help of a male breadwinner.

Meanwhile, divorce law's evolution confirmed many "responsible divorce" advocates' worst fears: easy exit from marital responsibilities without corresponding reforms to make the financial consequences of dissolution more equitable. Women who did marry their partners at least had a potential claim to property accumulated during marriage, though the value of that claim depended upon their husbands' wealth. Despite reforms that appeared friendlier to cohabiters, most unmarried women struggled to recover assets they helped to build during nonmarital relationships.

The result was that well-educated, professional women—and the wives of wealthy men—theoretically could access the benefits of formal sex equality in marriage. But marriage and divorce law proved only nominally more equal for most women, who continued to work a double shift or who found themselves "displaced homemakers" after a divorce. And for women who never married their partners or never put agreements in writing, even equitable distribution or equal division of marital property remained mostly out of reach. The feasibility of gender-egalitarian partnerships, then, often depended on two factors that increasingly intertwined: marital status and class privilege.

For some gay and lesbian couples, the very unavailability of marriage created a space for innovation. The real and perceived need for legal protection may have made these couples more likely to do what contracting proponents advised for all: put their intentions in writing.[205] But the limited reach of full formal sex neutrality took a toll, and not only on those who wished to marry or who sought legal relationship recognition: failure to extend sex discrimination laws to gay and lesbian Americans had ramification across all domains.

The modernization of marriage law thus changed the relationship between marriage and male privilege. Marriage and divorce law became more gender-neutral: function often replaced sex as the criterion for legal benefits and responsibilities. These transformations mostly eluded nonmarital partners, while gay and lesbian couples' efforts to secure marriage and other rights foundered. Courts became nominally more willing to consider functional roles as a basis for limited private legal rights at the end of nonmarital relationships. But efforts to blur the lines between married and unmarried couples, whether through contracting or ascription, largely sputtered. The privileging of marriage survived even as gender hierarchy—alive and well as a matter of social reality— faded from the formal law of marriage.

Some women and families surely benefited from greater sex neutrality in government benefits and in the laws of marriage and divorce. Still, the partial success of feminist reforms also helped to blunt the edges of abolitionist and liberationist critiques. Patriarchy no longer was inscribed so indelibly on the law of marriage, and the institution's advantages as a source of public and private legal benefits remained secure. The possibility of a truly equal partnership, stamped with the state's imprimatur and support, beckoned—however elusive it proved to be in practice. Some Americans instead looked beyond marriage and the nuclear family to realize their visions of equality and liberation.

CHAPTER FOUR

Redefining the Household
Communal Living, Government Benefits, and Housing

"THE WORD COMMUNE RAISES images in the average, middle-class American mind of 'wild sex-dope-rock-filth orgies,'" wrote Jonathan Shor, a law student, in 1972.[1] To critics, communes conjured a doomsday scenario for the nuclear family and conventional marriage: they thought communes took countercultural lifestyles to their logical extreme and concentrated all the debauchery and disorder of hippiedom into one mode of life.

In fact, communal living took many forms. In towns and cities, groups of young people lived together to save money on rent and utilities. Handfuls of families set up cooperatives where they divided cooking, housekeeping, and childcare responsibilities. Migrant workers shared lodgings as they moved from place to place to perform seasonal labor. "Hippie communes" attracted special ire because they visibly flouted social norms and conventional sexual morality. But to those alarmed by cultural change, communes symbolized a much larger, more disturbing phenomenon: a broad-based, if diffuse, effort to redefine the American household.[2]

As rates of divorce and nonmarital childbearing rose, the number of households headed by a single parent, usually a mother, soared. Heterosexual couples increasingly cohabited as a prelude or an alternative to marriage.[3] In smaller but significant numbers, gay men and lesbians lived together openly, sometimes after extricating themselves from marriages; some raised children together. Poor and low-income Americans had long pooled resources and provided care for relatives and fictive kin, relying on extended families and neighbors for support. They banded together in households to save money, as did young adults at odds with their parents. Older couples, widowed or divorced, lived together unmarried so they would not lose public and private sources of support. Other Americans constructed new household forms intentionally, reviving utopian projects that deliberately rejected the nuclear family model.[4] Such developments—inspired by motives pragmatic and idealistic—threatened a revolution in marital status law and in American family life. They strained against a legal system designed to bolster marital households headed by a husband/father/breadwinner and a wife/mother/homemaker.[5]

Not only communalists but all who departed from the marital nuclear family ideal—unmarried and divorced adults, single parents raising children, gay men and lesbians, nonmarital partners living together—faced pervasive discrimination. This chapter focuses on household definition, zoning, and housing, core sites of contestation over the rights of Americans who tried to make a home together outside of marriage.

As they had in other areas, advocates for nontraditional living arrangements turned to constitutional law and to legislation at all levels of government. Their attempts to revise legal definitions of "household" confronted familiar hurdles. At the federal level, judges and lawmakers adopted formal nondiscrimination rules based on race, sex, and eventually the presence of children. But they balked at demands to extend protection to communalists and to unmarried couples, and they repelled bolder theories of sexual and associational freedom. The Supreme Court's constitutional decisions left nonconforming Americans at the mercy of state and local laws and subject to a housing economy increasingly inhospitable to all but the affluent.

Communal Living and Food Stamp Eligibility

Intentional communes—religious, utopian, urban, rural, countercultural—attracted new attention in the 1970s.[6] Some communes practiced a modern version of free love—rejecting monogamy, exchanging sexual partners, and raising children collectively. Such a lifestyle made nonmarital sex the norm and displaced the family unit as the primary source of care and financial support. It conjured the specters of welfare dependency and communism in an era when critics' alarm about a government takeover of the family doomed attempts to achieve universal subsidized childcare, and proposals for a guaranteed minimum income failed.[7]

Their defenders sometimes protested that communes posed a lesser threat to public coffers than unwed mothers and divorced women with children. Even if a commune disbanded, the risk of needing government aid was no greater than when a traditional or nonmarital family dissolved, proponents insisted.[8] In an era of family instability, communes could provide more, not less, continuity of care and support.

Unsurprisingly, such arguments did not stave off anti-commune legislation.[9] Passage or selective enforcement of local ordinances and state laws targeting communes surged in the 1960s and 1970s. Concern about undeserving countercultural youth receiving public assistance swelled as the country descended into recession. In Massachusetts the decision to reinstate eligibility for AFDC benefits to communalists sparked public outcry in 1972, as some residents feared an onslaught of opportunistic hippies.[10] Press accounts of college students with affluent parents collecting food stamps only fueled the anger.

In 1971, Congress excluded from food stamps two groups: households containing persons who had been claimed as dependents by parents on the previous year's tax return, and individuals living only with others not related "by blood, affinity, or through a legal relationship sanctioned by State law."[11] The provision's sparse legislative history revealed a concern with "hippie communes"; press coverage suggested its targets also included "free-loading kids," college students, frat brothers, and unmarried mothers cohabiting with partners.[12] Critics considered these individuals morally corrupt, voluntarily poor, or both, and therefore undeserving of food assistance.

For civil libertarians, state-sponsored attacks on countercultural lifestyles and hippie communes infringed privacy and freedom of association, as well as the right to subsistence that welfare rights advocates tried and ultimately failed to obtain. The food stamp restrictions came to the ACLU's attention when the director of a Zen Buddhist society in Maui wrote to the national office in July 1971 fearing that residents of Peahi Chapel, a halfway house, would lose their benefits. Rather than the ACLU filing suit on behalf of the Maui Zendo, however, the Food Research and Action Center at the Center for Social Welfare Policy and Law in New York challenged the new provisions in court with the ACLU's assistance.

Advocates strategically emphasized fairness to poor families rather than freedom for hippie communalists. The ACLU's Sanford Rosen solicited "minority group members, or non-counter culture poor people" when he asked affiliates to identify potential plaintiffs.[13] Otto Zinke of the Arkansas ACLU suggested a young Fayetteville couple, Michael Alexi and Barbara McClelland, and noted in his postscript: "They are poor, but I am not sure of what you mean by non counter culture."[14]

Initially the status of unmarried couples under the amendment was unclear. By 1971, few states still recognized common law marriage, which typically required that a couple have an agreement to be married and hold themselves out to family, friends, and neighbors as husband and wife. In public comments on the changes to food stamp regulations proposed by the U.S. Department of Agriculture (USDA), critics objected that in most cases the draft rule would exclude couples living as spouses but not formally married. The final regulation therefore clarified that "a man and woman living as man and wife, if they are accepted as married in the community in which they live," would be eligible.[15] Since many cohabiting couples deliberately declined to marry and did not purport to be husband and wife, the regulation excluded most couples under age sixty who were "living in sin."

The complaint filed by Attorney Ronald Pollack in March 1972 featured a diverse array of households, none of them an unmarried couple. One household did contain two male roommates, nineteen-year-old David Durrant and twenty-eight-year-old David Kilmer, who lived together in Salt Lake City because their work in construction and odd jobs did not produce enough income for either man to live alone. The men "desperately need[ed]" food stamps "to obtain adequate nutrition."[16]

The named plaintiffs also included a group of unemployed job-seeking young people aged seventeen to twenty-four who moved in together in Columbia, South Carolina, "to reduce their expenses" but also because of their "strong social affinity."[17] One plaintiff, the eighteen-year-old Deborah Jirel, had left her parents' home due to discord over her political views. Another teenager, Michael Hoffman, moved out at his mother's request "because [of his] . . . political, social and racial beliefs which his parents could neither understand nor accept." Michael Gaddy, a Vietnam veteran, was a full-time university student. These plaintiffs emphasized that their "relationship [was] far deeper and stronger than the bonds between friends or between mere roommates." They "consider[ed] themselves a family not merely for the purposes of this lawsuit, but for *all* purposes." They shared financial resources and contributed to Gaddy's educational expenses. Without food stamps they faced "an extremely precarious economic position," since they were compelled "to feed themselves and obtain other necessities through the generosity of neighbors and other friends."[18] Affidavits implied that these plaintiffs were (white) civil rights sympathizers struggling to survive after being cast out by their families of origin, not hippies exploiting government largesse meant for genuinely poor people.

Of the five households, Pollack spotlighted the most clearly sympathetic plaintiffs. Victoria Keppler, a single mother in Oakland, California, moved in with a friend and her child, also AFDC recipients, so that Ms. Keppler's daughter could attend a school for the deaf. Keppler faced a "tragic dilemma": to relocate in "dilapidated housing considerably far away" from her daughter's school or remain in her new home and "continue to be deprived of health-vital food assistance." Sheliah and David Hejny and their three children were living with neither car nor telephone in a trailer in North Carolina when they took in a young woman whose mother had ordered her to leave home. Mr. Hejny's job as a pipelayer and Mrs. Hejny's income from babysitting did not begin to cover thousands of dollars in family medical expenses, much less adequate food. The food stamp program's relatedness requirement "denied [the Hejnys] . . . proper nutrition solely because they have been charitable enough to care and provide for a previously unwanted child."[19]

Pollack centered Jacinta Moreno, a fifty-six-year-old Mexican American woman whose diabetes cost her the use of her left leg and foreclosed work in the packinghouse where she had labored seasonally for nearly a decade. Mrs. Moreno lived with Ermina Sanchez and her family in Homestead, Florida, and stretched a monthly income of $75 to cover her share of rent and gas, transportation for hospital visits, and laundry expenses, with only $10 remaining for "food, hygienic items, clothes, and such."[20] Mrs. Sanchez and her three children, also migrants, subsisted on $133 per month in AFDC benefits and cared for Moreno, who helped with housework when she could but "sometimes [had] to spend several days in bed because of her condition."[21] Exhibits explained the "common practice for the very poor to 'move in' with friends during unemployment, or any type of crisis."[22]

These plaintiffs argued that an exclusion aimed at hippie communes in fact ensnared "the poorest of the poor"—innocent people brought together by mutual need and altruism. True hippie communalists could afford to "alter their living arrangements" to retain food stamp eligibility, but the deserving poor lacked the resources to live apart.[23] The *Miami News* reported in May 1972 that Mrs. Moreno had "some food in her Homestead quarters today, no thanks to the U.S. Department of Agriculture and its bureaucratic red tape." Moreno's "crime was moving in with another migrant family when she became too ill to work." The "Agriculture experts . . . were using the food stamps to express their disapproval of the life style of a few young people." The only "decent criterion" for eligibility was "poverty."[24]

Privacy and freedom of association claims headlined the plaintiffs' complaint in federal district court. Pollack relied upon *Griswold v. Connecticut* and *Stanley v. Georgia* to establish a right of privacy in the home, "traditionally . . . an exalted place in our Constitutional framework" that "remained inviolate from governmental interference." In 1972 *Eisenstadt v. Baird* applied the right to privacy to unrelated individuals.[25] Fourth Amendment search and seizure cases protected homes from governmental invasion, while cases such as *N.A.A.C.P. v. Alabama* (1958) secured the right to associate with others "to effectuate political purposes."[26] The food stamp rule distinguished between related and unrelated persons on "arbitrary, capricious, and irrational" grounds.[27]

A three-judge federal district court found for the plaintiffs in May 1972. Judge Carl McGowan wrote that the state could not "in the name of morality infringe the rights to privacy and freedom of association *in the home*."[28] Even if it could, the exclusion reached beyond the "households containing unrelated individuals of both sexes" that a morals regulation presumably would target.[29] On appeal to the Supreme Court, Pollack gave "traditional equal protection" claims pride of place, anticipating that the justices might prefer a narrower ruling, based on the tenuous relationship between means and ends.[30]

Justice Douglas thought *Moreno* should be decided on freedom of association grounds, perhaps with a dollop of privacy thrown in, and drafted an opinion to this effect.[31] But a skeptical Justice Blackmun wrote, "The privacy argument does not impress me—there is no invasion of privacy here." He thought the alleged infringement on "association rights—too far-fetched." Blackmun was mostly "disturbed" by how the amendment penalized "the deserving."[32] Powell, also in doubt, wavered at conference and then balked at joining Douglas's draft opinion.[33]

Brennan suggested that a more temperate approach might "command a majority," and Douglas reassigned the opinion to him. Brennan had hoped to use McGowan's reasoning, but the government had re-placed its "morality" justification with an "even less convincing" fraud-prevention rationale.[34] Brennan's draft applied rational basis review and emphasized the illegitimacy of the apparent congressional purpose to ex-clude "hippie communes."[35] Powell found Brennan's draft "fairly re-strained and persuasive."[36] Blackmun signed on as well.[37]

Brennan's final opinion included language that would be cited for decades to come: "If the constitutional conception of 'equal protection of the laws' means anything," he wrote, "it must at the very least mean that a bare congressional desire to harm a politically unpopular group cannot constitute a legitimate governmental interest."[38] Douglas, who converted his draft opinion into a concurrence, thought greater judicial scrutiny was in order: "Banding together to combat the common foe of hunger" fell on the "wide spectrum of human interests" "guaranteed by the First Amendment," Douglas wrote. "The right to invite the stranger into one's home is too basic in our constitutional regime to deal with roughshod."[39]

Moreno laid groundwork for later decisions that applied the "bare de-sire to harm a politically unpopular group" standard to laws that singled out gay and lesbian Americans for discriminatory treatment. But plaintiffs' more capacious constitutional claims languished. Had the Court's major-ity embraced the bolder theory that restrictive definitions of family vio-lated fundamental rights of privacy and freedom of association, all kinds of laws that excluded or penalized household arrangements outside the marital nuclear family norm would have been constitutionally suspect. In-stead, a narrow version of equal protection prevailed, one that applied only when lawmakers targeted a particular group with discriminatory ani-mus. Even then, such targeting triggered only a slightly more rigorous version of rational basis review, not the stronger sauce of strict scrutiny.

Pollack's *Moreno* strategy succeeded: both Brennan's and Douglas's opinions narrated in detail the heartrending stories of sympathetic plain-tiffs, "desperately poor people with acute problems."[40] Those who suf-fered deprivation because of the law were not hippie communalists or lazy middle-class college kids but society's most vulnerable.

Zoning Out Communalists

A cooler reception greeted plaintiffs in other communal-living cases. Following close behind *Moreno*, *Village of Belle Terre v. Boraas* chal-lenged a Long Island zoning ordinance that allowed no more than two persons not related by blood, marriage, or adoption to occupy homes in a small beachside enclave not far from the Stony Brook campus of the State University of New York (SUNY). In December 1971 Peter Boraas, a graduate student in sociology, rented a six-bedroom house from a married couple, Edwin and Judith Dickman, to share with five other students. Village authorities denied the students' application for beach privileges in the summer of 1972 and threatened legal action. In July, the Dickmans received a criminal summons: they faced a fine of up to $100 and imprisonment for up to sixty days for each day their tenants remained.[41]

Zoning laws like Belle Terre's had become commonplace by the early 1970s. Until the 1960s most courts looked askance at zoning regulations that restricted occupancy to "traditional" families. Now a growing share of localities prevented unrelated individuals from sharing a residence, citing a mixture of moral compunctions and instrumental concerns about property values.[42] The Bay Area community of Belmont, California, decided in 1969 to allow no more than three unrelated individuals to live together, a move "intended to give the city a lever to pry out any hippie-type communal living 'pads.'"[43] In 1971 a Mill Valley, California, proposal set the limit at five.[44] For Angelo Tullo, a councilman in Ramsey, New Jersey, "unrelated members of both sexes" sharing houses stymied "a healthy moral climate for our children" and brought "noise and filth," traffic, and parking woes.[45]

Unrelated persons limits cramped many living arrangements. In Rochester, New York, three married couples purchased "a large home in one of the city's wealthiest neighborhoods," "living as one, except for conjugal rights." This was in 1972, three years after they met through a community organization. The families chose city life "to be close to work, cultural events, and parks." Saving money was a factor, but the "single most overriding reason," explained one resident, Robert Warth, "was the desire to extend the nuclear family ... [to] share responsibilities." The couples—accountants, businesspeople, and engineers—split taxes, mortgage payments, household chores, and childcare equally. Their thirteen children, aged two to fourteen, shared bedrooms "according to sex and age."[46]

Another Rochester collective, inspired by the "utopian communal settlement" of B. F. Skinner's *Walden Two*, included four adults and one child. Martha Rush, a member of the household, thought it best if "the neighbors just know us as people. If we get the 'commune' label, it might be difficult." Rush emphasized "practical" benefits, including reduced costs, "less mundane work for each person," and the "social advantage of always having someone to talk to or go to the movies with."[47]

A shortage of affordable housing spurred communal living arrangements among renters, too. Communalists reaped social benefits, even if the "chief motivation" was "saving money." Diane Rabinowitz, a substitute teacher in San Francisco, lived in Mill Valley with two roommates, who provided companionship and pooled funds. "We were lucky to find rent as low as this in Marin County," she told a reporter.[48]

Saving on rent and sharing household and childcare responsibilities inspired groups of single mothers to rent homes together. In Marin County, Polly Leach launched three collectives in 1972 after unreliable babysitting arrangements forced her to leave her five-year-old alone while she worked as a waitress in San Francisco. Leach rented a house with two other single mothers, and a fourth provided childcare in exchange for rent. The arrangement supplied camaraderie and a sense of "family" for her son. "It was a wonderful atmosphere," Leach said. When she ran ads, "the phone [rang] constantly" with calls from women—usually divorced, sometimes never married—raising children "without child support." Susan Milman, who had a doctorate in psychology and a two-year-old, found the collective a desirable alternative to public assistance. "What these mothers really want to do is to get off welfare," Leach explained. "They want to be responsible for their own lives." She estimated that the three collectives saved Marin County $12,000 per month.[49]

Defenders of communal living extolled its virtues. Sharing household and childcare responsibilities across several adults alleviated the dilemmas of working parenthood and reduced burdens on the public fisc. Communal living conserved "finite resources" and promoted an "ecologically sound" lifestyle. Communalists learned how to get along with people of varied backgrounds and experiences, solve problems, and work toward common goals for mutual benefit—but without the high stakes of lifetime marital commitment. And communal living at its best assuaged loneliness and alienation.[50] Ross Speck, a Philadelphia psychiatrist who studied urban communes, argued that they could "help relieve . . . the deadness in nuclear family life."[51]

State and federal courts had mixed reactions to limits on unrelated persons. In 1966, the Illinois Supreme Court struck down a Des Plaines ordinance that restricted occupancy to related persons because the legislature had not authorized municipalities to "penetrate so deeply . . . into the internal composition of a single housekeeping unit."[52] The same year the Connecticut Supreme Court read "family" in a Westport zoning ordinance to foreclose a communal living arrangement between unrelated persons.[53]

Communal living suffered its first major constitutional defeat in
1970 when a federal court upheld a no-more-than-four ordinance
against a challenge by the Palo Alto Tenants' Union on privacy, freedom
of association, due process, and equal protection grounds.[54] Plaintiffs also
demanded freedom from "harassment" by local businesses and landowners.[55] In December 1970 the *San Francisco Examiner* reported that "Palo
Alto police have staged the first in a planned series of raids aimed at the
rising problem of hippie communes." Their first target: a home occupied
by the activist John Dolly; his wife, Jean; and Charles Noble, "leader
of the militant left Palo Alto White Panther Party," allies of the Black
Panthers.[56]

The seventy-year-old Eisenhower appointee who decided *Palo Alto
Tenants' Union v. Morgan*, Judge Albert C. Wollenberg, described himself
as a "moderate" with a "conservative bent."[57] Nevertheless, he had voted
to enjoin a one-year residency requirement for public assistance in 1968,
held that prisoners retained a constitutional right to read periodicals
while incarcerated, and exempted indigent candidates for citywide office
from filing fees.[58] Still, Wollenberg evinced little sympathy for communalists' claims to quasi-family status. He wrote:

> The traditional family is an institution reinforced by biological
> and legal ties which are difficult, or impossible, to sunder. It
> plays a role in educating and nourishing the young which, far
> from being "voluntary," is often compulsory. Finally, it has been a
> means, for uncounted millennia, of satisfying the deepest emo-
> tional and physical needs of human beings.

Not so for "communal living groups," which were "voluntary, with fluc-
tuating memberships who have no legal obligations of support or cohabitation" and who lacked "biological links which characterized most
families." Plaintiffs had no "right to insist that [they] . . . live under the
same roof, in any part of the city they choose."[59]

By the time the Ninth Circuit affirmed Wollenberg's ruling in 1973,
the uproar over hippie communes in Palo Alto had subsided.[60] Other
constitutional challenges flared, however, and the dispute in Belle Terre
reached the Supreme Court. Larry Sager, a young NYU law professor,
represented Boraas and his roommates on behalf of the New York Civil
Liberties Union. For Sager, *Belle Terre* joined a commitment to land
use reform in service of justice for low-income people and communities

of color with civil libertarian imperatives like privacy and freedom of association.[61]

The links between these causes were rich and numerous. The Supreme Court's most ambitious past attempts to curb property rights in the name of racial equality concerned restrictive covenants.[62] The leading freedom of association case upheld the NAACP's prerogative to shield its membership rolls from state scrutiny.[63] A constitutional right to travel was established when a young single mother of two lost AFDC benefits after moving from Boston, Massachusetts, to Hartford, Connecticut.[64]

Sager invoked each of these precedents in *Belle Terre*. Like exclusions based on race, religion, or political affiliation, unrelated persons limits restricted "the deeply personal choice of individuals to live together in a common household." Neither an aversion to communal living nor a preference for "neighboring households comprised of traditional families," the plaintiffs argued, could justify the ordinance. Belle Terre's blanket exclusion of unrelated co-residents conjured a dystopia that excluded "childless households" or "families with children," "the aged or the infirm," or "young, college-educated persons" and used state coercion to create "socially homogeneous enclaves." This kind of residential separation, Sager argued, was "drastically incompatible with the right to travel."[65]

The plaintiffs' privacy argument, too, further stretched precedent: earlier decisions largely concerned families and/or procreation. Sager emphasized the home as a protected "sanctuary of personal privacy" and characterized "decisions concerning one's household associations" as "of great personal importance and sensitivity." Certainly "feelings by persons in the community that only a narrow mold of household arrangement is socially desirable" could not justify exclusion.[66]

After a loss in federal district court, a Second Circuit panel ruled for the plaintiffs, deeming the rights infringed "unquestionably . . . important," if not quite "fundamental." The ordinance allowed "existing inhabitants to compel all others" wishing to live in Belle Terre "to conform to its prevailing ideas of lifestyle." Traditional zoning prerogatives—to control population density, noise, and traffic, to avoid rent escalation, and to foster stability of residency—could not justify the law.[67]

The Supreme Court's ruling in *U.S.D.A. v. Moreno* (1973) sent mixed signals to the *Belle Terre* plaintiffs. On one hand, the Court did not find that the relatedness requirement for food stamps infringed fundamental rights such as privacy or freedom of association. On the other hand,

Moreno scrutinized more closely laws reflecting animus toward a particular group. Excluding deserving poor families in an effort to target hippie communes appeared antithetical to the goal of providing food assistance to needy Americans. But zoning out unrelated households—especially large groups of students—to protect the quiet family ambience of a neighborhood might seem perfectly rational.

For its part, Belle Terre denied any animus toward "groupers." The village's lawyer, the law professor Bernard Gegan, defended the ordinance as pro-family (not anti-grouper) and compatible with affordable housing. The village meant to prevent overcrowding without excluding large families and to shield single-breadwinner households from the higher rents SUNY professors or other groups of wage-earners could afford. The *Belle Terre* plaintiffs were "numerous," "articulate," and "educated"—"the very opposite of the kind of helpless minority" entitled to invoke strict scrutiny.[68]

The swing justices were skeptical of the plaintiffs' claims.[69] One clerk noted that "the context within which the issue arises here is somewhat different" from *Moreno's*; Justice Powell crossed out "somewhat" and wrote "very."[70] At conference, only Brennan and Marshall voted to affirm. Justice Potter Stewart worried that ruling against Belle Terre would "upset every zoning law in [the] country." Blackmun called the right to travel claim frivolous; Powell saw "no discrimination here," observing that the "'family' concept has been fundamental to our society."[71]

Douglas's concurrence in *Moreno* and his history of siding with compatriots in unconventional living made his authorship of the majority opinion in *Belle Terre* startling. Douglas brushed aside the plaintiffs' litany of constitutional claims. The case was "not aimed at transients," and it concerned "no 'fundamental right' guaranteed by the Constitution" nor "any rights of privacy." The ordinance prohibited "no other forms of association" and addressed legitimate "urban problems." The "police power," Douglas concluded, "is ample to lay out zones where family values, youth values, and the blessings of quiet seclusion and clean air make the area a sanctuary for people."[72] The man *Time* magazine called "the most doctrinaire and committed civil libertarian ever to sit on the Court" endorsed unrelated persons limits in a decision one journalist dubbed an April Fool's trick.[73] Some observers thought Douglas's environmentalism overwhelmed his competing concern for individual freedom and economic justice in *Belle Terre*.[74]

Opponents of exclusionary zoning reacted to *Belle Terre* with despair and disbelief. Stephen Nagler, an ACLU lawyer, described the ruling as "a killer."[75] A California legal aid attorney, Grace Kubota, recalled, "I kept reading the decision over and over and I couldn't believe Douglas wrote it."[76] Richard F. Bellman, a lawyer challenging discriminatory zoning laws in several northeastern states, found a silver lining: the plaintiff students were neither poor nor of color so the key would be to limit *Belle Terre* to its particular facts.[77]

Nevertheless, new zoning laws multiplied around the country as municipalities watched potential constitutional challenges evaporate. The decision effectively killed some of the ongoing litigation to attack similar ordinances. The three families who challenged Rochester's unrelated persons limit, for instance, had "given up the fight": one family moved out of the shared house in anticipation of an adverse ruling; another was searching for a new residence.[78]

The Supreme Court's final word on zoning relatedness requirements, *Moore v. City of East Cleveland* (1977), reinforced the primacy of blood and marital ties over more inclusive definitions of family and household. Inez Moore, a sixty-four-year-old Black woman disabled by arthritis, faced criminal charges for living with two motherless grandsons in violation of a suburban zoning ordinance. The ordinance sought to maintain the "middle-class" character of a suburb after "white flight" and urban renewal opened new housing opportunities for Black city-dwellers.[79] The Moore household, comprised of Mrs. Moore, her daughter Carol, her son Dale Sr., and her grandsons Dale Jr. and John Jr., epitomized how extended families could offer a safety net of care and support to cope with poverty, unemployment, and maternal death.[80]

After negative rulings from Ohio's courts, Mrs. Moore appealed to the U.S. Supreme Court. Post–*Belle Terre*, references to the sanctity of family life and the rights to privacy and free association in the home paved the most plausible path to victory. "It's clear from [*Belle Terre*] that communities can regulate communes," Moore's lawyer, Francis Murtaugh, said. "But our case is distinct: it involves related people."[81] As "blood" relatives, the Moores fit the definitions of "family" that dominated zoning law. Mrs. Moore's lawyers characterized her relationship with her grandson John Jr. as akin to that of "the child's natural mother." They depicted extended families as integral to American life, proffering "services and emotional support seldom found in the nuclear family."[82]

Moore's brief drew from the burgeoning sociological literature extolling the centrality of extended families to poor Black and white ethnic "subcultures." In the early 1970s, a new generation of social scientists challenged the reigning consensus of Black family "pathology" epitomized by the Moynihan Report. A prominent strand of this literature emphasized the strengths and adaptive qualities of Black families. Some scholars highlighted working- and middle-class Black families who nurtured strong marriages and raised productive citizens despite racial oppression.[83] Others plunged into fieldwork with the "underclass" and emerged with nuanced depictions that spotlighted the resilience of families and social networks previously condemned as broken, hopeless, and disorganized.

Young Black sociologists eviscerated scholarship that measured Black families against a flawed patriarchal, white middle-class ideal, and they lauded single mothers' perseverance and ingenuity. Robert Staples's article "The Myth of the Black Matriarchy," published in 1970, debunked the notions that Black women "emasculated" or "dominated" men, thrived at men's expense, or transmitted a "pathology" of poverty to their fatherless children. Instead, women and girls faced racism, sexism, and capitalist exploitation with creativity and steadfastness, an "asset to Black survival."[84] Joyce Ladner's book *Tomorrow's Tomorrow* (1972) empathetically explored the lives of Black adolescent girls and young women.[85]

Extended family and kin networks fulfilled many of the functions that mid-century norms assigned to the nuclear family, scholars emphasized. Robert B. Hill's study *The Strengths of Black Families* (1972) cited "strong kinship bonds" and "adaptability of family roles," and it examined phenomena such as informal adoption.[86] The white anthropologist Carol Stack, a daughter of working-class Russian-Jewish immigrants, lived for three years with her young son in an impoverished midwestern Black neighborhood and published *All Our Kin* in 1974. Alongside Herbert Gutman's book *The Black Family in Slavery and Freedom* (1976), Stack's work showcased how reciprocity among kinfolk and fictive kin, as well as intergenerational family care and support, counteracted the legacies of enslavement and segregation.[87] By 1978, Elmer P. Martin and Joanne Mitchell Martin wrote that adherents of both the "pathology/disorganization" and the "strength/resiliency" perspectives agreed that kinship beyond the nuclear family shaped Black life across time and space.[88]

Inez Moore's lawyers drew on this body of scholarship, noting that "within the Black lower-class it has been quite common for several generations . . . to live together under one roof," often headed by a maternal grandmother.[89] Mrs. Moore's allies also invoked Douglas's paean to "family values" in *Belle Terre*, which recognized their "critical importance" as "particularly relevant in the context of zoning."[90]

Justice Powell, who had little patience for Boraas's claims, reacted viscerally to *Moore*. "I confess to being strongly 'result oriented' in this case." Powell called the ordinance "an extreme example of the idiocy of the city council. Grandparents, children, and grandchildren have resided together ... from the beginning of man's existence."[91] Powell found it "incredible" that East Cleveland officials would target "a grandmother and the grandson she has reared from infancy."[92] Powell drafted a dissent that later became the Court's plurality opinion.

Justice Blackmun also easily distinguished *Moore* from *Belle Terre*. "I have very little trouble with this case," Blackmun noted, preferring to rely on "the newly developing concept of privacy, and, in particular, privacy of the family."[93] A 5–4 majority initially supported the ordinance; Blackmun drafted a short dissent warning that this approach could allow a municipality to exclude all families with children. Blackmun worried that the Carter White House, with the president's sons and their wives and children residing together in the executive mansion, would be illegal in East Cleveland.[94]

Other swing justices expressed skepticism. Justice John Paul Stevens, Douglas's replacement, deemed *Moore* a "phony," "manufactured" case, and he resisted applying substantive due process analysis to a zoning dispute. He and Stewart found the city council's racial composition significant; Stewart called the ordinance's purpose "to prevent [the] city from becoming a slum" after its population went from "all-white to virtually all-Black." He warned that if the Court found an equal protection violation here, then "*every* definition of family will be suspect."[95] Chief Justice Warren Burger initially voted to reverse but later reconsidered. "Many family homes, my own included, often had a grandparent living in the household," he acknowledged, but "'nuclear' family," as the "basic building block of our society," seemed "a rational place to draw the line."[96]

Justice Marshall strongly disagreed. "I have seen too many situations where a strong grandparent literally held the family together and was responsible for the education and upbringing of decent, law-abiding youngsters," he responded to Burger. "The government has no business foisting" "a middle class norm" "on those to whom economic or psychological necessity dictates otherwise."[97] Justice Brennan, the son of Irish immigrants, raised in Newark with his parents, seven siblings, and paternal grandmother, objected vehemently as well: "The 'nuclear family' concept seems to me completely out of touch with the reality of a vast number of relationships in our society, including my own as a youngster growing up. . . . I cannot believe that the Constitution embraces . . . an affluent suburban concept of what is a family."[98]

Justice Stewart's draft majority opinion minimized any free association interest and reasoned that *Belle Terre* precluded claims based upon "general notions about the 'privacy of the home.'" The law "did not impede [Mrs. Moore's] choice to have or not to have children, and it did not dictate to her how her own children were to be nurtured and reared." In his view, "extended family" should not receive the same constitutional protection as marital and parental relationships. Stewart dismissively characterized Mrs. Moore's interest as "permanently sharing a kitchen and a suite of contiguous rooms with some of her relatives."[99]

Brennan drafted a blistering dissent. "Reaction to this decision must be one of shocked disbelief," he wrote. "The Court holds that the Constitution is powerless to prevent East Cleveland from prosecuting as a criminal and jailing a 63-year-old grandmother for refusing to expel from her home her now 10-year-old grandson who has . . . been brought up by her since his mother's death when he was less than one year old." The city could "prohibit groups of *unrelated* individuals from constituting a family." But limiting extended-family occupancy reflected "complete cultural myopia" and "depressing insensitivity about the human condition of a very large part of our society."[100]

Brennan pointedly noted Moore's race but stopped short of calling the law "racially discriminatory." He did warn, however, that a decision for East Cleveland "may encourage enactment elsewhere of similar ordinances that effectively exclude Blacks from single-family white neighborhoods."[101] Stewart prepared a retort: he saw nothing "racially discriminatory," noting that East Cleveland's population and leadership was "over ninety percent Negro." Brennan's draft "boils down to the proposition that the people of the Negro community of East Cleveland are prevented by the Constitution from trying to escape the racial stereotypes of the 'subculture' that his dissenting opinion describes."[102] This exchange remained out of the public eye because Stevens switched sides and Powell's draft dissent became a plurality opinion joined by Blackmun, Brennan, and Marshall.

Powell resisted any reference to race in *Moore*, as he had in earlier welfare and poverty cases. His notes indicate that he saw "no racial overtones" in the case and would decline to join any opinion that highlighted race.[103] Powell's opinion instead waxed eloquent about the value of extended family relationships in universalist terms. The "accumulated wisdom of civilization, gained over the centuries and honored throughout our history," supported due process protection for relatives who came together to support each other, especially in difficult times.[104] Brennan filed a concurrence, joined by Marshall, which emphasized the importance of extended kinship ties "for large numbers of the poor and deprived minorities of our society," especially Black families. Brennan borrowed statistics from Mrs. Moore's brief; quoted Ladner, Herbert Gans, and other scholars; and foregrounded the law's racial and economic impact.[105]

Mrs. Moore won not because the justices reached consensus on contentious questions of racial and economic justice or agreed on the meaning of privacy and freedom of association. Rather, she prevailed because she persuaded a plurality of the Court that East Cleveland's ordinance, by "slicing deeply into the family itself," belonged in an entirely different category from Belle Terre's restriction on unrelated persons. And Inez Moore functioned as a parent: as Marshall wrote to Burger, she undertook "the duties of a mother for her grandchildren."[106]

Belle Terre all but foreclosed federal constitutional challenges to occupancy limits for non-relatives. State constitutional challenges survived in several states, and unrelated persons limits remained contentious in some communities. For example, in Ramsey, New Jersey, Mayor Salvatore Burgio had suspended enforcement after hostile state court rulings; following *Belle Terre*, the Republican-dominated city council tightened the limit to two unrelated occupants, and similar ordinances passed in other northern New Jersey towns.[107] In 1975, a Superior Court judge struck down an anti-grouper law in Manasquan under the state constitution. A lawyer for the plaintiffs predicted that "unless a town can demonstrate circumstances identical to those in Belle Terre," ordinances in a half-dozen other shoreline communities would fall one after the other.[108]

In some communities, the zeal to ban countercultural living arrangements faded with time. By 1978 in Ramsey, a thirty-one-year-old city councilman, Michael Adams, campaigned against the no-more-than-two restriction. "Today's [college] student," he averred, in contrast to earlier notions of hippies and communes, "is stable and basically conservative." Adams, a high school guidance counselor, believed the ordinance unfairly excluded young college graduates who wished to return to Ramsey to settle down, as well as "divorced or separated persons who need at least three dwellers" to make rent and senior citizens pooling resources.[109]

The New Jersey Supreme Court revisited the issue in 1979, when Dennis Baker, a Presbyterian minister who lived with his wife and three children, an unrelated woman and her three children, and various other co-religionists, challenged Plainfield's no-more-than-four law. The court ruled that the city could not exclude from the definition of "single, non-profit housekeeping unit" a household that functioned as a "traditional extended family."[110]

The following year, California's highest court struck down Santa Barbara's no-more-than-five ordinance, challenged by Beverly Rysdale (Adamson). Rysdale usually bought, renovated, and sold homes at a profit, but she rented one house—a ten-bedroom French Normandy home of more than six thousand square feet—to a group of tenants who had developed a "bond closer to that of a family." The residents, who ranged in age from twenty-one to thirty-seven and included "a businesswoman, a graduate biochemistry student, a tractor-business operator, a real-estate woman, a lawyer," cooked and traveled together, with some contributing significant sums to the property's improvement. The threat of eviction disrupted this communal living arrangement. Rysdale said that the ensuing legal battle catalyzed her commitment to group living. She saw herself as "a community consultant . . . providing a space for people to live in and enjoy and experiment."[111] Rysdale's attorney, Ben Bycel, conceded that he could more easily challenge the unrelated persons ordinance if he were representing "two widows each with two children." Still, with amicus support from the ACLU, he successfully argued that the ordinance violated due process, equal protection, and a recent state constitutional amendment protecting a right of privacy.[112]

A handful of states joined New Jersey and California in the following years, but *Belle Terre* cast a long shadow.[113] In most U.S. jurisdictions the ability to live communally with non-relatives still was subject to local governments' discretion.[114] State supreme courts in more than a dozen states explicitly affirmed local prerogatives to define family narrowly or to limit the number of unrelated persons who could live together.[115] For instance, a Missouri court upheld the City of Ladue's ordinance preventing an unmarried couple from living together with their child; the highest courts in Maine and Delaware allowed ordinances precluding group homes for cognitively disabled residents; and the Colorado Supreme Court validated a Denver law that excluded two married couples and two other unrelated persons "seeking to live together as a communal family."[116]

Notably, municipalities that defined family more broadly still had the power to constrain household living arrangements. Whether a local government would consider a collection of individuals living together a "functional family" or a "single housekeeping unit" depended largely on how closely they resembled a traditional family structure.[117] Typical favored characteristics included "stability" and "permanence," financial interdependence, joint living and cooking, and no appearance of extra-marital intimacy or countercultural "lifestyles." Most zoning disputes never made it to court. Clashes between living preferences and local regulations played out in the shadow of the law, shaping how people imagined their options or made choices about where and how to live.

Even in the handful of states that took a broader view of constitutional rights, functional definitions of family nevertheless invited official scrutiny and judgment. For example, Michigan's highest court, which interpreted its due process guarantee to prohibit "arbitrary and capricious" applications of zoning law, explained that municipalities could prohibit living arrangements that produced "undesirable behavior." To draw the line at legally related persons, however, would not merely exclude "college fraternities, hippie communes, motorcycle gangs, and other loosely structured groups of people associating for the purpose of enjoying a purely licentious style of living": it would also fence out unrelated Christian adults living together to further their religious mission or a married couple fostering six disabled non-related children. Because these groups more closely resembled traditional families, exclusion did not serve the law's stated purposes: "preservation of traditional family values, maintenance of property values and population and density control."[118] Even where they allowed persons without formal legal ties to co-reside, localities and courts retained the power to decide who and what were "functional equivalents" of families.

Fair Housing and Family Status

In addition to relatedness requirements, high rents, urban renewal policies, other exclusionary zoning laws, and a shortage of affordable housing units plagued low- and middle-income Americans and further limited housing access for those who departed from the marital nuclear family norm. Private discrimination by landlords, lenders, sellers, and real estate agents also undermined fair housing efforts. In the years following the enactment of the Fair Housing Act of 1968, which barred discrimination based on race, color, and national origin, advocates confronted other forms of bias based on sex, marital and familial status, and sexual orientation.

Even white, middle- and upper-income heterosexual couples who deviated from a male-breadwinner/female-homemaker model encountered lenders who assumed that young married women would abandon their careers to raise children. Banks discounted wives' income when determining creditworthiness, even if it was vital to the family budget.[119] In 1971 a survey by the Federal Home Loan Bank Board found that one-quarter of lenders would count none of the income of a twenty-five-year-old wife with two school-age children and a full-time secretarial job, and a majority would count less than half of her income.[120]

Banks conducted invasive inquiries into young couples' reproductive plans. Public and private lenders compelled married women of reproductive age to provide a "baby letter" from a physician attesting to "her or her husband's sterility, their use of approved birth control methods, or their willingness to terminate a pregnancy."[121] Veterans Administration (VA) guidelines prompted lenders to "[demand] affidavits from wives stating that they were practicing birth control and did not intend to have children." In one notorious episode, the VA told a veteran and his wife applying for a GI loan in 1973 that they must specify their birth control method and promise to seek an abortion in case of pregnancy.[122]

Divorced and widowed women faced formidable barriers to homeownership. Wives' inability to establish credit in their own names meant that after a marriage ended in death or divorce women often lacked a credit history to qualify for home loans.[123] Lenders frequently refused to count alimony and child support as income and used credit scoring systems that assigned numerical values based on sex or marital status.[124]

More subtle prejudices about women's capacity to conduct their own affairs also infected lending decisions. Widows could often draw on life insurance proceeds or estate settlements for a down payment or income. But divorced women carried the stigma of psychological and financial instability. Young, never-married women, one broker told the Civil Rights Commission, had "the most trouble securing a mortgage," due to the "likelihood of marriage and pregnancy," while only a long-term professional career shielded older "spinsters" from virtually automatic credit denial.[125]

Advocates described a potent combination of intentional, overt discrimination and inadvertent or "unthinking" bias in the housing market.[126] In 1974 a report by the U.S. Commission on Civil Rights observed that "traditional mortgage lending criteria ... virtually *require* sex discrimination." Women seeking credit were "automatically considered suspect risks," and "sex discrimination [was] part and parcel of official bank policy."[127] Bank officials claimed that support payments from an ex-spouse might be unreliable and that lack of an independent credit history raised alarm bells. But banks struggled to produce hard evidence that discriminatory policies in fact prevented borrower defaults.

Women's organizations exposed and attacked barriers to credit of all kinds in the early 1970s. They lobbied successfully for passage of the federal Equal Credit Opportunity Act of 1974 (ECOA), which banned discrimination based on marital status as well as sex. But ECOA "helped married and formerly married women more than never-married women" and "did little for low-income women," since laws prohibiting discrimination in mortgage lending only aided those with the resources to purchase a home.[128] Nor did ECOA include race as a protected category until two years later, after congressional hearings highlighted that more Black than white married women worked outside their homes, that Black couples more frequently relied upon the wife's income, and that Black women were more likely to be single. Racial prejudice, poverty, and entrenched residential segregation exacerbated barriers to mortgage access, creating a "gross underrepresentation of minority and female-headed families" among homeowners.[129]

The many women who lacked the means to buy a home faced a tight, expensive market compounded by rampant discrimination. A dismal picture emerged from public hearings in Atlanta, St. Louis, San Antonio, New York, and San Francisco conducted by the National Council of Negro Women (NCNW) and the Department of Housing and Urban Development (HUD) in 1974. The study was led by Black women, including Dr. Gloria Toote, a HUD assistant secretary; the former NOW president Aileen Hernandez; Dovey Johnson Roundtree, a lawyer; and the civil rights leader Dorothy Height. The study's report, published in 1976, documented obstacles across the nation.[130]

The shortage of affordable rental housing disproportionately harmed single women, especially mothers. Landlord bias aggravated structural debilities such as the "feminization of poverty" and wage inequality. Some hostility was blatant; in St. Louis, for example, a prospective tenant was told that the landlord "won't rent to divorced women."[131] As one housing advocate put it, "Many landlords seem to buy the myth that divorced or separated women can't legally sign leases, won't be able to pay their rent, will have wild parties to entertain men, will have unruly children, and may be emotionally unstable."[132] Rental agents worried aloud that unattached women would bother landlords with routine maintenance tasks.[133] A New Jersey rental agent said, "A complex with a reputation for renting to single women attracts more prowlers," requiring "larger security forces."[134] Single female roommates also encountered suspicion: "The insinuation . . . is often that these two women who want to live together must be lesbians or . . . prostitutes," the NCNW reported.[135]

For many single Black women, prejudice against recipients of public assistance doomed rental prospects, whether or not the women in fact received government support. One New York City woman described how "when she wears her regular everyday clothing to apply for an apartment, the landlord says to her, 'We don't want any welfare mothers.' And when she got dressed up, he said, 'We don't want any hookers.'"[136] Landlords often viewed unmarried Black women as undesirable tenants even when they had no children and held middle-class professional jobs.[137]

Poor single mothers of color faced the highest hurdles.[138] In 1972, officials in Rockland County, New York, reported a surge of discrimination allegations by welfare recipients.[139] In Rhode Island the Providence Human Relations Commission and the local ACLU received dozens of such complaints each month in 1973. Carolyn Maldonado told the state senate's judiciary committee that "she was forced to live in a $90/month 'dump,'" because landlords told her, 'We don't want you, you're divorced, you're on welfare, you've got children.'"[140] A *Los Angeles Times* survey conducted in 1976 found that AFDC recipients were "relegated to the most rundown sections of the city" and "forced to live in substandard or unsuitable housing."[141] Lack of accessible public transportation and childcare forced many women to choose public assistance over gainful employment.[142] Long waiting lists even for dilapidated public housing coupled with suburban zoning ordinances that precluded higher-density housing exposed what the NCNW called the "demographic consequences of apartheid, American style."[143]

Assumptions that "the children of single-parent women are not disciplined and do not have the kind of supervision they need" led many landlords to reject nonmarital families or to require unaffordable deposits. For some, children were "not wanted unless there is a man in the family."[144] In 1969 a survey found that 66 percent of San Francisco apartment buildings banned children altogether.[145] A decade later, 62 percent of female renters in California had children, and families with children made up more than 40 percent of Black renters.[146] But 70 percent of Los

Angeles apartment buildings disallowed children, while another 16 percent excluded children in certain age groups.[147]

Lenders and landlords alike assumed that marriage conferred on
spouses financial stability and moral worthiness that justified discrimination in their favor.[148] Marital status was a time-honored, acceptable criterion, especially in mortgage lending, for identifying desirable applicants.
Testers who posed as prospective tenants or home buyers to expose discrimination based on race, religion, and even sex routinely used marital
status as a control variable, sending married white and Black couples or
single males and females to compare lender and landlord responses.[149]
Indeed, some lenders and real estate agents looked to marital status as a
putatively neutral alternative to newly prohibited factors such as race
and, later, sex. A system proposed in Pennsylvania in 1972 awarded
points based on "marital status," among other factors. Touted as the "ultimate answer" to housing discrimination, the plan garnered enthusiastic
support from the head of Philadelphia's Board of Realtors. "We used to
get a helluva lot of complaints about discrimination," he crowed. "Now
we have virtually none."[150]

Of these varieties of bias, sex discrimination sparked the most sustained, organized campaign in the early 1970s. By the time Congress
amended the Fair Housing Act (FHA) to include sex in 1974, approximately half the states had some form of prohibition on sex discrimination.[151] But unlike the Equal Credit Opportunity Act, the Fair Housing
Act did not protect against marital status discrimination, and thus it offered limited legal remedies for lower-income unmarried women who
could not afford to purchase a home.[152] And marital status discrimination
affected a range of individuals: single men, male roommates, cohabiting
gay and straight couples, as well as single women with or without children.

Some states and localities passed marital status anti-discrimination
laws in the 1960s and 1970s, thanks largely to zealous advocacy by wom-
en's organizations on behalf of married and divorced women.[153] But their
meanings were variable and contested.[154] Did marital status discrimination bans prohibit discrimination against unmarried *couples* who wished
to live together, or merely against *individuals* based on their status as single, married, divorced, widowed, or separated?

A handful of states, including Alaska, California, Massachusetts, and
New Jersey, embraced an expansive reading. In Washington, at the urging
of women's organizations the attorney general interpreted a 1973 law to
protect unmarried couples. Press accounts describe a "bitterly contested

case" in Spokane the following year. A Black man and a white woman rented an apartment after telling their landlord they planned to marry soon. Four months later, the landlord's superintendent "discovered the couple hadn't married and evidently didn't plan to do so." Explaining that "tenants with children had a right to expect that their children would not be exposed to a situation that apparently put the stamp of approval on unmarried cohabitation," the rental company served the couple with an eviction notice. After the state human rights commission upheld their complaint, the couple received one month's rent as compensation.[155]

Complaints from rental companies and landlords in Washington state about the mandate to rent to unmarried couples prompted legislative reconsideration, but not repeal.[156] In Oregon, by contrast, state legislators carved out a couples exception, and several other state attorneys general and courts followed suit.[157] By 1992, twenty-one states and the District of Columbia banned housing discrimination based on "marital status," but "only two federal courts, three state courts, and one state administrative agency ha[d] interpreted [those laws] to protect unmarried couples."[158] The persistence of laws that made nonmarital sex unlawful bolstered the narrower interpretation.[159]

The prospect of forcing landlords to rent to cohabiting couples often encumbered or derailed efforts to pass marital status discrimination laws in the first place. In Gainesville, Florida, Commissioner Joe Little dropped marital status from his proposed anti-discrimination bill for fear it "might ... condon[e]" cohabitation.[160] In 1973, this "monumental" issue caused Rhode Island legislators to drop a marital status discrimination ban.[161] In Lincoln, Nebraska, advocates secured passage only by assuring lawmakers that they would never ban discrimination in housing "against people who were illegally cohabiting."[162]

A few municipalities considered measures designed to cover unmarried couples, including, occasionally, same-sex couples. In Boulder, Colorado, officials specified in 1974 that to protect "homosexuals living together," marital status as well as sexual orientation discrimination must be proscribed.[163] Philadelphia's Commission on Human Relations confirmed that an amendment passed in 1980 included both "single parents" and unmarried persons "living together."[164] A handful of cities, including Detroit, passed bans on discrimination based on marital status and sexual orientation simultaneously to "prohibit housing discrimination against unmarried persons of either the same or different sex who want to live together."[165]

Elsewhere, the addition of sexual orientation threatened proposed legislation to ban other forms of discrimination. In Michigan, for instance, a lawmaker cautioned, "We don't want to lose coverage of [sex, age, and marital status] in order to have a Don Quixote run at [sexual orientation]."[166] California, by contrast, passed a sex and marital status discrimination bill in 1975 after proponents confirmed its applicability to couples, despite warnings that "it would eliminate the authority of landlords to refuse to rent to homosexuals."[167]

A smattering of localities addressed sexual orientation separately. In 1975, Yellow Springs joined Columbus, Ohio, in passing a prohibition drafted by Antioch College's Gay Rights Center and the village's Human Relations Commission.[168] A few municipalities—such as Washington, D.C. (1973 and 1977), Mountain View, California (1975), Champaign, Illinois (1977), Hartford, Connecticut (1977), Detroit (1977), and San Francisco (1978)—enacted laws covering public accommodations and education as well as housing and employment.[169]

These battles often dragged on for years. After a three-year effort was derailed on the final stretch by Catholic Church opposition, the New York City Council rejected an anti-discrimination ordinance in 1974.[170] A bill finally passed in 1986.[171] In Austin, Texas, a gay rights ordinance introduced in the early 1970s passed in 1982 after the defeat of an anti-gay referendum sponsored by fundamentalist Christian groups.[172] In Hawaii, the state House of Representatives passed a bill in 1976—albeit with one member voting for the bill "in a squeaky falsetto voice" to "chuckle[s]" from his colleagues—but it did not become law until 1991.[173] Anita Bryant's "Save Our Children" campaign defeated Dade County, Florida's anti-discrimination ordinance soon after its passage in 1977; several cities around the country followed suit and Florida prohibited same-sex marriage and adoption within weeks.[174]

The partial success of efforts to abolish marital status discrimination in public housing is telling. After federal legislation in 1976 made single persons eligible to apply, HUD issued a proposed rule that would allow low-income unmarried couples, regardless of sex, to live in public housing if they could demonstrate a "stable family relationship." The regulation took effect in 1977 with little fanfare, but weeks later congressional opposition flared. An amendment excluded same-sex couples entirely, while local authorities would have the discretion to accept or deny unmarried different-sex couples.[175] This resolution recalled HUD's policy toward mothers with nonmarital children: a functional standard partly replaced formal exclusion but left room for continued discrimination.

Under ECOA, too, a debate ensued about protection for nonmarried couples who sought to purchase homes together.[176] In 1974, Nancy Polikoff, then a law student and later a feminist lawyer, expressed optimism that ECOA would protect unmarried couples.[177] Some bank officials did interpret ECOA broadly. "Bankers, a conservative lot anyway, once held that unmarrieds were unstable, and, therefore, bad risks. These days, thanks in large part to [ECOA] . . . such thinking is a thing of the past."[178] A man who successfully qualified for a mortgage with his partner confirmed, "They don't seem to care if we're married or not. If you have some kind of substantial financial background, you're as good a risk as a married couple."[179]

But questions persisted about ECOA's coverage. Feminists argued unsuccessfully in 1975 for regulations that would force lenders to consider a couple's combined income, regardless of marital status. In 1976, an engaged couple, Marcia Harris and Jerry Markham, signed a contract to purchase property on Capitol Hill. But the lender rejected their application, saying their incomes could not be aggregated when determining creditworthiness. The couple sued. The federal district court held that ECOA allowed creditors to consider the "special legal ties created between two people by the marriage bond." The D.C. Circuit reversed, citing ECOA's "plain language."[180] One commentator warned that *Markham* could "have far-reaching consequences," supporting similar claims by "communal cohabitants" and "homosexual couples."[181]

Anecdotal evidence suggests a surge in unmarried individuals purchasing homes together in the late 1970s and 1980s. In Tucson, lenders reported that up to a quarter of home loans went to single people purchasing real estate together—two women, two men, siblings, and parent-child combinations among them. Some pooled resources out of financial necessity: almost 30 percent of homes sold by American savings and loan associations in 1981 went to unmarried individuals, pairs, or groups, but only an estimated one-fifth of these buyers were "shacking up."[182]

Publicly, lenders professed fidelity to the bottom line, rather than to traditional notions of marital superiority. But few court cases tested ECOA's application to discrimination against unmarried different-sex couples, much less same-sex couples or communalists. Their ambiguous legal status meant that cohabiting couples seeking mortgages could not be sure that the law would have their backs. And many who could not

afford to purchase homes remained at the mercy of landlords' willingness to rent to the unmarried.

The persistent shortage of affordable rental housing and the prolifera-
tion of "adults-only" policies spurred a growing movement to outlaw discrimination against families with children. Combating "familial status"
discrimination was a more politically palatable cause than legal protections for unmarried individuals or couples, gay and straight. A few states
already banned such discrimination: the earliest state laws appear to be
New Jersey's (1898) and Illinois's (1909). Post–World War I housing
shortages prompted similar enactments in New York and Arizona in
1921.[183] A second ripple of laws began in 1971, when Massachusetts and
Delaware enacted statewide familial status discrimination bans. A small
handful of localities followed suit.

Landlords complained that children's presence required safety pre-
cautions, incurred maintenance costs and property damage, and drove
away prospective tenants.[184] Other qualms included competing liberty
claims from the elderly and others who preferred not to have children as
neighbors. Some familial status discrimination bans therefore included
exemptions for housing meant solely for seniors or other specific demographic groups.[185]

Child exclusions also provided a pretext for racial discrimination.[186] "I
was recently told by an apartment building manager that she wouldn't rent
to me because I have a three-year-old child," wrote a "non-white" woman
to a Long Beach, California, newspaper in 1977. After learning that other
children lived in the building, the letter-writer "wonder[ed] if racial prejudice on the part of the white manager is involved."[187] A divorced mother
turned away from many San Francisco apartments could not be sure
"whether [it was] because she was a single mother, a welfare mother, a
black, or a black woman with a child of an interracial marriage."[188] Studies
found that child exclusion policies in rental housing were "designed" to
maintain school segregation. The concentration of adults-only housing in
predominantly white areas also limited residential integration.[189]

California became an early battleground for debates about familial
status discrimination.[190] Warning of a "city without children," in 1975 a
coalition of fifty San Francisco agencies drafted a familial status ordinance after failing to pass a similar law the year before.[191] The "controversial" measure passed by a vote of 9–1.[192] Lawmakers introduced
statewide legislation but it failed year after year.[193] Soon the state attorney

general issued a non-binding advisory opinion ruling that California law already prohibited landowners from discriminating against families with children.[194]

Housing advocates urged judges to follow suit. In 1976, Stephen Wolfson, an attorney, and his wife, Lois, received an eviction notice from their Marina del Rey landlord after the birth of their son, Adam. Unable to buy because of rising home prices, the couple struggled to find a desirable apartment. Lois recalled, "It was so unusual to be discriminated against. . . . It happens to others, not us. I grew up in a [white] middle-class family here, and having kids is what . . . was expected from me."[195]

Supported by housing groups and the ACLU, the Wolfsons brought a class action lawsuit charging that no-children policies violated state statutory and constitutional guarantees. Lower courts rejected their claims, but in 1982 the state supreme court ruled in the Wolfsons' favor.[196] Justice Matthew Tobriner's opinion dodged the constitutional questions but held that state law forbade "widespread, and potentially universal, exclusion of children from housing" just as it prohibited "arbitrary" discrimination against welfare recipients, "homosexuals," and students. The court refused to sanction "the sacrifice of the well-being of children on the altar of a landlord's profit, or possibly some tenants' convenience."[197]

As discrimination complaints poured in, Governor Jerry Brown and his successor, George Deukmejian, announced they would leave enforcement to private plaintiffs and local agencies. Advocates slowly made local headway, passing laws in Los Angeles and other, smaller cities. California courts extended familial status protection to condominiums and eventually mobile homes, but only after years of litigation.

Enforcement lapses blunted the effect of familial status laws that did pass.[198] Ignorance of the law plagued prospective tenants.[199] A year after Berkeley's enactment City Councilmember Carole Davis, a divorced Black parent of a six-year-old, reported: "I mentioned my son [to an apartment manager] and then the woman said, 'I'm sorry to inform you that we don't rent to people with children.'"[200] In 1983 a survey of eleven California municipalities showed that "39 percent of landlords excluded or imposed restrictions on children," contravening state court rulings.[201] In Connecticut a study conducted in 1986 found that child exclusion continued despite an anti-discrimination law enacted in 1981.[202] In one New Jersey county, at least half of the families receiving public services experienced discrimination based on familial status.[203]

A grim picture emerged of an exclusionary rental market that became tighter with each passing year. A HUD study found that child exclusion nationwide "jumped from an estimated 17 percent in 1974 to 26 percent in 1980."[204] Of approximately thirteen million two-bedroom rental units in the United States, one-quarter of them were unavailable to families with one child, one-third excluded families with more than one child, and 60 percent banned families with three or more children.[205] Much more dramatic figures described many cities. Landlords now were "more careful" about concealing exclusionary intent, instead enacting "one person per bedroom" rules, or restricting pool access for children to school hours, or asking questions designed to signal that children were unwelcome.[206]

The struggles of unhoused families shut out of the rental market made headlines.[207] Advocates catalogued the consequences, including limited access to childcare, employment, and transportation. Sympathetic press accounts featured families such as the Moraleses, a Mexican American immigrant couple with ten children, who depended on their fellow churchgoers and extended family to keep a roof over their heads.[208] The columnist Tom Elias excoriated Republicans for touting family values and law enforcement but withholding resources from familial status anti-discrimination efforts.[209]

In 1983, Congress began considering a familial status amendment to the Fair Housing Act.[210] Prospects improved when Democrats retook the Senate in 1986. Senator Edward Kennedy (D-MA) introduced a fair housing bill in February 1987, denouncing "American apartheid."[211] Advocates stressed that the original Fair Housing Act contained broad categorical protections but the act's feeble enforcement mechanisms and paltry remedies limited its efficacy. Housing discrimination was notoriously difficult to prove, and the absence of protections against child exclusion gave biased owners an easy alibi.

Supportive lawmakers noted the "racially discriminatory effect" of child exclusion policies.[212] Representative Ron Dellums (D-CA) called them "a smokescreen to exclude minorities from housing."[213] Congress members cited the growing number of unhoused families and a resultant rise in foster care placements.[214] Representative George Miller (D-CA) lamented, "When we see two [political] parties struggling to be profamily . . . say that somebody has a private right to discriminate against you because you had a child . . . That just cannot be." Miller shamed legislators who championed personal fiscal responsibility, noting that many parents who brought their children to homeless shelters were "working every day but they cannot find housing."[215]

The Reagan administration initially opposed the measure. The assistant attorney general, William Bradford Reynolds, warned in 1987, "No other federal civil rights statute prohibits discrimination based on familial status. Its intrusion in the Fair Housing Act would dramatically expand the reach of the federal government."[216] Opponents worried that "all-adult" communities, especially those serving the elderly, would unfairly be eliminated. An affordable housing shortage was the real culprit, these lawmakers argued. Rather than imposing a blanket federal ban on child exclusion, they said, "let state and local governments come up with appropriate laws."[217]

After years of opposition from the National Association of Realtors and conservative politicians, in 1988 advocates brokered compromise legislation that strengthened enforcement mechanisms and extended protections based on familial status and disability.[218] Proponents hailed the Fair Housing Amendments as the most important civil rights legislation in a generation. Phyllis Schlafly warned the measure would hurt "middle-aged and senior citizens" and force landlords to accept "AIDS patients" and "violent alcoholics."[219] But George H. W. Bush, the vice president and Republican presidential candidate, distanced himself from the Reagan administration's civil rights record by highlighting his support.[220] Reagan signed the bill into law following an overwhelming bipartisan vote in favor, declaring, "Discrimination is particularly tragic when it means a family is refused housing near good schools, a good job or simply in a better neighborhood to raise children."[221]

Congressional sponsors made clear, however, that the amendments did not encompass discrimination based on *marital* status. A leading authority on housing discrimination wrote in 1989 that "no serious effort has been mounted" to change their minds.[222] Barring discrimination against families with children provided a cause behind which liberals and conservatives could unite; ending bias against straight or gay unmarried individuals and couples did not.

From subversive communal experiments that deliberately tested the boundaries of constitutional freedom to desperate searches for shelter in exclusionary rental markets, Americans who explored new definitions of household in the 1970s encountered daunting obstacles. Once again, marital status law reforms successfully attacked the most objectionable aspects of marital supremacy—overt racial bigotry, discrimination against married women—as well as child exclusion. But they could not win broad constitutional protections for unconventional households or prevent state and private actors from enforcing distinctions based on marital status. At the federal level and in many states and localities, advocates succeeded mostly where they did not directly challenge the primacy of marital heterosexual nuclear families or proclaim bold visions of sexual and associational liberty. Focusing on harm to children, or sex discrimination, or racial animus remained a surer path to success than asserting the right to live with one's nonmarital partner, unrelated friends, or counterculture comrades. Similar constraints faced Americans who fought exclusions from public sector employment, as the next chapter details.

CHAPTER FIVE

Double Standards

Nonmarital Sex and Public Employment

S EAMAN ANNA FLORES, A twenty-three-year-old Mexican American woman from Dallas, Texas, was serving in the Communication Center at Whiting Naval Base in Pensacola, Florida, when she learned she was pregnant. Flores and her fiancé, an enlisted man, planned to marry on May 28, 1970. But instead of walking down the aisle, Flores spent her intended wedding day in a base dispensary, suffering a miscarriage. While recovering in the hospital Flores learned that she would be discharged from the Navy for becoming pregnant. A few weeks later her commanding officer denied Flores's appeal, despite her "excellent professional performance and her strong desire to remain in the Navy." Retention "would imply that unwed pregnancy is condoned and would eventually result in a dilution of the moral standards set for women in the Navy."[1]

Flores sent a flurry of letters—to Senator John Tower of Texas, to Representative Martha Griffiths of Michigan, to the deputy assistant secretary of defense (for civil rights) Frank W. Bender II, and, on the advice of the Equal Employment Opportunity Commission (EEOC)'s Sonia Pressman by way of a sympathetic Navy lawyer, the American Civil Liberties Union.[2] "Because I committed (to the Navy Department, at least) an unpardonable sin, I am to be banished from the service for no apparent reason other than I am, presumably, a tarnished woman."[3] Wrote Flores to Bender:

Sir, if a study was ever made of the sexual morality of the men and women comprising the military, and if those found guilty of transgressing the unwritten boundaries of unwed sex life [were excluded], we would have no military, at all ... there would scarcely be enough numbers left to man a decommissioned PT boat, let alone a ship of the line.[4]

"Have you ever heard of a father of an illegitimate child being discharged from the military?" Flores demanded of Senator Tower. "I haven't."[5] To apply a sexual double standard, Flores insisted, was "a direct and unthinkable violation of any woman's civil and human rights regardless if she wears a uniform or not."[6]

Tower intervened, and in August 1970 Flores's commanding officer revoked her discharge, saying that "the incidence of unwed pregnancy ... should not prejudice [Flores's] service career."[7] The ACLU's Betsy Nolan quipped to Attorney Chuck Morgan, "You've struck a real blow for equality, now WAVES can have a guy in every port."[8] The Associated Press reported that Flores "has fired a broadside for Women's Lib with a federal court suit claiming the Navy discharges pregnant service ladies, but takes no action against the sailors responsible for their pregnancies."[9] In fact, although Flores had won her own fight, the battle to change military policy was only just beginning.

In the early 1970s public employment became a key battleground for those who departed from heterosexual marital norms. Like Flores, individuals who wanted to join the military or maintain occupations such as schoolteacher and librarian faced especially daunting hurdles. After overt moralizing began to fade from other areas of the law, public employees in a position to influence children and young people still encountered deep-seated expectations about the state's prerogative to regulate their conduct. Unlike their private sector counterparts, however, they could invoke the constitution's protection.

By the end of the decade, as privacy, equality, due process, and liberty claims eased absolute bars to government employment, the prevailing constitutional standard allowed public employers to defend discrimination against unmarried pregnant, cohabiting, or gay individuals if they could demonstrate a *nexus* between an employee's identity or conduct and their ability to function effectively on the job. But the nexus standard, although an improvement over categorical exclusions, left many who did not or could not conform to ideals of marital heterosexuality without recourse.

Anna Flores's activism fueled a campaign against what advocates for women considered the discriminatory and hypocritical treatment of enlisted women and officers. Pregnancy had long been grounds for discharge, regardless of a servicewoman's marital status. Officials in the Department of Labor's Women's Bureau and representatives of the Florence Crittenton Association (FCA) demanded in 1970 that the Department of Defense review military policies toward unmarried mothers.[10] The FCA's challenge was hardly a full-throated endorsement of sexual liberty: "To discriminate because of what may well have been one brief indiscretion" and "to penalize those who through poverty and ignorance were unable to have an abortion or to use contraceptive measures" seemed "unjust."[11]

Internal military debates reveal a range of views on the exclusion of unmarried women who became pregnant. Some counseled a case-by-case approach. Others cautioned that retaining unmarried women who became pregnant would damage the military's reputation as a respectable pursuit for the educated, middle-class women the services wished to attract.[12] In 1970 a memo from Director of Women Marines Jeannette Sustad worried that "enlistment of women who have borne children out of wedlock could be interpreted by the public as a lowering of our moral standards."[13]

But military leaders could not ignore the growing legal vulnerability of policies permitting discharge for pregnancy. *Flores*, among the first of a series of constitutional challenges, involved discrimination based on marital status as well as sex. In 1971, the ACLU filed a class action complaint against the Navy, citing servicewomen's "right to be free of invasions of their right to privacy in their sexual relationships." Echoing Anna Flores, advocates decried a sexual double standard.[14] Navy men "have sexual intercourse with women to whom they are not married," "father children out of wedlock," and "incur in their sexual activities venereal disease," but they never were discharged or even investigated.[15]

Flores also challenged discrimination against unmarried women in particular. After the ACLU sued, the Navy claimed to consider requests for retention on a case-by-case basis, "regardless of marital status."[16] But Emily Carssow of ACLU's Atlanta office found that the Navy frequently granted married women's requests, while commanding officers almost never recommended retention of unmarried pregnant women—even though, unlike the married women, almost all chose abortion or adoption over raising a child.

Officials' reasoning continued to betray moral judgments about women's nonmarital sexual activity. Rear Admiral Douglas Plate, head of naval personnel, explained that a "specific pregnancy would not in itself render a woman morally unfit." However, circumstances that suggested "prostitution or blatant promiscuity" or a "serious moral dereliction" might prove disqualifying. Plate said "he would look to see whether the woman was 'the company whore' or whether her conduct would bring discredit to the Navy."[17]

Most of the women who became pregnant while unmarried expressed regret and shame. "I realize the wrong that I have done toward the reputation of the Navy Waves," said one characteristically apologetic supplicant. Servicewomen often emphasized that they became pregnant as the result of a one-time error. One woman averred: "I fully realize that the [pregnancy] was the result of my indiscretion and I truly regret it. However, I would like to point out that I am not a wanton, promiscuous girl. The sailor involved and I were thinking of marriage, and I truly believed I loved him at the time of intimacy." Another woman "stated that she made a mistake because she believed she was in love and allowed herself to be swayed by the protestations of a rather unscrupulous individual," a Marine.

Sometimes such repentant attitudes won a reprieve. A commanding officer described one woman as a "good worker . . . not considered to be promiscuous and feels guilt ridden for her mistake." He recommended discharge, with an opportunity to reenlist should she give her child up for adoption as planned. Another single woman, "remorseful and ashamed," obtained an abortion and was retained. Contrition, while necessary, often proved insufficient. To ACLU lawyers, the pattern was clear: the Navy accommodated married women's (often officers') pregnancies, but not those of unmarried enlisted women.[18]

Legal developments buoyed Flores's claims. The EEOC's Sonia Pressman noted that federal civil service regulations from 1966 contained anti-discrimination protections for sex and marital status. Furthermore, Pressman suggested, "premarital intercourse is such a common part of current American life," a custom "particularly common among women with their future marriage partners," that it was "questionable whether such conduct can properly be termed immoral."[19]

Some state legislatures and lower courts had begun to ease up on morals regulation, often influenced by the Model Penal Code, which recommended decriminalization of private, consensual adult conduct. This growing agreement among elite reformers, along with discreet homophile activism, spurred some states to reconsider their prohibitions on sodomy.[20] In 1969, reformers in Connecticut, following a similar effort in Illinois, successfully lobbied for decriminalization; by 1973, a total of eight states had repealed similar prohibitions and the American Psychiatric Association ceased to list homosexuality as a disorder in its diagnostic manual.[21]

Reformers made inroads in employment law too. The D.C. Circuit held in 1969 that homosexual conduct could not be grounds for automatic discharge of a government employee in the absence of "some ascertainable deleterious effect" on the civil service.[22] A federal district court in California ruled in 1970 that the U.S. Postal Service could not summarily terminate Neil Mindel for living unmarried with a woman.[23] With increasing success, feminists and civil rights lawyers pushed for interpretations of Title VII and other sex discrimination prohibitions that included discrimination based on pregnancy and marital status.[24] Some EEOC officials even read Title VII to cover discrimination against individuals because they were gay, lesbian, or "transsexual."[25]

Developments in the constitutional law of privacy also looked promising. In *Stanley v. Georgia* (1969), the Supreme Court ruled that states could not punish the possession of "obscene" materials at home.[26] When Pressman replied to a Navy lawyer's query concerning *Flores*, she enclosed a copy of the First Circuit's recent decision in *Baird v. Eisenstadt*, which challenged a Massachusetts statute that prohibited the dispensing of contraceptives to unmarried individuals. Dr. William Baird, a birth control activist, had witnessed the death of a Black single mother of nine from an attempted self-abortion in 1963. Four years later, he handed a package containing vaginal foam to a young woman and gave a fiery speech denouncing legal restrictions on contraception.[27] *Baird* asked the courts to step beyond *Griswold*, which had invalidated bans on contraceptives only for married couples. The First Circuit agreed: the law's mandate that "unmarried persons ... must risk for themselves, an unwanted pregnancy, for the child, illegitimacy, and for society a possible obligation of support" was contrary to "fundamental human rights."[28]

On appeal to the Supreme Court, Dr. Baird's supporters took a range of positions on the privileged status of marriage as a protected site for sexual privacy. Baird's brief did not challenge regulations to "diminish sexual promiscuity" but stated that banning birth control did not deter illicit sex. Instead, bans exacerbated the "tragic consequences that ensue from illegitimacy," including higher mortality rates for mothers and infants, stigma and poverty, overpopulation, pressure to abort illegally, and skyrocketing welfare costs.[29] "People are dying—the unwanted child (in many cases uncared for), is running amuck in the ghetto" (a barely veiled reference to race), "and the cost to the community is staggering."[30]

Others directly attacked the sexual double standard. Planned Parenthood's brief, authored by Harriet Pilpel, argued that the birth control ban "imposes a harsh penalty on women who violate the laws against fornication by putting them at risk of unwanted pregnancy, health hazards and the birth of illegitimate children, yet their male partners, equally guilty of fornication, are not burdened by forced conception in any comparable manner."[31] Human Rights for Women (HRW) challenged male supremacy and even marital privilege, invoking a "right of single persons to sexual relations without unwanted pregnancy." Denying such a right "works a particular hardship on single women," whose bedrooms, like the "sacred precincts of marital bedrooms" extolled in *Griswold*, "certainly . . . should be at least as private and free of state interference."[32] Moreover, the law "denied single women the equal protection of the law" based on both marital status and sex. HRW declared, *"A woman should not have to marry in order to exercise fundamental human rights."*[33]

The ACLU inched closer to but stopped short of asserting a right to sex outside marriage. Mel Wulf made sure the ACLU's brief did not endorse the constitutionality of laws prohibiting adultery and fornication.[34] The brief's final language made the state's prerogative to prohibit nonmarital sex conditional: "If the State does have a secure basis for a proscription of fornication it is the interest in reducing the birth rate of illegitimate children."[35] The ACLU used lower court decisions striking down abortion restrictions to argue that the "right of sexual privacy" protected in *Griswold* applied to "both married and single men and women."[36] But in *Eisenstadt*, the ACLU left the scope of this "right to sexual privacy" ambiguous.

So did the Supreme Court. Justice Brennan wrote for the majority: "The marital couple is not an independent entity with a mind and heart of its own, but an association of two individuals, each with a separate intellectual and emotional makeup." He continued: "If the right of privacy means anything, it is the right of the individual, married or single, to be free from unwarranted governmental intrusion into matters so fundamentally affecting a person as the decision whether to bear or beget a child."[37] Targeting unmarried individuals only, the majority said, did not serve the state's asserted interests in promoting health and preventing fornication since married persons would remain free to have extramarital sex without consequence.[38] "It would be plainly unreasonable," Brennan wrote, "to assume that Massachusetts has prescribed pregnancy and the birth of an unwanted child as punishment for fornication."[39] This focus on the relationship between means and ends—rather than on the legitimacy of legislating morality—allowed the justices to sidestep disagreements about the nature and scope of constitutional rights.[40]

Emboldened by *Eisenstadt*, ACLU lawyers asked the court in *Flores* to find that the "right of privacy protects a single individual's right to live with a member of the opposite sex," as well as "an unmarried individual's right to have children."[41] The Navy could not constitutionally discharge a woman "solely because of marital status and extramarital sexual relationships" or because of "the illegitimacy of her child."[42] The ACLU now came close to challenging the Navy's prerogative to punish nonmarital sexual activity at all where it did not harm the service's ability to carry out its mission. The records of single pregnant women failed to exhibit "the type of moral dereliction which is justification for discharging *either a male or a female* from the Navy."[43] By this reasoning, the Navy could not cure its policy's constitutional infirmity by applying the same stringent moral standard to men.

The ACLU read *Eisenstadt* to preclude the dismissal of servicemembers solely for having nonmarital sex, absent a compelling government interest. In cases involving sexual conduct, this interpretation had wider implications than a focus on equal protection for the married and unmarried: it could mean that everyone had a constitutional right to engage in sex, not merely that the government had to grant people the same rights regardless of marital status. At the same time, a general right to equal protection regardless of marital status could affect all kinds of laws, not just those related to sex or procreation. But if *Eisenstadt*'s ramifications for nonmarriage were confined to sex or procreation, then the decision did not necessarily call into question *all* legal distinctions between the married and unmarried.

In short, *Eisenstadt* opened tantalizing possibilities for sexual freedom and for those who would challenge marital status laws. But it remained far from clear whether or how the decision would extend to contexts beyond reproductive rights or to broader questions of marital primacy.[44]

Reading the constitutional writing on the wall, the government did not defend a sexual double standard in *Flores:* it argued instead that Navy policy no longer considered the moral status or implications of nonmarital pregnancy. None of the case histories from the first half of 1972 referred to servicewomen's "moral character," and Admiral Plate's successor, Admiral Robert B. Baldwin, gave "unequivocal" testimony that pregnant servicewomen would be judged based on *functional* factors: "the person's ability to do her job and cope with her physical condition." He also averred that "the same basic criteria" would apply "to both single and married pregnant women requesting retention."[45] The federal district court judge Winston Arnow accepted this defense.[46] He denied plaintiffs' request for a declaratory judgment to clarify that inquiries into moral character violated servicewomen's equal protection and privacy rights.[47]

Anna Flores's case faded into obscurity. Internal and external pressure, along with constitutional lawsuits, ultimately ended the military's automatic pregnancy discharge policies.[48] Sexual and reproductive privacy and liberty claims never came to fruition, and the military continued to penalize nonmarital sex in other ways without facing constitutional sanction. In catalyzing a shift from outright exclusion to a functional approach, *Flores* encapsulated developments in the constitutional law of nonmarital sex that presaged other cases examined in this chapter.

Many tributaries of advocacy and legal doctrine flowed into the river of 1970s litigation that challenged barriers to public employment for individuals who departed from conventional marital heterosexuality. Assisted by local ACLU lawyers and eventually by its national Sexual Privacy Project, gay and lesbian plaintiffs often led the way in creating precedents that unmarried pregnant women and heterosexual cohabitants put to use—despite important differences in the legal landscape each group confronted.

Sexual privacy was the common denominator in cases involving teachers and librarians, whose contact with children raised the stakes of morals regulation.[49] For all unmarried plaintiffs, the Supreme Court's decisions in *Eisenstadt v. Baird* (1972) and subsequently *Roe v. Wade* (1973) stretched the right of privacy beyond the marital bedroom and into a broader conception of autonomy. Advocates in public employment cases drew on *Eisenstadt* and *Roe* to argue that sexual privacy meant freedom to engage in nonmarital sex without losing one's job. The right to choose abortion even provided an analog for gay plaintiffs, who argued that compelling people to suppress their true sexual identities was comparable to forcing women to become mothers against their will.

Plaintiffs also made an array of equality arguments, with varying efficacy. Unmarried pregnant women attacked the sexual double standard Anna Flores cited in her battle with the Navy. Gay and cohabiting plaintiffs, in contrast, found little success describing the harm they suffered as sex discrimination. But gay teachers did use sex equality precedents like *Frontiero v. Richardson* (1973) to argue that sexual orientation should be considered a suspect classification subject to heightened judicial scrutiny. And cohabitants drew on *Eisenstadt*—with limited effectiveness—to argue that discrimination based on marital status violated equal protection. Some plaintiffs, especially those who could not or did not wish to hide their identities and ways of life, also invoked the First Amendment's protection of freedom of speech and association.

Plaintiffs and advocates articulated expansive claims: a constitutional right to engage in consensual nonmarital sex, to openly proclaim the worthiness of non-normative sexuality, and to freely associate with nonmarital partners without negative employment consequences.[50] In these cases, the law afforded some protection from categorical exclusion. However, the use of a functional standard—one that examined the impact of sexual identity or conduct on an individual's ability to perform the job in question—left the door open to discretionary decision-making by employers and courts that limited the scope and contours of sexual freedom and equality.

Gay and Lesbian Pioneers

The case that set the stage for the following decade's struggles over nonmarital sex and sexual privacy in public employment began with James Michael ("Mike") McConnell and Richard John ("Jack") Baker (whom we first encountered in chapter 3). The couple met in Oklahoma in 1966 and, after more than a year of "off and on" dating, "began thinking seriously about forming a permanent relationship." Baker proposed marriage on New Year's Eve, 1969. After moving to Minneapolis so that Baker could begin law school, both men joined the city's gay advocacy community. McConnell and Baker occupied the "militant middle" of a political spectrum that ranged from "liberal" to "revolutionary." Their application for a marriage license at the county clerk's office in May 1970 was simultaneously a sincere act of love and commitment, the launch of a deliberate legal strategy, and a theatrical attempt to publicize the cause of gay liberation.[51]

McConnell's marriage advocacy jeopardized his job offer from the University of Minnesota's library. After a hearing, the Board of Regents unanimously vetoed his appointment as head of cataloguing services. McConnell, assisted by local ACLU attorneys, filed suit in federal court. There, Regent John Yngve testified that "by seeking a marriage license, Mr. McConnell had signaled his intention to break the law by committing sodomy." McConnell denied this but remained unapologetic about his advocacy for equality.[52]

McConnell argued that "private consensual sexual conduct" was "not in itself a valid basis for exclusion from employment." The rarely enforced Minnesota sodomy statute criminalized both same-sex and different-sex conduct. "Suspected violations ... of a statute whose scope is appallingly broad, whose constitutionality is doubtful, and whose enforcement ... is impossible unless accomplished through shocking invasions of the right of privacy, afford a flimsy basis indeed for the deprivation of plaintiff's right to exercise his chosen calling," McConnell's attorneys contended. McConnell's activism also implicated freedom of speech and association: his application for a marriage license was "a dramatic gesture intended to call public attention to ... unjust legal discrimination," comparable to students wearing black armbands to protest the Vietnam War and other expression recently protected by the Court.[53]

The Minnesota ACLU's lawyers drew upon earlier decisions pertaining to civil service employment, which required a clear connection or "nexus" between an employee's status or conduct and his job performance.[54] The state, they insisted, could not bar McConnell's employment unless his conduct "impair[ed] his fitness to supervise the cataloging of books in the university library." Only public disapproval "so intense" that it created a real danger of ineffectiveness could justify his exclusion. They dismissed the notion that a gay employee "might corrupt the morals of his fellow employees or of students." Gay men were no more inclined toward predatory behavior than anyone else. McConnell's exclusion derived from "blind and unreasonable prejudice against homosexuals."[55]

The federal district court judge Philip Neville agreed with McConnell. Previously a respected trial lawyer who taught business law at the University of Minnesota, the sixty-one-year-old Neville was known for his scrupulous fairness. A former clerk recalled how, in the late 1960s, the judge

balked at a lawyer's courtroom appearance in a turtleneck but decided not
to mention this breach of "decorum." Only later, while discussing privately
the merits of the young attorney's arguments, did he suddenly exclaim: "I
decided that his turtleneck had nothing to do with his motion."[56]

In this weightier matter Neville concluded that McConnell's "public
profession" of homosexuality, the "rather bizarre occurrence" of applying
for a marriage license, and membership in Fight Repression of Erotic Expression (FREE) were irrelevant to his ability to serve as a competent
librarian. Significantly, he noted that McConnell's job would "not expose
him to children of tender years who conceivably could be influenced or
persuaded to his penchant." And unlike the "clandestine homosexuals" targeted for Cold War "purges" from federal government service, McConnell
was open about his "deviation," which made him impervious to blackmail.[57] Therefore, "what he does in his private life ... should not be his
employer's concern."[58]

Judge Neville's decision was not wholly without precedent. In 1969
the D.C. Circuit's ruling in *Norton v. Macy* established the nexus test for
federal civil service employees. The California Supreme Court ruled
later that year that the state could not revoke Marc Morrison's teaching
license based on a few episodes of sexual intimacy with a married male
friend without evidence that the conduct would "impair his function as a
teacher."[59]

Unlike those plaintiffs, however, McConnell proudly revealed his
sexual orientation, which proved to be his undoing. On one hand, Mc-
Connell's advocacy for gay equality and justice more clearly implicated
his First Amendment right of free speech. On the other hand, his out-
spoken defense of gay rights struck critics as provocative and embarrass-
ing for his employer and dangerous to the morals of university students
and co-workers. In 1971 the Eighth Circuit overturned Neville's ruling.
The Nixon appointee Judge Roy Laverne Stephenson distinguished
McConnell from more discreet plaintiffs. McConnell had attempted to
"foist tacit approval of this socially repugnant concept upon his employer." Stephenson concluded: "We know of no constitutional fiat or
binding principle of decisional law which requires an employer to accede
to such extravagant demands."[60]

Over the objection of Justice William O. Douglas, the U.S. Supreme
Court declined to hear McConnell's case in April 1972.[61] Still, McConnell's lawsuit blazed a path for nonconforming teachers to follow, even as

it provided a cautionary tale for those who would proudly proclaim their sexual identities.

Teachers had a tougher time in court, given the mission of educators to instill values and morals as well as knowledge in impressionable children. Traditionally, for school officials who wanted to dismiss or reject teachers because of "immorality," the bar had been low. But decisions such as Judge Neville's in *McConnell* provided an opening, and a handful of gay and lesbian schoolteachers challenged barriers to employment that frequently kept their peers out of the teaching profession or in the closet.

Peggy Burton, age twenty-five, received positive reviews during her first year of teaching science and coaching girls' sports at Cascade High School in a tiny farming town near Salem, Oregon. Burton, a self-described "small-town woman" from Missoula, Montana, "liv[ed] with a female partner, but was not out at work."[62] She later recalled: "One day out of thin air with no warning," Principal Leonard Federico told her he had "heard a rumor" that Burton "was a homosexual."[63] Burton replied, "So what? What does that have to do with teaching?" She recounted, "He fired me on the spot."[64] The school board quickly resolved that Burton's "contract be terminated because of her immorality of being a practicing homosexual."[65]

Burton's sudden unemployment in 1971 devastated her. "I cried for days. . . . It really did hurt. . . . I knew that I wasn't a bad person, and I decided to stand up for my rights."[66] Struggling to find an attorney, Burton approached the ACLU of Oregon, and Charlie Hinkle took her case.[67]

Hinkle marshalled a growing body of case law to argue that Burton's termination was unlawful. No one, he wrote, contended that her status affected "her *functioning* as a capable and adequate teacher." Burton had never revealed her sexual orientation to anyone other than close friends. A "blanket exclusion of homosexuals from public employment" offended the due process and equal protection clauses, and it violated the right to privacy protected by *Griswold* and *Eisenstadt*. Hinkle discussed *Norton v. Macy*, *Morrison*, and *Mindel* at length and cited other court decisions that overturned teacher terminations for private conduct unrelated to classroom performance. He noted that Oregon had recently repealed its prohibition on consensual sodomy, reflecting an emerging consensus that "private homosexual activity" was not "immoral."[68]

Burton's case established an important if narrow precedent: the federal district court judge Gus Solomon, a sixty-seven-year-old Truman appointee, ruled the statute authorizing her dismissal for "immorality" unconstitutionally vague and overbroad. By making school board members the "arbiters of morality for the entire community," the statute neglected "to give fair warning" to potential violators and allowed "erratic and prejudiced exercises of authority."[69] Solomon ruled on none of Burton's broader claims about privacy, due process, and equal protection.[70]

Burton paid a high price for her principled position. She "lost many friends and sometimes was screamed at and spat upon"; received threatening phone calls; and had to take a job for meager wages at a fish cannery, struggling to support herself and make payments on student loans. Her former students dedicated a yearbook page to Burton, but "school administrators vindictively confiscated all copies ... and tore the page out."[71] Judge Solomon did award Burton $10,523 in back pay and damages plus attorneys' fees, and he expunged Burton's record, but he refused to order her reinstatement as a teacher.[72]

Solomon understood that Burton's involuntary outing had doomed her teaching career: "Let's not kid ourselves. If any [school] district finds out that she is a lesbian, they are not going to hire her, no matter what the law is."[73] The judge scoffed at Hinkle's argument for wrongful termination damages: "She won't be able to get a job because she is a lesbian, not because she was fired. How long does that little school district have to pay because of her peculiar propensity?"[74] School board members said "they would be recalled and tarred and feathered" if they reinstated Burton.[75]

The Ninth Circuit upheld Solomon's denial of reinstatement over a vigorous dissent from the seventy-four-year-old judge J. Edward Lumbard, Jr., who protested that "if community resentment was a legitimate factor ... few Southern school districts would have been integrated."[76] The Supreme Court denied the ACLU's petition for certiorari on Burton's behalf. Even so, the *Advocate* called the invalidation of Oregon's "immorality" statute "a major advance for the cause of gay civil rights."[77]

Teachers who engaged in public advocacy still faced obstacles to legal redress, however. Joseph Acanfora III attended Penn State on a Navy ROTC scholarship after graduating as high school valedictorian. In 1970, a "Free University" course opened his eyes to others who struggled with sexual identity in a "rigidly straight society."[78] Acanfora relinquished his scholarship and changed his major to education. He came out to his friends and family in 1971 and joined the newly formed Homophile Organization of Penn State (HOPS). Acanfora temporarily lost his job as a student teacher for participating in a lawsuit that challenged the university's refusal to recognize HOPS, but a court injunction allowed him to complete the assignment.[79]

Officials grilled Acanfora about the "homosexual acts" he "prefer[red] to engage in" after he applied for a teaching certificate from the state. Acanfora demurred, citing personal privacy, but confirmed that he felt sexual and romantic attraction to men. Later, he "clarified that he had never engaged in any homosexual acts."[80] Acanfora emphasized his "strong belief that a student-teacher relationship ... is purely professional and academic." He believed that "no one should advocate homosexuality ... since each person's sexual orientation is a private matter."[81]

After the university declined to recommend Acanfora for a teaching certificate, he began teaching earth science at Parkland Junior High in Rockville, Maryland. Acanfora "intentionally did not disclose his homosexuality" or his membership in HOPS on his job application.[82] A few weeks into the school year, the *New York Times* reported that Pennsylvania had granted his certificate. Acanfora's preemptive disclosure of Pennsylvania's action to Parkland's principal alerted Maryland officials that he was gay.[83] Two days later, the school district transferred him to a nonteaching administrative position.

Even though most faculty members and nearly all his students signed a letter supporting Acanfora's reinstatement, officials were adamant. Superintendent Donald Miedema, who had "not knowingly hired homosexuals for employ as teachers" in the past, justified Acanfora's transfer by citing his "insubordination and misconduct" in not revealing that he was a "militantly activistic homosexual" on his employment application.[84]

Press coverage included an interview with Maury Povich and a twenty-minute segment on *60 Minutes*, as well as a public television program where Acanfora appeared with his supportive parents. His father, a truck driver, recalled that when Joe came out to him, he had replied: "I loved you then, I love you now, and I'll love you afterwards ... we're with you."[85] Joe's mother, Lee, once "had the same negative feelings everyone has" about homosexuality. "When Joe came out of the closet, I came out of the kitchen," she told a local paper. After long talks with her son and his friends, she realized that gay people were "not sick, they're oppressed."[86] The Acanforas hoped their unconditional, public support for Joe would help others understand homosexuality as a benign variation rather than a wicked pathology.

Acanfora emphasized that he "never brought [his] private life into the classroom." Still, he refused to conceal his sexuality from the world or temper his advocacy for equality. "I have every right to be what I am," Acanfora declared. "I have every right to be a teacher. And I plan on doing both."[87] Acanfora's stance attracted support from allies in the National Education Association (NEA) and sparked law reform efforts, including a successful local bid for protection against sexual orientation discrimination in employment by the Washington Gay Activists Alliance.[88]

But this publicity and activism also fueled school officials' outrage. They worried that Acanfora's open homosexuality would influence "impressionable male youths" and students "on the fence" about their lifestyle.[89] "There's always a touch of homosexuality in almost every individual," opined Dr. Reginald Lourie of George Washington University Medical School. "Nature allows this remaking period (adolescence) so that poor answers can be discarded."[90] Acanfora's apparent teaching skills and popularity only heightened the perceived danger.[91]

Acanfora called two experts to rebut the defense witnesses' testimony. Dr. William Stayton of the University of Pennsylvania School of Medicine suggested that a gay teacher would benefit students by "breaking down homosexual stereotypes" and "affirm[ing] the self-image" of those attracted to other boys.[92] The school board's closing argument, by contrast, dripped with derision, ridiculing Acanfora's "heartrending portrait of himself as a wretched homosexual . . . being stoned by an unfeeling press and having his very bread snatched from his mouth by his heartless Victorian employer," when he was instead "a militant homosexual and civil rights activist" who had asserted rights far beyond any yet declared by a court or legislature.[93]

The federal district court judge Joseph Young ruled against Acanfora in May 1973. Young, a decorated veteran of World War II, had co-chaired Maryland Lawyers for Nixon-Agnew in 1968, but he had also volunteered to represent protesters charged with looting and disorderly conduct following the assassination of Martin Luther King, Jr. Young's opinion reflected both relatively progressive views on the legal status of gay persons and deep ambivalence about Acanfora's activism. Notably, Young rejected blanket bans on employment. "Mere knowledge that a teacher is homosexual" could "not justify transfer or dismissal." A gay teacher "need not become a recluse, nor need he lie about himself." Indeed, Young declared that the "time has come today for private, consenting, adult homosexuality to enter the sphere of constitutionally protectable interests." Remarkably, he declared sexual orientation a suspect classification subject to strict scrutiny under the equal protection clause.

Young also appreciated that Acanfora's public advocacy for gay rights would normally fall within the protections of the First Amendment. Yet a public school teacher had a "duty" as well as a "right" of privacy, Young wrote. The potential dangers an openly gay teacher posed to adolescent students justified the school district's refusal to employ him. Acanfora's activism "exceed[ed] the bounds of reasonable self-defense" and would negatively affect the educational process.[94] Young had approached the constitutional precipice but pulled away at the last instant.

On appeal, the ACLU's new Sexual Privacy Project amplified Acanfora's rights to free speech, privacy, and equal protection.[95] *Eisenstadt* and *Roe* clarified that the right of privacy extended beyond the marital non-procreative sex shielded in *Griswold*, or privacy "in the narrow sense of protecting individuals from government snooping." The "right to choose" abortion, the ACLU explained, attached "equally to married and unmarried persons" and should be understood as "a right of autonomy—the right to make certain individual decisions free from unwarranted governmental intrusion or pressure." Like the inability to decide whether to become a mother, suppressing, denying, or attempting to alter one's sexual orientation would infringe fundamental constitutional guarantees.[96]

Acanfora also relied on the *Frontiero* (1973) plurality opinion, which provided a road map for upholding Judge Young's ruling that sexual orientation classifications should be suspect. Like Black Americans, gay people had been stigmatized and disadvantaged historically. Like sex and race, sexual orientation rarely was related to a legitimate state goal or to an individual's competency, and it was "beyond the power of the person to change."[97]

Finally, the First Amendment forbade the state to penalize Acanfora for bringing lawsuits "to vindicate" these "constitutional rights," argued the ACLU. The "message to the homosexual community" from a failure to protect plaintiffs from negative repercussions of their activism would be clear: "Stay in the closet." Activities outside of school were only relevant if authorities could show a "clear danger to order *in* the school"—in other words, if they affected a teacher's ability to function. The school board could not show a "substantial and material danger" that "Acanfora's presence in the classroom . . . would convert . . . students to homosexuality." Moreover, if homosexuality was constitutionally protected, then social prejudices could not justify continuing discrimination.[98]

In the end, the Fourth Circuit took Judge Young's opinion one step further and held that the First Amendment protected Acanfora's public advocacy for gay rights. Nevertheless, Acanfora's failure to disclose his membership in HOPS doomed his reinstatement claim.[99] Acanfora was damned if he disclosed his sexuality publicly and damned if he did *not* disclose it to a hostile prospective employer.

A Supreme Court denial of certiorari ended Joe Acanfora's brief teaching career, but not his activism.[100] He moved to California, where he spent twenty-five years as a university grant writer and administrator and fought for protections against sexual orientation discrimination. The cert denial in *Acanfora* may have been fortuitous: had the Court heard the case it likely would have rejected his claims.[101] Because the lower court rulings remained good law, *Acanfora*—like *Burton* and the civil service cases—provided a precedent that other teachers, gay and straight, put to use in their own legal battles in the coming years.

Pregnancy Without Marriage

Women who became pregnant outside of marriage seized upon these precedents as they tried to break the logjam that blocked them from employment as public school teachers. In the late 1960s and early 1970s, women of color had pioneered challenges to employment discrimination against mothers of nonmarital children.[102] Early plaintiffs who sued private employers under Title VII of the 1964 Civil Rights Act argued, with some success, that bans on unmarried mothers' employment unlawfully discriminated based on race and sex. Public school teachers faced more formidable hurdles. Until Title VII's application to government employers in 1972, they could rely only on the constitution; moreover, the prerogative of school districts to dismiss teachers for "immorality" persisted. Nevertheless, *Eisenstadt* and *Roe* provided potentially powerful new precedents—as did gay and lesbian teachers like Peggy Burton and Joe Acanfora.

Ilena DeVone Drake, a twenty-eight-year-old Black woman, worked as a schoolteacher in the small town of Florala, Alabama, and was engaged to be married to an enlisted man. Her troubles began in March 1973, when Mary Gilmer, a county bookkeeper, told Murray King, the white superintendent of Covington County's public schools, that Drake was pregnant and in the hospital.[103] Superintendent King called the hospital to ask if the rumor was true. Dr. Ray Evers, who had examined

Drake, informed King that "Miss Drake had asked him to do an abortion on her because she would lose her job if she had a baby." King then visited Drake in her hospital room and confirmed that a nonmarital pregnancy would indeed cost her her job.[104] Drake returned home the following day and continued to teach school.

Several weeks later, King notified Drake that the Board of Education was proposing to fire her for "immorality."[105] Drake's union assigned Solomon Seay to her case. Seay, the son of a prominent minister who had followed the Reverend Dr. Martin Luther King, Jr., as leader of the Montgomery Improvement Association, had already distinguished himself fighting racial segregation and discrimination in court.[106]

At a closed school board hearing in May, Drake testified that she could not have been pregnant in March, because her fiancé had by then been serving in Italy for four months. "Do you mean . . . that you had been having relations with your fiancé up until he left?" demanded the school district's attorney, Frank Tipler. When she hesitated, Seay instructed Drake to answer the question. "Okay. Yes, I'm twenty-eight years old, and I don't think the Board or anybody else can tell me what I can do with my private life."[107]

Drake expressed indignation at King's audacious invasion of her privacy. "I think that whatever I do after 3 o'clock is my business . . . as long as I teach those kids. . . . My private life is my private life," she emphasized. "I don't dig into Mr. King's private life." King, she charged, had made her intimate business the talk of Florala: "My moral stature . . . has been ruined, really." It "wasn't [King's] place to come to the hospital" or to insist on knowing the name of a doctor who had told her she wasn't pregnant. The racial overtones of King's intrusion compounded Drake's conviction that he treated her disrespectfully. In refusing to answer the superintendent's questions, Drake "wanted to show him just because my skin is black and his is white that he doesn't have the power."[108]

For his part King framed his visit to Drake's hospital room as an act of moral courage. "It might save an unborn child's life if I went to her in time," King explained: perhaps if Drake knew that she would lose her job either way, whether she had an abortion or gave birth, she would decide to continue the pregnancy. Ms. Drake denied that she had asked Dr. Evers about performing an abortion but clarified: "I told Mr. King . . . if I ever get pregnant, sure I would have an abortion. And there is no law against abortion."[109] In the spring of 1973, Drake's statement was true, but barely: the Supreme Court had decided *Roe v. Wade* on January 22.

In *Roe*, litigants and amici made creative arguments that implicated marital status. Nancy Stearns of the Center for Constitutional Rights argued that abortion bans' "incursions on the liberty of an unmarried woman who becomes pregnant are even more severe" than for married women. "She too may be fired from her job," denied public housing, and "compelled to discontinue her education." Without access to abortion, "she is often forced into marriage against her will and better judgment."[110] Advocates also refuted the argument that abortion bans deterred nonmarital sex or punished fornication. If that were the state's aim, then the statutes were overly broad: they included married women who, one amicus brief noted, had no legal right to refuse their husbands' sexual advances.[111]

The Court's 7–2 decision in *Roe* had little to say about marriage, or women's equality. In passing, Justice Blackmun's majority opinion noted "the additional difficulties and continuing stigma of unwed motherhood" that might aggravate the "distress" of an unwanted pregnancy.[112] As Blackmun acknowledged, the plaintiffs in *Roe* and other successful challenges to abortion restrictions included unmarried women.[113] Blackmun's opinion emphasized physicians' prerogatives rather than feminist themes of women's autonomy or racial and economic injustice. But *Roe* made clear that the right to abortion did not depend on marital status.

The decision in *Roe* apparently had not registered with the Florala school board attorney, who declared repeatedly that "abortion in Alabama is against the law." And even if individuals had a right to sexual privacy that encompassed nonmarital conduct, Attorney Tipler insisted that teaching was a privilege to be earned, not an unconditional right. As moral role models for students, teachers must adhere to higher standards of conduct than ordinary citizens.[114] And when conduct became public, the board could use its discretion to "balance educational interests versus the [individual] freedom of private sexual intercourse."[115]

Tipler freely admitted to Judge Frank M. Johnson, Jr., that he was no "constitutional expert." Seay was that, and a talented oral advocate. "Plaintiff's wholly private sexual orientation and conduct . . . cannot legitimately be made a subject of state concern, as a criteri[on] for public employment," Seay argued. Drake conceded pregnancy for the sake of argument, which "naturally implies sexual intercourse and because plaintiff has no child and is not now pregnant, then voluntary or involuntary abortion" (miscarriage). *Roe* clearly established that absent a compelling government interest, the state could not place restrictions on a woman's decision about whether to continue a pregnancy.[116]

Seay also argued that, like the Oregon law struck down in Peggy Burton's case, the Alabama statute that authorized the dismissal of teachers for "immorality" should be void for vagueness and overbreadth. Moreover, school officials had not shown any "rational nexus between the allegedly immoral conduct and job performance." Ms. Drake had returned to the classroom after her release from the hospital and taught until the end of the term without incident.[117]

Judge Johnson and Judge Richard Rives found Seay's vagueness argument compelling, and the opinion drafted by Rives's clerk, Craig Smith, maintained that morality was too subjective to be the basis for an employment exclusion.[118] By contrast, morality's contested nature "more firmly convince[d]" Judge Robert Varner, a recent Nixon appointee, "that local authorities, directly responsible to the people" were "in a far better position to determine" its contours than "a somewhat detached and isolated court."[119]

Ultimately, the judges' disagreement in *Drake* migrated to different terrain: the constitutional law of privacy. Johnson's clerk argued that "an unmarried woman's decision to have sexual relations" could not be denied under *Eisenstadt* and *Roe* or "left to society's notion of morality." "It would be ironic indeed . . . if the right to privacy covers an unmarried woman's use of contraceptives and her decision to abort her pregnancy, but does not cover the very conduct which makes these other actions necessary."[120]

Hoping for unanimity, Rives avoided passing judgment on the immorality provision's constitutionality.[121] Citing *Eisenstadt* and *Roe*, Rives and Johnson held that the school board had no evidence that "claimed immorality" "affected [Drake's] competency or fitness as a teacher." Drake's termination "on evidence growing out of her consultations with her physician" therefore amounted to "an unconstitutional invasion of her right to privacy."[122] The court ordered her reinstatement.[123]

Judge Varner objected strenuously in dissent. Once "rumor" of Drake's pregnancy reached the superintendent, she forfeited any privacy interest, in his view. By the time of the board's hearing, Drake's "morals were street talk in Florala." By discussing her nonmarital sexual activity and by engaging in intimacies in a car that could be "viewed by passersby," Drake waived any privacy claim, Varner thought. In any case, her privacy interest must give way to the "compelling State interest in the morality of the State's public school system." Drake's known pregnancy and the loss of student respect that it must have occasioned were "obviously a deterrent to [her] teaching ability."[124] As applied by Varner, a functional analysis would implicate community moral standards and doom Drake's effort to keep her job.

Drake never was visibly pregnant.[125] Her case was distinct from Joe Acanfora's in that school board officials themselves were wholly responsible for the "public" nature of her conduct. It also differed from most cases of pregnancy discrimination, since pregnancy often was difficult or impossible to conceal.

Historically, the visibility of pregnancy had been a workplace liability, but the rise of anti-discrimination law challenged this status quo. Soon after Title VII's passage women began to question employer policies and practices that discriminated based on pregnancy or reproductive capacity. Public employees used constitutional and, later, statutory law to argue that pregnancy discrimination was unlawful sex discrimination.

Seay did not raise sex discrimination arguments in Ilena Drake's case but others did. Barbara Jean Brown, for instance, became pregnant while serving as a probationary junior high science teacher in Omaha, Nebraska. At first, Brown's innovative pedagogy and rapport with students earned praise. Then, in April 1973, the school's principal learned from "unidentified sources" that Brown was pregnant.[126] The school board voted to terminate her contract because the very existence of "an unmarried lady, pregnant and expecting a baby" embodied "[in]appropriate moral conduct."[127]

Brown filed a sex discrimination charge with the Nebraska Equal Opportunity Commission (NEOC), represented by a local civil rights attorney, Clyde Christian. Discovery revealed that of a half-dozen employees terminated for "immorality," three were unmarried pregnant women and none were male teachers accused of becoming fathers outside of marriage.[128] But a state court overturned the NEOC's favorable sex discrimination ruling in a short, dismissive decision. Judge John C. Burke found that "school officials acted in a prudent, reasonable manner" and that Brown "was not discriminated against because she was a female." Burke had "searched the Statutes of Nebraska" but was "unable to find any authority which would allow [him] to repeal the biological laws of nature."[129]

Brown and Attorney Christian had reason to hope for a friendlier reception in federal court. In July 1973, Judge William Keady ruled in favor of Katie Mae Andrews and Lestine Rogers, Black women excluded from teaching positions by a rural Mississippi school district because they had given birth to nonmarital children years earlier (a case detailed in chapter 6). Thanks to zealous advocacy from their young attorney, Charles Victor McTeer, and from feminist lawyers at the Center for Constitutional Rights (CCR), Keady heard an array of race and sex discrimination arguments, as well as a robust defense of the right to procreate outside of marriage. The Drew school district's policy "constitutes an invidious and impermissible discrimination . . . against women and more specifically against black women," argued the CCR's Nancy Stearns and Rhonda Copelon. "Men who father out-of-wedlock children are neither identifiable nor identified to the same extent," and the "approximately ten-to-one ratio between out-of-wedlock children born to black and white women" made the policy's racial impact "inevitable."[130]

The CCR lawyers saw Andrews's case as an extension of women's right to reproductive autonomy and equality. The "liberty to have a child" could not "be conditioned on the relinquishment of liberty to follow one's chosen profession."[131] The civil rights icon Fannie Lou Hamer, a survivor of involuntary sterilization, testified in support of the plaintiffs. The social psychologist Kenneth Clark, whose testimony had been featured in *Brown v. Board of Education*, averred that policies punishing illegitimacy perpetuated "a long history of discrimination against females on matters of sex and sexual behavior . . . designed to subordinate females to an essentially inferior role."[132] Judge Keady found the conclusion "inescapable" that a policy forbidding the employment of unmarried parents would discriminate against women, who were "stuck with the result" of nonmarital sex.[133]

The Fifth Circuit panel sidestepped questions of sex and race discrimination, sexual privacy, and procreative liberty when it upheld Keady's ruling in 1975. Instead the court said that to entirely exclude "unwed parents . . . male or female" from employment "creates an irrational classification" insufficiently connected to the district's asserted objectives of promoting morality, providing positive role models, and preventing "schoolgirl pregnancies."[134] At the least, unmarried pregnant teachers were entitled to a hearing.[135]

Barbara Jean Brown had secured only short-term non-teaching jobs that forced her to rely on public assistance and support from family by the time she received such a hearing. The federal district court denied her claim. Chief Judge Warren K. Urbom affirmed "the school board's interest in conserving marital values, when acts . . . destructive of those values are revealed, verbally or nonverbally."[136] Urbom's ruling highlighted how the "nonverbal" revelation of pregnancy could take a teacher's sexual activities outside the protected realm of privacy.

Brown ultimately won a small victory in her case against the Omaha School Board: in 1977, the Eighth Circuit ruled that Brown should have received a hearing, awarded her the balance of her salary for the year, and ordered the school to expunge "any derogatory material from her personnel records."[137] In a concurring opinion, Judge Miller rested his decision on sex discrimination grounds. Miller did not question the board's prerogative to "conserve marital values." He did find that the "brunt" of the board's "undefined 'morality' standard's application appears to fall on the female gender."[138]

Even in the face of powerful sex discrimination arguments, however, many courts allowed school officials discretion to take action against teachers whose pregnancy became a topic of public debate. A nonmarital pregnancy might not automatically disqualify a teacher, but a functional inquiry into whether she could remain effective in the classroom despite community censure smuggled moral objections back into the analysis.

Harriet Wardlaw's case illustrates how the nexus standard diluted even formidable constitutional and statutory arguments. Wardlaw, a twenty-nine-year-old special education teacher at Austin's brand-new Lyndon Baines Johnson High School, became pregnant in 1974.[139] She wanted to share her happiness, assuage any worry, and forestall negative gossip.[140] Before she could disclose her pregnancy to her students, however, the news had spread. At her principal's request Wardlaw wrote to Superintendent Jack Davidson: "I am pregnant, and single. I intend to work throughout the school year."[141] Two weeks later, Davidson transferred her to a non-teaching librarian position at a junior high school.[142] In the meantime, without Wardlaw's knowledge, the school board chairman issued a press release and appeared in a television interview "announcing that there was an unwed pregnant school teacher at LBJ." A local journalist called Wardlaw, who "was horrified and absolutely refused to talk about her pregnancy with the press."[143]

Her young feminist attorneys, Carol Oppenheimer and Bobby Jane Nelson, saw Wardlaw as a victim of a sexual "double standard."[144] They requested a temporary injunction from a state court, citing the Texas Equal Rights Amendment and state anti-discrimination laws, and filed a complaint with the EEOC. Women's groups called Wardlaw's transfer "blatant discrimination" resulting from an "archaic mentality." One activist "wonder[ed] how many unwed fathers are teaching in the Austin schools." The Austin Right to Life Committee, too, supported "the continued employment of a pregnant woman without discriminatory action" and condemned "the rejection of society which forces many to choose . . . abortion."[145]

The state trial court judge James Meyer ruled that Wardlaw could not prove sex discrimination. "Presumably, male teachers do not reveal their fatherhood . . . out of wedlock" whereas "female teachers . . . necessarily reveal their motherhood." To Meyer, this fact was a liability rather than an asset in proving sex discrimination. "Discrimination in the availability of knowledge must be charged to nature," Meyer wrote, "not to [Superintendent] Davidson."[146] "Next we'll see poor old Mother Nature hauled into court on sex bias charges!" quipped one editorialist.[147]

Wardlaw could not avoid the media spotlight. Articles and editorials appeared in local and national newspapers; all three major networks aired evening news segments about her case. With her partner, Jim Cox, a divorced thirty-one-year-old graduate student and father of two, at her side, Wardlaw told NBC, "I certainly never expected to lose my job. Were I a man and fathering a child, this issue would never have come up. Because I am a woman, my condition would become apparent, and that's why I've been transferred."[148] Students offered their support. "It's not really anybody's business what she does outside of school," said one. Another insisted, "She can teach just as good when she's pregnant as when she's not."[149]

Wardlaw described her pregnancy not as a mistake or accident but as a planned, welcome event. She "did not want to deal with the institution of marriage," and news outlets reported that Wardlaw and Cox had no plans to formalize their union. "My students certainly understand that it is a personal decision of my choice, and certainly not binding on their behavior." Rather, Wardlaw explained, "I just feel like marital status is independent of teaching and should rightfully be so."[150]

School officials disagreed. Superintendent Davidson told ABC News that an individual "has a right to his own lifestyle. He or she ought to have the option to marry or not marry, to bear children or not." But school officials had a duty to act when a teacher's "lifestyle comes into conflict with the expectations of a community." The Austin school board sided with Davidson, 6–1, at a public hearing.

In court, school officials strained to depict Wardlaw's transfer as a case-specific decision based on educational concerns rather than what Cox described as "religious morality rules" about nonmarital pregnancy.[151] Defendants testified that the Austin Independent School District (AISD) had no blanket policy prohibiting the employment of "single parents," in contrast to the general and permanent ban in Drew, Mississippi. School officials cited complaints from parents and other "overwhelmingly negative" community reaction.[152] They also argued that Wardlaw's presence in the classroom would harm special education students, allegedly more vulnerable to "sex-related problems" and more apt to emulate their teachers.

Wardlaw's allies countered that the only educational disruption was students' distress at the removal of a beloved and trusted teacher from the classroom. Wardlaw herself testified that "one of the primary things she . . . taught her eight students" was "how to make individual, independent and self-reliant judgments." And "proselytizing any lifestyle would have flown in the face" of her "teaching technique and philosophy."[153] By transferring Wardlaw, the board put its "stamp of approval" on only one kind of role model for students, Oppenheimer said.[154]

Many constitutional arguments converged in *Wardlaw*. Borrowing liberally from the ACLU's brief in *Acanfora*, Wardlaw's attorneys, in cooperation with Marilyn Haft of the ACLU's Sexual Privacy Project, asserted a broad privacy right that "protects the choice not to marry, to procreate, and to have extra-marital sex."[155] Wardlaw emphasized that depriving women of their jobs for choosing to bear nonmarital children would not only deny them reproductive autonomy but also would lead to more abortions.[156]

Wardlaw advanced sex discrimination arguments under all available constitutional provisions and statutes.[157] She echoed Anna Flores and the Mississippi plaintiffs in arguing that the AISD policy "places a judicial stamp of approval on a double standard of morality."[158] And, like successful private sector claimants before her, Wardlaw argued that penalties for unwed pregnancy violated Title VII's prohibition on employment practices with an adverse impact on women. The school district's unwritten policy was "void . . . not so much for vagueness but for omission": Wardlaw received no notice that nonmarital pregnancy would lead to removal from the classroom. The AISD relied on an impermissible "irrebuttable presumption" that unmarried pregnant teachers were unfit. To penalize Wardlaw for publicity caused by others or by her lawsuit violated the First Amendment. Just as that provision should protect Acanfora's activism so too should it prevent the school board from discouraging or stigmatizing Wardlaw's constitutionally protected "choice to associate outside the classroom, with a man to whom she is not married, and to have a child with that man."[159]

None of these arguments, however, persuaded the federal district court judge Jack Roberts.[160] Wardlaw "presented ... absolutely no evidence that she was treated any differently" than "a single male teacher whose status as an expectant parent became known to school officials." Roberts cited the Supreme Court decision in *Geduldig v. Aiello* (1974), which said that "while it is true that only a woman can become pregnant ... not ... every ... classification concerning pregnancy is a sex-based classification."[161] Moreover, Roberts saw the district's decision as one made in good faith and out of concern for Wardlaw's ability to function in the classroom, not her status as an unmarried pregnant woman. The board's decision "in no way reflected upon the morality or propriety of Plaintiff's lifestyle," and it "reflects no punitive motivation." Roberts let it stand.[162]

By the mid-1970s, school district officials had learned that categorical exclusion of unmarried pregnant teachers likely would not pass constitutional muster. Instead, they turned to functional arguments. Teachers who became pregnant outside of marriage gained additional statutory and regulatory protections in the years that followed, but they never fully overcame the argument that discrimination could be justified when nonmarital pregnancy ostensibly affected job performance. Nonmarital cohabitants had an even more difficult time asserting a right to hold jobs in classrooms and libraries.

Nonmarital Cohabitation

As Harriet Wardlaw fought the Austin school board, Kathleen Sullivan battled a rural South Dakota school district for the right to live unmarried with her male partner and keep her job. Sullivan, a New Yorker, had moved to the tiny village of Union Center in the summer of 1974 to teach nine children in grades one through four in a two-room schoolhouse. No one questioned her pedagogical prowess; the unincorporated community of fewer than one hundred residents had difficulty finding highly qualified teachers given its size and remote location. The trouble began when Sullivan's boyfriend, Donald Dragon, moved into her mobile home. Sullivan did not, and probably could not, hide her living arrangements: several of her students lived in the same trailer park. In September, Sullivan and Dragon tried to rent a house owned by Mr. and Mrs. Ronald Opstedahl, the parents of one of her students.

The Opstedahls complained, and the school's principal, Wayne Musilek, "confronted" Sullivan and requested that she make other living arrangements. Sullivan declined, protesting the principal's intrusion into her private life. At a school board hearing, several parents testified that "since Ms. Sullivan's arrival, their children's interest in school and rate of learning had markedly improved."[163] Two sets of parents opposed her retention, and three other parents supported it. A petition organized by members of a church in a nearby rural community and signed by 140 people requested Sullivan's termination, even though Mr. Opstedahl, who circulated the petition, "conceded that his daughter idolized Ms. Sullivan and seemed to be learning very well."[164] One board member told Sullivan, "You could make the decision an awful lot easier for the board if you do one of two things—either get married or kick the guy out."[165]

Sullivan refused to respond to inquiries about their relationship or to live apart from Dragon, although she did offer to move farther from the school.[166] The board argued that Sullivan's "morality" was unacceptable to many and that her reputation would make it "extremely difficult for her to exert the proper authority" and to retain the respect of her students and the community that was crucial to "effectually carry out the school program.[167] After giving Sullivan another chance to change her mind, the board voted to terminate her employment in what one member called "the most difficult decision she had ever made."[168]

The federal district court judge Andrew Bogue affirmed the officials' prerogative to apply community standards to Sullivan's conduct. The board had given Sullivan adequate notice, which blunted her "void for vagueness" argument. Bogue agreed that public knowledge of Sullivan's cohabitation would compromise her effectiveness as a teacher.[169]

For the ACLU lawyers who handled Sullivan's appeal to the Eighth Circuit, the case tested many of the arguments gay and unmarried pregnant teachers had advanced in other lawsuits, as well as constitutional claims borrowed from other streams of litigation. Marilyn Haft of the ACLU's Sexual Privacy Project alerted the local ACLU attorneys, Steven Sanford and the University of South Dakota law professor John H. Davidson, Jr., to recent cases, including *Acanfora*, which modeled Sullivan's argument that the right to privacy shielded her from government interference in decisions about how and with whom she would live.[170]

Sanford thought *Acanfora* relevant to Sullivan's potential free speech claims as well: if Sullivan "had merely been caught with Don Dragon in a motel on a weekend" or hidden her relationship by "sneaking around" she would not have been fired, but instead she was "living with this fellow openly and refused to change"—this is what had "provoked the locals."[171] Like Acanfora's gay rights advocacy or Ilena Drake's "exercise [of] the right guaranteed to her under *Roe v. Wade*," Sullivan's "statements," "construed as a justification for extramarital sexual relations," were "clearly protected by the First Amendment."[172] Sanford also suggested that *McConnell v. Anderson*—the 1971 Eighth Circuit precedent—was ripe for reevaluation, and he noted that (unlike McConnell) Sullivan had not publicized or promoted her living arrangements.[173]

Sullivan's claims differed in important ways from the rights asserted by gay and unmarried pregnant teachers, however. Unlike homosexuality, "considered by most experts an involuntary condition," nonmarital cohabitation "involves a clearly voluntary association," as Sanford put it.[174] Sullivan's case did not directly concern reproductive freedom or even nonmarital sex, since Sullivan refused to discuss her intimate life.[175]

Sullivan also implicated privacy and freedom of association cases about the regulation of living arrangements. *Stanley v. Georgia* (1969), the Court decision overturning a man's conviction for the possession of "obscene" materials in his house, "adds an essential dimension to our argument," Sanford wrote, because it depicted the home "as a locus for the satisfaction of intellectual and emotional needs."[176] Haft encouraged Sanford to "play up" the Supreme Court decision in *U.S.D.A. v. Moreno* (1973), which invalidated a provision that denied food stamps to households containing individuals not related by blood, marriage, or formal adoption.[177] The district court's opinion in *Moreno* contained helpful language suggesting that the government "cannot in the name of morality infringe the rights to privacy and freedom of association *in the home*."[178]

However, the Court's decision in *Village of Belle Terre v. Boraas* (1974) complicated the arguments the ACLU could make in *Sullivan*.[179] In *Belle Terre* the ACLU had urged the Supreme Court to recognize that a local zoning ordinance could not prohibit more than two unrelated individuals from occupying a housing unit. Justice Douglas, usually an ACLU ally, wrote the majority opinion upholding the ordinance, although he strongly implied that a law prohibiting *two* unrelated persons from living together would not pass constitutional muster.[180] Ultimately, Sanford decided not to discuss *Belle Terre* in his brief, but he did argue that Sullivan's termination violated her right to freedom of association in intimate personal relationships.[181]

Cohabitation cases did not lend themselves as readily to sex discrimination arguments as those involving pregnancy. Haft saw sexual "immorality" regulations as subordinating women and "epitomizing the stereotypical double standard": "only women's sexuality is punished while men are praised for their sexual prowess."[182] Still, a sex discrimination argument would be tricky in the absence of a similarly situated male comparator who had lived with a woman outside of marriage, and Sullivan's attorneys did not attempt one.

Sullivan did spotlight the marital status classifications *Eisenstadt* had called into question. Sanford initially hesitated to include equal protection arguments based on marital status, but Haft strongly objected to this omission. Haft acknowledged that "we cannot claim marital status to be a suspect classification because of the voluntary nature of the condition," so the brief argued that Sullivan's firing lacked a rational basis.[183]

Sullivan's lawsuit ended anticlimactically. Because her attorney had withdrawn her request for reinstatement, on appeal her only remaining claim consisted of damages for a constitutional tort. The Eighth Circuit dodged "very difficult constitutional issues," ruling that even if "the right of a couple to live together without benefit of matrimony" meant that Sullivan was "constitutionally entitled to follow her own lifestyle," individual board members could not be held liable because they acted "in complete good faith and with concern for Ms. Sullivan's constitutional rights."[184] ACLU's legal director, Mel Wulf, deemed a cert petition to the Supreme Court "a futility."[185]

A case that presented similar questions did reach the Supreme Court the following year. The Carnegie Free Library in Connellsville, Pennsylvania, hired Rebecca Hollenbaugh as head librarian in 1969. In 1971, Fred Philburn joined the library staff as a janitor. Hollenbaugh, the only employee with a car, issued a standing invitation to drive her co-workers to buy lunch. Philburn joined these outings, and soon he and Hollenbaugh began seeing each other outside of work. Their relationship became serious and they discussed their mutual desire for children.

Hollenbaugh, age thirty-two, was divorced; Philburn, forty-seven, felt trapped in an unhappy marriage. A decorated veteran, Philburn spent six months as a German prisoner of war and returned from World War II with emotional and physical wounds. He had worked only sporadically in the years since, relying on veterans' disability benefits. To his distress, a quarter-century of marriage had produced no children; Philburn testified that his wife had refused to have intercourse for most of their union. He explored the possibility of divorce, but an attorney advised him that given his wife's medical conditions (including bone cancer), ending the marriage without her consent would be impossible.

In November 1972, Hollenbaugh discovered she was expecting. The couple welcomed this unplanned but much-wanted pregnancy, and Philburn moved into Hollenbaugh's home, although he continued to support his wife financially. In February 1973, Hollenbaugh requested and received a leave of absence from the library. A daughter, Barbara, was born to the couple in summer 1973. Shortly thereafter, Hollenbaugh approached the library's board of trustees about returning to work.

By then, word had spread of the couple's living arrangement. Two trustees visited Hollenbaugh at home and expressed "second thoughts" about retaining her. Only if she "regularized her position"—either married Philburn or stopped living with him—could she keep her job. Hollenbaugh indicated that the couple wished to marry and intended to do so as soon as they were able. At one point, a board member told Philburn that he could come back to work if he moved out; Philburn replied that he would not leave his child and her mother. In August 1973, the board dismissed both Hollenbaugh and Philburn.[186]

In proceedings before the federal district court judge Hubert Teitelbaum, defendants insisted that "openly adulterous cohabitation" was the sole motivation for Hollenbaugh's termination, while they cited substandard job performance as a reason for Philburn's firing. Plaintiffs contended that Hollenbaugh's pregnancy and decision to bear Philburn's child, as well as the couple's living arrangements, motivated the trustees' action. If the library fired Hollenbaugh because of her nonmarital pregnancy or childbirth, the plaintiffs could more easily argue sex discrimination and make privacy-as-reproductive-autonomy and right-to-procreate arguments based on *Griswold*, *Eisenstadt*, and *Roe*. The couple's desire to live together with their child and Philburn's inability to have children otherwise also invited greater compassion.

Judge Teitelbaum proved unsympathetic. The plaintiffs' lawyer, William Tantlinger, suggested that a hearing might have shown that Philburn's "conduct ... was not open lust" or "immoral" but rather "a considered decision by a man who is approaching the age where he couldn't have children." The judge interrupted him to point out that when Philburn started "fu[tz]ing around, he didn't know that the girl was going to have a baby" and to say that a "man's age doesn't have anything to do with his ability to have intercourse. ... Justice Douglas was about 78 and he married a woman [who was] 28." Tantlinger replied, "Justice Douglas is a phenomenal man in more ways than one," but he conceded the point.[187]

Teitelbaum agreed with defendants that "the sole reason" for Hollenbaugh's and Philburn's discharge "was that they were living together in 'open adultery.'" The judge rejected plaintiffs' equal protection and due process arguments, holding that "any rights plaintiffs have to live together must be balanced against" the board's concerns about adverse community reaction, Hollenbaugh's ability to perform a job that required significant contact with children, and the trustees' desire not to give "tacit approval" to the couple's lifestyle. Teitelbaum also held that the right to privacy protected "personal intimacies of the home, the family, motherhood, procreation, and child rearing"—not any right "for two persons, one of whom is married, to live together under the circumstances of this case."[188]

With the Pittsburgh ACLU on board, the plaintiffs had high hopes for their appeal to the Third Circuit, but these hopes proved unwarranted, and the Supreme Court declined to hear *Hollenbaugh*. Justice Brennan dissented from the denial of certiorari, and Justice Marshall wrote an opinion voicing his chagrin: the lower court's ruling "permits a public employer to dictate the sexual conduct and family living arrangements of its employees, without a meaningful showing" of "any relation to job performance." Marshall found "particularly invidious" the "hypocrisy" that the Carnegie Free Library enforced by objecting not "to furtive adultery, but only to petitioners' refusal to hide their relationship." Moreover, Hollenbaugh and Philburn's relationship clearly fell under the constitutional rights of privacy and family autonomy implicated in a laundry list of precedents. Pennsylvania's 1972 repeal of criminal sanctions for adultery and fornication and the absence of evidence that the plaintiffs' marital status impaired their job functions made the board's decision all the more galling.[189]

By 1978, Hollenbaugh and Philburn had built a life together with their now five-year-old daughter. Hollenbaugh performed clerical work for the Fayette County Redevelopment Authority, and the couple purchased a home on the outskirts of Connellsville. Philburn reveled in watching his daughter grow. The couple enjoyed a warm relationship with Katherine Philburn, to whom Fred remained legally wed. Despite their lack of a legal bond, Hollenbaugh and Philburn were committed life partners. Hollenbaugh reflected, "We may not have won the battle or the war, but it felt good to stand up and have . . . the ACLU fighting for our rights. There's a lot of satisfaction in that."[190] Philburn was less sanguine. He believed the litigation, along with his disabilities, prevented him from finding another steady job. He told the *Pittsburgh Press*, "I feel that Rebecca and I have been done a great injustice."[191]

The outcomes in cases such as *Sullivan* and *Hollenbaugh* underscore the unfulfilled promise of *Eisenstadt v. Baird* and other cases that challenged the constitutionality of laws and policies that invaded the private lives of individuals and allowed the government to discriminate based upon marital status. Much had changed since Anna Flores's 1970 discharge from the Navy for nonmarital pregnancy, but Americans who departed from conventional norms of marital heterosexuality still faced significant barriers to employment at the end of the decade. Especially daunting obstacles stood in the way of educators and others expected to serve as instructors and role models for young people.

The Nexus Standard

Plaintiffs and advocates made capacious constitutional claims in public employment cases: equal protection based on sex, sexual orientation, and marital status; sexual privacy and autonomy; freedom of speech and association. Still, even where courts recognized violations of constitutional rights, the nexus standard governed most cases throughout this period. In practice, this functional approach allowed school districts and other state employers ample discretion to bow to opposition from school administrators, parents, and community members.

Requiring that school officials justify a decision to fire, or not to hire, based on sexual conduct or orientation surely improved upon outright exclusion based on status. But the nexus standard led to uneven recognition and enforcement of constitutional rights. Jim Gaylord's case underscored this capriciousness and the persistent vulnerability of gay teachers. Gaylord compiled a sterling performance record as a teacher at Wilson High School in Tacoma, Washington, from 1959 until his abrupt dismissal in November 1972, merely for admitting to the vice principal that he was gay.

By 1977, when the Washington Supreme Court upheld Gaylord's discharge for "immorality," ACLU lawyers could point to a decade of legal and social change: the American Psychiatric Association no longer classified homosexuality as a mental illness; several lower courts had protected civil servants from summary termination; U.S. Civil Service Commission guidelines issued in 1975 affirmed that homosexuality alone could not be cause for termination of federal employment; Massachusetts and several major cities had enacted anti-discrimination laws covering sexual orientation.[192] Gay teachers, previously silenced or kept out of the profession altogether, organized with support from the National Education Association and more visibly asserted their rights.[193]

At the same time, however, a burgeoning conservative movement stoked fear and hostility toward gay Americans generally and teachers in particular. The "Save Our Children" campaign, launched in 1977 by the singer and beauty queen Anita Bryant, trumpeted the homophobic trope that gay men and lesbians posed a double-barreled threat to young people: as potential molesters and as transmitters of moral contagion.[194] In California, a state representative, John Briggs, led a campaign in 1978 to pass a ballot initiative to ban gay and lesbian teachers from public education.[195]

The Briggs initiative failed, but the support it attracted highlighted the wide spectrum of public opinion about the relationship between sexual orientation and fitness to teach school. Richard McWilliams of Sun City, California, represented one pole: he believed that "homosexuality is not and cannot be private" because "advocacy is primarily not in words as such but in subtle mannerisms; the very presence of such a person . . . exerts . . . the power to harm and convert lives to the desperate emotional needs of the homosexual to maintain his corrupted nature."[196] Others professed that gay Americans should be free to live and work in peace—except in the classroom. Some invoked parents' right to avoid perceived moral and physical dangers to their children; others distinguished between jobs that involved contact with young people and those that did not.

The nexus standard gave school boards discretion to defer to community objections, even when teachers like Jim Gaylord had done nothing to publicize their sexual orientation. The U.S. Supreme Court denied Gaylord's petition for certiorari, letting the state court's decision stand.[197]

Anti-discrimination laws and constitutional privacy protections did open some doors, to be sure. Plaintiffs often enjoyed greater success when they could claim that their employer had applied a sexual double standard or otherwise treated employees differently based on sex or race. For example, in 1975, the Pennsylvania Human Relations Commission extinguished a Pittsburgh-area school district policy denying maternity leave to unmarried women—effectively an automatic discharge for unwed teachers who gave birth during the academic year—on sex discrimination grounds. The state court acknowledged that the policy appeared to discriminate on the basis of marital status rather than sex but found "no evidence" that the district had "adopted a mandatory termination policy for unwed male teachers who have fathered illegitimate children or otherwise participated in extramarital sex."[198] In 1978, a Black teacher successfully sued an Arkansas school district that had used nonmarital pregnancy as a pretext for maintaining racial segregation.[199]

And the nexus standard sometimes protected plaintiffs. Teachers could prevail in some cases by convincing judges that employers had not provided sufficient evidence of impact on job performance to justify infringing upon constitutional rights. But as the experiences of Joe Acanfora and even his less vocal compatriots suggest, this showing proved challenging for many. Sexual orientation once revealed often provoked a hostile reaction that allowed officials to claim disruption; pregnancy was difficult to hide; and nonmarital cohabitation looked more like a voluntary choice than an immutable status. Many pregnant, cohabiting, and gay plaintiffs disclaimed any desire for publicity; indeed, some actively sought concealment. Others proudly proclaimed their identity, a move that implicated First Amendment rights but also trapped those who advocated for equality and justice only to find their words and acts turned against them in court. Visibility was a double-edged sword: a necessary step to expose the irrationality of discrimination, galvanize activism, and invoke First Amendment protection but an often-insurmountable barrier when framed as disruptive or "proselytizing."

For all that united them and intertwined their fates, unmarried pregnant women, cohabitants, and gay teachers differed in important ways. Gay teachers faced hostility heightened by the increasing visibility and activism of organized social movements for and against gay rights and liberation. Antipathy toward nonmarital pregnancy and cohabitation persisted and affected individuals' employment prospects. But it did not galvanize the same degree of political reaction and collective moral panic.

Further, unmarried pregnant teachers and gay educators both were outliers in the treatment of employees, but in different ways. In contexts other than education, unmarried pregnant employees won some protection from discrimination by the late 1970s. Rose Jacobs's case illustrates how plaintiffs prevailed in private sector jobs that—notably—did not involve contact with children. The Martin Sweets Company transferred and demoted Jacobs, a secretary, when she became pregnant while unmarried in 1972. The Sixth Circuit upheld a lower court ruling that the company violated Title VII, calling the employer's contention that it would have treated similarly a "male expectant parent" who engaged in nonmarital sex a "sophistry."[200]

In 1978, Congress, at the behest of a coalition that included feminist, labor, and anti-abortion organizations, passed the Pregnancy Discrimination Act (PDA), overturning the Supreme Court ruling in *Gilbert v. General Electric* (1976) that held Title VII inapplicable to pregnancy discrimination.[201] Defining sex discrimination to include pregnancy made it more difficult for judges to treat penalties for nonmarital pregnancy as the fault of "Mother Nature" or "biology." At least in Title VII cases not involving teachers, the PDA's protections applied regardless of marital status. By the end of the decade, to the extent that EEOC guidelines had not already done so, HEW regulations and the PDA largely brought the public and private sectors into rough parity. The nexus standard sporadically reared its head in both domains, but for employees who did not have contact with children or young people, the default was protection from discrimination based on pregnancy, regardless of marital status.[202]

By contrast, because the sex discrimination claims of gay and lesbian employees failed, federal employees enjoyed the *most* protection of any gay employees. It was not always clear that this would be so: in the early 1970s, regional EEOC offices processed and pursued some claims brought by individuals who alleged that employers discriminated "because of sex" when they excluded or discharged gay and lesbian applicants or employees. In 1971 the EEOC lawyer Sonia Pressman publicly suggested that Title VII's sex discrimination provision covered discrimination based on sexual orientation.[203] Not until 1975 did the EEOC say such discrimination fell outside Title VII's scope.[204]

Representative Bella Abzug (D-NY) and allies in Congress slowly began to marshal support for federal bills prohibiting sexual orientation discrimination, and advocates brought court cases—unsuccessfully—seeking to extend federal protections to gay and lesbian workers.[205] Most private sector and nonfederal public employees enjoyed little or no protection from discrimination based on sexual orientation.[206] The Supreme Court's decision in *Bowers v. Hardwick* (1986) confirmed that states remained free not only to discriminate against gay and lesbian Americans but to criminalize gay sex based on the belief that "homosexual sodomy" was "immoral and unacceptable." Justice White's opinion for a 5–4 majority decisively rejected the idea that "any kind of private sexual conduct between consenting adults is constitutionally insulated from state proscription."[207] For gay employees in most of the United States, the nexus standard applicable to federal employees and sometimes to teachers, with all its flaws and limitations, was the only game in town.

Unlike women and, increasingly, gay and lesbian Americans, cohabitants lacked a social movement pressing for recognition and inclusion.[208] They confronted less hostility and persecution than gay employees but enjoyed minimal legal protection. Courts often interpreted laws that prohibited marital status discrimination in employment narrowly, to exclude cohabitants. Of the twenty states that passed prohibitions on marital status discrimination in the 1970s and 1980s, only a handful extended protection to cohabiting couples or individuals living in nonmarital relationships. Rather, marital status discrimination laws primarily targeted discrimination against married women and were interpreted by courts to protect *individuals* against discrimination based on *status*—whether they were single or married or divorced.[209] Employers remained free, for the most part, to dismiss or otherwise penalize employees who lived with a partner unmarried: courts characterized cohabitation as *conduct* outside the scope of anti-discrimination protection.

The experience of public employees—in the military, classrooms, and libraries—who challenged state action that punished their departure from marital heterosexual norms reflects larger trends in the history of feminism and in the modernization of marital status law. Feminists eliminated most sex-based distinctions from the law but did not enact the ambitious versions of freedom and equality they envisioned. And while some of the most egregious injustices subsided, marital privilege endured in law and practice. Sex discrimination arguments sometimes succeeded where other legal pathways failed. Unmarried pregnant women could in some cases rely on the protection of sex discrimination laws; for gay and cohabiting workers, legal protections were confined to a few domains.

The emergence of the nexus requirement reflected a shift from moralistic formalism to functional standards in the treatment of Americans who did not conform to marital heterosexuality. Privacy, equality, and liberty claims weakened categorical exclusions based on absolutist sexual morality. In theory, no longer could public employers per se refuse to hire all gay and lesbian applicants or fire employees solely for nonmarital pregnancy or cohabitation. Rather, constitutional norms forced them to justify exclusionary decisions by showing how non-normative sexuality infringed on individuals' abilities to function as effective teachers or librarians or military servicemembers.

But the old morality resurfaced in the functional nexus standard. Community reactions to gay, unmarried pregnant, and cohabiting persons frequently became the measure of ability to perform jobs that involved contact with children. Often, only by hiding their identity or conduct could teachers and librarians protect themselves. But being discreet was impossible or undesirable for many pregnant and gay individuals.[210] Public employers' and courts' discretion to consider moral objections under the guise of measuring job performance and protecting children limited the efficacy of the constitutional claims that civil libertarians and feminists advanced.

The mixed outcomes of 1980s litigation underscored the stakes of these judgments. Gay and lesbian teachers remained at the mercy of school officials' and judges' discretion. The Court's approval of laws criminalizing sodomy in *Bowers* aggravated this problem. Heterosexual cohabitants, too, risked their jobs in many communities, sometimes backed by criminal prohibitions on adultery and fornication that seldom were enforced directly but cast a shadow over nonmarital conduct.[211]

Public school teachers who became pregnant outside of marriage continued to enjoy somewhat greater constitutional and statutory protections now that federal law defined discrimination based on pregnancy as sex discrimination. Principal Hattie Webb told Pamela Ponton that she must "resign, get married, or take a leave of absence" when she became pregnant in 1983 while teaching vocational education at a public magnet school in Newport News, Virginia. Webb testified in court that "when we are addressing the concern of teenage pregnancy and unwed mothers, it would be inappropriate to have a single pregnant teacher in the classroom. Teachers are role models." Under questioning in federal district court by Judge Robert Merhige, Webb confirmed that she would not have so treated a married teacher or an unmarried father.[212] Merhige, who had issued some of the earliest rulings in favor of pregnant plaintiffs, had no trouble seeing Ponton's treatment as sex discrimination under the equal protection clause and Title VII.[213]

Still, other courts gave wide leeway to private employers who made similar arguments in cases involving young unmarried Black women like Ponton who taught or counseled children. Paula Harvey, a twenty-two-year-old program director at the Charlotte YWCA, became pregnant in 1976. Executive Director Micki Riddick, also a Black woman, told Harvey she could resign or be fired; Harvey replied that she could offer teen girls a positive example of how to make an "alternative lifestyle" work.[214] By the time her race and sex discrimination case went to trial in 1982, Paula Harvey Todd was married and working for the EEOC. She lost:

Judge Robert Potter held that the YWCA should not be forced to employ a person who would promote a "lifestyle which is abhorrent to [its] ideals and goals."[215]

Crystal Chambers, a twenty-two-year-old art teacher at the Omaha Girls' Club, faced a similar fate after she became pregnant later that year.[216] Board members, who were mostly white, fired Chambers as an unfit role model for the club's teenage students, 90 percent of whom were Black. Chambers, too, lost her race and sex discrimination case.[217] Her defeat, critically dissected by the legal scholar Regina Austin in her classic article "Sapphire Bound!" (1989), became an emblem of Black women's struggle to redefine racial, economic, and sexual citizenship.[218] How that struggle unfolded in the long 1970s is the subject of the next chapter.

PART III

CHAPTER SIX

Single Mothers and Responsible Citizenship

L YING IN THE MATERNITY ward of a Philadelphia hospital in 1967, Lois Fernandez felt boundless joy at becoming a mother. She soon learned that the state of Pennsylvania did not share her enthusiasm. Maternity health insurance benefits only covered married women, a nurse informed her, and Fernandez's unmarried status meant that her newborn son, Adeyemi, would not be issued a birth certificate.[1] Instead, she could pay two dollars for a short form that confirmed his birth but listed neither mother nor father.[2] Fernandez refused on principle to purchase such a document and began to research birth status law. She discovered that in Pennsylvania, a child born to unmarried parents could become "legitimate" only if his parents married each other.[3] In 1971, Fernandez launched a letter-writing campaign that spurred state representatives to introduce legislation to formally abolish discrimination against nonmarital children.[4] "To give birth is human, not illegitimate," she insisted.[5]

One of ten surviving children of a Black American mother and a Bahamian immigrant father who admired Marcus Garvey, Fernandez saw her campaign as part of a larger commitment to racial justice and cultural pride. Her mother, a South Philadelphia Democratic committeewoman who migrated from Alabama as a child, was aghast when Lois—inspired by the South African singer Miriam Makeba and awakening to a lost African heritage—stopped straightening her hair and wearing "high-fashion" clothing.[6] Mrs. Fernandez, a clerk at the Bureau of Vital Statistics who issued the unequal birth certificates her daughter fought against, raised her children as "high-church" Episcopalians. She also encouraged them to "take a stand," but Mrs. Fernandez expressed skepticism that Lois could "change that white man's law" after "200 years."[7]

Undaunted, Lois Fernandez litigated, lobbied, spoke on local television and radio shows, and enlisted the help of allies at the National Urban League and beyond. She fought against the sexual double standard that persistently stigmatized unmarried mothers. The "question of the fathers never came up," she later recalled. Mothers "were considered 'whores,' or 'illicit women,' and then there were the children, who were considered 'bastards,' 'illegit.' I just couldn't accept that."[8] She resented "the stereotype of mothers of out-of-wedlock children as promiscuous" and recoiled when family and friends expected her children to have their fathers' surnames rather than her own.[9] Fernandez considered her decision to become a single mother a deliberate step that she was proud of, and not an unfortunate, inadvertent, or shameful fate. "To have a child without a husband was my choice," she said. "I made the decision with pride; I did not worry about societal pressures. To give birth is one of the most beautiful experiences I have ever had."[10]

Fernandez celebrated single motherhood as a valid, voluntary lifestyle choice. At the same time, Fernandez's status as a worker, property holder, and taxpaying citizen countered demeaning ideas about "unwed mothers" as "lazy welfare chiselers." As a reporter wrote in 1971, "That picture hardly fits Lois. She has only one child"—Fernandez later gave birth to a second—"and she works as hard as anyone else to support him." Alongside her job with the youth conservation service of the public welfare department, she earned a college degree in library technology and co-chaired the Parents' Union for Public Schools. Fernandez observed that her son had "no birth certificate and no inheritance rights, [but] he can still be drafted." As a "working mother" and a "homeowner," Fernandez insisted that she and her family deserved better.[11]

With the help of Community Legal Services and the Women's Law Project, Fernandez challenged the constitutionality of Pennsylvania's discriminatory laws in court. Her lawyers, including the prominent feminist attorney and professor Ann Freedman, argued that state laws that prevented nonmarital children from inheriting from fathers who died intestate (without leaving a will) and that taxed bequests to nonmarital children at a higher rate were unconstitutional sex discrimination. These laws exacerbated women's economic disadvantage, her lawyers maintained, for mothers were "burdened with the far more onerous task of supporting a child who has no claim against his or her father's estate." Advocates made similar arguments in other cases challenging sex and birth status discrimination in inheritance and child support laws.[12]

In some ways, these arguments built on Sylvester Smith's challenge to Alabama's substitute father rule discussed in chapter 2. *King v. Smith* prefigured an alternative, feminist approach that emphasized how marital status laws foisted upon mothers the care and support of nonmarital children. These laws shamed and punished women for illicit sex while allowing men to escape consequences with impunity. They restricted women's reproductive autonomy by penalizing their decision to bear and raise nonmarital children. The state invasively patrolled *women*'s personal lives by conditioning sustenance on the disclosure of sexual relationships or paternity.

Feminists had long resisted these unfair burdens, but emerging sex equality principles now provided a sturdier legal basis for their complaints. In the late 1960s, the Supreme Court had yet to find a sex-discriminatory law unconstitutional under the equal protection clause. Feminists already were making creative constitutional arguments in adjacent realms: they argued, for example, that abortion restrictions violated equality principles because they infringed women's bodily autonomy and disproportionately burdened poor women and women of color.[13] As the increasingly conservative composition of the Supreme Court made arguments about disparate impact based on race and poverty less potent, sex discrimination claims gained ground. In the early 1970s, feminists reframed laws that imposed disadvantages on nonmarital parents and children as *unconstitutionally* injurious to women.

Feminist arguments, fortified by new sex equality precedents, clashed with the prevailing approach, exemplified by Harry Krause's focus on establishing legal paternity to secure father-child relationships and private financial support. "Punitive statutes directed at illegitimate mothers" like suitable home and substitute father laws, Krause agreed, "ultimately fell upon the child," and "reprehensible activities by welfare bureaucrats have come under just scrutiny." Nevertheless, Krause believed poverty lawyers were too preoccupied with "eliminating interference with the welfare mother." Social services directed at children, including a more robust response to child abuse and neglect, were imperative: "Whether or not society owes adults a living, the child is owed a chance," Krause concluded his 379-page tome, *Il-legitimacy: Law and Social Policy* (1971). As we saw in chapter 2, the Supreme Court embraced Krause's approach in birth status cases, condemning the punishment of blameless children for parental transgressions.[14]

However, in the 1970s, a new generation of lawyers and advocates challenged this dominant orthodoxy on explicitly feminist grounds. Patricia Tenoso and Aleta Wallach denounced Krause's "dogged" devotion to "the holy principle of paternity." Illegitimacy, Tenoso and Wallach argued, only posed a "problem" because law and social norms made it so. Krause's proposed Uniform Legitimacy Act "merely substitute[d] paternity for marriage" as the basis for classifying children, reinforcing the importance of birth status. He neglected to "treat the mother as an economic resource" by tackling discriminatory hiring, unequal pay, and lack of affordable childcare. Moreover, Krause failed to consider "adequate governmental support of all unmarried mothers and their children" as an alternative. Tenoso and Wallach, by contrast, rejected any presumption of marital primacy and questioned a legal regime that privatized support in the nuclear family.[15]

Tenoso and Wallach advanced instead "an independent justification for abolition of illegitimacy: the right of women to self-determination requires that they be free from all forms of male domination."[16] They condemned the valorization of the marital family that "relegated to inferior status" unmarried mothers and their children.[17] Feminists sought to unsettle the patriarchal family ideal and empower women as independent economic, social, and sexual actors.

Like the wide-ranging conceptions of sexual autonomy, liberty, and economic citizenship advanced by Mrs. Sylvester Smith and the welfare rights leader Johnnie Tillmon, feminist critiques of marital status law did not translate neatly into legal or constitutional claims. To realize the "abolition of illegitimacy," let alone women's "right to self-determination," would require revolutionary societal transformation. What Tenoso and Wallach demanded—an overthrow of hierarchies based on gender, race, and class—arguably threatened the foundations of late-industrial capitalist society.[18]

Some feminists on the left, particularly those influenced by Marxism, did indeed seek the end of capitalism, but the benefits of social democracy—family allowances and universal health care, education, and childcare—would have satisfied most feminist law reformers. After the passage of Medicare and Medicaid, such policy innovations seemed possible if not likely in a future Democratic administration. Indeed, two policy initiatives that failed in the early 1970s, Nixon's proposed Family Assistance Plan and the Comprehensive Child Development Act he ultimately vetoed, suggested that these reforms remained just barely out of reach.[19]

Economic justice for single mothers and children awaited sweeping social legislation. In the meantime, single mothers of color used newly available constitutional sex equality principles to redefine the contours of responsible citizenship by challenging marital and birth status discrimination against women as well as children. These women did not speak with one voice, nor did they advance a singular vision. Some sought to conform to existing normative ideals; some rejected the politics of respectability altogether; and still others tried to reconfigure conventional values by providing an affirmative account of virtuous single motherhood. Their allies (and occasional antagonists) spanned a wide spectrum of feminism, civil libertarianism, and advocacy for racial justice and child welfare.

Single mothers' struggles for what Black feminists later named reproductive justice enjoyed only mixed success, as this chapter describes. Unmarried mothers who asserted their prerogative to earn a living rather than depend on public assistance sometimes persuaded courts that employment exclusions imposed unconstitutional sexual and racial double standards. When single parents sought the right to join the Army and Air Force, however, they laid claim to more than just a job: a burgeoning military welfare state offered myriad benefits to married male servicemen and their wives and dependents just as the civilian welfare state crumbled. And indigent mothers who resisted state pressure to identify their children's paternity had an even steeper climb: women who relied on welfare could not portray themselves as self-sufficient, responsible citizens able to support their nonmarital children without any help from the state. The success of challenges to marital primacy often tracked their fiscal impact: the state safely could ignore marital status when doing so helped to privatize dependence in the family.

Working Motherhood

To make "working motherhood" a reality, unmarried mothers of color, especially, had to surmount overt and covert employment discrimination. Until the late 1960s, few doubted that private employers could lawfully exclude women who became pregnant or gave birth outside of marriage.

Employers cited morality and worker morale as rationales, but a racial subtext often lurked beneath the surface. The NAACP Legal Defense Fund sued Southwestern Bell in 1968 for excluding unmarried mothers, a policy that bore "more heavily upon Negroes than upon whites." Judge Jesse Smith Henley, who had struck down a similar ban in Little Rock public housing, in this case believed the phone company's "good faith" policy to be lawful even if it "bears more heavily on an underprivileged ethnic or racial group." An employer, Henley believed, had a "legitimate interest . . . in the sexual behavior of its employees and their morale while at work." Even if "certain classes of Negroes have a different attitude toward extramarital sex than do most white people," Title VII did not "require an employer to conform his standards to the Negro attitude."[20]

In 1970, the EEOC disagreed, ruling in favor of a Black woman denied a job as a telephone operator because she had nonmarital children.[21] In 1971, the Supreme Court ruled that plaintiffs could bring disparate impact claims under Title VII without proving discriminatory intent.[22] Later that year, a New York court had no trouble finding that the New York Police Department discriminated based on race and sex in denying Sofia Cirino a job as crossing guard because as "the mother of eight children by five different fathers" she did not exhibit the requisite "moral character." In an impoverished Puerto Rican community where a quarter of births occurred outside of marriage, the judge wrote, Cirino's "lifestyle" was "too prevalent . . . to reflect against her 'character.'" A public assistance recipient, Cirino "want[ed] to work, and does when work is available." Indeed, she had a "glowing letter of reference" from her previous job as a substitute teacher's aide. Cirino's desire to earn a living and sterling employment record evinced "competence and character" irrespective of her marital status or poverty.[23]

Such disparate views collided in Katie Mae Andrews's lawsuit challenging the exclusion of unmarried mothers from employment as public school teachers in rural Mississippi.[24] The Drew school district, introduced in chapter 5, was a long-standing battleground in the struggle for desegregation and voting rights. At the behest of Superintendent George F. Pettey, officials denied four Black women positions as teachers or teachers' aides because they had nonmarital children. One of them, the twenty-three-year-old Katie Mae Andrews, knocked on Charles Victor McTeer's door in 1973. McTeer, a twenty-eight-year-old Baltimore native and a protégé of the civil rights lawyer Morty Stavis of New York's Center for Constitutional Rights (CCR), had just arrived in Mississippi.

The ensuing litigation featured characters who represented Mississippi's past, present, and future. Judge William Keady, a Mississippi native, became a judge in 1968, the day after the assassination of Dr. Martin Luther King, Jr., and presided over school desegregation. Champ Terney, son-in-law of the segregationist senator James O. Eastland, represented the school district. McTeer enlisted the support and testimony of the local civil rights icons Fannie Lou Hamer and Mae Bertha Carter.[25] The social psychologist Kenneth Clark—who co-authored with Mamie Phipps Clark the "doll studies" cited by the Supreme Court in *Brown v. Board of Education* to establish the psychological harm of racial segregation—testified by deposition from New York. So did Ernest van den Haag, a Dutch-born former communist who survived imprisonment in fascist Italy and became a defender of racial segregation and genetic theories of intelligence in his adopted country.[26] Feminist lawyers from CCR, as well as the ACLU and Equal Rights Advocates, the EEOC, and the Child Welfare League, contributed briefs and legal counsel to the plaintiffs.

McTeer argued that the "Pettey rule" excluded and stigmatized Black families, in purpose and effect. An estimated 30 to 40 percent of Black children in the Drew school district were born to unmarried parents. Even the more open-minded white teachers and school officials warned that allowing mothers of nonmarital children to teach would extinguish already waning white support for the now majority-Black public schools.[27] Pettey insisted he only wished to maintain high standards of moral character among adults who had daily contact with children, regardless of race or sex. Pettey conceded that identifying unmarried fathers would be difficult since only "the unwed mother is stuck with the result."[28] The white woman charged with making hiring recommendations acknowledged that, in practice, the exclusion affected only Black women.[29]

In Judge Keady's courtroom a vigorous debate unfolded over morality and character. The school district defended marital supremacy, arguing that "those who do not conform to the institution of marriage 'are legitimately made to suffer some disadvantages,'" in van den Haag's words.[30] Drew's Black community initially divided over the wisdom of opposing the Pettey rule. Some preferred not to air "dirty laundry" in public for fear of reinforcing damaging stereotypes and undermining a fragile racial peace.[31]

The women turned away for being unmarried parents did not speak with one voice on sexual morality. Violet Burnett, who had lost her job as a teacher's aide, defiantly embraced sexual freedom. "Do you personally feel that it's moral or immoral for an unmarried person to have sexual intercourse?" she was asked by the school district's lawyer on cross-examination. "I feel like as an individual a person ... has the freedom to do anything they want to as long as it's not hurting anyone," Burnett replied. Would she advise a teenaged student in her charge to have sexual intercourse with her boyfriend? "I would tell her if that's what she wanted ... go right ahead." Did she plan to have any more children outside of marriage? No. Why? "Because taking care of one is hard enough." The plaintiff Lestine Rogers, too, saw nonmarital sex as an individual decision: "I can't say it's right and I can't say it's wrong. Because I think it's left up to you as long as you are not hurting anyone else."[32]

Katie Mae Andrews presented herself as a churchgoing woman who had become pregnant due to a lack of knowledge about and access to contraception. Andrews considered premarital sex "a sin" but insisted, "The Bible says ... [y]ou can repent for your sin and be forgiven." She did not intend to have any more children before getting married. She also refused to apologize for her decision to give birth. "I mean, God put us here on earth and ... I feel that we should have them. ... If we try to get rid of it, as most people do, that's killing it. Well, you know where we would wind up then." And she defended her prerogative to marry only "when I meet the right person to marry."[33] Indeed, by the time her case reached the Supreme Court in 1975, Ms. Andrews had become Mrs. Katie Mae Peacock.

Some of Andrews's allies emphasized that equal employment opportunity was essential to ensure private sources of support for families. Andrews had graduated from Mississippi Valley State College and earned money as a factory worker in Cleveland, Mississippi, while raising her son with the help of her mother and siblings, with whom she lived. Without a school district job, Andrews would be "consigned to unemployment or welfare or relegated to marginal employment, often available only at a distance from her home and child."[34] Exclusion perpetuated the "cycle of poverty" that Andrews had escaped through her hard work.[35] Fannie Lou Hamer testified: "I know so many young women that after having one child, go back to school, finish school and yet not marry." Single mothers able to find good jobs could support their children and lift them out of poverty.[36]

Hamer explained that Sunflower County's Black community viewed the choice that Andrews and her compatriots made—to keep, care for, and support their children—as evidence of strong character, not immorality or irresponsibility. Women like Andrews *were* admirable role models: college graduates who sought meaningful employment to overcome poverty and achieve economic self-sufficiency. Hamer admonished school officials, "you always tell us . . . we have got so many kids on the welfare roll, 'Why don't you get up and do something?' And then when we start doing something, 'You don't have any business being that high.'" If the school district excluded all employees, she continued, white and Black, who engaged in nonmarital sex, then "lock up the doors. There won't be any school."[37]

Kenneth Clark's testimony confirmed that Black and white Americans alike regularly defied proscriptions against sex outside marriage. Lack of access to contraception and information, not racially specific moral codes, explained disparate nonmarital pregnancy rates. Clark argued that Drew officials were the ones acting immorally by "pry[ing] into the personal or sex life of other individuals . . . [and] impos[ing] their personal sexual patterns or gratifications upon others."[38] Mae Bertha Carter, a married mother of thirteen children who had integrated the Drew public schools a decade earlier, testified that she would be proud to see Andrews teach her children.[39]

Feminists at CCR used *Andrews* to promote broader claims of reproductive autonomy. Jan Goodman explained, "We are arguing that all women should have the freedom to choose, and that they not be penalized whatever the choice is—to bear the child or to abort" without giving up their career aspirations.[40] The Pettey rule "encourage[d] abortion," they charged, "a practice that offends the moral sensibility of a significant segment of American society," as well as the personal moral and religious beliefs of both Andrews and Hamer.[41]

Feminists also made constitutional sex equality arguments.[42] The ACLU/Equal Rights Advocates brief called the Pettey rule "an unwarranted return to the times during which stigmatization of unwed mothers was a tool, along with forced pregnancy, compulsory marriage and deprivation of birth control information, by which women were kept in their legal and societal place." These amici emphasized how employment exclusions "deprived [unmarried mothers] of economic self-sufficiency" and prevented women from "making the contribution to society that [their] work affords." Only implicitly did they invoke the specter of welfare costs, noting that families whose "sole breadwinners are females" comprised a "most economically needy group."[43]

Both sides in the Mississippi litigation professed to have children's best interests at heart. The school district presented testimony about the importance of role models for impressionable students, especially disadvantaged children of color.[44] White parents, the district intimated, would not condone such moral disintegration, causing all children to suffer from the withdrawal of financial support for the public schools.[45]

The plaintiffs offered a very different assessment of children's welfare. Clark scoffed at the notion that a teacher who bore a nonmarital child would influence students' sexual conduct or likelihood of becoming pregnant. Instead, the plaintiffs argued, the Pettey rule "dehumanize[d] and stigmatize[d]" children, "branding them as inferior to their 'legitimate' classmates."[46] The Child Welfare League of America charged that the policy deprived children of "adequate food, shelter, clothing, and medical care." Such hardship threatened that children would be removed from their parents for "neglect" and that unmarried mothers would relinquish their children for adoption—or, more likely, foster care—rather than raise them.[47] Penalties for nonmarital childbearing, they argued, hurt children at least as much as their mothers: they threatened family separation as well as poverty.

Military Service

Family separation and poverty also stalked single mothers who tried to join the military. In 1976, two young Black New Yorkers spoke with an Army recruiter on a Bronx street corner. Not long after, on Mother's Day, the sisters, Thelma Barnes and Shirley Concepcion, applied to enlist in the Army Reserve, sat for a test, and were sworn in. Barnes, a commissions analyst at New York Life Insurance, disclosed to the recruiter that she had a young child, and his advice mirrored Katie Mae Andrews's decision: don't mention the kid on the application form.

After she received instruction in marching, shooting an M-16 rifle, and filling out forms "the Army way," Barnes was told that she must transfer legal guardianship of her daughter before attending basic training in North Carolina. Barnes paid a lawyer $300 to file a guardianship petition on her mother's behalf, but shortly before her scheduled departure the Army informed her that she should not have been allowed to enlist unless she surrendered her child for adoption. "I told them, 'No way, that's my baby,'" Barnes later recounted.[48] Her commanding officer, loath to lose a capable reservist, asked Barnes to continue to attend drills, but his superiors voided her enlistment retroactively in December 1976.[49] She refused, on principle, to return her Army Reserve salary.

Concepcion also had a child when she enlisted, and she even shared a caregiver with Barnes: the women's mother took care of her grandchildren in her home. But Concepcion was married, and that made all the difference. Litigation and feminist pressure had compelled the military to rescind policies that justified the automatic discharge of pregnant servicewomen in the years since Anna Flores had sued the Navy. Women who became parents no longer faced inevitable separation from the military, nor did parents who became single through divorce or the death of a spouse. Enlistment was another story. The Army, Air Force, and their respective Reserves barred "accessions" of single parents with custody of a minor child.

Just a few years earlier, government officials had defended discrimination against unmarried mothers on grounds of morality, morale, and the armed forces' reputation. The ascendant doctrines of sex equality and sexual privacy, as we have seen, made such justifications constitutionally vulnerable. Anti-discrimination law had replaced sexual moralizing with a functional standard: now the government said that parents with sole responsibility for children simply did not make good recruits. They were unreliable, required costly accommodations, and could not handle irregular duty assignments, much less deployment abroad.[50]

The military, government lawyers contended, was "*not* concerned with morality, the welfare of the children or emotional trauma caused by family separation other than as traumas impact the service." The sole purpose of the regulations was to "preclude the enlistment of persons who, because of their solitary responsibilities and natural instincts, may prove to be less attentive and more disruptive soldiers than others, regardless of their inherent abilities."[51] The Army and Air Force redrew the line of ineligibility at "sole parenthood" rather than sex or marital status—a functional rather than formal exclusion that had nearly identical effects.

Thelma Barnes could not serve, whereas her sister's marital status meant that Concepcion faced no obstacles to pursuing a military career, even when she and her husband later separated.[52] Over the next several years, Concepcion reenlisted many times and earned a promotion to the rank of sergeant. "But for the single parent role," Barnes concluded, "I . . . would have had a similar career."[53]

Barnes and several other Black single mothers filed a class action lawsuit against the Department of Defense in 1976. Carlene Mack, a twenty-three-year-old never-married mother of two boys, applied in 1974 to enlist in the Army, but she was turned away because of her single-parent

status despite meeting all other requirements.[54] Shirley Stukes, also a
Black never-married mother of two, resided with one of her children in
Rochester, New York, and attended Monroe Community College. A federal grant paid her tuition; her only other source of income was public
assistance of less than $300 a month. In 1974, Stukes applied to the Air
Force and was denied enlistment when she refused to relinquish legal
custody and guardianship of her child.[55] The plaintiffs Maxine McNeill,
Patricia Ramsure, and Queen Esther Taylor, all single Black mothers,
were inducted into the Army Reserve in 1976. They submitted documents indicating that their children's grandparents would provide childcare, but the Army eventually voided their inductions, too, because they
refused to give up custody or guardianship.[56]

Represented first by the ACLU and the Greater Upstate (New York)
Legal Assistance Project (GULP) and later by attorneys at the National
Center for Women and Family Law, the plaintiffs in *Mack v. Rumsfeld* advanced three constitutional arguments. First, the enlistment restrictions
burdened the plaintiffs' "fundamental right to have and raise a family" by
forcing them to relinquish custody to enlist. Second, the military impermissibly favored the marital nuclear family based on spurious moral
judgments and "a stereotypical view of families." Third, the restrictions
violated equal protection. Single parent exclusions, plaintiffs said, were
motivated by a discriminatory purpose—keeping women out of the military. And the policy disproportionately burdened women, who were far
more likely than men to act as "sole parents" to minor children.[57]

None of the original named plaintiffs gave up custody of their children—but others did. A former New York family court judge averred that
she had "presided over numerous petitions seeking to transfer custody in
order to enlist in the military."[58] The family law scholar Carol Bruch—the
first single mother to clerk for a Supreme Court justice—wrote a report
detailing the difficulty of regaining custody once it had been relinquished.[59]

Plaintiffs' attorneys also sought testimonials from women who had
given up custody only to find that they had unwittingly sacrificed parental rights more permanently.[60] Geraldine Schmidt, a twenty-three-year-
old white woman who dropped out of high school at fourteen and gave
birth at fifteen, worked as a waitress to support her child. At seventeen,
when her daughter was two years old, Schmidt decided to enlist in the
Air Force. A recruiter told her she would have to relinquish custody to
enlist, but that she could regain custody immediately thereafter. "Relying
on his advice," Schmidt recalled, "I went to family court in Phoenix and

transferred custody ... to my parents." Upon learning that she would be giving up custody for the duration of her service, three years, Schmidt changed her mind, but her parents "refused to give [her daughter] back."[61] Over the next several years, Schmidt worked various jobs as a security guard, truck loader, cocktail waitress, and shipping clerk—but none paid enough for her to demonstrate she could support her daughter and regain custody.[62] Another single mother, Trina Lewis, put the matter succinctly: "I don't want to give up my son just to serve Uncle Sam."[63]

Like the aspiring Mississippi schoolteachers, single mothers seeking military careers protested how the enlistment restrictions placed unconstitutional burdens on their right to marry, or not, as they chose. Sarah Caldwell of Proctor, Vermont, age thirty-three, arranged for her fifteen-year-old son to stay with her fiancé while she was on active Army Reserve duty but declared herself "unwilling to speed up her marriage in order to qualify for military service." Caldwell declared, "I don't need the government to tell me when to get married."[64] Plaintiffs echoed Katie Mae Andrews's suggestion that punishing nonmarital childbearing encouraged abortion; lawyers folded this concern into a broader right to bear and raise children outside of marriage, free from job repercussions.[65]

The *Mack* plaintiffs also confronted function-based doubts about single parents' ability to be effective servicemembers. In response, they highlighted Black single mothers' particular experience and expertise in balancing work and family duties. The pioneering Black social worker and professor Patricia Morisey provided an expert report detailing how Black single mothers "receive support in regard to childcare from an extended network of relatives even if the single parent is a substantial distance away and needs help for an extended period of time."[66] Each of the named plaintiffs in *Mack* had parents willing and able to care for grandchildren while their daughters fulfilled their military duties. "Contrary to defendants' stereotyped notions about single mothers, they are able to arrange childcare ... and to meet their full-time work/school responsibilities."[67]

In addition to the social scientific literature that celebrated kin networks in Black communities, plaintiffs could point to the Supreme Court's recognition of the importance of extended family ties in *Moore v. City of East Cleveland* (1977), discussed in chapter 4. Inez Moore had faced criminal charges for violating the city's zoning law by taking her grandson, John Moore, Jr., into her home after his mother's death. Justice Lewis F. Powell, Jr., wrote for a plurality of the Court: "Ours is by no means a tradition limited to respect for the bonds uniting members of the nuclear family. The tradition of uncles, aunts, cousins, and especially grandparents sharing a household with parents and children has roots equally venerable and deserving of constitutional recognition."[68]

The plaintiffs also underscored the value of military service as a path out of poverty. "For low income Black families it is especially important that the single mother receive the salary, skill training, and PX privileges of being in the military. These advantages accrue to the extended family as a whole," wrote Professor Morisey.[69] Plaintiffs noted that "single mothers are the poorest group" in the United States, and "Black single mothers, who comprise 35 percent of single mothers, are even poorer."[70]

The plaintiffs laid claim to the benefits of the "military welfare state" at a time when the civilian welfare state was under sustained attack.[71] Military service offered an "unparalleled" bundle of benefits that was "especially valuable" to Black single mothers, their lawyers said. Servicemembers could "receive training," "make a reasonable salary that is not reduced by sex discrimination, and ... avoid the vicissitudes of unemployment." They could invoke "special rights" such as veterans' preferences and "extensive education, health, disability, and pension benefits."[72] Indeed, the plaintiffs argued that support services such as childcare centers, increasingly available on military bases, should mitigate any difficulties single parents might encounter in the event of overseas deployment or stateside assignments involving irregular hours.[73]

Government lawyers strenuously objected: the "business of the military services is not to run extensive networks of childcare centers; it is national defense."[74] The government condemned the plaintiffs' "characterization of military service as a public benefit existing to provide jobs and training to needy members of our society."[75] Major Roger S. Almquist put the matter bluntly. Reciting a litany of complaints about pregnant and "sole parent" servicewomen under his Army command, he wrote: "My tongue is not quite firmly in cheek when I suggest that I command a birth control clinic/maternity ward/pediatrics clinic/nursery/babysitting service that passes itself off as a Rapid Deployment Force Unit."[76] The solution, Almquist believed, was to allow commanding officers to "involuntarily separate pregnant women and nondeployable sole parents" and to "reduce the real problem by severely curtailing female enlistments, appointments, and commissions." He concluded: "The Army's business is martial, not maternal."[77]

Lawyers for Mack and her co-plaintiffs suspected that many military officials shared Almquist's diagnosis of "the real problem."[78] Press accounts of growing dissension about women in the military reinforced these suspicions.[79] Officials expressed particular disenchantment with servicewomen who became single parents while serving.[80] Military discourse often linked the "problem" of single parenthood to women, but because only a small fraction of servicemembers were female, the majority of single parents already *in* the military were men.[81] In 1980 a newspaper profile of the Marine staff sergeant Brad Babayco, who had sole custody of his young daughter, reported that an increasing number of single fathers chose to remain in the military rather than seek a "humanitarian discharge." Babayco was stationed in Orange County, California, where an onsite day care center cared for three-year-old Trishia between 7:30 a.m. and 4:30 p.m., and Babayco's parents flew down from Sacramento to take over her care when he departed for a six-month tour of duty in Okinawa.[82]

The flattering profile of Babayco contrasted sharply with articles about single servicewomen who reported for emergency drills with young children in tow. "Girl Soldiers Bring Babies Along on Duty" read one disapproving headline in 1978.[83] By then, an Army survey estimated that 7 percent of servicewomen and almost 2 percent of servicemen were sole parents of minor children. Single fathers did not escape censure, to be sure. Supply Sergeant Charles Haskins, a divorced Black father who unexpectedly won custody of his daughter after ten years in the Army, received numerous reprimands for bringing three-year-old Natalie to physical training. Army officials confirmed that single parents continued to suffer from a chronic childcare shortage.[84]

Because single women in the United States were more than ten times more likely than single men to have custody of children, restrictions on single parents' enlistment affected women disproportionately.[85] Phyllis Gelman, a lawyer for the *Mack* plaintiffs, told the *New York Times* in 1984 that the restrictions had ensnared an estimated eleven thousand single mothers, more than thirty-five hundred of them Black, since 1976.[86] Detailing the military's long history of discrimination against women generally and unmarried mothers in particular, plaintiffs charged intentional, as well as de facto, discrimination. "Traditional views of the 'proper' role of women and families" littered the record.[87] The sociologist and expert witness Kurt Lang observed "a persistent tendency to associate the problem [of single parents] with illegitimacy and a generally dissolute lifestyle."[88] Moral judgments about unwed mothers lurked beneath a façade of neutral, functional standards, plaintiffs charged.

Mandatory Paternity Disclosure

Women seeking gainful employment or military service could emphasize that they wanted to escape "dependence" on welfare. And they could portray their children's interests as aligned with their own as well as the government's. Poor and low-income women who did receive public assistance could do neither. After the campaign for a constitutional right to subsistence failed, welfare advocacy at the national level largely focused on struggles over legislation and regulation.[89] Constitutional claims did not disappear, however. Low-income women continued to challenge invasions of privacy and denials of due process and equal protection by welfare policymakers and administrators. Like their counterparts who sought employment opportunities, they defended single mothers' moral character, right to privacy, and prerogative to make decisions in their children's best interests.

States' efforts to identify fathers and pursue child support intensified in the 1960s and 1970s. Many states tried to condition AFDC receipt on mothers' cooperation with paternity determinations, but courts ruled, as they had in *King v. Smith*, that needy children could not be deprived of benefits because of their parents' conduct. To circumvent these rulings some states imposed penalties directly on mothers.[90] In 1971, Connecticut passed an especially draconian law compelling unmarried mothers to disclose the names of their children's fathers on pain of fines and imprisonment of up to one year.

Connecticut's law, in theory, applied to wives whose children were "found not to be issue of the marriage" and to unmarried mothers regardless of eligibility for public assistance. In practice it targeted poor unmarried mothers, disproportionately Black women. "Welfare mothers of illegitimate children" brought a class action lawsuit in 1973, claiming that the law violated their rights to privacy, due process, and equal protection. The state defended the law as necessary to protect not only the state's financial resources but also the interests of children who otherwise would be deprived of a relationship with their fathers. Officials described unwilling mothers as "recalcitrant," "obstinate," and "primarily concerned with their own welfare."[91]

Mothers insisted that their families' safety and well-being depended upon keeping paternity private. Rena Roe (a pseudonym) of Willimantic averred that the father of her child "has threatened [her] with physical harm if she divulges his name. He has never shown any interest in his child and has consistently denied fathering the child." Mildred Walter of Rockville explained she had declined to initiate paternity proceedings because she lived in "fear of this man . . . due to the beatings and physical abuse he inflicted on me," including dragging her by the hair and kicking her down the street while she was nine months pregnant. Walter declared, "I cannot testify or sign papers that may place my life and that of my child in danger."[92]

Others feared that disclosure would undermine or destroy positive relationships with their children's biological fathers and other potential father figures. Sharon Roe of New Haven testified that her daughter's father "has started to develop a good relationship with her; he plays with her. If I were to give his name he would leave the state and break off the relationship."[93] A woman named only as "A" in court records explained her "fear that if she disclosed [her fiancé's] name, subsequent legal action could jeopardize their relationship and the possibility of marriage."[94] Several mothers noted the slim likelihood of recovering any financial support from the fathers of their children. And even if support could be collected, it would "reimburse" state coffers, not benefit families.[95]

Plaintiffs also invoked women's right to shield their intimate lives from scrutiny. As they argued to the Supreme Court, "Even if successful, [a paternity suit] may not be worth the price" of damaged relationships or the "humiliating and degrading experience" of invasive questioning.[96] Sharon Roe listed "first" among her reasons for silence that "the question of with whom I have had sexual intercourse is private; I don't feel I should be forced to tell any government agency that."[97] Pressed repeatedly by a judge to "stop playing games," Rosalyn Carr replied that she did not know the father's name, and even if she did she "would consider it a gross intrusion of my privacy to have to give the name. . . . Even having to be here is a gross intrusion of my privacy."[98] Lawyers for the mothers—now armed with what appeared to be more potent constitutional precedents than those available to Mrs. Smith in the late 1960s—asserted a "constitutional zone of privacy."[99]

The plaintiffs also secured testimony from child welfare experts to counter the state's contention—following Harry Krause—that involuntary paternity disclosure served children's best interests. The pediatric psychiatrist Albert Solnit, co-author of the influential *Beyond the Best Interests of the Child*, testified that forcing an unwilling mother to identify her child's father would cause material and psychological harm to the child that would rarely, if ever, be outweighed by any financial or psychic benefits. Incarcerating a mother, usually the primary parent, would be "catastrophic." Solnit also backed mothers' assertions that a paternity action would likely destroy existing positive relationships between fathers and children.[100]

Welfare advocates like Herb Semmel disagreed with the stringent approach to child support enforcement that Connecticut's policy reflected. Semmel, who argued the contemporaneous, unsuccessful constitutional challenge to unmarried mothers' exclusion from Social Security survivor benefits in *Califano v. Boles* (discussed in chapter 3), joined the anthropologist Carol Stack to tell Congress in 1973 that most poor fathers of color lacked the resources to make more than sporadic monetary and in-kind contributions. "Aggressive enforcement efforts would discourage support of many kinds that might otherwise be given" and would do "little or nothing to help dependent AFDC children." Ultimately, Stack and Semmel concluded—channeling the welfare rights leader Johnnie Tillmon—that "a national income maintenance program should offer assistance to all needy persons," regardless of marital or birth status or the presence of children.[101]

Civil libertarians also objected strongly to Krause's prescription. John C. Gray, Jr., the Norman Dorsen protégé who had worked on the early birth status litigation examined in chapter 2, bluntly criticized Krause's naivete about the law in poor people's family life. It was "not the status of illegitimacy which most harms poor children," Gray argued, "but the resulting denial of government benefits." Further, Krause's recommendation that authorities use abuse and neglect charges to "protect" children belied the reality that "public interference in the lives of poor families tends to destroy the very family structure (though not a white, middle class one)" that Krause was "at pains to encourage."[102] Since the 1960s, reformers had expressed growing alarm at high rates of child removal from the homes of parents based on poverty and bias rather than abusive conduct.[103]

Critics mobilized to support the plaintiffs in *Roe v. Norton*. Justine Wise Polier had recently retired from a thirty-eight-year career as a family court judge to head the Juvenile Justice Project at the newly launched Children's Defense Fund (CDF).[104] *Roe v. Norton* tested what most disturbed Polier about Krause's "judgmental approaches to the responsibilities of the 'man in the house'" and his "insistence that unmarried mothers be forced to name the natural father through court action."[105]

Polier strategized with a group of concerned advocates, including Elizabeth Wickenden and Norman Dorsen. The resulting amicus brief detailed the irreparable psychological and material damage Connecticut's law visited upon children. A child, they insisted, possessed the right to be raised by his "natural parents," unless those parents endangered the child's welfare. Incarcerating a mother for up to a year threatened permanent separation, given the difficulty of regaining guardianship after a child's placement in foster care. To divest a child of her mother's care absent abuse or neglect constituted "cruel and unusual punishment." Even the threat of imprisonment could damage children by heightening mothers' anxiety.[106] The law, they insisted, was antithetical to women's *and* children's welfare, and to racial and economic justice.

Not all child welfare advocates sided with the Children's Defense Fund. Rena Uviller of the ACLU's Juvenile Rights Project dissented from the organization's position as a "'conscientious objector'" who "did not agree with any position that interfered with the right of a child to have support from a putative father."[107] Feminists, too, divided over the trend toward more aggressive modes of child support enforcement. Federal legislation enacted in 1975 caused a rift within NOW, with the head of its marriage and family task force, Elizabeth Coxe Spalding—a white Republican divorcée who counted the Bushes as family friends—in favor but her co-chair, Norma Card, along with members of NOW's task force on women and poverty, vehemently opposed.[108] For feminists primarily concerned with middle-class women newly impoverished by divorce, better child support guidelines and enforcement promised more equitable outcomes after dissolution. Many low-income women and men simply lacked adequate resources to support a child, placing that kind of gender equitable outcome out of reach. And poor mothers would be better off receiving support directly from fathers, bypassing the state.

Redefining Responsible Sexual Citizenship

Of the claimants described in this chapter, only the would-be teachers prevailed. Judge Keady decided *Andrews* in May 1973, finding for the plaintiffs. In 1975, the Fifth Circuit affirmed Keady's decision in a terse opinion that avoided questions of race and sex discrimination. The Supreme Court granted certiorari but eventually dismissed the writ as improvidently granted, letting the appellate ruling stand.

Initially, the *Andrews* plaintiffs successfully framed their constitutional injury as one of sex discrimination. Judge Keady rested his decision on twin "unconstitutional vice[s]": the state could not presume a "parent's immorality or bad moral character from the single fact of a child born out of wedlock," and the rule had an "inescapable" and "essentially discriminatory effect ... upon unmarried women."[109] In the end, though, statutory and regulatory nondiscrimination rules allowed the Supreme Court to avoid a constitutional ruling.[110] Justices eager to avoid the thorny constitutional questions raised in *Andrews* pounced on the National Education Association's argument that the exclusion of unmarried mothers from teaching violated new federal regulations that prohibited "school districts from making marital, parental or family status a criterion for employment unless that criterion is 'essential to successful operation of the employment function concerned.'"[111] *Roe v. Norton* also reached the Supreme Court, only to be sent back to the lower courts for reconsideration in light of amendments to the Social Security Act.

Mack v. Rumsfeld dragged on for a decade, concluding with a court ruling for the government.[112] By the mid-1970s, the *Flores* litigation (described in chapter 5) and developments in anti-discrimination law taught military officials and their lawyers to articulate functional rather than moral rationales for single parents' exclusion and to apply their rule on a facially sex-neutral basis. Fathers with custody of minor children could not enlist either. Readiness and deployability concerns, not sexual mores, now excluded "sole parents."

Additionally, conservative retrenchment in constitutional doctrine hindered the *Mack* plaintiffs' arguments. The Court's decision in *Personnel Administrator v. Feeney* (1979) confirmed that even the most dramatic and foreseeable disparate impact on women would not render a policy constitutionally vulnerable without evidence of discriminatory intent.[113] *Rostker v. Goldberg* (1981) upheld the male-only draft and reinforced courts' traditional deference to military judgments about personnel and readiness questions, even when they involved overt sex-based classifications.[114]

Poor unmarried mothers struggled to mobilize sex discrimination arguments at all in the mandatory paternity disclosure cases. On its face, the Connecticut law applied only to mothers, not to fathers of nonmarital children abandoned by their mothers. The Connecticut Civil Liberties Union lawyer Frank Cochran initially argued that the law therefore included two "suspect" classifications: sex and birth status. Lawyers from the ACLU Women's Rights Project reviewed some of Cochran's submissions, but welfare advocates and poverty lawyers drove the litigation.[115] The briefs devoted relatively little space to the sex discrimination argument.[116]

The sexual double standard argument, too, was less clearly applicable to mandatory paternity disclosure requirements. Like substitute parent laws, efforts to identify fathers targeted both partners.[117] Moreover, for poor mothers, concerns about sexual morality fused with larger questions of political economy: mothers and children untethered to a male breadwinner endangered not only social and religious order but the public fisc. Antidiscrimination laws had largely banished moralistic arguments from the employers' arsenal and replaced them with functional rationales. But the government retained the prerogative to enact welfare and family policies that promoted marriage and punished adults for nonmarital childbearing.

The state's moralizing rhetoric in *Roe v. Norton* focused not on penalizing women for nonmarital sex per se but on "recalcitrant" mothers' putative disregard for their children's welfare. In *Andrews* and *Mack*, mothers' interest in obtaining decent employment dovetailed with their children's interest in a parent's support and care. Although mothers believed, with good evidence, that they acted in their children's best interest when they resisted paternity disclosure, the state successfully pitted mothers against their children in *Roe v. Norton*. The federal district court judge M. Joseph Blumenfeld opined in 1973 that the statute "operates prophylactically against the adverse differential treatment which the unwed mothers would impose on their children."[118] Blumenfeld, a Kennedy appointee who was later remembered as "one of the state's most lenient and liberal Federal judges,"[119] dismissed the mothers' privacy, equal protection, and due process claims in a decidedly unsympathetic opinion.[120]

Invasive inquiries into unmarried mothers' sexual encounters and limits on their parental autonomy did trouble the federal appellate judge Jon O. Newman. Newman had grown up in a mostly secular Jewish home, attended Hotchkiss, Princeton, and Yale Law School, and clerked for Chief Justice Earl Warren. Newman had been a top aide to Abe Ribicoff, who served as governor of Connecticut, secretary of HEW, and U.S. senator.[121] After helping to draft the Civil Rights Act of 1964, Newman returned to Connecticut to serve as U.S. Attorney; Nixon appointed him to the federal bench in 1971. Newman immediately immersed himself in constitutional privacy doctrine when feminists challenged Connecticut's abortion prohibition: in 1972 his opinion in the case colloquially known as *Women v. Connecticut* laid groundwork for Justice Blackmun's majority opinion in *Roe v. Wade*.[122]

Newman suggested in his *Roe v. Norton* concurrence that, in at least some cases, compelling paternity disclosure would infringe a mother's privacy and family rights. It seemed "obvious" to Newman that the privacy rights recognized in *Griswold* and *Roe v. Wade* "carry with them concomitant rights to maintain secrecy concerning sexual intimacies." And a mother's decision about paternity disclosure was "certainly an important aspect of child-rearing" that "would plainly seem to enjoy . . . constitutional protection."[123] Newman suggested that state judges should exercise discretion to decide, on a case-by-case basis, whether the state's interest in recovering child support from the father outweighed the mother's privacy right.[124]

Newman's proposed balancing test reflects that, unlike the aspiring schoolteachers, indigent single mothers faced a formidable obstacle: a decision in their favor would impose public responsibility for their children's support. Allies of Katie Mae Andrews and Lestine Rogers could emphasize how exclusion from employment in the school system would force them to take low-wage menial jobs and to depend on Mississippi's meager public assistance benefits. Andrews and Rogers insisted that the state should allow them access to jobs for which they were fully qualified, jobs that would pay them the decent wage they deserved as upstanding young women striving to support themselves and their children.

The boldness of this claim should not be underestimated, given the history of disenfranchisement and racial violence in Sunflower County, Mississippi.[125] Fears of sexual contagion and immorality fed resistance to school desegregation around the nation; local critics of Judge Keady's ruling in *Andrews* expressed their disgust in crude and denigrating terms.[126] It is also true, however, that Andrews's ability to invoke other tenets of respectable, responsible citizenship likely aided her cause and that of other mothers of nonmarital children seeking a right to freedom from discrimination in employment.

The plaintiffs in *Mack v. Rumsfeld* followed a similar cultural script: they sought the right to serve their country and to secure employment that would spur social and economic mobility. They upended tropes about Black family dysfunction, arguing for a model of extended family care that promoted economic self-sufficiency. But the plaintiffs in *Mack* also highlighted the distinctive social supports—housing, medical, and childcare—of military service. These benefits became increasingly generous in the 1970s as imperatives of maintaining an all-volunteer force.[127] Single mothers seeking to enlist were laying claim to perquisites that many viewed as a scarce commodity to be made available only to the most deserving.[128]

The plaintiffs in *Roe v. Norton* sought public assistance from the state, but by refusing to reveal fathers' identities they also ostensibly deprived the government of reimbursement for that aid. The case's inconclusive outcome spawned years of wrangling over federal regulations. Advocates secured a "good cause" exception to be invoked when paternal identification conflicted with a child's best interests. But they struggled against narrow administrative interpretations, states' spotty implementation, and bureaucratic foot-dragging. Time and again, welfare advocates submitted detailed comments on proposed rules, lobbied legislators and administrators, celebrated small victories, and lamented their limitations. Poor unmarried mothers' inability to secure constitutional protections against mandatory paternity disclosure left them at the mercy of government officials.[129]

Meanwhile, the Supreme Court made clear that states had no obligation to make real for poor women the right to reproductive autonomy and sexual privacy. In Connecticut, for instance, several women challenged the state's denial of Medicaid funding for abortion care in 1974. Their attorneys presented the named plaintiffs as single mothers and unmarried teenagers who wished to terminate pregnancies in part to achieve economic self-sufficiency.[130] The sixteen-year-old Mary Poe "desired an abortion so that she could complete high school, obtain a job, and terminate her dependence on public assistance." The eighteen-year-old divorcée Barbara Bye did "not wish to bear an illegitimate child, who would then become dependent for its support on public assistance."[131] Carol C., a divorced working mother of three who received AFDC, averred that "if I do not have another child, I can improve my earning capacity and become independent of public assistance."[132] The plaintiffs argued that funding medical care for poor patients who carried pregnancies to term but not those who chose abortion infringed on reproductive freedom. It could not be justified by fiscal concerns, since pregnancy and childbirth cost the state much more than termination.[133]

Like their counterparts in similar lawsuits against other states, the Connecticut plaintiffs won in the lower courts: in 1975 Judge Newman and two colleagues ruled unconstitutional the state's refusal to pay for indigent women's first-trimester abortions when they were not certified by a physician as "medically necessary."[134] But in *Maher v. Roe* (1977), Justice Powell wrote for a 6–3 majority that poverty, not Connecticut law, prevented indigent women from terminating pregnancies: the state "imposed no restriction on access to abortion that was not already there."[135]

In 1980, the Supreme Court upheld the 1977 Hyde Amendment, which prohibited any use of federal funds for abortion care except when a woman's life was in danger. Advocates protested that policies denying abortion care coerced poor women of color into seeking sterilizations they did not want—but that, unlike abortions, were federally funded.[136] Nevertheless, Justice Stewart wrote in *Harris v. McRae* that "it simply does not follow that a woman's freedom of choice carries with it a constitutional entitlement to the financial resources to avail herself of the full range of protected choices."[137] The abortion funding decisions haunted future challenges to federal laws that infringed on reproductive autonomy and allowed states discretion to deny to poor women the means to exercise ostensibly protected constitutional rights.

Protecting the Public Fisc

By the early 1980s, Harry Krause's vision prevailed over that of his feminist challengers. Even the Supreme Court's reaffirmation of a constitutional right to marry first recognized in *Loving v. Virginia* (1967) came in a case about child support enforcement and protection of public resources. In *Zablocki v. Red Hail* (1978), Roger Red Hail, a member of the Oneida Nation living outside Milwaukee, challenged a Wisconsin statute that required parents who owed child support arrears or whose children might later rely on public assistance to obtain judicial permission to marry.[138] Red Hail could not get a marriage license because he owed nearly $4,000 for the support of a nonmarital child who was, as Justice Powell put it, "a public charge, living on welfare benefits."[139]

Powell and his colleagues offered various constitutional rationales for the Court's 8–1 decision striking down the Wisconsin law.[140] But all agreed that the statute burdened the right to marry without accomplishing the (wholly legitimate) objective of recovering child support from parents.[141] As Powell's clerk, Sam Estreicher, put it, the state could employ "more direct means" to that end: "contempt proceedings, imprisonment or conditional probation, wage attachment, etc." And "even if a legal marriage is blocked, cohabitation and childbirth out of wedlock will continue unabated."[142] In fact, marriage to a solvent spouse could *help* a debtor like Red Hail meet his obligations.[143] Justice Marshall's opinion for the Court noted that "since the support obligation is the same whether the child is born in or out of wedlock, the net result of preventing the marriage is simply more illegitimate children."[144] To prevent indigent parents from marrying seemed irrational as well as unjust if the law served no debt collection aim.

In the years that followed, similar logic supported unmarried mothers in a series of successful lawsuits that attacked statutes of limitation on paternity establishment. Texas had imposed a one-year time limit in "grudging" compliance with the Court's decision in *Gomez v. Perez* (1973) that made fathers liable for the support of nonmarital children.[145] To the surprise of Justice Powell, accustomed to 5–4 decisions on birth status claims, the conference vote in the first of these cases, *Mills v. Habluetzel* (1982), was unanimous.[146] The justices sided with Lois Mae Mills, a twenty-five-year-old white cocktail waitress. Mills was raising five-year-old Robert and three-year-old Archie while living with her own parents in Ingleside, Texas, and receiving public assistance. Archie's alleged father, Dan Habluetzel, owned a local garage and could afford to help support him, argued the legal aid lawyer Michael Mankins.[147] "After one year, the father [of a nonmarital child] is free forever," Justice Brennan observed, whereas legitimate children could establish paternity any time before they reached the age of majority. Moreover, the "substantial state interest" in extracting support for minor children and advances in the accuracy and availability of blood tests belied the state's avowed concerns about problems of proof.[148]

Justice Rehnquist almost never sided with plaintiffs in birth status or sex equality cases. But here he wrote sympathetically of "the obstacles . . . that confront unwed mothers during the child's first year," including "financial difficulties caused by child-birth expenses or a birth-related loss of income, continuing affection for the child's father, a desire to avoid disapproval of family and community, or the emotional strain and confusion that often attend the birth of an illegitimate child."[149]

Justice Powell sought a more robust statement of the Texas law's constitutional infirmity than Rehnquist's first draft provided, given the "very strong—if not compelling" state interests at stake.[150] "In modern society where, in some environments, children born out of wedlock outnumber those blessed by marital vows, there is every reason to compel a father to support children he brings into this world," Powell wrote to Rehnquist. "Otherwise, taxpayers support them."[151] Indeed, Attorney Mankins estimated that at least eighty thousand children receiving AFDC benefits in Texas should instead be supported by their putative fathers.[152] In concurrence, Justice Sandra Day O'Connor emphasized that the state's interest in establishing paternity "stems not only from a desire to see that 'justice is done' but also ... to reduce the number of individuals forced to enter the welfare rolls."[153] The one-year cut-off, that is, not only disserved both mothers and children but also shortchanged the state.

Over the next several years, the Court unanimously struck down increasingly lengthy statutes of limitations. Tennessee's two-year limitation fell in 1983, when Frances Pickett brought suit against Baxter Brown, who she believed had fathered her child. Pickett's case was especially sympathetic: Tennessee law already allowed AFDC-eligible mothers to petition for paternity until their children reached age eighteen, while a woman who could support herself and her child had only two years. "She knew she could have quit her job and gone on welfare, and the courts would have heard her claim," emphasized Pickett's attorney.[154]

By the early 1980s, bolder welfare rights and feminist arguments likely seemed futile. Ronald Reagan won the presidency in 1980 after campaigning against "welfare queens" and promising to rein in the perceived excesses of Great Society policies and the civil rights revolution. Against this backdrop of conservative retrenchment, a brief from the Children's Defense Fund and the Women's Legal Defense Fund framed mothers' rights, children's interests, and fiscal concerns as complementary. Ineffectual child support enforcement was "a major contributing factor to the 'feminization of poverty.' "[155] If fathers had no duty of legal support, "women suffer clear economic disadvantage," "burden[ing] ... the mother's constitutionally protected right to the companionship, care, and custody of the child." Further, "women ... bear a greatly disproportionate share ... of the stigma, impaired social position, condemnation, and punishment" visited upon nonmarital parents.[156]

Like its decisions concerning birth status discrimination, the Court's opinions in the paternity cases did not incorporate even the more limited feminist themes introduced by advocates. Notwithstanding evidence that mothers often had good reasons not to bring paternity actions, O'Connor opined in her influential *Mills* concurrence that some mothers' "unwillingness to file suit underscores that the mother's and child's interests are not congruent."[157] In *Pickett v. Brown*, Justice Brennan wrote that the exception for children who otherwise would depend on public assistance did not save the statute, because "an illegitimate child has an interest not only in obtaining paternal support, but also in establishing a relationship to his father."[158] Harry Krause could not have said it better.

By 1988, when Cherlyn Clark challenged Pennsylvania's six-year limit, a brief signed by several feminist organizations focused almost entirely on how weak child support enforcement harmed children, deepened the poverty of female-headed households, and burdened the welfare system. Clark's story underscored the precarity of nonmarital motherhood: her daughter Tiffany's biological father, Eugene Jeter, who was married to another woman, allegedly threatened and choked her when she refused to obtain an abortion. Clark listed a fictitious name on Tiffany's birth certificate because she feared his violent reaction.[159] The women's organizations' brief in *Clark v. Jeter* included a lengthy excerpt from the Senate's debates in 1984 over child support enforcement legislation, elaborating the "strong link between female-headed households, poverty, welfare recipiency and child support."[160] The senator quoted therein was Daniel Patrick Moynihan.

Constitutional claims allowed Black single mothers to advance new visions of sexual and economic citizenship in the long 1970s. But at the same time that courts began to recognize sex discrimination as a constitutional problem, anti-welfare sentiment intensified and more expansive conceptions of racial and economic justice ran aground.[161] To the extent single mothers succeeded, then, their victories rarely left a constitutional legacy. When federal constitutional doors closed, single mothers' fate lay in the hands of legislators, regulators, and bureaucrats at all levels of government. Lois Fernandez's decade of advocacy produced legislative results: in 1978 Governor Milton Shapp signed into law a statute that eliminated many legal distinctions between legitimate and illegitimate children in Pennsylvania.[162] But despite renewed efforts to frame marital status laws as affronts to reproductive autonomy, sexual privacy, and now women's equality under the law, single mothers' challenges succeeded mostly when they could provide care and support to their children without any help from the state.

CHAPTER SEVEN

Unmarried Fathers and
Sex Equality

I N A CLASS ACTION lawsuit filed in 1974, single fathers raising children on their own challenged provisions of the Immigration and
Nationality Act (INA) that denied them beneficial exemptions
available to mothers and their nonmarital children as well as to
marital families. The named plaintiffs included the Dominican national
Ramon Fiallo-Sone, whose son Ramon Martin Fiallo was a U.S. citizen
but could not facilitate his father's legal residency or confer on him exemption from immigration quotas—which he could have done if his parents had married or if the noncitizen parent in question had been his
mother. Another plaintiff, Serge Warner, was the West Indian–born son
of a naturalized U.S. citizen father, Cleophus Warner, who could not bypass the quota system to become a permanent resident, as he could have
done if his mother, instead, had been a U.S. citizen or if his parents were
married. The teenaged plaintiffs Trevor and Earl Wilson were permanent U.S. residents whose Jamaican father, Arthur Cecil Wilson, could
not obtain a visa to move to the United States after their mother's death,
even though their mother or a "legitimate" father could have done so.[1]

Like the married couples represented by Ruth Bader Ginsburg in
constitutional sex equality litigation around the same time, the parents in
these cases had taken on nontraditional gender roles. Fiallo-Sone became the "primary caretaker and constant companion" shortly after his

son was born in New York in 1971, while the child's mother, Celia Rodriguez, "assumed the role of bread-winner." By 1974, the toddler Fiallo
was very attached to and dependent on his father, with whom he lived in
Brooklyn. Rodriguez continued to support the family financially and felt
the arrangement was in her child's best interests. There was no path to
"legitimation" short of Fiallo-Sone adopting his son or marrying Rodriguez. The parents did not wish to marry for unspecified personal reasons, and adoption by Fiallo-Sone might have required Rodriguez to
relinquish her own parental rights. Because he could not avail himself of
the INA provisions, Fiallo-Sone would have to obtain a labor certification to remain in the United States with his son—a feat all but impossible for a worker without special skills. Fiallo-Sone eventually obtained a
stay of deportation, but he learned of it too late: he and his son had already left for the Dominican Republic.[2]

Just as Stephen Wiesenfeld sought Social Security survivor benefits to
care for his newborn after his breadwinning wife, Paula, died in childbirth,
the Jamaican citizen Arthur Cecil Wilson wanted to move to the United
States to care for his teenaged sons Trevor and Earl after the death of their
mother, Leony Moses. Wilson had lived with and supported his sons until
they were eleven and nine years old. The children then moved with Moses
to New York, where they became legal permanent residents. Granted a
temporary emergency visa to visit his sons, Wilson was denied further ex-
tensions and returned to Jamaica, where he could find work legally and
help support the children. Like Fiallo-Sone, Wilson, a handyman, stood no
chance of obtaining the required labor certification to work in the United
States. In the meantime, Trevor and Earl lived with their mother's sister.

The plaintiff Serge Warner came to the United States at age nine to
visit his father, Cleophus, who had "always supported and maintained
him"; shortly thereafter, his mother married another man and asked Cleophus, a naturalized U.S. citizen, to "keep their son." Cleophus and Serge
lived together in Queens thereafter; a defeat in court, they said, would
mean Serge would "be forced to return to a country where there is no one
to care for him." Because Serge was older than fourteen, Cleophus—like
Arthur Wilson—could not become a "parent" for the purposes of exemption from the immigration quota system, even though he was Serge's
biological father. Neither man could "cure" his son's "illegitimacy" by
marrying the children's mother.

National origin, gender, family status, and class together prevented
these fathers from obtaining the relief from immigration restrictions that

would have enabled them to care for their children in the United States. The plaintiffs' attorneys, led by Janet Calvo of the Legal Aid Society, focused primarily on discrimination based on sex and birth status. They drew on empirical studies to argue that unmarried fathers frequently developed strong bonds with their children and that nonmarital pregnancies often emerged out of lasting and exclusive relationships. The challenged regulations, they insisted, unconstitutionally "stereotyped" unwed fathers as uninvolved and uncaring when in fact the opposite was true in the plaintiffs' lives.[3]

In *Fiallo*, as in *Wiesenfeld*, a decision in favor of the fathers would dovetail with feminists' vision of shared parenting and equal social and economic citizenship. The *Fiallo* plaintiffs' brief noted that although the "primary sex discrimination imposed by the challenged provisions is against illegitimate children and their fathers," the law "discriminated against women as well." A citizen or permanent resident father could rest assured that if he could not care for his nonmarital child, "that child can be united in this country with the other parent, the mother." A U.S. citizen or permanent resident mother "has no similar assurance . . . since the father is effectively barred from entering this country." As a result, Trevor and Earl Wilson's mother "could not be assured that upon her death her children would be supported and cared for in this country "by their surviving parent."[4]

This brief reference gave a tantalizing hint of a more robust argument that citizenship laws discriminated against mothers as well as fathers. Ruth Bader Ginsburg, general counsel for the ACLU and founder of its Women's Rights Project, must have recognized *Fiallo* as the mirror image of *Wiesenfeld*—her "ideal case." Like Paula Wiesenfeld, whose contributions to Social Security yielded benefits worth less to her family than a husband's would have been, Leony Moses could not rely on her U.S. citizenship to guarantee her children the care of their "sole surviving parent." Ginsburg very much wanted to file an amicus brief in *Fiallo*, but despite her repeated entreaties and support from Norman Dorsen and Janet Calvo, Mel Wulf, the ACLU's legal director, rejected the idea.[5]

The fathers in *Fiallo*—poor and working-class men of color who defied traditional gender roles—advanced a vision of nonmarital parenthood that flouted foundational assumptions of marital status law in the United States. Their lawsuits took Stephen Wiesenfeld's challenge a step further: not only did they dispute mothers' monopoly on caregiving and assert fathers' capacity for nurturance, but they also attacked the legal significance of marital status in determining parental rights and citizenship itself.

These men joined a growing contingent—diffuse and unorganized—of fathers who sought a new nonmarital bargain as developments in the law of sex equality and birth status lent credence to their claims. Sometimes, as in *Fiallo*, mothers' and fathers' interests aligned; other times, nonmarital fathers' assertion of parental rights clashed with mothers' wishes and exposed deep fissures among feminists and other progressive advocates. As biological paternity became increasingly knowable with the advent of more accurate testing technologies, functional definitions of fatherhood competed with genetic and marital ties for preeminence.[6]

Discovering Unmarried Fathers

In the 1960s experts began to investigate the emotional, psychological, and social needs of young unmarried fathers. An early pilot program in Los Angeles, launched in 1963 and funded by the U.S. Children's Bureau, studied almost one hundred young men receiving services formerly reserved for mothers from a Jewish agency. "The unwed father," Reuben Pannor, a social work researcher, told a regional conference of the Child Welfare League of America in 1965, "has traditionally been the forgotten man. But he needs help, and it's about time we started giving it to him."[7]

Pannor's experience counseling young fathers led him to reject the common trope of "wicked older men" "seducing" innocent young girls only to abandon them. Instead, he believed most fathers were no more than two or three years older than their partners and just as "panicky and frightened as the girl." Nonmarital pregnancies resulted not from casual sexual encounters but from "meaningful," long-term relationships.[8] Teenaged boys experienced genuine distress because of both nonmarital pregnancies and the prospect of losing their children: "Some fathers," reported the Brooklyn social worker Joe Barton, "come close to nervous collapse when their girlfriends give their babies up for adoption," as three-quarters of these young women did.[9]

Pannor perceived typical (white) teenaged fathers as the product of "homes that are female-dominated due to divorce or desertion," where "the adult father had abdicated his responsibility as head of the household." The cure for the "weak or distorted masculine identity" this matriarchal family structure produced, young fathers told Pannor, included "better relationships with their own fathers," who should "wear the pants in the family."[10] For his part, Pannor prescribed more comprehensive sex education. Knowledge about contraception did not translate into reliable use: young adults associated babies with marriage and felt reluctant to interrupt the "spontaneity" and "romance" of sexual intimacy. If anything, boys often assumed that girls were responsible for contraception. Parents, schools, and professionals should address both the biological and emotional aspects of sex and pregnancy, Pannor argued.[11]

Other experts concurred with Pannor. In 1966 an influential study by Mignon Sauber and Elaine Rubinstein concluded that "a majority of young men who get girls pregnant out of wedlock are neither irresponsible nor casual about their obligations to the girls and their babies."[12] Social workers at a 1970 workshop on unmarried teenage parents "testified that not only did the mothers want to keep their babies but that unmarried fathers were also very concerned about what happened to their children."[13] These studies "triggered a chain reaction among social welfare people across the country," spawning local programs that provided counseling to young unwed fathers, often headed by a male caseworker.[14]

Press coverage of these efforts frequently blurred distinctions between white middle-class fathers and the impoverished fathers of color whom sympathetic urban social welfare professionals urged states and localities to support. In 1960 the White House Conference on Children and Youth called for "medical, psychiatric, casework, group work, legal, and financial services, vocational guidance, education, living arrangements, and early planning for the baby" to be "extended to the biological father" as well as the "unmarried mother."[15] A handbook on unmarried parents published by HEW's Children's Bureau in 1961 recommended that "the father should, if possible, have access to the same social agency as the mother so his interests and responsibilities may be established."[16] Services, in HEW's view, "should be based on a philosophy of help, rather than punishment."[17]

By the late 1960s, programs originally established for unmarried mothers of color in urban, high-poverty areas began outreach efforts that encompassed fathers too. In 1969, the Harlem social worker Frances Peterson told the *New York Times* that work with fathers had become fashionable.[18] These fathers trod a different path from Pannor's subjects. Caseworkers in Harlem reported that they rarely attempted to persuade couples to marry, and adoption services remained largely unavailable to young people of color.[19] Rather, social workers emphasized both psychological and material assistance: "giv[ing] the boys the chance to bring any feelings of guilt and confusion they may have about their situation out into the open" and "helping the boys find jobs or return to school." Young men enrolled in the federally funded Harlem program expressed a desire to be involved fathers. Calvin Gentry (a pseudonym) told a reporter that he might someday marry his girlfriend, who lived with her mother and infant son, "but right now I'm in no position financially to marry." Still, Gentry planned "to be around a lot so the baby will see that he has a father," explaining that his own father had long ago "left home" and "I hardly ever see him."[20]

Unmarried fathers, long typecast as sexual exploiters of vulnerable young women who cared nothing for their children, began to appear in more varied guises: the cohabiting parent-partner, functionally indistinguishable from his married counterpart but barred from a licit relationship because of an inability to end a prior marriage; the well-intentioned young man willing to marry the mother of his child but rejected by her; the poor but sympathetic teenage boyfriend, suffering from a dearth of parental supervision and paternal role models; the father hoping to maintain a relationship with his child after the breakdown of a romance; the eager father bereft over a mother's decision to give up her child for adoption.[21] No longer "elusive ghosts" or dispensable derelicts, unmarried fathers emerged as stakeholders in a modernizing American family.

As social scientists and social work professionals began to show greater interest in unmarried fathers, the sociologist Clark Vincent predicted that legal rights could not be far behind. "As the father is given greater public visibility and receives some services," Vincent wrote, "greater attention will be given to his 'rights,' legal and otherwise."[22] Vincent forecasted a development aided by larger social and legal shifts in the second half of the 1960s. Slowly but surely, some state social welfare departments began to advise agencies not to disregard unmarried fathers' parental rights. Once fathers ceased to be nameless, faceless nonentities but instead appeared as clients in need of assistance, social welfare professionals began to see them as deserving of some voice in decision-making about their children's futures.

Commentators, especially lawyers, also tied parental rights to financial responsibilities. Freda Jane Lippert, an attorney with HEW, wrote in 1968 that "where there is an obligation there is generally a corresponding right." Nearly all states imposed upon putative fathers a statutory or common law duty of support, so Lippert believed they "should have some reciprocal rights in the child," if compatible with the child's best interests.[23] Harry Krause concurred: "No rational legislative reason justifies not hearing the interested father who fairly and regularly contributes to the support of his child on issues such as the child's general welfare, including his custody and education."[24]

This argument gained more traction as efforts to identify biological fathers intensified and technologies to do so accurately developed apace. Krause's Uniform Legitimacy Act, first proposed in 1966, inspired a "revolutionary" law reform effort that culminated in the promulgation of the Uniform Parentage Act (UPA) in 1973.[25] The UPA's guiding principle was "full equality for all children, legitimate and illegitimate, in their legal relationship with both parents."[26] The model law sought to rationalize the process of establishing paternity through blood-group testing, to enable child support enforcement, and to comply with new federal constitutional mandates against birth status discrimination.

At the same time, feminist attacks on stereotypes about women's natural superiority as mothers undermined the notion that only mothers could nurture and form strong psychological bonds with children. As chapter 3 described, some feminists, including leading legal scholars and strategists, promoted a sex-neutral approach: they argued that men and women should be free to defy traditional gender roles and build egalitarian partnerships where partners shared breadwinning and caregiving responsibilities. In these years, feminism and the unprecedented influx of married women and mothers into the workforce "prompted a far-reaching cultural debate about fatherhood never before known in American history."[27]

New visions of fatherhood also surfaced in post-divorce custody deliberations, where the default maternal preference increasingly came under attack.[28] Influenced by trends in family psychology, many law reformers believed that the bonded relationships children developed with adults should sometimes trump formal legal status. The family law scholars Henry Foster and Doris Freed wrote in 1964 that preferences for mothers over fathers and parents over nonparents resulted in the "rigid" application of rules that privileged formal legal categories and blood relationships over "de facto" family bonds born of "established rather than theoretical ties of love and affection."[29] Foster and Freed favored a flexible, multifactor custody standard in lieu of presumptions.[30] Courts, too, began to question mothers' inherent superiority as post-divorce custodians. The Missouri Supreme Court opined in 1968, "What a mother's

care means to her children has been so much romanticized and poeti-
cized that its reality and its substance have sometimes been lost in the
flowers of rhetoric."[31] In child custody, as in marriage and divorce law,
function increasingly replaced sex.

To some feminists, maternal preferences that applied regardless of
who performed the actual day-to-day work of childcare reinforced wom-
en's subordinate domestic roles and discouraged men from undertaking
the joys and burdens of caregiving. The anthropologist Margaret Mead
called these preferences "a mere and subtle form of anti-feminism by
which men—under the guise of exalting the importance of maternity—
are tying women more tightly to their children."[32] In 1973, the New York
family court judge Sybil Hart Kooper, a self-described feminist (and a divorced, remarried mother of three), cited Mead alongside constitutional
sex equality principles when she jettisoned the "tender years" doctrine
(which preferred mothers as custodians of young children) as "based on
outdated social stereotypes rather than on rational and up-to-date consideration" of children's well-being.[33]

Others believed that the conditions created by divorce required a re-
evaluation of maternal superiority. A trio of lawyers writing in 1972
questioned whether a presumption in favor of maternal custody served
children's best interests given the "post-divorce reality where the mother
must assume both a mother's and a father's role."[34] They applauded recent decisions by states such as New York, Wisconsin, and Florida to give
divorcing mothers and fathers "equal consideration" in awarding custody.[35] Advocates for fathers' rights urged the importance of maintaining
existing paternal relationships after a marriage broke down, often repur-
posing the rhetoric of sex equality to serve their own ends.[36] The Uniform Marriage and Divorce Act, drafted in 1970, emphasized children's
best interests, rather than parental sex, as the paramount consideration in
custody decisions.[37]

Even the more progressive wing of the divorced fathers' movement
did not seek to overthrow the gendered division of family labor but
rather to expand fathers' prerogatives. Fathers' rights activists' partial
and opportunistic alliance with feminist law reformers enjoyed considerable success in unseating the maternal presumption through court decisions and legislative reforms. By the end of the 1970s, twenty-one states
had abandoned it.[38] Instead, most used a best-interest-of-the-child standard, which gave courts discretion to determine which parent should
have primary custody.

As post-divorce custody law edged closer to sex neutrality, fathers of nonmarital children likewise challenged the legal presumption that *unwed* fathers were unfit until proven otherwise. If divorced fathers received equal treatment with mothers under liberalizing state laws and possessed due process rights to be notified of a pending adoption, then why not never-married fathers? A smattering of courts agreed, some invoking children's rights and interests. In 1966, Judge Morrie Slifkin of the Westchester County, New York, family court called for the elimination of distinctions based on birth status in child custody decision-making. Illegitimate children, Slifkin wrote, deserved the same best-interests consideration as their legitimate counterparts.[39] Parental function, in other words, should prevail over marital status as well as sex.

The growing instability of marital families also unsettled legal assumptions about fatherhood. The no-fault divorce revolution created a contingent of noncustodial fathers whose varying levels of post-divorce contact with their children belied any correlation between a child's birth status and a father's engagement. Further, as the "best interests of the child" standard began to displace maternal preferences, the definition of those best interests evolved. A growing body of literature suggested that a child's relationship with the "natural" father was crucial to psychological health. The fiscal imperative to secure all available private sources of support for nonmarital children fused with a growing sense that nonmarital fathers could provide less tangible benefits to their offspring—an intact sense of self, a stable authority figure, even an occasional caregiver.

By the early 1970s, then, many policymakers and social work professionals agreed that nonmarital fathers warranted further study and regulation.[40] But there was little consensus about legal reform. Most could agree on the desirability of securing financial support, though they struggled over the practicalities of holding impecunious fathers responsible. Custody and control of children were another matter. Should the law continue to assume that nonmarital fathers would routinely shirk their parental obligations, rendering them presumptively unfit to participate in their children's upbringing? Or did changing family structures warrant a rethinking of nonmarital fathers' roles? What would nonmarital fathers' rights mean for adoption law and practice? How should disputes between unmarried parents be adjudicated? And what did parental sex equality require in the absence of marriage?

Marital Status and Fatherhood

Nonmarital fathers who embraced a parental role navigated an uneven legal landscape in the early 1970s. As the maternal preference began to erode in post-divorce custody decision-making, it survived in cases involving nonmarital children.[41] And while divorced fathers generally enjoyed visitation rights, only a handful of states granted visitation to nonmarital fathers over mothers' objections.[42] State laws usually presumed husbands to be the legal fathers of any children born during marriage. In contrast, both legal and practical obstacles impeded a biological father's voluntary "legitimation" of a child against the mother's wishes.[43]

A father's influence in adoption cases also depended on marital status. The Supreme Court ruled in 1965 that a divorced father must receive notice and the opportunity to object to the adoption of a child born during marriage.[44] A nonmarital father, by contrast, often lacked the power to veto an adoption by strangers or a prospective stepfather or even the right to be notified of his biological child's birth. Disregard for unwed fathers' parental rights largely reflected a concern that paternal consent requirements would harm nonmarital children by thwarting their adoption into two-parent marital families and would burden the state with welfare costs.

Even Oregon, the first state to abolish distinctions based on birth status, allowed mothers unilaterally to choose adoption. The Oregon statute expressed "the majority position" circa 1970: "The consent of the mother is sufficient. . . . [T]he father of the child shall be disregarded just as if he were dead."[45] Justine Wise Polier, all too familiar with the broken, abusive, and discriminatory foster care system from her decades as a family court judge, worried that an emphasis on biological fathers' rights would stymie adoptions without yielding any benefit for most nonmarital children, whose fathers lacked the ability or desire to assume custody.[46]

Increasingly, nonmarital fathers challenged the notion that they were unfit, uninterested, and incapable parents. Jerry Rothstein and Karen Lewis were living together in Denver in the late 1960s when she became pregnant. Lewis wanted to marry Rothstein, but he initially refused, accusing Lewis of having intimate relations with other men. Lewis moved to Wisconsin to stay with relatives and began proceedings to place the child with adoptive parents through Lutheran Social Services. Rothstein apparently reconsidered, but before he could locate Lewis, she had given birth to a son and a LaCross county court terminated both birth parents' rights. By the end of 1970, circumstances had changed for the now twenty-nine-year-old Rothstein: he had moved to Milwaukee, taken a job as a clerk-driver with the local newspaper, and begun studying to become a flight instructor. He had married, his wife was expecting a baby, and Rothstein wanted to raise the child he had conceived with Lewis.

The Wisconsin Supreme Court rejected Rothstein's claim that nonmarital fathers deserved to participate in the decision to relinquish a child for adoption. The majority ratified the presumption that most nonmarital fathers had no interest in acknowledging their children, much less supporting or raising them. Justice Leo B. Hanley wrote that few "would be able to present anything like a rational argument that the child's best interests would be served by recognizing the father's desire to obtain custody of the child."[47] Rothstein appealed to the U.S. Supreme Court, determined to vindicate "the chance for thousands of illegitimate children to grow up in homes with natural fathers." Such a ruling could "unite many children who are homeless with fathers they otherwise may never know," the Associated Press reported.[48]

Rothstein's suit, however, did not produce the first Supreme Court pronouncement on the parental rights of unmarried fathers. That came instead in Peter Stanley's case. Less than two years after the death of his partner of eighteen years and mother of his three children, Stanley looked on helplessly as a judge declared his two younger children wards of the state, condemning them to a series of foster placements and their father to years of legal turmoil. In Illinois the legal definition of "parent" excluded "natural" fathers of illegitimate children, denying Stanley even a hearing to determine whether he was fit to parent the children he loved and had helped to raise from birth.

These were the stark facts that Peter Stanley's lawyers presented to the Court in 1971. The reality of Stanley's legal status and of his record as a father was more complicated; in fact, his parental fitness had been questioned.[49] But if Stanley had been a woman, married or unmarried, or if he had been able to produce proof of a valid marriage to the children's mother, then he would have been their legal parent and almost certainly would not summarily have lost his parental rights.

To many observers, Peter Stanley's case exemplified "sex discrimination in reverse."[50] Stanley's lawyers emphasized that Illinois singled out unwed fathers for discriminatory treatment.[51] Illinois's defense, likewise, entwined marital status and sex. Mothers' and married fathers' assumption of parental duties justified granting them the "full range of parental rights." Mothers, the state held, generally assumed legal and social responsibility for their children regardless of birth status.[52] Mothers were present from birth—and unlike fathers, committed a crime if they abandoned their baby.[53] And "mothering," the state contended, "is the result of the primary sexual drives of females."[54] Fathers, on the other hand, required a state-sanctioned legal structure to impress them into the bonds of parenthood. To accomplish this feat, "the chosen institution of the state is marriage," Illinois concluded.[55] To earn equal status with a child's mother, a father had to demonstrate his commitment to the family by marrying her.[56]

Stanley asked the Court to overturn long-established precedent denying any protected legal relationship between a father and his illegitimate child. He attacked the presumption that marital status was a proxy for paternal fitness. Still, Stanley did not radically challenge the primacy of marriage. His attorneys emphasized how Peter and Joan Stanley had lived together in a marriage-like relationship, referring to Joan as Peter's "common-law wife."[57] Peter's relationship with Joan and their children functioned no differently from that of a husband and legitimate father, they said; it was irrational to treat him as if he were uninterested and irresponsible.[58] Indeed, cohabiting couples differed from men and women whose casual liaisons produced children. "Except for the legal factor, this may be a family like any other."[59]

An early draft opinion by Justice White embraced sex neutrality and a more functional definition of parenthood: "On the death of a spouse, unwed fathers lose their children but unwed mothers suffer no diminution of control. This discrimination between natural parents according to the superficial mother/father dichotomy unnecessarily ignores and impermissibly overrides the relevant criterion of a parent's capacity to raise his child. Under this standard, capable men . . . are separated from [their children], simply because they are men."[60]

Justice Douglas disagreed. He saw the Illinois law not as "an invidious discrimination against unwed fathers, but rather a protection of illegitimate children." Most unmarried fathers, Douglas wrote in his first draft, "are not present at their children's births and like hit-and-run drivers are difficult to locate." Douglas thought the Illinois scheme reasonable given children's interest in "swift and certain placement in adoptive homes," and prospective parents' likely reluctance to adopt if a father might "later demand custody or visiting privileges." Even in cases where unwed fathers came forward to volunteer for parental status, Douglas suspected their motives might be more pecuniary—a ploy to receive government benefits—than paternal.[61]

Douglas's draft cast unmarried fathers as callous, irresponsible, and opportunistic. Justice Marshall's draft opinion reflected a different understanding of nonmarital parenthood. Marshall attacked "stereotypes" that presumed a father's "weak emotional and practical ties to his children." The "many reasons for illegitimacy" included the "structure of . . . welfare programs" that "provide financial assistance only to children in one-parent households." In such circumstances nonmarriage reflected a father's concern for his children's well-being.[62] Douglas envisioned the prototypical unwed father as a potential obstruction to a socially desirable adoption, an option primarily open to white families; Marshall likely imagined an unwed father's role in many poor families of color.[63]

But even Marshall did not embrace White's full-blown sex discrimination theory. Taken to its logical conclusion, White's draft opinion implied that mothers and fathers should have fully equal rights with respect to their children, perhaps even regardless of marriage or other factors. A formal sex equality principle as applied to nonmarital parenthood did not command support on the Court. The justices were not prepared to jettison all distinctions based on marital status. Nor were they ready to create a robust substantive due process right to custody of one's "natural" child.[64]

In the end, Marshall joined White's majority opinion, the final version of which nimbly dodged these and other contentious points. The Court found that the Illinois statute violated unmarried fathers' procedural due process rights and affirmed Stanley's "interest . . . in the children he has sired and raised" but left open many questions about the ruling's scope and ramifications. White affirmed the "familial bonds" of nonmarital families as "warm, enduring, and important." He wrote that even if granting procedural protections to unmarried fathers would be costly and time-consuming, "the Constitution recognizes higher values than speed and efficiency."[65] Whether *Stanley* portended more than nominal parental rights for unmarried fathers, however, remained to be seen.[66]

Stanley raised serious questions for established adoption law and practice. Some state officials read the decision to require a dramatic expansion of unmarried fathers' procedural rights, and they worried about its impact on adoptions. Indeed, after *Stanley* the plight of (mostly white) nonmarital fathers denied the right to object to a newborn's adoption by strangers did spur state legislative campaigns for greater procedural protections.

For instance, Michael Neal, a twenty-something aspiring musician, protested Los Angeles County's placement of his biological son in an adoptive home in 1972. Neal preferred to marry the child's mother or alternatively to provide him a home, together with his own mother and sister. But the child's seventeen-year-old mother did not "want anything more to do with me or our baby." Authorities confirmed that Neal had "expressed an interest in the child," but the mother "was very adamant that she did not want the baby placed with him," and under California law, Neal had "no legal rights" since he had not "legitimated" the child. "If we can't resolve the differences between the mother and father, we have to go by what the mother wants," explained Lenore Campbell, a county official.[67]

Neal found an ally in Reuben Pannor, who thought the legal bar to taking a child from a competent and willing biological father should be high. Hoping to recruit similarly situated men to his cause, Neal founded a group called Loving and Fit Fathers and publicized his case in local media.[68]

Stanley held out the initial promise of procedural reforms to address Neal's plight, as state officials scrambled to understand and comply with its constitutional mandate. In California, a task force convened to propose legislation that would allow men to register their desire to parent a nonmarital child with the state. They hoped to avoid the chaos *Stanley* initially produced in Los Angeles and elsewhere: delays and instability for children stuck in limbo as adoption agencies combed through government records, interviewed neighbors, and placed newspaper ads in a desperate effort to locate putative fathers. Social workers, already concerned about "a near-fad among adolescent mothers to try to raise youngsters by themselves," worried about "forcing mothers to keep their illegitimate babies against their will" when the prospect of the biological father or his relatives raising the child caused mothers to withhold their consent to an adoption.[69] The California task force hoped that a registration option that expired thirty days after a baby's birth would alleviate these pressures.

The California legislation enjoyed bipartisan support and, like the UPA, attempted to balance the rights of mother, father, child, and prospective adoptive parents. Not everyone endorsed procedural reforms, however. Attorney David Keene Leavitt, who represented the adoptive parents in Michael Neal's case and many others, argued that granting rights to unmarried fathers over the objection of mothers worked "the rankest kind of injustice." Leavitt argued that absent "affection and cooperation between the two [parents]," "someone has got to have the rights and it has got to be [the mother]." Leavitt warned, "A man can have seven minutes of pleasure with a girl and then come back later and ruin her life and that of the child."[70] Leavitt's position dovetailed with Chief Justice Burger's view, expressed in dissent in *Stanley*, that states should be free to decide, "on the basis of common human experience, that the biological role of the mother in carrying and nursing an infant creates stronger bonds . . . [than those] resulting from the male's often casual encounter."[71]

In the end, states scrambling to comply with *Stanley* implemented a patchwork of requirements that replicated the heterogeneity of paternal rights generally. Almost half of U.S. states required notice only to fathers who were "either known, identified by the mother, or ha[d] acknowledged the child." A few removed formal distinctions between legitimate and illegitimate children for adoption purposes. In practice, some jurisdictions developed procedures to bypass paternal consent. California, for instance, retained a requirement that a biological father "received the child into his home and openly held out the child as his natural child" in order to object to an adoption. The adoption expert Ruth-Arlene Howe wrote that despite the initial panic and temporary halt in adoptions post-*Stanley*, by the end of the 1970s "the vast majority of states" placed on the unmarried father "the burden . . . to affirmatively assert his paternal interests in the child" to gain the right to notice and a hearing in an adoption proceeding.[72]

New Models of Nonmarital Fatherhood

The poor and working-class fathers Justice Marshall likely envisioned when he wrote his draft opinion in Peter Stanley's case began to present diverse examples of nonmarital fatherhood and to articulate new conceptions of parental rights. Nonmarital fathers of color, especially, used the courts to make claims upon the state for recognition of their rights as parents. Unlike the divorced fathers who mobilized during this period, they lacked organizational might and depended largely on legal aid and civil liberties lawyers' willingness to champion their cause. Unlike the predominantly white working- and middle-class men who sought a right to veto adoptions, these fathers frequently encountered the limitations of the law *after* they had developed meaningful relationships with their nonmarital children.

Among other models of nonmarital parenthood that emerged in legal and public consciousness in the 1970s were fathers who provided care and support to children without ever living with the children's mothers; parents who lived together for a time with their children but then separated and established new partnerships; single fathers who raised children alone, with little or no maternal involvement; and families in which grandparents provided care while both parents worked and lived separately.

Fiallo, the lawsuit challenging sex and marital status discrimination in immigration and naturalization, presented among the most sympathetic scenarios: nonmarital fathers who had served as primary caregivers but were deprived of legal benefits available to married parents and to unmarried mothers. Like Peter Stanley, these fathers were opposed by the government, not their children's mothers. The remedy they sought—an extension of benefits—stood to benefit parents regardless of sex: like Stephen Wiesenfeld, they fought both *for* legal recognition of paternal involvement and caregiving duties and *against* the assumption that mothers should assume sole legal and social responsibility for nonmarital children.

Some did view the citizenship laws' distinctions between maternal and paternal relationships with nonmarital children as "totally arbitrary sex discrimination." Justice Powell's clerk, J. Philip Jordan, also called the government's concern that fathers might bring unlimited numbers of nonmarital children into the United States "a bunch of *crap!*" In the end, however, Powell wrote the *Fiallo* majority opinion upholding the challenged provisions, citing Congress's virtually unfettered authority to determine who is admissible to the United States.[73] Another clerk, Gene Comey, urged Powell to omit language about "the perceived absence in most cases of close family ties" between fathers and their nonmarital children. Comey saw "no reason to rely on this somewhat 'distasteful' argument," since "legitimate and illegitimate families . . . have a strong degree of family intimacy and unity."[74] Powell apparently rejected this advice. In dissent, Justice Marshall condemned the law's "invidious and irrational" discrimination against nonmarital fathers and children and its abridgment of constitutionally protected family freedoms.[75]

In *Fiallo*, fathers' and mothers' interests coincided, but cases involving parental rights often pitted parents against each other. As mothers more frequently kept and raised nonmarital children rather than marrying their children's fathers or placing babies for adoption (mostly an option for white women), a third alternative emerged: marriage to another man who would adopt the child, thereby "legitimating" him and providing a two-parent marital family. The two stepfather adoption cases that reached the Supreme Court in the late 1970s featured fathers of color who had formed relationships with their children that stepfather adoption threatened to sever.

In 1976, Leon Quilloin, a sometime nightclub manager and fisherman in Savannah, Georgia, fought to retain his parental rights despite an adoption petition by Randall Walcott, who had married the mother of Leon's eleven-year-old son, Darrell. Quilloin came from a politically active family: his mother, Mabel Dawson, took part in voter registration drives, and his sister Carolyn had participated in lunch counter sit-ins to protest segregation as a high school student in the early 1960s. Quilloin's lawsuit was no test case, however. Like other nonmarital fathers who fought for parental rights in the 1970s, Quilloin sued because he found himself in danger of losing all access to his child.

Unlike Peter Stanley, Quilloin had an opportunity to be heard regarding his request that the judge deny Walcott's adoption petition and grant Quilloin "partial custody, in the form of visitation privileges." The hearing before Judge Elmo Holt in Fulton County Superior Court revealed that Darrell's mother, Ardell, gave birth on Christmas Day, 1964. For the first year of his life Darrell lived with his mother and maternal grandmother in Savannah, and Quilloin contributed some financial and in-kind support, including paying for surgery to repair a hernia. Then Ardell moved to New York to find work, and for the next four years Darrell continued to reside in Savannah, cared for by Quilloin's mother, Darrell's maternal grandmother, and Quilloin himself. Quilloin testified that he purchased milk and clothing for Darrell and arranged for him to start kindergarten early at a local Catholic school. Quilloin recounted how he had built a soundproof nursery in the nightclub he managed so that his son could spend time with him at work, and he said that he arranged for Darrell's transportation to and from school. Quilloin's mother told the judge that the two grandmothers cooperated with Darrell's parents to take care of the boy's needs and that Quilloin supplemented the money Ardell sent home for Darrell's care. "On both sides the family has always been agreeable," Ms. Dawson testified.[76]

In 1969, five-year-old Darrell joined Ardell in New York, where she had a new husband and a baby son. There was some dispute about the length and frequency of Darrell's subsequent visits in Georgia, but all agreed that Quilloin had given him several gifts, including a new bicycle. Believing that Quilloin's visits and expensive presents were "disruptive" to family harmony and desiring that Darrell share the Walcott surname, the Walcotts petitioned for Randall to adopt Darrell.

Darrell himself expressed a desire to continue seeing Quilloin *and* to be adopted by Walcott. In a poignant exchange at the hearing, he seemed not to understand that the two might be mutually exclusive. If Walcott adopted Darrell and became his legal father, the judge would terminate Quilloin's parental rights, and the Walcotts could deny Quilloin any opportunity to see his son. Quilloin's lawyer tried to ask Darrell whether he understood that "in the event the Court were to approve the adoption . . . you might never be able to see Mr. Quilloin again?" But the Walcotts' attorney objected, and Judge Holt disallowed the question.[77]

Quilloin did not seek full equality with Darrell's mother, and he did not bring a sex discrimination claim. He "honestly believe[d] that [Darrell's] rightful place is with his mother" and sought visitation, not custody. He simply wished to be treated, as his lawyer put it, "like a de facto divorced father." Quilloin speculated: "Maybe if I had a father . . . I [would have gone] on and finished school." He conceded the superiority of a two-parent home for Darrell: "I'm not married, so . . . with me, he's in a broken home more or less. I don't have any objection to her keeping him. It's just a matter of, it's a little bond between the kid and myself, seldom as it's been."[78]

Judge Holt acknowledged Darrell's wish to maintain a relationship with his biological father, but he decided that Walcott's adoption, not legitimation and visitation by Quilloin, was in the child's best interest. The state defended its decision to allow mothers but not fathers of illegitimate children to veto adoptions.[79] The Georgia Supreme Court upheld Holt's ruling. "To further the protection and care of its children," Justice Harold Nelson Hill, Jr., wrote for the majority, "Georgia favors and encourages marriage and child rearing in a family relationship," and the "placing of full parental power in the mother" served these state interests.[80] The court deemed Quilloin's action too little, too late, as he had not taken steps to "legitimate the child or support him" before the proposed adoption.[81]

As Quilloin's appeal headed to the U.S. Supreme Court, lawyers in the ACLU's national offices debated his cause. Initially, the general counsel voted to file an amicus brief supporting Quilloin, and the task fell to Rena K. Uviller, head of the Juvenile Rights Project (JRP), and Martin Guggenheim, then a staff attorney. Uviller, born Rena Katz in Detroit, was a "classic 1960s poverty lawyer" who moved quickly up the ranks of the Legal Aid Society, eventually heading its criminal appeals division. Uviller served as a "law guardian" representing the interests of children and their parents in family courts, including Judge Polier's, where Uviller often recommended against government intervention and championed family integrity.[82] Under her leadership the JRP fought for greater due process protections for parents and children threatened with terminations of parental rights.[83]

In Leon Quilloin's case, competing principles vied for Uviller's allegiance. The JRP believed that terminating the parental rights of adults who were willing and able to care for their children devastated families and mistook poverty for neglect.[84] Uviller testified along these lines in congressional hearings on the Indian Child Welfare Act (ICWA) held in August 1977, noting the inappropriate standards of "questionable constitutionality" imposed on poor families through the "tyranny of social work."[85] The state, JRP lawyers believed, should provide resources to alleviate poverty and support services to keep families together, rather than severing family ties and consigning children to group homes or foster care. And as a feminist, Uviller believed that mothers and fathers should share caregiving and breadwinning responsibilities equally. Indeed, one of her first ACLU cases challenged Utah's maternal presumption in child custody.[86]

Uviller and Guggenheim consulted with lawyers from the Women's Rights Project, and several voiced "strong objections."[87] To be sure, siding with Quilloin jibed with the ACLU's critique of classifications based on sex and birth status and its view that child-parent relationships "should not be permanently severed for reasons less serious than abandonment or child neglect." Nevertheless, "serious feminist considerations" weighed "against participating in this case." Uviller wrote to the ACLU's legal director, Bruce Ennis: "There is a concern that we ought not be arguing that adoption decisions of unmarried mothers who have borne sole responsibility for their children be subject to the veto of men who have not assumed any meaningful responsibility. Notwithstanding the rhetoric of equality, the only real advantage that women have in this society is their children and even this advantage was a hard-won feminist battle." Taking Quilloin's side "could seriously harm the credibility of ACLU with the feminist movement." Further, "it could help solidify the opposition of traditional housewives to women's rights, and give them the feeling that 'women's lib' is for professional women and against traditional women," jeopardizing ERA ratification.[88]

Ennis felt torn.[89] He believed that the "civil liberties argument" on behalf of Quilloin was "extremely strong" and that "giving fathers greater control over the adoption and placement of their children . . . may in fact liberate women" from their principal role as mother. He also understood that "as a practical matter, because of pervasive discrimination against women, true equality is not possible at the present time, and theoretical equality between men and women . . . will in fact disadvantage women." Ultimately, Ennis concluded, the "social and political consequences" of a victory for Quilloin were "extremely difficult to predict" and this, combined with internal dissension, counseled against the ACLU's participation.[90]

It is impossible to say whether Quilloin's claims would have fared better with the ACLU's support. Quilloin earned some sympathy: Powell's clerk Jim Alt agreed with Quilloin's attorneys that it was "irrational to give the divorced father a voice in the adoption decision, but not the father who never married." He noted that fathers like Quilloin "had no reason to go to court" to seek formal legal status "when, in practice, his relationship with his son was satisfactory."[91] At oral argument, however, the justices expressed skepticism, even scorn, toward Quilloin's claim, repeatedly noting his failure to "legitimate" or provide consistent financial support for Darrell.[92]

In the end, Justice Marshall's opinion for a unanimous Court upheld Walcott's adoption of Darrell and the termination of Quilloin's parental rights. Marshall wrote the opinion narrowly, leaving the door open to future challenges. But the decision rejected Quilloin's argument that he should be treated like a "de facto divorced father." Unlike a father who had married the mother or lived in the same household with his family, Quilloin had never taken legal or actual responsibility for his son. Georgia, therefore, "was not foreclosed from recognizing" the difference between a divorced and a never-married father's "extent of commitment to the welfare of the child."[93]

Abdiel Caban had greater success presenting his claim to the justices the following year.[94] Caban had lived with his two children and their mother, Maria, for several years, and had since married another woman, Nina. Even so, a New York court interpreted state law to mean that Caban could only prevent Maria's husband, Kazim Mohammed, from adopting Brian and Linda if he could demonstrate that remaining with the Mohammeds was contrary to the children's best interests. Bruce Ennis noted that unlike *Quilloin*, *Caban* presented "ideal facts," in that the "father has had a significant relationship with his children." The case offered the ACLU an excellent chance to combat the "alarming trend" toward removing children from their parents in the name of children's "best interests."[95]

This time, Uviller and Guggenheim co-authored an amicus brief supporting nonmarital fathers' rights. Caban's supporters made equal protection and substantive due process arguments. They emphasized how legal and social changes undermined the case for treating nonmarital fathers as second-class parents.[96] After experimenting with full formal equality for mothers and fathers, Justice Powell's opinion for a narrow majority embraced sex neutrality only in circumstances where a nonmarital father had developed a relationship with his children comparable to their mother's. Dissenters from the 5–4 ruling—including John Paul Stevens, an adoptive father himself—reiterated the concern that rights for nonmarital fathers would jeopardize adoptions, especially of newborns.[97]

Another 5–4 decision issued the same day underscored divisions among the justices about the meaning of sex equality for nonmarital parents. *Parham v. Hughes* rejected the claim of a nonmarital father who had developed a close bond with his son while sharing parenting duties. After an automobile accident killed six-year-old Lemuel Parham and his mother, Cassandra Moreen, Mr. Parham sued for his son's wrongful death. Curtis Parham did not live with Lemuel and his mother, but he had supported Lemuel financially, visited him daily, and taken care of him on many weekends. Parham signed his son's birth certificate but never completed the paperwork required to legitimate him.[98] The Richmond County, Georgia, Superior Court judge Franklin H. Pierce wrote that Parham had "in every respect treated [Lemuel] as his own."[99]

A decade earlier the U.S. Supreme Court had recognized a mother's right to sue for the death of her illegitimate child.[100] Yet in *Parham* Justice Stewart wrote for a plurality that the Georgia law that allowed mothers but not fathers to sue for an illegitimate child's wrongful death did not offend the constitutional principle of sex equality.[101] *Parham* continued the pattern, begun in *Fiallo*, of rejecting fathers' sex discrimination claims precisely where fathers' and mothers' interests in sex neutrality most clearly converged. No feminist dilemma clouded Curtis Parham's claim; indeed, depriving him of the right to sue perpetuated mothers' primary responsibility for nonmarital children by devaluing fathers' caregiving relationships.

Fathers like Parham and Quilloin had another trait in common: they could have taken steps to "legitimate" their children—thereby creating a legal support obligation—but did not seize the opportunity. When a state provided no easy legal path to legitimation, the Court often had greater sympathy. Jessie Trimble, a Black mother in Chicago, claimed for her young daughter Deta Mona a constitutional right to inherit from the child's biological father, Sherman Gordon, the victim of a homicide who died without leaving a will. In *Trimble v. Gordon* (1977), Justice Powell acknowledged the state's interest in avoiding the difficulties of proving the paternity of a deceased putative father. But here paternity was not in question: Sherman Gordon had acknowledged and supported Deta Mona. Illinois could not exclude all "illegitimate" children from inheritance but provide no way to legitimate a child other than marrying her mother.[102]

Curtis Parham, in contrast, was not a child, "for whom the status of illegitimacy is involuntary and immutable," so it was "neither illogical nor unjust for society to express its 'condemnation of irresponsible liaisons beyond the bonds of marriage'" by excluding fathers from recovery.[103] Moreover, Parham, like Quilloin, "was responsible for conceiving an illegitimate child and *had the opportunity to legitimate the child but failed to do so*."[104] That missed chance to confer formal legal status and enable the state to impose financial responsibility doomed his claim. In refusing to allow Parham to seek compensation for his son's death, the Court again denied constitutional recognition to nonmarital fathers of color whose bonds with their children were neither speculative nor in tension with mothers' interests. Marital status mattered less mostly when recognizing functional relationships between father and child secured paternal financial support.

Feminism, Equality, and Marital Primacy

Rena Uviller's reservations about an ACLU intervention in *Quilloin* presaged a more sweeping critique of sex neutrality in the law of parenthood that emerged in the late 1970s and early 1980s. Uviller worried that feminists had put the cart before the horse. "If sex-neutral custody laws presently either reflected a reality of pervasive shared childcare during marriage or helped eliminate persistent sexual stereotyping in the job market, they would be a legitimate feminist objective," she wrote in 1978. However, equality had not yet come to pass either in employment or in family care. Uviller detected "misogynist overtones" in fathers' rights advocates who castigated wives as "blood-sucking parasites" and called alimony an "undiluted evil." "At this point in history," Uviller concluded, "the law should recognize a woman's option to keep the children whose daily care she has so disproportionately assumed." For poor and low-income mothers especially, she believed, shared parenting was "sheer abstraction."[105]

Uviller's position echoed earlier critiques of the no-fault revolution. Some feminists had long worried that allowing for easier divorce without property and alimony reform would undercut women's negotiating position. The decline of the maternal presumption in child custody, they feared, would further undermine women who had given up career opportunities for childrearing only to find that a sex-neutral best-interests standard devalued their caregiving work.

In the late 1970s and early 1980s that maternal preference continued to erode and joint custody gained ground in many states.[106] For feminists, joint custody could relieve divorced mothers of sole responsibility for childcare, undermine stereotypes about motherhood as women's primary destiny, and incentivize fathers to care for children during marriage.[107] For fathers' rights activists, joint custody cemented the new "divorce bargain," as the legal historian Deborah Dinner has shown, in which fathers received custody rights in exchange for child support or in lieu of more generous payments. But while divorced fathers fought for a categorical presumption of joint custody, feminists only favored the presumption when both parents agreed. Without this crucial caveat, feminists worried that the devaluation of women's caregiving during marriage would reduce their bargaining power at divorce, harming both women and children.[108]

These feminists saw their worst fears confirmed by the early 1980s. Reforms that treated divorcing husbands and wives as if they were fungible spouses could not produce equality of results, wrote the feminist legal scholar Martha Fineman in 1983.[109] Feminists critical of ostensibly gender-neutral rules argued that they devalued mothers' caregiving labor and held fathers to a "different, much less demanding standard."[110] Nancy Polikoff, writing in 1982, proposed a "primary caretaker" presumption for child custody decision-making. This functional standard would benefit mothers and children in most cases but would also protect fathers who provided "primary nurturance and care during the ongoing marriage."[111]

In the early 1980s a new generation of women in law emerged, galvanized by the conservative ascendency that fueled Ronald Reagan's election to the presidency. No longer wary of ideas that might undermine the now-vanquished ERA's chances of success, feminists began to own publicly bolder visions of sex equality and sometimes to criticize earlier legal strategies. Against this backdrop the dissension that had simmered beneath the surface in the early nonmarital fathers' cases burst into the open in a case from rural Nebraska.

Donald Kirkpatrick and Laura S. began an intimate relationship when he was twenty-two and she was fourteen. At fifteen, Laura became pregnant, and she decided, in consultation with her parents, to place the child for adoption. An adoptee herself, Laura "had great concern for the stigma attached to a child born out of wedlock in a small town." She did what many white girls in her situation had done for generations: entered a home for unwed mothers and remained there until she gave birth. Kirkpatrick proposed marriage when Laura told him of the pregnancy, but she declined. In Texas, where the baby was born, putative fathers were entitled to receive notice of adoption proceedings but could not veto an adoption and take custody unless a court agreed that legitimation was in the child's best interests.

Supporters said Kirkpatrick was a responsible, upstanding young man devoted to his daughter and eager to marry her mother. Detractors claimed he was an irreligious statutory rapist with inconstant paternal instincts who planned to turn the baby over to the care of his female relatives.[112] Both characterizations enjoyed some support in the record. Laura testified that Kirkpatrick was a "wonderful man" but said that, at fifteen, she was not ready to marry and start a family. Laura also felt strongly that her daughter should be raised by "two Christian parents."[113]

Texas courts had not been friendly to the claims of men like Kirkpatrick in the past.[114] In 1980 the state supreme court explained in another case: "While the mother who is unmarried and pregnant is trying to figure out what she will do with the child, the father is totally free from any responsibility. . . . To classify him as a parent simply because he is a biological father would give him a powerful club with which he could substantially reduce the options available to the unmarried mother."[115] There was "a rational basis for the State to distinguish" between "a sperm donor, a rapist, a 'hit and run' lover, an adulterer and the like" and "the father who has accepted the legal and moral commitment to the family."[116]

When the U.S. Supreme Court declined to hear *Kirkpatrick*, three justices—Brennan, Marshall, and White—objected. A trial court denied Donald Kirkpatrick's petition, a state appellate court affirmed, and Kirkpatrick appealed again to the U.S. Supreme Court. It seemed as if the justices might finally decide the long-simmering question of sex equality in newborn adoptions.[117]

After "an apparently bitter internal dispute" the ACLU's Children's Rights Project (CRP, formerly JRP) agreed to represent Kirkpatrick before the Court.[118] The CRP focused on limiting the state's ability to terminate parental rights, promoting family reunification, and achieving institutional reforms to state foster care systems.[119] Its interest in Donald Kirkpatrick's case stemmed from the conviction that "best interests of the child" standards were "so vague as to be without any substantive meaning." They permitted "trial judges to intrude the government into family decisions by making judgments based on individual or community prejudice and bias." Such judgments, "virtually impossible for a parent to defend," underpinned the unnecessary "destruction of a parent-child relationship."[120]

The CRP's mission to oppose unwarranted government intervention in poor families won the day. Its brief also criticized the Texas law as "freighted with the 'baggage' of sexual stereotypes so often condemned by this Court." The injury to fathers was obvious. Equally harmful if less obvious was "the harm done to women," who were "inevitably locked into the childcare role, unable to share childrearing responsibilities equally with men."[121]

The feminist attorney and law professor Nancy Erickson viewed the "harm done to women" very differently. Erickson, active in abortion rights movements and women's liberation generally, counted among her mentors Ruth Bader Ginsburg and Rhonda Copelon.[122] Erickson applauded the advances feminists had won and lamented the shortcomings of the Court's "formal equality" jurisprudence: its failure to recognize pregnancy discrimination and restrictions on reproductive freedom as sex discrimination; its narrow interpretation of equal pay laws; and its insistence on proof of discriminatory intent and failure to provide adequate redress against laws that disproportionately harmed women.[123]

On nonmarital parenthood, though, Erickson, like Uviller and skeptics in the ACLU, departed from the conventional wisdom that sex neutrality advanced feminist aims. Erickson authored an amicus brief, after soliciting anonymous letters from mothers who had faced dilemmas similar to Laura S.'s.[124] D. H. explained that her husband abandoned his family a few months after the birth of her first child but refused to pay child support; she was now expecting a second child but lacked the resources to care for another baby properly. "If the father will not give his consent," she wrote, "I will be *forced* to keep this child despite my feelings that it would be in the child's best interest to be adopted." Another woman, who had placed her child for adoption, wrote that she would have made a very different decision if the baby's biological father had threatened to seek custody, perhaps to keep a child she did not wish to raise.[125]

To Erickson, true reproductive freedom required women's autonomy to decide between abortion, adoption, and childrearing, regardless of her sexual partner's preferences. A consent requirement would allow men to use their sexual partners as involuntary surrogate mothers. "Not even a pregnant woman's husband may demand" that a woman terminate a pregnancy or carry a fetus to term against her wishes, Erickson pointed out.[126] S. J. wrote Erickson from a Texas maternity home that she might have terminated her pregnancy if adoption were not available: "I don't think I could go through a full-term pregnancy on my own, knowing I never could provide the kind of life I want for [the child]."[127] Marriage, cohabitation with the intent to co-parent, or a co-parenting agreement, Erickson argued, should be required for a putative father to claim custody rights or veto an adoption over a mother's wishes.[128]

Erickson denied that Texas law promoted gender bias or stereotypes. Kirkpatrick himself seemed to assume that his mother, his sister, his grandmother, and now his wife, described as a full-time homemaker, would care for the baby if he were to obtain parental rights and custody. Erickson, like Uviller, embraced the goal of greater paternal involvement in the care of children but worried about the effects of formal legal equality on unequal social circumstances. "Our desires, as feminists, to see men assume the parental duties that in the past they have abandoned to women should not prevent us from recognizing that a legal rule granting an unwed father exactly the same rights as an unwed mother could lead to extreme oppression of women," Erickson wrote.[129]

Justice White again championed fathers' rights on sex equality grounds. Since writing *Stanley*, White had dissented in *Roe v. Wade* (1973): he objected to the majority's view, in his words, that "the Constitution values the convenience, whim, or caprice of the putative mother more than the life or potential life of the fetus."[130] White also wrote for the majority in *Washington v. Davis* (1976), holding that evidence of discriminatory intent, not disparate impact alone, was required to prove an equal protection violation.[131] White felt that *Kirkpatrick* presented the "weighty equal protection claim" that Texas's laws were "based simply on the sexual stereotype that women can be more trusted with children than men."[132]

White persuaded three of his colleagues to hear Kirkpatrick's appeal, but the Court sidestepped the thorny questions of equal protection and due process by remanding the case on a question of state law. The Texas courts upheld their original ruling against Kirkpatrick. By then, Kirkpatrick's daughter had lived with adoptive parents for more than a year, and another appeal would likely have meant years of additional litigation. Not wishing "to subject his child to that kind of uncertainty," Kirkpatrick's attorneys reached an agreement with the adoption agency that allowed him to contact his daughter once she reached a specified age.[133]

Instead of *Kirkpatrick*, the Court decided Jonathan Lehr's case. Lehr and Lorraine Martz met after Lorraine's father was killed in Vietnam and Jonathan's mother, Helen, took the troubled teenager, estranged from her mother and stepfather, into her care. Jonathan and Lorraine became intimately involved and lived together sporadically along with Lorraine's child, Renee, from a previous relationship. Their daughter, Jessica, was born in 1976, and at one point the couple was engaged. Lehr visited Lorraine and Jessica in the hospital after the birth but did not accede to Lorraine's request that they marry.[134]

What happened next was the subject of vigorous dispute. Lehr maintained that he did everything in his power to ascertain Lorraine's whereabouts when she moved with her children to another part of New York state and then married Richard Robertson. Lorraine insisted that Lehr showed no interest in Jessica until Richard commenced adoption proceedings, although Lehr did visit Renee on several occasions after Jessica's birth.[135] Lehr's petition for paternity and visitation was not one of the seven circumstances that entitled a putative father to notice and a hearing in New York adoption proceedings. Although all parties, including the judge, were aware of Lehr's paternity suit, the court approved Richard's adoption of Jessica, foreclosing Lehr's parental rights.[136]

The judge's apparent eagerness to finalize the adoption despite his knowledge of Lehr's paternity filing disturbed several of the justices.[137] A majority nevertheless agreed that Lehr's failure to comply with the statute's requirement was fatal to his claim. Chief Justice Burger assigned the opinion to Justice Stevens, whose first draft endorsed "formal family and recognized family relationships" as superior.

Stevens quoted at length a recent article by Bruce Hafen, a family law scholar and elder in the LDS church who co-founded the law school at Brigham Young University (BYU).[138] Hafen was the father of seven children; his wife, Marie, stayed home when they were young and then resumed teaching English and religion at BYU in 1980. The Hafens modeled a middle ground between feminist egalitarianism and traditionalist wifely submission: they emphasized husbands' and wives' complementary and interdependent roles.[139]

Hafen's reading of recent jurisprudence also embraced a kind of intermediate position. The Court, in Hafen's view, had not effected a revolutionary change in the laws of reproduction and the family in the 1970s.[140] The justices eased some legal burdens on nonmarital children and their parents, legalized contraception and abortion, and removed many sex-based classifications from the law, but the Court never dethroned the marital family or formal family relationships. Notwithstanding much wishful and creative thinking by liberal constitutional lawyers and scholars (and a few lower court judges), "marriage and kinship are still the touchstones of constitutional adjudication in family-related cases," Hafen concluded. "The Court has limited some traditional policies, but has done so only in an effort to remedy exceptional inequities." And critically: "Even [in] the exceptional cases . . . constitutional protection has not been extended to relationships between unmarried adults."[141]

Stevens's majority opinion in *Lehr* ratified Hafen's account, even after the justice removed the long quotations at colleagues' request.[142] Stevens made another change to assuage Justice O'Connor's concerns about his treatment of the sex-based equal protection issue. He had written in an early draft: "Before birth, the mother carries the child; it is she who has the constitutional right to decide whether to bear it or not. And from the moment the child is born, the mother always has a relationship of legal responsibility toward the child. Because the natural father of an illegitimate child can often be legally and practically anonymous if he chooses, responsibility does not devolve upon him in the same way."[143]

O'Connor found this discussion "disturbing." She agreed that, "as a practical matter, it is easier for the natural father of an illegitimate child to evade legal responsibility because of his anonymity." She continued: "I recognize that the clause 'responsibility does not devolve upon him in the same automatic fashion' is probably intended to be descriptive only. Nevertheless, the language contains connotations of approval of a scheme that imposes less legal responsibility on the natural father, and I would prefer to avoid any implication of that kind."[144]

Stevens revised the draft accordingly: he relied instead on Lehr's failure to establish a relationship with Jessica.[145] But none of the justices disputed the majority's ruling that unmarried mothers and fathers could be treated differently in adoption proceedings if the father had not formed a significant relationship with his biological child and the mother had.[146] *Lehr* confirmed that marital status was a legitimate basis for sex-differentiated parental rights and responsibilities. Mothers' husbands were presumed fathers until proven otherwise. Nonmarital fathers, by contrast, must "seize the opportunity" afforded by their genetic tie.

Lehr freed states to maintain varied approaches to nonmarital bio-logical fathers' assertion of parental rights. Some required that fathers file a voluntary acknowledgment of paternity form; initiate a court action to "legitimate" the child; or anticipate that a child might result from in-tercourse and sign up for a putative father registry. To have standing to object to an adoption, some states said that a father must live with the child for a requisite period and hold the child out as his own. Others em-phasized the importance of providing financial support during pregnancy and after birth. Many states recognized an unmarried mother's right to custody automatically, while fathers had to petition a court to gain access to a child born outside of marriage. At the same time, federal and state governments stepped up child support enforcement for all fathers, re-gardless of marital status—and often notwithstanding the inability of low-income fathers to pay.[147] Marriage mattered less, in short, where a functional definition of parenthood conserved the public fisc.

In the 1970s, constitutional claimants articulated far-reaching visions of nonmarital fathers' parental rights and duties. In cases such as *Fiallo* and *Parham*, where fathers sought legal recognition of established, caring re-lationships, feminist principles aligned with nonmarital fathers' rights and their challenge to the legal primacy of marriage. To recognize the fa-ther-child relationship here was to validate parental caregiving regardless of marital status or sex, alleviating mothers' sole responsibility for chil-dren born outside of marriage.

In adoption cases, by contrast, parental rights were a zero-sum game, and there feminists divided painfully. On one hand, poverty lawyers cha-grined by rising rates of child removal and terminations of parental rights in poor families favored robust substantive due process rights for biological parents. On the other hand, granting parental rights to non-marital fathers often meant thwarting the wishes of mothers: those who preferred to relinquish babies for adoption but might feel compelled to keep and raise them if the alternative was paternal custody; and those who wished to marry a different man and enable their new husbands to forge a legal parent-child bond.

Marriage stood in complicated relationship to these competing val-ues. For advocates concerned about unjust child removal, the legal pref-erence for placement with a two-parent marital family with financial means threatened to extinguish birth parents' rights unfairly and to undermine the integrity of non-normative, often nonmarital families—disproportionately poor and of color. Feminists who favored equal treatment for fathers hoped women would benefit from countering gendered assumptions about parental responsibility. They joined others who sympathized with nonmarital fathers in protesting the law's elevation of a mother's marital tie over a biological father's genetic and relational bond.

But for feminists concerned about mothers' autonomy in a world where women usually bore burdens of care and support as well as pregnancy and childbirth, marriage's primacy had a more complex valence. Whereas adoption advocates—and several of the justices—worried primarily about preserving a smooth path to adoption of infants by two-parent marital families, feminists guarded *mothers'* prerogative to make decisions without interference from the state or from nonmarital fathers.

For some feminists on either side of the fathers' rights question, marital status seemed largely irrelevant. Most feminists neither assumed the moral superiority of marital families nor prized the efficiency of adoption procedures, except to the extent that they vindicated a mother's truly voluntary decision to relinquish her child. And these feminists often harbored similar qualms about custody decision-making at divorce—their concerns about fairness to women did not depend on parents' marital status.

Justices and feminists who believed marital status *was* significant differed as to why. For justices who were skeptical of nonmarital fathers' rights, formal marriage signaled a man's commitment to accept all of the responsibilities of fatherhood—especially the obligation to provide financial support. In exchange he deserved the full complement of parental rights. Feminists who sought to preserve legal distinctions between divorced and nonmarital fathers did so, instead, to safeguard mothers' autonomy. For them, marriage was morally significant, but not because it confirmed a *man's* commitment to fatherhood. Rather, marriage signaled a *woman's* consent to her partner's parental rights—and nonmarriage its absence.

The constitutional standard for nonmarital fathers' parental rights announced in *Lehr* came to be known as "biology-plus." Marital status or biology alone guaranteed equal parental rights for married and divorced fathers. In contrast, unmarried biological fathers also had to establish a relationship with their children to be constitutionally entitled to notice and a chance to object to a stranger or stepfather adoption. Courts and legislatures already looked beyond marriage to establish paternal *obligations*. Now they would also look beyond formal indicia to establish parental *rights*. In this way, the nonmarital fathers' cases joined the larger movement toward functional definitions of family. But the Court applied functional definitions selectively, often to reward fathers who seized opportunities to "legitimate" and to assume legal financial responsibility for their children. More capacious visions of nonmarital fatherhood pioneered by low-income men of color recognized caregiving and affective bonds fathers formed—or might form—with their children. Even when these claims complemented mothers' rights and feminist visions of egalitarian parenting, though, the Court often proved less sympathetic.

The unmarried fathers cases helped to cement a federal constitutional regime that permitted significant legal distinctions based on marital status and sex. In the following years, the locus of innovation shifted to states and localities, now free to experiment with varied approaches to the legal recognition of partners and parents.

PART IV

CHAPTER EIGHT

The Functional Family

I‌N 1979, PRESIDENT JIMMY Carter convened a White House Conference on Families to explore how the government could help to absorb "successive waves of deep and often unpredictable change." Even the use of "families" rather than "the family" ignited controversy: conservatives recoiled at the implication that cohabiting partners, unmarried mothers, and gay and lesbian couples deserved equal billing with the marital nuclear family.[1] New Right leaders fought back hard. The chair of Ronald Reagan's presidential campaign, Senator Paul Laxalt (R-NV), introduced a Family Protection Act that would bar federal spending on sex education, school desegregation, and legal services for divorce, abortion, or gay rights cases. Conservatives accused feminists of plotting to "destroy the family as we know it."[2]

Feminists, meanwhile, held their own National Assembly on the Future of the Family. Sponsored by NOW's Legal Defense and Education Fund, the gathering featured panels about single-parent, minority, and "nontraditional" families along with parental leave, childcare, Social Security, and marriage as an economic partnership.[3] The "overriding theme," one reporter wrote, "was that the 'typical' family does not exist" and lawmakers "should stop passing laws that benefit the so-called nuclear family and penalize" other family forms.[4] The lesbian feminist lawyer Nancy Polikoff wished that the keynote panel on egalitarian (heterosexual) marriage had also featured "single-parent living with children, a gay family, communal family, an extended household." Polikoff craved an affirmative vision of family political economy that grappled with the constraints of a capitalist system, "an analysis of what we want to see and how we are going to get there." But she concurred with the assembly's conclusion that the *"function of family relationships,"* rather than their formal structure, should be the basis for allocating benefits and privileges.[5]

Less than a year later, Ronald Reagan—a divorcé who as governor of California had liberalized abortion and signed a pathbreaking no-fault divorce law—won the presidency with the support of the ascendant New Right. Reagan's election buoyed a "family values" movement that promoted sharply differentiated gender roles, compulsory heterosexuality, traditional marriage, a stingy welfare state, and civil rights retrenchment.

By the early 1980s, campaigns for federal constitutional change in marital status law had run their course. As decisions about how the law would define and structure family status reverted to state and local governments, some jurisdictions clung to formal categories such as marriage and biology. Others embraced the movement toward functional standards and definitions, designed to include the diverse family forms Polikoff prized.

In the 1980s and 1990s, family pluralism persisted on the ground. "Chosen" families unrelated by blood, marriage, or adoption became increasingly visible—and crucial—as gay men and lesbians confronted HIV/AIDS. More nonmarital cohabitation caused adults to form nurturing relationships with children to whom they had no legal tie. Growing numbers of parents with nonmarital partners raised questions about how sex outside of marriage related to parental fitness. State intervention in the name of child welfare separated birth parents from children; changing conditions of foster care and adoption intersected with theories of functional parenthood to unsettle the permanence and singularity of parental rights. Even long-standing patterns of informal and intergenerational caregiving gave rise to new dilemmas about whether and how the law should recognize nonparents who cared for children.

Americans thrust by intention or happenstance into caregiving relationships beyond the marital nuclear family often found themselves on the defensive. Chapter 4 described how, in the 1970s and into the 1980s, they sought relief from restrictive zoning laws and discriminatory practices of landlords and lenders. This chapter focuses on quests for affirmative recognition in the 1980s and 1990s. Local activists, often led by gay and lesbian advocates seeking recognition for relationships with chosen family, fought for domestic partnership legislation.[6] Many of these proposed laws contemplated unmarried couples in long-term committed relationships. But a handful went beyond the quasi-marital model to encompass "alternative families," collections of individuals who lived in mutually supportive and caring relationships beyond the nuclear family.

This chapter considers advocacy around the formation and recognition of nonmarital and chosen family relationships; their dissolution; and the parentage and custody of children who lived in "nontraditional" households. In each of these major facets of a relationship, advocates promoted functional definitions and standards in the final decades of the twentieth century, with varying degrees of success. Functional approaches occasionally replaced but more often supplemented formal categories such as marriage and biology.

Without legal recognition, the law treated life partners, extended and chosen family members, and others who lived outside the marital nuclear norm as legal strangers with no rights or responsibilities. Functional standards and family definitions instead examined how relationships worked in practice. Extending legal recognition to functional relationships could confer previously unavailable rights and benefits—parentage and custody, financial support, job security, social insurance, government assistance—on people who did not conform to the marital ideal. The emergence of HIV/AIDS and the growing numbers of unmarried partners—gay and straight—raising children heightened the urgency of these efforts.

The meaning and impact of functional definitions and standards depended on context: who created and used them, when, how, and for what purpose. Functional approaches often improved conditions for those at society's margins by relaxing rigid per se rules of exclusion. They inspired fruitful coalitions between disparate groups who lived outside the marital nuclear family. As we have seen in other contexts, functional approaches also entailed trade-offs. More so than clear formal rules, they delegated discretion to officials, who could exercise that discretion unpredictably so as to produce similarly exclusionary results. Functional approaches established qualifications for legal recognition that shaped behavior and granted legitimacy to certain conduct or relationships over others. They encountered fierce opposition on moral, fiscal, and practical grounds—and not only from conservatives.

"Alternative Families"

As marital nuclear families became less dominant, progressive municipalities and organizations promoted law and policy reform to support inclusive definitions of family.[7] In 1989, a California legislative committee described family in terms of function rather than formal legal ties. San

Francisco's task force on family policy, convened the same year, characterized "family" as "a unit of interdependent and interacting persons, related
together over time by strong social and emotional bonds *and/or* by ties of
marriage, birth, and adoption, whose central purpose is to create, maintain, and promote the social, mental, physical and emotional development
and well-bring of each of its members."[8] The Los Angeles task force on
family diversity extolled the virtues of family pluralism and urged government officials to define family as inclusively as possible.[9] Reformers
recommended expansion of supports for diverse families, including affordable housing, accessible transportation, and provision of elder- and
childcare.

Even cities on the leading edge of open-ended family definitions,
however, often concluded that extending legal recognition beyond unmarried *couples* would strain public coffers and squander political capital.
Berkeley was one of the first to enact domestic partnership legislation. In
1983, Berkeley's Human Relations and Welfare Commission (HRWC)
heard testimony about the many government and employer benefits
available only through marriage.[10] The HRWC considered allowing "unrestricted choice" of domestic partners. But expanding benefits beyond
couples, the commissioners worried, "would change the basic 'philosophy' on which benefits are extended" to a "loosely defined conception of
need" that would "entail enormous expense." The Berkeley commission's
report set aside such profound re-examination for another day in favor of
addressing sexual orientation discrimination only.[11]

The Berkeley report recommended "equalization," not "liberalization," of the benefit eligibility criteria. Rather than making domestic
partnership "substantially easier," reformers sought criteria that were
"functionally equivalent" to marriage, entailing a "degree of 'seriousness'
and 'commitment' approximately as great as the marriage criterion requires of opposite-gender couples."[12] They were acutely aware that the
"'loosening' of a criterion costs money."[13] By requiring that partners cohabit and "share the common necessities of life" Berkeley made domestic
partnership criteria even more rigorous than marriage.[14] The HRWC
was agnostic about whether to extend benefits to different-sex couples;
the ordinance enacted in 1985 allowed pairs of any sex to register. By
1989 Berkeley reported 108 registered couples, 85 percent of whom
were "heterosexual."

One member dissented from the Berkeley recommendations: the gay
activist Bobby Hilliard believed that access to benefits should not be

contingent upon relationships of any kind.[15] But other early adopters similarly narrowed their definition of domestic partnership to include cohabiting pairs in committed relationships that resembled marriage. In San Francisco, Supervisor Harry Britt proposed in 1982 to "end the city's discrimination with regard to employment benefits, to increase awareness about non-traditional relationships, and point out that marriage is not, by itself, a valid condition for the availability of such basic needs as medical care, visiting or caring for a loved one."[16]

Mayor Dianne Feinstein vetoed the bill, calling its scope, cost, and consequences "vague and unclear."[17] Many suspected that Catholic Church–led opposition derailed Britt's bill, but Feinstein's veto signaled that proponents would have to account for exactly who could register as domestic partners, the legal rights and responsibilities partners would assume, and the costs of expanding health insurance coverage and other employee benefits.

Feinstein convened a task force to consider these questions in 1983. San Francisco, like Berkeley, considered allowing a city employee to designate any health insurance beneficiary, related or not, of any age or sex.[18] The group quickly concluded that the likelihood of adverse selection— incentives for employees to designate high-needs beneficiaries and for younger, healthier employees to opt for private coverage—made an unrestricted definition infeasible. Instead, the task force recommended extending benefits to the "principal partner of city employees of the same sex with whom there is a continuing financial and emotional involvement residing in the same household."[19] Such a measure would capture the "symbolic benefits" of "equal pay for equal work" for gay and lesbian employees without straining public funds.[20]

When San Francisco enacted its first domestic partnership ordinance in 1989, Britt acknowledged that the law offered "very little real benefits," given that employees paid their own health insurance premiums, but did address the basic problem of discrimination against same-sex couples.[21] By 1987 an internal ACLU memo observed that "the most commonly applied definition of domestic partner runs parallel to that of cohabiting spouses and is sometimes referred to as 'spousal equivalent.' "[22]

In a few outlier jurisdictions, however, expansive definitions of family survived the initial study phase. In Madison, Boston, and Washington, D.C., proposals included not only same-sex couples but also extended family members, individuals with disabilities and their caregivers, single parents banding together to raise children in one household, elderly friends, communalists, and other so-called alternative families. Legal recognition, advocates hoped, could enable these families to live together without violating single-family zoning laws, visit one another in hospitals and jails, authorize emergency medical treatment, jointly make medical and educational decisions about children, and obtain employment benefits such as health insurance and bereavement leave traditionally available to legally married spouses. The experience of these exceptional jurisdictions sheds light on the diverse coalitions that supported expanded definitions of family and the daunting obstacles that stood in their way.

In Madison, the Equal Opportunities Commission (MEOC) formed a task force on "alternative family rights" in 1983 to study possible avenues for legal recognition. Backed by the Madison Institute for Social Legislation (MISL), a "broad-based," "gay-led coalition," Barbara Lightner, a local lesbian feminist lawyer and self-described agitator, urged Barbara Cox, the head of the University of Wisconsin Law School's legal writing program and the task force co-chair, to promote domestic partnership legislation.[23] Lightner thought this would be a small project, but it catalyzed six years of advocacy in Madison and propelled Cox into the animating struggle of her career.[24]

The task force adopted a broad working definition of family: "Two *or more* unmarried, legally adult persons involved in a mutually supportive, committed relationship who are registered publicly as 'domestic partners' in order to be considered, under municipal ordinance, as a 'family.' "[25] This definition would redress zoning regulations that excluded from single-family housing persons not related by blood, marriage, or adoption. It also protected cooperative living arrangements of elderly and disabled people; extended family such as grandparents, aunts, uncles, cousins, nieces, and nephews; and people like Judy Popham, who lived with her female partner and two children as well as another lesbian couple and their children.[26]

Task force members knew they took a serious political risk when they recognized families that included more than two adults.[27] In April 1984, the task force considered a motion to limit the number of adults to four. Cox and Bob West voted in favor on prudential grounds, but the other four members present voted to retain the "two or more" language.[28] The task force did make one early concession to political reality: employees would need to designate a "spouse equivalent" as sole beneficiary of health insurance and pension plans.[29]

Task force members also considered restricting recognition to unrelated adults, as other jurisdictions had, but ultimately decided to "err on the side of inclu[sion]."³⁰ The task force heard testimony from Doug Meyer, who lived with his children—both single parents—and their children, a household that was "denied a lot of the rights of a normal nuclear family."³¹ When the question resurfaced members again decided to retain the "two or more" definition and include related as well as unrelated adults.³²

Hospital visitation and the authority to make medical decisions figured prominently in the Madison deliberations. When Judy Popham's son was hospitalized, chosen family could not visit him in the hospital together. Kate Nolan, a task force member and also a lesbian co-parent, recounted how her lover had to rush across town and fetch Kate to authorize emergency medical care when their daughter became seriously ill at school. Even though Kathy Patrick's female partner had explained their relationship to doctors and assigned power of attorney to Patrick before undergoing surgery, the ICU nurse would speak only with her partner's mother.³³ Trudy Dyreson wrote that her exclusion from the hospital room where her stepson Michael lay critically ill caused her so much distress that she lost a much-wanted pregnancy.³⁴

Alternative families also sought access to health insurance and other employment benefits. Cheri Maples testified that her inability to cover her recently unemployed female partner and nonbiological children on her own health insurance plan cost the family almost a quarter of their annual household income of $10,000.³⁵ A local ordinance could not alter or emend legal parentage, custody, or visitation. But it could provide some benefits to unrecognized co-parents who otherwise could not authorize medical care or access health or educational records. For instance, even though Janice Czyscon shared fully in the care and support of her partner's two daughters, her employer denied her sick leave to care for the children when they were ill. Czyscon worried about losing them entirely should something happen to her partner.³⁶

Employment benefits for nonmarital partners attracted union support but a mixed response from local businesses.³⁷ Insurance companies worried that employees would select their sickest family member or friend as "spousal equivalent," which would drive up costs.³⁸ In response, MISL's Barbara Lightner testified that "one . . . cannot put a price on civil rights" and that the ordinance simply "redistribute[d]" costs "equitably, with those in committed relationships no longer having to subsidize those within marriage."³⁹

Ordinance supporters pragmatically emphasized economic and fiscal benefits. Restrictive zoning laws precluded single mothers or the elderly from sharing expenses in lieu of relying on "taxpayer-subsidized" forms of assistance, wrote Margaret McMurray, president of NOW's Madison chapter.[40] Ellen Magee could not insure her nonmarital male partner with the city's family health plan, so "taxpayers ended up paying [his medical bills] anyhow" through AFDC.[41]

Moral and religious disapproval animated some opponents, who pointed to an erosion of the "traditional nuclear family structure," the need for "opposite sex" parents to model appropriate gender roles, and biblical proscriptions against homosexuality.[42] Some spewed hateful and crude invective. One anonymous opponent wrote: "I am tired of paying for the fags' and lesbos' free ride through society at my expense. They are nothing but the diseased crud of humanity."[43] Several grouped together "adultery, fornication, and homosexuality," explicitly or implicitly: "Couples have lived a decent married life for generations. . . . Why encourage this animal-like behavior? It is no wonder this world is going to hell with all this disgusting goings on."[44]

Opponents often used "taxpayer citizenship" rhetoric, lamenting the cost to what one foe called "the white, traditional average taxpayer" of covering insurance for women, people of color, and the disabled.[45] Another wrote, "There is enough fraud in welfare, food stamps, etc. I feel this would only add to the working taxpayers' burden of supporting those who don't want to conform to society's rules."[46] Others distinguished between deserving and undeserving recipients of legal recognition, with the poor, those with physical disabilities, and widows as examples of the former and gays and lesbians exemplifying the latter.[47] Indeed, some skeptics saw the inclusion of other family forms as a smokescreen for a nefarious "homosexual agenda."[48]

Notwithstanding this opposition the task force ultimately recommended to the MEOC the "two or more" definition of alternative family and the extension of legal recognition for credit, employment nondiscrimination, hospital visitation, medical and educational decision-making, leave for illness and bereavement, access to family memberships at public accommodations, and single-family residential housing.

After two years of deliberations, however, the MEOC backed away from the "two or more" language and narrowed the definition of alternative families to include only those who lived together in a single housekeeping unit. The commission's report attributed the first change to objections from realtors and landlords who worried about "groups of college students" circumventing zoning laws and the second to a desire to "help prevent abuse of the proposed alternative family rights."[49] The bill now required extension of health benefits to city employees only: Madison would gather data on costs before imposing a mandate on private businesses.[50]

But even this narrower ordinance did not win approval from the Madison Common Council. Instead, proponents achieved more modest victories: the redefinition of "family" for zoning purposes to include "two unrelated adults and the minor children of each" and the extension of leave to city employees to care for or mourn alternative family members.[51] "After six years of work . . . this piecemeal adoption of two minor sections of the proposed ordinance was a disappointing result," Barbara Cox wrote in 1989.[52]

The achievement of minor successes sapped momentum in both directions: it satisfied some activists while others emerged disgusted and exhausted.[53] The outcome, after years of work, left Cox disillusioned—and radicalized. Temporarily freed from the constraints of political battles, Cox presented the Madison fight as a quest to throw off the yoke of patriarchy. Seeking sexual intimacy, caregiving, and sustenance outside of marriage flouted a system premised upon women's dependence on men, and on racial and economic subordination. As Cox saw it, Madison ultimately had done little more than define "alternative family" as a facsimile of the "traditional nuclear family"; it excluded extended or chosen family and communal forms of living more typical in poor and working-class families, especially among people of color. Instead of placating insurance companies, she thought, activists should fight for state-supported universal health care. Cox could "no longer pretend that working within the legal system will result in extensive meaningful change."[54]

Madison deliberated against the backdrop of a long-simmering debate among lesbian and gay advocates over marriage that boiled over in 1989 in a famous exchange between Paula Ettelbrick, a lawyer with the Lambda Legal Defense and Education Fund, and Tom Stoddard, Lambda's executive director. Stoddard, a student of Norman Dorsen's, had long believed that society should help gay relationships achieve "greater stability."[55] He acknowledged critiques of marriage as patriarchal and oppressive; nevertheless, Stoddard maintained that "the gay rights movement should aggressively seek full legal recognition for same-sex marriages." Whatever its dubious historical pedigree, marriage conferred "substantial economic and practical advantages" inaccessible through other legal instruments. Creative workarounds, such as relationship contracts and powers of attorney, left gay and lesbian Americans vulnerable to unsympathetic officials. Many couples could not afford the legal representation necessary to build a relationship piecemeal. And only marital status could provide certain crucial federal benefits such as immigration preferences and Social Security.[56]

The symbolic resonance of marriage also moved Stoddard. Because marriage was "the centerpiece of our entire social structure," denying "entry to this 'noble' and 'sacred' institution" implied that "gay relationships are somehow less significant, less valuable."[57] Domestic partnership would always be the equivalent of second-class citizenship.[58]

Ettelbrick disagreed. "I do not want to be known as 'Mrs. Attached-To-Somebody-Else,' " she wrote.[59] "Nor do I want to give the state the power to regulate my primary relationship." Marriage furthered an assimilationist project antithetical to lesbian and gay liberation, she argued, and would "result, at best, in limited or narrowed 'justice' for those closest to power at the expense of those who have been historically marginalized."[60] Advocates would insist that gay and lesbian relationships resembled normative heterosexuality rather than celebrating diverse sexualities and ways of living. Marriage legalization could stigmatize and even outlaw gay nonmarital sex "just as sexually active non-married women face stigma and double standards."

Further, Ettelbrick feared that gay marriage would reward the privileged minority who could afford health insurance, worked in a job that provided benefits, or had a spouse who did. This description might apply to wealthy white gay men but not to many women, people of color, or the working class. Prioritizing marriage, Ettelbrick worried, would sap the momentum of progressive movements that sought to expand the definition of family and extend health care and basic subsistence guarantees to all.

Ettelbrick saw both promise and peril in the movement for domestic partnership. On one hand, it could validate nonmarital relationships, especially those that were not "sexual or romantic." On the other hand, she cautioned, activists must "avoid the pitfall" of framing domestic partnership as "a stepping stone to marriage."[61]

That pitfall would prove difficult to sidestep. The quest for legal recognition of domestic partnerships for same-sex couples had an ambivalent relationship to marriage as an institution, as Douglas NeJaime has argued. Even marriage skeptics who advocated for nonmarital recognition in California found themselves constrained by the centrality of marriage in both the legal infrastructure and cultural script of relationships.[62]

But advocates did not give up on the more transformative project Ettelbrick envisioned. A Committee for Family Protection convened in Boston in 1989–90 to draft legislation that recognized not only unmarried couples but also "extended family" members, related or not, who lived together in mutually supportive relationships. The city's first openly gay councilman, David Scondras, a Harvard graduate, former social worker, and local gay rights advocate, introduced the bill in March 1991.[63]

Scondras sought not an equivalent to marriage but a redefinition of family. "Merely creating a marriage bill for gays and lesbians is a narrow approach," he told the *Boston Globe* in 1991. Demanding "a total revision of the entire idea of formalizing relationships," he said neither church nor state should determine how or with whom individuals chose to live.[64] Scondras had resided at various times with "grandparents, uncles, and from time to time friends, all of whom [he] considered [his] 'family.'" A friend of his "lived with two men, had a child from each, and all five lived for decades together, nurturing each other as a family."[65]

Known locally for providing advice and sometimes shelter for friends and acquaintances in need, Scondras understood how indispensable chosen families were, especially for gay men with HIV rejected by their families of origin.[66] Scondras represented "people who were told they could not see their dying partners at a hospital, often left to die of AIDS alone"; "women co-parenting children denied access to school records"; "gay couples denied mortgages"; and "children trying to care for their aging parents at home [whose] workplace did not consider their own parents to be part of a 'real family.'"[67]

Scondras's Family Protection Act (FPA) cheekily shared a name with the federal legislation designed to preserve the traditional marital family. It recognized "domestic partners" and extended family members who "share basic living expenses" and "assume responsibility for the welfare of the other members of the extended family and any dependents."[68] The bill would grant hospital and jail visitation rights and access to children's educational records, and it would give city workers in domestic partnerships and extended families the same benefits, including health insurance, as spouses and dependents of married employees.

A similar cocktail of fiscal and moral concerns as had hampered Madisonians impeded Boston's FPA. Councilor Albert O'Neil vowed to "destroy" the bill. "If they want to be gay, be gay! If you want to be a lesbian, be one! . . . But I'm not going to pay for your medical and health benefits by the taxpayers of this city," he exclaimed in a 1991 radio ad.[69]

Councilor James Kelly of South Boston, formerly an anti-busing crusader, also warned of FPA's cost.[70] Religious groups divided: Episcopalian,
Reform Jewish, and Unitarian clergy supported the bill while the Catholic Church remained vehemently opposed.[71]

In Boston, public debate and media coverage often discussed the
FPA primarily as a gay rights measure despite its wider applicability. As
in Madison, several progressive groups and union locals backed the FPA,
touting its benefits beyond gay and lesbian couples. Ellen Zucker, president of the Boston chapter of NOW, said the FPA conferred "the respect
that all families in the city of Boston deserve, whether it's elderly sisters
living together to take care of each other or a same-sex couple living together and raising kids." Scondras, too, emphasized the bill's reach to "all
non-traditional families."[72]

The FPA came tantalizingly close to enactment. On June 19, 1991,
an estimated ninety-four thousand people marched in Boston's Gay
Pride parade, with Scondras leading a chant at City Hall for the FPA's
passage.[73] On June 26 the *Boston Globe* reported that nine of thirteen
council members had agreed to support a version of the bill that omitted
health coverage to assuage budgetary concerns.[74] Still, the measure went
down to defeat, 7–6.[75] Scondras vowed to make the FPA an election issue
in November.[76] By 1993, the FPA had won enough support to pass by a
council vote of 7–5, but Mayor Raymond Flynn unexpectedly vetoed the
measure, citing a conflict with state laws that restricted city employee
benefits to spouses and dependents. A much narrower bill that gave unmarried couples who registered with the city "largely symbolic" benefits
such as hospital visitation rights became law. In November 1993, Scondras lost to Thomas Keane in an election that produced a "more moderate city council" with a "middle class agenda."[77]

By 1995, domestic partnership in Boston became a second-best marriage substitute rather than an opportunity to transform the definition of
family. An implicit bargain narrowed the definition of domestic partner
to include only same-sex couples in exchange for the health insurance
benefits withheld two years earlier. Councilor Keane reasoned that unmarried heterosexuals did not need city health benefits: they could marry.
Todd Fernandez, a local gay rights leader and formerly a leading FPA
sponsor, made the shift plain: "Limited domestic partnership benefits to
gays and lesbians is essential to preserve the focus on obtaining equal
rights for a group that the current law excludes. Our fight is for equality,
not to change the category of families recognized under current law."[78]

Washington, D.C., went furthest toward expanding "family" beyond unmarried couples. In 1989, the district convened feminist, labor, senior citizen, religious, and gay and lesbian representatives to work with city leaders to draft legislation extending employee health benefits.[79] Modeled on Madison's original proposal, the commission's definition of "alternative family" encompassed "a variety of family members, including siblings, grandparents, grandchildren, nieces and nephews."[80] Chairman John A. Wilson, the Black civil rights veteran who sponsored the measure in the D.C. City Council, called it "a terrible misconception that it is just a gay issue."[81] Advocates identified key beneficiaries as "a disabled person who cannot live alone," "two sisters or brothers, living together and raising their children together," "a grandchild and a grandparent, each taking care of the other," "two widows or widowers, making a common household," "elderly people or single mothers living together to save money," "displaced homemakers," and "heterosexual couples who decide not to marry" alongside "gay couples who cannot marry."[82]

The usual attacks ensued once the D.C. city government passed the ordinance and sought congressional approval. Both the House and Senate overwhelmingly voted against funding the health insurance benefits provided to domestic partners under the D.C. enactment. Mayor Sharon Pratt Kelly told city officials to continue registering domestic partners, but their status remained symbolic.[83] In 1993 conservative Republicans offered an amendment to the D.C. appropriations bill barring the city from enforcing a law that "erodes the legal status of the family" and "violates the sanctity of marriage."[84] Gary Bauer, president of the Family Research Council and former Reagan adviser, warned that the "law highjacks the moral capital of marriage by making other 'lifestyles' seem equally valuable and worthy of societal support." Bauer cautioned that "given the District's enormous number of broken families and the resultant crime and societal pathologies ... the institution of marriage should be supported, not defined so broadly as to become meaningless."[85]

Fiscal appeals also pervaded opposition talking points.[86] Leaders of the Christian Coalition, for example, wrote that "it is simply outrageous to ask that hard-pressed taxpayers pay for employee benefits for unmarried 'partners' of D.C. employees. We cannot afford to subsidize 'alternative' lifestyles."[87] Representative Clyde Holloway (R-LA) warned of a "slippery policy slope, financial slope, and moral slope."[88]

In response, D.C. proponents, even more so than in Madison or Boston, spotlighted the law's broad reach and support: from the Gray

Panthers, the AFL-CIO, the D.C. Nurses Association, and several churches. The Reverend John Mack, a Black civil rights leader and pastor, declared, "Many of us would not be here were it not for the loving and sturdy family care given us by grandparents, god-parents, extended family and friends."[89] Mack's op-ed on behalf of an ecumenical group of clergy depicted a D.C. police officer whose health insurance could not cover a sister's child who was in intensive care after being struck by a car, even though they had all lived together as an extended family unit.[90]

Headlined "Extended Families in the Minority Communities and Senior Citizens Are the Largest Groups of Beneficiaries Under the Law," a widely circulated flyer explained that "D.C.'s law was specifically amended to focus on extended families in the African-American, Latino and Asian-American communities," which distinguished the D.C. statute "from every other domestic partnership law in the country." "D.C.'s law," the flyer concluded in bold capital letters, "does not require physical or sexual intimacy of any kind in order to become a domestic partner."[91] And D.C.'s benefits—an employer health care deduction, hospital visitation, family and sick leave, and health insurance for city employees—fell far short of "all of the rights, privileges, and benefits of marriage."[92] Chairman Wilson renamed his bill the Health Care Benefits Expansion Act and added a last-minute amendment to allow unmarried relatives living together to register as domestic partners.[93] The Gay and Lesbian Activists Alliance mounted a publicity campaign targeting senior citizens and attendees at the Black Family Reunion on the Mall.[94]

The law's encompassing reach stemmed from motives both sincere and strategic. Charles Gossett, a political scientist and member of the commission, noted the desire of both labor unions and senior citizens' groups to include "the types of living relationships that their members frequently had" and the instrumental value of including constituencies beyond "homosexual and unmarried heterosexual couples."[95] Supporters touted the law's privatization of support and avoided public discussion of costs associated with benefit eligibility expansion.[96]

The D.C. domestic partnership skirmish became entangled with a larger battle over home rule. Congressional disapproval reenacted the spectacle of white congressmen denigrating decisions ratified by mostly Black officials—many of them long-time civil rights and feminist leaders—in a majority-Black city.[97] Pairs could register as domestic partners beginning in June 1992, but for a decade Congress refused to appropriate any funds to implement the law's grant of health insurance benefits to the part-ners of D.C. employees.

By the mid-1990s, the window of opportunity for a wholesale revision of nonmarital legal recognition appeared to have closed. In hindsight, Mad-ison, Boston, and Washington, D.C., look like the exceptions that prove the rule: by and large, domestic partnership legislation—whether framed as a nonconformist alternative to marriage for all couples or as a second-best interim step on the road to equality for gay and lesbian Americans (or both)—became synonymous with unmarried *couples'* quest for a sub-set of benefits previously available only through marital or biological ties.

Barbara Cox personified this transformation. In 1989, after six years of mostly unrequited effort in Madison, Cox saw marriage as a tool of op-pression and domestic partnership as a pale imitation of a discredited in-stitution. She despaired of using the law to make meaningful change. But Cox subsequently embraced domestic partnership and, eventually, mar-riage. By the mid-1990s, she had moved to San Diego and helped to se-cure employee benefits for same-sex partners at her new university. Cox now tackled questions such as whether domestic partnership might offer a "'parallel' or 'equivalent' alternative to marriage" and issues like interstate recognition of same-sex unions.[98] Alternative statuses, she concluded in the end, could not replicate the benefits of marriage. Cox later reflected that despite the "disdain for marriage" held by many activists, "we began to realize that winning the freedom to marry would be the only way to end [the] discrimination" faced by same-sex couples.[99] Boston's David Scondras remained far less sanguine. The pursuit of a narrower version of domestic partnership left him disappointed in "the powerful tendency to-ward assimilationism" that later culminated in marriage equality.[100]

As these stories illustrate, gay and lesbian activists differed in the de-gree to which they aspired to a more radical restructuring of family, as opposed to the inclusion of same-sex couples in the existing benefits of marriage. Key players in each of the cities that pursued more inclusive family definitions clearly sought to decenter marriage and the nuclear family, not merely to sweeten the pot for political allies of convenience. These all-embracing family definitions proved politically double-edged. They raised the specters of adverse selection and moral hazard, intensify-ing fiscal concerns. But they also created a much larger potential consti-tuency and dovetailed with movements for racial, gender, and economic justice. This breadth could be a liability if associated with radical feminist and sexual liberationist challenges to the traditional family, or it could be an asset: alliances between gay and lesbian advocates, Black and feminist lawmakers, the elderly, unions, and religious organizations spurred the kind of success in the D.C. council that proved elusive in Madison and Boston.

Securing equality in public employee benefits for "spouse equivalents" by itself proved daunting: opponents attacked any move that threatened the legal primacy of marriage or a marriage-like status for same-sex couples. Where domestic partnership laws succeeded, hard-won anti-discrimination laws and policies enabled advocates to make a narrower argument: to deny limited legal recognition for spouse-like partners was to discriminate against individuals and couples based on sexual orientation, sometimes in violation of nascent local laws.

The narrower version of domestic partnership that prevailed provided a genuine alternative to marriage for some. Domestic partnership laws that included unmarried different-sex pairs made room for couples who could marry but deliberately chose not to do so and for same-sex couples who would have avoided marriage in any event. Elderly people often served as the sympathetic face of these initiatives, but marriage-averse younger heterosexual couples could and did utilize them.[101]

Some who fought for domestic partnership viewed marriage *and* alternative statuses as desirable options that should be available to all regardless of sex.[102] Advocates wary of or opposed to marriage as an institution recognized domestic partnerships' potential either to unsettle or to reify marital primacy—or to do both simultaneously. Ultimately, domestic partnership legislation fell far short of what activists such as Cox, Scondras, and Ettelbrick initially hoped to achieve: a holistic revisioning of the family that demoted marriage, patriarchy, and heteronormativity in favor of chosen family, extended kinship, communal living, and sexual freedom. It was, nonetheless, a step toward allowing couples and occasionally other adult pairs to opt for legal recognition of their families based on function, rather than marriage.

Domestic Partnership Ascription

The concentration of domestic partnership options in progressive cities and states, the narrow range of benefits they provided, their limited uptake, and the legal and financial barriers to private relationship contracting meant that most unmarried couples, gay and straight, lacked legal recourse in the event of a partner's death or the dissolution of a long-term union.[103]

Since the 1970s, private family law had allowed for some recognition of nonmarital relationships at dissolution. But by the mid-1980s, advocates concerned about unmarried women left destitute at the end of a long relationship doubted the efficacy of existing remedies, as we saw in chapter 3. The few states that retained common law marriage required evidence of a mutual agreement between partners to be married. Even states that recognized implied contracts between nonmarital partners or equitable doctrines such as unjust enrichment rarely followed through in practice. And very few couples made express relationship agreements before living together unmarried. Meanwhile, same-sex couples could not obtain the full bundle of rights and responsibilities reserved for marriage in any state. The reformers who drafted the Principles of the Law of Family Dissolution for the American Law Institute (ALI) eventually tackled both dilemmas.[104]

Charged with recommending best practices to states with diverse family law regimes, scholars and practitioners puzzled over how the law should treat not only the dissolution of marriages but also never-formalized adult relationships. Minutes from the first convening of the ALI's ad hoc committee on family law in 1985 described "a general consensus" that laws concerning domestic relationships were inadequate and unfair, owing to their outmoded notions of family.[105] Members eventually agreed that to align the law with greater heterogeneity in domestic relationships the ALI should tackle both traditional and unconventional family structures.[106] Judith Areen and Margo Melli hoped the ALI could address the "feminization of poverty" and "the large number of mother-headed, single parent families," who were twelve times more likely to rely on public assistance after a divorce.[107]

Reformers understood family law to be in "such a state of flux" that a common work product of ALI, the "restatement" of existing law, would be incoherent at best and instantly obsolete at worst.[108] "Would you pay an architect $20,000 to design a sandcastle?" asked the legal scholar Robert Mnookin.[109] Model legislation, in the form of principles to guide courts and legislatures, seemed a more realistic goal.[110]

The project launched in earnest in 1989, with Melli, a law professor at the University of Wisconsin, as the official reporter. Melli tried to dodge controversial subjects such as same-sex marriage in favor of the "problems of family dissolution" for both "formally married" couples and those cohabiting outside of marriage, regardless of sex.[111] But those questions proved contentious enough. Over the next decade, an evolving cast of characters refined a set of principles for dissolving adult relationships.

They began with married couples, asking what role fault should play in determining ease of marital exit, property distribution, and spousal support (none, the ALI ultimately concluded); what principles should govern those financial allocations; and how courts should treat contractual agreements between engaged couples and spouses. Rationales for alimony, too, seemed undertheorized. Historically, states made alimony nominally available to "innocent" wives, but in practice relatively few, mostly affluent, women received awards. "Today," Melli wrote, "gender-based rules are out of fashion, fault often is no longer a factor to be considered, and women are expected to work and support themselves." Stark inequities persisted, especially when women's investment in caregiving reduced their earning potential after divorce.[112]

Reformers eventually settled upon a property division scheme that included a presumption of equal division of marital assets and debts (with departures for specific equitable reasons) and detailed guidelines for how to distinguish between separate and marital property.[113] Rather than "alimony" or "maintenance" or even "support," the ALI Principles "refocus[ed] the legal inquiry from need to loss," as the co-reporter Ira Ellman put it in 1993.[114] "Compensatory spousal payments" aimed directly to reimburse partners who had provided primary care for children or who had suffered a loss of earning power during the marriage for other reasons.[115] The ALI Principles substituted partners' functional roles for sex, need, or innocence from fault as the basis for spousal support.

As for nonmarital relationships, Melli's background memo in 1989 on the "Dissolution of Informal Intimate Relationships" posed the questions that divided reformers. She queried whether nonmarital partners' ability to contract should be limited in any way; what evidence should be required to find an implied contract; and whether long-term cohabitants should have lasting "economic obligations."[116]

The ALI's approach dated back to earlier writings of the co-reporter Grace Ganz Blumberg, who joined Ellman in drafting a chapter initially entitled "De Facto Spouses" and later "Domestic Unions." Blumberg, a law professor at the University of California, Los Angeles, made her name challenging the gendered division of family labor in public law. Her 1971 article "Sexism in the Code" examined federal income tax provisions that favored breadwinner/homemaker couples and penalized those with more equal earning power.[117] In 1980, she explained how a patchwork of derivative Social Security benefits ill-served working wives, divorced women, widows, and dual wage-earning couples, and she proposed egalitarian reforms.[118]

Blumberg first tackled cohabitation in 1981. She observed that despite its growing prevalence, the state recognized nonmarital relationships primarily to the detriment of unmarried couples.[119] Most benefits available to spouses, surviving widows and widowers, and occasionally divorced individuals remained unavailable to the nonmarried. But cohabitation provided grounds for termination or reduction of public assistance, spousal workers' compensation, and alimony from a previous marriage.[120] Blumberg recommended the extension of Social Security survivor insurance and workers' compensation benefits to cohabitants in "marriage-like" unions, defined as relationships of economic interdependence.

Nonmarital recognition based on economic integration departed from the dominant contract-based approach—in Blumberg's view, desirably so. In other domains, progressive legal authorities recognized contract as an "intensifier of human disadvantage by which the wealthy and powerful exploit the poor and weak." Feminist proposals for divorce reform wisely counteracted "gender-related differences in wealth and power" through equitable distribution of marital property, rehabilitative alimony, and the revaluation of homemakers' contributions. When it came to cohabitants, though, many of the same feminist reformers "heralded" contract as a "harbinger of freedom of choice, mobility, and economic well-being."[121]

Blumberg strongly disagreed with the opt-in approach to obligations. Most male-female relationship contracts entailed "the man giv[ing] up wealth that would otherwise accrue to him in order to insure the woman some semblance of economic dignity." Rational "self-interest" would "lead the man to give up as little as possible," and a woman had "scant leverage . . . to persuade him otherwise." Treating romantic partners like commercial actors negotiating at arm's length obscured "emotional factors" that inhibited the search for a better bargain: a woman who had invested in a specific relationship could not just shop for another suitor offering a superior post-dissolution financial arrangement.[122]

Blumberg catalogued the drawbacks of contracting "on the eve of cohabitation about future circumstances that can be only dimly foreseen." For one thing, "domesticity and maternity surprise and alarm even the most astute women," their expectations of "a life of achievement and independence" mugged by reality. And unmarried couples almost never memorialized their agreements in writing or with specificity. Further, the available remedies even under the most generous doctrines undervalued women's homemaking and caregiving work and sacrifice.[123]

Blumberg suggested a "simple solution": treat cohabitants like spouses when a relationship ended or one partner died. Couples who lived together for two years or more, or who had a child together and shared a residence for any length of time, should be subject to financial allocation as if they had formally married. Cohabitants could still contract around divorce laws if they wished, but the default rule would be full marital rights and responsibilities rather than none.[124]

In the years that followed, cohabitation burgeoned and became more socially acceptable. Fifteen years later, ALI's draft principles resembled Blumberg's earlier recommendations. Reformers thought property accumulated during a relationship should "certainly" be subject to division, with post-dissolution support "possibly, but less certainly" available to nonmarital partners.[125] The draft laid out functional criteria to determine "whether persons have treated each other as spouses," including "oral or written statements or promises made to one another, or representations jointly made to third parties"; "the degree to which the parties intermingled their finances" or "took other steps to formalize their responsibilities to one another, such as by naming the other as the primary beneficiary of life insurance or . . . an employee benefit plan"; "the procreation of, or joint assumption of parental functions toward, a child"; and "participation in some form of marriage or commitment ceremony."[126]

Later, the framers added even more spouse-like elements: the extent to which "the parties engaged in conduct and assumed specialized or collaborative roles in furtherance of their life together"; the degree to which "the relationship wrought change in the life of either or both parties"; whether "the parties' relationship was . . . qualitatively distinct from the relationship either party had with any other person"; the measure of "emotional or physical intimacy"; and "the parties' community reputation as a couple."[127]

Blumberg hoped that, in most cases, domestic partnership status would attach to long-term unmarried cohabiting couples unless the parties agreed otherwise.[128] Couples who shared a primary residence and had a child together usually qualified automatically, regardless of how closely their partnership resembled marriage. Persons who "maintained a common household" for a requisite period would be presumed domestic partners, "rebuttable by evidence" that they "did not share life together as a couple."[129]

The stakes felt high: the ALI Principles made domestic partners eligible for compensatory spousal payments and equal division of property at dissolution. A headline in *USA Today* summarized: "After 10-Year Study, Judicial Group Equates Married, Non-Married Couples." Blumberg told reporters, "If it looks like a marriage, it should be treated like one."[130]

David Blankenhorn of the Institute for American Values condemned the domestic partnership provisions. "Children do best in a society that recognizes and supports marriage" and that keeps marriage distinct and special, he maintained.[131] Lynn Wardle, a law professor at Brigham Young University, found the domestic partner provisions hostile toward marriage and wildly overinclusive.[132]

The ALI's proposal also attracted criticism from the left and center. Marsha Garrison castigated its false "equivalence of marriage and cohabitation."[133] Her influential critique contrasted spouses' and cohabitors' expectations and touted the superiority of marriage for both adults and children. The ALI's recommendation "would undermine the consistency, fairness, and integrity of family law," she warned. Requiring "individualized, post-relationship litigation" over the nature of a couple's relationship would "virtually ensure expense, fraud, loss of privacy, and uncertainty."[134]

Even less critical scholars shared Garrison's concerns.[135] Margaret Brinig thought women would be "better protected" by the government and third-party recognition afforded by marriage or common law marriage.[136] Elizabeth Scott proposed instead that couples who lived together for five years automatically assume obligations to one another when a relationship dissolved, unless they had agreed otherwise.[137] Scott favored a "modest" legal privileging of marriage that did not unduly stigmatize or disadvantage the nonmarried. She hesitated to jettison a contractual approach to nonmarital relationships. Marriage entailed a quid pro quo—benefits in exchange for a stable bundle of obligations—that perhaps counseled against allowing spouses to contract for a different arrangement. But it seemed "illiberal, coercive, and paternalistic" to impose such duties on short-term partners without their consent.[138]

For same-sex couples who sought relationship recognition and a path to marriage, the ALI Principles would improve upon the status quo in nearly all states by imposing domestic partner status regardless of sex.[139] Some gay and lesbian advocates who prioritized marriage viewed the ALI's proposal, like domestic partnership statutes and civil unions, as a "second-best solution," just "a waystation on the road to full marriage rights," as Terry Kogan put it.[140]

Even marital primacy's detractors divided over the ALI's proposal. Nancy Polikoff applauded the principles for "making marriage matter less" and recognizing non-sexual and/or non-monogamous relationships. Polikoff hoped eventually to move away from involuntary ascription of domestic partner status, but she called the ALI Principles "one step in the right direction."[141] Others viewed the provisions as an assimilationist trap that disciplined and domesticated queer relationships. Professor Katherine Franke worried that the ALI proposal "enlarge[ed] the shadow of marriage" by foisting obligations on unwilling individuals and circumscribing possibilities for more liberatory ways of living.[142] To Franke, the proposal was less a departure from the privileging of marriage than an extension of it.

The ALI's defenders had answers to some of these objections at the ready. Blumberg and Ellman insisted that ascription *encouraged* marriage by removing incentives for financially advantaged partners to avoid tying the knot. Those who wished to dodge post-dissolution obligations could marry and simply contract around the default rules, which would apply even if they never formalized their relationship. ALI supporters also questioned the assumption that cohabitants eschewed marriage to avoid future legal obligations. Studies showed that couples were largely oblivious to the financial consequences of marriage, divorce, or cohabitation. Since most couples did not enter into formal agreements, supporters argued, better to place the burden on the economically advantaged partner to contract around a default rule of sharing.

But objections from critics reflected deeper differences even among those who shared the ALI's desire to make relationship dissolution more equitable for women and children and for same-sex couples. For some, marriage rightfully retained a special status, and domestic partnership, whether ascribed or freely chosen, should remain a second-best alternative. For others, nonmarital recognition was more than a temporary expedient to rescue women who had sacrificed for their partners and gay couples who couldn't marry: it could protect a wider range of relationships beyond the romantic and conjugal. Or, alternatives to marriage might further entrench the law's imposition of support obligations on family members and ease the pressure on government to provide universal benefits regardless of family status.

Functional Parenthood

By the early 1990s, questions about parental recognition loomed large on the ALI reformers' agenda. For more than a decade, sex equality norms had prompted courts to reconsider maternal preferences in child

custody disputes.[143] Efforts to hold fathers liable for child support regardless of marital status sparked a reconsideration of who deserved the
rights and prerogatives of parenthood, as we saw in chapter 7. Beginning
in the early 1970s, custody disputes involving women who formed post-
divorce relationships with other women attracted growing attention to
the legal treatment of parents' nonmarital sexual conduct generally and
lesbian motherhood in particular.

At mid-century, visible nonmarital intimacy often rendered a divorced mother presumptively unfit, especially if a court saw her as a re-
peat offender, insufficiently contrite, or notorious in the community. By
the early 1970s many courts had begun to require some showing of harm
to children to disqualify an otherwise fit mother.[144] To be sure, women
still suffered harsh consequences for nonmarital sex.[145] In 1979 an Illinois
decision sanctioned Jacqueline Jarrett, a divorced mother whose boyfriend moved in with Jarrett and her children, with loss of custody.[146] But
judges often applied a functional standard, requiring proof of negative
impact before denying custody or restricting visitation.[147]

For mothers in relationships with women the landscape also began
to shift, although same-sex intimacy often received a chillier judicial reception. The standard announced by courts, be it a per se rule that automatically denied custody based on sexual orientation or a nexus test that
required a showing of harm to children, may have influenced outcomes
to some degree. Still, because custody determinations followed the "best
interests of the child," judges had virtually limitless discretion with few
checks on judicial bias.[148]

Surveying the field in 1976, the lesbian feminist lawyers Nancy Polikoff and Nan Hunter emphasized that while it beat automatic disquali-
fication, a "nexus requirement" left plenty of room for degrading
assumptions.[149] Lesbian and gay parents battled a hydra of allegations
and moral judgments in custody disputes—moral contagion; community
ostracism; revulsion at displays of same-sex affection or intimacy; and
fears about drawing children into a "homosexual lifestyle," non-normative gender roles, or gay activism. Judges confronted with competing
claims from disapproving relatives sometimes ignored the traditional
presumption that preferred fit "natural" parents over nonparents.[150]
Often, courts merely "inched beyond the point of treating the *status* of
lesbianism as per se unfitness to the point of treating the *practice* of lesbianism as per se unfitness," Hunter and Polikoff observed.[151]

Many judges who did allow custody or visitation imposed onerous conditions: third-party supervision, regular home visits from social services,

termination of any same-sex conduct or cohabitation, and concealment of parents' intimate lives from children and the community.[152] In one high-profile case, Sandy Schuster and Madeleine Isaacson obtained custody of the children from their marriages over the fathers' objections, on the condition that the women cease living together. They moved into "adjoining apartments" with their eight children and functioned as a single household; eventually their years-long custody battle culminated in a narrow victory in the state supreme court.[153] Others could not circumvent court-ordered conditions. In one typical case, Jane Irish unsuccessfully appealed a Michigan trial court's finding that because her "lesbian relationship was detrimental to the health and upbringing" of her children, Irish could not engage in any "intimate sexual conduct" or have her partner stay overnight during visitation.[154]

Lesbian mothers faced a minefield of potential incursions by hostile relatives and state actors. Some hid their same-sex desire.[155] But concealing one's sexuality, an inviting short-term expedient, could later support a successful change of custody motion. In one highly publicized case, Mary Jo Risher easily obtained custody of her two sons as her fourteen-year marriage ended, but when her former husband, Doug, now remarried, learned that she had moved in with another divorced mother, he pounced. In 1975, a Dallas jury heard testimony on questions such as whether Risher had multiple sexual partners, loved her partner more than her young son, or expressed physical affection in his presence. Lawyers probed whether lesbian mothers could raise "masculine" boys or model stereotypical male adult roles. The trial culminated in a heart-wrenching scene captured on camera: Mary Jo weeping inconsolably after the verdict in Doug's favor was read.[156]

Lesbianism was a tempting cudgel even for a tolerant father, not to mention a hostile ex-spouse or relative. Rosalie Davies's role as a "public lesbian activist" haunted her efforts to obtain more than a few weeks' annual visitation when her ex-husband remarried and attempted to move with their two children and his new wife to Canada from Pennsylvania in 1974. "It was too late to pretend heterosexuality," "too late to promise to be good," she recalled. And the "average judge" would not accept lesbianism as a "positive behavior" deserving of equal treatment.[157] Davies's children voluntarily returned to her the following year, but "the moment of loss was irreparable." Her travails led Davies to found Custody Advocacy for Lesbian Mothers (CALM), earn a law degree, and devote her career to helping similarly situated women. Other grassroots support and legal defense groups emerged across the country.[158]

Given steep odds in court, Hunter and Polikoff advised lesbian parents to avoid a custody trial while keeping an eye on potential future litigation.[159] Sue Overstreet's marriage disintegrated in the early 1980s, and she negotiated in vain before relinquishing custody of her children, two and six years old, to her estranged husband in exchange for visitation rights, fearful that a "prolonged court battle would have ended similarly, if not worse." Even after her ex-husband's sexual abuse of their older daughter came to light, she faced an uphill battle to regain custody when he told police that she was a lesbian. Overstreet "testified for hours" in a courtroom "circus" about the most intimate details of her life. The fight made Overstreet "the relentless warrior" she "had always wanted to be," and she eventually prevailed.[160]

Many others were not so fortunate. Minnie Bruce Pratt's wrenching poem "The Child Taken from the Mother," published in 1986, described her decision to relinquish custody of two children in the mid-1970s. She feared losing all access to her sons if she fought her ex-husband in court, and running away with them seemed like "no way for children to live." She wrote: "I did the best I could. It was not enough."[161] For some mothers, not much had changed even two decades later. In 1995, Mary Ward lost custody to her ex-husband, who had served prison time for killing his first wife, because a Florida judge thought Ward's eleven-year-old daughter "should be given the opportunity and the option to live in a non-lesbian world."[162]

Often lesbian mothers avoided court for fear that ensuing publicity would mean the loss of jobs, family support, and access to their children altogether.[163] If a trial was unavoidable, Hunter and Polikoff urged mothers to focus on evidence about the quality of their parent-child relationships and the harm a separation would cause their children. Invoking constitutional arguments about discrimination or the civil rights of gay and lesbian Americans only invited trouble. Litigate motherhood, not lesbianism, the advocates cautioned. Notwithstanding this advice some gay and lesbian parents did make constitutional claims: they argued that denying them access to their children violated due process, equal protection, family privacy, and freedom of association.[164]

Lesbian mothers, like their straight counterparts, stood to benefit from assumptions about the primacy of the mother-child bond. And because mothers usually received custody, they could invoke continuity of care, a mainstay of best-interests analysis. But the same feminist currents that weakened restrictive gender norms and challenged the constraints of marital heterosexuality also helped to erode courts' maternal preference. As fathers' claims to sex-neutral custody determinations and to presumptions in favor of joint custody gained traction, formal equality ill-served mothers who had invested disproportionately in family caregiving. In 1982, Polikoff, by then a staff attorney with the Women's Legal Defense Fund, refuted the contention of fathers' rights activists that custody decisions favored mothers.[165] In fact, fathers won close to half of the few contested cases because of superior financial resources, new marriages to wives who could provide primary childcare, and bias against working mothers. Polikoff favored a "sex-neutral primary caretaker standard" that prioritized parents who functioned as chief caregivers.[166]

This primary caretaker standard—which looked to parents' functional roles—could improve upon both maternal preference and the highly discretionary best-interests inquiry. Polikoff harbored no illusions of functionalism as a panacea, however. By the mid-1980s, about half of U.S. states had adopted a nexus test for adjudicating custody disputes involving lesbian and gay parents.[167] But even the friendlier jurisdictions pressured lesbians to conform to patriarchal norms or lose their children. Polikoff wrote candidly in 1986 that zealous representation entailed compromises: "middle-class values, middle-of-the-road political beliefs, repressed sexuality, and sex-role-stereotyped behavior" won custody disputes, while "communal child-rearing arrangements, radical feminist activism, [and] sexual experimentation" doomed lesbian mothers in court. When empirical studies showed that lesbians' "sex-role behavior and attitudes toward ideal child behavior" differed little from those of straight mothers, Polikoff's "immediate response as a lawyer was to be elated. . . . But as a lesbian, a feminist, and a mother with a vision of an entirely different way of raising our children, I was horrified." Polikoff feared that her "role within the system" had "a conservatizing effect on all gay and lesbian people."[168]

Affirmative steps would be necessary to protect lesbians' parental rights, Polikoff argued: foremost among them, paving an independent path to parenthood for lesbian and gay adults. Before 1980, most conflicts over lesbian parenthood arose after a marriage ended and the father challenged a mother's right to custody when she began a relationship with another woman. Though these disputes still arose, another scenario became increasingly common: through insemination, adoption, in vitro fertilization, and occasionally intercourse with men, lesbian couples formed intentional families in a "gayby boom" that accelerated in the 1980s and 1990s.

These couples could not establish formal parent-child bonds for both partners through genetics or gestation or marriage, nor were they permitted to jointly adopt children. Even in California, the vanguard of family law innovation, official state policy prohibited adoption by unmarried couples until 1999.[169] Co-parents therefore remained legal strangers to their children even when they assumed an equal or greater caregiving role. This meant not only that they lacked parental rights during a relationship but also that co-parents lost any right to see their children after a relationship ended or the legally recognized parent died.

Just as lawyers urged couples to use private instruments such as contracts, power of attorney, and joint property ownership to compensate for their inability to marry, they also encouraged lesbian mothers to create legal documents such as wills and trusts, guardianship, and co-parenting agreements as proof of a parent-like relationship.[170] Such partial, piecemeal solutions required resources and left many co-parents unprotected. Further, for most unrecognized co-parents—unlike couples who welcomed alternatives to marriage such as domestic partnership—incomplete simulations of legal parenthood amounted to precarity, not liberation.

A co-parent's plight worsened if calamity befell her partner or their relationship. Susan Hamilton's death in a car crash in 1989 left her partner of twelve years, Susan Bellemare, fighting for custody of their fourteen-month-old son, Collin. Hamilton's will, executed while she was trying to become pregnant, stipulated that Bellemare should be the legal guardian of her future child. After Bellemare recuperated from her own injuries, Hamilton's parents contested the will and sought permanent custody. An initial hearing gave Bellemare temporary custody based on her earlier agreement with the Hamiltons that they care for Collin only until she recovered, but it took more than two years of litigation to secure legal guardianship and primary custody. Co-parents whose partners passed away often lost custody during protracted legal disputes, even if they eventually encountered sympathetic judges.[171]

Nonbiological parents faced especially steep odds when relationships dissolved, because the law favored a child's "natural" parent. Battles between estranged mothers began to appear on the dockets of organizations such as the National Center for Lesbian Rights (NCLR) and Lambda Legal in the 1980s and 1990s. A small cadre of advocates—including Polikoff, now a law professor at American University, Paula Ettelbrick at Lambda, and Roberta Achtenberg at NCLR—strategized in

D.C., New York, and San Francisco, while a handful of courts began to grant second-parent adoptions on an ad hoc basis.

Lack of a marital or biological tie prompted co-parents' reliance on functional definitions of parenthood.[172] In loco parentis, a common law doctrine used mostly to recognize stepparents' visitation rights, required a showing that a nonparent stepped voluntarily and intentionally into a parental role. Equitable estoppel, invoked to prevent mothers from excluding nonbiological fathers from their children's lives and to impose support obligations on men not recognized as legal fathers, looked to evidence that parties relied on the adult in question to play a parental role. Lawyers also creatively used the nonmarital fathers cases to argue that biology should not trump intent and function in determining parentage.[173]

In the 1990s additional functional parenthood definitions emerged, variously labeled "de facto" or "equitable" or "psychological" parenthood. Standards varied in whether they required a prospective parent to reside with the child, stipulated a particular relationship duration, emphasized caretaking tasks versus emotional bonds or financial support, or mandated consent by the legal parent(s) to the formation of a parent-child relationship.[174] The stakes of recognition also spanned a spectrum, from a right to visitation only where its denial would cause substantial harm to the child all the way up to full parental status and the ability to petition for sole physical and legal custody.

Functionalism's rise called into question parenthood's exclusivity and indivisibility. Previously, lawmakers and judges often assumed that a child should have no more than two legal parents, each with a full complement of rights and duties. Adoption of infants traditionally entailed the termination of birth parents' rights as well as measures to conceal their identity and vest adoptive parents with the prerogatives of natural parents. Most states allowed the spouses of legal parents to adopt only on the condition that the second biological parent's rights terminated.

Gradually, the hegemony of these assumptions began to wane. In 1984, an influential article by the legal scholar Katharine Bartlett, "Rethinking Exclusive Parenthood," endorsed recognition of "de facto parenting relationships without severing the child's relationship with natural or legal parents."[175] Recognition for multiple parents could allow a biological father to remain a legal parent after a stepfather adoption; birth parents could avoid termination of parental rights and banishment from an adopted child's life; and a lesbian co-parent could gain legal recognition while maintaining legal ties between the child and the biological or adoptive mother.

In 1989 a Supreme Court case that pitted a prospective stepfather against a biological father underscored the costs of exclusive parenthood. In *Michael H. v. Gerald D.*, Michael Hirschensohn fought for parental rights over his biological daughter, Victoria, after her mother, Carole, married Gerald Dearing, who sought a stepparent adoption. In the case of *Lehr v. Robertson* (1983), discussed in chapter 7, the mother had prevented the biological father from establishing a relationship with their child. By contrast, both Hirschensohn and Dearing had lived with and "held out" Victoria as their own. A guardian ad litem argued that allowing both men to maintain a parental relationship would best serve Victoria's interests, but a divided Court upheld the California law that preferred Gerald as Victoria's sole legal father. Justice Antonin Scalia rejected in scathing terms any constitutional right for a nonmarital father to disrupt the integrity of an "intact marital family." The Court assumed that either Gerald or Michael, but not both, could be Victoria's legal father and that only her legal father had any claim to access.[176]

Michael H. was a battle between marriage and biology, with intricate collateral consequences for nonbiological parents. On one hand, Scalia credited Gerald's victory to his marital status—and marriage remained out of reach for many seeking to gain or retain parental rights over a child they helped raise, including lesbian and gay co-parents. On the other hand, *Michael H.* confirmed that biology did not always trump the relationship between a legal parent and her partner. Read together with *Lehr*, which established that biology alone did not require states to recognize a nonmarital father's legal parentage, *Michael H.*—despite its strident rhetoric valorizing the traditional marital family—ironically provided a legal opening for lesbian and gay co-parents to argue that functioning as a parent might be more important than a genetic tie.[177]

Recognition of nonbiological parents suffered a setback in 1991, when the New York Court of Appeals rejected Alison Davis's bid for legal recognition of her relationship to Alex, the biological son of Davis's former partner, Virginia Martin. Paula Ettelbrick, Davis's attorney, believed *Alison D.* had strong facts: Davis and Martin had planned Alex's conception and raised him together alongside his sister Avery, Davis's biological child, from birth to age six, including for a time after the couple separated.[178] Furthermore, in 1989 New York's highest court had ruled in *Braschi v. Stahl Associates* that a deceased tenant's same-sex life partner should be considered "family" for purposes of retaining his rent-controlled apartment.[179] Heralded as a landmark case for gay rights, *Braschi* embraced a functional definition of family: the court looked to the couple's financial interdependence, mutual care and support, and reputation as lifelong companions.[180]

However, two years later, the New York court rejected Ettelbrick's de facto parenthood, in loco parentis, and equitable estoppel arguments—based on "functional indicia"—over a lone dissent.[181] A similar decision in California denied parental rights to Micki Graham in 1991 despite her role as primary parent to Kate and Micah, the biological children of her former partner Nancy Springer, with tragic results: only after Springer's 1997 death in a car accident and protracted legal proceedings was Graham able to establish guardianship. The precedent likely denied hundreds of lesbian co-parents access to the children they had raised.[182]

This unreliable patchwork of legal doctrines, capricious judicial assessments, and the practical and dignitary harms of parenting without legal status led advocates to seek a way to establish a legal parent-child relationship *before* disaster or dissolution struck. If states allowed a second mother or father to adopt a child they planned to co-parent, nonbiological parents would have the full complement of parental rights. Again, existing law provided some precedent: stepparents could petition to adopt their spouses' children without terminating the spouse's parental rights, for example, and married couples could jointly adopt. But because every state had its own body of complex and idiosyncratic adoption laws and practices and no statute contemplated the possibility of same-sex co-parents, couples litigated second-parent adoption cases state by state too.

In theory, second-parent adoption promised formal legal recognition that would shield co-parents from questioning by school officials, doctors, nurses, and bureaucrats and obviate the need to apply a functional standard at death or dissolution. In practice, couples endured the same intrusive assessments of their personal lives that applied to prospective parents seeking to adopt a child with whom they had no pre-existing relationship. A letter from the New York attorney Betty Levinson to prospective lesbian and gay clients posed forty-two discrete questions about ethnic heritage, religious practices, immigration, military service, physical and mental health, income and financial status, the physical appearance of house and person, and the reactions of relatives and friends. Levinson requested "a fairly specific narrative of your family life—such as whether Jane acted as Jill's Lamaze coach, the nature of your daughter/son's current relationship with extended family, and the social network in which you live." "Be overinclusive," Levinson encouraged.[183]

Lesbian parents then faced a phalanx of evaluators. Typical state adoption regulations required a pre-placement inquiry that included a home visit and personal interview in addition to inquiries on topics such as those Levinson outlined.[184] Valerie C. and Diane F., who obtained New York's first second-parent adoption in 1992, enlisted a social worker to conduct a home study; Surrogate (Judge) Eve Preminger appointed the feminist law professor Sylvia Law of NYU as guardian ad litem for the couple's son, Evan, and asked a second social worker to "conduct an independent investigation" and write yet another report on the suitability of their home.[185]

Couples appeared before judges who exercised virtually unchecked discretion to grant or deny a second-parent adoption. Briefs detailed how both parents decided together to conceive or adopt; provided daily support and care to their children; engaged in joint medical and educational decision-making; and functioned interchangeably and irreplaceably as parents. Polikoff's forty-four-page submission to the D.C. Superior Court in one early case recounted a decade of "love, empathy, partnership and commitment" between Laura Solomon and Victoria Lane, special education professionals with two children. Solomon gave birth to Tess and Lane adopted Maya through a family connection in Nicaragua.[186] The couple had exchanged wedding rings in a 1983 ceremony, purchased a home together, and joined a local group of lesbians considering motherhood. During Solomon's pregnancy the couple "signed a contract detailing their commitment to joint childrearing." This case underscored the critical importance of second-parent adoption: Lane died two years later in a car accident that otherwise would have left Maya an orphan.[187]

Lane and Solomon were among a small but growing number of lesbian and gay co-parents who obtained second-parent adoptions.[188] These victories came at a cost even to the families who ultimately prevailed, and especially to those who did not—or never tried. Expense and hassle discouraged many couples. Even some with the wherewithal to hire an attorney and other experts recoiled at the prospect of inviting the state into their homes to inspect their living arrangements and family dynamics. "Lesbians in functioning family units, suffering no state intervention, are unlikely to want to draw attention to their families by entering the adoption system," as Polikoff wrote in 1990.[189]

Especially for those without means, state oversight and intervention could easily backfire. In Black, Indigenous, and poor communities, home visits from social workers and other professionals raised the specter of child removal. And even if states had routinely granted second-parent adoptions, many co-parents could not or would not obtain formal legal recognition in advance. The availability of functional parent doctrines, however imperfect, remained crucial to the many co-parents who never formalized a parent-child relationship.

At the same time, functional definitions developed for different purposes translated awkwardly and sometimes painfully into this context. Some lesbian mothers chose known sperm donors who developed relationships with the children they helped to conceive. In one high-profile case, Robin Young and Sandy Russo each gave birth to a daughter using different donors, determined to form a family unit defined by relationships, not biology. The donor for their second child, Ry, was Tom Steel, a prominent gay lawyer for gay clients. Young, Russo, and Steel agreed that Steel would have no parental rights or responsibilities; the mothers wished to be the girls' only parents. Steel, his partner Milton, and Milton's son visited the Russo-Young family several times beginning when Ry was five, and Steel formed what he considered to be a parental bond. After the adults disagreed about Steel's role, he sued to establish parentage—a move that Ry's mothers perceived as endangering not only their own family but all lesbian co-parents and children.

The dispute between Steel and the Russo-Youngs highlighted how functional parent standards—and, moreover, the recognition of multiple parents—could cut both ways: Russo had acted as Ry's parent since birth, but Steel arguably could claim both a biological connection and an established relationship with Ry under the "biology-plus" standard articulated in *Lehr*. And without marriage, an impossibility at the time, Russo could not invoke *Michael H.*'s protection for the marital family unit. Some advocates and families sought more flexible and inclusive standards that might recognize more than two legal parents, or at least afford visitation rights to adults other than a child's primary parental figures. Others, like the Russo-Youngs, prized exclusive parental status and invoked family privacy to protect their prerogatives. Lesbian parents, Russo and Young insisted, should have the same right to exclude interlopers as any other "nuclear family."[190]

"We must remember," Polikoff wrote in 1986, "that our efforts are not made in a vacuum."[191] That functional definitions cut both ways is illustrated by the Supreme Court case *Troxel v. Granville* (2000). After the death of her children's (nonmarital) father, Brad Troxel, Tommie Granville objected to Troxel's parents' proposed visitation plan and challenged a Washington statute that allowed nonparents wide latitude to petition for visitation.[192] Such liberal visitation laws benefited lesbian co-parents who lacked legal ties to their partners' biological children. But these laws also opened the door for grandparents and other disapproving relatives to undermine gay and lesbian parents' rights. Polikoff recommended a "strong preference for parents over non-parents"—a functional parenthood that would recognize gay and lesbian co-parents without diluting parental prerogatives or providing an intermediate quasi-parental status.[193]

Advocates continued to worry that prioritizing functional relationships over biological ties could undermine family reunification in cases where the state had separated families of origin in the name of child welfare.[194] Favoring those who had provided a child's daily care most consistently and recently might enable foster parents or other temporary caregivers to prevail over birth parents accused of neglect, struggling with substance use, or living with a disability. Joseph Goldstein, Anna Freud, and Albert Solnit argued that custody should be awarded to the "psychological parent": "one, who on a continuing day to day basis, through interaction, companionship, interplay, and mutuality, fulfills the child's psychological needs for a parent, as well as the child's physical needs." This individual could be "a biological, adoptive, foster, or common-law parent, or any other person."[195]

Native American advocates recognized the danger immediately: in 1976 the book *Indian Family Defense* warned of psychological parenthood's potentially catastrophic implications for Native families.[196] *Smith v. Organization of Foster Families for Equality and Reform (OFFER)* (1977) showcased the complicated politics of functional standards: even advocates who usually agreed that birth parents' prerogatives deserved priority disagreed about whether foster parents should have the right to a hearing before a child could be transferred from their home.[197]

Peggy Cooper Davis wrote in 1984 of her increasing unease during three years as a New York family court judge about how courts and social workers applied the concept of psychological parenthood.[198] Goldstein, Freud, and Solnit had cautioned against unnecessary state intervention in families: only under extreme circumstances, they said, should children be permanently separated from their parents.[199] But between 1968 and 1980, parental rights terminations in New York increased more than eighteenfold, as courts interpreted state law to mandate termination after as little as a year in foster care "without satisfactory progress toward return to the biological home."[200] Such interpretations, combined with unchecked discretion of government agents, likely distorted psychological parenthood's intended application.[201]

Davis's concerns grew as she watched a birth mother with schizophrenia fight valiantly to retain her parental rights, interviewed "children who had been in care for years but were nevertheless adamant in their wish to return to or maintain contact with their biological families," and heard from foster parents who "empathized with biological parents" and "were comfortable with the continuation of multiple attachments and dependencies." Ironically, Davis observed, whereas conventional wisdom increasingly favored contact with noncustodial parents post-divorce as "essential to emotional adjustment," authorities often discounted the damage done to children when removal undermined family bonds and stability in a child's primary attachments.[202]

Polikoff, too, flagged the "frightening" danger of misuse: psychological parenthood was "used against mothers, mostly poor ones, who require the extensive assistance of relatives, friends, or even baby sitters."[203] She and Nan Hunter emphasized the importance of seeing lesbian mothers' rights as part of a larger struggle: in 1979, they wrote of "millions of women ... who also face a daily threat of losing custody ... welfare mothers, incarcerated mothers, politically radical mothers, heterosexual mothers who are not married to their sexual partners, or even sometimes mothers with jobs outside their homes."[204]

Lesbian co-parents' fight intersected with the growing conflict between a movement for "children's rights" and the struggles of marginalized parents to keep their children. Many advocates strategically spotlighted the impact on children of losing important relationships to adults rather than the rights (constitutional or otherwise) of those adults. An amicus brief in support of Alison Davis filed by the law professors Martha Minow and David Chambers proposed a functional standard that centered children's interest in maintaining established relationships with parent-like adults regardless of marital status or sexual orientation.[205] Polikoff and Hunter, too, capitalized on courts' solicitude for children when they counseled litigants to emphasize mother-child relationships rather than parents' constitutional prerogatives. A focus on children could backfire, however. If a dispute came down to a child's birth parents—whom decision-makers might perceive as deviant or troubled—versus caregivers with greater social and financial capital or more conventional lifestyles, then functional standards might redound to parents' detriment.[206]

Some feminists also worried that functional standards could empower men to use parental rights as a weapon of control over women.
Mothers already feared that a man's biological tie to a child might grant
him parental prerogatives and leverage in a violent relationship. Now
male partners who could invoke relationships developed with genetically
unrelated children while living together might threaten mothers with loss
of custody or obtain visitation rights that enabled continued abuse and
harassment.[207] Functional parenthood proponents disagreed, too, about
what bundle of rights and responsibilities should adhere to individuals
who did obtain legal parental recognition.

Advocates responded variously to these challenges. Ettelbrick suggested functional doctrines tailored to lesbian couples who intentionally
planned families, rather than all-purpose standards that might short-
change lesbians or endanger straight women.[208] Polikoff proposed a general designation of equitable parenthood that any adult could invoke,
but she emphasized the importance of requiring that the existing legal
parent(s)—biological, adoptive, or otherwise—had consented to the other
adult's formation of a parent-child relationship.[209]

Polikoff's vision influenced deliberations by the ALI as reformers
fashioned functional parent categories. An early draft of the ALI's Principles of the Law of Family Dissolution granted full parental status to "a
person whose parental relationship . . . arose because the person lived in
a same sex relationship with the child's legal parent."[210] A revised version
provided instead that "a person, who has lived in a family relationship
with a child and the child's parent and . . . has sole physical custody of a
child and either sole or shared parental authority, may be treated as a
stepparent . . . when the family relationship dissolves." The drafters decided to treat nonmarital cohabitants and marital partnerships similarly
because "psychological ties" between adults and children did not depend
upon the adults' horizontal relationships or co-parents' sex; "continuity
of care by a primary caretaker" was what mattered.[211]

Critics objected to the ALI's proposals on various grounds. Professor
Robin Fretwell Wilson worried that mothers' boyfriends and new husbands would exploit de facto parent doctrines to prey upon children.[212]
John DeWitt Gregory, a law professor, former NAACP leader, and welfare
rights and legal aid lawyer, feared that custody or visitation rights for nonparents would undercut already fragile family autonomy, especially in poor
and low-income communities. Gregory valued "the once sacrosanct authority of parents to make decisions with respect to the control and care of

their children" and sought to extend those rights beyond the "intact family" to include unmarried parents.[213]

The conservative scholar Lynn Wardle, by contrast, expressed "serious reservations" about including gay and lesbian partners. He cited AIDS, the "rampant" "breakdown of families," "gender confusion," and what he called "disturbing evidence" of "disproportionate promiscuity and pedophilia among homosexuals."[214] Like many opponents on the right, Wardle branded "homosexual parenting" (as well as same-sex marriage) as dangerous to children's welfare.[215] More generally, Wardle condemned the assertion in a 1992 ALI draft that "for the child, the parental relationship is the same whether or not the adults were married."[216] To Wardle and other social conservatives, nothing could be further from the truth.

Functional parenthood, like domestic partnership, had a complex relationship to marriage's legal primacy. Douglas NeJaime has shown that in California during the 1990s advocates used same-sex couples' marriage-like relationships to bolster nonbiological, nonmarital claims to parentage. In so doing, they redefined parenthood more generally to focus on intent and function rather than marriage, biology, and gender difference. These strategies could just as easily blur the lines between marriage and non-marriage as reinforce them.[217] And progressive outcomes remained contingent upon courts' and lawmakers' openness to revising the legal and social meanings of parenthood. Moreover, functional standards had conservative and assimilationist as well as subversive elements: making marriage and biology matter less did not necessarily expand possibilities for families that transgressed existing norms.

As in debates over "alternative families" ordinances, reformers faced a choice between including gay and lesbian partners and parents in existing structures of family or redefining those structures. In both contexts, external constraints limited their options: formidable opponents who resisted both marriage equality and a broader redefinition of family, for one. Even modest steps toward extending benefits beyond the nuclear family ran aground because of their fiscal as well as moral implications.

Internal tensions also littered the path to reform. Some reformers worried about well-intentioned efforts to create universal categories of partnership and parentage that encompassed both different-sex and same-sex couples. It was one thing to create a stopgap measure for gay and lesbian couples, but another to ascribe domestic partner status to those who could marry but didn't. It was one thing to develop functional definitions of parenthood to accommodate nonbiological lesbian co-parents, and another to open the door to a mother's ex-boyfriend who might exploit de facto parent status to abuse his former partner or her children.[218]

Functional definitions also preserved and extended the privatization of support within families: indeed, for the ALI and many reformers this was a feature, not a bug. By the end of the twentieth century, states, spurred by federal mandates and incentives, imposed financial support obligations on nonmarital and divorced fathers. Revisions to the Uniform Parentage Act (UPA) in 2000 and 2002 extended assisted reproduction protocols to unmarried different-sex couples; recommended mechanisms for the voluntary establishment of paternity; and reinstated provisions that recognized as parents men who "held out" nonmarital and potentially nonbiological children as their own.

The UPA drafters left "issues relating to same-sex couples . . . to another day."[219] The American Law Institute, by contrast, fashioned sex-neutral functional parent categories that triggered the right to petition for access to children. The final ALI Principles, promulgated in 2002, recommended "de facto parenthood" for an adult who, with the consent of a legal parent (or because of the parent's incapacity), assumed equal or greater caregiving responsibility, not for financial compensation, while living with the child for at least two years. "Parenthood by estoppel" encompassed individuals who were liable for child support or who "assumed full and permanent parenting responsibilities with the agreement of the child's legal parent(s)." Courts often used doctrines of estoppel to impose support obligations on adults; the ALI's usage enabled adults who functioned as caregivers and/or providers to receive an allocation of custodial time.[220] In effect, the ALI's definitions proposed that all functional parents—regardless of sex, marital status, or genetic tie—should be able to claim parental rights as well as obligations.

Of all the efforts described in this chapter, functional definitions of parenthood enjoyed the most success, followed by domestic partnership laws that allowed nonmarried couples to register voluntarily for a subset of rights and obligations previously reserved for the married. The ALI's proposal to ascribe domestic partnership to couples who met marriage-like criteria faced objections across the ideological spectrum. The greater willingness to impose duties on parents than on partners tracked their different fiscal impacts. Imposing parental obligations obviated the need for state support of children, whereas a refusal to recognize obligations adults owed to one another often did not require the state to step in instead. Children should not be punished for the sins of their parents, but adults could pay for their failure to secure the benefits of marriage.

The use of functional definitions of parenthood to enforce parental obligations highlighted a larger truth about efforts to expand the definition of family. Even if "marriage mattered less," as Polikoff put it, family relationships—formal or functional—remained primary as a source of financial support and of social and economic benefits. And broadening who counted as family had limited impact on larger distributive inequalities. Race and class as well as gender and sexual orientation affected who had a parent or a partner who was able to provide financial support.

For those who yearned for more transformative change, reform of inter se legal rights and responsibilities always came up short. Even if states adopted the ALI Principles wholesale (none did, or even came close), neither third parties nor the government would be obliged to recognize domestic partners for purposes of allocating benefits or otherwise. Rules about property division and spousal support meant little to couples who had few assets and little human capital to share. Expanding the definition of family to include nonconjugal relationships and alternative household configurations only went so far. Redistribution within families at dissolution might privatize dependency within the family but did little to address inequality between families or to improve life prospects for poor and low-income Americans, as reformers themselves recognized. To address the inequities that increasingly correlated with marital status, an expansion of societal responsibility for public welfare and the disestablishment of family relationships as the basis for distribution would be necessary. Developments at the federal level, however, pointed in the opposite direction.

CHAPTER NINE

Securing Marital Privilege

"ARRIAGE IS THE FOUNDATION of a successful society," proclaimed the preamble to the welfare reform bill that President Bill Clinton signed into law in 1996. The Personal Responsibility and Work Opportunity Reconciliation Act (PRWORA) posited welfare largesse and nonmarital childbearing as drivers of poverty curable by mothers' employment, fathers' financial support, and, most of all, marriage. Lawmakers recited a litany of pathologies traceable, in their view, to AFDC's shortcomings: "teen pregnancy," "out-of-wedlock" births, absent fathers, and inadequate child support orders; lower birth weights, inferior cognitive abilities, violent crime, juvenile incarceration, and welfare "dependency"—often intergenerational. Strikingly, PRWORA's three single-spaced pages of findings mentioned no causes of poverty and associated social ills other than childbearing outside of marriage.[1]

PRWORA replaced the beleaguered AFDC program with Temporary Assistance to Needy Families (TANF), which incorporated new time limits, work requirements, and childbearing disincentives. The law delegated to states discretion to determine eligibility and spending priorities, but it pushed them to promote marriage and adoption and to reduce nonmarital births. The act blessed policies that discouraged childbearing by poor mothers by limiting cash assistance for children born to families already receiving aid. PRWORA also strengthened sanctions for mothers who did not cooperate with authorities in establishing paternity and obtaining child support.[2]

PRWORA withdrew statutory entitlement to public assistance (minimal as it had been) based on need. The law's time-limited aid forced mothers to find employment or alternative sources of funds—ideally husbands or former sexual partners—or to go without. Critics charged that lawmakers discounted barriers such as intimate partner violence, the dearth of jobs that paid a living wage, lack of affordable childcare and transportation, as well as individual preferences about marriage and family formation.

This conception of poverty's relationship to family political economy was decades old, but never had welfare laws been so overtly focused on the promotion of marriage as the primary cure for poverty. Not since the 1960s had the federal government allowed, much less encouraged, the denial of cash assistance to needy children because of their parents' sexual and marital behavior.

PRWORA was only the most visible piece of federal legislation that intensified marital privilege in the 1990s. Federal laws enacted between 1993 and 1997 raised the stakes of marital status and intensified disparities between married haves and unmarried have-nots. The Family and Medical Leave Act of 1993, the Defense of Marriage Act of 1996, the Adoption and Safe Families Act of 1997, and major crime and immigration legislation bolstered marital status law's function as an engine of inequality.

The triumph of marital primacy reflected not only conservatives' ascendancy but also enduring disagreements on the center-left about gender, marriage, work, and poverty. The statutes' immunity to constitutional challenge, too, was a legacy of the history recounted here. Had advocates prevailed on earlier constitutional claims to sexual privacy, reproductive freedom, and equality, many of the 1990s laws that reinforced marital privilege would have been vulnerable to attack. Courts' earlier failure to embrace advocates' expansive and creative arguments haunted their legatees.

By the turn of the century, then, a regime of marital privilege solidified, imposing ever-greater costs on those who did not or could not marry. As the price of nonmarriage grew steeper, the marriage gap widened: marital status increasingly correlated with race, socioeconomic status, and education.[3] Progressives generally, and gay and lesbian advocates in particular, still disagreed about whether winning a right to marry should be a central goal. But movement leaders' strategic choice to embrace marriage equality is understandable: by the end of the twentieth century, challenges to marital primacy likely seemed futile—and the dignitary, legal, and material benefits of marriage irresistible.

Raising the Stakes of Marital Status

In 1990 Representative Marge Roukema (R-NJ), a co-sponsor of the Family and Medical Leave Act (FMLA), described the proposed legislation as "a bill so minimal it's almost an embarrassment to present it."[4] The FMLA, the product of a decade of advocacy by women's organizations and their allies, was filled with compromises.[5] In its final form, the act provided covered employees with twelve weeks of unpaid annual leave to care for themselves, a newborn or adopted child, or another immediate relative with a serious medical condition, without losing their jobs. The FMLA afforded less time off for new mothers than the period provided in most other developed countries and offered no paid leave. The act covered only those who had worked full-time for most of the preceding year in businesses with more than fifty employees. The law formally excluded at least 40 percent of the labor force: those who worked part-time, held multiple part-time jobs, switched jobs frequently, or worked for a smaller business. As a practical matter, even eligible low-income workers rarely could afford to take unpaid leave.

The FMLA's definition of family also limited its scope: the act confined "immediate family members" to a "spouse, child, or parent." The law most obviously excluded unmarried partners of any sex and all same-sex partners, who could not marry. It also left out adults who acted as co-parents or even primary caregivers but were not legally recognized as parents. Less visibly, the FMLA provided fewer benefits to the children of solo parents: whereas children with two legal parents might benefit from the care of two adults with a total of twenty-four weeks of leave each year, children with only one eligible parent would receive a maximum of twelve.[6] Children cared for primarily by adults with whom they did not have a legal parental relationship were even worse off. As Roukema put it, the FMLA "is about kids. It's about grandma and grandpa. ... It's about the two-worker family and what it means to be middle-class in America."[7]

In short, the FMLA placed a premium on marriage, shortchanged employees who lived outside marital nuclear families, and excluded the most vulnerable workers from coverage. Low-income workers—disproportionately people of color, women, and individuals with disabilities or marginalized sexualities—were more likely to need caregiving and medical leave but far less likely to receive it. They more often lived outside of marriage and cared for or relied on care from chosen or extended family. The FMLA joined other federal laws such as Social Security that conditioned benefits on conformity to heterosexual marital norms and excluded those who most needed state support.

FMLA proponents saw the law as a start—a floor of benefits that would prompt employers to compete for workers by voluntarily offering more. But conditions for low-income families and communities improved little. Large employers seeking to attract "skilled" or professional labor did offer benefits beyond the FMLA, but only a fraction of Americans enjoyed significantly more leave than it provided, and most low-income workers received less. As the share of unionized workers continued to fall, fewer Americans could collectively bargain for a better deal, and proposed federal paid leave legislation languished.

The failure of universal health care reform in the months after the FMLA's passage further entrenched marital privilege. The Health Security Act, proposed in November 1993 by Hillary Rodham Clinton's task force, not only required employers to heavily subsidize their employees' coverage but also insured adults who lacked a job or an employed spouse.[8] Opposition from conservatives, insurance companies, and other key interest groups derailed this effort, a casualty of what the sociologist and Clinton advisor Paul Starr called "one of the great lost political opportunities in American history."[9]

The reality that access to health insurance continued to depend mostly on employment and marriage impelled gay and lesbian Americans to fight for nondiscrimination laws covering both. First introduced in 1974 by Representative Bella Abzug (D-NY), an omnibus bill that would have added sexual orientation, sex, and marital status to all provisions of the Civil Rights Act of 1964 was eventually renamed the (proposed) Employment Nondiscrimination Act (ENDA), which covered only sexual orientation and employment. Congress held hearings in 1980 and 1982. After a long hiatus in which gay activists focused on the AIDS crisis but gathered crucial support from civil rights groups, Bill Clinton's election in 1992 boded well. A debate over military service swallowed ENDA in 1993, but when the bill was reintroduced in 1994 with the support of the Leadership Conference on Civil Rights, headlined by Coretta Scott King, it attracted bipartisan support. After a hearing in September 1994 the bill seemed "in striking distance" of passage in the House and of the sixty votes needed to overcome a Senate filibuster.[10]

The GOP's takeover of Congress in November 1994 abruptly halted ENDA's momentum. Meanwhile, an unexpected legal victory shifted public attention to same-sex marriage: the Hawaii Supreme Court ruled in *Baehr v. Lewin* that the denial of marriage licenses to same-sex couples violated the state constitution's ban on sex discrimination.[11]

Although Hawaii lawmakers moved swiftly to define marriage as exclusive to different-sex couples, *Baehr* spurred conservatives to use the threat to traditional marriage for political gain. The ensuing backlash produced discriminatory measures including the federal Defense of Marriage Act (DOMA).[12] DOMA's definition of marriage as a union between a man and a woman for purposes of federal law meant that gay and lesbian couples validly married in a jurisdiction that allowed same-sex marriage (none did, as of 1996) could not receive the hundreds of federal benefits tied to marriage.[13] A second provision allowed state governments to deny recognition to marriages conducted in other states.

In May 1996 the Supreme Court's ruling in *Romer v. Evans* provided a glimmer of hope. Justice Anthony Kennedy wrote for a 6–3 majority that Colorado could not amend its constitution to ban laws intended to protect residents from discrimination based on sexual orientation.[14] Kennedy relied on the principle articulated in *U.S.D.A. v. Moreno* (1973): "A bare desire to harm a politically unpopular group" could not sustain an exclusionary law.[15] Just as congressional animus against "hippie communes" did not justify denial of food stamps to unrelated persons living together, legislators could not act solely based upon antipathy toward homosexuality.[16] Such animosity suffused the DOMA hearings, where proponents compared same-sex marriage to bestiality and warned of its threat to "the moral and spiritual survival of this nation."[17]

As the Senate debated DOMA, Senator Ted Kennedy (D-MA) negotiated a freestanding vote on the employment measure. ENDA had the necessary fifty votes to pass with Vice President Al Gore poised to break the tie, but a son's hospitalization sidelined Senator David Pryor (D-AR) and ENDA lost by one vote. DOMA, on the other hand, passed by a wide margin, 86–14, with thirty-five senators voting for both bills.[18] Clinton signed DOMA—a bill he had called "divisive and unnecessary"—into law in the middle of the night on September 21, 1996.[19] DOMA's speedy passage with veto-proof congressional majorities reflected heterosexual marriage's position as a commonsense fixture of American political life.

The support in Congress for both DOMA and ENDA mirrored public opinion polls. Only 27 percent of respondents favored same-sex marriage in 1996, yet 84 percent said gay and lesbian Americans should have "equal rights" to job opportunities.[20] Kennedy reassured

Pryor that "there will be another day" when the senator missed the ENDA vote to be at his son's bedside, but that day never came.[21] Instead, gay and lesbian Americans preemptively lost marriage rights they had not yet won and remained unprotected from employment discrimination in most jurisdictions.

Among the many federal benefits unavailable to gay and lesbian couples and others who could not marry were family preferences in immigration and citizenship law. Here, too, legislation raised the stakes of marital and socioeconomic status in the 1990s. Most federal benefits never included the undocumented, but PRWORA restricted *lawful* immigrants' access to public assistance as well. The law denied Medicaid benefits to noncitizens who immigrated legally after August 1996; severely limited immigrants' eligibility for TANF during their first five years in the United States; and withheld food stamps and Supplemental Security Income (SSI) from most noncitizens. A few states created substitute health insurance programs for some immigrants, but most did not; activism by immigrants' rights organizations restored SSI benefits to immigrants already receiving them and to pre-1996 arrivals who later became disabled.[22] Health care utilization by immigrants fell in subsequent years.[23]

Changes to immigration law also altered conditions for noncitizens and citizens with needy family members seeking to relocate to the United States for reasons of economic hardship, political repression, or family reunification. Just one month after PRWORA's enactment, President Clinton signed the Illegal Immigration Reform and Immigrant Responsibility Act (IIRIRA), which enhanced penalties for noncitizens who overstayed visas or who entered the United States without authorization. IIRIRA also discouraged immigration by those who might call upon the government for support and by family members of impoverished U.S. residents. For instance, the law upped the earnings requirement to sponsor family members and required affidavits guaranteeing that relatives, not the state, would bear responsibility for the immigrants' support. A rule that persons "likely to become a public charge" could not immigrate to the United States operated not only to exclude the poor but also to chill access to public benefits: reliance on cash assistance raised a red flag that could render individuals ineligible for entry or legal permanent residency.[24]

Because marriage to a U.S. citizen provided a unique path to naturalization, the ability to marry conferred a singular immigration privilege. Reforms in the 1980s and 1990s strengthened this marital privilege for some and weakened it for others. DOMA excluded same-sex couples from all of marriage's federal benefits, including immigration preferences. For different-sex couples, the ability to immigrate depended more than ever on economic self-support. A "dual system for dealing with immigrant spouses in need of aid" emerged: those in the United States less than two years could be deported if not self-sufficient, and immigrants who procured legal residency through their sponsoring spouses became legally dependent upon them regardless of whether those spouses in fact provided support.[25]

Surveillance and regulation of poor families in the name of child welfare also intensified. A confluence of developments in the mid-1990s encouraged swifter removal of children from the homes of "neglectful" parents. The law promoted adoption by two-parent marital families, rather than support for birth parents, as the solution. At the same time, the substitution of TANF for AFDC itself made subsistence more difficult for poor single mothers, increasing their vulnerability to charges of child neglect. PRWORA also contained incentives for TANF-eligible parents to relinquish their infants for adoption: a few states even offered cash assistance bonuses for doing so.[26]

Other federal legislative developments encouraged parental rights terminations and adoptions. The Multi-Ethnic Placement Act of 1994 eased the way for white married couples to adopt children of color, and a 1996 amendment facilitated the placement of foster children into adoptive homes. The Adoption and Safe Families Act of 1997 (ASFA) conditioned federal funding for child welfare on a requirement that, in most instances, states initiate proceedings to terminate parental rights when a child had been in foster care for fifteen of the past twenty-two months. And though attempts to repeal the Indian Child Welfare Act of 1978 (ICWA) failed, removal rates for Native children continued to rise.[27]

Intended to rescue children from purportedly dangerous conditions in birth or foster homes and "free" them for adoption by loving two-parent marital families, these policies often severed ties between birth parents and children without achieving either family reunification or a permanent adoption placement. As the Black feminist scholar Dorothy Roberts later wrote, "The coincidence of the welfare and adoption laws marked the first time in US history that the federal government mandated that states protect children from parental neglect but failed to guarantee a minimum economic safety net for impoverished families."[28] At the same time, enthusiasm across much of the political spectrum for tough-on-crime initiatives accelerated mass incarceration and intensified policing of communities of color, placing marriage further out of reach for many Americans and cementing its relationship to racial and economic privilege.[29]

Welfare Reform, Marriage, and Single Motherhood

Welfare reform, the most visible legislative sign of marriage's ascendancy, reflected the GOP's conservative bent and the emergence of the New Democrats. Bill Clinton and the Democratic Leadership Council denounced both "tax-and-spend" liberalism and "do-nothing" conservative government. From micro-lending to housing policy to welfare reform, the Clintons and their allies countered stereotypes about low-income Black single mothers with policies designed to showcase how the right incentives and public-private partnerships could empower individuals to overcome their "dependency" on government. Critics worried that those who could not marry, find a job, become an entrepreneur, or keep their relatives out of jail now ostensibly had only themselves to blame when they lost welfare benefits or public housing. Meanwhile, underlying structural inequalities went unaddressed.[30]

As Arkansas governor and presidential candidate, Clinton made welfare reform a centerpiece of his New Democratic platform and styled himself as a champion of the middle class and of hard-working, law-abiding Americans. The Republican takeover of Congress in 1994 virtually ensured that more progressive visions of government aid to the poor would face steep odds, but Clinton had long insisted that the government should abandon "handouts" and reward remunerative work and "personal responsibility."[31] In June 1994, the White House had proposed legislation that embraced this now-dominant ethos. The bill, headlined "No More Something for Nothing," included a lifetime benefit limit, mandatory paternity testing, and the "Toughest Child Support Laws Ever Proposed." This first draft also cut immigrants' benefits to fund childcare for parents, who would now be required to seek and obtain work outside the home.[32]

The GOP's counterproposals, part of its "Contract for America," went further. Republicans doubled down on the punitive elements of New Democrats' proposals and omitted health insurance expansion, childcare subsidies, and guarantees of jobs for parents who no longer qualified for cash assistance. House Speaker Newt Gingrich's suggestion that the children of young unmarried mothers should be removed from their homes and consigned to orphanages exemplified the debate's harshening tone.[33] Anti-welfare political momentum left dissenters with little more than the vain hope that Republicans would not produce a bill that Clinton could sign.

The final version of PRWORA contained many provisions familiar to those who fought the legal battles of earlier decades. For instance, families' eligibility for TANF hinged on mothers' efforts to help identify and locate biological fathers; uncooperative mothers could not receive aid.[34] Like earlier paternity disclosure mandates, the law required mothers who needed public assistance to provide personal information about their past sexual activities and relationships that nonpoor women would never be obliged to divulge. Most putative fathers of TANF-eligible children could not afford to reimburse the state for welfare expenditures, much less provide additional support, so mothers' cooperation often provided no benefit to their families. The law contained a "good cause" exception for survivors of domestic violence but allowed states to decide whether and how to implement it.[35] The act promised bonuses to states that improved their child support collection records and threatened loss of federal funds for those that did not.[36]

Rhetoric that touted welfare policy consensus across the ideological spectrum concealed enduring disagreements.[37] The strongest opposition to punitive proposals came from feminists in the welfare rights tradition.[38] Their legislative leader, Representative Patsy Takemoto Mink (D-HI), convened a conference in 1993 to air the concern that reforms attacked poor women rather than poverty. Representative Mink's counterproposal rejected the premise that mothers of young children should be forced to work outside the home and insisted that adequate childcare and access to good jobs accompany any work requirements.[39] In 1995, a coalition of "grassroots welfare rights activists, social justice advocates in mainstream women's organizations, and feminist academics" pressed President Clinton to veto PRWORA. The newly formed Women's Committee of 100 declared that "a war against poor women is a war against all women" and lobbied lawmakers, to no avail.[40]

PRWORA's feminist opponents proposed their own approach to welfare reform that valued poor single mothers' caregiving *and* paid work outside the home. But as they had in the past, advocates for women often disagreed among themselves about whose welfare to prioritize and how. Gwendolyn Mink (the daughter of Representative Mink and a political scientist) captured this dynamic in a 1998 essay detailing how many (mostly white) female Democratic lawmakers and organizations dominated by middle-class and professional women failed to appreciate the value of poor women's caregiving labor or of the government benefits on which they relied. Indeed, many believed that "poor single mothers should move from welfare to work and into financial relationships with their children's fathers."[41] The result, said Mink, was that middle-class women retained sexual and reproductive privacy rights and the ability to decide whether to marry or involve fathers in their children's lives while poor mothers were compelled "to reveal the details of intimate relationships in exchange for survival" and to "make room for biological fathers in their families."[42]

The federal child support enforcement regime augmented by PRWORA ensnared not only "uncooperative" mothers and "deadbeat" dads who could afford to pay support but didn't.[43] "Dead-broke" fathers, too, faced wage garnishment, driver's license rescission, even incarceration for nonpayment, despite courts' ostensible obligation to consider ability to pay. A complex web of interstate statutes and government agencies surveilled fathers' incomes and movements.[44] A concession won by a bipartisan coalition of women's organizations and lawmakers was telling: PRWORA's "family first" policy provided that once a family no longer received public assistance, paternal support would go to families rather than to the government as reimbursement for past expenditures. But strikingly, even this income transfer to mothers and children came at the expense of poor fathers, not the state.[45]

Familiar, too, were the objections of many liberal policymakers and advocates who opposed PRWORA primarily because the law would abandon children to poverty in the name of controlling their parents' behavior. Marian Wright Edelman, a civil rights leader, Children's Defense Fund founder, and mentor to a young Hillary Rodham, wrote an open letter to the president in November 1995. She foresaw "irreparable damage" to children if Clinton abandoned the "fundamental moral principle that an American child, regardless of the state or parents the child chanced to draw, is entitled to protection of last resort by his or her national government."[46] Her husband, Peter Edelman, and a fellow welfare policy expert, Mary Jo Bane, resigned in protest from their posts at the Department of Health and Human Services (HHS) after Clinton signed PRWORA into law in September 1996.[47]

Indeed, even key architects of earlier welfare reform and child support enforcement efforts recoiled from this more extreme retrenchment for similar, child-focused reasons. By 1990, Harry Krause, long a champion of paternal accountability, had second thoughts about policymakers' overreliance on private sources of support for impoverished children. "Looking carefully at statistics and reality," Krause concluded that "many fathers are unable to provide the support their children need to get a decent start in life, even if many try." Child support collection had become "an income transfer from poor fathers to lawyers and welfare bureaucrats," and enforcement "has not significantly improved the poorest children's lot!" In fact, half of Black children under age six lived below the federal poverty line in 1987. Children, Krause worried, had been "privatized." Taxpayers, he contended, should share with poor fathers the child support burden as a matter of fairness and self-preservation.[48]

PRWORA's preamble extolling marriage effectively codified the 1965 Moynihan Report, and many provisions echoed earlier reforms that its author had championed. But strikingly, Moynihan assailed the legislation. He continued to see rising rates of "out-of-wedlock" births and single-mother families as the leading indicator and cause of social dysfunction. Yet PRWORA's abolition of a federal entitlement to assistance, Moynihan feared, would relegate children to the vagaries of states' political whims and overwhelm local charities just as nonmarital childbearing sent more into poverty.[49]

Notably, many prominent liberal critics of TANF applauded the anti-"illegitimacy" and marriage-promotion initiatives of the early years of George W. Bush's administration. In 2001 Wendell Primus, who resigned from HHS in protest of PRWORA in 1996, co-authored an Urban Institute study that heralded a "decline in single-parent families" and an "increase in marriage and cohabitation, particularly among lower income blacks."[50] Others embraced the goal of promoting "healthy" marriages among low-income parents. Theodora Ooms of the Center for Law and Social Policy favored a "marriage-plus" model that acknowledged structural barriers to family flourishing and emphasized relationship quality rather than promoting marriage at all costs.[51] Even liberals whose antipathy toward PRWORA persisted often took for granted the marital family's normative status. Peter Edelman continued to pillory the law but agreed that "we need to be promoting responsible fatherhood, marriage, and two-parent families."[52]

The implementation of PRWORA only confirmed feminist critics' worst fears. By 2003, twenty-four states had enacted family cap or child exclusion provisions, which limited aid to children born while a family received assistance.[53] Whereas in 1996 about 70 percent of families living below the federal poverty line received cash assistance, by 2001 only 40 percent did.[54] States with higher proportions of Black families eligible for aid maintained the lowest benefit levels and most stringent eligibility requirements.[55]

Instead, states spent TANF funds on marriage education, efforts to reduce "out-of-wedlock" pregnancies, and abstinence-only sex education curricula. The act even funded a competition among states to reduce nonmarital births: states that achieved the greatest reductions without increasing the abortion rate could receive a $20 million to $25 million "bonus."[56] Teen pregnancy prevention earned a special pot of money. TANF funded an array of public and private institutions, sometimes—as in public school sex education—reaching beyond poor families to target the sexual behavior of all young people.[57]

Feminist welfare advocates continued to protest these developments.[58] As the federal government's promotion of marriage and "responsible fatherhood" accelerated in the early 2000s, the feminist scholars Martha Fineman, Gwendolyn Mink, and Anna Marie Smith published "No Marriage Promotion in TANF." They excoriated the denigration of nonmarital families; demonization of single motherhood; diversion of resources from the poor to religious, anti-feminist, and anti-gay organizations; and failure to address the root causes of poverty.[59]

This critique reflected Fineman's conviction that the "caregiver-dependent dyad" (often but not always a mother and child) rather than the conjugal couple should be the core family unit supported by law and public policy. Instead of privileging marriage, Fineman argued, government should bolster nurturing relationships of care and dependency. She believed the state should subsidize single motherhood as socially valuable labor, not its antithesis.[60]

Representative Mink proposed a sweeping overhaul that would have eliminated most time limits on TANF receipt; repealed family caps and mandatory paternity and child support cooperation; guaranteed child-care for employed recipients; counted the pursuit of higher education as well as care for pre-school-aged, disabled, and ill children as "work"; banned the withholding of assistance from children because of a parent's rule-breaking; and required states to redress violence, mental health and substance abuse challenges, and disability.[61] Representative Mink's counterproposal attracted significant co-sponsorship in 2002, but the main Democratic bill tweaked rather than transformed PRWORA.[62]

Opponents' inability to unite behind an alternative to PRWORA reflected not only a shift to the right within the Democratic Party but also basic differences that had long divided center-left reformers. Many liberals lionized the two-parent marital family ideal and lamented welfare reform's failure to invest in it. Even some self-described feminists fought for paternal responsibility and credited women's work outside but not inside the home. Only where welfare justice and feminist sensibilities intersected did activists insist upon the value of poor mothers' caregiving and reproductive autonomy. Their ethos echoed Johnnie Tillmon, Mrs. Sylvester Smith, and the mothers who resisted mandatory paternity disclosure decades earlier.[63]

Family Caps and Reproductive Justice

Courts' failure in the 1960s and 1970s to accept advocates' constitutional claims stalked those who dissented from the consolidation of marital privilege in the 1990s. As we saw in earlier chapters, the Court sometimes protected "hapless, innocent children" from punishment for their parents' "sins." But the justices sustained state prerogatives to encourage marriage, contain dependency within the nuclear family, and penalize nonconforming adults.

The strongest affirmations of welfare rights in the 1960s rested entirely on statutory interpretation. PRWORA therefore not only repealed AFDC but also nullified court decisions that provided a modicum of protection to families who relied on public assistance. Most obviously, PRWORA rendered moot the ruling in *King v. Smith* (1968) that the Social Security Act's overriding purpose was to provide subsistence to needy children, regardless of their parents' conduct.[64] Less often recognized are the efforts of women who challenged mandatory paternity disclosure in the 1970s.[65] Courts' rejection of these constitutional claims, or their resolution on other grounds, enabled such policies to thrive before and after PRWORA.[66]

Earlier decisions that allowed the government to deny public funding for abortions also hampered efforts to assert a broad right to sexual and reproductive autonomy. In *Planned Parenthood v. Casey* (1992), plaintiffs challenged several Pennsylvania laws that restricted access to abortion care. Reproductive rights advocates emphasized the burden these restrictions placed on poor and rural women who could not afford the costs of transportation, lodging, childcare, and time off from work entailed in compliance with statutory strictures. The Third Circuit upheld a twenty-four-hour waiting period and parental consent requirement for minors anyway. But the court struck down Pennsylvania's mandate that women notify their husbands before seeking an abortion, over a dissent from Judge Samuel Alito. As a young lawyer in Reagan's Department of Justice, Alito had helped hatch the anti-abortion strategy tested in *Casey:* chip away at *Roe v. Wade* until there was nothing left. Now, Alito judged the burden on wives with abusive husbands insufficiently weighty to violate the constitution.[67]

Most observers expected *Roe* to meet its final demise when *Casey* reached the Supreme Court. Instead, in a surprise opinion co-authored by Justices Anthony Kennedy, Sandra Day O'Connor, and David Souter, the majority reaffirmed *Roe's* core holding. Unlike *Roe*, *Casey* framed reproductive rights as essential to sex equality: "The ability of women to participate equally in the economic and social life of the Nation has been facilitated by their ability to control their reproductive lives," said the majority.

Casey also rejected the "common law" view of women as subservient wives and mothers. To force a woman to notify her husband would "empower him with [a] troubling degree of authority over his wife." The requirement was "repugnant to our present understanding of marriage. . . . Women do not lose their constitutionally protected liberty when they marry."[68] But the majority did not grapple with the racial and class dimensions of reproductive decision-making. The Court upheld all of the other Pennsylvania restrictions despite their disparate impact on poor women and women of color, who disproportionately sought abortion care.

The challenges to welfare family caps that proliferated in the 1990s and 2000s also faced strong constitutional headwinds. Family caps, the latest effort to deter nonmarital childbearing among poor women of color, implicated what Black feminists now called reproductive justice: the right not just to end a pregnancy but also to have and raise children with adequate resources to care for and support them.[69]

Poor women's already limited access to reproductive health care aggravated the impact of family caps. In many states public funding was available for abortion only if a pregnant patient's life was in danger. Barriers multiplied after *Casey's* replacement of strict scrutiny with a more lenient "undue burden" standard eased the way for increasingly stringent state regulations.[70]

But as advocates for reproductive justice insisted, abortion—though crucial—was only one component of a much larger set of unmet needs. Family caps strained underfunded family planning services, which already failed to meet the demand among low-income women for lower-cost contraception.[71] Advocates worried that women desperate to avoid pregnancy would undergo permanent sterilization or use long-acting contraception with dangerous side effects.[72] They also suspected that family caps intentionally coerced welfare recipients to relinquish their newborn children to foster care or adoption.[73]

The fight against family caps began before PRWORA. In 1993, feminist and legal aid organizations brought a lawsuit attacking New Jersey's denial of additional benefits for children born while a family received assistance.[74] The plaintiffs argued that family caps penalized childbearing in violation of the right to reproductive and family privacy, equal protection, and the First Amendment. They used the birth status cases to argue the "irrationality" of "punish[ing] needy children" for "parental behavior over which the child has no control."[75] Advocates also reprised earlier sex equality arguments against illegitimacy penalties.[76] Family caps unfairly ensnared women who became pregnant through rape and incest (including two of the plaintiffs) and mothers who could not work, while they ignored the fathers' role and responsibility.[77]

A bipartisan coalition defended family caps' efficacy and constitutionality.[78] The Democratic assemblyman Wayne Bryant, a Black lawmaker who sponsored the original New Jersey legislation, admonished, "We have allowed people to hide behind their children. . . . If you have a child, take the responsibility."[79] The conservative organizations American Legislative Exchange Council and Independent Women's Forum (along with four Black women identified as "New Jersey recipients of AFDC and enthusiastic participants" in the state's reformed program) accused plaintiffs of engaging in an "ideological campaign to transform welfare into a legal right" and to perpetuate welfare's "poverty trap" and "disincentives to marriage."[80]

Opponents of family caps, too, forged unlikely alliances. Pro-choice challengers emphasized how family caps not only infringed reproductive autonomy but also forced women "to choose between their religious beliefs and the benefits they need to raise a child." One plaintiff, L. W., "became pregnant with her second child while using birth control," but her Catholic faith precluded abortion.[81] New Jersey Right to Life blasted the law's "[coercion] of women into killing their unborn children." Family caps, they argued, violated both children's Fourteenth Amendment rights, which "began at conception," and those of "our society's most vulnerable women," whose abortions the state funded.[82] When advocates tried to repeal New Jersey's family cap, Assemblywoman Charlotte Vandervalk (R-Bergen) worried about the reduction in funds available to children and the "dramatic difference" in abortion rates; Bear Atwood, president of New Jersey NOW, agreed: "If we force one woman to have an abortion, that's frightening to me."[83]

Empirical evidence about family caps' efficacy cut both ways. If family caps in fact lowered nonmarital birth rates, then the government could argue that the policy was reasonably related to a legitimate government objective. But if family caps influenced pregnant women's decisions about whether to use contraception, terminate a pregnancy, or bear a child, then they might implicate constitutional rights to make autonomous decisions about procreation and trigger more rigorous judicial scrutiny.[84]

Early research on impact produced ambivalent results. In 1997 a study at Rutgers compared a "treatment group" to whom the family cap applied with a "control group" to whom it did not: 40 percent of respondents said the family cap was "an 'important' consideration in their decision to avoid pregnancy." But between 1990 and 1995 births among recipients declined overall, with no significant difference between mothers who did or did not receive benefits for an additional child.[85] Sherry Leiwant, an attorney with NOW's Legal Defense and Education Fund, said the results showed the family cap's inefficacy in lowering nonmarital birth rates, while Human Services Commissioner William Waldman thought "both groups heard the state's message—it's time to take responsibility for yourself and your family."[86]

By the late 1990s, however, the effectiveness of family caps—now enacted in some twenty states—seemed beside the point. New Jersey's Waldman insisted that the "intent of the family cap policy was not to reduce the birthrate or to save money"; rather, the aim was to "get welfare women to work" and send "a social message" that women should only have as many kids as they can "afford," as the American Enterprise Institute's Doug Besharov put it.[87] And as a constitutional matter, if family caps did not trigger heightened judicial scrutiny then the government need only show that lawmakers might reasonably have believed them effective.

Judges had little sympathy for the New Jersey plaintiffs' arguments. The federal district court judge Nicholas Politan, a Reagan appointee, wrote that the state's "failure to subsidize a recipient's reproductive choice" did not "[intrude] upon . . . reproductive freedom."[88] He cited the Supreme Court's decision to uphold Maryland's limit on benefits regardless of family size or need in *Dandridge v. Williams* (1970) and the Court's acceptance of federal restrictions on abortion funding in *Harris v. McRae* (1980).[89] Little empirical evidence supported a causal relationship between family caps and nonmarital births, but the rational basis standard required none.[90] The Third Circuit affirmed Politan's ruling days before Clinton signed PRWORA into law.[91]

Earlier precedents obstructed these challenges. The federal constitution, courts had ruled in the 1970s, foreclosed states from prohibiting abortion and required due process before terminating public assistance benefits.[92] Yet it contained no positive rights to reproductive health care or to a minimum level of subsistence.[93] Family caps, like all welfare retrenchments, disproportionately affected women and families of color. Case law, also from the 1970s, hampered federal constitutional challenges to that disparate impact: the Court required a showing of racially discriminatory intent to prove an equal protection violation and failed to see discrimination based on pregnancy as sex discrimination.[94] By the 1990s promoting marriage over single parenthood and work over welfare barely raised a constitutional eyebrow. Advocates largely abandoned race- and wealth-based discrimination arguments as futile.

Inhospitable federal courts spurred advocates to turn to state constitutions. They enjoyed some success in challenging state abortion funding restrictions. For instance, in *Doe v. Maher* (1986), Catherine Roraback, who had represented Estelle Griswold two decades earlier, persuaded a state court that Connecticut's Equal Rights Amendment required Medicaid funding of therapeutic abortion care.[95] A few other courts located the same right in state due process and equal protection clauses.[96]

Attorneys with NOW's Legal Defense and Education Fund hoped to replicate these successful attacks in family cap litigation. New Jersey again looked promising: courts had interpreted the state constitution to require public funding for abortion and to invalidate a parental notification requirement.[97] Twenty-one-year-old Sojourner A., a mother who lived with two children in one room of her grandparents' home, averred that the family cap "prompted her to abort two pregnancies because of the financial burden."[98] She gave up her job in a packing plant when she became pregnant again to avoid fumes she worried would harm her child. To attend mandatory "work preparation" classes, Sojourner A. had to use part of her monthly cash benefit to pay for childcare.[99]

Another plaintiff, Angela B., had dropped out of high school and married at eighteen. She so feared her violent husband of eleven years that she relinquished her newborn son for adoption before taking her three daughters to live with relatives, friends, and in shelters.[100] The plaintiff Crystal D. had previously been employed, but her caseworker told her she could not receive childcare assistance as an SSI recipient. Crystal's religious beliefs and a traumatic non-consensual abortion in her youth led her to continue her second pregnancy. After leaving her abusive partner, Crystal lived in dilapidated housing, unable to provide healthful food for her children.[101]

Plaintiffs argued first that the family cap violated state constitutional equal protection guarantees by discriminating against children—based upon the timing of their birth, their siblings' receipt of benefits, and their parents' conduct.[102] They cited a 1971 New Jersey ruling that the state could not prosecute parents for fornication based upon their admission to nonmarital sex in a support proceeding because the state constitution foreclosed "impoverishment" of children as a punishment for "erring mothers and fathers."[103] Plaintiffs also invoked a more comprehensive right to privacy under New Jersey's constitution than that protected by the federal constitution.[104] The state, they argued, could not "condition receipt of government benefits on a woman's foregoing" the "right to choose whether and when to conceive and bear a child."[105]

Plaintiffs fought an uphill battle. The Superior Court judge Anthony Iuliani ruled that the state interest "in promoting self-sufficient citizens, diminishing the dependency upon welfare, and creating [parity] between welfare recipients and working people . . . greatly outweighs [the] slight imposition . . . on plaintiffs' right to privacy."[106] The appellate judge Michael Winkelstein relied on U.S. Supreme Court rulings from the 1970s to conclude that the family cap did "not place a direct legal obstacle in the path of a woman's decision to have additional children."[107] Rather, it "merely introduces one of many factors that a woman considers when deciding whether to become pregnant and carry the child to term; a choice that remains hers and hers alone."[108]

Opponents thought New Jersey's supreme court might see family caps as infringing fundamental constitutional rights. Chief Justice Deborah Poritz, a former English professor and state attorney general who earned her law degree at age forty, led a court that often found robust individual rights in the state constitution.[109] But not here. Poritz wrote for a unanimous court that "even if we assume that procreative choices are influenced" by a family cap, "we do not feel that influence to be undue or that a new burden is thereby created."[110] And the court rejected plaintiffs' argument that family caps harmed innocent children. The money New Jersey saved went to childcare, job training, and other initiatives to promote "self-sufficiency and decreased dependency on welfare," which the court agreed would improve children's lives.[111] After this decision, creative arguments applying state equal rights amendments to family caps never came to fruition.[112] Their constitutional challenges stymied, opponents turned to the "arduous" process of state-by-state legislative repeal.[113]

Nonmarital Fatherhood and Citizenship

Nor did constitutional law provide recourse for the immigrants, noncitizens, and their families whose statutory rights contracted further in the 1990s. Laws that had long discriminated based on sex and family status remained on the books, artifacts of the Court's rejection of plaintiffs' claims in *Fiallo v. Bell* (1977). In the 1990s, constitutional challenges to classifications based on sex, marital status, or birth status more directly surfaced the sex equality arguments that Ruth Bader Ginsburg, now a justice, had wanted to make in *Fiallo* two decades earlier. But precedents established by the nonmarital fathers cases discussed in chapter 7 stood in the way.

Lorelyn Penero Miller and her father, Charlie Miller, challenged a statutory provision that imposed more rigorous derivative citizenship requirements on the foreign-born children of nonmarital U.S. citizen fathers than on children of nonmarital U.S. citizen mothers. Lorelyn, born in 1970 in the Philippines to Luz Penero, a Filipina national, and Charlie Miller, an American servicemember, unsuccessfully applied for U.S. citizenship in 1992.[114] Charlie's failure to establish both a "biological" and a "personal" relationship with Lorelyn prior to her twenty-first birthday as required under Section 1409 of the Immigration and Nationality Act (INA) doomed her application.[115] Had Luz Penero and not Charlie Miller been her sole U.S.-citizen parent, Lorelyn would have been a citizen from birth.

Unlike the plaintiffs in *Fiallo*, nonmarital fathers of color who provided primary care for their children, Charlie Miller, who was white, appeared to exemplify the American serviceman who fathered a child abroad and then left, never to return. Often these men married American women and started "legitimate" families in the United States, leaving their nonmarital children behind to be raised by their mothers. Concern about granting U.S. citizenship to the multiracial children of military personnel likely animated lawmakers who strengthened requirements for passing citizenship from nonmarital fathers to children, such as the one that stood in the Millers' way.[116]

Charlie had in fact departed the Philippines for the last time in 1970, the year of Lorelyn's birth, and Lorelyn grew up and attended school there. By the time she was twenty-one, Lorelyn had moved to the United States and lived briefly in Tyler, Texas, with Charlie, who was not married and had no other children.[117] Charlie signed a voluntary paternity decree in 1992, which under Texas law "legitimated" Lorelyn since birth. But it was too late. Authorities at the U.S. embassy in Manila denied Lorelyn's application to register her U.S. citizenship and obtain a passport.[118]

Section 1409 appeared vulnerable to attack as both sex and birth status discrimination. Donald R. Patterson, the local attorney who represented the Millers, at first focused primarily on unjust harm to children who could not control their parents' conduct.[119] He drew upon a federal district court decision from 1991, *LeBrun v. Thornburgh*, a case involving the adult daughter of a U.S. soldier who fought in France during World War II. In *LeBrun*, Judge Lee Sarokin held that the INA's extra hurdle for children of nonmarital fathers "discriminates against 'illegitimate' children" in violation of the equal protection clause.[120] Sarokin cited *Plyler v. Doe*, the 1982 case striking down a Texas statute that denied state funding to, and allowed school districts to exclude, undocumented children. *Plyler*, a 5–4 decision authored by Justice Lewis F. Powell, Jr., relied on *Weber v. Aetna Casualty* (1972), Powell's seminal opinion explaining why punishing children for their parents' actions was "illogical and unjust." Sarokin also called "wrong" and "sexist" a nonmarital father's "unilateral ability to confer or deny citizenship to his daughter."[121]

In *Miller*, the D.C. Circuit considered only Lorelyn's claims and found them foreclosed under *Fiallo*. Judges James Buckley and Karen Henderson, appointed by Ronald Reagan and George H. W. Bush respectively, called the distinction between nonmarital fathers and mothers "entirely reasonable," since "a mother is far less likely to ignore the child she has carried in her womb than is the natural father, who may not even be aware of its existence." The fact that Lorelyn "was fathered by a U.S. serviceman while he was serving a tour of duty overseas" made the distinction "especially warranted" in her case.[122]

Judge Patricia Wald regretfully concurred. Wald, who was raised in a "crowded [working-class] Irish-American household with an extended family of mostly women after her father left home when she was 2," graduated from Yale Law School in 1951. Wald paused her career to raise five children to school age and then served in various public interest law and government positions before her appointment to the D.C. Circuit in 1979.[123] Wald thought the challenged law was based on stereotypes and considered *Fiallo* "a precedent whose time has come and gone," but she felt constrained to deny Lorelyn's claim.[124]

The Supreme Court, of course, faced no such constraint. As Wald noted, the Court's equal protection jurisprudence had evolved significantly since 1977. Decisions in the late 1970s and early 1980s clarified that nonmarital fathers who had established relationships with their children could not be presumed inferior to mothers based only on sex.[125] In 1996, Justice Ginsburg had authored a landmark decision that applied "skeptical scrutiny" to invalidate the Virginia Military Institute's exclusion of women and required an "exceedingly persuasive justification" for sex-based classifications.[126] Attorneys from NOW's Legal Defense and Education Fund and the ACLU filed an amicus brief urging the Court to abandon *Fiallo*'s "offensive stereotyping," which cemented women's role as primary homemakers and caregivers and shortchanged men capable and desirous of an active parental role. DNA testing—which much more accurately verified genetic ties—had eliminated any concerns about fraudulent assertions of paternity that might justify a sex-based distinction.[127]

The Supreme Court's splintered ruling in *Miller v. Albright* (1998) left Lorelyn unable to claim U.S. citizenship through Charlie. Justice John Paul Stevens's opinion, joined by Chief Justice William Rehnquist, rejected the plaintiffs' sex discrimination arguments. Stevens's opinion relied less on *Fiallo*, which rested on Congress's plenary power to regulate immigration, and more on the Court's decision in *Lehr v. Robertson* (1983). There, the Court upheld a New York statutory scheme that required a nonmarital father to register potential paternity with the state to merit notice and a hearing when another man sought to adopt his biological child. Here, similarly, differential requirements for fathers and mothers reflected not harmful stereotypes but the "fact" of "biological differences." Stevens elaborated the views he first expressed in his 1979 dissent in *Caban v. Mohammed*: a mother inevitably would be present at her child's birth to establish a legal parent-child relationship, whereas a nonmarital father might never know of his child's existence, much less have the "opportunity to develop a caring relationship with the child."[128] Four justices concurred in the judgment denying Lorelyn citizenship, but on other grounds.

The same provision came before the Court again three years later in *Nguyen v. Immigration and Naturalization Service (INS)*. Tuan Anh Nguyen, a Vietnamese-born U.S. legal permanent resident, had lived with his father, Joseph Boulais, "from early infancy." Boulais's relationship with Tuan Ahn's mother, Hung Thi, ended shortly after their son's birth. Boulais later married another Vietnamese national, whose family helped Tuan Anh escape after the fall of Saigon to North Vietnam in 1975.[129] A few months later, the six-year-old entered the United States as a refugee and reunited with Boulais and his stepmother. The family never knew whether Hung Thi survived the war. Tuan Anh grew up in Houston and never returned to Vietnam.[130]

Boulais's parental involvement and Nguyen's vulnerability to deportation to an unfamiliar land because of his conviction on sexual assault charges in 1992 underscored the high stakes of assuming a lack of connection between fathers and nonmarital children. Nevertheless, Nguyen lost in the lower courts, and a 5–4 majority of the Supreme Court upheld the disparate requirements for nonmarital fathers on grounds similar to those in *Miller*.[131]

The Court had largely ignored feminist arguments in the nonmarital fathers cases of the 1970s and 1980s; by the turn of the twenty-first century, the Court's first two female justices made them in dissent. In *Miller*, Ginsburg lambasted the law's generalization that "mothers, as a rule, are responsible for a child born out of wedlock; fathers unmarried to the child's mother, ordinarily, are not."[132] Scholars and advocates buttressed Ginsburg's critique. Kristin Collins, at that time a law student, demonstrated that reliance on "biological" difference obscured how stricter requirements for nonmarital fathers perpetuated a gendered division of labor in nonmarital families that harmed mothers at least as much as fathers.[133]

O'Connor had persuaded Stevens to omit language about mothers' inevitable responsibility for nonmarital children eighteen years earlier in *Lehr*. Now, armed with quotations from the 1930s National Woman's Party leaders—supplied by Collins via an amicus brief from feminist legal organizations—O'Connor wrote in her *Nguyen* dissent that the law was "paradigmatic of a historic regime that left women with responsibility, and freed men from responsibility, for nonmarital children."[134] After completing his prison sentence, Tuan Anh Nguyen faced deportation to a country in which he had not set foot since early childhood. Justice Kennedy, who wrote the majority opinion, called this outcome "unfortunate, even tragic."[135] Nguyen's attorney Nancy Falgout lamented, "He doesn't know anybody at all in Vietnam. He looks very Western. He doesn't speak the language well. He would be totally out of place there, like a Martian."[136]

Lorelyn Penero Miller's story ended very differently. Her marriage to a U.S. servicemember afforded a path to citizenship, and her two daughters enjoyed a close relationship with their grandfather Charlie until his death in 2017.[137] A news report in 2015 described how Lorelyn's husband surprised their ten-year-old daughter at school on her birthday, only the fourth he had spent with her after deployments kept him abroad for months at a time. Chief Electronic Technician Jeremy Burleson of the U.S. Navy told the local newspaper, "I'm real lucky. My family's been real supportive. I don't have to worry about a lot of things back home, because they're taking care of everything. It's a nice feeling to be able to focus on your job, and not have to think of everything going on back home."[138] Military service and paternal absence inflected Lorelyn's adult life, too—but marriage shaped their meaning.

Religious Freedom and the Marriage Movement

The shortfalls of earlier campaigns also affected disputes over marital status discrimination in the 1990s. As we saw in chapter 4, advocates who fought marital status discrimination in the 1970s and 1980s achieved only partial success. When Congress added "familial status" to the federal Fair Housing Act in 1988, lawmakers protected families with children, not unmarried couples (straight or gay). In the states and localities that did prohibit "marital status" discrimination, officials often interpreted statutes to exclude cohabiting couples.

These mixed results persisted. The highest court in Massachusetts ruled in 1989 that state law precluded the exclusion of unmarried couples from public housing. Alaska's supreme court reached a similar conclusion when a landlord refused to rent to an unwed couple and their infant.[139] Other courts interpreted state nondiscrimination laws narrowly, holding that they applied to *individuals'* marital *status* but not to a *couple's* nonmarital sexual *conduct*. Wisconsin's supreme court, for instance, refused to enforce a local ordinance prohibiting marital status discrimination because the state's family code expressly promoted marriage.[140]

In the 1990s, the debate evolved, thanks to a burgeoning movement to exempt individuals and businesses with religious objections from anti-discrimination laws. The effort stemmed from an unexpected source. In *Employment Division v. Smith* (1990), the Supreme Court ruled that generally applicable laws could constitutionally burden religious practices unless they intentionally targeted religion.[141] Congress responded by passing the Religious Freedom Restoration Act of 1993 (RFRA), which restored strict scrutiny for laws challenged in free exercise cases.[142] RFRA, viewed as a protection for religious minorities—such as Native Americans who used peyote in rituals—garnered bipartisan support.

But the political valence of RFRA, and similar state statutes, shifted.[143] Landlords fighting bans on marital status discrimination were on the front lines of a battle waged by Christian conservatives.[144] Evelyn Smith, a landlord in Chico, California, believed that "God will judge her if she permits people to engage in sex outside of marriage in her rental units," jeopardizing Smith's ability to reunite with her husband "in the hereafter."[145] Two brothers in Montague, Massachusetts, Paul and Roland Desilets, refused to lease an apartment to Mark Lattanzi and Cynthia Tarail because Catholic beliefs proscribed facilitating "sinful conduct."[146] In Anchorage, Alaska, Tom Swanner maintained a policy against renting to unmarried men and women living together because his Christian faith regarded "even a non-sexual living arrangement by roommates of the opposite sex" as "sinful" because it created "an appearance of immorality."[147]

Landlords claimed that the First Amendment, state constitutional protections for religious free exercise, and state RFRAs shielded them from liability. Their claims differed from those that had motivated the federal Religious Freedom Restoration Act, designed to protect the rights of minority religious groups whose rituals or practices ran afoul of the criminal law or employers' policies. Exempting landlords from anti-discrimination laws, in contrast, would infringe the rights of minorities who were vulnerable to exclusion based on prejudice.[148]

Both sides understood the high stakes. Jay Sekulow of the American Center for Law and Justice, a conservative Christian organization founded in 1990, defended the Desilets brothers; Catholic and evangelical Protestant groups, Concerned Women for America, and Focus on the Family filed amicus briefs on their behalf. The Massachusetts Civil Liberties Union, the Center for Constitutional Rights, gay rights organizations, and feminist groups weighed in on the tenants' side. A brief from Gay and Lesbian Advocates and Defenders (GLAD) and the Women's Bar Association in *Desilets* warned that religious exemptions would validate intrusions into the "intimate details" of individuals' lives. Access to jobs, housing, credit, and public accommodations were threatened by conservative religious beliefs about "homosexuality, sexual relations outside of marriage, divorce, birth control practices, interracial . . . or interdenominational relations."[149]

The religious liberty defense met a mixed reception. The California Supreme Court was unwilling to "sacrifice the rights of [Smith's] prospective tenants to have equal access to public accommodations and their legal and dignity interests in freedom from discrimination based on personal characteristics."[150] Alaska's highest court reasoned similarly.[151] The Massachusetts Supreme Judicial Court more ambivalently overturned a ruling for the Desilets brothers. The majority called marital status discrimination "not as intense a State concern as . . . other classifications," such as race, sex, color, religion, and national origin, all of which the state's constitution explicitly protected.[152] A dissenting opinion excoriated the majority for requiring a trial to determine "whether the defendants may lawfully be forced to choose between violating their religiously informed consciences or withdrawing from their commercial endeavors."[153] Justice Clarence Thomas, too, objected when the U.S. Supreme Court refused to hear the Alaska appeal.[154]

Other states embraced broad readings of religious liberty protections and narrow interpretations of marital status discrimination laws. Justice Larry Yetka, a former Democratic state legislator and confidant of Hubert Humphrey, was known for progressive rulings protecting civil rights and the environment. Yetka wrote for the Minnesota Supreme Court: "Before abandoning fundamental values and institutions, we must pause and take stock of our present social order: millions of drug abusers; rampant child abuse; a rising underclass without marketable job skills; children roaming the streets; children with only one parent or no parent at all; and children growing up with no one to guide them in developing any set of values." Yetka asked: "How can we expect anything else," when "the state itself contributes" (by arguing that landlords must rent to cohabitants) "to further erosion" of marriage and family, which "formed the foundation of our civilization for centuries?" The court ruled that state law did not prohibit housing discrimination against unmarried couples, and, even if it did, Minnesota's constitution protected landlords' right to object on religious grounds.[155]

Justice Yetka was far from alone among liberals in his vehement defense of marriage as a foundation of civilization. At the turn of the twenty-first century, a "marriage movement" united some progressives and centrists with conservatives concerned about the impact of high divorce and non-marital childbearing rates, low marriage rates, and a widening "marriage gap" between rich and poor. The *Statement of Principles* issued in 2000 by the Institute for American Values (IAV) declared: "Marriage, a rich gen-erator of social and human capital, must not become the private hoard of the upper-middle class, creating a new, disturbing marital divide between the haves and have-nots in America." Racial and economic equality, as well as the health and welfare of children, depended upon the restoration of marriage.[156]

An eclectic group, the signatories to the *Statement of Principles* leaned center-right, with a few left-liberal clergy sprinkled in. The IAV founder David Blankenhorn, a self-described liberal New Yorker from Mississippi who was married to a Jewish woman, made his name as an advocate for responsible fatherhood. Enola Aird, a former Children's Defense Fund lawyer, had left her corporate law job in the mid-1980s to "devote her time and energies to her children." Aird was jolted by the loss of the ex-ternal validation offered by professional life; her experience of "devalua-tion" "led her to a new calling as an activist mother" committed to transforming a culture distorted by "radical individualism, relentless competition, and materialism."[157] Aird's own marriage to Stephen Carter, a Yale law professor, public intellectual, and author of mystery novels starring elite New England Black families, modeled a devoutly religious yet cosmopolitan partnership iconoclastic in its conventionality.

Another signatory, Maggie Gallagher, discovered Ayn Rand as a Yale undergraduate in the late 1970s, became pregnant and gave birth to a son while unmarried, recommitted to Catholicism, and became a conser-vative culture warrior. Gallagher argued firmly against gender neutrality and supported Vice President Dan Quayle when, during the 1992 presi-dential campaign, he criticized the fictional character Murphy Brown (the protagonist of a television sitcom) for having a child out of wedlock. Gallagher's marriage in 1993 to her fellow conservative Raman Sristav endured rough patches they apparently surmounted. Although Sristav had been raised by Hindu parents, the couple sent their second son to a boys' school affiliated with the ultra-conservative Catholic group Opus Dei.[158] By contrast, Rabbi Michael Lerner, a former leader in the Berke-ley Free Speech movement and Students for a Democratic Society (SDS), edited the progressive Jewish magazine *Tikkun* and collaborated with the philosopher and African American studies professor Cornel

West. Some signatories, like Wade Horn, were fixtures in the social conservative movement; others, such as Judith Wallerstein, had gained prominence as critics of the effects of divorce on children; the family scholars David Popenoe and Barbara Dafoe Whitehead also joined.

Marriage movement adherents differed in their views about gender roles within marriage and the proper place of government; they also varied in their partisan, religious, and ethnic affiliations. Later, some parted ways over same-sex marriage.[159] Still, a wider consensus about marriage's public importance coalesced at the turn of the century, as battles for inclusion awakened Americans to the many rights and benefits available only through marriage. An influential book by the historian Nancy Cott, *Public Vows: A History of Marriage and the Nation* (2000), spotlighted the rhetorical, religious, economic, and political roles of marriage since the founding. Marriage equality advocates quickly enlisted her expert testimony in state legislatures and eventually in court.[160]

Cott's research reinforced two essential themes. First, she showed how marriage had become a more internally egalitarian institution over time, as barriers to interracial marriage, divorce, and women's rights fell. On this view, same-sex marriage would be less a sudden transformation than the capstone to an incremental evolution. Of course, these egalitarian trends threatened conservative defenders of marriage, who saw easy divorce and the demise of differentiated sex roles as an indictment rather than an inducement to recognition of same-sex marriage. Cott's second point proved less controversial: marriage served as a gateway—to government benefits essential to social and economic citizenship, to rights and duties within families—and as a primary unit of policymaking and regulation.[161] Marriage's fiercest critics acknowledged this truth: indeed, the primacy of marriage remained the central object of their ire.

Marriage and (In)equality

For gay and lesbian advocates and their civil libertarian and feminist allies, prioritizing access to marriage remained controversial. They had long presented a unified front against sodomy laws; even when seldom enforced, criminalization of sexual conduct cast a long shadow over gay life, haunting family law, employment, education, access to housing and public accommodations, military service, and political participation. But the campaign for marriage rights divided activists such as Nan Hunter and Nancy Polikoff, close allies in the fight for lesbian mothers' parental rights. Hunter argued that "same-sex marriage would move beyond the formalistic equality in marriage law that has been achieved to date" and could "expose and denaturalize the historical construction of gender."[162] Polikoff retorted: "We Will Get What We Ask For." She warned that same-sex marriage would replicate conventional gender roles and "valorize the *current* institution of marriage," blocking more universal solutions to social inequities.[163] Polikoff continued to hope for a reconstruction of intimate and other caring relationships that stripped marriage of its superior position in American law and life.

Proponents hoped that marriage's proven ability to change and adapt meant it could evolve further toward an egalitarian ideal once gender difference was no longer a requirement for entry. And attacks that impugned the dignity and moral worth of gay and lesbian love demanded an answer. Many gay and lesbian couples yearned for legal as well as social recognition of their intimate relationships, given the myriad symbolic, dignitary, and material benefits of marriage. Without marriage equality, Barbara Cox wrote in 1997, gay and lesbian Americans could "not be equal members of the polity."[164]

The appeal of marriage to ordinary gay and lesbian couples led formerly reluctant organizations such as Gay and Lesbian Advocates and Defenders in Boston to pursue marriage at the state level, and they began to make headway in the early 2000s. Two court victories in 2003 suggested different paths forward for marital status law. In *Lawrence v. Texas*, the U.S. Supreme Court declared anti-sodomy laws unconstitutional. *Lawrence* overruled *Bowers v. Hardwick* (1986) and vindicated decades of advocacy that already had decriminalized same-sex sexual conduct in thirty-one states, eleven since *Bowers*.[165] Then, in *Goodridge v. Department of Public Health*, the Massachusetts Supreme Judicial Court ruled that the state constitution prevented the exclusion of same-sex couples from the many legal benefits associated with marriage.

The decisions shared much in common: both emphasized the equal dignity of intimate relationships regardless of sex and described how the law had changed in response to evolving understandings of freedom and equality.[166] Both relied on principles of substantive due process, privacy, and liberty; both featured a concurring opinion based on equal protection; and both acknowledged strong moral and religious convictions on the other side.[167]

In other ways, the decisions diverged—most obviously, in their relationship to marriage. The opinions in *Lawrence* "shadowboxed" with the looming question of same-sex marriage.[168] Justice Kennedy's majority opinion implied that the *non*marital nature of the defendants' relationship helped to render their sexual conduct private and beyond the reach of the state. Justice O'Connor's concurrence, too, distinguished marriage: she noted that "other reasons exist to promote the institution of marriage beyond mere moral disapproval of an excluded group."[169] Justice Scalia scoffed in dissent at the majority's claim that its ruling had nothing to say about "state laws against bigamy, same-sex marriage, adult incest, prostitution, masturbation, adultery, fornication, bestiality, and obscenity"—all of which, he warned, *Lawrence* put at risk.[170]

The Court's detachment of a right to engage in private, consensual sex from a right to marriage—once the only site of licit sexual activity—contained liberatory possibilities. Some critics thought *Lawrence* offered only a "domesticated liberty," in Katherine Franke's words.[171] But Melissa Murray later argued that the decision opened an "interstitial space where intimate acts and choices are neither valorized as marital . . . nor vilified as criminal."[172] Whatever the majority claimed not to be saying about *Lawrence*'s collateral consequences, the decision called other laws penalizing nonmarital sex into question and left a tantalizing "middle ground between criminalization and assimilation."[173]

Goodridge, by contrast, emphasized the centrality of marriage to government, society, and full citizenship, as well as to individuals, families, and communities.[174] Marriage was "among life's momentous acts of self-definition," wrote Chief Justice Margaret H. Marshall, and it remained "a social institution of the highest importance" that "anchors an ordered society by encouraging stable relationships over transient ones."[175] She enumerated the many "legal, social, and economic" advantages marriage conferred on families, especially children.[176] Echoing the arguments of marriage equality advocates, Marshall invoked the "family stability and economic security" that was "largely inaccessible . . . to nonmarital children," including "enhanced approval" and "greater ease of access to family-based State and Federal benefits."[177]

Skeptics objected to the centrality of marriage as a movement goal. Polikoff wrote that what children needed was not access to the scarce commodity of marital privilege but rather laws that recognized and supported families regardless of marital or birth status.[178] Franke recoiled at how rapidly gay and lesbian advocates shifted from "mutual contempt, distrust and fear" of the government to the "powerful desire for recognition by and identification with the state." Franke mourned the loss of alternative sociabilities and sexualities that flourished before marriage took center stage.[179]

Critics also discerned a troubling racial subtext beneath debates over marriage equality. Opponents' rhetoric occasionally veered into overt white nationalism: in 2004 Maggie Gallagher testified in a California case that the survival of Europeans and Euro-Americans depended upon encouraging heterosexual marriage and childbearing.[180] But even liberal proponents of same-sex marriage sometimes adopted what Franke termed "Moynihan-esque" arguments, in which nonmarital parenthood appeared as "a site of pathology, stigma, and injury to children."[181] Mattie Udora "Matt" Richardson, a queer Black feminist scholar, wrote in 2004 of how Black Americans historically were measured against "an impossible standard of two-parent nuclear household." The normative status of marriage devalued queer people's chosen and extended families, nonexclusive intimate partnerships, and "bodies that are not exclusively male or female."[182]

The gender studies scholar Priya Kandaswamy saw race, not marital status, as the primary obstacle to family integrity, observing that "being married doesn't protect straight black families from having their children taken away" by authorities in the name of child protection. Kandaswamy castigated marriage for treating women as property, maintaining families' monopoly on material wealth, and "preserv[ing] white privilege." Rather than pursuing marriage rights as a path to U.S. citizenship, Kandaswamy called for a "radical queer politics" to resist "racist state policies that criminalize immigrants."[183]

Marriage abolitionism had evolved: by the early twenty-first century, critics saw marriage as part of a larger system that reproduced structural and systemic injustice on many fronts.[184] The queer activist and writer Mattilda Bernstein Sycamore summarized: "Gay assimilationists have created the ultimate genetically modified organism, combining virulent strains of nationalism, patriotism, consumerism, and patriarchy and delivering them in one deadly product: state-sanctioned matrimony." Sycamore advocated "fighting for the abolition of marriage (duh), and universal access to the services that marriage can sometimes help procure."[185]

In 2006, a group of LGBT and allied activists articulated "a new strategic vision" that went "beyond marriage" to call for "the separation of benefits and recognition from marital status, citizenship status, and the requirement that 'legitimate' relationships be conjugal." They demanded universal health care, affordable housing, social insurance, and public assistance for the poor along with legal recognition for all relationships that provided mutual care and sustenance. Prioritizing marriage, these activists warned, compromised opportunities for coalition with the many Americans living outside marital nuclear families; inflamed right-wing opposition; and distracted from the larger injustices in need of remedy: "corporate greed" and the "increasing shift of public funds from human needs into militarism, policing, and prison construction," which exacerbated income and wealth inequities.[186]

Marriage's defenders made very different assumptions about the relationship between marriage's primacy and inequality, and their voices often drowned out those of skeptics. As the likelihood of marriage increasingly followed indices of race, education, income, and wealth, many law- and policymakers equated correlation with causation: they saw marriage as a solution to societal inequalities that the privileging of marriage helped to sustain. Social scientists, too, often viewed nonmarital childbearing and single parenthood as routes to poverty and social immobility.[187]

Some observers questioned the premise that marriage was a viable option for low-income Americans or that nonmarital childbearing resulted from a devaluation of marriage. In 2005 an influential ethnography by Kathryn Edin and Maria Kefalas of more than one hundred fifty poor single mothers in eight communities concluded that these young women had not "given up" on marriage. Instead, like better-off Americans, they postponed marriage unless and until they achieved financial stability and found partners worthy of a long-term commitment.[188]

These results resonated with an observation by the sociologist Andrew Cherlin that Americans' high regard for marriage produced unrealistic expectations of happiness and individual fulfillment that often led to disillusionment and divorce.[189] Paradoxically, individual Americans' investment of symbolic importance in marriage primed them for disappointments that undermined marital stability.

A similar story could be told about marriage and political economy writ large. Groaning under the burden of social and economic inequalities, marriage could not bear the weight Americans asked it to carry. Even so, at the dawn of the twenty-first century, marital privilege appeared stronger and more resilient than ever, and prospects for challenging marriage's supreme status ever more remote.

Conclusion

IN OCTOBER 2005, DELEGATE Eleanor Holmes Norton (D-D.C.) testified before Congress in support of Marriage Development Accounts (MDAs), designed to "promote and save marriages by eliminating finances as a factor for low-income D.C. residents." MDAs, a brainchild of Senator Sam Brownback (R-KS), would "fund engaged or married couples on a three to one federal match basis to save for home purchases, education and small business expenses" and provide "marriage and relationship counseling on a voluntary basis." Norton, touted as a long-time "leader on Black family issues," warned that with 70 percent of Black children now born to "never-married mothers," "the issue is in an extreme state—not family dissolution or divorce, but the failure to form families at all through marriage, often with devastating consequences for Black children."[1]

Norton and Brownback agreed on little else: their views on government spending, domestic partnership, feminism, gay rights, religious liberty, gun safety, taxation, school vouchers, and D.C. home rule diverged dramatically. Still, both believed marriage worth subsidizing in America's poorest communities.[2] Norton's alliance with one of the most conservative members of the U.S. Senate to promote an initiative associated with the "traditional family values" of the Right dismayed some of her feminist compatriots. But this priority was not new.

In 1985, on the twentieth anniversary of the Moynihan Report, Norton had called on policymakers and Black leaders to address head-on the "growth of poor, alienated female-headed households," not only among Black Americans but, increasingly, among families generally. She acknowl-

edged the sensitive nature of her mission. Valid concern about perpetuat-
ing racist tropes or victim-blaming had choked off public discussion of
Black family disintegration, she wrote. But the contemporaneous rise of
a Black middle class bolstered by strong nuclear and extended family
bonds augured a growing intraracial class divide.[3]

Some interpreted Norton's analysis as an admission that "Moynihan
was right" or as a retreat from her earlier views.[4] In fact, Norton's position
remained largely consistent.[5] The "traditional Black family" Norton sought
to resurrect was not Moynihan's male-breadwinner/female-homemaker
ideal. Rather, she endorsed "the values of the black working poor and
middle class—where husbands often work two jobs, wives return to work
almost immediately after childbirth and extended families of interdependent kin are still more prevalent than among whites."[6] Welfare, a "brilliant
innovation" in its time, had become "*the* way to take care of poor women
with children" and mitigate "structural unemployment of black men."[7]
Norton's solutions—education and decent jobs for Black men *and* women,
funding for childcare and health insurance, and a renewed commitment to
strong male-female partnerships—echoed her earlier emphasis on egalitarian marriage and equal employment opportunity.

Norton's own marriage, held up as a model of gender egalitarianism
in the 1970s, ended in the early 1990s just as her long career as a non-
voting member of Congress began. Later, Norton held welfare reformers
to account for failing to provide supports that would allow single mothers to find gainful employment and care for their children.[8] But she also
lent her voice to the chorus of policymakers who promoted marriage and
work as salves for social and economic ills.

Norton's stance reflected both her own long-held beliefs and the political reality she—and her antagonists across the political spectrum—
helped to shape. By the twenty-first century, changes to marital status
law had blunted some of the critiques that besieged marriage in the late
1960s and amplified others. Important progressive reforms had succeeded. No longer did the law of marriage explicitly impose unequal status on men and women or condemn children to second-class citizenship
based solely on birth status. The state could not impose differential penalties for nonmarital sex or exclude couples from marriage based solely
on race. But the government retained the prerogative to promote marriage, channel key benefits through marriage, and contain support obligations within the family. The persistence of marital primacy did not
induce more Americans to marry, nor did it reduce childbearing outside

of marriage. And so, as marriage declined among less affluent Americans, marital status law intensified racial and economic inequality.

Activists, reformers, legal decision-makers, and ordinary people fought over how the laws of marriage and nonmarriage should respond to the tectonic shifts in American family life that marked the last four decades of the twentieth century. Those who challenged the legal primacy of marriage did so not in a single coordinated movement but rather in more diffuse, piecemeal efforts that overlapped—but never perfectly— with other causes. They made creative, ambitious claims to equality and autonomy under the federal constitution and sought legislative and administrative reforms at all levels of government.

Challenges to marital primacy faced formidable obstacles. Marriage undergirded a New Deal welfare state that rewarded households headed by a breadwinning husband and father whose wife cared for home and children. Religious, moral, and fiscal concerns had long motivated the containment of sex and childbearing within marriage. Marriage, in short, performed crucial work for the state and at mid-century also anchored cultural commitments to capitalist democracy and anti-communism.

A temporal disjuncture also plagued the boldest bids for sexual liberation, gender equality, and reproductive justice. Possibilities for progressive federal constitutional change peaked during the Warren Court's heyday in the 1960s. But so too did what the historian Robert Self calls "breadwinner liberalism," which rested upon the breadwinner/homemaker model of household political economy. In the late 1960s, breadwinner liberalism was under siege by feminism, gay liberation, anti-war and countercultural movements. But broader legal and constitutional arguments for sexual privacy, sex equality, gay rights, and reproductive autonomy had only just begun to emerge.

Moreover, the most ambitious of these arguments faced a skeptical judicial audience that soon became downright hostile. The Warren Court (1953–69), receptive to some civil rights, civil liberties, and economic justice advocacy, rejected or ignored even the nascent feminist and sexual liberty claims presented to it. By the time advocates had laid groundwork for more capacious arguments, the political and legal ground had shifted. The Burger Court (1969–86) rejected welfare rights, foreclosed constitutional disparate impact claims, declined to apply heightened scrutiny to wealth-based classifications, and declared that discrimination based on pregnancy was not necessarily sex discrimination that violated the equal protection clause. Anti-feminist and anti-gay movements helped to unite social and economic conservatives around a New Right agenda that dominated national politics in the 1980s. By then, efforts at federal constitutional change had run out of steam. Most challenges to marital primacy now played out at the state and local levels.

Under pressure from social and legal movements of the 1960s and 1970s, the regime of marital supremacy gave way to one of marital privilege. Contestation between radical, reformist, and conservative advocates produced important legal and constitutional change. The rise of a limited right to privacy restrained some government intrusion and regulation of sex and family life. But mostly it shielded those who did not stray far from heterosexual marital norms or make too many demands on the state. Equality principles removed overt race-based distinctions from the face of the law. Marriage law no longer starkly distinguished the roles of husbands and wives. In some domains, formal and categorical exclusions gave way to functional definitions and standards.

Dual imperatives—to comply with nondiscrimination norms and to rely on the nuclear family for economic sustenance—propelled a modernization of family status laws.[9] The legal regime of marital supremacy had failed effectively to deter nonmarital sex, relationships, and childbearing. Now the state would overlook marital status when doing so saved the public money, for instance, by holding parents accountable for the support of children. Marital privilege, despite its newfound facial neutrality, more than ever entwined with racial and class advantage. Marital status still determined who could access the many public and private benefits channeled through marriage, who could invoke principles of gender neutrality when relationships ended, and who could claim a right to be free from government interference in their intimate lives.

By the end of the 1970s, feminists such as Eleanor Holmes Norton and Ruth Bader Ginsburg largely succeeded in writing their vision of gender-egalitarian marriage into law, a profound change from 1960. Gone was the old marital bargain, in which husbands provided financial support for wives who took care of home and children, and men reigned supreme as heads of households while women labored under the remnants of coverture. Husbands and wives became interchangeable spouses, equally responsible—as a matter of formal law—for breadwinning and caregiving. Wives could provide military, Social Security, and survivor benefits to their husbands, widowers, and children. Married women could contract, own property, and apply for credit in their own names—names the state could no longer legally compel them to change upon marriage. In theory, married couples could negotiate any division of labor they wished without government placing a thumb on the scale. Function largely replaced sex as the determinant of legal treatment: the roles performed by each spouse, rather than their identity as husband or wife, shaped rights and duties during and after marriage. These were significant changes, real progress for those in a position to take advantage of their egalitarian promise.

Divorce law, too, became increasingly sex-blind, at least on the surface. As no-fault laws spread, exit grew easier for both spouses. In states where division of property at divorce had been based on title, feminists fought for equitable distribution laws that valued homemakers' labor. Husbands now could receive alimony, and, in most states, courts could not explicitly favor mothers in post-divorce child custody disputes. Divorced fathers' activism produced joint custody laws in many jurisdictions. Feminists, divorce reformers, and fiscal conservatives allied to strengthen enforcement of child support awards against "deadbeat dads."

Like the doctrine of colorblindness, which suffused American law during the same period, sex-blind laws produced formal, not substantive, equality. Still-dominant custom and sentiment, as well as social practice—how families actually functioned—lagged far behind the liberal feminist ideal of egalitarianism in work and family life. Women still performed the lion's share of caregiving labor, and workplace discrimination limited their employment opportunities. Women who had invested in caregiving were less willing than men to risk losing their children, leading to concerns that gender-neutral standards caused mothers to trade financial entitlements for custody. By the mid-1980s, the economic toll of divorce on women and children alarmed even optimistic reformers who wagered that egalitarian marriages would obviate the need for anything more than temporary, "rehabilitative" post-divorce spousal support.

Even formal sex neutrality eluded couples who lived together or had children outside of marriage. Feminists hoped that bespoke contracts could make couples' relationships more equitable for women, especially upon dissolution. Many courts proved nominally willing to recognize property-sharing contracts between cohabitants, but few couples made such agreements. And unmarried women who functioned as wives often were left with nothing—or, presumably, stayed in unhappy or abusive relationships for lack of other viable options.

In the law of relationship dissolution, marital status now mattered both more and less, in ways that disparately affected couples with and without means. Marriage mattered more for affluent couples, because wives divorcing at the end of long marriages could hope to share more equally in their family's accumulated wealth—through property distribution as a matter of right, not merely alimony as a discretionary matter of need and desert.[10] At the same time, courts' greater willingness to enforce relationship contracts meant that wealthy spouses could leave homemakers in the lurch. Indeed, some judges enforced premarital and cohabitation agreements that limited post-dissolution sharing as if they were commercial contracts. In a famous ruling from 1990, the Pennsylvania Supreme Court reasoned that women liberated from the constraints of coverture and fully equal before the law had only themselves to blame if they agreed to a lopsided prenuptial bargain.[11] And when, a decade later, the American Law Institute recommended the default ascription of domestic partner status to couples who lived together and functioned like spouses, not a single state adopted the idea.[12]

By contrast, lawmakers and judges granted greater legal recognition to nonmarital children. The Uniform Parentage Act encouraged states to create better systems of "legitimation." No longer could states prevent "illegitimate" children from suing for the wrongful death of their parents, for workers' compensation, or for child support. Many more federal government benefits became available, but—as with state inheritance rights—not always on the same terms as marital children enjoyed. Antidiscrimination norms modernized "illegitimacy": rather than excluding children based on formal birth status, laws looked instead to the father's functional role. If a nonmarital child could prove she depended upon her father for support, she might be eligible for survivor benefits upon his death though her parents had never married—but not if her mother supported and cared for her on her own.

Advocates succeeded in establishing that laws could not punish innocent children for the "sins" of their parents. But courts ignored or rejected more expansive constitutional arguments about sexual liberty, reproductive freedom, and racial and economic justice for adults. After welfare rights advocates failed to win a constitutional right to subsistence, they hoped that claims of disparate racial impact could address the "dual system" that subjected poor nonmarital families to government intrusion and offered minimal public benefits. Instead, courts allowed states great leeway in resource allocation and insisted upon evidence of intentional racial discrimination. States could limit grant amounts and treat mostly white beneficiaries of old age and disability benefits better than mostly nonwhite AFDC recipients so long as officials did not speak racist motives aloud. Moreover, lawmakers could encourage—even coerce—marriage and employment over single motherhood and reliance on public assistance without running afoul of the constitution.

Marital primacy's most intrepid challengers were those who fought for what Black feminists eventually named reproductive justice: the right to have children as well as not to have them, and to parent with safety and support rather than punitive surveillance—regardless of marital status. Led by Black women, single mothers fought to redefine responsible citizenship. They fared best when seeking reforms that enabled them to support and care for their families without any help from the state. Women with nonmarital children gained greater protection from employment discrimination, especially when they exposed employers' sexual or racial double standards of morality. Functional inquiries that examined whether nonmarital sexual conduct affected an employee's ability to perform her job replaced per se exclusion of pregnant single women. Mothers vanquished statutes of limitations on lawsuits seeking to establish paternity of their nonmarital children. Single mothers and their children won some protection from overt discrimination in the housing rental market.

Single mothers' constitutional claims foundered, however, when they called upon the state for support—when they claimed entitlement to public assistance without naming their children's fathers, or to Social Security survivor benefits available to widowed spouses, or to serve in the armed forces and access the military welfare state.[13] These dashed constitutional hopes left single mothers without recourse when lawmakers later repealed poor children's statutory entitlement to assistance, allowed states to place severe time and other limits on aid, strengthened paternity disclosure requirements, imposed family caps, and spent scarce funds on marriage promotion.

Fathers, too, renegotiated the boundaries of nonmarital parenthood. Their efforts sometimes complemented and other times clashed with feminist, anti-poverty, and child welfare advocacy. In contests between husbands and biological fathers for parental rights, states retained the prerogative to make marriage to a child's mother the trump card. Even where nonmarital fathers' rights did not contradict mothers' wishes, courts often denied their constitutional claims to equal parentage. But if the alternative was the unmarried mother's reliance on public assistance, the marital status of the putative father did not matter: the government stepped up child support enforcement efforts for divorced as well as never-married fathers, irrespective of whether parents were "deadbeats" or "dead-broke."

Again, functional definitions of family flourished where they ensured private sources of support. A single mother could claim child support from her children's father to reduce their reliance on public assistance. But AFDC (and later TANF) benefits were never available to adults in their own right, so the state had no obligation to support a woman (or man) left destitute at the end of a relationship. In other words, the state could indemnify cohabitors against responsibility for their former partners without risking much public expenditure. The alternative to "palimony" was not welfare at government expense but employment or poverty—often both.

Gay and lesbian Americans' relationship to marriage and marital primacy wound a circuitous path. For many activists, especially gay men, decriminalization of same-sex sexual conduct, an end to police surveillance and violence, and protection from discrimination in employment, housing, and public accommodations took precedence over relationship recognition. For others, especially lesbian mothers, child custody and parentage dominated the agenda. Some gay liberationists and lesbian feminists expressed hostility toward marriage as an institution. Others prized the legal, material, and symbolic benefits of marital status. Many felt ambivalent. For some, marriage was—for better and worse—the ultimate badge of societal acceptance and full citizenship. Others believed that gay and lesbian couples could change marriage for the better, upending traditional gender roles and sexual norms and exploring new modes of living.

Alternative forms of legal protection and relationship recognition beckoned. Just as Black feminists led the way toward gender-egalitarian marriage and single parents of color pioneered claims on behalf of nonmarital families, lesbians and gay men launched legal campaigns that paved the way for others who veered from the marital path. Individuals fired for being gay made the first inroads in turning back per se exclusions from government employment for nonmarital sexual conduct. Lesbian and gay advocates led domestic partnership efforts that often included unmarried heterosexual couples and, occasionally, extended and chosen families. Different-sex couples rarely took up the feminist challenge to craft relationship contracts with equitable divisions of labor and decision-making power. Gay and lesbian couples more frequently turned to private agreements out of necessity. And efforts by lesbian and gay co-parents to claim legal parentage underwrote new definitions of parenthood that relied upon intent and function rather than just marriage and biology, with ramifications for all families.

The advocacy of gay and lesbian workers and parents, partners and lawyers, stood in complicated relationship to other intertwined causes. Gay government employees, teachers, and librarians laid constitutional groundwork for cohabitors and for women who became pregnant outside of marriage. Gay advocates collaborated with feminists, civil rights activists, and labor leaders to promote "alternative" families initiatives, and they joined forces with organizations representing the elderly to advance domestic partnership legislation—sometimes in exchange for the political cover offered by these more established interest groups. Same-sex couples' inability to marry spurred legal innovations in private relationship contracting more generally.

Advocacy for lesbian and gay parents did not occur "in a vacuum," as Nancy Polikoff took care to note. The functional standards and definitions that replaced per se exclusion often proved double-edged, not only for gay and lesbian Americans but for all whose lives they touched. The "nexus" standard in public school teaching and child custody cases left great discretion to local school officials and courts to impose community norms and individual biases in the name of children's best interests. Functional definitions of partnership and parenthood threatened similar disciplinary and assimilative effects for families already marginalized by poverty, race, family status, gender identity, or sexual orientation.

The tension between protecting the rights of birth parents and expanding the indicia of parenthood beyond marital, biological, and adoptive ties long had plagued poverty lawyers and family law reformers concerned about government intervention in poor families of color. By the early twenty-first century, debates about racial disproportionality—high rates of child removal, foster and juvenile system involvement, and parental rights terminations in Black and Indigenous communities—reached a fever pitch. *Shattered Bonds* (2002), Dorothy Roberts's study of Black Chicago mothers who lost children to the child welfare system, offered a powerful rejoinder to works such as Elizabeth Bartholet's *Nobody's Children* (1999), which encouraged speedier removal of children and easier adoption placements.[14]

Advocates for lesbian and gay parents, too, recognized the high stakes of disputes over the rights of birth parents: extending rights to adults other than "natural" parents could help nonmarital, nonbiological gay and lesbian parents obtain access to children they helped raise—but could also fortify additional rights for disapproving relatives who sought to exclude a parent's same-sex partner.

Like those of feminists and single parents of color, the efforts of gay and lesbian advocates enjoyed varying degrees of success. Federal civil rights legislation to prohibit discrimination based on sexual orientation and marital status proved elusive. State and local efforts bore greater fruit, gradually producing scattered oases of legal protection. A permissive constitutional regime allowed for local experimentation with broader anti-discrimination laws and more inclusive definitions of family. But courts' failure to embrace advocates' expansive visions of liberty, equality, and reproductive justice also sanctioned aggressive promotion of marriage and punitive treatment of unmarried parents and nonmarital families. And this failure left untouched and untouchable the suite of federal legislation—on welfare, work, crime, adoption, immigration, and family leave—that intensified marital, racial, and class privilege at century's end.

The shift over time from marital supremacy to marital privilege reflected and fed larger trends in American law and life. In law, it accompanied a shift toward color- and sex-blindness in the long 1970s that removed some of the most egregious discriminations and opened opportunities for those already advantaged along other dimensions, especially class. When the background reality of structural inequality made ignoring race or sex a recipe for injustice, neutrality could have perverse consequences. In marital status law, selectively blurring the boundaries between marriage and nonmarriage, legitimacy and illegitimacy also had multi-valent effects. Marriage entailed duties and burdens as well as rights and benefits— and legal changes made marital status less relevant when it came to the former but more important for the latter. The law cared little about marital status when enforcing child support obligations, but a lot when allocating government benefits to adults. And state actors often justified both the imposition of parental responsibility and the privileging of marriage as necessary to children's welfare. Marital status neutrality therefore often applied in ways that aggravated inequities under cover of promoting equality.

The evolution of marital status law in the late twentieth century exemplifies elements of what the legal scholar Reva B. Siegel calls "preservation through transformation"—reforms that change the justificatory rhetoric underpinning a contested legal regime without fundamentally altering underlying status hierarchies.[15] When constitutional rulings forbade discrimination against nonmarital children, state actors increasingly rationalized policies that penalized their parents in terms of child welfare and fiscal prudence rather than morality. The partial and uneven decriminalization of nonmarital sex gave way to subtler penalties: disadvantages woven into the fabric of everything from family and employment law to government benefits, immigration, and citizenship. The emergence of sex equality and privacy norms, on this view, cleansed family status law of its most offensive elements: overt white and male supremacy and distinctions based on marital and birth status that punished children for their parents' conduct. But these reforms arguably legitimized marital privilege in ways that deepened structural inequalities based on gender, race, and class.

The story told here also departs from other instances of preservation through transformation. Unlike phenomena such as racial segregation and domestic violence, no consensus emerged about the wrongfulness of elevating marriage in the law. By the late twentieth century most legal decision-makers, regardless of ideology, generally disavowed white and male domination. But judges, lawmakers, administrators, and even many law reformers rarely questioned the government's ability to promote and privilege marriage.

Marital primacy, firmly entrenched by the end of the twentieth century, claimed adherents across the political spectrum, a key if often unspoken element of the prevailing neoliberal consensus. Antagonists in the debate over marriage equality, as divisive an issue as any at the turn of the twenty-first century, agreed on one descriptive premise: the enduring, privileged status of marriage. That status was so deeply embedded that marriage provided a language and a vehicle for gay and lesbian Americans to claim full social and economic citizenship and to combat dehumanization. Many who critiqued the elevation of marriage over other family forms and the channeling of public and private benefits through conjugal relationships nevertheless endorsed marriage equality.[16] In a society that placed a legal and cultural premium on marriage, the injustice of excluding same-sex couples was undeniable. As advocates and law reformers directed their energies toward the battle over marriage equality, the same pull of inclusion and nondiscrimination that softened the edges of marital supremacy helped marital privilege endure.

Epilogue

HEN THE U.S. SUPREME Court heard arguments in *Obergefell v. Hodges* in April 2015, several justices asked how the constitution could require Americans to abandon the age-old definition of marriage as a union between a man and a woman. Justice Ruth Bader Ginsburg interjected to emphasize how marriage had transformed from a "dominant and subordinate" to an "egalitarian" relationship. Mary Bonauto, an attorney with Gay and Lesbian Advocates and Defenders (GLAD), agreed: "All of those gender differences in the rights and responsibilities of the married pair have been eliminated. And that, of course, is a system in which committed, same-sex couples fit quite well."[1]

Arguments for same-sex marriage had seemed revolutionary, even outlandish, thirty years earlier. Now they garnered majority support, among the public and on the Court. "Marriage," Justice Anthony Kennedy wrote, is "a keystone of our social order," a "building block of our national community," a pinnacle of personal intimacy and spiritual fulfillment. To deprive gay and lesbian couples of the fundamental right to marry caused "a grave and continuing harm" inimical to liberty and equality.[2]

Obergefell's words—and silences—recapitulate many of this book's themes. The history Kennedy recounted, of how marriage's meaning evolved to embrace race and sex equality, cast the inclusion of gay and lesbian couples as the logical next step. The marriage equality movement that flowered in the early twenty-first century had made newly visible the institution's unique legal benefits. Still, the opinion's treatment of nonmarriage recalled older tropes. "Without the recognition, stability, and predictability marriage offers," Kennedy wrote, "children suffer the stigma of knowing their families are somehow lesser." Echoes of "hapless, innocent children" infused his recitation of the "significant material costs of being raised by unmarried parents, relegated to a difficult and uncertain family life."[3] Thanks to skillful advocacy, children's well-being—long a conservative weapon against gay rights—had become an argument for inclusion in marriage.[4] But *Obergefell* did not disturb states' prerogative to treat *non*marital sex and relationships less favorably.

Advocates for freedom and social justice found much to celebrate in *Obergefell*'s affirmation of gay and lesbian love and dignity. On the steps of the U.S. Supreme Court, Bonauto told a jubilant crowd, "This is a momentous decision ... for equality, for liberty, for justice under law." LGBT Americans could now "marry the person they love and make that unique commitment, take on that unique responsibility." Children would "no longer have to question why their parents were deemed unworthy of marriage" and could enjoy "the same security and protections that marriage provides to families."[5] President Barack Obama, who had embraced marriage equality in 2012, hailed the "slow, steady effort" of advocates like Bonauto, "rewarded with justice that arrives like a thunderbolt."[6]

Even some conservatives switched sides. In 2010, David Blankenhorn testified in favor of bans on gay marriage because he believed that "children have the right ... to know and to be cared for by the two parents who brought them into this world." Two years later, he pledged to "build new coalitions" among gay and straight Americans who wanted to shore up marriage and discourage nonmarital cohabitation and childbearing.[7] Same-sex couples' quest for inclusion, gay conservatives had long argued, reflected reverence for a venerable institution under threat.[8] Jonathan Rauch declared of *Obergefell*, "The conservative marriage narrative has won."[9] Others on the right remained steadfastly opposed. In dissent, Justice Samuel Alito warned that "Americans who do not hide their adherence to traditional religious beliefs about homosexual conduct will be 'labeled as bigots and treated as such' by the government."[10]

On the left, many who supported marriage equality as a matter of basic civil rights worried that *Obergefell* left behind those who could not or did not wish to marry. Justice Kennedy's opinion glorified the "nobility and dignity" of marriage at the expense of other family forms, wrote Melissa Murray.[11] It ignored how marital status law subordinated people of color and "diminished Black dignity and citizenship," in Robin Lenhardt's words.[12] Nan Hunter, who once hoped gay and lesbian couples could make marriage more gender-egalitarian, feared that *Obergefell* "elevates traditionalist concepts of marriage."[13] Katherine Franke cautioned that winning the right to marry could ensnare queer Americans in a web of punitive state regulation and surveillance.[14] Legal marriage, Nancy Polikoff warned, would not solve and could exacerbate racial and class divides: women in the top 5 percent of household income were now the only group of Americans to marry at higher rates than they had in 1970.[15] Critics worried that the hard-won triumph of marriage equality might drain momentum from crucial fights against oppression and violence and for liberation.[16]

In the following years, advocates, scholars, and LGBTQ+ Americans continued to debate the political valence of marriage equality.[17] Some mourned the loss of alternatives such as domestic partnerships and civil unions and resisted new social pressure to marry.[18] Others insisted that marriage need not displace nonmarital recognition.[19] Some warned that legal regulation of nonmarital sex continued unabated, with government and private actors no less free to discriminate on that basis.[20] At the same time, many rejoiced at how legal marriage made their relationships newly legible to family and friends, as well as governments and employers. A study conducted between 2015 and 2019 revealed nuanced views among racially diverse LGBTQ+ respondents, who often connected marriage equality to "their ability to combat stigma . . . in domains that extend beyond marriage."[21]

Obergefell could be read to entrench marital privilege but also to open new possibilities. A half-century earlier, *Griswold v. Connecticut* had established a constitutional right to privacy first grounded in the sanctity of marriage but soon extended to the unmarried. The principles of liberty and equality that animated the recognition of same-sex marriage could also apply to discrimination against nonmarital families. Courtney Joslin, who had argued landmark cases recognizing legal rights for lesbian parents, saw promise for nonmarital relationships in *Obergefell*'s expansion of constitutional protection to match evolving social norms.[22]

The relationship between marriage equality and marital status law more generally remained complicated. Greater acceptance of committed, marriage-like gay relationships sometimes made authorities more receptive to diverse family forms and less concerned with marital status and blood ties.[23] Would-be parents emphasized the similarities between nonmarital same-sex and marital different-sex relationships to argue for parental recognition. Lesbian mothers' committed relationships with partners as well as children bolstered their intent- and function-based claims to parentage.²⁴

For others, the availability of marriage made its absence legally significant, to the detriment of the unmarried. Karah Fisher and Lorrena Thompson met in 2004.²⁵ The couple initially "agreed they did not want to seek a legal relationship" because they "shared a common belief in freedom *from* marriage." Later, they held a commitment ceremony and registered as domestic partners. In 2008, Lorrena was inseminated with sperm from one of Karah's brothers and from a friend; both women adopted a new surname to share with the baby. But when the couple later separated, Lorrena claimed she was the child's only parent. Karah argued that Oregon's marital presumption, applied to a same-sex spouse in a prior case, should make Karah a mother too. But a state court ruled in 2015 that partners like Karah would automatically gain parental rights only if they married—or would have married had it been legal to do so.²⁶

After *Obergefell*, federal constitutional law limited states' ability to discriminate against same-sex *spouses*, at least in theory. But in some states, even marriage was insufficient. The U.S. Supreme Court soon weighed in. When Terrah Pavan gave birth in Arkansas in 2015, the state refused to add her wife, Marisa, to their baby's birth certificate, even though a male spouse would have been listed regardless of genetic ties. The Court ruled that Arkansas must provide same-sex couples "the constellation of benefits the states have linked to marriage."²⁷

Even so, when Andrew Dvash-Banks, a U.S. citizen, and his Israeli husband, Elad, had twins through surrogacy in 2016, American consular officials refused to grant U.S. citizenship to the twin who was not genetically related to Andrew—treating him as if he were born outside of marriage despite precedents conferring citizenship on nonbiological parents in married different-sex couples. It took two years for the couple to win a favorable federal court ruling.²⁸ And such decisions did not reach unmarried partners or nonmarital children. Had the Dvash-Bankses not been married, Andrew could not have passed citizenship to his nonbiological son without formally adopting or "legitimating" him.

Citizenship law did edge a step closer to sex neutrality for nonmarital biological parents in *Sessions v. Morales-Santana* (2017). Luis Morales-Santana, the son of a U.S. citizen father, had lived in the United States since age thirteen. When he faced deportation because of several criminal convictions, Morales-Santana challenged a law that gave U.S. citizen mothers—but not fathers—a shortened residency period to pass citizenship to nonmarital children. Once in dissent, Justice Ginsburg now wrote for the majority: "Hardly gender-neutral, [the law] conforms to the long-held view that unwed fathers care little about, indeed are strangers to their children." The law rested on two "now untenable" premises: "In marriage, husband is dominant, wife subordinate; unwed mother is the natural and sole guardian of a nonmarital child." Such "familiar stereotype[s]" could not withstand modern equal protection scrutiny.[29]

Unfortunately for Morales-Santana and other unmarried parents, the Court remedied this discrimination by subjecting all parents to the same stringent residency requirement.[30] Moreover, myriad immigration and citizenship laws continue to depend on adults' marital status, including the ability to help one's spouse—but not a nonmarital partner—to immigrate and naturalize. Thousands of other federal benefits still turn on marital or birth status, many of them reliant on state definitions of "legitimacy."[31] For unmarried parents and children, family status often depends on the idiosyncrasies of state law and officials' discretion.

And the role of marital status in parentage law varies widely by state. States differ in the requirements they impose on nonmarital biological fathers to assert parental rights or to object to a child's adoption; how marital presumptions are applied; whether marital status is a relevant category in assisted reproduction statutes; the availability of functional parenthood doctrines; and whether a child can have more than two legal parents. More than half of U.S. states lack a second-parent adoption statute that applies to unmarried couples, and many states make joint adoption difficult for unmarried partners.[32] Advocates still encourage even married nonbiological co-parents to seek a second-parent adoption. When her wife, Whitney, gave birth, Nikki Graf adopted their daughter, Logan, because the Minnesota statute governing assisted reproduction applied only to "husbands."[33]

Such inequities spurred revisions to the Uniform Parentage Act. Amendments in 2017 made its provisions neutral as to marital status and sex, and expanded intent-based and functional parenthood. The UPA now recognizes "individuals" who intend to be parents through assisted reproduction and extends voluntary acknowledgments of parentage to all, regardless of biology, sex, or marital status. The revised UPA also includes a new "de facto parent" category.[34] An optional provision allows for recognition of more than two parents when non-recognition would be detrimental to a child.[35] As of 2024, eight states had enacted the revised UPA.

States continue to take divergent approaches to nonmarital adult relationships, too. The ALI's domestic partnership provisions, which ascribed status to couples based on functional criteria, never caught on.
Some states refuse to grant any rights to unmarried couples. Jane Blumenthal and Eileen Brewer raised three children together and commingled their lives and finances during a twenty-six-year relationship.
Though Illinois had not legalized same-sex marriage until 2014, in 2016
the state supreme court—invoking *Obergefell*'s homage to marriage—
held that Brewer could not claim a share of Blumenthal's lucrative medical practice because *any* nonmarital recognition would undermine formal
marriage.[36] Other states recognize agreements between cohabitants, but
recovery remains rare.[37] In 2021, reformers drafted a Uniform Cohabitants' Economic Remedies Act (UCERA), which rejects the ALI's ascriptive approach but promotes the enforcement of oral, written, express,
and implied-in-fact agreements.[38]

Dissension about functional family definitions persists. The debate
over UCERA featured enduring disagreements about whether and when
unmarried cohabitants should have reciprocal obligations. Some were
sympathetic to functional definitions as a stopgap for same-sex partners
and parents but withdrew their support when marriage and second-
parent adoption became available. Critics continue to worry that functional parenthood doctrines authorize state intrusions on familial privacy
and integrity, violate the rights of existing legal parents, invite judicial
bias, empower abusive partners, open the floodgates to bogus claims of
parentage, and aggravate family conflict to children's detriment.[39]

Based on their study of 669 published court decisions between 1980
and 2021, Courtney Joslin and Douglas NeJaime argue that such concerns reflect inaccurate empirical assumptions. In the "overwhelming
majority" of cases, the functional parent had been a primary caregiver to
the child. In many cases, the legal parent—if involved in the child's life—
had not been providing day-to-day care. Same-sex partners comprised
less than one-fifth of a data set dominated by relatives, especially grandparents, as well as different-sex partners. These families often faced economic hardship, health challenges, poverty, and housing insecurity.
Functional parent doctrines usually provided continuity in existing living
arrangements, preserved children's relationships with existing legal parents, and avoided the need for further state intervention.[40]

The use of functional doctrines to impose support obligations also
divides progressive reformers. In *Elisa B. v. Superior Court*, the California

Supreme Court held a lesbian co-parent to account after she stopped providing for twins she had raised with her former partner. The majority relied on precedents involving nonmarital, nonbiological fathers who held themselves out as parents.[41] Many saw *Elisa B.*, one of three companion cases that recognized rights as well as duties for lesbian co-parents, as a signal victory. Elisa earned nearly six figures; her ex-partner Emily supported the state's efforts to recoup support. Others worried that, like poor single mothers with male sexual partners, lesbian mothers would be subject to mandatory (m)aternity disclosure and child support obligations regardless of ability to pay.[42]

Marriage equality held out the promise of a more gender-egalitarian division of labor between partners. Some early returns suggest that gay and lesbian couples continue to divide work and care responsibilities more evenly than their heterosexual counterparts. Others indicate that marriage and/or parenting correlates with greater specialization even among same-sex partners.[43]

Either way, twenty years after *Goodridge*, marriage equality appeared to have bolstered the institution. In 2024 a Rand Corporation study concluded that marriage enhanced the well-being of same-sex couples and may have increased different-sex couples' interest in marrying.[44] These results backlit a now-familiar eruption of anxiety about the decline of marriage, captured in the title of a book published in 2023 by the economist Melissa Kearney, *The Two-Parent Privilege: How Americans Stopped Getting Married and Started Falling Behind.*[45]

Americans continue to harbor complex and divergent views about marriage and nonmarriage. Support for same-sex marriage grew sharply in the early twenty-first century, increasing from 27 percent in 1996 to 70 percent in 2021.[46] Public opinion about nonmarital childbearing and cohabitation improved much more modestly.[47] The share of Americans who agreed that single parents could raise children as well as two parents rose from 35 percent in 1994 to 48 percent in 2012, and the number who disagreed declined slightly. In 2015, however, two-thirds of Americans said that more single women having children without a partner was bad for society and almost half felt the same way about unmarried couples with children.[48] Discrimination based on marital status still is legal in most jurisdictions.[49]

To improve the legal treatment of nonmarital families, state and local efforts have remained necessary. Advocates worked doggedly to repeal family caps on public assistance, and by 2020 ten of twenty-two states had done so.[50] As of early 2024, seven states maintained a family cap.[51] States and localities continued to innovate more comprehensive family definitions. About a dozen states enacted paid family leave laws in the twenty-first century, often expanding eligibility beyond the narrow ambit of the Family and Medical Leave Act (FMLA). Some states allow employees compensated time off to care for extended, functional, or chosen family members.[52]

Some jurisdictions maintained civil union and domestic partnership laws after marriage equality, but nonmarital relationships still are not recognized by the federal government for purposes of benefit eligibility. In 2020, Somerville, Massachusetts, became the first municipality to allow more than two people to form domestic partnerships, and the city soon passed an anti-discrimination ordinance covering polyamorous residents. Alexander Chen of Harvard's LGBTQ+ Advocacy Clinic said such laws should appeal to conservatives who complain that liberals too often "look to the state" for care solutions. "If people want to take legal responsibility for each other," he said, "that's a good thing."[53]

Ten days before the *Obergefell* decision, Donald Trump descended an escalator at Trump Tower and announced his presidential candidacy. His victory the following year transformed the American political and legal landscape. Among his lasting legacies was the transformation of the federal judiciary. The Republican-led Senate had refused to consider President Obama's Supreme Court nominee, giving President Trump the chance to appoint Neil Gorsuch in 2017. Brett Kavanaugh replaced Justice Kennedy in 2018. After Justice Ginsburg's death in September 2020, Republicans rushed to confirm Amy Coney Barrett.

Breakthroughs in 2020 gave progressives hope. In *Bostock v. Clayton County*, the Supreme Court interpreted Title VII's sex discrimination provision to cover sexual orientation and gender identity.[54] The murders of George Floyd and Brenna Taylor energized the Movement for Black Lives and prompted a racial reckoning. Calls grew louder to end mass incarceration, to abolish the police, to transform immigration and customs enforcement, and to dismantle the system of family regulation that separated families in the name of child welfare. Democrats narrowly won the presidency and both houses of Congress in November.

When President Joe Biden took office, he issued a series of executive orders that undid some of the Trump administration's worst abuses and extended *Bostock*'s anti-discrimination protections to immigration, health care, and education. The COVID-19 pandemic's devastating impact, especially on communities of color, inspired the expansion of the child tax credit to give unconditional aid to lower-income families. For single mothers like Anique Houpe, forced by the pandemic to quit her $18-per-hour job at a suburban Atlanta post office to care for two children, monthly payments of $500 kept at bay poverty, homelessness, and food insecurity.[55] For a brief time, it seemed that Trump's incitement of an insurrectionist mob that attacked the Capitol on January 6, 2021, might break his hold on the Republican Party.

But resistance from right-wing countermovements swiftly followed. As the federal judiciary lurched further to the right, religious liberty and free speech challenges endangered prohibitions on discrimination, and the wall between church and state crumbled.[56] Exemptions for individuals and corporations that opposed birth control, abortion, nonmarital sex, and rights for LGBTQ+ Americans threatened to swallow constitutional and statutory protections. "Don't Say Gay" laws, attacks on "critical race theory" and diversity initiatives, and assaults on the rights of transgender children and adults proliferated in the following years. The Equality Act—which would prohibit discrimination based on sex, sexual orientation, and gender identity across a range of domains—stalled in Congress. The expanded child tax credit expired, felled by familiar arguments that it discouraged work and marriage.[57] And in June 2022, the Supreme Court overruled *Roe v. Wade* (1973) and *Planned Parenthood v. Casey* (1992), eliminating the federal abortion right.[58]

Dobbs v. Jackson Women's Health Organization represented a triumph for conservatives decades in the making, with devastating implications for individuals and families. But the rights that the decision threatened to erase had always fallen short of what advocates sought. Challenges to marital supremacy were a key battlefield on which Americans fought for more capacious visions of reproductive and sexual freedom, racial and economic justice, and gender equity. Understanding how marital primacy withstood these challenges recasts this latest constitutional rupture as a moment of continuity as well as change.

Against the backdrop of the history told here, *Dobbs* represents both departures and throughlines. It repudiated any role for changing social values in constitutional interpretation and instead enshrined a narrow version of "history and tradition" as the measure of today's rights. In so doing, *Dobbs* called into question nearly every major federal constitutional precedent discussed in this book, from *Griswold* to *Obergefell*.[59] At the same time, *Dobbs* intensified pre-existing reproductive injustices. It exacerbated disparities between rich and poor, red and blue states. It weakened a body of privacy and equality law that always had been less available to those marginalized by poverty, race, sex, and marital status. The further criminalization of pregnancy echoed earlier campaigns of reproductive control, which fell most heavily on single mothers of color. By unchaining government's ability to prioritize embryos and fetuses over living human beings—especially their own parents—*Dobbs* reinforced familiar ideas about children's innocence and adult culpability.

The resistance to *Dobbs*, too, reflected continuity and change. In the twentieth century, struggles for what Black feminists named reproductive justice—the right to have children, or not; the resources to raise flourishing families; protections for bodily autonomy and family integrity—often took the form of challenges to marital supremacy. But constitutional doctrines came up short. *Dobbs*, the legal scholar Kimberly Mutcherson wrote, could be a "catalyst for reproductive justice."[60] Many of the same states that had punished "illegitimacy" in the service of white supremacy still maintained family caps on public assistance to discourage nonmarital childbearing, limited sex education and access to contraception, and now banned abortion. The acute visibility of reproductive injustice and its impact on otherwise privileged Americans might elevate the broader agenda feminists of color had long championed.

No longer obliged to defend flawed precedents, advocates revitalized creative strategies, leaned into equality arguments, and harnessed burgeoning public support for reproductive autonomy. Advocates resisted narratives that pitted women against their existing and future children, and they fought for a pregnant person's right to receive lifesaving and health-preserving medical care. They spotlighted the hypocrisy of lawmakers who claimed to protect maternal health and potential life but failed to provide the most basic supports to living parents and families. With federal constitutional protections stripped away, states became laboratories for new legislation and state constitutional provisions to protect a broader range of rights and freedoms.

Two years after *Dobbs*, the Supreme Court's decision in *Department of State v. Muñoz* cast another ominous shadow. Sandra Muñoz, a prominent Los Angeles workers' rights attorney, married Luis Asencio-Cordero, an undocumented immigrant from El Salvador, in 2010. After they lived together in California for five years and had a child, the couple sought legal permanent residency for Luis—a privilege for which he was eligible as the spouse of a U.S. citizen. But when Luis returned to San Salvador to apply for a visa, the U.S. consulate denied his application without explanation. Luis had no criminal record, but just in case he "renounced any [gang] affiliation" and obtained a supportive letter from Representative Judy Chu (D-CA). The State Department again denied his application, and Muñoz sued. She argued that the government's refusal to provide any reason for excluding her spouse infringed upon her own fundamental right to marry.

The Court rejected Muñoz's claim in a "needlessly sweeping" decision.[61] The majority could simply have said that Sandra eventually received an explanation for the visa denial (suspicion that Luis's tattoos were gang-related) and was entitled to nothing more. Instead, Justice Barrett's opinion reached out to decide that no fundamental liberty interest was implicated at all because the right to live together with one's spouse in the United States is not "deeply rooted in the nation's history and traditions."[62]

The case's outcome was devastating for Sandra and Luis, separated since 2015 and now forced to expatriate if they wished to raise their child, a U.S. citizen, together. Same-sex couples unable to marry or even live together safely abroad, the dissenters noted, faced even greater peril. And that was not all. Justice Sotomayor decried the majority's striking disregard for more than a century of precedent that "vindicated the expansiveness of the right to marriage." The Court, she implied, not only denied the privileges of marriage to citizens with foreign-born partners and parents but also threatened the right to marry, and possibly other fundamental rights and freedoms. Less than a decade after *Obergefell*, marriage equality—and so much else—once again hung in the balance.[63]

Notes

Abbreviations
Individuals

BRW	Justice Byron R. White
HAB	Justice Harry A. Blackmun
JPS	Justice John Paul Stevens
LFP	Justice Lewis F. Powell, Jr.
PS	Justice Potter Stewart
SOC	Justice Sandra Day O'Connor
TM	Justice Thurgood Marshall
WEB	Chief Justice Warren E. Burger
WHR	Justice William H. Rehnquist
WJB	Justice William J. Brennan, Jr.
WOD	Justice William O. Douglas

Organizations and Government Agencies

ACLU	American Civil Liberties Union
ALI	American Law Institute
CLASP	Center for Law and Social Policy
CORE	Congress of Racial Equality
LDF	NAACP Legal Defense Fund, Inc.
NAACP	National Association for the Advancement of Colored People
NCLR	National Center for Lesbian Rights
NCWFL	National Center on Women and Family Law
NOW	National Organization for Women
NOW LDEF	NOW Legal Defense and Education Fund
PPFA	Planned Parenthood Federation of America

Archival Sources

ACLU Records	Records of the American Civil Liberties Union, Mudd Library, Princeton University, Princeton, N.J.
ALI Records	Archives of the American Law Institute, Biddle Law Library, University of Pennsylvania Carey Law School, Philadelphia, Pa.
BB Papers	Betty Blaisdell Berry Papers, Schlesinger Library, Radcliffe Institute, Harvard University, Cambridge, Mass.
BRW Papers	Justice Byron R. White Papers, Manuscripts Division, Library of Congress, Washington, D.C.
CG Papers	Charles Gossett Papers, ONE Archives, Los Angeles, Calif.
FMJ Papers	Frank M. Johnson, Jr., Papers, Manuscripts Division, Library of Congress, Washington, D.C.
HAB Papers	Justice Harry A. Blackmun Papers, Manuscripts Division, Library of Congress, Washington, D.C.
HRW Papers	Human Rights for Women Papers, Schlesinger Library, Radcliffe Institute, Harvard University, Cambridge, Mass.
JWP Papers	Justine Wise Polier Papers, Schlesinger Library, Radcliffe Institute, Harvard University, Cambridge, Mass.
LFP Papers	Justice Lewis F. Powell, Jr., Archives, Washington and Lee University School of Law, Lexington, Va.
ME Papers	Mary Eastwood Papers, Schlesinger Library, Radcliffe Institute, Harvard University, Cambridge, Mass.
NARA	National Archives and Records Administration (College Park, Md.; Kansas City, Mo.; Fort Worth, Tex.; New York City, N.Y.; Philadelphia, Pa.; Seattle, Wash.)
NCWFL Papers	National Center on Women and Family Law Papers, Schlesinger Library, Radcliffe Institute, Harvard University, Cambridge, Mass.
ND Papers	Norman Dorsen Papers, Tamiment Library and Robert F. Wagner Labor Archives, Elmer Holmes Bobst Library, New York University, New York, N.Y.
NOW Papers	National Organization for Women Papers, Schlesinger Library, Radcliffe Institute, Harvard University, Cambridge, Mass.
NOW LDEF Papers	NOW Legal Defense and Education Fund Papers, Schlesinger Library, Radcliffe Institute, Harvard University, Cambridge, Mass.
PCSW Papers	President's Commission on the Status of Women Papers, Schlesinger Library, Radcliffe Institute, Harvard University, Cambridge, Mass.
PE Papers	Paula L. Ettelbrick Papers, Division of Rare and Manuscript Collections, Cornell University Library, Ithaca, N.Y.

PM Papers   Pauli Murray Papers, Schlesinger Library, Radcliffe
                   Institute, Harvard University, Cambridge, Mass.
RBG Papers   Justice Ruth Bader Ginsburg Papers, Manuscripts
                   Division, Library of Congress, Washington, D.C.
TM Papers   Justice Thurgood Marshall Papers, Manuscripts Division,
                   Library of Congress, Washington, D.C.
WCK Papers   William C. Keady Papers, Special Collections, Mississippi
                   State University Library, Mississippi State, Miss.
WJB Papers   Justice William J. Brennan, Jr., Papers, Manuscripts
                   Division, Library of Congress, Washington, D.C.
WOD Papers   Justice William O. Douglas Papers, Manuscripts Division,
                   Library of Congress, Washington, D.C.

Periodicals and News Services

ANP   Associated Negro Press
AP   Associated Press
LAT   *Los Angeles Times*
NYT   *New York Times*
UPI   United Press International
WP   *Washington Post*

Introduction

1. Dobbs v. Jackson Women's Health Organization, 142 S. Ct. 2228 (2022).
2. Ari Shapiro et al., "HRC President Reacts to Respect for Marriage Act Ahead of Signing," National Public Radio, Dec. 12, 2022.
3. Respect for Marriage Act, Pub. L. 117–228, 136 Stat. 2305 (2022). The act repealed what remained of the 1996 Defense of Marriage Act and required states to recognize valid marriages conducted in other states.
4. "HRC's Kelley Robinson Talks Family, Fighting Back, and the Future," *Mombian*, Jan. 12, 2023.
5. "Robinson: Respect for Marriage Act 'An Important Step' in Journey to Freedom and Equality," MSNBC, Dec. 3, 2022.
6. Iker Seisdedos, "President of the Human Rights Campaign," *El Pais*, Dec. 24, 2022.
7. Dana Rudolph, "HRC's First Black Queer Woman Leader," *Dallas Voice*, Jan. 13, 2023.
8. Sheila B. Kamerman, "Gender Roles and Family Structure Changes in the Advanced West: Implications for Social Policy," in *Poverty, Inequality, and the Future of Social Policy*, ed. Katherine McFate et al. (Russell Sage, 1995); Janet C. Gornick and Marcia K. Meyers, *Families That Work: Policies for Reconciling Parenthood and Employment* (Russell Sage, 2003); Vanier Institute, "Facts and Stats: Married and Common Law Couples in Canada," May 30, 2023.

9. Valerie Schweizer, "Marriage: More than a Century of Change, 1900–2018," Family Profile No. 21, 2020; President's Commission on the Status of Women, *American Women* (1963), 18.

10. Elaine Tyler May, *Homeward Bound: Families in the Cold War Era* (Basic Books, 2008). See also Stephanie Coontz, *Marriage, a History: How Love Conquered Marriage* (Penguin Books, 2006), chapters 13-14.

11. May, *Homeward Bound*, 2–3.

12. The first use of the term "marital supremacy" that I am aware of came in Elizabeth Pleck, *Not Just Roommates: Cohabitation After the Sexual Revolution* (University of Chicago Press, 2012).

13. Margot Canaday, "Heterosexuality as a Legal Regime," in *Cambridge History of Law in America*, ed. Michael Grossberg and Christopher Tomlins (Cambridge University Press, 2008); Nancy F. Cott, *Public Vows: A History of Marriage and the Nation* (Harvard University Press, 2000); Alice Kessler-Harris, *In Pursuit of Equity: Women, Men, and the Quest for Economic Citizenship in Twentieth-Century America* (Oxford University Press, 2001); Linda Gordon, *Pitied But Not Entitled: Single Mothers and the History of Welfare, 1890–1935* (Harvard University Press, 1998).

14. Gordon, *Pitied But Not Entitled*; Jill Quadagno, *The Color of Welfare: How Racism Undermined the War on Poverty* (Oxford University Press, 1996); Michael Katz, *The Undeserving Poor: America's Enduring Confrontation with Poverty* (Oxford University Press, 1989).

15. Canaday, "Heterosexuality as a Legal Regime."

16. "Marriage is not merely a private contract between the parties," the court said, "but creates a status in which the state is vitally interested." Graham v. Graham, 33 F. Supp. 936, 937–38 (E.D. Mich. 1940).

17. Reva B. Siegel, "'The Rule of Love': Wife-Beating as Prerogative and Privacy," 105 *Yale L. J.* 2117 (1996); Linda Gordon, *Heroes of Their Own Lives: The Politics and History of Family Violence* (University of Illinois Press, 2002).

18. Jill E. Hasday, "Contest and Consent: A Legal History of Marital Rape," 88 *Calif. L. Rev.* 1373 (2000).

19. Wives also stood to lose government benefits if they divorced. See Suzanne Kahn, *Divorce, American Style: Fighting for Women's Economic Citizenship in the Neoliberal Era* (University of Pennsylvania Press, 2021).

20. Pleck, *Not Just Roommates*; Joanna L. Grossman and Lawrence M. Friedman, *Inside the Castle: Law and the Family in Twentieth-Century America* (Princeton University Press, 2011); Peggy Pascoe, *What Comes Naturally: Miscegenation Law and the Making of Race in America* (Oxford University Press, 2010).

21. Canaday, "Heterosexuality as a Legal Regime"; Margot Canaday, *The Straight State: Sexuality and Citizenship in Twentieth-Century America* (Princeton University Press, 2009); William N. Eskridge, Jr., *Gaylaw: Challenging the Apartheid of the Closet* (Harvard University Press, 1999); William Eskridge, Jr., *Dishonorable Passions: Sodomy Law in America, 1861–2003* (Viking, 2008); Anna Lvovsky, *Vice Patrol: Cops, Courts, and the Struggle over Gay Life Before Stonewall* (University of Chicago Press, 2021).

22. Walter O. Weyrauch, "Informal and Formal Marriage: An Appraisal of Trends in Family Organization," 28 *U. Chicago L. Rev.* 88, 98 (1960). On common law marriage as a means of privatizing dependency, see Ariela R. Dubler, "Governing Through Contract: Common Law Marriage in the Nineteenth Century," 107 *Yale L. J.* 1885 (1998).

23. See, for example, Leigh Ann Wheeler, *How Sex Became a Civil Liberty* (Oxford University Press, 2012); Risa Goluboff, *Vagrant Nation: Police Power, Constitutional Change, and the Making of the 1960s* (Oxford University Press, 2016).

24. Sara Evans, *Tidal Wave: How Women Changed America at Century's End* (Free Press, 2003); Ruth Rosen, *The World Split Open: How the Modern Women's Movement Changed America* (Penguin Books, 2006); Keeanga-Yamahtta Taylor, *How We Get Free: Black Women and the Combahee River Collective* (Haymarket Books, 2017); Linda K. Kerber, *No Constitutional Right to Be Ladies: Women and the Obligations of Citizenship* (New York: Hill & Wang, 1998); Serena Mayeri, *Reasoning from Race: Feminism, Law, and the Civil Rights Revolution* (Harvard University Press, 2011).

25. See, for example, Tomiko Brown-Nagin, *Courage to Dissent: Atlanta and the Long History of the Civil Rights Movement* (Oxford University Press, 2011); *The Black Power Movement: Rethinking the Civil Rights–Black Power Era*, ed. Peniel Joseph (Routledge, 2006).

26. Premilla Nadasen, *Welfare Warriors: The Welfare Rights Movement in the United States* (Routledge, 2004); Felicia Kornbluh, *The Battle for Welfare Rights: Politics and Poverty in Modern America* (University of Pennsylvania Press, 2007); Karen M. Tani, *States of Dependency: Welfare, Rights, and American Governance, 1935–1972* (Cambridge University Press, 2016); Annelise Orleck, *Storming Caesars Palace: How Black Mothers Fought Their Own War on Poverty* (Beacon Press, 2005); Martha F. Davis, *Brutal Need: Lawyers and the Welfare Rights Movement, 1960–1973* (Yale University Press, 1993).

27. Lillian Faderman, *The Gay Revolution: The Story of the Struggle* (Simon & Schuster, 2015); Eskridge, *Gaylaw;* Margot Canaday, *Queer Career: Sexuality and Work in Modern America* (Princeton University Press, 2023); Marie-Amélie George, *Family Matters: Queer Households and the Half-Century Struggle for Legal Recognition* (Cambridge University Press, 2024).

28. Natasha Zaretsky, *No Direction Home: The American Family and the Fear of National Decline, 1968–1980* (University of North Carolina Press, 2007); Alison Lefkovitz, *Strange Bedfellows: Marriage in the Age of Women's Liberation* (University of Pennsylvania Press, 2018); Rebecca L. Davis, *More Perfect Unions: The American Search for Marital Bliss* (Harvard University Press, 2010), chapter 6.

29. Sally C. Curtin and Paul Sutton, "Marriage Rates in the United States, 1900–2018," National Center for Health Statistics, April 2020; Stephanie J. Ventura and Christine A. Bachrach, "Nonmarital Childbearing in the United States, 1940–1999," National Vital Statistics Reports, vol. 48, no. 16,

Oct. 18, 2000; Catherine Fitch et al., "The Rise of Cohabitation in the United States: New Historical Estimates," Minnesota Population Center, 2005; Sheela Kennedy and Steven Ruggles, "Breaking Up Is Hard to Count: The Rise of Divorce in the United States, 1980–2010," *Demography*, vol. 51, no. 2 (April 2014): 587–98.

30. Pew Research Center, "The American Family Today," Dec. 17, 2015. The median age at first marriage rose from twenty for women and about twenty-three for men in 1960 to about twenty-five for women and twenty-seven for men in 2000. U.S. Census Bureau, "Median Age at First Marriage: 1890 to Present" (2024).

31. Schweizer, "Marriage"; Julissa Cruz, "Marriage: More than a Century of Change," *Family Profile*, No. 13, 2013. See also Naomi Cahn and June Carbone, *Marriage Markets: How Inequality Is Remaking the American Family* (Oxford University Press, 2014).

32. As I discuss in the book's conclusion, this trajectory resembles but also departs from the phenomenon of "preservation through transformation" identified by Reva Siegel. See, for example, Siegel, "'Rule of Love'"; Reva Siegel, "Why Equal Protection No Longer Protects: The Evolving Forms of Status-Enforcing State Action," 49 *Stanford L. Rev.* 1111 (1997).

33. On the artificial narrowness of "family law" as a category, see Jill Hasday, *Family Law Reimagined* (Harvard University Press, 2014); Janet Halley, "What Is Family Law? A Genealogy, Part I," 23 *Yale J. L. & Hum.* 1 (2011).

34. Like resistance to vagrancy laws in the 1960s, reforms to marital status law "resulted more from convergence than coordination." Goluboff, *Vagrant Nation*, 7.

35. Loretta Ross and Rickie Solinger, *Reproductive Justice: An Introduction* (University of California Press, 2017).

36. I borrow this term from Reva Siegel's classic article on an earlier period, "The Modernization of Marital Status Law: Adjudicating Wives' Right to Earnings, 1860–1930," 82 *Georgetown L. J.* 2127 (1994).

37. On uneven decriminalization, see Pleck, *Not Just Roommates;* Cynthia Grant Bowman, *Unmarried Couples, Law, and Public Policy* (Oxford University Press, 2010); JoAnn Sweeny, "Undead Statutes: The Rise, Fall, and Continuing Uses of Adultery and Fornication Criminal Laws," 46 *Loyola Univ. Chi. L. J.* 127 (2014).

38. On the conservatism of liberals during this period, see, for example, Lily Geismer, *Left Behind: The Democrats' Failed Attempt to Solve Inequality* (Hachette Books, 2022); Naomi Murakawa, *The First Civil Right: How Liberals Built Prison America* (Oxford University Press, 2014); Elizabeth Hinton, *From the War on Poverty to the War on Crime: The Making of Mass Incarceration* (Harvard University Press, 2016); Julilly Kohler-Hausman, *Getting Tough: Welfare and Imprisonment in 1970s America* (Princeton University Press, 2017); Marisa Chappell, *The War on Welfare: Family, Poverty, and Politics in Modern America* (University of Pennsylvania Press, 2010).

39. Marital households form "the central pivot of intimate governance," a key "site of both privilege and regulation." Introduction to *Intimate States: Gender, Sexuality, and Governance in Modern U.S. History*, ed. Margot Canaday, Nancy F. Cott, and Robert O. Self (University of Chicago Press, 2021), 3.

40. On family law's historical and contemporary role in privatizing dependency, see, for example, Dubler, "Governing Through Contract"; Melissa Murray, "Family Law's Doctrines," 163 *U. Pa. L. Rev.* 1985 (2015).

41. On how the marital household has been "deeply embedded in the legal substructure of the social and economic order," see Canaday, Cott, and Self, "Introduction," 3.

42. Andrew Cherlin, *The Marriage Go-Round: The State of Marriage and the Family in America Today* (Doubleday, 2010).

43. See Robert O. Self, *All in the Family: The Realignment of American Democracy Since the 1960s* (Hill and Wang, 2012); Melinda Cooper, *Family Values: Between Neoliberalism and the New Social Conservatism* (Princeton University Press, 2017); Brent Cebul, "Afterword: Frugal Governance, Family Values, and the Intimate Roots of Neoliberalism," in Canaday et al., *Intimate States*, 325–36.

Chapter 1. Challenging Marital Supremacy

1. On the Louisiana crisis, see, for example, Lisa Levenstein, "From Innocent Children to Unwanted Migrants and Unwed Moms: Two Chapters in Public Discourse on Welfare in the United States, 1960–61," *Journal of Women's History*, vol. 11, no. 4 (Winter 2000); Taryn Lindhorst and Leslie Leighninger, "'Ending Welfare as We Know It' in 1960: Louisiana's Suitable Home Law," *Social Service Review* (December 2003): 564–84; Andrew Pope, "Making Motherhood a Felony: Activism in New Orleans and the End of Suitable Home Laws, 1959–1962," *Journal of American History*, vol. 105, no. 2 (September 2018): 291–310.

2. Pope, "Making Motherhood a Felony."

3. George Sherman, "Louisiana Shocked By British Offer," *The Observer* (London, England), Sept. 11, 1960.

4. Pope, "Making Motherhood a Felony," 291–94.

5. Anders Walker, *The Ghost of Jim Crow: How Southern Moderates Used* Brown v. Board of Education *to Stall Civil Rights* (Oxford University Press, 2009).

6. Martha F. Davis, *Brutal Need: Lawyers and the Welfare Rights Movement, 1960–1973* (Yale University Press, 1993), 9.

7. Walker, *Ghost of Jim Crow*.

8. Anders Walker, "Legislating Virtue: How Segregationists Disguised Racial Discrimination as Moral Reform Following *Brown v. Board of Education*," 47 *Duke L. J.* 399 (1997).

9. Serena Mayeri, "Marital Supremacy and the Constitution of the Nonmarital Family," 103 *Calif. L. Rev.* 1277 (2015) (n. 30); Rickie Solinger, *Wake Up*

Little Susie: Single Pregnancy and Race Before Roe v. Wade (New York: Rout-
ledge, 1992); Rebecca M. Kluchin, *Fit to Be Tied: Sterilization and Reproductive
Rights in America, 1950–1980* (Rutgers University Press, 2009); Alexandra
Minna Stern, *Eugenic Nation: Faults and Frontiers of Better Breeding in Modern
America* (University of California Press, 2005).

10. Roger Greene (AP), "Storm of Controversy Develops as Illegitimacy Hits
New High," *Argus-Leader* (Sioux Falls, S.Dak.), Aug. 9, 1959.

11. See, for example, Jackson Daily News, "The Cost of Illegitimacy," *Daily Herald*
(Biloxi, Miss.), Apr. 17, 1959 (describing Detroit study); "Commission Makes
Illegitimacy Report," *Richmond Times-Dispatch*, Nov. 21, 1959 (describing Vir-
ginia Commission). Maryland's 1961 commission is described in chapter 2.

12. See, for example, Dean G. B. Hancock, "Illegitimacy a National Problem,"
ANP, *Louisiana Weekly*, June 20, 1959; Dean G. B. Hancock, "Our Worsen-
ing Problem," ANP, *Alabama Tribune*, Dec. 14, 1962; Clifton R. Jones, Letter to the Editor, *Baltimore Sun*, July 26, 1960.

13. Blanche Crozier, "Marital Support," 15 *Boston Univ. L. Rev.* 28, 28 (1935).

14. Dr. George Gallup and Evan Hill, "The American Woman," *Saturday Evening Post*, Dec. 22, 1962, at 24–28. See also Stephanie Coontz, *A Strange
Stirring: The Feminine Mystique and American Women at the Dawn of the
1960s* (Basic Books, 2011), 1–3.

15. Homer H. Clark, Jr., "The Legal Position of Married Women Under Modern Statutes," in *The Law of Domestic Relations* (West, 1968), 223–24.

16. "Marriage is not merely a private contract between the parties," the court
said, "but creates a status in which the state is vitally interested." Graham v.
Graham, 33 F. Supp. 936, 937–38 (E.D. Mich. 1940).

17. Hoyt v. Florida, 368 U.S. 57 (1961).

18. State v. Hall, 187 So.2d 861, 863 (Miss. 1966).

19. For more, see Serena Mayeri, "After Suffrage: The Unfinished Business of
Feminist Legal Advocacy," *Yale L. J. Forum*, Jan. 20, 2020; Linda K. Kerber,
No Constitutional Right to Be Ladies: Women and the Obligations of Citizenship
(New York: Hill & Wang, 1998), chapter 4.

20. Alice Kessler-Harris, *In Pursuit of Equity: Women, Men, and the Quest for Economic Citizenship in Twentieth-Century America* (Oxford University Press,
2001); Nancy F. Cott, *Public Vows: A History of Marriage and the Nation* (Harvard University Press, 2000).

21. Margot Canaday, "Heterosexuality as a Legal Regime," in *Cambridge History
of Law in America*, ed. Michael Grossberg and Christopher Tomlins (Cambridge University Press, 2008), 453.

22. Cott, *Public Vows*, 167.

23. Kessler-Harris, *In Pursuit of Equity*.

24. Canaday, "Heterosexuality as a Legal Regime," 457.

25. On the roots of this exclusion, see, for example, Mary Poole, *The Segregated
Origins of Social Security: African Americans and the Welfare State* (University
of North Carolina Press, 2006).

26. U.S. Department of Commerce, Bureau of the Census, "Female Family Heads," Series P-23, No. 50, July 1974; Deborah Gray White, *Too Heavy A Load: Black Women in Defense of Themselves, 1894–1994* (W.W. Norton, 1999).

27. Cynthia Harrison, *On Account of Sex: The Politics of Women's Issues, 1945–1968* (University of California Press, 1988), 154–55.

28. Harrison, *On Account of Sex*, 156, 157–58.

29. President's Commission on the Status of Women, *American Women*, 47; Harrison, *On Account of Sex*, 156.

30. PCSW, *American Women*, 47–48; Betty Friedan, *The Feminine Mystique* (W.W. Norton, 1963); Coontz, *A Strange Stirring*.

31. ADC became AFDC in 1962.

32. Jennifer Mittelstadt, *From Welfare to Workfare: The Unintended Consequences of Liberal Reform* (University of North Carolina Press, 2005), 137–39.

33. Mittelstadt, *From Welfare to Workfare*, 124, 139–41.

34. Daniel P. Moynihan, *The Negro Family: The Case for National Action* (U.S. Department of Labor, 1965); Serena Mayeri, "Historicizing 'The End of Men': The Politics of Reaction(s)," 93 *Boston Univ. L. Rev.* 729 (2013).

35. Adam Clymer, "Daniel Patrick Moynihan Is Dead; Senator from Academia was 76," *NYT*, Mar. 27, 2003; Douglas E. Schoen, "A Place Called Hell's Kitchen: The Boyhood Myth that Helped Make Moynihan," *NYT*, Apr. 6, 2003.

36. On this liberal consensus, see, for example, Marisa Chappell, *The War on Welfare: Family, Poverty, and Politics in Modern America* (University of Pennsylvania Press, 2010), 37; Ruth Feldstein, *Motherhood in Black and White: Race and Sex in American Liberalism, 1930–1965* (Cornell University Press, 2000), 144–52; Serena Mayeri, *Reasoning from Race: Feminism, Law, and the Civil Rights Revolution* (Harvard University Press, 2011), 23–26, 41–42.

37. Quoted in Lee Rainwater and William L. Yancey, *The Moynihan Report and the Politics of Controversy* (MIT Press, 1967), 185. On Murray, see Rosalind Rosenberg, *Jane Crow: The Life of Pauli Murray* (Oxford University Press, 2017); Mayeri, "After Suffrage." On Black women's activism in the early 1960s, see Paula Giddings, *When and Where I Enter: The Impact of Black Women on Race and Sex in America* (William Morrow, 1984); White, *Too Heavy a Load*, chapter 6; Brittney Cooper, *Beyond Respectability: The Intellectual Thought of Race Women* (University of Illinois Press, 2017).

38. Pauli Murray, "Memorandum in Support of Retaining the Amendment to H.R. 7152, Title VII (Equal Employment Opportunity) to Prohibit Discrimination in Employment Because of Sex," 14 April 1964, PM Papers: Series II, 1935–1984, Box 85, Folder 1485, Schlesinger Library, Radcliffe Institute, Harvard University. For more, see Serena Mayeri, "Intersectionality and Title VII: A Brief (Pre-)History," 95 *Boston Univ. L. Rev.* 713 (2015).

39. Murray, Title VII memo, 21, 23.

40. Dorothy Height and Caroline Ware, "To Fulfill the Rights of Negro Women in Disadvantaged Families," A Statement for the White House Conference "To Fulfill These Rights," June 1–2, 1966, Prepared by a Task Force on the Disadvantaged Family at the Request of the Citizens' Advisory Council on the Status of Women.

41. On Height's evolution on this question, see White, *Too Heavy a Load*.

42. See Karen M. Tani, *States of Dependency: Welfare, Rights, and American Governance* (Cambridge University Press, 2016); Davis, *Brutal Need*; Karen M. Tani and Felicia Kornbluh, "Siting the Legal History of Poverty: Above, Below, and Amidst," in *A Companion to American Legal History*, ed. Sally E. Hadden and Alfred Brophy (Wily-Blackwell, 2013); Marie A. Failinger and Ezra Rosser, eds., *The Poverty Law Canon: Exploring the Major Cases* (University of Michigan Press, 2016).

43. Felicia Kornbluh, "The Untold History of American Equality: Jacobus ten-Broek, Blind People's Politics, and Legal Rights, 1945–1954," unpublished paper, https://www.scribd.com/document/157675710/.

44. Joseph Tussman and Jacobus tenBroek, "The Equal Protection of the Laws," 37 *Calif. L. Rev.* 341 (1949).

45. Davis, *Brutal Need*, 20.

46. Jacobus tenBroek and Richard B. Wilson, "Public Assistance and Social Insurance," 1 *UCLA L. Rev.* 237 (1954).

47. Jacobus tenBroek, "California's Dual System of Family Law: Its Origin, Development, and Present Status: Part III," 17 *Stanford L. Rev.* 614, 624 (1965).

48. "A Celebration of the Life of Hazel tenBroek," *Braille Monitor*, August/September 2006.

49. TenBroek, "Dual System," Part III, 624.

50. TenBroek, "Dual System," Part III, 649.

51. TenBroek, "Dual System," Part III, 619. California was one of the first states to abolish common law marriage, in 1895.

52. TenBroek, "Dual System," Part III, 658–59. Notice to Law Enforcement Officials (NOLEO) required "prompt notice," a practice criticized as punitive and counterproductive. See Joel F. Handler, "Controlling Official Behavior in Welfare Administration," 54 *Calif. L. Rev.* 479 (1966); Elizabeth D. Katz, "Criminal Law in a Civil Guise," 86 *U. Chicago L. Rev.* 1241 (2019).

53. Tussman and tenBroek, "Equal Protection," 353.

54. TenBroek, "Dual System," Part III, 641–42.

55. "Harry D. Krause," 1997 *U. Ill. L. Rev.* 667.

56. See Michael Grossberg, *Governing the Hearth: Law and the Family in Nineteenth-Century America* (University of North Carolina Press, 1987), chapter 6.

57. Harry D. Krause, "Bringing the Bastard into the Great Society—A Proposed Uniform Act on Legitimacy," 44 *Texas L. Rev.* 829 (1966).

58. Harry D. Krause, "Equal Protection for the Illegitimate," 65 *Mich. L. Rev.* 477, 484 (1967).

59. Only two states, Arizona and Oregon, even attempted to eliminate discrimination based on birth status. Editorial Notes, "Illegitimacy," 26 *Brooklyn L. Rev.* 45 (1959).
60. Krause, "Bringing the Bastard into the Great Society."
61. Krause, "Bringing the Bastard into the Great Society," 831; Herbert Semmel, "Social Security Benefits for Illegitimate Children After *Levy v. Louisiana*," 19 *Buffalo L. Rev.* 289, 295–96 (1970).
62. Semmel, "Social Security Benefits," 294.
63. The legislative history of this amendment is sparse. See Senate Report No. 404, 89th Cong., 1st Sess., 109–10 (1965).
64. Senate Report No. 404, at 110.
65. In 1966 the cost of this change was estimated as $10 million, a relatively small amount.
66. Semmel, "Social Security Benefits," 296.
67. House Report No. 544, 90th Cong., 1st Sess. Social Security Amendments of 1967, August 7, 1967, at 53.
68. House Report No. 544, at 96; House Report No. 544, at 97; Premilla Nadasen, *Welfare Warriors: The Welfare Rights Movement in the United States* (Routledge, 2004), 49.
69. House Report No. 544, at 100.
70. Joanne L. Goodwin, "'Employable Mothers' and 'Suitable Work': A Re-Evaluation of Welfare and Wage-Earning for Women in the Twentieth-Century United States," *Journal of Social History*, vol. 29, no. 2 (Winter 1995).
71. See Deborah Dinner, "The Universal Child Care Debate: Rights Mobilization, Social Policy, and the Dynamics of Feminist Activism, 1966–1974," *Law and History Review*, vol. 28, no. 3 (August 2010).
72. House Report No. 544, at 102.
73. TenBroek, "Dual System," Part III, 644; Gideon v. Wainwright, 372 U.S. 335 (1963); Griffin v. Illinois, 351 U.S. 12 (1956).
74. Krause, "Equal Protection for the Illegitimate," 488.
75. Nandor Fodor, "Emotional Trauma Resulting from Illegitimate Birth" [1945], 54 *Archives of Neurology and Psychiatry* 581 (1954).
76. Krause, "Equal Protection for the Illegitimate," 488–89.
77. Joyce Antler, *The Journey Home: How Jewish Women Shaped Modern America* (Schocken, 1998), 190.
78. On Polier's opposition to religious matching, see Ellen Herman, "The Difference Difference Makes: Justine Wise Polier and Religious Matching in Twentieth-Century Child Adoption," *Religion and American Culture*, vol. 10, no. 1 (Winter 2000): 57–98.
79. Justine Wise Polier, "What's Your Name If You Have a Name?" (1947), 9a, JWP Papers, MC 413, Box 558.
80. Justine Wise Polier, "Laws and Practices Affecting the Child Born Out of Wedlock," JWP Papers, MC 413, Box 578.

81. See, e.g., Justine Wise Polier to Florence Kelley, "Memorandum on the City-Wide Filiation Team," 1966, JWP Papers, MC 413, Box 578.
82. Polier, "What's Your Name."
83. Regina M. Kunzel, *Fallen Women, Problem Girls: Unmarried Mothers and the Professionalization of Social Work, 1890–1945* (University of California Press, 1993); Solinger, *Wake Up Little Susie.*
84. [Name obscured] to Justine Wise Polier, August 2, 1947, JWP Papers, MC 413, Box 558; Ann Fessler, *The Girls Who Went Away: The Hidden History of Women Who Surrendered Children for Adoption in the Years Before* Roe v. Wade (Penguin, 2006).
85. Justine Wise Polier, "Problems Involving Family and Child," 66 *Columbia L. Rev.* 305 (1966).
86. Polier, "Problems Involving Family and Child."
87. Solinger, *Wake Up Little Susie.*
88. Krause also saw the focus on mothers as a "white" framing of the problem. In his view, for Black Americans, "the socially fatal situation of the illegitimate welfare child wholly overshadows the mother's concerns." Krause, *Illegitimacy: Law and Social Policy* (Bobbs-Merrill, 1971), 295; Martha F. Davis, "Male Coverture: Law and the Illegitimate Family," 56 *Rutgers L. Rev.* 73, 98 (2003).
89. Justine Wise Polier, Book Review of Harry D. Krause, *Illegitimacy: Law and Social Policy,* in *Child Welfare,* Nov. 1972.
90. Polier, "Problems Involving Family and Child," 310–15.
91. Elizabeth Wickenden, "The Constitutional Rights of Assistance Recipients," Mar. 24, 1963, JWP Papers, MC 413, Box 140.
92. Tani, *States of Dependency,* 237–44.
93. Hoyt v. Florida, 368 U.S. 57 (1961).
94. Peggy Pascoe, *What Comes Naturally: Miscegenation Law and the Making of Race in America* (Oxford University Press, 2010); Jane Dailey, *White Fright: The Sexual Panic at the Heart of America's Racist History* (Basic Books, 2020).
95. Elaine Tyler May, *The Pill: A History of Promise, Peril, and Liberation* (Basic Books, 2011).
96. Linda Gordon, *The Moral Property of Women: A History of Birth Control Politics in America* (University of Illinois Press, 2002); Leigh Ann Wheeler, *How Sex Became a Civil Liberty* (Oxford University Press, 2012).
97. On the legal history of the Comstock laws and resistance to them, see Reva B. Siegel and Mary Ziegler, "Comstockery: How Government Censorship Gave Birth to the Law of Sexual and Reproductive Freedom and May Again Threaten It," *Yale L. J.* (forthcoming, 2024).
98. David Garrow, *Liberty and Sexuality: The Right to Privacy and the Making of* Roe v. Wade (University of California Press, 1998).
99. Garrow, *Liberty and Sexuality,* 172; Wheeler, *How Sex Became a Civil Liberty,* 100.
100. Wheeler, *How Sex Became a Civil Liberty,* 94–95.

101. See Reva B. Siegel, "'The Rule of Love': Wife-Beating as Prerogative and Privacy," *105 Yale L. J.* 2117 (1996).

102. Quoted in Garrow, *Liberty and Sexuality*, 161.

103. Garrow, *Liberty and Sexuality*, 172.

104. Melissa Murray, "Overlooking Equality on the Road to *Griswold*," *124 Yale L. J. Forum* 324, 326 (2015).

105. Murray, "Overlooking Equality," 325–27.

106. Quoted in Garrow, *Liberty and Sexuality*, 195.

107. Poe v. Ullman, 367 U.S. 497, 522 (1961) (Harlan, J., dissenting).

108. Garrow, *Liberty and Sexuality*, 201.

109. Marc Stein, *Sexual Injustice: Supreme Court Decisions from* Griswold *to* Roe (University of North Carolina Press, 2010), 98, quoting Linda Gordon, *Woman's Body, Woman's Right: A Social History of Birth Control in America* (Grossman/Viking, 1976)); see also Gordon, *Moral Property of Women*, 298.

110. Garrow, *Liberty and Sexuality*, 206. See also Stein, *Sexual Injustice*, chapter 3 on advocates' and amici's emphasis on marital rights in *Griswold*.

111. Garrow, *Liberty and Sexuality*, 237.

112. Griswold v. Connecticut, 381 U.S. 479, 484 (1965).

113. *Griswold*, 381 U.S. at 486.

114. WOD, Draft Opinion, *Griswold*, Apr. 22, 1965, at 5, WOD Papers, Box 1347.

115. *Griswold*, 381 U.S. at 486–87. Siegel and Ziegler point out that police had done just that under the federal Comstock law. Siegel and Ziegler, "Comstockery."

116. *Griswold*, 381 U.S. at 498–99 (Goldberg, J., concurring).

117. David J. Garrow, "The Tragedy of William O. Douglas," *The Nation*, April 14, 2003.

118. "September Song," *Time*, July 29, 1966.

119. *Griswold*, 381 U.S. at 498–99 (Goldberg, J., concurring).

120. William O. Douglas, Conference Notes, No. 496—Griswold, Apr. 2, 1965; Garrow, *Liberty and Sexuality*, 244.

121. Melissa Murray, "Sexual Liberty and Criminal Law Reform: The Story of *Griswold v. Connecticut*," in *Reproductive Rights and Justice Stories*, ed. Melissa Murray, Katherine Shaw, and Reva B. Siegel (Foundation Press, 2019), 23.

122. Brief for Appellants, *Griswold*, 79.

123. Murray, "Sexual Liberty," 17–20; Risa Goluboff, *Vagrant Nation: Police Power, Constitutional Change, and the Making of the 1960s* (Oxford University Press, 2016), 49–50; David Minto, "Perversion by Penumbras: Wolfenden, *Griswold*, and the Transatlantic Trajectory of Sexual Privacy," *American Historical Review*, October 2018. On the racially disparate results of sexual liberalization during this period, see Anne Gray Fischer, *The Streets Belong to Us: Sex, Race, and Police Power from Segregation to Gentrification* (University of North Carolina Press, 2022), chapter 3.

124. Wheeler, *How Sex Became a Civil Liberty*.
125. Brief Amicus Curiae of the ACLU and CCLU, *Griswold*, 1965 WL 92600, *16.
126. Justice Brennan had asked during oral argument whether the plaintiffs were challenging Connecticut's effective health exception for men (who could purchase condoms at drugstores) but not women (who could not obtain diaphragms or oral contraceptives from their physicians). Neil S. Siegel and Reva B. Siegel, "Contraception as a Sex Equality Right," 124 *Yale L. J. Forum* 349, 354 (2015).
127. Olive Byrne Richard to WOD, June 9, 1965, WOD Papers, Box 1347, No. 496—Griswold. See also Murray, "Overlooking Equality"; Siegel and Siegel, "Contraception."
128. Lawrence Livingston to Mel Wulf, May 19, 1964, ACLU Records, Mudd Library, Princeton, Box 1412, Folder: Griswold v. Connecticut.
129. Fred P. Graham, "Court Bans Birth Control Curbs," *NYT*, June 13, 1965.
130. For more on the facts and social context of *McLaughlin*, see Elizabeth Pleck, *Not Just Roommates: Cohabitation After the Sexual Revolution* (University of Chicago Press, 2012), chapter 2.
131. Pascoe, *What Comes Naturally*, 252.
132. See Dailey, *White Fright*.
133. In the 1940s and 1950s the NAACP ceded the field to organizations such as the ACLU and the Japanese-American Citizens League (JACL), which focused their efforts on western states and carefully avoided representing Black male/white female couples. Pascoe, *What Comes Naturally*, 199.
134. Naim v. Naim, 87 S.E.2d 749 (Va. 1955), vacated and remanded, 350 U.S. 891 (1955), aff'd, 90 S.E.2d 849 (Va. 1955), motion to recall mandate denied and appeal dismissed, 350 U.S. 985 (1956).
135. More generally, leading liberal legal authorities called laws against adultery and fornication anachronistic relics that provided a cover for discriminatory and selective prosecution. Pascoe, *What Comes Naturally*, 254.
136. Pascoe, *What Comes Naturally*, 262–64.
137. WOD, Handwritten Conference Notes, *McLaughlin*, Oct. 16, 1964, WOD Papers, Box 1330. (Both Douglas and Warren mistakenly thought the parties were common law married).
138. Evan L. Schwab, Memo on Jurisdictional Statement, *McLaughlin*, Dec. 23, 1963, WOD Papers, Box 1330.
139. McLaughlin v. Florida, 379 U.S. 184, 189 (1964), overruling Pace v. Alabama, 106 U.S. 583 (1883).
140. Reva B. Siegel, "Equality Talk: Anticlassification and Antisubordination Values in Constitutional Struggles Over *Brown*," 117 *Harvard L. Rev.* 1470 (2004).
141. *McLaughlin*, 379 U.S. at 193.
142. Ariela R. Dubler, "From *McLaughlin v. Florida* to *Lawrence v. Texas*: Sexual Freedom and the Road to Marriage," 106 *Columbia L. Rev.* 1165 (2006); Pleck, *Not Just Roommates*, chapters 2 and 10.

143. Loving v. Virginia, 388 U.S. 1, 12 (1967).

144. Robert F. Drinan, "The *Loving* Decision and the Freedom to Marry," 29 *Ohio St. L. J.* 358 (1968).

145. Drinan also discussed *Loving*'s potential impact on marriage restrictions based on consanguinity, affinity, age, and disability, as well as statutes that made marriage a defense for men who seduced women with the false promise of marriage. Drinan, "*Loving* Decision."

Chapter 2. Hapless and Innocent Children

1. Appendix of Appellants Barbara Jean Cager, Doris L. Patterson, and Brenda LaVerne Jackson, *In re Cager*, in the Court of Appeals of Maryland, September Term, 1967, at 78a (hereinafter *Cager* Appendix). Barbara Jean Cager was 15 when her first child was born in 1963. The fathers of her four children were aged 27, 29, 21, and 24, respectively. *Cager* Appendix, 69a-71a.

2. *Cager* Appendix, 78a-79a.

3. Peter A. Jay, "Illegitimacy-Neglect Ruling: Is It Wise or Fair? Prince George's Decision Can Have National Impact," *WP*, Sept. 24, 1967.

4. "Sterilize Unwed Mothers, States' Lawmakers Urge," *WP*, Feb. 13, 1960.

5. Per capita welfare receipt in Maryland declined overall between 1940 and 1960. Laurence M. Stern, "Maryland's Illegitimacy Rate Reported Climbing," *WP*, Nov. 24, 1960; AP, "Is Illegitimacy a Racket? Some Marylanders Think So," *WP*, Feb. 24, 1960.

6. Editorial, "Scarlet Letter," *WP*, Feb. 27, 1960.

7. Eve Edstrom, "Maryland Considers Forced Reporting of Illegitimate Births," *WP*, December 30, 1961.

8. Edstrom, "Maryland Considers." On the different moral constructions of Black and white unmarried mothers during this period, see Rickie Solinger, *Wake Up Little Susie: Single Pregnancy and Race Before* Roe v. Wade (University of California Press, 1993).

9. See Claudia Lawrence-Webb, "African-American Children and the Modern Child Welfare System: A Legacy of the Flemming Rule," in *Serving African American Children: Child Welfare Perspectives*, ed. Sondra Jackson and Sheryl Brisset-Chapman (Routledge, 1998); Laura Briggs, *Somebody's Children: A History of Transnational and Transracial Adoption* (Duke University Press, 2012).

10. Obituary, "Perry Gray Bowen, Jr.," *Recorder* (Calvert County, Md.), Mar. 14, 2018; Opinion of the Court, In re Cager, Excerpts from Trial Transcripts, *Cager* Appendix,1a.

11. Opinion of the Court, *Cager* Appendix, 5a.

12. Opinion of the Court, *Cager* Appendix, 11a-12a.

13. "Charges of Neglect Planned in County Illegitimacy Cases," *WP*, Sept. 23, 1967.

14. *Cager* Appendix, 52a.

15. Fred P. Graham, "Mothers Warned on Illegitimacy," *NYT*, Sept. 22, 1967; Opinion of the Court, *Cager* Appendix, 5a-6a.

16. "Charges of Neglect Planned in County Illegitimacy Cases," *WP*, Sept. 23, 1967.

17. Hobson called an emergency meeting of the state's Welfare Board, but "held out little hope for stopping Marshall's crackdown." "Charges of Neglect Planned in County Illegitimacy Cases," *WP*, Sept. 23, 1967.

18. "Child Neglect Ruling Attacked," *WP*, Sept. 28, 1967.

19. "Illegitimacy Cases Face Court Action Warning," *WP*, Sept. 27, 1967.

20. "Legislators Weigh Stiff Welfare Rules as Illegitimacy Curbs," *WP*, Oct. 22, 1967.

21. Editorial, "Off With Their Heads!," *WP*, Sept. 25, 1967.

22. Judith M. Waby, Letter to the Editor, *WP*, Oct. 1, 1967.

23. Virginia Phillips, Letter to the Editor, *WP*, Oct. 1, 1967. See also John W. Porter, Jr., Judge, County Court of Muskogee, Oklahoma, Letter to the Editor, *WP*, Oct. 1, 1967, F6; Walter Green, Letter to the Editor, *WP*, Oct. 1, 1967.

24. Willa Pierce, Letter to the Editor, *WP*, Oct. 1, 1967. For other views, see Richard Mattis, Letter to the Editor, *WP*, Oct. 1, 1967; Edwin A. Lahey, "Crackdown on Illegitimate Births," *Herald-News* (Passaic, N.J.), Oct. 5, 1967.

25. George Gallup, "Unwed Mother Aid Vastly Disapproved," *Tennessean*, Jan. 27, 1965.

26. See, for example, Peter A. Jay, "In Judge's Opinion, 2 Illegitimacies Proof of Neglect," *WP*, Sept. 2, 1967.

27. Leroy D. Clark, NAACP LDF, to Thomas Asher, ACLU, Oct. 10, 1967, Re: In re Cager, ACLU Records, Box 1135, Folder: 4.

28. Brief of Appellants Barbara Jean Cager, Doris L. Patterson, and Brenda LaVerne Jackson, in the Court of Appeals of Maryland, September Term 1967, No. 353, Filed Feb. 23, 1968, In re: Barbara Jean Cager et al., 15–16.

29. The brief cited Armstrong v. Manzo, 380 U.S. 545 (1965).

30. Brief of Appellants Barbara Jean Cager et al., *Cager*, 31–33.

31. Brief of Appellants Barbara Jean Cager et al., *Cager*, 35–37, 40.

32. Brief for Appellants, In re Cager et al., in the Court of Appeals of Maryland, No. 353, September Term, 1967, Appeal from the Circuit Court for Prince George's County (Perry G. Bowen, Judge) (hereinafter Brief for Appellants—Children).

33. Brief for Appellants—Children, *Cager*, 23, 26–29, 34.

34. In 1961 Maryland's Commission to Study Problems of Illegitimacy had rejected proposals to legalize abortion and sterilization in order to stem the tide of "illegitimacy."

35. "Unwed Mothers Plan Too Limited—Murphy," *Baltimore Afro-American*, June 6, 1964.

36. "Compulsory Birth Control Is Unconstitutional: Group," *Chicago Defender*, Jan. 30, 1968; Cathy Aldridge, "Court Threatens Unwed Moms in Birth Control Test Case," *New York Amsterdam News*, Feb. 3, 1968. On Black Americans' relationship to birth control advocacy, see, for example, Dorothy Roberts, *Killing the Black Body: Race, Reproduction, and the Meaning of Liberty* (Penguin, 1997), chapter 2; Mary Ziegler, *After* Roe: *The Lost History of the Abortion Debate* (Harvard University Press, 2015); Linda Gordon, *The Moral Property of Women: A History of Birth Control Politics in America* (University of Illinois Press, 2002).

37. Brief as Amici Curiae for Planned Parenthood Federation of America et al., In the Matter of Barbara Jean Cager et al., ND Papers, Box 32, Folder 4 (hereinafter PPFA Brief), 9.

38. PPFA Brief, *Cager*, 14.

39. PPFA Brief, *Cager*, 12, 14, 16–17.

40. In re Cager, 248 A.2d 384 (Md. Ct. App. 1968).

41. Quotes are from Alfred Klimcke, "13 Mothers Sue Housing Authority," *Philadelphia Inquirer*, May 8, 1968.

42. A 1957 list of disqualifying attributes for Philadelphia public housing included "any unmarried mother of two or more children evidencing irresponsibility and a continuing illegitimacy pattern." Lisa Levenstein, *A Movement Without Marches: African American Women and the Politics of Poverty in Postwar Philadelphia* (University of North Carolina Press, 2009), 98–99.

43. Barbara S. Williams, "CORE Seeks Housing Picketing," *Courier-Post* (Camden, N.J.), June 2, 1966; "Housing Unit May Ease Unwed Policy," *Courier-Post*, Oct. 6, 1966.

44. Robert Hummerstone, "Race Bias Charge May Be Filed Against New Bern's Public Housing," *Charlotte Observer*, Mar. 4, 1966.

45. "Illegitimacy Problem for Housing," *Morning News* (Wilmington, Del.), Sept. 15, 1961; "Housing Agency Has Evicted 6," *News Journal* (Wilmington, Del.), Jan. 30, 1963. See also John Finley, "Legal Aid Counsel's Talk Brings Barbed Response," *Courier-Journal*, Feb. 8, 1969.

46. Opponents of illegitimacy exclusions countered authorities' claims that public housing residents themselves approved such policies. "Poll Backs City Housing for Unmarried Mothers," *Courier-Journal*, Sept. 20, 1968.

47. AP, "Public Housing Morals Issue in Court Case," *Danville Register*, Mar. 5, 1969.

48. "5 Suits Challenge Housing Agency's Regulations on Illegitimate Children," *Courier-Journal* (Louisville, Ky.), Aug. 25, 1967; "Who's to Live in Public Housing?," *New Era* (Lancaster, Pa.), Dec. 4, 1965.

49. "Editorial: Responsibility Is Needed," *DelCo Times*, Jan. 31, 1963; see also Frank J. Orpe, "NAACP Protests Loom If Unwed Mother Evicted," *Morning Call*, Oct. 11, 1966.

50. "Underlying Problem Explored," *Star-Gazette*, Feb. 24, 1968.

51. "Unwed Mother's Cause Taken to Housing Unit," *Morning Call* (Bethlehem, Pa.), Sept. 20, 1966.

52. Frank J. Orpe, "NAACP Protests Loom If Unwed Mother Evicted," *Morning Call*, Oct. 11, 1966.

53. "Unwed Mother's Cause Taken to Housing Unit," *Morning Call*, Sept. 20, 1966.

54. "Underlying Problem Explored," *Star-Gazette*, Feb. 24, 1968.

55. "NAACP Threatens Suit on Eviction of Mothers," *Evening Journal* (Wilmington, Del.), Feb. 13, 1963, at 3. Stanley F. Branche, executive director, Chester branch, NAACP, and Monroe C. Beardsley, chairman, Delaware County chapter, ACLU, "NAACP, ACLU Protest Editorial," Letter to the Editor, *DelCo Times*.

56. Stanley F. Branche, executive director, Chester branch, NAACP, and Monroe C. Beardsley, chairman, Delaware County chapter, ACLU, "NAACP, ACLU Protest Editorial," Letter to the Editor, *DelCo Times*; "CHA Refuses to Soften Policy on Illegitimacy," *DelCo Times*, Jan. 30, 1963.

57. "NAACP Threatens Suit on Eviction of Mothers," *Evening Journal* (Wilmington, Del.), Feb. 13, 1963, at 3; "Public Housing May Be Sought for Elderly," *Courier-Journal*, Aug. 21, 1968; "14 Mothers Join Suit to Gain Public Housing," *Courier-Journal*, Aug. 27, 1969.

58. "CHA Refuses to Soften Policy on Illegitimacy," *Delaware County Daily Times* (Chester, Pa.), Jan. 30, 1963.

59. "5 Suits Challenge Housing Agency's Regulations on Illegitimate Children," *Courier-Journal* (Louisville, Ky.), Aug. 25, 1967; John Finley, "Legal Aid Counsel's Talk Brings Barbed Response," *Courier-Journal*, Feb. 8, 1969.

60. Fred Minshall, "Court Upholds Illegitimacy Limit," *Courier-Journal*, May 10, 1968.

61. AP, "Eviction Upheld for Unwed Mothers in Richmond Court," *Progress-Index*, July 28, 1967.

62. Brief for Plaintiffs on their Motion for Summary Judgment, *Thomas v. Housing Authority of Little Rock*, Civil Action No. LR-66-C-230 (E.D. Ark.), Feb. 23, 1967, at 26–27, NARA-Ft. Worth, RG 21, Box 518, Folder 66C230 (hereinafter Plaintiffs' Brief, *Thomas*); Plaintiffs' Memorandum in Reply to Defendants' Brief in Support of Its Motion for Summary Judgment, *Thomas v. Housing Authority of Little Rock*, Civ. Action No. LR-66-C-230 (E.D. Ark.), May 23, 1967, at 6, NARA-Ft. Worth, RG 21, Box 518, Folder 66230 (citing *Griswold*); see also Plaintiffs' Brief, *Thomas*, 31.

63. Thomas v. Housing Authority of Little Rock, 282 F. Supp. 575, 580 (E.D. Ark. 1967).

64. *Thomas*, 282 F. Supp. at 580–81.

65. *Thomas*, 282 F. Supp. at 581.

66. Judge Henley also dismissed the plaintiffs' racial discrimination claims. *Thomas*, 282 F. Supp. at 581–82.

67. Jerry Sapenza, "WHA Says Known Illegitimacy Rises," *News Journal* (Wilmington, Del.), Mar. 16, 1967.

68. "Rules Changed on Housing Tenants," *Lancaster New Era*, Mar. 1, 1966; Bob Kozak, "Public Housing Policies Under Fire at Forum," *Lancaster New Era*, Jan. 29, 1966.

69. The circular provided that local housing authorities "shall not establish policies which automatically deny admission or continued occupancy to a particular class, such as unmarried mothers, families having one or more children born out of wedlock, families having police records or poor rent-paying habits, etc." HUD Circular: Admission and Continued Occupancy Regulations for Low-Rent Public Housing, Dec. 17, 1968, quoted in Florence Wagman Roisman, "Right to Public Housing," 39 *Geo. Wash. U. L. Rev.* 691, 694 (1970).

70. Frank Orpe, "BHA's Role as Landlord a Trial," *Morning Call*, Sept. 4, 1971.

71. "1 Housing Battle Won; Still Some Erratic Fire," *Star-Gazette*, Aug. 3, 1968.

72. Mike King, "Louisville Housing Authority Attorney Criticizes Press Reports on Recent Suits," *Courier-Journal*, July 19, 1972 (emphasis added).

73. Alfred Klimcke, "Phila. Housing Authority Drops Its Ban on Unwed Mothers," *Philadelphia Inquirer*, May 21, 1968.

74. Premilla Nadasen, "Expanding the Boundaries of the Women's Movement: Black Feminism and the Struggle for Welfare Rights," *Feminist Studies*, vol. 28, no. 2 (January 2010): 277–78.

75. This description of Tillmon is drawn from Annelise Orleck, *Storming Caesars Palace: How Black Mothers Fought Their Own War on Poverty* (Beacon Press, 2005), 108–9.

76. Orleck, *Storming Caesars Palace*, 109.

77. Quoted in Premilla Nadasen, *Welfare Warriors: The Welfare Rights Movement in the United States* (Routledge, 2004), 145, n. 107.

78. Quoted in Nadasen, "Expanding the Boundaries," 282.

79. Brief for Appellees, *King v. Smith*, *2; Winifred Bell, *Aid to Dependent Children* (Columbia University Press, 1965), chapter 5.

80. On state regulation of men's sexuality through substitute father laws and other man in the house rules, see Alison Lefkovitz, "Men in the House: Race, Welfare, and the Regulation of Men's Sexuality in the United States, 1961–1972," *Journal of the History of Sexuality*, vol. 20, no. 3 (2011): 594–614.

81. Martin Garbus, *Ready for the Defense* (Carroll & Graf, 1987), 148.

82. Garbus, *Ready for the Defense*, 148–49.

83. Quoted in Walter Goodman, "The Case of Mrs. Sylvester Smith: A Victory for 400,000 Children," *NYT*, Aug. 25, 1968, SM28. See also Rickie Solinger, "The First Welfare Case: Money, Sex, Marriage, and White Supremacy in Selma, 1966: A Reproductive Justice Analysis," *Journal of Women's History*, vol. 22, no. 3 (2010): 20.

84. Quoted in Solinger, "The First Welfare Case," 20.
85. Garbus, *Ready for the Defense*, 149.
86. Deposition of Sylvester Smith, in Appendix, King v. Smith, 392 U.S. 309 (1968) (hereinafter Smith deposition).
87. Garbus, *Ready for the Defense*, 148.
88. Smith deposition, *King v. Smith* Appendix , vol. II, 257–58.
89. See Nadasen, "Expanding the Boundaries"; Nadasen, *Welfare Warriors*.
90. See Solinger, "The First Welfare Case"; Joanne Goodwin, "'Employable Mothers' and 'Suitable Work': A Reevaluation of Welfare and Wage-Earning for Mothers in the Twentieth-Century United States," *Journal of Social History*, vol. 29, no. 12 (Winter 1995): 253–74.
91. Garbus, *Ready for the Defense*, 153.
92. Brief of Appellees, *King v. Smith*; Plaintiffs' Trial Brief of Fact and Law at 13–15, Smith v. King, Civ. Action No. 2495-N (M.D. Ala.), FMJ Papers, Box 46, Folder 5 (hereinafter Plaintiffs' Trial Brief).
93. Plaintiffs' Trial Brief, *Smith v. King*, 92.
94. Brief of Appellees, *King v. Smith*, 1968 WL 112516, at *57.
95. See Louis B. Schwartz, "Morals Offenses and the Model Penal Code," 63 *Columbia L. Rev.* 669 (1963).
96. Brief for Appellant, *King v. Smith*, 50. See also Serena Mayeri, "The State of Illegitimacy after the Rights Revolution," in *Intimate States: Gender, Sexuality, and Governance in Modern U.S. History*, ed. Margot Canaday, Nancy F. Cott, and Robert O. Self (University of Chicago Press, 2021), 239–41.
97. Brief of Appellees, *King v. Smith*, *73. Garbus cited to *Parrish v. California*, 66 Cal.2d 253 (1967) (midnight raids) and to a dissenting opinion in *Snell v. Wyman*, C.A. 67–2676 (S.D.N.Y. Feb. 29, 1968). See also Brief of Appellees, *King v. Smith*, *72; Plaintiffs' Trial Brief, *King v. Smith*, 13–14.
98. Martha F. Davis, *Brutal Need: Lawyers and the Welfare Rights Movement, 1960–1973* (Yale University Press, 1993), 36.
99. Norman Dorsen and David Rudovsky, "Equality for the Illegitimate," *Welfare Law Bulletin*, May 1967.
100. Petition for Writ of Certiorari and Review to the Court of Appeal, Fourth Circuit, State of Louisiana, 7–8, Levy v. State (La. 1967) (No. 48518), ND Papers, Box 32, Folder 14 (hereinafter Petition).
101. Melissa Murray, "What's So New About the New Illegitimacy," 20 *American Univ. J. of Gender, Social Policy, & Law* 387 (2012); Serena Mayeri, "Marital Supremacy and the Constitution of the Nonmarital Family," 103 *Calif. L. Rev.* 1277, 1290–91 (2015).
102. Petition, *Levy*, 4.
103. Petition, *Levy*, 4.
104. Quoted in John Witte, Jr., *The Sins of the Fathers: The Law and Theology of Illegitimacy Reconsidered* (Cambridge University Press, 2009), 141.
105. Jonah Engel Bromwich, "Norman Dorsen, Tenacious Civil Rights Advocate, Dies at 86," *NYT*, July 2, 2017.

106. Atticus Gannaway, "NYU Law's First Citizen," *NYU Law Magazine*, Sept. 1, 2017.

107. Bromwich, "Norman Dorsen."

108. The group also included the Poliers, Mel Wulf, Ed Sparer, and Charles Reich. Davis, *Brutal Need*, 84. On the turn to law by welfare rights advocates, see Davis, *Brutal Need*; Karen M. Tani, *States of Dependency: Welfare, Rights, and American Governance, 1935–1972* (Cambridge University Press, 2016).

109. Norman Dorsen, "Poverty, Civil Liberties, and Civil Rights: A Symposium," 41 *NYU L. Rev.* 328 (1966).

110. Mel Wulf to Norman Dorsen, Nov. 20, 1967, ND Papers, Box 32, Folder 11. Dorsen also participated in *Cager*. See Brief for Appellants, In re Cager, No. 353 (Md. Ct. App. 1967).

111. Winifred Bell, *Aid to Dependent Children* (Columbia University Press, 1965).

112. Mel Wulf, Memorandum from the ACLU on Louisiana Plan for Aid to Dependent Children, Filed with the Department of Health, Education, and Welfare, at 3 (Nov. 22, 1960), ND Papers, Box 32, Folder 11 (hereinafter Wulf memo); Henry Freedman, "Sylvester Smith, Unlikely Heroine," in *The Poverty Law Canon: Exploring the Major Cases* (University of Michigan Press, 2016), ed. Marie A. Failinger and Ezra Rosser, 51–52.

113. Leroy Clark to Harry Krause, Dec. 4, 1967, ND Papers, Box 32, Folder 13; "LDF Mourns the Loss of Leroy D. Clark," Dec. 6, 2019, NAACPLDF.org.

114. "A high percentage (70%) of white illegitimate children are adopted . . . whereas very few (3–5%) Negro illegitimates find adoptive parents." Brief for the NAACP LDF, *Levy v. Louisiana*, 1968 WL 112827, at *18; Brief for the NAACP LDF, *Levy*, at *20.

115. Wulf memo, 3.

116. Wulf memo, 5.

117. On the limitations of the "illegitimacy" cases, see also Martha F. Davis, "Male Coverture: Law and the Illegitimate Family," 56 *Rutgers L. Rev.* 73 (2003); Murray, "What's So New About the New Illegitimacy"; Mary Ziegler, "The Non-Right to Sex," 69 *Univ. Miami L. Rev.* 631 (2015); Susan Frelich Appleton, "Illegitimacy and Sex, Old and New," 20 *American Univ. J. of Gender, Social Policy, & Law* 347 (2012); Mayeri, "Marital Supremacy."

118. Brief for Appellant, *Levy*, 1967 WL 113865, at *20.

119. Lois P. Sheinfeld to Norman Dorsen, re: Levy: Punishment of Status, Nov. 22, 1967, ND Papers, Box 32, Folder 17; Risa Goluboff, *Vagrant Nation: Police Power, Constitutional Change, and the Making of the 1960s* (Oxford University Press, 2016).

120. Sylvia Law, Notes on Reply Brief to Louisiana Attorney General, Feb. 22, 1968, ND Papers, Box 32, Folder 15 (emphasis added).

121. Glona v. American Guarantee & Liability Ins. Co., 379 F.2d 545 (1967).
122. Brief for the Attorney General, State of Louisiana, *Levy*, 1968 WL 112828, at *3–5, 7.
123. Appendix, *King v. Smith*, 77.
124. Levy v. Louisiana, 391 U.S. 68, 70–71 (1968).
125. *Levy*, 391 U.S. at 72.
126. Glona v. American Guarantee & Liability Insurance Co, 391 U.S. 73, 75 (1968) (echoing appellant's brief).
127. Semmel, "Social Security Benefits for Illegitimate Children After *Levy v. Louisiana*," 19 *Buffalo L. Rev.* 289, 290 (quoting Harlan dissent on "brute force"); WOD, First Circulated Draft of *Levy* Decision, 1, WOD Papers, Box 1423, Folder 508.
128. The court made clear that "this decision should be and will be designed to ensure to the benefit of all needy children regardless of their race or color." Slip op., Smith v. King, 7–8, n.7, FMJ Papers, Box 46.
129. Judge Virgil Pittman to Judge John Godbold, Oct. 20, 1967, FMJ Papers, Box 46 (emphasis in original).
130. Smith v. King, 277 F. Supp. 31, 37 n. 7, 39–40 (M.D. Ala. 1967) (emphasis added).
131. King v. Smith, 392 U.S. 309, 325 (1968).
132. King v. Smith, 392 U.S. at 333–34.
133. On the import of *King v. Smith*, see Karen M. Tani, "Administrative Equal Protection: Federalism, the Fourteenth Amendment, and the Rights of the Poor," 100 *Cornell L. Rev.* 824 (2015); Freedman, "Sylvester Smith: Unlikely Heroine"; Davis, *Brutal Need*. See also Solinger, "The First Welfare Case"; Alison Lefkovitz, *Strange Bedfellows: Marriage in the Age of Women's Liberation* (University of Pennsylvania Press, 2018), chapter 4.
134. King v. Smith, 392 U.S. at 336 (Douglas, J., concurring).
135. *Levy*, 391 U.S. at 78, 80 (Harlan, J., dissenting).
136. Donald E. Walter to WOD, June 6, 1968, WOD Papers, *Levy*, at 3.
137. Robert Byrn, "Demythologizing Abortion Reform," *Catholic Lawyer*, vol. 14 (1968), 183. For more, see Mary Ziegler, *Personhood: The New Civil War Over Reproduction* (Yale University Press, 2025).
138. Byrn, "Demythologizing," 183.
139. John C. Gray, Jr., and David Rudovsky, "The Court Acknowledges the Illegitimate: *Levy v. Louisiana* and *Glona v. American Guarantee and Liability Insurance Co.*, 118 *U. Pa. L. Rev.* 1, 15–17 (1969).
140. Marie Failinger, "A Tragedy of Two Americas: *Jefferson v. Hackney*," in *Poverty Law Canon*, 175; Brief for Appellants, *Jefferson*, 7.
141. Brief for Appellants, *Jefferson*, 15.
142. Davis, *Brutal Need*, 134.
143. Brief for Appellants, *Jefferson*, 9.
144. Failinger, "*Jefferson v. Hackney*," 173–74.
145. Brief for Appellants, *Jefferson*, 10, 21, 30–36, 69.

146. Welfare strategists hoped to bring the Texas case, with its stark racial disparities and stingy benefit levels, to the Court first. Instead the justices first decided challenges to state aid cuts in Maryland and New Jersey, as discussed below. Davis, *Brutal Need*, 127–28.

147. Brief Amicus Curiae of the Center for Social Welfare Policy and Law, *Dandridge*, quoted in Davis, *Brutal Need*, 131. See also Wendy A. Bach, "Litigating in the Zeitgeist: *Rosado v. Wyman* (1970)," in *Poverty Law Canon*; and Julie A. Nice, "A Sweeping Refusal of Equal Protection: *Dandridge v. Williams* (1970)," in *Poverty Law Canon*.

148. Quotes are from Davis, *Brutal Need*, 132. The majority refused to see Maryland's scheme as depriving an innocent child of aid; rather, "the lot of the entire family is diminished." Dandridge v. Williams, 397 U.S. 471, 477 (1970).

149. *Dandridge*, 397 U.S. at 487 n.17 (1970).

150. See New Jersey Welfare Rights Organization (hereafter NJWRO) v. Cahill, 349 F. Supp. 491 (D. N.J. 1972).

151. See Leontine Young, *Wednesday's Children: A Study of Child Neglect and Abuse* (McGraw-Hill, 1964).

152. Trial Transcript, NJWRO v. Cahill, Civil Action No. 879–71, NARA, New York, Cahill file.

153. Social workers testified that their Black clients were less likely to secure divorces so they could marry new partners because of lack of funds and aversion to "courts of law" and "officialdom." Trial Transcript, *Cahill*.

154. Such an assertion would perhaps have been unwise, given that fornication remained a criminal offense under New Jersey law. John Wilson, a seasonally employed construction worker and father of eleven children aged twelve and under, explained that he had tried and failed to obtain a divorce from his legal wife, who had left him fifteen years earlier in Miami.

155. Affidavit of Nicholas Elliott Borg and Ronald Hine, members of the Board of Directors of Self-Help, NJWRO v. Cahill, NARA-NY.

156. Affidavit of Lucy Santiago, Puertorriqueños Asociados for Community Organization, NJWRO v. Cahill, NARA-NY.

157. In 1973, the Court also rejected once and for all the argument that wealth was a suspect classification subject to strict scrutiny. See San Antonio v. Rodriguez, 411 U.S. 1 (1973).

158. Weber described herself as his "common law wife," although Stokes remained married to his children's mother and Louisiana did not recognize common law marriage.

159. Stokes v. Aetna Casualty & Sur. Co., 242 So. 2d 567 (La. 1970).

160. Labine v. Vincent, 401 U.S. 532, 538 (1971).

161. *Labine*, 401 U.S. at 541 (Brennan, J., dissenting).

162. Boddie v. Connecticut, 401 U.S. 371, 374 (1971).

163. Gary Gerstle, *The Rise and Fall of the Neoliberal Order* (Oxford University Press, 2022), 109.

164. At conference, six of the nine justices voted to reverse. Burger may have voted with the majority so that he, rather than Douglas, could assign the opinion.

165. Powell "did not question the importance" of the state's interest in "regulat[ing] and protect[ing] the family unit," but only the relationship between means and ends. Weber v. Aetna Casualty, 403 U.S. 164, 173 (1972) (quoting *Glona*).

166. *Weber*, 403 U.S. at 175–76.

167. Vanue Lacour to Mel Wulf, Nov. 16, 1971, ND Papers, Box 35, Folder 12. On Lacour, see Russell L. Jones, "African American Legal Pioneers: A Biography of Vanue Lacour," 23 *Southern Univ. L. Rev.* (1995).

168. Hamilton P. Fox, Bench Memo, Jefferson v. Hackney, LFP Papers, Box 370, Folder 28; Serena Mayeri, "Intersectionality and the Constitution of Family Status," 32 *Constitutional Commentary* 377, 385 (2017).

169. Jefferson v. Hackney, 406 U.S. 535, 547 (1972).

170. *Jefferson*, 406 U.S. at 575–76 (Marshall, J., dissenting).

171. Glenn Feldman, "Southern Disillusionment with the Democratic Party: Cultural Conformity and 'The Great Melding' of Racial and Economic Conservatism in Alabama During World War II," *Journal of American Studies*, vol. 43, no. 2 (August 2009): 206.

172. "Legal Aid Clinic Headed by Samford," *Montgomery Advertiser*, Oct. 5, 1970, at 9.

173. Whitfield v. King, 364 F. Supp. 1296, 1298 (M.D. Ala. 1973) (three-judge court). Whitfield v. King was one of several similar federal lawsuits filed against states to challenge the adequacy of welfare payments. For more, see Davis, *Brutal Need*; Tani, *States of Dependency*.

174. Robert D. McFadden, "Frank M. Johnson, Jr., Judge Whose Rulings Helped Desegregate the South, Dies at 80," *NYT*, July 24, 1999.

175. Whitfield v. King, 364 F. Supp. 1296 (M.D. Ala. 1973).

176. Melvin Wulf, Legal Director, to Laughlin McDonald, ACLU Foundation, Southern Regional Office, Dec. 17, 1973 (copied to Frank Samford, Harvard Law School).

177. Plaintiffs' Supplemental Brief of Equal Protection Issues, April 11, 1974, Whitfield v. King, FMJ Papers, Box 66, Folder 2 of 6.

178. Deposition of Ruben King, quoted in Plaintiffs' Supplemental Brief of Equal Protection Issues, at 23, Whitfield v. King, FMJ Papers, Box 66, folder 2 (hereinafter King Deposition).

179. King deposition, *King v. Smith* Appendix, 22.

180. Whitfield v. Oliver, 399 F. Supp. 348 (M.D. Ala. 1975).

181. Plaintiffs' Reply to Defendants, Whitfield v. Oliver, Nov. 14, 1975, at 15, FMJ Papers, Box 65, Folder 6.

182. Order (per curiam), Whitfield v. Oliver, Nov. 10, 1976, at 3, FMJ Papers, Box 65, Folder 6.

183. RM, Handwritten Note, May 9, 1977, on Preliminary Memorandum, Whitfield v. Burns, No. 76–6413, for May 12, 1977, Conference, HAB Papers, Box 871, Folder 5.

184. Whitfield v. Burns, 431 U.S. 910 (1977) (summary affirmance).

185. NJWRO v. Cahill, 349 F. Supp. 501 (D. N.J. 1972).

186. Marshall L. Small, "William O. Douglas Remembered: A Collective Memory of WOD's Law Clerks," *Journal of Supreme Court History*, vol. 32, no. 3 (2007): 297–334.

187. Bruch recalled her clerkship as a boon to her professional career but also an experience marred by the justice's personal unkindness toward her. James Bow, "Douglas: Personal View of an Impersonal Judge," *Sacramento Bee*, Nov. 24, 1975.

188. Carol S. Bruch to WOD, Apr. 10, 1973, WOD Papers, Cahill file.

189. NJWRO v. Cahill, 411 U.S. at 620 (quoting *Weber*).

190. Harry D. Krause, *Illegitimacy: Law and Social Policy* (Bobbs-Merrill, 1971), Appendix; Deanna L. Pagnini and Ronald R. Rindfuss, "The Divorce of Marriage and Childbearing: Changing Attitudes and Behavior in the United States," *Population and Development Review*, vol. 19, no. 2 (June 1993), 333–41.

191. On this historical phenomenon more broadly, see Linda Gordon, "The Perils of Innocence, or What's Wrong with Putting Children First," *Journal of the History of Childhood and Youth*, vol. 1, no. 3 (Fall 2008): 331–50.

192. See affidavits contained in Appendix, *Wyman v. James*, May 5, 1970.

193. Appendix; Brief of Appellees, *Wyman v. James*; Minutes of Hearing, June 30, 1969, S.D.N.Y., in Appendix, *Wyman v. James*, at 88–92. Michele Estrin Gilman, "Privacy as a Luxury Not for the Poor," in *Poverty Law Canon*, 160. See also Elizabeth Pleck, *Not Just Roommates: Cohabitation After the Sexual Revolution* (University of Chicago Press, 2012), chapter 3; Khiara M. Bridges, *The Poverty of Privacy Rights* (Stanford University Press, 2017); Tarek Ismail, "Family Policing and the Fourth Amendment," 111 *Calif. L. Rev.* 1485, 1511-18 (2023).

194. Essentially, New York "claim[ed] that receipt of public assistance results in the loss of parental rights protected by the Constitution!" protested Mrs. James's lawyers. Brief of Appellees, *Wyman v. James*, at 10; Memorandum re NOLEO [Notice to Law Enforcement Officials] Provisions, Appendix, *Wyman v. James*, at 112.

195. Memorandum re NOLEO Provisions, Appendix, *Wyman v. James*, at 113–14 (citing *Armstrong v. Manzo*).

196. James v. Goldberg, 303 F. Supp. 935, 945 (S.D.N.Y. 1969) (three-judge court).

197. Brief for the Legal Aid Society of San Mateo County as Amicus Curiae, *Wyman v. James*, at 11–13.

198. Wyman v. James, 400 U.S. 309, 317–19, 323 (1971).

199. The Supreme Court held in *Lewis v. Martin* (1970) that states could not count the income of a male cohabiting partner of a mother receiving public assistance in determining her children's grant unless he, as the children's biological father, had a legal support obligation.
200. Ismail, "Family Policing," 1518.
201. Johnnie Tillmon, "Welfare Is a Women's Issue," *Ms.*, Spring 1972. On welfare rights leaders' attitudes toward marriage, see Lefkovitz, *Strange Bedfellows*, chapter 4; Nadasen, *Welfare Warriors*, 145–46; Nadasen, "Expanding the Boundaries," 279–81.
202. Chappell, *The War on Welfare*, 105; Lefkovitz, *Strange Bedfellows*, 121–29.

Chapter 3. Making Marriage Safe for Equality

1. Ti-Grace Atkinson to Mary Eastwood, July 14, 1968, ME Papers, MC 596: 2.
2. The Feminists, Inc., Draft: An Emancipation Proclamation for Women, ME Papers, MC 596: 55a.
3. Alice Echols, *Daring to Be Bad: Radical Feminism in America, 1967–1975* (University of Minnesota Press, 1989), 148 (emphasis added). On feminist critiques of marriage, see Alison Lefkovitz, *Strange Bedfellows: Marriage in the Age of Women's Liberation* (University of Pennsylvania Press, 2018), chapter 1; Kirsten Swinth, *Feminism's Forgotten Fight: The Unfinished Struggle for Work and Family* (Harvard University Press, 2018).
4. Patricia Mainardi, "The Marriage Question," in *Feminist Revolution* (Redstockings, 1975), 122.
5. Jessie Bernard, *The Future of Marriage* (Yale University Press, 1972), 289.
6. Natasha Zaretsky, *No Direction Home: The American Family and the Fear of National Decline, 1968–1980* (University of North Carolina Press, 2007); Kirsten Swinth, "Post-Family Wage, Postindustrial Society: Reframing the Gender and Family Order Through Working Mothers in Reagan's America," *Journal of American History*, vol. 105, no. 2 (2018): 311–335.
7. Robert O. Self, *All in the Family: The Realignment of American Democracy Since the 1960s* (Hill and Wang, 2012); Serena Mayeri, "Family Matters: The Sexual Revolution in American Politics," *Jotwell*, Feb. 18, 2013.
8. See Serena Mayeri, "After Suffrage: The Unfinished Business of Feminist Legal Advocacy," *Yale L. J. Forum*, Jan. 20, 2020, and sources cited therein.
9. Kenneth M. Davidson, Ruth Bader Ginsburg, and Herma Hill Kay, *Sex-Based Discrimination: Text, Cases, and Materials* (West, 1974).
10. Aleta Wallach, Book Review, 10 *Harvard Civil Rights–Civil Liberties L. Rev.* 252 (1975).
11. Grace Ganz Blumberg, Book Review, 53 *Texas L. Rev.* 1354, 1368 (1974); Barbara Allen Babcock, Ann E. Freedman, Eleanor Holmes Norton, and Susan Deller Ross, *Sex Discrimination and the Law: Causes and Remedies* (Little, Brown, 1975).

12. Bernard, *Future of Marriage*; Rebecca L. Davis, *More Perfect Unions: The American Search for Marital Bliss* (Harvard University Press, 2010), 184.

13. Bernard, *Future of Marriage*, 14, 24, 289; Swinth, *Feminism's Forgotten Fight*, 37–39.

14. Swinth, *Feminism's Forgotten Fight*, chapter 3.

15. Feminists successfully attacked laws that distinguished between young men and women with respect to their parents' support obligations in *Stanton v. Stanton*, 421 U.S. 7 (1975).

16. Alice Kessler-Harris, *In Pursuit of Equity: Women, Men, and the Quest for Economic Citizenship in Twentieth-Century America* (Oxford University Press, 2001); Nancy F. Cott, *Public Vows: A History of Marriage and the Nation* (Harvard University Press, 2000); Margot Canaday, "Heterosexuality as a Legal Regime," in *Cambridge History of Law in America*, ed. Michael Grossberg and Christopher Tomlins (Cambridge University Press, 2008).

17. Mailer, a noted novelist and intellectual, was remembered as a misogynist, homophobe, and domestic abuser. In 1960, for example, he was arrested for stabbing his wife, Adele Morales, in a drunken rage, nearly killing her. See Joan Smith, "Farewell to Norman Mailer, a Sexist, Homophobic Reactionary," *Guardian*, Nov. 13, 2007.

18. Herma Hill Kay, "Making Marriage and Divorce Safe for Women," 60 *Calif. L. Rev.* 1683, 1690–94 (1972).

19. Swinth, *Feminism's Forgotten Fight*, 73.

20. See Ruth Feldstein, *Motherhood in Black and White: Race and Sex in American Liberalism, 1930–1965* (Cornell University Press, 2000); Marisa Chappell, *The War on Welfare: Family, Poverty, and Politics in Modern America* (University of Pennsylvania Press, 2010).

21. The discourse about equality in marriage cultivated by Black authors had long outpaced comparable writing by white commentators. See Christina Simmons, *Making Marriage Modern: Women's Sexuality from the Progressive Era to World War II* (Oxford University Press, 2009).

22. See Serena Mayeri, *Reasoning from Race: Feminism, Law, and the Civil Rights Revolution* (Harvard University Press, 2011), chapter 2; Serena Mayeri, "Historicizing 'The End of Men': The Politics of Reaction(s)," 93 *Boston Univ. L. Rev.* 729 (2013).

23. Quoted in Caroline Bird, "Black Womanpower," *New York Magazine*, Mar. 10, 1969; Mayeri, *Reasoning from Race*, 48.

24. Quoted in Ann Scott and Lucy Komisar, *And Justice For All: Federal Equal Opportunity Enforcement Effort Against Sex Discrimination* [1971], 14, NOW Papers, 72–8-82-M211, Carton 18, Folder: NOW Compliance for Affirmative Action; Mayeri, *Reasoning from Race*, 48.

25. Barbara Kashian Gubbins, "Eleanor Holmes Norton, Human Rights Commissioner," *Chicago Tribune*, Nov. 24, 1974, K9; see also Enid Nemy, "Feminist? Definition Varies with the Woman," *NYT*, Nov. 8, 1975; Marylin

Bender, "Black Woman in Civil Rights: Is She a Second-Class Citizen?," *NYT*, Sept. 2, 1969.

26. Quoted in Charlayne Hunter, "Many Blacks Wary of 'Women's Liberation' Movement in U.S.," *NYT*, Nov. 17, 1970.

27. Eleanor Holmes Norton, "For Sadie and Maude," 25 *Rutgers L. Rev.* 23 (1970). Eleanor H. Norton, "For Black Women, Opportunities Open," *NYT*, Jan. 10, 1971.

28. Pauli Murray, "Why Negro Girls Stay Single," *Negro Digest*, July 1947; Sarah Azaransky, *The Dream Is Freedom: Pauli Murray and American Democratic Faith* (NYU Press, 2011); Rosalind Rosenberg, *Jane Crow: The Life of Pauli Murray* (Oxford University Press, 2017).

29. For more, see Joan Steinau Lester, *Fire in My Soul: The Life of Eleanor Holmes Norton* (Simon & Schuster, 2004). On the struggles to balance work and family faced by the pioneering civil rights lawyer, public official, and judge Constance Baker Motley, see Tomiko Brown-Nagin, *Civil Rights Queen: Constance Baker Motley and the Struggle for Equality* (Penguin Books, 2022).

30. On Ginsburg's use of male plaintiffs, see Joan Williams, *Unbending Gender: Why Family and Work Conflict and What to Do About It* (Oxford University Press, 1999); Serena Mayeri, "Reconstructing the Race-Sex Analogy," 49 *Wm. & Mary L. Rev.* 1789 (2009); Cary Franklin, "The Anti-Stereotyping Principle in Constitutional Sex Discrimination Law," 85 *NYU L. Rev.* 83 (2010).

31. See Jane S. DeHart, *Ruth Bader Ginsburg: A Life* (Alfred Knopf, 2018).

32. On employment discrimination laws and their enforcement during this period, see Nancy MacLean, *Freedom Is Not Enough: The Opening of the American Workplace* (Harvard University Press, 2006); Katherine Turk, *Equality on Trial: Gender and Rights in the Modern American Workplace* (University of Pennsylvania Press, 2016); Mayeri, *Reasoning from Race*.

33. See Brief for Appellant, *Reed v. Reed*, 404 U.S. 71 (1971); Mayeri, *Reasoning from Race*, 61.

34. The fourth category was discrimination in the criminal law. Almost all of the appendix's "small sample" of discriminations against women in state law involved marriage; see also Jurisdictional Statement, *Reed v. Reed*, 10.

35. Pauli Murray, "A Proposal to Reexamine the Applicability of the Fourteenth Amendment to State Laws and Practices Which Discriminate on the Basis of Sex Per Se," 1 December 1962, Box 8, Folder 62, PCSW Records, 1961–1963, Schlesinger Library, Radcliffe Institute, Harvard University (hereinafter PCSW memo).

36. Murray, PCSW memo, 8–9.

37. Swinth, *Feminism's Forgotten Fight*, 87–90; Franklin, "Anti-Stereotyping Principle."

38. Brief for the ACLU as Amicus Curiae, *Frontiero v. Richardson*, No. 71–1694, at 24.

39. ACLU Brief, *Frontiero*, 26–27; Brief for Appellees, *Frontiero*, No. 71–1694, 1972 WL 137566, at * 11–12. On *Frontiero*, see Serena Mayeri, "The Story of *Frontiero v. Richardson*," in *Women and the Law Stories*, ed. Elizabeth M. Schneider and Stephanie Wildman (Foundation Press, 2009).

40. Frontiero v. Richardson, 411 U.S. 677 (1973).

41. Fred Strebeigh, *Equal: Women Reshape American Law* (W.W. Norton, 2009), 72.

42. Brief for Appellee, *Weinberger v. Wiesenfeld*, No. 73–1892, 1974 WL 186057.

43. Brief for Appellee, *Wiesenfeld*, 17–18 (emphasis added); see also Brief for Amicus Curiae Center for Constitutional Rights, *Wiesenfeld*, 1974 WL 186058, *8.

44. Quoted in Linda Greenhouse, "The Evolution of a Justice," *NYT Magazine*, April 10, 2005.

45. Nancy Axelrad Comer, "Working Mothers: How They Juggle Their Lives," *Mademoiselle*, May 1975.

46. The former clerk had unsuccessfully recommended several women to Brennan. See Strebeigh, *Equal*.

47. Seth Stern and Stephen Wermiel, *Justice Brennan: Liberal Champion* (Houghton Mifflin, 2010), 399–400.

48. Strebeigh, *Equal*, 75.

49. Weinberger v. Wiesenfeld, 420 U.S. 636, 648–49 (1975).

50. *Wiesenfeld*, 420 U.S. at 652.

51. John C. Jeffries, Jr., *Justice Lewis F. Powell, Jr.: A Biography* (Scribner's, 1994), 503.

52. See Mayeri, "Reconstructing the Race-Sex Analogy."

53. Strebeigh, *Equal*, 75.

54. Califano v. Goldfarb, 430 U.S. 199 (1977).

55. See Serena Mayeri, "Marital Supremacy and the Constitution of the Nonmarital Family," 103 *Calif. L. Rev.* 1277 (2015).

56. Stanley v. Illinois, 405 U.S. 645 (1972).

57. Eisenstadt v. Baird, 405 U.S. 438, 453–54 (1972).

58. Roe v. Wade, 410 U.S. 113 (1973).

59. John O. Noonan, "The Family and the Supreme Court," 23 *Catholic Univ. L. Rev.* 255, 273–74 (1973).

60. A result of the 1967 Social Security Amendments, which rolled back the 1965 amendments to the definition of "child." See chapter 1.

61. See Griffin v. Richardson, 346 F. Supp. 1226, 1228–29 (D. Md. 1972).

62. Griffin v. Richardson, 346 F. Supp. 1226 (1972).

63. Jimenez v. Weinberger, 417 U.S. 628 (1974). For more, see Mayeri, "Marital Supremacy," 1323–25.

64. See Carol B. Stack and Herbert Semmel, "The Concept of Family in the Poor Black Community," in Joint Economic Committee, Congress of the United States, Studies in Public Welfare, Paper No. 12 (Part II): The Family, Poverty, and Welfare Programs—Household Patterns and Government

275 (Joint Committee Print 1973); Harry D. Krause, "Child Welfare, Parental Responsibility, and the State," 6 *Fam. L. Q.* 377 (1972), reprinted in Studies in Public Welfare, Paper No. 12 (Part II), 255. On Semmel's life, see "Herbert Semmel, 73, Lawyer in Civil Rights Suits," *NYT*, Feb. 10, 2004. On CLASP, see Alan Houseman, "A Historical Perspective on the Center for Law and Social Policy," 26 *Clearinghouse Rev.* 32 (1992).

65. Herbert Semmel, "Social Security Benefits for Illegitimate Children After *Levy v. Louisiana*," 19 *Buffalo L. Rev.* 289, 297 (1970).

66. Gregory Sr. had begun gathering the documents necessary for his son to receive a dependent child's military allotment, but he "failed . . . to complete the required procedures before he was killed." Norton v. Mathews, 427 U.S. 524, 525–26 (1976).

67. Rhode Island was one of only a handful of states that still recognized common law marriage in 1975.

68. Mayeri, "Marital Supremacy," 1324–25.

69. Mathews v. Lucas, 427 U.S. 496, 506 (1976).

70. Mathews v. Lucas, 427 U.S. at 523 (Stevens, J., dissenting).

71. Rosemary Beales, "Illegitimate Children's Mothers Gain Benefits," *Austin American-Statesman*, June 24, 1978.

72. Semmel, "Social Security Benefits," 300.

73. Boles v. Califano, 464 F. Supp. 408, 411 (W.D. Tex. 1978).

74. If a nonmarital father "did not choose voluntarily to support the unmarried mother, in most states she had no legal recourse to compel him to do so." Transcript of Oral Argument, Califano v. Boles, 443 U.S. 282 (1979) (No. 78-808).

75. Mathews v. DeCastro, 429 U.S. 181 (1976). For more, see Suzanne Kahn, *Divorce, American Style: Fighting for Women's Economic Citizenship in the Neoliberal Era* (University of Pennsylvania Press, 2021), chapter 5.

76. Califano v. Jobst, 434 U.S. 47 (1977). John Jobst eventually was able to receive a lesser Social Security benefit, but as he noted, the new program disincentivized work in addition to providing a significantly lower monthly benefit. George E. Curry, "Asserts U.S. Penalized Him for Marrying," *St. Louis Post-Dispatch*, Nov. 15, 1977.

77. I use similar language in Serena Mayeri, "The State of Illegitimacy After the Rights Revolution," in *Intimate States: Gender, Sexuality, and Governance in Modern U.S. History*, ed. Margot Canaday, Nancy F. Cott, and Robert O. Self (University of Chicago Press, 2021), 248.

78. Stephen Vider, *The Queerness of Home: Gender, Sexuality, and the Politics of Domesticity After World War II* (University of Chicago Press, 2021), 29–30.

79. Vider, *Queerness*, 30–31.

80. Kate Millett, *Sexual Politics* (Doubleday, 1970), 85–86; Michael Boucai, "Glorious Precedents: When Gay Marriage Was Radical," 27 *Yale J. L. & Hum.* 1, 16–17 (2015). See also Cary Franklin, "The Anti-Stereotyping

Principle in Constitutional Sex Discrimination Law," 85 *N.Y.U. L. Rev.* 83, 112 (2010); Lefkovitz, *Strange Bedfellows*, chapter 1.

81. Stephanie Gilmore and Elizabeth Kaminski, "A Part and Apart: Lesbian and Straight Feminist Activists Negotiate Identity in a Second-Wave Organization," *Journal of the History of Sexuality*, vol. 16, no. 1 (January 2007): 95–113. On NOW, see Katherine Turk, *The Women of NOW: How Feminists Built an Organization that Transformed America* (Farrar Straus & Giroux, 2023).

82. See, for example, Boucai, "Glorious Precedents"; Eskridge and Riano, *Marriage Equality*; Vider, *Queerness of Home.*

83. Sandra Stencel, "Homosexual Legal Rights," *Alabama Journal*, Apr. 4, 1974.

84. Jeffrey Escoffier, "Straw Men," *Gay Alternative*, issue 9, 1975, at 28–29 (Independent Voices) (reviewing several books).

85. Lotti B. Benker, "Gay Article Not the True Picture," *Democrat and Chronicle* (Rochester, N.Y.), Jan. 7, 1973.

86. Evan Mills, "Homosexual Marriage," *The Phoenix*, vol. 2, issue 6, July 1967.

87. "Church Considers Gay Marriage Legitimate," *Standard Speaker* (Hazleton, Pa.), June 30, 1977.

88. Grace Lichtenstein, "Gay Marriages Set Off Legal Debate," *Independent Press* (Long Beach, Calif.), Sept. 25, 1975.

89. "Gay Marriage," *Detroit Liberator*, vol. 1, issue 4, August 1, 1970.

90. John Carman, "Lesbian Confronts Myths, Talks of Life," *Minneapolis Star*, Nov. 11, 1977.

91. "Marriage Vows," *Echo of Sappho*, vol. 1, issue 2, August/September 1972, at 8.

92. Phil Mullen, "Love Between Men," *Gay Alternative*, issue 3, 1973, at 11 (Independent Voices).

93. Don Borbe, "Celebrating Gay Marriages," *New Gay Life*, vol. 2, issue 5, May 1978, at 10, 26.

94. "Marriage Vows," *Echo of Sappho*, vol. 1, issue 2, August/September 1972, at 11. For more, see Elise Chenier, "Love-Politics: Lesbian Wedding Practices in Canada and the United States from the 1920s to the 1970s," *Journal of the History of Sexuality*, vol. 27, no. 2 (May 2018).

95. Boucai, "Glorious Precedents."

96. Boucai, "Glorious Precedents."

97. See William Eskridge and Christopher Riano, *Marriage Equality: From Outlaws to In-Laws* (Yale University Press, 2020), chapter 1.

98. Singer quoted in Boucai, "Glorious Precedents," 6; Eskridge and Riano, *Marriage Equality*, 22–24.

99. Eskridge and Riano, *Marriage Equality*, 5–9, 13–17, 26–27.

100. AP, "Homosexuals Visit Agency in Attempt to Adopt Child," *Bismarck Tribune* (N.Dak.), May 15, 1974, at 33; AP, "Gay Activist Files Discrimination Suit in St. Paul in Attempt to Adopt Child," *Argus-Leader* (Sioux Falls,

S.Dak.), Oct. 22, 1974, at 8. McConnell also filed a petition to legally adopt Baker. "Gay Lib Leader to Speak," *Oshkosh Northwestern*, Sept. 27, 1973; Eskridge and Riano, *Marriage Equality*, 31–33.

101. "He's Not Spouse, Says VA," *Sioux City Journal*, Nov. 20, 1974.

102. AP, "Minneapolis Couple Files Joint Tax Return," *Argus-Leader* (Sioux Falls, S.Dak.), Apr. 19, 1974.

103. Gwyneth Jones, "Gay Couple Sues to Keep Income Tax Refund," *Minneapolis Star*, Oct. 17, 1978.

104. "A Year in Jail for Trespassing!" *Lesbian Tide*, vol. 6, issue 3, November-December 1976, at 22.

105. Susan Edwards, "Never the Twain Shall Meet," *Lavender Woman*, vol. 4, issue 5, December 1975.

106. Edwards, "Never the Twain Shall Meet," 1, 4.

107. Lefkovitz, *Strange Bedfellows*, 155–63.

108. Barbara A. Brown et al., "The Equal Rights Amendment: A Constitutional Basis for Equality for Women," 80 *Yale L. J.* 871 (1971); Reva B. Siegel, "Constitutional Culture, Social Movement Conflict, and Constitutional Change: The Case of the De Facto ERA," 95 *Calif. L. Rev.* 1323 (2007).

109. [S. T. Perkins and A. J. Silverstein,] Note, "The Legality of Homosexual Marriage," 82 *Yale L. J.* 573, 574 (1973).

110. See Marjorie Spruill, *Divided We Stand: The Battle Over Women's Rights and Family Values That Polarized American Politics* (Bloomsbury, 2017); Jane Sherron De Hart and Donald Mathews, *Sex, Gender, and the Politics of ERA: A State and the Nation* (University of North Carolina Press, 1991).

111. For more, see Mayeri, "After Suffrage"; Mayeri, *Reasoning from Race*; Siegel, "De Facto ERA"; De Hart and Mathews, *Sex, Gender*; Self, *All in the Family*; Lefkovitz, *Strange Bedfellows*, chapter 3.

112. Siegel, "De Facto ERA." See, for example, Rep. John Wargo (Columbiana County), Letter to the Editor, *Evening Review* (East Liverpool, Ohio), Apr. 3, 1973; Paul Scott, "Equal Rights Amendment Would Okay Marriages for Homosexual Couples," *Lebanon Daily News* (Pa.), Sept. 25, 1974.

113. Quoted in Sasha Gregory Lewis, "Phyllis Schlafly and the Right-Wing Connection," *Lesbian Tide*, vol. 8, issue 5, March/April 1979. Schlafly's charges did not prevent feminists from achieving formal legal equality between husbands and wives within marriage, but they did discipline claims about the nondiscrimination principle's reach. Siegel, "De Facto ERA."

114. Lefkovitz, *Strange Bedfellows*, 101, 93–95.

115. Ruth Bader Ginsburg, "Observation, Ratification of the Equal Rights Amendment: A Question of Time," 57 *Texas L. Rev.* 919, 937 (1979); for more, see Siegel, "De Facto ERA."

116. "The ERA Kill Bill," *The Rag*, vol. 9, issue 24, April 24, 1975, at 10.

117. Jurisdictional Statement, *Baker v. Nelson*, No. 71–1027, 409 U.S. 810 (1972).

118. Baker v. Nelson, 291 Minn. 310 (1971).

119. The Washington court rejected the plaintiffs' analogy to *Loving v. Virginia*. Singer v. Hara, 522 P. 2d 1187 (Wash Ct. App. 1974).

120. Lefkovitz, *Strange Bedfellows*, 158–60.

121. See Kirchberg v. Feenstra, 450 U.S. 455 (1981).

122. Orr v. Orr, 440 U.S. 268 (1979).

123. On how men fought back against alimony awards in the 1970s, see Lefkovitz, *Strange Bedfellows*, chapter 2.

124. Reva B. Siegel, "'The Rule of Love': Wife-Beating as Prerogative and Privacy," 105 *Yale L. J.* 2117, 2188–96 (1996); Jill Elaine Hasday, "Contest and Consent: A Legal History of Marital Rape," 88 *Calif. L. Rev.* 1373 (2000).

125. Grace Blumberg, "Sexism in the Code: A Comparative Study of Income Taxation of Working Wives and Mothers," 21 *Buff. L. Rev.* 49 (1971). See also Cott, *Public Vows*, 192–93.

126. Cf. Reva Siegel, "Why Equal Protection No Longer Protects: The Evolving Forms of Status-Reinforcing State Action," 49 *Stanford L. Rev.* 1111 (1997).

127. Cf. Siegel, "'The Rule of Love'"; Hendrik Hartog, *Man and Wife in America: A History* (Harvard University Press, 2000).

128. On the anti-ERA movement, see Siegel, "De Facto ERA"; Mary Frances Berry, *Why ERA Failed: Politics, Women's Rights, and the Amending Process of the Constitution* (Indiana University Press, 1988); Jane J. Mansbridge, *Why We Lost the ERA* (University of Chicago Press, 1986); De Hart and Mathews, *Sex, Gender*; Spruill, *Divided We Stand*. On men's rights advocates, see Deborah Dinner, "The Divorce Bargain: The Fathers' Rights Movement and Family Inequalities," 102 *Virginia L. Rev.* 79 (2016); Lefkovitz, *Strange Bedfellows*, chapter 2. On reforms to the public law of divorce, see Suzanne Kahn, *Divorce, American Style: Fighting for Women's Economic Citizenship in the Neoliberal Era* (University of Pennsylvania Press, 2021).

129. On common law marriage, see Ariela R. Dubler, "Governing Through Contract: Common Law Marriage in the Nineteenth Century," 107 *Yale L. J.* 1885 (1998); Cynthia Grant Bowman, "A Feminist Proposal to Bring Back Common Law Marriage," 75 *Oregon L. Rev.* (1996).

130. On cohabitation, see Grace Ganz Blumberg, "Cohabitation Without Marriage: A Different Perspective," 28 *U.C.L.A. L. Rev.* 1125 (1981); Elizabeth Pleck, *Not Just Roommates: Cohabitation After the Sexual Revolution* (University of Chicago Press, 2012); Cynthia Grant Bowman, *Unmarried Couples, Law, and Public Policy* (Oxford University Press, 2010).

131. Some gay and lesbian Americans married, but to be legally recognized, those marriages had to be male-female unions.

132. On how Schlafly and other conservatives "blam[ed] feminists for the fragile family," see Lefkovitz, *Strange Bedfellows*, chapter 3.

133. See Lisa Levenstein, "'Don't Agonize, Organize!': The Displaced Homemakers Campaign and the Contested Goals of Postwar Feminism,"

Journal of American History, vol. 100, no. 4 (March 2014): 1114–38; Mary Ziegler, "An Incomplete Revolution: Feminists and the Legacy of Marital Property Reform," 19 *Mich. J. Gender & L.* 259 (2013); Lefkovitz, *Strange Bedfellows*, chapter 2; Swinth, *Feminism's Forgotten Fight*, chapter 4; Kahn, *Divorce*.

134. Kahn, *Divorce*, 121.

135. Kahn, *Divorce*, 137.

136. Kahn, *Divorce*, 136–38, 141–43. As Kahn notes, Congress did not take the cheapest way out, as conservatives and sometimes President Jimmy Carter suggested they do. Rather, they acted consistently to shore up the breadwinner/dependent model of marriage even when it cost the government somewhat more.

137. Kahn, *Divorce*, 118.

138. Kahn, *Divorce*, 146.

139. Because Kahn has provided a comprehensive and persuasive analysis of feminist divorce reforms in public law, I have briefly summarized her findings here and focused my research elsewhere.

140. Equal Partnership in Marriage: History and Statement of Policy of the Task Force on Marriage, Divorce, and Family Relations, BB Papers, MC 506, Box 2, Folder 6 (containing NOW resolutions presented by the TF, 1967–71).

141. In 1968, she envisioned a "type of life insurance" with a "certain percentage of the policy . . . earmarked for contingency." Betty Berry, History of Marriage and Divorce Insurance (June 1972), BB Papers, MC 506, Box 2, Folder 13. For more on Berry's divorce insurance proposals, see Kahn, *Divorce*, chapter 2.

142. In 1966, New York expanded the grounds for divorce to include a two-year legal separation and fault-based grounds beyond adultery, previously the only basis for exiting a marriage.

143. Marriage, Family Relations, Divorce, 22, Washington Conference (NOW), Feb. 15–17, 1973, BB Papers, MC 506, Box 2, Folder 8.

144. See Herma Hill Kay, "Equality and Difference: A Perspective on No-Fault Divorce and Its Aftermath," 56 *U. Cinn. L. Rev.* (1987); Herma Hill Kay, "Making Marriage and Divorce Safe for Women, Revisited," 32 *Hofstra L. Rev.* 71 (2003).

145. Marriage, Family Relations, Divorce, 21, Washington Conference (NOW), Feb. 15–17, 1973, BB Papers, MC 506, Box 2, Folder 8.

146. Marriage and Divorce Workshops; Legislative Recommendations (1971) (helpful summary) (Women's Unit, Governor [Rockefeller]'s Office/NY State Legislative Conference, Nov. 13, 1971, NYC), BB Papers, MC 506, Box 4, Folder 5 (Gov. Rockefeller's Conference, 1971).

147. Equal Partnership in Marriage: History and Statement of Policy of the Task Force on Marriage, Divorce, and Family Relations, BB Papers, MC 506, Box 2, Folder 6. For more, see Kahn, *Divorce*, chapter 2.

148. Nora Lavori, *Living Together, Married or Single: Your Legal Rights* (Harper & Row, 1976), 18.

149. See Alix Kates Shulman, *A Marriage Agreement and Other Essays* (Open Road Media, 2012); Swinth, *Feminism's Forgotten Fight*, 70–73, 81–82.

150. Davis, *More Perfect Unions*, 185–86.

151. Norman Sheresky and Marya Mannes, "A Radical Guide to Wedlock," *Saturday Review*, July 29, 1972 (emphasis added). The article was adapted from their book, *Uncoupling*.

152. Goals of Committee on Sex and Domestic Relations (Atlanta NOW), August 1972, BB Papers, Box 2, Folder 9; Eliza Paschall to Betty Berry, BB Papers, Box 6, Folder 9.

153. Some contracting proponents did not consider themselves feminists at all. See Richard Neely, "Marriage Contracts, for Better or for Worse," in *Marital and Non-Marital Contracts: Preventive Law for the Family*, ed. Joan M. Krauskopf (ABA, 1979), 1; Karl Fleischmann, "Marriage Contract: Defining the Terms of the Relationship," 8 *Fam. L. Quarterly* 27 (1974). Marriage counselors, historically among the most ardent promoters of traditional gender roles, saw therapeutic value in contracting for troubled couples. See Davis, *More Perfect Unions*.

154. Weitzman and Goode married in 1978, a union that endured until Goode's death in 2003. Goode had two children from previous marriages. He, too, had published on divorce's consequences for women. Wolfgang Saxon, "William Goode, Scholar of Family Life and Divorce, Dies at 85," *NYT*, May 8, 2003.

155. Lenore J. Weitzman, A Proposal for Legal Partnerships (Marriage Contract), March 1972, BB Papers, Box 12, Folder 2.

156. Weitzman, Proposal, 1.

157. Weitzman, Proposal, 2.

158. Lenore Weitzman, "Legal Regulation of Marriage: Tradition and Change: A Proposal for Individual Contracts and Contracts in Lieu of Marriage," 62 *Calif. L. Rev.* 1169, 1187 (1974). Weitzman cited reports from the Citizens' Advisory Council on the Status of Women; later, she co-authored a study of the "alimony myth." Lenore Weitzman and Ruth B. Dixon, "The Alimony Myth: Does No-Fault Divorce Make a Difference?," 14 *Fam. L. Quarterly* 141 (1980). See also Doras Jonas Freed and Henry H. Foster, Jr., "Economic Effects of Divorce," 7 *Fam. L. Quarterly* 275 (1973).

159. Weitzman, "Legal Regulation," 1249.

160. Weitzman, "Legal Regulation," 1253.

161. See, for example, Margaret G. Sokolov, "Marriage Contracts: Is There a Need?," in Krauskopf, *Marital and Non-Marital Contracts*, 15.

162. "Pre-Marital Contracts Within the Patriarchy," *New Women's Times*, vol. 3, issue 6, June-July 1977, at 12.

163. Weitzman, "Legal Regulation," 1257. The Uniform Partnership Act was originally promulgated by the National Conference of Commissioners on

Uniform State Laws (NCCUSL) in 1914, and it was adopted by every U.S. state except Louisiana; several updated versions subsequently were adopted by many states.

164. See Marjorie M. Shultz, "Contractual Ordering of Marriage: A New Model for State Policy," 70 *Calif. L. Rev.* 207 (1982).

165. Lenore Weitzman, *The Marriage Contract: Spouses, Lovers, and the Law* (Free Press, 1981), 242.

166. Marsha Garrison, "Marriage: The Status of Contract," 131 *U. Pa. L. Rev.* 1039, 1045 (1983).

167. Orr v. Orr, 440 U.S. 268 (1979); Kirchberg v. Feenstra, 450 U.S. 455 (1982).

168. See Lefkovitz, *Strange Bedfellows.*

169. Garrison, "Marriage," 1046–48. Thomas Oldham predicted that marriage contracts would "remain the province of the upper middle class, the wealthy, and the previously married." J. Thomas Oldham, Book Review, 54 *U. Colo. L. Rev.* 469–487 (1983).

170. Lenore J. Weitzman, *The Divorce Revolution* (Free Press, 1985). See also Martha Albertson Fineman, *The Illusion of Equality: The Rhetoric and Reality of Divorce Reform* (University of Chicago Press, 2d ed., 1994).

171. Dinner, "Divorce Bargain"; Lefkovitz, *Strange Bedfellows.*

172. Kahn, *Divorce.*

173. Barbara B. Hirsch, *Living Together: A Guide to the Law for Unmarried Couples* (Houghton Mifflin, 1976), 96. Lavori, *Living Together, Married or Single,* 111.

174. Toni Ihara and Ralph Warner, *The Living Together Kit,* 2d ed. (First Fawcett Press, 1978), 50.

175. Ihara and Warner, *Living Together Kit,* 65.

176. In re Marriage of Cary, 109 Cal. Rptr. 862, 863 (Ct. of App., 1st Dist. 1973).

177. Cary, 109 Cal. Rptr. at 867.

178. Herma Hill Kay and Carol Amyx, "*Marvin v. Marvin:* Preserving the Options," 65 *Calif. L. Rev.* 937, 952 (1977).

179. H. Jay Folberg and William P. Buren, "Domestic Partnership: A Proposal for Dividing the Property of Unmarried Families," 12 *Willamette L. J.* 453, 481, 484 (1976).

180. Carol S. Bruch, "Property Rights of De Facto Spouses Including Thoughts on the Value of Homemakers' Services," 10 *Fam. L. Quarterly* 101 (1976).

181. In re Estate of Thornton, 81 Wash. 2d 72 (1972).

182. Marvin v. Marvin, 557 P.2d 106 (Cal. 1976). Michelle Marvin herself did not recover.

183. Hewitt v. Hewitt, 394 N.E.2d 1204 (Ill. 1979); Pleck, *Not Just Roommates.*

184. See Ann Laquer Estin, "Ordinary Cohabitation," 76 *Notre Dame L. Rev.* 1381 (2001); Pleck, *Not Just Roommates,* chapter 7; Grossman and Friedman, *Inside the Castle.*

185. Kay and Amyx, *"Marvin v. Marvin,"* 952.
186. Martha L. Fineman, "Law and Changing Patterns of Behavior: Sanctions on Non-Marital Cohabitation," 1981 *Wisc. L. Rev.* 275, 325.
187. Pleck, *Not Just Roommates*, chapter 6.
188. Cf. Boucai, "Glorious Precedents"; Douglas NeJaime, "Before Marriage: The Unexplored History of Nonmarital Recognition and Its Relationship to Marriage," 102 *Calif. L. Rev.* 87 (2014).
189. AP, "Lesbian Family Reunited," *News-Palladium* (Benton Harbor, Mich.), Oct. 23, 1973.
190. R. James Kellogg to Abigail Van Buren, Dear Abby, *Indiana Gazette* (Pa.), May 7, 1980.
191. Curry and Clifford quoted in Mickey Friedman, "A Legal Guide for Gay Couples," *S.F. Examiner*, Apr. 14, 1981.
192. Lesbian Law Section Collective, "Legal Planning for Lesbian Partnerships," in *Our Right to Love: A Lesbian Resource Book*, ed. Ginny Vida (NGTF, 1978), 216.
193. Harry Johansen, "S.F. Gays Take Heart Over New Ruling: Property Rights for Unmarrieds Must Apply to All, They Feel," *S.F. Examiner*, Dec. 29, 1976.
194. See, e.g., Judith Michaelson, "The Marvin Case Revisited," *Spokesman Review*, May 24, 1979 (mentioning San Diego case); George P. Ritter, "Property Rights of a Same-Sex Couple: The Outlook After *Marvin*," 12 *Loyola L.A. L. Rev.* 409, 419 (1979).
195. Bob Greene, "Lesbian Couple Seeks 'Divorce,'" *Times and Democrat* (Orangeburg, S.C.), July 3, 1978; UPI, "Lesbian Told to Aid Wife, Share Military Pension," *LAT*, June 6, 1978.
196. Greene, "Lesbian Couple," 6.
197. Ted Vollmer, "Lesbian Must Pay Support to Her 'Wife,'" *LAT*, June 7, 1978.
198. Vollmer, "Lesbian Must Pay Support," 29.
199. See Rhonda R. Rivera, "Queer Law: Sexual Orientation Law in the Mid-Eighties," 11 *Univ. Dayton L. Rev.* 275 (1986).
200. The book included various "models" of contractual arrangements that largely mirrored Weitzman's contemporaneous volume. Hayden Curry and Denis Clifford, *A Legal Guide for Lesbian and Gay Couples* (Nolo Press, 1980), 28.
201. Lesbian Law Section Collective, "Legal Planning," 217.
202. Drawing up one contract for "financial and property arrangements" and another for "housekeeping arrangements, fidelity, child care, etc.," would ensure the enforceability of the former. Lesbian Law Section Collective, "Legal Planning," 217.
203. Lesbian Law Section Collective, "Legal Planning," 218–19.
204. Dinner, "The Divorce Bargain"; Lefkovitz, *Strange Bedfellows*.

205. While empirical confirmation is difficult to come by, anecdotal evidence suggests that gay and lesbian couples were more likely to turn to contracting, albeit unlikely to call upon courts for enforcement.

Chapter 4. Redefining the Household

1. Jonathan Shor, "All in the Family: Legal Problems of Communes," 7 *Harvard Civil Rights–Civil Liberties L. Rev.* 393, 393 (1972).
2. Laura Kalman, *Right Star Rising: A New Politics, 1974–1980* (W.W. Norton, 2010), 75.
3. "The number of single women raising children nearly doubled between 1965 and 1990." Robert O. Self, *All in the Family: The Realignment of American Democracy Since the 1960s* (Hill and Wang, 2012), 323. As of 1968, 12 percent of single parents in the United States were fathers. Gretchen Livingston, "The Changing Profile of Unmarried Parents," Pew Research Center, Apr. 25, 2018. See also Elizabeth Pleck, *Not Just Roommates: Cohabitation After the Sexual Revolution* (University of Illinois Press, 2012).
4. Natasha Zaretsky, *No Direction Home: The American Family and the Fear of National Decline, 1968–1980* (University of North Carolina Press, 2007); Self, *All in the Family: The Realignment of American Democracy.*
5. Alice Kessler-Harris, *In Pursuit of Equity: Women, Men, and the Quest for Economic Citizenship* (Oxford University Press, 2001); Alison Lefkovitz, *Strange Bedfellows: Marriage in the Age of Women's Liberation* (University of Pennsylvania Press, 2018); Nancy F. Cott, *Public Vows: A History of Marriage and the Nation* (Harvard University Press, 2000); Suzanne Kahn, *Divorce, American Style: Fighting for Women's Economic Citizenship in the Neoliberal Era* (University of Pennsylvania Press, 2021).
6. See, e.g., Rosabeth Moss Kanter, *Communes: Creating and Managing the Collective Life* (Joanna Cotler Books, 1973). By the early 1970s, Americans had established upward of two thousand communes in thirty-four states.
7. Deborah Dinner, "The Universal Child Care Debate: Rights Mobilization, Social Policy, and the Dynamics of Feminist Activism, 1966–1974," *Law and History Review*, vol. 28, no. 3 (August 2010): 577–628; Marisa Chappell, *The War on Welfare: Family, Poverty, and Politics in Modern America* (University of Pennsylvania Press, 2010).
8. See, e.g., Shor, "All in the Family."
9. See Zaretsky, *No Direction Home.*
10. AP, "Welfare Aid for Commune Residents Termed Calculated Risk By Minter," *Berkshire Eagle* (Pittsfield, Mass.), May 31, 1972.
11. Persons older than sixty were exempt. After notice and comment, the final rule provided: "'Related' means related by blood, affinity, or through a legal relationship sanctioned by State law. Persons shall also be considered related for purposes of the program if they are (1) a man and woman living as man and wife, and accepted as such by the community in which they live, or

(2) legally adopted children, legally assigned foster children, or other children under the age of 18, when an adult household member (18 years of age or older) acts in loco parentis to such children."

12. See, e.g., "Coupons Allow More Food for Less Money," *Lansing State Journal*, June 4, 1972.

13. Sanford Rosen to Affiliates, Dec. 8, 1971, Re: Food Stamp Restrictions, ACLU Records, Box 1555, Folder: Moreno, 1972.

14. Otto Henry Zinke, ACLU of Arkansas, to Sanford Rosen, Jan. 11, 1972, ACLU Records, Box 1555, Folder: Moreno, 1972.

15. 36 Fed. Reg. 20145, Oct. 16, 1971.

16. Complaint, Moreno v. U.S. Dept of Agriculture, 11, Joint Appendix, USDA v. Moreno.

17. Complaint, *Moreno*, 11.

18. Complaint, *Moreno*, 38–41.

19. Complaint, *Moreno*, 8–10.

20. Complaint, *Moreno*, 8; AP, "U.S. Facing Lawsuit Over Food-Stamp Cut-off," *Miami Herald*, Mar. 31, 1972.

21. Complaint, *Moreno*, 8; AP, "U.S. Facing Lawsuit Over Food-Stamp Cut-off," *Miami Herald*," Mar. 31, 1972. Refused food stamps, Mrs. Moreno sought help from the Florida Rural Legal Assistance Program. Connie Standish, "Suit Seeks to End Food Stamp Denial," *Miami News*, Apr. 3, 1972.

22. Robert V. Carleson, Director of Social Welfare, to Kenneth Schlossberg, Staff Director, Select Committee on Nutrition and Human Needs, Nov. 15, 1971, in Appendix "A" to Memorandum of Law filed March 30, 1972, Appendix, *Moreno*, 43.

23. Carleson to Schlossberg, Appendix, *Moreno*, 43.

24. "Criterion for Poverty," Editorial, *Miami News*, May 9, 1972.

25. Eisenstadt v. Baird, 405 U.S. 438 (1972).

26. Pollack thought the plaintiffs' equal protection claims stronger. Ronald Pollack, Center on Social Welfare Policy & Law, to Norman Dorsen, March 30, 1972, ACLU Records, Box 1555, Folder: Moreno, 1972.

27. Memorandum of Law in Support of Plaintiffs' Motion for a Preliminary Injunction and Temporary Restraining Order, *Moreno*, 27–34, (D.D.C. 1972), ACLU Records, Box 1555, Folder: Moreno, 1972.

28. Moreno v. U.S. Dept of Agriculture, 345 F. Supp. 310, 314 (D. D.C. May 26, 1972).

29. *Moreno*, 345 F. Supp. at 315. The government's lawyer contended that support for the "traditional family unit" motivated the amendment.

30. Brief of Appellees, *Moreno*, 15–16 (citing *Weber*). See Gerald Gunther, "The Supreme Court, 1971 Term—Foreword: In Search of Evolving Doctrine on a Changing Court: A Model for a Newer Equal Protection," 86 *Harvard L. Rev.* 1 (1971).

31. 1st (2nd?) Draft of USDA v. Moreno and USDA v. Murry (Memorandum from WOD), circulated May 9, 1973, WOD Papers, Box 1613.

32. HAB, Conference Notes, *Moreno*, Apr. 23, 1973, HAB Papers, Box 168, Folder 1.
33. [J. Harvie Wilkinson] to LFP, Re: USDA v. Moreno, LFP Papers.
34. WJB, Case History of USDA v. Moreno, WJB Papers, II:6.
35. WJB, First Draft of USDA v. Moreno, circulated June 5, 1973, WOD Papers, Box 1613.
36. LFP, handwritten notes on WJB, First Draft of USDA v. Moreno, June 5, 1973, LFP Papers.
37. WJB, Case History of USDA v. Moreno, WJB Papers, II:6.
38. USDA v. Moreno, 413 U.S. 528, 535 (1973).
39. *Moreno*, 413 U.S. at 543, 553–55 (Douglas, J., concurring).
40. *Moreno*, 413 U.S. at 541 (Douglas, J., concurring).
41. Complaint, *Boraas v. Belle Terre*, in Appendix, A17.
42. Kate Redburn, "Zoned Out: How Zoning Law Complicates Family Law's Functional Turn," 128 *Yale L. J.* 2122 (2019).
43. "A Long Journey for Belmont Council," *The Times* (San Mateo, Calif.), June 10, 1969.
44. George Nevin, "Anti-Commune Zoning Ordinance May Be Case of Overkill," *Daily Independent Journal* (San Rafael, Calif.), Jan. 22, 1971. See also, for example, Larson v. Mayor and Council of Spring Lake Heights, 99 N.J. Super. 365 (L. Div. 1968).
45. Angelo Tullo, Councilman, Ramsey, Letter to the Editor, *Sunday News*, Sept. 8, 1974; George Nevin, "Anti-Commune Zoning Ordinance May Be Case of Overkill," *Daily Independent Journal* (San Rafael, Calif.), Jan. 22, 1971; Editorial, "Defining the Family Unit," *The Record*, Apr. 2, 1973; see also Jeff Greer, "Mill Valley Leaders Split on Communes," *Daily Independent Journal*, Feb. 4, 1971. Other cities, such as Rochester, New York, dusted off and enforced older ordinances. Kathy O'Toole, "Commune Tests City Zone Law," *Rochester Democrat and Chronicle*, Sept. 16, 1973.
46. Kathy O'Toole, "Commune Tests City Zone Law," *Rochester Democrat and Chronicle*, Sept. 16, 1973.
47. O'Toole, "Commune Tests City Zone Law."
48. Rebecca Larson, "Living Together Because They Like Each Other," *Daily Independent Journal*, Mar. 6, 1974.
49. Rebecca Larsen, "Single Mothers Face the Loss of Home," *Daily Independent Journal*, Dec. 3, 1974.
50. See, for example, Mace M. Bowen, Letter to the Editor, *Ames Daily Tribune* (Iowa), Apr. 5, 1974.
51. Pamela Warrick and Jim Scovel, "Can Social Mores Be Imposed Through Housing Regulations?," *Courier Journal*, Feb. 10, 1974.
52. City of Des Plaines v. Trottner, 216 N.E.2d 116, 120 (Ill. 1966).
53. Planning and Zoning Commission v. Synanon Foundation, Inc., 153 Conn. 305 (1966). Such interpretations of state law avoided the constitutional questions presented. For more, see Redburn, "Zoned Out."

54. Palo Alto Tenants' Union v. Morgan, 321 F. Supp. 908 (N.D. Cal. 1970).

55. Toni Klimberg, Note, "Excluding the Commune from Suburbia: The Use of Zoning for Social Control," 23 *Hastings L. J.* 1459, 1462 (1972) (citing Brief for Appellants, 7–8, Palo Alto Tenants' Union v. Morgan, 321 F. Supp. 908 (N.D. Cal. 1970)).

56. "1st Raid on Palo Alto Communes," *S.F. Examiner,* Dec. 1, 1970.

57. UPI, "Judge Albert C. Wollenberg Dies," *Petaluma Argus-Courier,* Apr. 20, 1981; Albert C. Wollenberg (Obituary), *S.F. Examiner,* Apr. 20, 1981.

58. Burns v. Montgomery, 299. F. Supp. 1002 (N.D. Cal. Apr. 17, 1968). The ruling was upheld by the U.S. Supreme Court in *Shapiro v. Thompson* (1968); see also "Judge Upheld Plea for Mickey Mouse," *LAT,* Apr. 27, 1981.

59. Nor had they presented evidence of unreasonable harassment or searches. *Palo Alto Tenants,* 321 F. Supp. at 911–12.

60. Don West, "Palo Alto Issues Commune Controls," *S.F. Examiner & Chronicle,* Nov. 18, 1973.

61. See Lawrence Sager, "Tight Little Islands: Exclusionary Zoning, Equal Protection, and the Indigent," 21 *Stanford L. Rev.* 767 (1969). Sager had also been on the *Cager* litigation team (see chapter 2).

62. Buchanan v. Warley, 245 U.S. 60 (1917); Shelley v. Kraemer, 334 U.S. 1 (1948).

63. NAACP v. Alabama, 357 U.S. 449 (1958).

64. Shapiro v. Thompson, 394 U.S. 618 (1969).

65. Brief for Appellees, *Belle Terre,* 16–17.

66. Brief for Appellees, *Belle Terre,* 23–25.

67. Boraas v. Village of Belle Terre, 476 F.2d 806, 813–18 (2d Cir. 1973).

68. Supreme Court Oral Argument Transcript, *Belle Terre.*

69. Justices Marshall, Stewart, and Brennan initially voted to affirm the Second Circuit's ruling and avoid a decision on the merits.

70. Richter, Preliminary Memo, Village of Belle Terre v. Boraas, No. 73–191, Sept. 25, 1973, LFP Papers. See also Memorandum from John C. Jeffries, Jr., to LFP, Feb. 15, 1974, Re: Village of Belle Terre v. Boraas, LFP Papers. Jeffries's co-clerk Jack Owens thought "it would be wise not to take" the case. Jack B. Owens to LFP, Re: Village of Belle Terre v. Boraas, No. 73–191, Oct. 14, 1973, LFP Papers.

71. LFP Conference Notes, *Belle Terre,* Feb. 19, 1974, LFP Papers.

72. Village of Belle Terre v. Boraas, 416 U.S. 1, 7–9 (1974).

73. "The Court's Uncompromising Libertarian," *Time,* Nov. 24, 1975; Sharon Rosenhause, "Two's Company, Six Is Unlawful," *The Record* (Hackensack, N.J.), Apr. 25, 1974.

74. See, for example, Louis Kohlmeier, "Zoning Rights and Communes," *Chicago Tribune,* May 23, 1974; Frank J. Tysen, "Commune Ruling Hits Individual Rights," *LAT,* May 12, 1974.

75. Douglas Clancy, "Those 'Unrelated Persons' Laws," *The Record,* Oct. 1, 1976.

76. "Banning Communes," *Emporia Gazette* (Kansas), Feb. 3, 1975.

77. Further, Belle Terre was a tiny enclave.

78. "Supreme Court Upholds Single-Family Zoning," *Rochester Democrat and Chronicle*, Apr. 2, 1974.

79. "Between 1965 and 1967 . . . the East Cleveland public schools shifted from 10% Black (1965) to 59% Black (1967)." Brief for Appellant, *Moore v. City of East Cleveland*, 1976 WL 178722, at *45.

80. On the *Moore* case, see Peggy Cooper Davis, "*Moore v. City of East Cleveland:* Constructing the Suburban Family," in *Family Law Stories*, ed. Carol Sanger (Foundation Press, 2007); Fordham Law Review Symposium (2017); R. A. Lenhardt, *Race, Law, and Family in an American City* (forthcoming).

81. "Court to Rule If Grandchild Is 'Family,'" *Indianapolis Star*, Oct. 31, 1976.

82. Brief for Appellant, *Moore*, 1976 WL 178722, at *10.

83. Andrew Billingsley with Amy Tate Billingsley, *Black Families in White America* (Prentice-Hall, 1968).

84. Robert M. Staples, "The Myth of the Black Matriarchy," *Black Scholar*, Jan.-Feb. 1970.

85. Joyce Ladner, *Tomorrow's Tomorrow: The Black Woman* (Anchor, 1972).

86. Robert B. Hill, *The Strengths of Black Families: A National Urban League Research Study* (Emerson Hall, 1972).

87. Herbert Gutman, *The Black Family in Slavery and Freedom, 1750–1925* ([1976] Vintage, 1977); Carol B. Stack, *All Our Kin: Strategies for Survival in a Black Community* (Harper & Row, 1974).

88. Elmer Martin and Joanne Mitchell Martin, *The Black Extended Family* (University of Chicago Press, 1978).

89. Brief for Appellant, *Moore*, *11–13.

90. Brief of the ACLU as amicus curiae, *Moore*, *13.

91. LFP, Notes, *Moore*, 1, LFP Papers.

92. Handwritten note on Bench Memo from Dave Martin to LFP, Re: Moore, Oct. 18, 1976, LFP Papers.

93. HAB, Memo to the file re: *Moore*, 6, Oct. 27, 1976, HAB Papers, Box 249, Folder 7.

94. 2nd Draft of HAB dissent, *Moore*, circulated Feb. 17, 1977, withdrawn. See, e.g., Laura Foreman, "Carter's Extended Family Puts Southern Tradition to Work," *NYT*, May 29, 1977.

95. LFP, Conference Notes, *Moore*, Nov. 5, 1976, LFP Papers.

96. LFP, Conference Notes, *Moore*, Nov. 5, 1976, LFP Papers; WEB, Memorandum to the Conference, Re: *Moore*, Nov. 22, 1976, LFP Papers.

97. TM to Chief, Re: *Moore*, Nov. 23, 1976, LFP Papers.

98. WJB to Chief, Re: *Moore*, Nov. 23, 1976, LFP Papers.

99. 1st draft of PS opinion for the Court, *Moore*, Feb. 10, 1977, Box 249, Folder 7.

100. 2nd draft of WJB dissent, *Moore*, Feb. 17, 1977, at 1, HAB Papers, Box 249, Folder 7.
101. 2nd draft of WJB dissent, *Moore*, Feb. 17, 1977, at 6, HAB Papers, Box 249, Folder 7.
102. PS, Memorandum to the Conference, re: *Moore*, Feb. 16, 1977, HAB Papers, Box 249, Folder 7.
103. LFP, Handwritten Notes on WJB's First Draft of Dissenting Opinion in Moore v. City of East Cleveland, 431 U.S. 494, 506 (1977), LFP Papers, Box 458, Folder 16; Serena Mayeri, "Intersectionality and the Constitution of Family Status," 32 *Constitutional Commentary* 377, 401 (2017); R. A. Lenhardt, "The Color of Kinship," 102 *Iowa L. Rev.* 2071 (2017).
104. Moore v. City of East Cleveland, 434 U.S. 494 (1977).
105. *Moore*, 434 U.S. at 510–13 (Brennan, J., concurring).
106. TM to Chief, Re: *Moore*, Nov. 23, 1976, LFP Papers; Melissa Murray, "*Obergefell v. Hodges* and Nonmarriage Inequality," 104 *Calif. L. Rev.* 1207, 1238–39 (2016).
107. Including Teaneck, Northvale, and Hackensack.
108. Judy Russell, "Shore Town Ban on Group Rentals Cut Down," *Daily News*, June 27, 1975.
109. Stuart Margulies, "Tough Living Under Ramsey's Housing Law," *Morning News*, Mar. 8, 1978.
110. State v. Baker, 81 N.J. 99 (1979). Lower courts had already overturned ordinances in Bergen and Atlantic counties.
111. City of Santa Barbara v. Adamson, 27 Cal. 3d 123 (1980); John Hurst, "Landlady Fights for Her 'Family,'" *LAT*, Dec. 26, 1979; K. Connie Kang, "High Court Voids a Santa Barbara Single-Dwelling Family Law," *S.F. Examiner*, May 15, 1980.
112. Hurst, "Landlady Fights for Her 'Family.'" The amendment was the result of a 1972 ballot initiative. Adamson prevailed despite opposition from officials in many of the thirty-seven California cities with similar laws.
113. See Redburn, "Zoned Out" (summarizing post–*Belle Terre* state approaches).
114. See Stephen Vider, "What Happened to the Functional Family?," in *Intimate States: Sexuality and Governance in Modern America*, ed. Margot Canaday, Nancy F. Cott, and Robert O. Self (University of Chicago Press, 2021).
115. Redburn, "Zoned Out," 2453.
116. City of Ladue v. Horn, 720 S.W.2d 745 (Mo. Ct. App. 1986); Penobscot Area Housing Dev. Corp. v. Brewer, 434 A.2d 14 (Me. 1981); Hayward v. Gaston, 542 A.2d 760 (Del. 1988); Rademan v. Denver, 526 P.2d 1325 (Colo. 1974). See also, for example, Dinan v. Board of Zoning Appeals of Stratford, 595 A.2d 864 (Conn. 1991).

117. On the double-edged nature of functional family definitions, see chapter 8 of this volume; Melissa Murray, "Family Law's Doctrines," 163 *U. Pa. L. Rev.* 1985 (2015); Martha Minow, "Redefining Families—Who's In and Who's Out," 62 *U. Colo. L. Rev.* 269 (1991).

118. Charter Township of Delta v. Dinolfo, 419 Mich. 253, 270, 277–78 (1984).

119. U.S. Commission on Civil Rights, "Mortgage Money: Who Gets It?: A Case Study in Mortgage Lending Discrimination in Hartford, Connecticut," June 1974, at 18 (hereinafter Hartford Mortgage Study).

120. Hartford Mortgage Study, 21, 23.

121. Hartford Mortgage Study, 23.

122. Credit Discrimination Hearings Before the Subcommittee on Consumer Affairs, 378.

123. Lenders required male co-signers or rejected mortgage applications outright. See Courtney Joslin, "Discrimination In and Out of Marriage," 98 *Boston Univ. L. Rev.* 1 (2018); Chloe N. Thurston, *At the Boundaries of Homeownership: Credit, Discrimination, and the American State* (Cambridge University Press, 2018).

124. See Nancy D. Polikoff, "Legislative Solutions to Sex Discrimination in Credit: An Appraisal," 2 *Women's Rights Law Reporter* 26, 26 (1974).

125. Hartford Mortgage Study, 27.

126. National Council of Negro Women, *Women and Housing: A Report on Sex Discrimination in Five American Cities*, Department of Housing and Urban Development (U.S. Government Printing Office, 1976), at 68 (hereinafter NCNW Study).

127. Hartford Mortgage Study, 18.

128. Kahn, *Divorce*, 72.

129. Kahn, *Divorce*, 91; Hartford Mortgage Study, 20, 8; NCNW Study, 71.

130. AP, "Government to Curb Sex Discrimination in Housing," *Fort Myers News-Press*, Aug. 31, 1974; NCNW Study.

131. NCNW Study, 35.

132. "Women Face Discrimination in Housing," *Evening Herald*, Mar. 8, 1977.

133. Bill Cryer and Wanda Pryor, "Subtle Sort of Housing Discrimination Lingers," *Austin American-Statesman*, Sept. 13, 1976 (quoting Robert Quinonez).

134. Jane Stuart, "Where Shall We Live?," *The Record* (N.J.), May 25, 1969.

135. NCNW Study, 45.

136. NCNW Study, 36.

137. Stuart, "Where Shall We Live?" The NCNW documented that women, who were "three times as likely to be single" as men, faced assumptions that they had "unstable incomes" or would "bring men into the house," "overuse the facilities," or "get pregnant and lose their jobs." NCNW Study, 41.

138. As the historian Keeanga-Yamahtta Taylor has shown, low-income single Black mothers also faced predatory lending practices enabled by the federal government itself. Keeanga-Yamahtta Taylor, *Race for Profit: How*

Banks and the Real Estate Industry Undermined Black Homeownership (University of North Carolina Press, 2019).

139. Diana L. Hurley, "Rights Unit Cup Is Full," *Journal News*, May 28, 1972.

140. "Rhode Island Bill Is Aimed at Ending Sex, Income Housing Bans," *Biddeford-Saco Journal*, April 12, 1973.

141. Geri Sherwood, "Housing Discrimination in California," *Hanford Sentinel*, July 28, 1977; Leslie Berkman, "Fair Housing: Once-Mute Council Finds Its Voice," *LAT*, Nov. 29, 1977.

142. NCNW Study, 36–40.

143. NCNW Study, 84.

144. NCNW Study, 38.

145. Dexter Waugh, "Dramatic Proposals in S.F. Fair Housing Study," *S.F. Examiner*, Sept. 24, 1973 (study by Department of City Planning).

146. This finding was reported in a survey conducted by Los Angeles's Fair Housing Project. Cary D. Lowe and Dora Ashford, "Bill Would Bar Rental Discrimination Against Family with Children," *Fresno Bee*, Jan. 27, 1980.

147. Mark Forster, "Campaign Against 'Adults-Only' Housing Growing in California," *LAT*, Oct. 14, 1979.

148. Richard Willing, "Housing Patterns Hurting 'Deprived,'" *Journal News*, Oct. 10, 1973.

149. See, e.g., Valeria Robinson, "Housing Discrimination Checked," *Daily Press* (Newport News, Va.), Nov. 8, 1971.

150. Other factors included "income and employment, credit and rental references, the size of unit [sought,] … and housekeeping habits." "Housing 'Point' Made," *Pocono Record*, Oct. 30, 1972.

151. NCNW Study, 171.

152. Fair lending advocates found ECOA's enforcement wanting. See, e.g., Scott Ilgenfritz, "The Failure of Private Actions as an ECOA Enforcement Tool: A Call for Active Government Enforcement and Statutory Reform," 36 *U. Fla. L. Rev.* 447 (1984).

153. Joslin, "Discrimination In and Out of Marriage"; Pleck, *Not Just Roommates*.

154. See, e.g., "Feminist Victories," Editorial, *Baltimore Sun*, Feb. 17, 1974.

155. Gordon Coe, "Marital Status Factor in Housing Law," *Spokane Chronicle*, Nov. 14, 1974.

156. Gordon H. Coe, "Landlords Are Critical of Discrimination Laws," *Spokane Chronicle*, Nov. 16, 1974.

157. Editorial, "Marital Status Shouldn't Be an Issue in Housing," *Capital Journal*, Oct. 14, 1976; Matthew J. Smith, "The Wages of Living in Sin: Discrimination in Housing Against Unmarried Couples," 25 *U.C. Davis L. Rev.* 1055, 1068 n. 57 (1992).

158. Most of the state court decisions cited by Smith are from the 1980s and early 1990s. Smith, "Wages," 1077–78.

159. For more, see Deborah Widiss, "Intimate Liberties and Antidiscrimination Law," 97 *Boston Univ. L. Rev.* 2083 (2017).
160. "Housing Law Bans Sex Discrimination," *Orlando Sentinel*, Jan. 9, 1974.
161. "Rhode Island Bill Is Aimed at Ending Sex, Income Housing Bans," *Biddeford-Saco Journal*, April 12, 1973.
162. Donna Karnes, Lincoln/Lancaster Commission on the Status of Women, "Human Rights," Dec. 17, 1977.
163. AP, "Boulder Sets Discrimination Hearing Tuesday," *Daily Sentinel*, Feb. 18, 1974. Some believed that state sex discrimination prohibitions covered discrimination based on sexual orientation, but early test cases suggested otherwise. See, e.g., "Anti-Bias Law OKd," *Dayton Daily News*, July 8, 1975.
164. "Gays Can't Grace Florida Apartments," *Philadelphia Daily News*, July 24, 1980.
165. Robert Ostmann, Jr., "Civil Rights Ordinance Gets Support at Council Hearing," *Detroit Free Press*, Jan. 25, 1977.
166. AP, "State Civil Rights Measure May Be Headed for Problems," *Times Herald*, July 8, 1974; Jim Weaver, "'Ignored' Minorities Attack Proposal," *Lansing State Journal*, July 3, 1974 (quoting Democratic state representative John Otterbacher of Grand Rapids). Mark F. Rohner, "Protection for Homosexuals Changed," *Iowa City Press-Citizen*, Mar. 22, 1977; "Council Okays Rights Law," *Iowa City Press-Citizen*, April 20, 1977.
167. UPI, "Housing Bill Given Okay," *Berkeley Gazette*, Sept. 15, 1975; "So Now We're Anti-Almost Everything," *Mendocino Coast Beacon*, July 10, 1975; Dorothy Townsend, "Younger Urges Sex Bias Ban in Housing Rentals," *LAT*, Mar. 19, 1975. The bill was part of an agenda created by a 1974 Women's Rights Task Force. In 1982, a lower state court interpreted California's fair housing law to prohibit housing discrimination based on sexual orientation. Hubert v. Williams, 184 Cal. Rptr. 161 (App. Dept. Super. Ct. 1982).
168. "Anti-Bias Law OKd," *Dayton Daily News*, July 8, 1975, 17.
169. William N. Eskridge, Jr., *GayLaw: Challenging the Apartheid of the Closet* (Harvard University Press, 1999), 356, Appendix B2. Berkeley's 1978 ordinance covered private employment education and housing. Beginning in 1974, Rep. Bella Abzug and others introduced federal legislation that would extend the protections of the Civil Rights Act (including Title VIII, the Fair Housing Act) to sexual orientation. The first version of the bill included marital status as well; the marital status provision was later dropped.
170. Not all Catholic Church officials were opposed to anti-discrimination laws protecting gay people; the archdiocese of San Francisco, also in 1974, expressed support for such a law. "Gay Group Seeks Rights Law," *The Times* (Redwood City, Calif.), June 21, 1974.
171. UPI, "Gay Rights Bill Barely Defeated," *Greenville News*, May 24, 1974; Joyce Purnick, "Homosexual Rights Bill Is Passed by City Council in 21-to-14 Vote," *NYT*, Mar. 21, 1986. Mayor John Lindsay outlawed sexual

orientation discrimination in New York City employment by executive order in 1972.

172. Carolyn Bobo, "Relations Chief Calls for Housing Ordinance," *Austin American-Statesman*, Sept. 25, 1973.

173. "House OKs Homosexuals Protection," *Tribune-Herald* (Hilo, Hawaii), Mar. 16, 1976.

174. Including Eugene, Oregon; St. Paul, Minnesota; and Wichita, Kansas. Miami-Dade County did not outlaw sexual orientation discrimination again until 1998. Mireya Navarro, "Two Decades On, Miami Endorses Gay Rights," *NYT*, Dec. 2, 1998.

175. Lefkovitz, *Strange Bedfellows*, 174–75; Judy Burke, "HUD to Allow Gays, Unmarried Couples in Public Housing," *WP*, May 28, 1977, A2.

176. Mildred Hamilton, "Why Women Homebuyers Get Hassled," *S.F. Examiner*, July 21, 1976.

177. Quoted in "Sex Bias in Credit Waning," *Asbury Park Press*, Dec. 11, 1974.

178. "Unmarried Couples Buy Homes," *Great Falls Tribune* (Minn.), Nov. 26, 1979; Neil Skene, "Living Together Gains Acceptance But It's Still Against the Law," *Tampa Bay Times* (St. Petersburg, Fla.), Jan. 8, 1978. See also, for example, Kelly Scott, "Singles Are Taking the Big Step Up to Homeowner," *St. Petersburg Times*, July 6, 1980, 1-D; Jim Reid, "Singles Purchasing Homes Together in Increasing Numbers," *Daily Oklahoman*, Mar. 8, 1981; Pam Leucke, "Single Women Discovering Home Ownership's Benefits," *Hartford Courant*, Feb. 27, 1977 (noting that Hartford-area lenders found increasing numbers of single women and unmarried couples buying homes).

179. Polly Pendleton Brown, "You Can Qualify—Married or Not," *Palm Beach Post*, Feb. 11, 1979. For more on ECOA, see Kahn, *Divorce*.

180. Markham v. Colonial Mortgage Service Co., 605 F.2d 566 (D.C. Cir. 1979).

181. "Protection of Unmarried Couples Against Discrimination in Lending Under the Equal Credit Opportunity Act: Markham v. Colonial Mortgage Service Co.," 93 *Harvard L. Rev.* 430, 432 (1979). Another observer feared that "competition from unmarried couples" might unintentionally harm single women on the mortgage market. Susan Smith Blakely, "Credit Opportunity for Women: The ECOA and Its Effects," 1981 *Wisc. L. Rev.* 655, 693 (1981).

182. Dan Sorenson, "Buy a House with a Friend, and Mingle," *Tucson Citizen*, Dec. 11, 1982.

183. Dennis H. Shaw, "Housing Discrimination Against Children: The Legal Status of a Growing Social Problem," 16 *J. Fam. L.* 559, 567–68 (1977).

184. See, for example, "Bill Would Prohibit 'Adult-Only' Housing," *Auburn Journal*, Aug. 1, 1977; Dick Alexander, "Why the Landlords Don't Want Kids," *S.F. Examiner*, Apr. 9, 1975.

185. "Family Renters," *LAT*, June 27, 1978; James Morales, "Use of the Fair Housing Act to Redress Housing Discrimination Against Families with Children," 17 *Clearinghouse Review* 736 (1983).

186. Plaintiffs sometimes challenged child exclusions as racial discrimination. See, for example, Betsey v. Turtle Creek Associates, 736 F.2d 983 (4th Cir. 1984); Morales, "Use of the Fair Housing Act," 738.

187. "Action Line: Housing Discrimination," *The Independent* (Long Beach, Calif.), Jan. 25, 1977.

188. Dick Alexander, "Rejected by Landlords," *S.F. Examiner*, April 8, 1975. A local housing advocate warned, "As long as people have a legal right to say, 'No families with kids,' it is impossible to screen out racial discrimination." Alexander, "Rejected by Landlords," 20.

189. *A Sheltered Crisis: The State of Fair Housing in the Eighties*, Presentations at a Consultation sponsored by the U.S. Commission on Civil Rights, Washington, D.C., Sept. 26–27, 1983, 130.

190. California also had a checkered history with fair housing laws, however. In 1964, Proposition 14 nullified the state's fair housing law, which was later reinstated by the California Supreme Court (and affirmed by the U.S. Supreme Court). See Reitman v. Mulkey, 387 U.S. 369 (1967). On sexuality and housing policy in the Bay Area, see Clayton Howard, *The Closet and the Cul-de-Sac: The Politics of Sexual Privacy in Northern California* (University of Pennsylvania Press, 2019); Clayton Howard, "Building a Family-Friendly Metropolis: Sexuality, the State, and Postwar Housing Policy," *Journal of Urban History*, vol. 39, issue 5 (2013): 933-55.

191. Dick Alexander, "A City Without Children? New S.F. Battle Over Housing," *S.F. Examiner*, Apr. 7, 1975.

192. AP, "S.F. Landlord Must Rent to Families with Children," *Santa Cruz Sentinel*, June 19, 1975.

193. "Housing Bill Introduced by Wornum," *Daily Independent Journal* (San Rafael, Calif.), Apr. 21, 1975; Sherwood, "Housing Discrimination in California," *Hanford Sentinel*, July 28, 1977.

194. "Landlords Can't Ban Children," *Daily Independent Journal*, Sept. 11, 1975; Sherwood, "Housing Discrimination in California," *Hanford Sentinel*, July 28, 1977. Proponents came close to victory in 1978 but the bill failed on a 17–17 tie. "Family Renters," *LAT*, June 27, 1978.

195. Barry Siegel, "Adults-Only Apartments Challenged in Court," *LAT*, Sept. 23, 1977.

196. See Marina Point, Ltd. v. Wolfson, 98 Cal. App. 3d 140 (Ca. Ct. App. 2d Dist. 1979).

197. Marina Point, Ltd. v. Wolfson, 30 Cal.3d 721, 744-45 (1982). Some sources suggest that the state legislature took action shortly thereafter. Lawmakers paused their efforts to pass a state law in the hope that the court ruling would provide greater protection. See "Housing Bias on Families with Children to Be Enforced," *Press-Democrat* (Santa Rosa, Calif.), May 17, 1984; Thorne Gray, "Housing Agency Delays Action on Child Discrimination Cases," *Sacramento Bee*, Sept. 6, 1984.

198. Early state laws imposed modest fines and left enforcement to local officials. Leonard Groupe, "Can Landlords Legally Bar Children?," *S.F. Examiner*, Aug. 6, 1980.

199. Kenneth J. Fanucchi, "Family Housing Gains—On Paper," *LAT*, Sept. 18, 1983.

200. Eleanor Edwards, "City Acts to Stop Housing Discrimination," *Berkeley Gazette*, Jan. 13, 1978.

201. Kenneth J. Fanucchi, "Family Housing Gains—On Paper," *LAT*, Sept. 18, 1983.

202. Connecticut Commission on Human Rights and Opportunities, Housing Discrimination and Opportunities in the State of Connecticut, 18 (1986), cited in Morales, "Use of the Fair Housing Act," 745.

203. Fair Housing Amendments Act of 1988, House Report, 20.

204. R. Marans and M. Colten, "A Report on Measuring Restrictive Rental Policies Affecting Families with Children: A National Survey," U.S. Dept. of Housing and Urban Development (1980), cited in Carol Golubock, "Housing Discrimination Against Families with Children: A Growing Problem of Exclusionary Practices," in *Sheltered Crisis*, 128.

205. Sue A. Marshall, "Women with Children in Today's Housing Market," in *Sheltered Crisis*, 112.

206. "Child Discrimination Still Occurs, Housing Group Says," *Californian*, Apr. 9, 1984; see also D'Arcy Fallon, "Marin Landlords Don't Like Kids, Survey Finds," *S.F. Examiner*, Nov. 7, 1986.

207. Editorial, "Unfair to Families," *LAT*, Apr. 14, 1987.

208. Roberto Robledo, "Sympathetic Landlord Ends Family's Long Housing Search," *Salinas Californian*, Feb. 18, 1982.

209. Tom Elias, "Administration Doesn't Defend Renter Families," *Hanford Sentinel*, Sept. 25, 1984.

210. Carol Golubock, "Housing Discrimination Against Families with Children: A Growing Problem of Exclusionary Practices," in *Sheltered Crisis*, 132.

211. Claude Lewis, "Toward Fairer Housing," *Central New Jersey Home News*, Feb. 24, 1987.

212. Fair Housing Amendments Act of 1988, House Report 100–711, at 21.

213. Cong. Rec. 15860 (statement of Rep. Ron Dellums). See also Cong. Rec. 15857 (June 23, 1988) (Rep. Morella); Cong. Rec. 15855 (June 23, 1988) (Rep. Schroeder); Cong. Rec. 15858, 15863 (June 23, 1988) (Rep. Pelosi).

214. See, for example, Cong. Rec. 15857 (June 23, 1988) (Rep. Morella and Rep. Miller [D-CA]).

215. Cong. Rec. 15858 (June 23, 1988) (Rep. Miller).

216. George E. Curry, "Fair Housing in Next Rights Push," *Chicago Tribune*, Mar. 28, 1988.

217. Fair Housing Amendments Act of 1988, House Report 100–711, at 84 (Objections of Rep. Henry Hyde et al.).

218. Earlier attempts were vanquished by the National Association of Realtors and by a filibuster by Sen. Orrin Hatch (R-UT). Ralph Neas of the Leadership Conference on Civil Rights described how the compromise was brokered with the National Association of Realtors here: www.c-span.org /video/?4267-1/fair-housing-amendments-1988. In 1988 both presidential candidates supported the compromise legislation, which helped to pressure conservative Republicans. The amendments eventually passed the House (376–23) and Senate (94–3) with bipartisan support.

219. Phyllis Schlafly, "Fair Housing Policy Isn't Very Fair," *Standard-Speaker* (Hazleton, Pa.), Aug. 23, 1988.

220. Negotiators in Congress took advantage of battle fatigue on the part of the administration after losses in the Bork hearings, as well as a desire not to air the administration's civil rights record on the eve of an election. See C-SPAN panel at 1:24, www.c-span.org/video/?4267-1/fair-housing-amendments-1988.

221. AP, "Open-Housing Law Gets Teeth," *Sacramento Bee*, Sept. 14, 1988.

222. Smith, "Wages," 1072 (quoting James A. Kushner, "The Fair Housing Amendments Act of 1988: The Second Generation of Fair Housing," 42 *Vand. L. Rev.* 1049, 1107 (1989)).

Chapter 5. Double Standards

1. ACLU Records, Box 3765, Flores v. Secretary of Defense.
2. Sonia Pressman, Senior Attorney, Office of the General Counsel, EEOC, to Douglass L. Custis, Lieutenant, JAGC, USNR, Legal Officer, July 20, 1970, ACLU Records, *Flores*; Anna Flores to Frank W. Bender II, Deputy Assistant Secretary of Defense (Civil Rights), Aug. 10, 1970 (describing correspondence), ACLU Records, *Flores*.
3. Flores to Bender, 1.
4. Flores to Bender, 1–2.
5. Anna Flores to Senator John G. Tower, July 22, 1970, ACLU Records, *Flores*.
6. Flores to Bender, 1.
7. *Chicago Tribune* Press Service, "Unwed WAVE Wins Fight on Pregnancy," *Chicago Tribune*, Sept. 1, 1970.
8. Betsy Nolan to Chuck Morgan, Aug. 1970, ACLU Records, *Flores*.
9. AP, "Equal Rights Asked on Navy Pregnancies," *Tampa Times*, Aug. 26, 1970. Flores's ACLU lawyers alleged that "numerous male members of the U.S. Navy (A) have sexual intercourse with women to whom they are not married and are not discharged, (B) father children out of wedlock and are not discharged, (C) incur in their sexual activities venereal disease and are not discharged, (D) are not subjected to the 'moral standards set for women in the Navy.'" Quoted in UPI, "WAVE Fights to Bar Ouster for Pregnancy," *Tampa Tribune*, Aug. 26, 1970.

10. The FCA, founded as an organization of maternity homes, had evolved into a maternal and child welfare advocacy group as young women increasingly kept and raised their nonmarital children. Mary Watson Palmer, PR Director, Florence Crittenton Association of America, to Lt. Colonel Lucille B. Dion, USAF, Exec Sec to DACOWITS, July 20, 1970, Mack v. Rumsfeld, NARA-NYC.

11. See Palmer to Dion, July 20, 1970; Lt. Colonel Lucille B. Dion, USAF, Exec Sec to DACOWITS, to Mrs. Mary Watson Palmer, PR Director, Florence Crittenton Association of America, Aug. 13, 1970, Mack v. Rumsfeld, NARA NYC. The FCA also worried about the welfare of the children of servicewomen should they succeed in gaining permission to serve.

12. On policies toward pregnancy and parenthood in the military, see Kara Dixon Vuic, "Reproduction in Combat Boots," in *Managing Sex in the U.S. Military: Gender, Identity, and Behavior*, ed. Beth Bailey et al. (University of Nebraska Press, 2022), chapter 5.

13. Memorandum from Director of Women Marines to Executive Secretary, DACOWITS, 1970.

14. Complaint, *Flores v. Secretary of Defense*, 5–6.

15. Complaint, *Flores*, 4.

16. The regulation addresssed "[p]regnancy, regardless of marital status, upon determination by a naval medical officer or, if not available, by a medical officer of another armed force of the United States. The type of discharge shall be as warranted by her service record regardless of marital status. If pregnancy is terminated prior to separation, a full report of the circumstances shall be submitted to the Chief of Naval Personnel including whether the termination was a result of a spontaneous or therapeutic abortion or a still birth, or if there is evidence of nontherapeutic abortion, together with the servicewoman's desires as to retention in the service and the commanding officer's recommendation thereon." Similar regulations obtained in the military's other branches.

17. Plaintiffs' Proposed Findings of Fact, *Flores*. For men, adultery, rape, and sodomy—but not fathering a nonmarital child—provided grounds for discharge.

18. Some COs saw the regulation as designed to protect married women who were career servicemembers, not unmarried women, who tended to be young and lack seniority.

19. Sonia Pressman to Douglass Custis, July 20, 1970, ACLU Records, *Flores*.

20. See William N. Eskridge, Jr., *Dishonorable Passions: Sodomy Laws in America, 1961–2003* (Penguin, 2008), chapter 5.

21. Eskridge, *Dishonorable Passions;* Brief for the ACLU as Amicus Curiae, *Acanfora*, 15 (listing states) in n. 2.

22. Norton v. Macy, 417 F. 2d 1161 (D.C. Cir. 1969).

23. Mindel v. U.S. Civil Service Commission, 312 F. Supp. 485 (N.D. Cal. 1970). The court used the Ninth Amendment analysis pioneered in birth control cases.

24. On the implementation of Title VII during this period, see Nancy MacLean, *Freedom Is Not Enough: The Opening of the American Workplace* (Harvard University Press, 2006); Katherine Turk, *Equality on Trial: Gender and Rights in the Modern American Workplace* (University of Pennsylvania Press, 2016); Serena Mayeri, *Reasoning from Race: Feminism, Law, and the Civil Rights Revolution* (Harvard University Press, 2011).

25. Brief of Historians as Amici Curiae in Support of Employees, Bostock v. Clayton County, Altitude Express, Inc. v. Zarda, and R. G. & G. R. Harris Funeral Homes v. EEOC, Nos. 17–1618, 17–1623, and 18–107 (U.S. July 3, 2019).

26. Stanley v. Georgia, 394 U.S. 557 (1969) (unanimous).

27. Barbara Love, ed., *Feminists Who Changed America, 1963–1975* (University of Illinois Press, 2006), 25.

28. Baird v. Eisenstadt, 429 F.2d 1398, 1402 (1st Cir. 1970).

29. Brief for Appellee, *Eisenstadt*, No. 70–17, 405 U.S. 438, at 7–11.

30. Brief for Appellee, *Eisenstadt*, 43–44; Brief for Planned Parenthood Federation of America as Amicus Curiae, *Eisenstadt*, 17 (hereinafter PPFA Brief); Brief for the ACLU as Amicus Curiae, *Eisenstadt*, 20 (hereinafter ACLU Brief).

31. PPFA Brief, *Eisenstadt*, 38.

32. Brief for Human Rights for Women as Amicus Curiae, *Eisenstadt*, 3 (hereinafter HRW Brief).

33. HRW Brief, *Eisenstadt*, 7 (emphasis added).

34. On the ACLU's deliberations, see Marc Stein, *Sexual Injustice: Supreme Court Decisions from* Griswold *to* Roe (University of North Carolina Press, 2010), 113–23.

35. ACLU Brief, *Eisenstadt*, 10–11.

36. "The claims of single women were expressly before the Courts and encompassed in their favorable rulings" in these cases. ACLU Brief, *Eisenstadt*, 11 n.*.

37. Eisenstadt v. Baird, 405 U.S. 438, 453 (1972).

38. Justice Brennan expressed skepticism that deterring fornication was in fact the law's objective. *Eisenstadt*, 405 U.S. at 448–50.

39. *Eisenstadt*, 405 U.S. at 440.

40. See Gerald Gunther, Foreword, The Supreme Court, 1971 Term, "In Search of Evolving Doctrine on a Changing Court: A Model for a Newer Equal Protection," 86 *Harv. L. Rev.* 1 (1972).

41. Trial Memorandum, Flores v. Secretary of Defense, Civil Action No. 2276, ACLU Records, *Flores*.

42. Plaintiffs' Proposed Conclusions of Law, Flores v. Secretary of Defense, Civ. Action No. 2276, ACLU Records, *Flores*.

43. Trial Memorandum, *Flores*, 6, 9.

44. Cf. Susan Frelich Appleton, "The Forgotten Family Law of *Eisenstadt v. Baird*," 28 *Yale J. L. & Fem.* 1 (2016).

45. Flores v. Secretary of Defense, 355 F. Supp. 93, 95–96 (N.D. Fla. 1973).
46. Arnow agreed with the ACLU's analysis of the Navy's 1971 retention decisions but ruled in January 1973 that new leadership and policy had transformed the processing of retention requests. Arnow ruled in *Flores* exactly one week before the Supreme Court's decision in *Roe v. Wade*. For more, see Wolfgang Saxon, "W. E. Arnow, Judge in Antiwar Trial, Dies at 83," *NYT*, Dec. 1, 1994.
47. *Flores*, 355 F. Supp. at 96.
48. The best known of these cases is Struck v. Secretary of Defense. See Neil S. Siegel and Reva B. Siegel, "Struck by Stereotype: Ruth Bader Ginsburg on Pregnancy Discrimination as Sex Discrimination," 59 *Duke L. J.* 771 (2010); Mayeri, *Reasoning from Race*, chapter 2; De Hart, *Ruth Bader Ginsburg: A Life* (Alfred Knopf, 2018), 179–88.
49. On the multi-valent meanings of sexual privacy during this period, see Clayton Howard, *The Closet and the Cul-de-Sac: The Politics of Sexual Privacy in Northern California* (University of Pennsylvania Press, 2019).
50. Cf. Melissa Murray, "Rights and Regulation: The Evolution of Sexual Regulation," 116 *Columbia L. Rev.* 573 (2016).
51. Quotations and facts are from Michael Boucai, "Glorious Precedents: When Gay Marriage Was Radical," 27 *Yale J. L. & Hum.* 1 (2015).
52. "Homosexual Wins a Suit Over Hiring," *NYT*, Sept. 20, 1970.
53. Memorandum of Law on Behalf of Plaintiff, 7–11, McConnell v. Anderson, Civil Action File No. 4–70 Civ. 297, Sept. 14, 1970 (D. Minn.), ACLU Records, Box 1531.
54. On the activism that produced these early civil service rulings, see Margot Canaday, *Queer Career: Sexuality and Work in Modern America* (Princeton University Press, 2023), chapter 3; see also William N. Eskridge, Jr., *Gaylaw: Challenging the Apartheid of the Closet* (Harvard University Press, 1999), 125–27.
55. Memorandum of Law, *McConnell*, 5–8.
56. Remarks of Alan Weinblatt, Memorial Service for Honorable Philip Neville, U.S. District Court for the District of Minnesota, May 3, 1974, www.minnesotalegalhistoryproject.org/assets/Philip%20Neville=HH.pdf.
57. McConnell v. Anderson, 316 F. Supp. 809, 815 (D. Minn. 1970).
58. *McConnell*, 316 F. Supp. at 814.
59. Morrison v. State Board of Education, 1 Cal. 3d 214 (Ca. 1969).
60. McConnell v. Anderson, 451 F.2d 193, 196 (8th Cir. 1971).
61. McConnell v. Anderson, 405 U.S. 1046 (Apr. 3, 1972). Minnesota's highest court derided McConnell's and Baker's lawsuit challenging their marriage license denial, and in October 1972, the U.S. Supreme Court dismissed the couple's appeal. Baker v. Nelson, 409 U.S. 810 (Oct. 10, 1972). See also chapter 3.
62. A friend of Burton's partner told her mother, and word traveled fast. Charles Hinkle and George T. Nicola, "Queer Heroes NW 2012: Peggy

Burton," Gay and Lesbian Archives of the Pacific Northwest, www.glapn. org/6316PeggyBurton.html; Ron Cowan, "Cascade Teacher, Fired as Homosexual, Brings Suit," *Statesman Journal* (Salem, Ore.), May 3, 1972.

63. Randy Shilts, "The Final Appeal and the Aftermath," *Advocate*, Dec. 3, 1975.

64. Hinkle and Nicola, "Queer Heroes."

65. Complaint, *Burton v. Cascade School Dist.*, Civ. No. 72–334 (D. Ore.), May 2, 1972, at 3, NARA-Seattle.

66. Jackie M. Blount, *Fit to Teach: Same-Sex Desire, Gender, and School Work in the Twentieth Century* (SUNY Press, 2005), 102.

67. Hinkle and Nicola, "Queer Heroes"; Larry Roby, "Homosexual Teacher Sues to Retain Her Job," *Capital Journal* (Salem, Ore.), May 2, 1972.

68. Plaintiff's Memorandum of Law in Support of Motion for Summary Judgment, 3, 21–24, 15–17, *Burton v. Cascade*, Civ. No. 72–334 (D. Ore.), Dec. 15, 1972, NARA-Seattle.

69. *Burton v. Cascade School Dist. Union High School No. 5*, 353 F. Supp. 254 (D. Or. Jan. 18, 1973).

70. "Court Ruling Favors Homosexual Teacher," *Capital Journal* (Salem, Ore.), Jan. 19, 1973; Letter to the Editor, *Capital Journal*, Jan. 26, 1973. The Supreme Court's decision in *Papachristou v. Jacksonville*, declaring a vagrancy ordinance unconstitutionally vague, laid constitutional groundwork. 405 U.S. 156 (1972). For more, see Risa Goluboff, *Vagrant Nation: Police Power, Constitutional Change, and the Making of the 1960s* (Oxford University Press, 2016).

71. Shilts, "The Final Appeal."

72. The damage award was the equivalent of Burton's remaining salary for the 1970–71 school year and half of the following year. Feb. 2, 1973, Hearing Transcript, *Burton*, 8, 3, NARA-Seattle.

73. Solomon speculated that if Burton "was married and had two children, despite this thing, she could probably get a job." Feb. 2, 1973, Hearing Transcript, *Burton*, 4.

74. Feb. 2, 1973, Hearing Transcript, *Burton*, 7.

75. "Lesbian Teacher Wins Case but Loses Her Job, Anyway," *Capital Journal* (Salem, Ore.), Feb. 2, 1973. See also "Remain Silent?," Letter to the Editor, *Capital Journal*, Feb. 13, 1973; "Enlightenment," Letter to the Editor, *Capital Journal*, Feb. 15, 1973.

76. *Burton v. Cascade School Dist. Union High School No. 5*, 512 F2d 850 (9th Cir. 1975).

77. Petition for a Writ of Certiorari, *Burton v. Cascade*, ACLU Records; "High Court Denies Appeal," *The Advocate*, Nov. 5, 1975; Shilts, "The Final Appeal"; Blount, *Fit to Teach*, 102; Audrey Rayner, "Witnesses Back Bill to End Job Bias Against Homosexuals," *Statesman-Journal* (Salem, Ore.), May 3, 1973.

78. Craig Simpson, "MoCo Gay Teacher Fired 1972; Justice Denied for 40 Years," *Washington Area Spark*, https://washingtonareaspark.com/2012/12/20 /moco-gay-teacher-fired-1972-justice-denied-for-40-years/.

79. Brief of the American Civil Liberties Union, Amicus Curiae, 3, Acanfora v. Board of Education, No. 73–1788 (4th Cir. Sept. 10, 1973) (hereinafter ACLU Brief), NARA-Kansas City; UPI, "Homosexual Teacher Fights Removal from Classroom," *Syracuse Herald-Journal*, Apr. 14, 1973.

80. Blount, *Fit to Teach*, 105.

81. Affidavit of Joseph Acanfora, Acanfora v. Board of Education, No. 72–1136Y, Jan. 23, 1973, at 5, NARA Philadelphia, 105–1-05.

82. ACLU Brief, *Acanfora*, 4.

83. Edward Walsh, "Homosexual Teacher Fights to Return to the Classroom," *WP*, Apr. 13, 1973.

84. Simpson reports that "61 of 83 teachers signed; 140 students at the school signed a student petition." Simpson, "MoCo Gay Teacher"; Affidavit filed by Donald Miedema, Superintendent of Montgomery County Public Schools, *Acanfora*, Feb. 8, 1973, at 2, NARA Philadelphia, 105–1-07.

85. Simpson, "MoCo Gay Teacher" (quoting *Advocate*).

86. Quoted in Jim Gallagher, "When Joe Came Out of the Closet, I Came Out of the Kitchen," *News Tribune*, Apr. 12, 1973 (Woodbridge, N.J.).

87. 60 Minutes, quoted in Acanfora v. Montgomery County Board of Education, 359 F. Supp. 843, 846 (D. Md. 1973).

88. Blount, *Fit to Teach*, 117.

89. Miedema affidavit, *Acanfora*, 3; Memorandum in Support of Defendants' Motion for Summary Judgment, Acanfora, NARA Philadelphia, 105–1-08; Brief for Defendants, *Acanfora*, 11–12, NARA Philadelphia, 105–1-12.

90. Philip A. McCombs, "Homosexual Teacher a Hazard in Class, Psychiatrist Says," *WP*, Apr. 14, 1973.

91. See Post-Trial Brief for Plaintiff, Acanfora, No. 72–1136Y, May 4, 1973, NARA–Philadelphia, 105–1-11; Walsh, "Homosexual Teacher Fights to Return to the Classroom," *WP*, Apr. 13, 1973.

92. Grayson Mitchell, "2 Say Homosexual Teacher Would Benefit Male Pupils," *WP*, Apr. 15, 1973.

93. Points and Authorities in Opposition to Plaintiff's Motion for Summary Judgment, and Renewal of Defendants' Motion to Dismiss, 6, *Acanfora*, NARA Philadelphia, 105–1-07.

94. Acanfora v. Montgomery County Board of Education, 359 F. Supp. 843, 857 (D. Md. 1973).

95. NEA sponsorship meant that Acanfora was ably represented at trial by a respected plaintiff-side labor law firm. The ACLU participated as amicus.

96. ACLU Brief, *Acanfora*, 30–31.

97. ACLU Brief, *Acanfora*, 38–39.

98. ACLU Brief, *Acanfora*, 17–18, 24–26, 33–35 (emphasis added).

99. Acanfora v. Board of Ed. of Montgomery County, 491 F.2d 498, 504 (4th Cir. 1974).

100. Acanfora v. Board of Education of Montgomery County, 419 U.S. 836 (1974) (denying certiorari).

101. See Eskridge, *Dishonorable Passions*, chapter 6, for an assessment of the justices' individual attitudes toward homosexuality in the mid-1970s.
102. See Mayeri, *Reasoning from Race*, 145–67; Serena Mayeri, "Intersectionality and Title VII: A Brief Pre-History," 95 *Boston Univ. L. Rev.* 713 (2015).
103. Judith Helms, "Judges Hear How Pregnant Teacher Tales Spread," *Alabama Journal*, Jan. 7, 1974.
104. Another (male) school district official accompanied King.
105. He had "a physician's certificate stating that [Drake] became pregnant during the current school year at which time [she was] a single unmarried person." Superintendent Murray King to Miss Ilena Drake, April 27, 1973, FMJ Papers, Box 89, Folder 3.
106. See Solomon Seay, Jr., with Delores Boyd, *Jim Crow and Me: Stories from My Life as a Civil Rights Lawyer* (University of Georgia Press, 2008).
107. Transcript of May 23 hearing, Drake v. Covington County Board of Education, 19, FMJ Papers, Box 89, Folder 3.
108. Transcript of May 23 hearing, *Drake*, 25.
109. Transcript of May 23 hearing, *Drake*, 31–32.
110. Motion for Permission to File Brief and Brief Amicus Curiae on Behalf of New Women Lawyers et al., *Roe*, 1971 WL 134283, at *22–24. On creative arguments before *Roe*, see Linda Greenhouse and Reva B. Siegel, "The Unfinished Story of *Roe v. Wade*," in *Reproductive Rights and Justice Stories*, ed. Melissa Murray, Katherine Shaw, and Reva B. Siegel (Foundation Press, 2019); Linda Greenhouse and Reva B. Siegel, *Before* Roe v. Wade: *Voices That Shaped the Abortion Debate Before the Supreme Court's Ruling* (Yale University Press, 2012).
111. Motion for Leave to File Brief Amici Curiae on Behalf of Organizations and Named Women in Support of Appellants in Each Case, and Brief Amicus Curiae, Roe v. Wade, Nos. 70–18, 70–40, 1972 WL 126045, at *29–30. For an argument that the briefs in *Roe* "privileged marital reproduction," see Stein, *Sexual Injustice*, 127–32.
112. Roe v. Wade, 410 U.S. 113, 153 (1973).
113. As did lawsuits challenging the military's pregnancy discharge cases beyond *Flores*, such as *Struck v. Secretary of Defense*.
114. Memorandum of Law, Drake v. Covington County Board of Education, Civil Action File No. 4144-N (M.D. Ala. Oct. 31, 1973), FMJ Papers, Box 89, Folder 4.
115. Memorandum of Law, *Drake*, 8.
116. Plaintiff's Memorandum in Support of Motion for Summary Judgment, 12–14, Drake v. Covington County Board of Education, Oct. 26, 1973, FMJ Papers, Box 89, Folder 4 (emphasis added).
117. Plaintiff's Memorandum, *Drake*, 19–20.
118. Tentative Draft submitted by Craig E. Smith, Law Clerk to Judge Rives, n.d., FMJ Papers, Box 89, Folder 4.
119. Memorandum from Judge Varner to Judges Rives and Johnson, Dec. 29, 1973, Re: Drake v. Covington County Board of Education et al., FMJ Papers, Box 89, Folder 4.

120. Ken to Judge Johnson, Nov. 5, 1973, Re: Drake v. Covington County Board of Education, FMJ Papers, Box 89, Folder 3.

121. Rives strove to "confine the effect of our decision in this case to as narrow limits as I can find possible." Judge Richard Rives to Judges Johnson and Varner, Jan. 7, 1974, FMJ Papers, Box 89, Folder 3.

122. Drake v. Covington County Board of Education, 371 F. Supp. 974 (M.D. Ala. 1974).

123. "Unwed Mother-Teacher Gets Job Reinstatement," *Anniston Journal*, Jan. 25, 1974; Judith Helms, "Teacher Ordered Reinstated," *Alabama Journal*, Jan. 24, 1974; "School Teachers Announced," *Florala News*, Aug. 14, 1975.

124. *Drake*, 371 F. Supp. at 983 (Varner, J., dissenting); Ken to Judge Johnson, Nov. 5, 1973, Re: Drake v. Covington County Board of Education, FMJ Papers, Box 89, Folder 3.

125. Reporters interpreted Seay's comments at the federal district court hearing to mean that Drake obtained an abortion. Judith Helms, "Judges Want More Information in Dismissed Schoolteacher's Case," *Alabama Journal*, Nov. 8, 1973; Judith Helms, "Judges Hear How Pregnant Teacher Tales Spread," *Alabama Journal*, Jan. 7, 1974; Judith Helms, "Teacher Ordered Reinstated," *Alabama Journal*, Jan. 24, 1974.

126. When Brown confirmed that she was seven months pregnant, district officials suspended her with pay, but they neglected to tell Brown that she must request a hearing in order to make her case to the school board.

127. Quoted in Brief of Appellant, 5, Brown v. Bathke, No. 76–2073 (8th Cir. Feb. 24, 1977). The school board relied on a Nebraska statute that authorized termination of a teacher's contract for "immorality."

128. The others had been dismissed for offenses including shoplifting and sexual relationships with students.

129. Omaha Public Schools v. Brown, No. 686 NO. 331, 1976, at *1 (Neb. Dist. Ct. Feb. 26, 1976).

130. Brief of Amicus Curiae, Center for Constitutional Rights, *Andrews*, Mar. 30, 1973 (N.D. Miss.), WCK Papers.

131. Brief of Amicus Curiae, Center for Constitutional Rights, Andrews, Mar. 30, 1973 (N.D. Miss.), WCK Papers.

132. Mayeri, *Reasoning from Race*, 151 (quoting Appendix, *Andrews*).

133. Andrews v. Drew Municipal Separate School Dist., 371 F. Supp. 27, 36 (N.D. Miss. 1973).

134. Andrews v. Drew Municipal Separate School Dist., 507 F.2d 611, 614 (5th Cir. 1975). The policy created an impermissible "irrebuttable presumption" akin to the mandatory maternity leave policy the Supreme Court had recently invalidated. See Cleveland Board of Education v. LaFleur, 411 U.S. 947 (1974); Deborah Dinner, "Recovering the *LaFleur* Doctrine," 22 *Yale J. L. & Fem.* 343 (2010).

135. Andrews v. Drew Municipal Separate School Dist., 507 F.2d 611, 616–17 (5th Cir. 1975).

136. Urbom found that the board's prerogative outweighed Brown's "interest in determining her familial relationships." Brown v. Bathke, 416 F. Supp. 1194, 1198 (D. Neb. 1976).

137. Brown v. Bathke, 588 F.2d 634, 636 (8th Cir. 1978).

138. Brown v. Bathke, 566 F.2d 588, 594–95 (8th Cir. 1977).

139. Wardlaw was concerned that, as her pregnancy became evident, she would undermine the students' trust if she did not explain that she was expecting a baby. Trial Transcript, *Wardlaw*, vol. 1, 12.

140. Ann Arnold, "Pregnant? Yes; Marriage? No!" *Chicago Defender* (UPI), Jan. 25, 1975, at 10.

141. Harriet Wardlaw to Mr. [Jack] Davidson, Nov. 21, 1974, ACLU Records, Box 1823, *Wardlaw*.

142. Brief of Plaintiff-Appellant, 10, Wardlaw v. Austin Independent School Dist., No. 75–2275 (5th Cir.), ACLU Records.

143. Brief of Plaintiff-Appellant, *Wardlaw*, 8–9.

144. See, for example, John Sutton, "Wardlaw Decision Due Monday," *Austin American-Statesman*, Jan. 18, 1975.

145. Lynne Flocke, "LBJ Teacher Supported," *Austin American-Statesman*, Jan. 9, 1975.

146. Wardlaw v. Davidson, No. 227, 991, 1975 WL 13889, at *1 (Tex. Dist. Jan. 20, 1975).

147. "Editorial," *Lubbock Avalanche-Journal* (Tex.), Jan. 24, 1975.

148. NBC News, Vanderbilt Archive; ABC News, Vanderbilt archive.

149. UPI, "Pregnant Teacher Ruling Due," *Napa Valley Register*, Jan. 17, 1975.

150. *Wardlaw* Hearing Transcripts, ACLU Records, Box 1823.

151. Jane Fries, "U.S. Judge Hears Suit by Wardlaw," *Austin American-Statesman*, Mar. 4, 1975.

152. *Wardlaw* Hearing Transcripts, ACLU Records, Box 1823.

153. Brief of Plaintiff-Appellant, *Wardlaw*, 18, 14, 19.

154. Lynne Flocke, "Wardlaw Eyes Federal Court," *Austin American-Statesman*, Feb. 1, 1975.

155. Brief of Plaintiff-Appellant, *Wardlaw*, 23.

156. The superintendent was "saying to all single women teachers that if they find themselves pregnant they ought to either quit their jobs or get an abortion," she told NBC. NBC News Report (Jan. 1975).

157. Brief of Plaintiff-Appellant, *Wardlaw*, 65. Wardlaw brought claims under the federal equal protection clause, Title VII, and Texas's state ERA and anti-discrimination laws.

158. Her lawyers cited *Flores*, too. Brief of Plaintiff-Appellant, *Wardlaw*, 68; UPI, "Court to Hear Unwed Pregnant Teacher's Suit," *Bonham Daily Favorite*, Mar. 2, 1975.

159. Brief of Plaintiff-Appellant, *Wardlaw*, 38, 76, 80.

160. Roberts decided *Boles v. Califano*, discussed in chapter 3.

161. Wardlaw v. Austin Independent School Dist., 1975 WL 182, *3 (W.D. Tex. 1975) (quoting Geduldig v. Aiello, 417 U.S. 484, 496 n.20 [1974]).

162. *Wardlaw*, 1975 WL 182, *4–5.

163. Sullivan v. Meade Independent School Dist., 530 F.2d 799, 804 (8th Cir. 1976).

164. *Sullivan*, 530 F. 2d at 804.

165. Quoted in Ted Gest, "Teacher Challenges Ouster Over Living with Her Boyfriend," *St. Louis Post-Dispatch*, Feb. 15, 1976.

166. Quoted in Sullivan v. Meade County, 387 F. Supp. 1237, 1240–41 (D. S.D. 1975).

167. *Sullivan*, 387 F. Supp. at 1242; *Sullivan*, 530 F.2d at 803–04.

168. The ground was "incompetence." *Sullivan*, 530 F.2d at 803.

169. Gest, "Teacher Challenges Ouster Over Living with Boyfriend," *St. Louis Post-Dispatch*, Feb. 15, 1976, 4A.

170. Marilyn G. Haft to John Davidson, University of South Dakota School of Law, Mar. 11, 1975, ACLU Records, Box 1722.

171. Steven W. Sanford to John Davidson, Mar. 21, 1975, Re: Sullivan, ACLU Records, Box 1722.

172. Memorandum from Steven W. Sanford, Re: Sullivan v. Meade Independent School District #101—Outline for Brief [March/April 1975], ACLU Records, Box 1722.

173. Brief of Appellant, Sullivan v. Meade Independent School District No. 101 et al., No. 75–1315, U.S. Court of Appeals for the Eighth Circuit, 1975, ACLU Records, Box 1722.

174. Memorandum from Steven W. Sanford, Re: Sullivan v. Meade Independent School District #101—Outline for Brief [March/April 1975], ACLU Records, Box 1722.

175. Ted Gest, "Teacher Challenges Ouster Over Living with Boyfriend," *St. Louis Post-Dispatch*, Feb. 15, 1976.

176. Memorandum from Steven W. Sanford, Re: Sullivan v. Meade Independent School District #101—Outline for Brief [March/April 1975], ACLU Records, Box 1722.

177. U.S.D.A. v. Moreno, 413 U.S. 528 (1973).

178. Moreno v. U.S. Dept. of Agriculture, 345 F. Supp. 310, 314 (D. D.C. 1972).

179. Boraas v. Village of Belle Terre, 476 F.2d 806, 816 (2d Cir. 1973). *Moreno* and *Belle Terre* are discussed in detail in chapter 4.

180. Village of Belle Terre v. Boraas, 416 U.S. 1, 8 (1974).

181. Brief of Appellant, Sullivan v. Meade Independent School District No. 101 et al., No. 75–1315 (8th Cir. 1975), ACLU Records, Box 1722.

182. Marilyn Haft to John H. Davidson, Jan. 27, 1975, Re: Sullivan v. Meade County, ACLU Records, Box 1722. Haft referred to related arguments in State v. Devall, 302 So.2d 909 (La. 1974).

183. Brief of Appellant, *Sullivan*, 18.

184. Sullivan v. Meade County Independent School District, 530 F. 2d 799 (8th Cir. 1976).

185. Mel Wulf to Steven W. Sanford, June 8, 1976, ACLU Records, Box 1722.

186. The facts in preceding paragraphs are taken from Depositions of Rebecca S. Hollenbaugh and Fred K. Philburn, Hollenbaugh v. Carnegie Free Library, Civil Action File No. 74–827 (W.D. Pa., Feb. 21, 1975), NARA-Philadelphia.

187. Transcript of Hearing on Motion to Dismiss, *Hollenbaugh*, NARA Philadelphia 2281-1-38.

188. Hollenbaugh v. Carnegie Free Library, 409 F. Supp. 629 (W.D. Pa. 1975).

189. Hollenbaugh v. Carnegie Free Library, 439 U.S. 1052, 1053–57 (1978) (Marshall, J., dissenting from denial of certiorari).

190. Joyce Gemperlein, "Living in Sin? 'It's Our Business,' Fayette Couple Insist," *Pittsburgh Post-Gazette*, Dec. 16, 1978.

191. Judy Vollmer, "Top Court Denial Disappoints Pair in Adultery Case," *Pittsburgh Press*, Dec. 17, 1978.

192. Petition for Certiorari, *Gaylord v. Tacoma*, 17–18.

193. See Canaday, *Queer Career*, chapters 3–4.

194. On Florida's "purge" of gay and lesbian teachers in the decades before Anita Bryant's campaign, see Karen L. Graves, *And They Were Wonderful Teachers: Florida's Purge of Gay and Lesbian Teachers* (University of Illinois Press, 2009). On the regulation of teachers' sexuality in California during this period, see Howard, *The Closet and the Cul-de-Sac*, chapter 2.

195. For more on the Bryant campaign and the Briggs initiative, see Lillian Faderman, *The Gay Revolution: The Story of the Struggle* (Simon & Schuster, 2015).

196. Letter to the Editor, *LAT*, Oct. 21, 1977.

197. Gaylord v. Tacoma School District No. 10, 88 Wash. 2d 286 (1977), cert. denied, 434 U.S. 879 (1977). Gaylord took a job with the American Federation of Teachers.

198. Leechburg Area School District v. Human Relations Commission, 339 A.2d 850 (Pa. Cmmwlth. Ct. 1975).

199. See Cochran v. Chidester School District of Ouachita County, 456 F. Supp. 390 (W.D. Ark. 1978); Moore v. Board of Education of Chidester School District No. 59, 448 F. 2d 709 (8th Cir. 1971).

200. Jacobs v. Martin Sweets Co., 550 F. 2d 364 (6th Cir. 1977). The Supreme Court denied cert., 431 U.S. 917 (1977).

201. Gilbert v. General Electric, 429 U.S. 125 (1976).

202. Some employers succeeded in arguing business necessity, see, e.g., *Harvey v. Y.W.C.A.*, discussed below.

203. Brief of Historians as Amici Curiae in Support of Employees, Bostock v. Clayton County, Altitude Express, Inc. v. Zarda, and R. G. & G. R. Harris Funeral Homes v. EEOC, Nos. 17–1618, 17–1623, and 18–107 (U.S. July 3, 2019) (based on research by Margot Canaday).

204. For a detailed account of how this came to be, see Canaday, *Queer Career*, chapter 3.

205. Chai Feldblum, "The Federal Gay Civil Rights Bill: From Bella to ENDA," in *Creating Change: Sexuality, Public Policy, and Civil Rights*, ed. Urvashi Vaid (St. Martin's Press, 2000); Katherine Turk, "Our Militancy Is in Our Openness: Gay Employment Rights Activism in California and the Question of Sexual Orientation in Sex Equality Law," 31 *L. & Hist. Rev.* 423 (2013).

206. The exceptions to this were a few local ordinances prohibiting sexual orientation discrimination in private employment, a small number of state laws that covered state employment, and a growing collection of large cities that prohibited such discrimination in municipal jobs. See Eskridge, *Gaylaw*, appendix b.

207. Bowers v. Hardwick, 478 U.S. 186, 219, 191 (1986).

208. See Elizabeth Pleck, *Not Just Roommates: Cohabitation After the Sexual Revolution* (University of Illinois Press, 2012).

209. Courtney Joslin, "Marital Status Discrimination 2.0," 95 *Boston Univ. L. Rev.* 805 (2015); Courtney Joslin, "Discrimination In and Out of Marriage," 98 *Boston Univ. L. Rev.* 1 (2018).

210. On gay and lesbian workers' complicated negotiation of visibility and discretion at work, see Canaday, *Queer Career*.

211. See, for example, Yanzick v. School Dist. No. 23, Lake County Mont., 196 Mont. 375, 641 P.2d 431, 2 Ed. Law Rep. 1179 (1982). For overviews of 1980s litigation in this area, see Melnick and Twyman, "Teacher as Exemplar: Freedom in Private Life," 59 *Clearing House* 301 (1986); Kenneth Karst, "Law, Cultural Conflict, and the Socialization of Children," 91 *Calif. L. Rev.* 967, 993 (2003). On gay teachers in particular, see Merri Schneider-Vogel, "Gay Teachers in the Classroom: A Continuing Constitutional Debate," 15 *J. L. & Educ.* 285 (1986); William D. Valente, "*Bowers v. Hardwick* and the Homosexual Teacher," 35 *West's Education Law Reporter* 1–8 (1987); John. C. Walden and Renee Culverhouse, "Homosexuality and Public Education," 55 *West's Education Law Reporter* 7 (1989); "Developments in the Law: Sexual Orientation and the Law: Part IV. Sexual Orientation and the Public Schools," 102 *Harvard L. Rev.* 1584 (1989).

212. Pamela Posey, "Ruling Delayed on Teacher Dismissal," *Daily Press* (Newport News, Va.), Jan. 29, 1986.

213. Ponton v. Newport News School Board, 632 F. Supp. 1056 (E.D. Va. 1986).

214. Marilyn Mather, "Woman Testifies She Lost YWCA Job When She Became Pregnant," *Charlotte Observer*, Jan. 12, 1982.

215. Marilyn Mather, "Court: YWCA Was Unbiased in Firing Pregnant Worker," *Charlotte Observer*, Feb. 10, 1982; Harvey v. Young Women's Christian Ass'n, 533 F. Supp. 949 (W.D. N.C. 1982).

216. AP, "Unwed Mothers' Firing Challenged," *Lincoln Journal*, Dec. 2, 1982.

217. Chambers v. Omaha Girls' Club, 629 F. Supp. 925 (D. Neb. 1986), aff'd, 834 F. 2d 697 (8th Cir. 1987).
218. Regina Austin, "Sapphire Bound!," 1989 *Wisc. L. Rev.* 539.

Chapter 6. Single Mothers and Responsible Citizenship

1. In another recollection, Fernandez traced her realization to a later point—when she did not receive notification of her son's birth in the mail as her married friends had. Lois Fernandez, *Legitimate* (Cowbird, Nov. 26, 2013). See also Lois Fernandez, *Recollections (Part 1)*, ed. Debora Kodish (2016), 49.
2. Pamela J. Smith, "Lois Fernandez: Because of Her There Are No More 'Illegitimate Children,'" *Philadelphia Tribune*, Jan. 2, 1979; Kendall Wilson, "A Mother's War on 'Illegitimate,'" *Philadelphia Tribune*, Dec. 9, 2003.
3. This was a recent reform of a law that had previously required a mother's husband to adopt the child. Sarah C. Casey, "He Has No Father . . . That Makes Him 'Different,'" *Philadelphia Inquirer*, Dec. 4, 1971.
4. Fernandez first wrote to the state representative Hardy Williams: "It is the feeling today that you can take a life legally (abortions), but to give life is illegitimate." Casey, "He Has No Father."
5. Wilson, "A Mother's War."
6. Garland L. Thompson, "26 Years of ODUNDE: One Woman's Vision Fulfilled," *Philadelphia Tribune*, June 12, 2001.
7. Serena Mayeri, "Race, Sexual Citizenship, and the Constitution of Nonmarital Motherhood," in *Heterosexual Histories*, ed. Rebecca L. Davis and Michele Mitchell (NYU Press, 2021).
8. Fernandez, *Legitimate*.
9. Stephen Franklin, "Mother Wins Fight to End Stigma of Illegitimacy," *The Bulletin*, Dec. 10, 1978.
10. Smith, "Lois Fernandez"; Wilson, "A Mother's War."
11. Wilson, "A Mother's War."
12. For more, see Serena Mayeri, "Marital Supremacy and the Constitution of the Nonmarital Family," 103 *Calif. L. Rev.* 1277 (2015).
13. See Reva B. Siegel, "Sex Equality Arguments for Reproductive Rights: Their Critical Basis and Evolving Constitutional Expression," 56 *Emory L. J.* 815 (2007); Felicia Kornbluh, *A Woman's Life Is a Human Life: Mother, Our Neighbor, and the Journey from Reproductive Rights to Reproductive Justice* (Grove Press, 2023).
14. Harry D. Krause, *Illegitimacy: Law and Social Policy* (Bobbs-Merrill, 1971), 294–95.
15. Patricia Tenoso and Aleta Wallach, Book Review, 19 *UCLA L. Rev.* 845, 851, 865, 850 (1972).
16. Patricia Tenoso and Aleta Wallach, "A Vindication of the Rights of Unmarried Women and Their Children: An Analysis of the Institution of Illegiti-

macy, Equal Protection, and the Uniform Parentage Act," 23 *U. Kansas L. Rev.* 23, 25 (1974).

17. Tenoso and Wallach, Book Review, 852; Tenoso and Wallach, "Vindication," 28.

18. Tenoso and Wallach, "Vindication," 23 n.1.

19. Deborah Dinner, "The Universal Child Care Debate: Rights Mobilization, Social Policy, and the Dynamics of Feminist Activism, 1966–1974," *Law and History Review*, vol. 28, no. 3 (August 2010).

20. Parham v. Southwestern Bell Telephone Co., 1969 WL 109, *9.

21. EEOC Dec. No. 71–332, September 28, 1970, 1970 WL 3569.

22. Griggs v. Duke Power Co., 401 U.S. 424 (1971).

23. 321 N.Y.S. 2d 493, 450, 451 (N.Y. Sup. Ct., Apr. 30, 1971). Similar paragraphs appeared in Serena Mayeri, *Reasoning from Race: Feminism, Law, and the Civil Rights Revolution* (Harvard University Press, 2011), 153–54.

24. Anders Walker, *The Ghost of Jim Crow: How Southern Moderates Used* Brown v. Board of Education *to Stall Civil Rights* (Oxford University Press, 2009).

25. On Fannie Lou Hamer, see Keisha N. Blain, *Until I Am Free: Fannie Lou Hamer's Enduring Message to America* (Beacon Press, 2021); Chana Kai Lee, *For Freedom's Sake: The Life of Fannie Lou Hamer* (University of Illinois Press, 2000). See also Chris Myers Asch, *The Senator and the Sharecropper: The Freedom Struggles of James O. Eastland and Fannie Lou Hamer* (University of North Carolina Press, 2011).

26. For more on van den Haag, see Nancy MacLean, *Freedom Is Not Enough: The Opening of the American Workplace* (Harvard University Press, 2006).

27. See testimony of Ruby Nell Stancil, Joint Appendix, *Andrews v. Drew Municipal Separate School District*, No. 74-1318.

28. Joint Appendix, *Andrews*, 39.

29. Joint Appendix, *Andrews*, 54.

30. Brief for Petitioners, *Andrews*, 6 (quoting van den Haag).

31. Charles Victor McTeer, telephone conversation with the author, September 2012.

32. Joint Appendix, *Andrews*, 84.

33. Joint Appendix, *Andrews*, 94–95.

34. Brief of Respondents, *Andrews*, 54.

35. Brief of Respondents, *Andrews*, 55. See also Brief Amicus Curiae Child Welfare League of America, *Andrews*, 8–9.

36. Joint Appendix, *Andrews*, 104.

37. Joint Appendix, *Andrews*, 104, 109.

38. Joint Appendix, *Andrews*, 195.

39. Brief for Petitioners, *Andrews*, 28.

40. Interview with Nancy Stearns, Rhonda Copelon Schoenbrod, and Janice Goodman, 1 *Women's Rights Law Reporter* 20, 35 (1974).

41. Brief of Respondents, *Andrews*, 53, 40.

42. Joint Appendix, *Andrews*, 188; Brief of Amicus Curiae ACLU Women's Rights Project and Equal Rights Advocates, *Andrews*, 10–12, 33–34.

43. ACLU/Equal Rights Advocates Brief, *Andrews*, 46–47, 26–27.

44. Brief for Petitioners, *Andrews*, 9–10.

45. The district's arguments recalled Alabama officials' claims that white taxpayers would not willingly subsidize public assistance to nonmarital Black families (see chapter 2).

46. Brief for Respondents, *Andrews*, 22 (quoting Kenneth B. Clark).

47. Brief Amicus Curiae of Child Welfare League of America, *Andrews*, 11–12.

48. David Margolick, "Single Mothers Join Suit to Enlist in the Military," *NYT*, Dec. 25, 1984, p. 30.

49. Barnes's commanding officer recommended that she be retained. Commander Carroll C. Wilson to Commander, First U.S. Army, Re: Retention within USAR Program, Sept. 14, 1976, Joint Appendix, Mack v. Rumsfeld, 409.

50. See West v. Brown, 558 F.2d 757 (5th Cir. 1977). See also Defendants' Memorandum of Points and Authorities in Support of Motion to Dismiss, Mack v. Rumsfeld, NARA; Affidavit of Lieutenant General Kenneth Tallman, Mack v. Rumsfeld, May 24, 1976, ACLU Records, Box 4842, Folder 4; Lieutenant General Kenneth Tallman, Memorandum for General Slay (AF), Re: Dependent Qualifications for Enlistment, ACLU Records, Box 4842, Folder 4.

51. Defendants' Memorandum of Points and Authorities in Support of Motion to Dismiss, 22–23, *Mack v. Rumsfeld*, NARA-NYC (emphasis mine).

52. Margolick, "Single Mothers Join Suit."

53. Affidavit of Named Plaintiff Thelma Barnes, in Opposition to Defendants' Renewed Motion for Summary Judgment and in Support of Plaintiffs' Motion for Summary Judgment, *Mack v. Rumsfeld*, NARA-NYC.

54. Plaintiffs' Memorandum in Opposition to Defendants' Renewed Motion for Summary Judgment, 1, *Mack*, NARA-NYC. Mack had arranged for her mother to care for her sons while she performed her military duties. Amended Complaint, *Mack*, 15.

55. Affidavit of Shirley Stukes, *Mack*, NARA-NYC. Stukes's older child, Teresa, had lived with Stukes's mother since she was four months old.

56. Plaintiffs' Memorandum in Opposition, *Mack*, 2–4.

57. Plaintiffs' Memorandum in Opposition to Defendants' Renewed Motion for Summary Judgment, Mack v. Rumsfeld, No. 76–22 (W.D.N.Y. Feb. 14, 1984).

58. Phyllis Gelman to Hon. John T. Curtin, Re: Mack v. Rumsfeld, Feb. 21, 1985.

59. Because of the value placed on continuity of care, the best interests of the child standard strongly favored incumbent custodians. See Memorandum from Carol Bruch to Phyllis Gelman, quoted in Plaintiffs' Memorandum, *Mack*, 40.

60. "Gresham Needs Witnesses: Single Parents in the Military," GULP Newsletter, vol. 5, no. 5, NCWFL Papers.

61. Affidavit of Geraldine Schmidt, *Mack*. See also, for example, Robert L. Ray to Laurie Woods, National Center on Women and Family Law, October 2, 1980, NCWFL Papers, Folder: Custody—Single Parents—Enlistment (describing similar policy of Tennessee National Guard); Lynn B. Montgomery, Memphis Area Legal Services, to Laurie Woods, NCWFL, June 25, 1980 (similar); Amy Hirsch, Staff Attorney, Jacksonville Area Legal Aid, Inc., to NCWFL, May 13, 1980 (similar); Cecilia Rodriguez, "A Mother's Problem in Joining the Army," *S.F. Chronicle*, Aug. 3, 1978; Legal Aid Society of Alameda County to Legal Officer, California National Guard, March 7, 1978, NCWFL Papers (requesting clarification of policy).

62. Affidavit of Geraldine Schmidt, Mack v. Rumsfeld, No. 76–22 (W.D.N.Y. Feb. 15, 1983), NARA-NYC.

63. Trina Lewis to Hon. John T. Curtin, Oct. 24, 1984; Brief for Plaintiff-Appellants, Mack v. Rumsfeld (2d Cir.), 19.

64. Quoted in "Single Parents Want to Serve," *Bangor Daily News*, May 21, 1980.

65. See also Affidavit of Regina Livingston, *Mack*, No. 76–22.

66. Quoted in Plaintiffs' Memorandum in Opposition to Defendants' Renewed Motion for Summary Judgment and in Support of Plaintiffs' Motion for Summary Judgment, 36, *Mack*, No. 76–22 (W.D.N.Y. Feb. 14, 1984), NARA-NYC.

67. Plaintiffs' Memorandum in Opposition, *Mack*, 36–40.

68. Moore v. City of East Cleveland, 431 U.S. 494 (1977).

69. Patricia Garland Morisey, "The Special Strengths of Extended Families Enable Single Mothers in the Armed Forces to Provide Adequate Child Care for Their Children," Jan. 10, 1984, NARA-NYC.

70. Plaintiffs' Memorandum in Opposition, *Mack*, 43; Richard Levine and Katherine Roberts, "Single Mothers and the Military," *NYT*, Dec. 30, 1984.

71. Jennifer Mittelstadt, *The Rise of the Military Welfare State* (Harvard University Press, 2015).

72. Petition for a Writ of Certiorari, *Mack*, 6–7.

73. The military now permitted servicemen and -women who became single parents while in the military to stay on, but this change had resulted in some complaints from officers. See, for example, "Babysitting Problem Bugs Single Soldiers," *Montreal Gazette*, Jan. 8, 1979.

74. Defendants' Response to Plaintiffs' Cross Motion for Summary Resolution of the Controversy, 43, *Mack*, No. 76–22 (W.D.N.Y. June 26, 1984).

75. Defendants' Response, *Mack*, 6.

76. Maj. Roger Almquist, Memorandum for Colonel Elden H. Wright, Re: Sole Parents/Women in the Army, *Mack*, NARA-NYC.

77. Almquist, "Memorandum."

78. See Plaintiffs' Memorandum in Opposition to Defendants' Renewed Motion for Summary Judgment, *Mack*, 88–90.

79. See, for example, "Army Wants Fewer Women, Restricts Jobs," *Spokane Chronicle*, Aug. 27, 1982; Editorial Research Reports, "Another Look at Women in the Military," *Toledo Blade*, Aug. 7, 1981; AP, "Pentagon to Reagan: Cut Back Recruiting of Women," *Free-Lance Star*, Jan. 21, 1981.

80. In 1979, General Bernard Rogers, chief of staff for the U.S. Army, "ordered all 15,000 single parents in the enlisted ranks to come up with a 'dependent care plan' suitable for all occasions, including emergencies, or be booted out of the service." "Babysitting Problem Bugs Single Soldiers." See Women in the Army Study Group Report (1981), Joint Appendix, *Mack*, 439.

81. Audit of Enlisted Women in the Army, April 1982, Report No. HQ 82, Joint Appendix, *Mack*, vol. II. Other studies found, however, that enlisted men incurred significantly more "lost time" than women. See Linda Bird Francke, *Ground Zero: The Gender Wars in the Military* (Penguin Books, 1997). See also Mittelstadt, *Rise of the Military Welfare State*, 85.

82. Marcia Dodson, "Military Answers a Call to Arms: Single Parents in the Service," *LAT*, Aug. 27, 1980.

83. Raymond Coffey, "Girl Soldiers Bring Babies Along on Duty," *Montreal Gazette*, Nov. 9, 1978. The same article ran in the St. Petersburg *Independent* under the headline "Soldier-Mothers and Their Children Are Worrying the Army" (Nov. 2, 1978). See also Raymond Coffey, "Babes and Arms: Soldier-Mother Dilemma," *Chicago Tribune*, Oct. 29, 1978 (same article, different headline).

84. Molly Moore, "Single Parents Struggle in Military," *WP*, Sept. 3, 1986.

85. A study commissioned by the plaintiffs' attorneys estimated that women were fourteen times more likely than men to be single parents.

86. David Margolick, "Single Mothers Join Suit to Enlist in the Military," *NYT*, Dec. 25, 1984. See Joint Appendix, *Mack*, 301.

87. Brief of Plaintiff-Appellants, *Mack*, 37.

88. Brief of Plaintiff-Appellants, *Mack*, 39–40, quoting Joint Appendix, 325 (Kurt Lang, Draft Summary Evaluation of Scientific Evidence for Claims in Defendants' Briefs, Dec. 30, 1983).

89. Welfare rights advocacy continued at the local level as well. See, for example, Annelise Orleck, *Storming Caesars Palace: How Black Mothers Fought Their Own War on Poverty* (Beacon Press, 2005).

90. Federal regulations enacted in 1973 explicitly permitted states to withhold benefits from mothers who failed to cooperate with authorities in identifying their children's biological fathers. Federal courts invalidated state laws to this effect, too, reasoning that withholding benefits from a mother harmed her children by reducing the total amount of funds available to the household.

91. Doe v. Norton, 256 F. Supp. 202, 206 n.6 (D. Conn. 1973); Doe v. Norton, 365 F. Supp. 65, 72, 79 n.23 (D. Conn. 1973); Mayeri, "Marital Supremacy," 1320–21.

92. Affidavit of Mildred Walter, Joint Appendix, *Roe v. Norton*, 41; see also Affidavit of Sharon Roe, Joint Appendix, *Roe v. Norton*, 51.

93. Affidavit of Rena Roe, Joint Appendix, *Roe v. Norton*, 37.

94. Affidavit, of "A," Joint Appendix, *Roe v. Norton*, 39. See also Affidavit of "M," Joint Appendix, *Roe v. Norton*, 45; Affidavit of Donna Doe, Joint Appendix, *Roe v. Norton*; Affidavit of Mary Brown, Joint Appendix, *Roe v. Norton*.

95. See Affidavits of Sharon Roe, Linda Loe, Rena Roe, Dorothy Poe; Brief for Appellants, *Roe v. Norton*, 43.

96. See Affidavits of Dorothy Poe, "D."

97. Affidavit of Sharon Roe, Joint Appendix, *Roe v. Norton*, 51.

98. Appendix of Brief of Children of Appellants, *Roe v. Norton*, 14a.

99. Brief for the Appellants, *Roe v. Norton*, 10–11. See also Affidavits of Katherine Lopes, Joint Appendix, *Roe v. Norton*.

100. Deposition of Albert J. Solnit, M.D., Appendix, *Roe v. Norton*, 69; see also Appendix, *Roe v. Norton*, 62–71; Mayeri, "Marital Supremacy," 1321; Brief of Appellants, *Roe v. Norton*.

101. Carol B. Stack and Herbert Semmel, "The Concept of the Family in the Poor Black Community," in Studies in Public Welfare, Paper No. 12 (Part II): The Family, Poverty, and Welfare Programs, Senate Committee on Fiscal Policy, 93rd Cong., 294 (Committee Print 1973).

102. John C. Gray, Jr., Book Review, 46 *NYU L. Rev.* 1210, 1234 (1971).

103. Elizabeth Wickenden, "The Constitutional Rights of Assistance Recipients," March 25, 1963, JWP Papers. For a mid-1970s assessment, see, e.g., Judith Areen, "Intervention Between Parent and Child: A Reappraisal of the State's Role in Child Neglect and Abuse Cases," 63 *Georgetown L. J.* 887 (1975).

104. Polier retired from the bench in 1973 and joined the New York staff of the Children's Defense Fund, newly launched by Marian Wright Edelman.

105. Justine Wise Polier, Book Review of Harry D. Krause, *Illegitimacy: Law and Social Policy*, in *Child Welfare*, Nov. 1, 1972. For a detailed discussion of the *Roe v. Norton* litigation, see Stephen D. Sugarman, "*Roe v. Norton:* Coerced Maternal Cooperation," in *In the Interest of Children: Advocacy, Law Reform, and Public Policy*, ed. Robert H. Mnookin (W.H. Freeman, 1985), Part VI.

106. Brief Amicus Curiae of the Children's Defense Fund et al., *Roe v. Norton*.

107. Justine Wise Polier, Memorandum to Files, Re: Doe v. Norton, Mar. 12, 1974, JWP Papers (summarizing conversation with ACLU's Mel Wulf).

108. On the disagreement, see Suzanne Kahn, *Divorce, American Style: Fighting for Women's Economic Citizenship in the Neoliberal Era* (University of Pennsylvania Press, 2021), 54–56; Marisa Chappell, *The War on Welfare: Family, Poverty, and Politics in Modern America* (University of Pennsylvania Press, 2010), 173–74; see also Libby Adler and Janet Halley, "'You Play, You Pay': Feminists and Child Support Enforcement in the United States, in *Governance Feminism: Notes from the Field*, ed. Janet Halley, Prabha Kotiswaran,

Rachel Robouché, and Hila Shamir (University of Minnesota Press, 2019), 287.

109. Andrews v. Drew Municipal Separate School District, 371 F. Supp. 27, 30 (N.D. Miss. 1973).

110. By 1975, Title IX regulations prohibited pre-employment inquiries about marital status.

111. Brief Amicus Curiae of the National Education Association, *Andrews*, No. 76–1310, *3–5.

112. Mack v. Rumsfeld, 609 F. Supp. 1561 (W.D.N.Y. 1985), affirmed, 784 F. 2d 438 (1986), cert. denied sub. nom. Mack v. Weinberger, 479 U.S. 815 (1986).

113. Personnel Administrator v. Feeney, 442 U.S. 256 (1979). On *Feeney*, see Linda K. Kerber, *No Constitutional Right to Be Ladies: Women and the Obligations of Citizenship* (Hill & Wang, 1998); Mayeri, *Reasoning from Race*, chapter 4.

114. Rostker v. Goldberg, 453 U.S. 57 (1981). On *Rostker*, see Kerber, *No Constitutional Right to Be Ladies*; Mayeri, *Reasoning from Race*, chapter 6; Jill Hasday, "Fighting Women: The Military, Sex, and Extrajudicial Constitutional Change," 99 *Minn. L. Rev.* 96 (2008).

115. Ruth Bader Ginsburg read Cochran's preliminary outline and remarked to colleagues that "he seems to be doing fine on his own."

116. The limited argument on sex discrimination might have been a response to *Geduldig v. Aiello* (1974), where the Court had cast doubt on whether classifications based on "natural" or "biological" sex differences such as pregnancy and childbirth were subject to sex equality analysis at all. Geduldig v. Aiello, 417 U.S. 484 (1974).

117. On how welfare regulated fathers, see Alison Lefkovitz, *Strange Bedfellows: Marriage in the Age of Women's Liberation* (University of Pennsylvania Press, 2018), chapter 4.

118. Doe v. Norton, 356 F. Supp. 202, 206 n.6 (D. Conn. 1973).

119. See Alfonso Narvaez, "M. Joseph Blumenfeld, Judge, 84," *NYT*, Nov. 6, 1988.

120. Joined by Second Circuit Judge William H. Timbers, a Nixon appointee.

121. These biographical details are taken from Jon O. Newman, *Benched* (Hein, 2017).

122. Reva B. Siegel, "Roe's Roots: The Women's Rights Claims That Engendered Roe," 90 *Boston Univ. L. Rev.* 1875 (2010).

123. Doe v. Norton, 365 F. Supp. 65, 85 (D. Conn.) (Newman, J, concurring).

124. Doe v. Norton, 365 F. Supp. at 85–86.

125. Just two years before Katie Mae Andrews filed suit, a young Black woman was killed on her graduation day from Drew High School. See Keisha N. Blain, "They Called Her 'Black Jet,'" *Atlantic*, April 28, 2022.

126. For more, see Mayeri, *Reasoning from Race*, 157.

127. The Army "wanted the white middle class back." Mittelstadt, *The Rise of the Military Welfare State*, 99.

128. See Mittelstadt, *The Rise of the Military Welfare State.*

129. For more, see Sugarman, "*Roe v. Norton.*"

130. The plaintiffs' attorneys included Catharine Rohrback, who had helped litigate the early Connecticut birth control cases in the 1960s (see chapter 1); the feminist attorney Ann Hill of New Haven; and Lucy V. Katz, who argued the case in the lower courts and in the U.S. Supreme Court. Sylvia Law wrote an amicus brief for several women's and public health/medical organizations supporting the plaintiffs.

131. Barbara Bye (pseudonym), Affidavit in Support of Motion for Temporary Restraining Order, Sept. 19, 1975, Appendix to Brief of Appellant, Maher v. Roe, No. 75–1440, ACLU Records.

132. Affidavit of Carol C., Sept. 23, 1975, Maher v. Roe, ACLU Records. Her attorneys wrote that Carol C. "was attempting to complete her nursing education so that she could end her dependence on public assistance." Brief of Appellees, Maher v. Roe, 1976 WL 181642, at *6-*8. Susan Roe, an unmarried mother of three and an AFDC recipient, felt another child would render her unable to care for her medically fragile infant.

133. Brief for Appellees, Maher v. Roe, *11-*12.

134. Roe v. Norton, 408 F. Supp. 660 (D. Conn. Dec. 31, 1975). Newman acknowledged that *Dandridge v. Williams* (1970) foreclosed a constitutional right to welfare but said that if the state funded childbirth for indigent women, it could not refuse to fund abortion without infringing women's fundamental rights under *Roe v. Wade* and *Doe v. Bolton* (1973).

135. Maher v. Roe, 432 U.S. 464, 474 (1977).

136. Khiara M. Bridges, "Elision and Erasure: Race, Class, and Gender in *Harris v. McRae*," in *Reproductive Rights and Justice Stories*, ed. Melissa Murray, Katherine Shaw, and Reva B. Siegel (Foundation Press, 2019). See also Khiara M. Bridges, *The Poverty of Privacy Rights* (Stanford University Press, 2017).

137. Harris v. McRae, 448 U.S. 297, 316 (1980).

138. Zablocki v. Redhail, 434 U.S. 374 (1978). For background on the case, see Tonya Brito, R. Kirk Anderson, and Monica Wedgewood, "Chronicle of a Debt Foretold: *Zablocki v. Red Hail* (1978)," in *The Poverty Law Canon: Exploring the Major Cases*, ed. Marie A. Failinger and Ezra Rosser (University of Michigan Press, 2016).

139. LFP, Aid to Memory Memo to File, Zablocki, Milwaukee County Clerk v. Redhail, No. 76–879, LFP Papers, Box 473, Folder 10. Red Hail's child was born in 1971, while Red Hail and the child's mother were high school students.

140. Handwritten note from LFP to TM, on TM, Memorandum to the Conference, Nov. 16, 1977, LFP Papers. Four separate opinions in addition to Rehnquist's dissent were eventually issued.

141. LFP, Aid to Memory Memo to File, Zablocki v. Redhail, No. 76–879, LFP Papers, Box 473, Folder 10. Powell thought the law had no rational basis.

LFP Conference Notes, 10/7/77, Zablocki v. Redhail, No. 76–879, LFP Papers, Box 473, Folder 12.

142. Sam Estreicher, Bench Memo to LFP, Sept. 22, 1977, Zablocki v. Redhail, No. 76–879, LFP Papers, Box 473, Folder 11. Powell adopted this view in his own oral argument notes. LFP, Handwritten Notes, Zablocki v. Redhail, No. 76–879, Argued 10/4/77, LFP Papers, Box 473, Folder 12.

143. Sam Estreicher, Bench Memo to LFP, Sept. 22, 1977, Zablocki v. Redhail, No. 76–879, LFP Papers, Box 473, Folder 11.

144. Zablocki v. Redhail, 434 U.S. 374, 390 (1978).

145. Gomez v. Perez, 409 U.S. 535 (1973).

146. LFP, Conference Notes, *Mills v. Habluetzel*, No. 80–6298, LFP Papers.

147. Elaine Ayala, "Archie's Case Could Upset Paternity Law," *Corpus Christi Caller Times*, May 24, 1981.

148. LFP Conference Notes, *Mills*, LFP Papers.

149. WHR, First Draft of Opinion for the Court in *Mills v. Habluetzel*, No. 80–6298, LFP Papers.

150. See also Kit Kinports to HAB, Re: No 80–6298—*Mills v. Habluetzel*, Feb. 12, 1982, at 2, HAB Papers, Box 357, Folder 2.

151. LFP to WHR, Feb. 11, 1982, Re: 80–6298: *Mills v. Habluetzel*, LFP Papers.

152. Ayala, "Archie's Case Could Upset Paternity Law."

153. Mills v. Habluetzel, 456 U.S. 91, 103 (1982) (O'Connor, J., concurring).

154. Mary Deibel, "Judging the Law," *Memphis Commercial Appeal*, Apr. 24, 1983.

155. The brief was signed by Jim Weill, his wife, Judith Lichtman, and Marian Wright Edelman. Weill had worked with Jane Greengold Stevens on *Jimenez v. Weinberger* (1974). See chapter 3.

156. Brief Amicus Curiae of Children's Defense Fund and Women's Legal Defense Fund 5–6, *Pickett v. Brown*, No. 82–5576, 462 U.S. 1.

157. *Mills*, 456 U.S. at 105 n.4 (O'Connor, J., concurring).

158. Pickett v. Brown, 462 U.S. 1, 14 n.13 (1983).

159. Affidavit in Support of Answer to Motion to Dismiss Complaint and Enter Judgment in Favor of Defendant, in Joint Appendix, *Clark v. Jeter*, *10–12.

160. Brief Amici Curiae for the Women's Legal Defense Fund et al., *Clark v. Jeter*, 1988 WL 1031608 n.19.

161. For more on the relationship between race and sex in 1970s constitutional doctrine, see Mayeri, *Reasoning from Race*.

162. Act 1978–288, *Laws of Pennsylvania*, General Assembly 1978 (vol. II), 1216 (Nov. 26, 1978).

Chapter 7. Unmarried Fathers and Sex Equality

1. I have discussed the *Fiallo* case in Serena Mayeri, "Foundling Fathers: (Non-)Marriage and Parental Rights in the Age of Equality," 125 *Yale L. J.* 2292, 2327–30 (2016); Serena Mayeri, "Intersectionality and the Constitu-

tion of Family Status," 32 *Constitutional Commentary* 377, 405–7 (2017); Serena Mayeri, "Marital Supremacy and the Constitution of the Nonmarital Family," 103 *Calif. L. Rev.* 1277, 1327–31 (2015). The legal scholar Kristin Collins is the foremost authority on the case and its history. See Kristin A. Collins, "Illegitimate Borders: Jus Sanguinis Citizenship and the Legal Construction of Family, Race, and Nation," 123 *Yale L. J.* 2134 (2014); Kristin A. Collins, "Deference and Deferral: Constitutional Structure and the Durability of Gender-Based Nationality Laws," in *The Public Law of Gender*, ed. Kim Rubenstein and Katharine Young (Cambridge University Press, 2016).

2. The law of Guadalupe only allowed legitimation through marriage of the parents. See Brief of Appellants, Ramon Martin Fiallo, etc., et al. v. Edward H. Levi, individually and as Attorney General of the United States, et al., No. 75–6297, 1976 WL 181344 (U.S. [August 23, 1976]) (hereinafter Brief of Appellants).

3. Brief of Appellants, *Fiallo*.

4. Brief of Appellants, *Fiallo*, 24 n. 17.

5. Mayeri, "Marital Supremacy," 1329; Martha F. Davis, "Male Coverture: Law and the Illegitimate Family," 56 *Rutgers L. Rev.* 73, 99 (2003).

6. See Nara B. Milanich, *Paternity: The Elusive Quest for the Father* (Harvard University Press, 2019).

7. Quoted in Ellen Schulte, "Help Urged for Unwed Father," *LAT*, April 2, 1965.

8. Lynn Lilliston, "A Counselor Looks at the Unwed Father," *LAT*, August 17, 1967; Reuben Pannor, Fred Massarik, and Byron W. Evans, *The Unmarried Father: New Approaches for Helping Unmarried Young Parents* (Springer Pub. Co., 1971), 44–63.

9. Judy Klemesrud, "The Unwed Father, Long Ignored, Now Gets Counseling, Too," *NYT*, July 25, 1969.

10. Lilliston, "A Counselor Looks at the Unwed Father."

11. Schulte, "Help Urged for Unwed Father."

12. See Mignon Sauber, "The Role of the Unmarried Father," 4 *Welfare Review* 15 (1966); "Unemployment a Factor in Illegitimate Births," *N.Y. Amsterdam News*, Mar. 18, 1967; Klemesrud, "The Unwed Father."

13. Deirdre Carmody, "Council Studying Teen-Age Parents," *NYT*, Feb. 8, 1970.

14. Klemesrud, "The Unwed Father."

15. Illegitimacy, Conference Proceedings (Washington, D.C.: Golden Anniversary White House Conference on Children and Youth, 1960), 286.

16. Reba E. Choate and Ursula M. Gallagher, *Unmarried Parents: A Guide for the Development of Services in Public Welfare*, U.S. Department of Health, Education, and Welfare, Bureau of Family Services, Children's Bureau (Washington: U.S. Government Printing Office, 1961).

17. Choate and Gallagher, *Unmarried Parents*, 36–37.

18. Klemesrud, "The Unwed Father," 56.
19. See Rickie Solinger, *Wake Up Little Susie: Single Pregnancy and Race Before Roe v. Wade* (University of California Press, 1993); Nina Bernstein, *The Lost Children of Wilder: The Epic Struggle to Change Foster Care* (Vintage Books, 2002).
20. Klemesrud, "The Unwed Father."
21. See, for example, Pannor et al., *Unmarried Father*, at 15; Elizabeth Herzog, "Some Notes about Unmarried Fathers," *Child Welfare*, April 1966, at 195; Lynn Lilliston, "Now What About the Unwed Father?," *WP*, Aug. 27, 1967; Lynn Lilliston, "A Father Vies for Custody of His Baby," *LAT*, Aug. 31, 1972.
22. Clark E. Vincent, "Illegitimacy in the Next Decade: Trends and Implications," 43 *Child Welfare* 513, 518 (1964); see also Rita Dukette and Nicholas Stevenson, "The Legal Rights of Unmarried Fathers: The Impact of Recent Court Decisions," 47 *Soc. Serv. Rev.* 1, 1 (1973) (quoting Vincent, supra).
23. Freda Jane Lippert, "The Need for a Clarification of Putative Fathers' Rights," 8 *J. Fam. L.* 398, 400 (1968).
24. Harry D. Krause, "Legitimate and Illegitimate Offspring of Levy v. Louisiana—First Decisions on Equal Protection and Paternity," 36 *U. Chi. L. Rev.* 338, 358 (1969).
25. The American Bar Association approved the UPA in 1974. See Harry D. Krause, "The Uniform Parentage Act," 8 *Fam. L. Quarterly* 1 (1974). Krause, who served as its "reporter-draftsman," hoped the UPA would "fill [the] vacuum" left by state legislatures' sluggish response to reforming laws that discriminated against children based on birth status. Krause, "The Uniform Parentage Act," 8.
26. Krause, "The Uniform Parentage Act," 9; see also Harry D. Krause, "Child Welfare, Parental Responsibility, and the State," 6 *Fam. L. Quarterly* 377, 391–92 (1972).
27. Robert L. Griswold, *Fatherhood in America: A History* (Basic Books, 1993), 244–45; Kirsten Swinth, *Feminism's Forgotten Fight: The Unfinished Struggle for Work and Family* (Harvard University Press, 2018), chapter 2.
28. For a trenchant analysis, see Deborah Dinner, "The Divorce Bargain: The Fathers' Rights Movement and Family Inequalities," 102 *Virginia L. Rev.* 79 (2016). On child support, see also Libby Adler and Janet Halley, "'You Play, You Pay': Feminists and Child Support in the United States," in *Governance Feminism: Notes from the Field*, ed. Janet Halley, Prabha Kotiswaran, Rachel Rebouché, and Hila Shamir (University of Minnesota Press, 2019); Jyl Josephson, *Gender, Families, and the State: Child Support Policies in the United States* (Rowman & Littlefield, 1997); Jocelyn Elise Crowley, *The Politics of Child Support in America* (University of Chicago Press, 2003).
29. Henry Foster and Doris J. Freed, "Child Custody, Part I," 39 *NYU L. Rev.* 423, 437 (1964).
30. Foster and Freed, "Child Custody, Part I."

31. Stanfield v. Stanfield, 435 S.W.2d 690, 692 (Mo. 1968).

32. Margaret Mead, as quoted in State ex rel. Watts v. Watts, 77 Misc. 2d 178, 182 (N.Y. 1973).

33. Kooper, newly appointed by Mayor John Lindsay, had successfully settled a sex discrimination lawsuit against the Metropolitan Trial Lawyers' Association for refusing her admission. State ex re. Watts v. Watts, 350 N.Y.S.2d 285 (Fam. Ct. 1973). See also Eric Pace, "Sybil Kooper, 66, Former Justice in New York Appellate Division," *NYT*, Dec. 13, 1991.

34. Ralph J. Podell, Harry F. Peck, and Curry First, "Custody—To Which Parent?," 56 *Marquette L. Rev.* 51, 53 (1972).

35. Podell et al., "Custody," 55–57.

36. See Dinner, "Divorce Bargain"; Alison Lefkovitz, *Strange Bedfellows: Marriage in the Age of Women's Liberation* (University of Pennsylvania Press, 2018).

37. The omission of sex as a factor reflected the "overlapping goals of fathers' rights and feminist legal activism in the early 1970s." Dinner, "Divorce Bargain," 115.

38. Dinner, "Divorce Bargain," 115.

39. Godinez v. Russo, 266 N.Y.S. 2d 636 (Westchester Cty. Fam. Ct. 1966).

40. See Pannor et al., *Unmarried Father*; Harry D. Krause, "The Bastard Finds His Father," 3 *Fam. L. Quarterly* 100 (1969); Pearl S. Weisdorf, "Illegitimacy: Data and Findings for Prevention, Treatment, and Policy Formulation," 40 *Soc. Serv. Rev.* 112 (1966) (book review); Deborah Shapiro, "Effective Services for Unmarried Parents and Their Children: Innovative Community Approaches," 43 *Soc. Serv. Rev.* 109 (1969) (book review).

41. Norman Gardner Tabler, Jr., "Paternal Rights in the Illegitimate Child: Some Legitimate Complaints on Behalf of the Unwed Father," 11 *J. Fam. L.* 231, 242–43 (1971).

42. Tabler, "Paternal Rights," 231–32.

43. Tabler, "Paternal Rights," 236.

44. Armstrong v. Manzo, 380 U.S. 545 (1965).

45. Tabler, "Paternal Rights," 245.

46. Polier, Book Review of Harry D. Krause, *Illegitimacy: Law and Social Policy*, in *Child Welfare*, Nov. 1972.; Bernstein, *The Lost Children of Wilder.*

47. State ex rel. John Thomas Lewis et al. v. Lutheran Social Services of Wisconsin and Upper Michigan, 47 Wis. 2d 420, 433 (1970).

48. AP, "Court Asked to Rule for Unmarried Fathers," *LAT*, Dec. 26, 1970.

49. For more on the Stanley case, see Mayeri, "Foundling Fathers," 2309–24; Josh Gupta-Kagan, "*Stanley v. Illinois*: The Untold Story," 24 *Wm. & Mary Bill of Rts. J.* 773 (2016).

50. John P. MacKenzie, "Supreme Court Rules for Working Mothers," *WP*, Jan. 26, 1971; Memorandum from Robert E. Gooding, Jr., Law Clerk, to Justice Harry A. Blackmun (Nov. 18, 1970), HAB Papers, Box 143, Folder 1.

51. *Stanley* Oral Argument, at 14:31.

52. Brief for Respondent, *Stanley*, 25–27.

53. A mother who abandoned her child at birth without arranging for its care committed a crime; fathers of nonmarital children did the same with impunity. Brief for Respondent, *Stanley*, 15–16.

54. Brief for Respondent, *Stanley*, 27 n. 25.

55. Brief for Respondent, *Stanley*, 26.

56. Brief for Respondent, *Stanley*, 27–29.

57. Illinois had abolished common law marriage in 1905. See *Stanley*, 405 U.S. at 663–64 (Burger, C.J., dissenting).

58. Brief for Petitioner, *Stanley*, 23; Mayeri, "Foundling Fathers," 2314. See also Melissa Murray, "What's So New About the New Illegitimacy," 20 *American Univ. J. of Gender, Social Policy, & Law* 387 (2012).

59. Brief for Petitioner, *Stanley*, 22 (quotation marks omitted).

60. BRW, Second Draft Opinion for the Court in *Stanley*, 8, Nov. 18, 1971, BRW Papers, Box 227, Folder 8; Mayeri, "Foundling Fathers," 2320–21.

61. Dissenting opinion of WOD, 2nd draft, Nov. 4, 1971, WOD Papers.

62. TM, Draft Opinion in *Stanley*, 5, Nov. 1971, TM Papers, Box 91, Folder 5.

63. For more, see Mayeri, "Intersectionality and the Constitution of Family Status," 399–400.

64. Barbara Underwood to TM, Feb. 4, 1972, TM Papers, Box 91, Folder 5.

65. Stanley v. Illinois, 405 U.S. 645, 656 (1972).

66. See Mayeri, "Foundling Fathers."

67. Facts in this paragraph come from Lynn Lilliston, "Father Vies for Custody of His Baby," *LAT*, Aug. 31, 1972.

68. See Lilliston, "Father Vies for Custody."

69. Lynn Lilliston, "Bill Spells Out Unwed Fathers' Rights," *LAT*, July 8, 1974.

70. Lilliston, "Bill Spells Out."

71. *Stanley*, 405 U.S. at 665 (Burger, C.J., dissenting).

72. Ruth-Arlene W. Howe, "Adoption Practice, Issues, and Laws 1958–1983," 17 *Fam. L. Quarterly* 173, 186–87 (1983).

73. Fiallo v. Bell, 430 U.S. 787 (1977).

74. Gene Comey, Bobtail Bench Memorandum, No. 75–6297, Fiallo v. Levi, Dec. 6, 1976, at 4, LFP Papers; Mayeri, "Marital Supremacy," 1330 n. 334.

75. *Fiallo*, 430 U.S. at 800 (Marshall, J., dissenting).

76. These facts are taken from the Transcript of Hearing, Quilloin v. Walcott, No. C-18673 (Ga. Sup. Ct. July 12, 1976), in Joint Appendix, Quilloin v. Walcott, 424 U.S. 246 (1978) (No. 76–6372). See also Mayeri, "Foundling Fathers," 2335–37.

77. Joint Appendix, *Quilloin*, 59.

78. Joint Appendix, *Quilloin*, 57.

79. Gayle White, "Who'll Rescue the Children in Limbo?," *Atlanta Constitution*, Jan. 5, 1979, 1B; Brief of the State of Georgia in Support of Appellee's Motion to Dismiss, *Quilloin*.

80. Quilloin v. Walcott, 238 Ga. 230, 232 (1977).

81. The very same year Georgia revised its law to allow fathers to petition for legal parental status after the filing of an adoption petition. The change came too late, however, for Quilloin.

82. See Daniel Ross, Note, "Rethinking the Road to *Gault:* Limiting Social Control in the Juvenile Court, 1957–1972," 98 *Virginia L. Rev.* 455 (2012); Christopher Manfredi, *The Supreme Court and Juvenile Justice* (University Press of Kansas, 1997).

83. Memorandum from Rena K. Uviller, Director, Juvenile Rights Project, ACLU, to Affiliates, Re: Juvenile Rights Docket, July 22, 1974, at 1–6, ACLU—Juvenile Rights Project Folder.

84. Between 1961 and 1974, the number of children in foster care in the United States tripled. See David Chambers and Michael S. Wald, "Part III: Smith v. OFFER: The Setting," in *In the Interest of Children: Advocacy, Law Reform, and Public Policy*, ed. Robert H. Mnookin (W.H. Freeman, 1985), 69.

85. Indian Child Welfare Act of 1977: Hearing on S. 1214 Before the U.S. Senate Select Committee on Indian Affairs, 95th Cong. 184 (1977) (statement of Rena Uviller, Director, Juvenile Rights Project, ACLU).

86. Arends v. Arends, 517 P.2d 1019 (Utah 1974); see JRP Docket, 12.

87. Tom Goldstein, "Melvin L. Wulf Quits as Legal Director of ACLU," *NYT,* Jan. 13, 1977.

88. Memorandum from Rena Uviller to Bruce Ennis, 1–2, July 7, 1977, ACLU Records, Box 2881, Folder: Quilloin.

89. See Wolfgang Saxon, "Bruce J. Ennis, 60, Lawyer Who Fought for Civil Liberties," *NYT,* Aug. 2, 2000.

90. Memorandum from Bruce J. Ennis to General Counsel Mailing List, 2–3 (July 6, 1977), ACLU Records, Box 2881, Folder: Quilloin.

91. Jim Alt to LFP, Nov. 7, 1977, LFP Papers, Box 196; Mayeri, "Foundling Fathers," 2340.

92. Oral Argument at 10:45, Quilloin v. Walcott, 434 US 246 (1978) (No. 76–6372), www.oyez.org/cases/1977/76–6372 [https://perma.cc/2JLE-JRQ5].

93. Quilloin v. Walcott, 434 U.S. 246, 256 (1978).

94. On the differences between the Court's approaches to *Quilloin* and to *Caban*, see Murray, "What's So New About the New Illegitimacy."

95. Ennis memo, 3; Mayeri, "Foundling Fathers," 2343.

96. Brief of the American Civil Liberties Union, Amicus Curiae, *Caban*, No. 77–6431, 1978 WL 207160.

97. Caban v. Mohammed, 441 U.S. 380 (1979) (Stevens, J., dissenting).

98. Parham v. Hughes (Ga. Super. Ct. Richmond Cnty. Sep. 13, 1977), in Appendix at 3, Parham v. Hughes, 441 U.S. 347 (No. 78–3).

99. Order, Parham v. Hughes, in Joint Appendix, *Parham*, 6.

100. Glona v. American Guarantee, 391 U.S. 73 (1968); see chapter 2.

101. Parham v. Hughes, 441 U.S. 347, 355–56 (1979).

102. Trimble v. Gordon, 432 U.S. 762 (1977).

103. *Parham*, 441 U.S. at 353. I describe *Parham* in similar terms in Serena Mayeri, "The State of Illegitimacy After the Civil Rights Revolution," in *Intimate States: Gender, Sexuality, and Governance in Modern U.S. History*, ed. Margot Canaday, Nancy F. Cott, and Robert O. Self (University of Chicago Press, 2021), 243–44.

104. *Parham*, 441 U.S. at 353 (emphasis added). See also Lalli v. Lalli, 439 U.S. 259 (1978).

105. Rena Uviller, "Fathers' Rights and Feminism: The Maternal Presumption Revisited," 1 *Harvard Women's L. J.* 107, 117, 116, 130 (1978). "The vast majority of mothers below the poverty line are single, either never married, separated, or divorced," Uviller wrote. "For them, the notion of shared child care . . . is sheer abstraction." Uviller, "Fathers' Rights," 119.

106. Dinner, "Divorce Bargain," 121–22.

107. Dinner, "Divorce Bargain," 122–23.

108. Dinner, "Divorce Bargain," 129–35.

109. Martha L. Fineman, "Implementing Equality," 1983 *Wisc. L. Rev.* 789.

110. Martha L. Fineman and Ann Opie, "The Uses of Social Science Data in Legal Policymaking: Custody Determinations at Divorce," 1987 *Wisc. L. Rev.* 107, 119. For a summary of these critiques, see Dinner, "Divorce Bargain," 142–44.

111. Nancy D. Polikoff, "Why Are Mothers Losing?: A Brief Analysis of Criteria Used in Child Custody Determinations," 7 *Women's Rights Law Reporter* 235, 237 (1982).

112. Appendix, *Kirkpatrick v. Christian Homes of Abilene*, No. 82-647, 103 S.Ct. 1760 (1983), 191a.

113. Appendix, *Kirkpatrick*, 151a, 191a.

114. In re K., 535 S.W.2d 168, 171 (Tex. 1976).

115. In re T.E.T., 603 S.W2d 793, 797 (Tex. 1980).

116. In re T.E.T., 603 S.W2d 793, 797 (Tex. 1980).

117. Mayeri, "Foundling Fathers," 2354–58.

118. Nancy S. Erickson, "The Feminist Dilemma over Unwed Parents' Custody Rights: The Mother's Rights Must Take Priority," 2 *Law & Inequality* 447, 454 (1984).

119. See ACLU Children's Rights Project Report (1983), 1–5.

120. The CRP believed such terminations to be equally destructive to the child as to the parent. ACLU CRP Report (1983), 14–16.

121. Brief for the Petitioner, *Kirkpatrick*, 31–32, 70–71.

122. Nancy S. Erickson, "The Other One: Life as a Feminist/Female Law Professor, 1975–1987," 80 *UMKC L. Rev.* 683 (2012).

123. See, for example, Nancy S. Erickson, "Equality Between the Sexes in the 1980s," 28 *Cleveland State L. Rev.* 591 (1979).

124. Brief of Nancy S. Erickson et al. as Amici Curiae on Behalf of Unwed Mothers, *Kirkpatrick*, 460 U.S. 1074 (No. 82-647).

125. Erickson, "Feminist Dilemma," 459, 463.

126. Erickson, "Feminist Dilemma," 465, 460.

127. Quoted in Erickson, "Feminist Dilemma," 460. And she asserted a woman's right to maintain anonymity when relinquishing her child for adoption. Erickson, "Feminist Dilemma," 462.

128. Erickson, "Feminist Dilemma," 455.

129. Erickson, "Feminist Dilemma," 470–71, 455.

130. Roe v. Wade, 410 U.S. 179, 221 (1973) (White, J., dissenting).

131. Washington v. Davis, 426 U.S. 229 (1976).

132. BRW, Draft Dissent from Denial of Certiorari in Kirkpatrick v. Christian Homes of Abilene, 2, Jan. 11, 1983, No. 82–647, LFP Papers, Box 250. For more on the Court's internal machinations over *Kirkpatrick*, see Mayeri, "Foundling Fathers," 2357–58.

133. ACLU Children's Rights Project Report, Appendix: Current Docket and Related Activities.

134. Appendix, Lehr v. Robertson, 1981 U.S. Briefs Lexis 1756, at *13–14.

135. *Lehr* Appendix, *88-*90.

136. *Lehr* Appendix, *63.

137. LFP, handwritten annotations to Memorandum from D. Rives Kistler to LFP, 1 (Dec. 6, 1982), LFP Papers.

138. JPS, First Draft Opinion in Lehr v. Robertson, 8 n.12 (Oct. 1983) (No. 81–1756).

139. Elder Bruce C. Hafen and Marie K. Hafen, "Crossing Thresholds and Becoming Equal Partners," *Ensign*, August 2007.

140. Bruce C. Hafen, "The Constitutional Status of Marriage, Kinship, and Sexual Privacy—Balancing the Individual and Social Interests," 81 *Mich. L. Rev.* 463, 495 (1983).

141. Hafen, "Constitutional Status," 544, 471.

142. Hafen's assessment was shared by some liberal legal scholars, such as Thomas Grey, spouse of the feminist law professor Barbara Babcock. See Thomas C. Grey, "Eros, Civilization and the Burger Court," 43 *Law & Contemp. Probs.* 83 (1980).

143. JPS, First Draft Opinion in *Lehr v. Robertson*, No. 81–1756, at 19 (Oct. 1983) (citation omitted), BRW Papers, box I-600, folder 81–1756. The discussion in Stevens's *Lehr* draft is remarkably similar to his opinion in *Miller v. Albright* fifteen years later (discussed in chapter 9). See Miller v. Albright, 523 U.S. 420, 436 (1998). See also Kristin A. Collins, "When Fathers' Rights Are Mothers' Duties: The Failure of Equal Protection in *Miller v. Albright*," 109 *Yale L. J.* 1669 (2000).

144. SOC to JPS, 2 (May 23, 1983), LFP Papers.

145. See JPS, Second Draft Opinion in *Lehr v. Robertson*, 19 (May 25, 1983), LFP Papers.

146. Lehr v. Robertson, 463 U.S. 248, 267 (1983).

147. See Ron Haskins et al., "How Much Child Support Can Absent Fathers Pay?," *Policy Studies Journal*, vol. 14, no. 2 (1985): 201–22; Clare Huntington, "Post-Marital Family Law: A Legal Structure for Nonmarital Families," 67 *Stanford L. Rev.* 167, 205–8 (2016).

Chapter 8. The Functional Family

1. Marjorie Spruill, *Divided We Stand: The Battle Over Women's Rights and Family Values That Polarized American Politics* (Bloomsbury, 2017), 299.

2. Robert O. Self, *All in the Family: The Realignment of American Democracy Since the 1960s* (Hill & Wang, 2012), 336.

3. Marta Martinez-Aleman, "Families Face Challenges in '80s," *Herald-Statesman* (White Plains, N.Y.), Nov. 23, 1979.

4. John T. McGowan, "NOW Hits Laws That Penalize New Style Families," *Courier-News*, Nov. 23, 1979.

5. "Assembly Removes Family Issue From the Right, But . . .," *Off Our Backs*, vol. 10, no. 3 (March 1980), 12. See NOW Legal Defense and Education Fund, *National Assembly on the Future of the Family: A Report*, Nov. 19, 1979, at 23.

6. On the role of HIV/AIDS in the movement for marriage equality, see George Chauncey, *Why Marriage?: The History Shaping Today's Debate Over Gay Equality* (Basic Books, 2005).

7. See, for example, Los Angeles Task Force on Family Diversity, Final Report: "Strengthening Families: A Model for Community Action," 3; Thomas F. Coleman, "The Family Is Changing and We Should Admit It," *LAT*, July, 26, 1989. On domestic partnerships in California, see Douglas NeJaime, "Before Marriage: The Unexplored History of Nonmarital Recognition," 102 *Calif. L. Rev.* 87 (2014); Melissa Murray, "Paradigms Lost: How Domestic Partnership Went from Innovation to Injury," 37 *NYU Rev. L. & Social Change* 291 (2013); William Eskridge and Christopher Riano, *Marriage Equality: From Outlaws to In-Laws* (Yale University Press, 2020), 65–69; Marie-Amélie George, *Family Matters: Queer Households and the Half-Century Struggle for Legal Recognition* (Cambridge University Press, 2024), chapter 3.

8. Final Report of the Mayor's Task Force on Family Policy, Approaching 2000: Meeting the Challenges to San Francisco's Families, June 13, 1990, at 1, ACLU Records (emphasis added).

9. L.A. Task Force Report, 18–21, 81–85.

10. Memorandum from the Human Relations and Welfare Commission to the Honorable Mayor and Members of the City Council, Re: Proposed Policy Establishing "Domestic Partnerships," July 17, 1984, at 4 (hereinafter Berkeley Report).

11. Berkeley Report, 16, 10.

12. Berkeley Report, 16–18. The commission saw its role as "responding to a particular set of complaints about unequal treatment," not "to make the benefits programs generally better."

13. Domestic partners also could not be wed to anyone else. Berkeley Report, 17.

14. Berkeley Report, 17. In order to disband one partnership and enter into another, couples had to wait a comparable period to that required for a married couple to divorce. Berkeley Report, 18.

15. The following year, Hilliard would appear on the cover of *Newsweek* with his partner Bobbi Campbell. Campbell and Hilliard died of AIDS within months of each other in 1984.

16. Harry Britt, to Friends, Oct. 20, 1982.

17. Mayor Dianne Feinstein to the Board of Supervisors, Dec. 9, 1982, at 2.

18. Report to the Mayor from the Mayor's Health Benefits Task Force, July 1984, at 7.

19. Report to the Mayor, 8–11.

20. Unmarried heterosexual partners could marry if they wished to obtain benefits, they reasoned.

21. Robert Chow, "S.F. Supervisors OK 'Domestic Partner' Law," *LAT*, May 23, 1989. On San Francisco, see David L. Chambers, "Tales of Two Cities: AIDS and the Legal Recognition of Domestic Partnerships in San Francisco and New York," 2 *Law & Sexuality* 181 (1992). Los Angeles, too, framed its proposed legislation as equalizing benefits between employees (of any sex, romantic partners or not) who could marry and those who could not "but who nevertheless live in a marriage-like family relationship." LA Task Force Report, 7, 17.

22. Richard Green, Domestic Partner Benefits: A Status Report to the ACLU, Lesbian and Gay Rights Project, ACLU, June 1987. By 1994, the political scientist Charles Gossett found that legislation required that domestic partners conform to nearly all eligibility requirements for marriage, plus additional requirements such as sharing a residence. Charles W. Gossett, "Domestic Partnership Benefits," *Review of Public Personnel Administration*, vol. 14, no. 1 (1994): 64–84.

23. See Barbara Lightner oral history index, https://minds.wisconsin.edu/handle/1793/82601.

24. Barbara Cox, "'The Little Project': From Alternative Families to Domestic Partnerships to Same-Sex Marriage," 15 *Wisc. Women's L. J.* 77 (2000); Barbara J. Cox, "Choosing One's Family: Can the Legal System Address the Breadth of Women's Choices in Intimate Relationships?," 8 *St. Louis U. Pub. L. Rev.* 299 (1989); Barbara J. Cox, "Alternative Families: Obtaining Traditional Family Benefits Through Litigation, Legislation, and Collective Bargaining," 2 *Wisc. Women's L. J.* 1 (1986).

25. EOC Alternative Family Rights Task Force Minutes, Nov. 17, 1983, at 2; amended slightly in EOC Alternative Family Rights Task Force Minutes, Jan. 19, 1984, at 2.

26. EOC Alternative Family Rights Task Force Minutes, April 10, 1984, at 2; EOC Alternative Family Rights Task Force Minutes, March 15, 1984, at 2.

27. EOC Alternative Family Rights Task Force Minutes, April 10, 1984, at 1.

28. Cox worried that the city council might amend the zoning law to allow for smaller alternative families but not an unlimited number of co-residents; EOC Alternative Family Rights Task Force Minutes, April 10, 1984, at 3.

29. EOC Alternative Family Rights Task Force Minutes, May 17, 1984.

30. EOC Alternative Family Rights Task Force Minutes, April 10, 1984; Cox, "Choosing One's Family," 315–16; EOC Alternative Family Rights Task Force Minutes, July 19, 1984, at 2; EOC Alternative Family Rights Task Force Minutes, July 19, 1984, at 3.

31. Transcript of Public Hearing, 19; Alternative Family Rights Supported—Written Testimonies, 3. Joyce Wells "felt [the broader definition] allows individual[s] to *choose* to form a family and this is a new and precious thing" she was loath to give up. EOC Alternative Family Rights Task Force Minutes, November 15, 1984, at 2.

32. John F. Dolm, Madison Apartment Association, to EOC Task Force, Re: Alternative Family Definition, Feb. 15, 1985.

33. Transcript of Public Hearing, 30.

34. Trudy Dyreson to Whom It May Concern, Dec. 13, 1983; Transcript of Public Hearing, 55.

35. Transcript of Public Hearing, 17.

36. Cox, "Choosing One's Family," 312–13.

37. The bill was supported by AFSCME and 1199W/United Professionals.

38. Transcript of Public Hearing, 54.

39. Lightner estimated a cost increase of no more than 1 or 2 percent. Transcript of Public Hearing, 25–27.

40. Transcript of Public Hearing, 40–41; Margaret McMurray, President, Madison NOW, to the Madison Equal Opportunities Commission, May 24, 1985, at 1–2.

41. Alderman James McFarland, Proposed Alternative Family Rights Ordinance, Report of the MEOC, Oct. 21, 1987.

42. The Reverend Richard E. Pritchard, a local white minister who had once marched with Martin Luther King, Jr., spouted disparaging and dehumanizing rhetoric that alienated his former civil rights allies. See, for example, AP, "Cleric Fights Sex Bill, Loses Liberal Support," *Marshfield News Herald* (Wisc.), May 4, 1983.

43. Quoted in Memorandum from Madison Institute for Social Legislation to Madison Equal Opportunities Commission, Participating Labor Union Locals, June 20, 1985, Re: Alternative Family Survey to Madison Labor Unions (Labor Unions Survey Memo).

44. Transcript of Public Hearing, 43; Labor Unions Survey Memo.

45. I borrow the term "taxpayer citizenship" from Camille Walsh, *Racial Taxation: Schools, Segregation, and Taxpayer Citizenship, 1869–1973* (University of North Carolina Press, 2018).

46. Labor Unions Survey Memo; Bill Taylor to MEOC, Oct. 15, 1984.

47. Labor Unions Survey Memo.

48. Transcript of Public Hearing, 61; Cox, "Choosing One's Family," 314.

49. Alderman James McFarland, Proposed Alternative Family Rights Ordinance, Report of the MEOC, Oct. 21, 1987, at 1.

50. McFarland, 5–7. The report estimated that the cost to the city would be approximately $42,000.

51. Cox, "Choosing One's Family," 320.

52. Compare Cox, "Alternative Families," 5.

53. Cox, "Choosing One's Family," 321–22, passim.

54. Cox, "Choosing One's Family?," 335; see also Stephen Vider, "What Happened to the Functional Family," in *Intimate States: Gender, Sexuality, and Governance in Modern U.S. History*, ed. Margot Canaday, Nancy F. Cott, and Robert O. Self (University of Chicago Press, 2021).

55. David W. Dunlap, "Thomas Stoddard, 48, Dies; An Advocate of Gay Rights," *NYT*, Feb. 14, 1997; Eskridge and Riano, *Marriage Equality*, 59–60.

56. Tom Stoddard, "Why Gay People Should Seek the Right to Marry," *OUT/Look*, Fall 1989, at 11–12.

57. Stoddard, "Why Gay People," 12.

58. Stoddard, "Why Gay People," 13. Stoddard married his partner shortly before dying of AIDS in 1997. Eskridge and Riano, *Marriage Equality*, 79–80.

59. Paula Ettelbrick, "Since When Is Marriage the Path to Liberation?," *OUT/Look*, Fall 1989, 16.

60. Ettelbrick, "Since When," 14, 16.

61. Ettelbrick, "Since When," 17; Eskridge and Riano, *Marriage Equality*, 76–77.

62. NeJaime, "Nonmarital Recognition."

63. Shortly after he was first elected in 1983, Scondras had unsuccessfully requested city health insurance benefits for his "partner and legal companion . . . and . . . spouse." Brian C. Mooney, "Four Councilors Say They'd Back Benefits for Unmarried Pairs," *Boston Globe*, July 26, 1989. Scondras sponsored the successful effort to add sexual orientation to the city's antidiscrimination law in 1985. By 1989, the city council's composition had shifted, and he led a "Gang of Four" that supported a bill to extend city employee benefits to unmarried couples.

64. Kay Langcope, "Gay Couples Fight For Spousal Rights," *Boston Globe*, Mar. 4, 1991.

65. David Scondras, *Angels, Liars, and Thieves, Book 3: The Coup*, 1st ed. (self-published, 2016), 44.

66. See Adrian Walker, "Scondras Riding Out Personal Storms," *Boston Sunday Globe*, April 4, 1993.

67. Scondras, *The Coup*, 133–34.

68. Committee for Family Protection, Summary: The Family Protection Act, [n.d., 1990?], Cornell Human Sexuality Collection, #7644, Domestic Partners folder.

69. Don Aucoin, "Not Confused with 'The Quiet Man,'" Notes from the Hill and the Hall, *Boston Globe*, Oct. 31, 1991.

70. AP, "'Domestic Partners' Act Passed," *The Transcript* (North Adams, Mass.), Jan. 28, 1993.

71. Kay Longcope, "Religious Leaders, Gay Groups, Back Bill to Redefine 'Family,'" *Boston Globe*, May 16, 1991; Kay Longcope, "Council Expected to Take Up Matter of Defining Family Unit," *Boston Globe*, June 26, 1991. On Reform Jewish leaders and marriage equality in Massachusetts, see Sarah Barringer Gordon, *The Spirit of the Law: Religious Voices and the Constitution in Modern America* (Harvard University Press, 2010).

72. AP, " 'Domestic Partners' Act Passed," *North Adams (Mass.) Transcript*, Jan. 28, 1993. For more on the FPA, see Committee for Family Protection, Summary: The Family Protection Act, [n.d., 1990?], Cornell Human Sexuality Collection, #7644, Domestic Partners folder.

73. Scondras, *The Coup*, 135.

74. Longcope, "Council Expected to Take Up Matter of Defining Family Unit."

75. Kay Longcope, "Domestic Partnership Bill Defeated," *Boston Globe*, June 27, 1991, at 31.

76. Longcope, "Domestic Partnership Bill Defeated."

77. "New City Council Eyes a Middle Class Agenda," *Boston Globe*, Jan. 3, 1994.

78. Adrian Walker, "Coverage Proposed for Gay City Workers' Partners," *Boston Globe*, Feb. 14, 1995.

79. The commission included three members each from those constituencies, along with five non-voting members from city government. Eleven of the commission's twenty-five members identified as gay or lesbian, though only three represented gay organizations. See Handwritten notes, n.d., CG Papers, Folder: DC: Domestic Partners; Franklin Kameny to James Mercer, Deputy Director, D.C. Office of Human Rights, Jan. 1, 1990, CG Papers.

80. District of Columbia Commission on Domestic Partnership Benefits for D.C. Government Employees, Final Report and Recommendations, July 1990, Volume 1, at 2, 10, ACLU Records.

81. Rene Sanchez, "Wilson Proposes Domestic Partners Bill with DC Benefits," *WP*, Mar. 28, 1991, C1.

82. The District of Columbia's Health Care Benefits Expansion Act of 1992, ACLU Records.

83. Kent Jenkins, Jr., "Kelly Defies Congress on Partners Law," *WP*, Oct. 4, 1992, A12.

84. Rep. Ernest Istook et al., to Colleagues, Re: Support the Istook Amendment to Block D.C.'s "Domestic Partners" Law, June 28, 1993, ACLU Records, Box 4383, Folder: DC: Domestic Partners.

85. Gary Bauer, President, Family Research Council, to Members of Congress, June 25, 1993, ACLU Records, Box 4383, Folder: DC: Domestic Partners; Urvashi Vaid, *Virtual Equality: The Mainstreaming of Gay and Lesbian Liberation* (Anchor, 1995), 191.

86. Rev. Louis P. Sheldon, Traditional Values Coalition, Chairman, June 24, 1993, ACLU Records, Box 4383, Folder: DC: Domestic Partners.

87. Marshall Wittmann, Director, Legislative Affairs, and Heidi Scanlon, Director, Governmental Affairs, Christian Coalition, to Members of Congress, June 25, 1993, ACLU Records, Box 4383, Folder: DC: Domestic Partners.

88. Testimony of U.S. Rep. Clyde C. Holloway Before the Subcommittee on Fiscal Affairs and Health, June 4, 1992, ACLU Records, Box 4383.

89. Statement of Reverend John Mack, First Congregational Church of Christ, for Concerned Clergy of Washington, D.C., June 2, 1992, ACLU Records, Box 4383.

90. Rev. John Mack, "Health Benefits Bill Is Pro-Family," *Washington Blade*, n.d., ACLU Records, Box 4383; Statement of the Reverend Gigi Conner, Assistant Rector, St. Paul's Episcopal Church, Rock Creek, May 26, 1992, ACLU Records, Box 4383.

91. "DC's Health Care Benefits Expansion Act," ACLU Records, Box 4383.

92. Mack, "Health Benefits Bill Is Pro-Family."

93. Rene Sanchez, "D.C. Moves to Give Unmarried Couples Legal Recognition, Expanded Benefits," *WP*, Mar. 4, 1992, A1; Handwritten Notes, n.d., CG Papers.

94. Maggie S. Tucker, "DC Domestic Partners Go On the Record Despite Law's Limits," *WP*, June 29, 1993, B1. Mark D. Agrast, Secretary, National Lesbian and Gay Law Association, to Members, Friends, and Affiliates of NLGLA, May 6, 1992, ACLU Records, Box 4383.

95. Handwritten Notes, n.d., CG Papers.

96. See Mack, "Health Benefits Bill Is Pro-Family." As Gossett confided, though, the expansion of benefit eligibility to adult relatives beyond "spouse equivalents" threatened a significant additional fiscal burden that supporters avoided discussing publicly. Handwritten Notes, n.d., CG Papers.

97. Congresswoman Eleanor Holmes Norton News, Press Release, "Norton Seeks Repeal of Ban on D.C. Abortion Funding and Domestic Partnership ..." Feb. 3, 1993, ACLU Records, Box 4383; Tim McFeeley, Executive Director, Human Rights Campaign, to President George H. W. Bush, April 22, 1992, ACLU Records, Box 4383. Not all supporters of home rule endorsed the domestic partners law. See Maggie S. Tucker, "DC Domestic Partners Go On the Record Despite Law's Limits," *WP*, June 29, 1993, B1; Lou Chibbaro, Jr., "Activists Work to Block Anti-Gay Amendment," *Washington Blade*, July 1, 1994.

98. Cox, "'The Little Project,'" 86.

99. Barbara Cox, "From One Town's 'Alternative Families' Ordinance to Marriage Equality Nationwide," 42 *California Western L. Rev.* 65, 70 (2015).

100. Scondras, *The Coup*, 135.

101. See Elizabeth Pleck, *Not Just Roommates: Cohabitation After the Sexual Revolution* (University of Illinois Press, 2012), chapter 10; NeJaime, "Nonmarital Recognition"; George, *Family Matters*, chapter 3.

102. Scott Cummings and Douglas NeJaime, "Lawyering for Marriage Equality," 57 *UCLA L. Rev.* 1235, 1257–58 (2013).

103. See, for example, Paula Ettelbrick, "Domestic Partnership, Civil Unions, or Marriage: One Size Does Not Fit All," 64 *Albany L. Rev.* 905, 914 (2001).

104. The legal scholars Linda McClain and Doug NeJaime argue that the ALI's family law Principles are "an important authority that, operating in dialogue with courts, legislatures, advocates, and scholars, has contributed to and advanced a progressive agenda in family law." Linda C. McClain and Douglas NeJaime, "The ALI Principles of the Law of Family Dissolution: Addressing Family Inequality Through Functional Regulation," in *The American Law Institute: A Centennial History*, ed. Andrew S. Gold and Robert W. Gordon (Oxford University Press, 2023).

105. Minutes of Meeting of ALI Ad Hoc Committee on Family Law, Oct. 25, 1985 (prepared by Michael Greenwald), 2. In attendance were Geoffrey Hazard, Robert Burt, David Chambers, Mary Ann Glendon, Herma Hill Kay, Patricia King, Robert Levy, Marygold Melli, Martha Minow, Frank Sander, and Lenore Weitzman. All ALI documents are from the collection in Biddle Law Library, University of Pennsylvania Carey Law School.

106. With an eye toward "responsibilities as well as rights." Minutes of Meeting of ALI Ad Hoc Committee on Family Law, Oct. 25, 1985 (prepared by Michael Greenwald), 3.

107. Judith Areen to Geoffrey Hazard, July 30, 1985, at 3; Memorandum from Margo S. Melli to Geoffrey Hazard, June 14, 1985, Re: Some Thoughts on the Scope of a Restatement of the Law of Family Relationships, 4.

108. See, for example, Memorandum from Jack Coons to Herma Kay, Oct. 9, 1985, Re: "Restatement" of Family Law, 1; Memorandum from Marygold S. Melli, Reporter for Project on Principles of Law Governing Family Dissolution to Participants in Conference on the Law and Public Policy of Family Dissolution, Re: Agenda for meeting on November 16–18, 1989, at Wingspread, Racine, Wisconsin, October 12, 1989.

109. Memorandum from Robert Mnookin to Geoffrey Hazard and Ad Hoc Committee on Family Law, October 12, 1985, Re: October 25 meeting.

110. Memorandum from Marygold S. Melli, Reporter for Project on Principles of Law Governing Family Dissolution to Participants in Conference on the Law and Public Policy of Family Dissolution, Re: Agenda for meeting on November 16–18, 1989, at Wingspread, Racine, Wisconsin, October 12, 1989.

111. Joan F. Kessler, "Oral History of Marygold S. Melli," Fall 2005, ABA Senior Lawyers Division, Women Trailblazers in the Law, 59. On Melli, see Herma Hill Kay, *Paving the Way: The First American Women Law Professors* (University of California Press, 2021), chapter 6.

112. [Marygold Melli], Background Paper, Conference on the Law and Public Policy of Family Dissolution, [Nov. 1989?], at 9.

113. For more, see McClain and NeJaime, "ALI Principles," 341–45.

114. Ira Ellman, ALI Council Draft No. 1, Nov. 22, 1993.

115. These proposals did not go as far as feminist reformers such as Carol Bruch would have liked. See McClain and NeJaime, "ALI Principles," 345.

116. [Marygold Melli], Background Paper, Conference on the Law and Public Policy of Family Dissolution, [Nov. 1989?], 15–16.

117. Grace Ganz Blumberg, "Sexism in the Code: A Comparative Study of Income Taxation of Working Wives and Mothers," 21 *Buffalo L. Rev.* 49 (1971).

118. Grace Ganz Blumberg, "Adult Derivative Benefits in Social Security," 32 *Stanford L. Rev.* 233 (1980).

119. Grace Ganz Blumberg, "Cohabitation Without Marriage: A Different Perspective," 28 *UCLA L. Rev.* 1125 (1981).

120. Blumberg, "Cohabitation," 1138–39.

121. Blumberg, "Cohabitation," 1160–63.

122. Blumberg, "Cohabitation," 1160, 1163–64.

123. Of *quantum meruit*, which measured a woman's reimbursable contributions by the cost of outsourcing them, Blumberg wrote: "she is valued at a maid's salary," a "degrading or useless formulation of the role and value of a homemaker." Blumberg, "Cohabitation," 1164–66.

124. Blumberg, "Cohabitation," 1167.

125. ALI Prelim Draft No. 6, Aug. 8, 1996. The qualifying duration would be determined by each jurisdiction/state.

126. ALI Prelim Draft No. 6, Aug. 8, 1996.

127. ALI Principles, Section 6.03.

128. Blumberg characterized the domestic partnership factors as a "long list of rarely required proof criteria" that would apply only to individuals who had *not* "maintained a common household with a common child." Memo from Grace Blumberg, Sept. 24, 1999, re: Ch. 6 on DPs, ALI Prelim Draft No. 9, Sept. 30, 1999.

129. ALI Principles, section 6.03.

130. Karen S. Peterson, "After 10-Year Study, Judicial Group Equates Married, Non-Married Couples," *USA Today*, Dec. 6, 2002.

131. Peterson, "After 10-Year Study."

132. Lynn D. Wardle, "Deconstructing Family: A Critique of the American Law Institute's 'Domestic Partners' Proposal," 2001 *BYU L. Rev.* 1189 (2001); see also McClain and NeJaime, "ALI Principles," 349–50. On Wardle's opposition to same-sex marriage, see Eskridge and Riano, *Marriage Equality*, 92–94.

133. Garrison had long criticized the "conscription" of cohabiting couples into marriage. See chapter 3.

134. Marsha Garrison, "Marriage Matters: What's Wrong with the ALI's Domestic Partnership Proposal," in *Reconceiving the Family: Critique on the American Law Institute's Principles of the Law of Family Dissolution*, ed. Robin Fretwell Wilson (Cambridge University Press, 2006), 305.

135. David Westfall, "Forcing Incidents of Marriage on Unmarried Cohabitants: The American Law Institute's Principles of the Law of Family Dissolution," 76 *Notre Dame L. Rev.* 1467 (2001).

136. Margaret F. Brinig, "Domestic Partnership: Missing the Target?," 4 *J. L. & Fam. Stud.* 19, 35 (2002).

137. Elizabeth S. Scott, "Marriage, Cohabitation and Collective Responsibility for Dependency," 2004 *U. Chi. Legal Forum* 225.

138. Elizabeth S. Scott, "Domestic Partnerships, Implied Contracts, and Law Reform," in Wilson, *Reconceiving the Family*, 345, 349.

139. Mark Strasser, "A Small Step Forward: The ALI Domestic Partners Recommendation," 2001 *BYU L. Rev.* 1135, 1136.

140. Terry S. Kogan, "Competing Approaches to Same-Sex Versus Opposite-Sex, Unmarried Couples in Domestic Partnership Laws and Ordinances," 2001 *BYU L. Rev.* 1023.

141. Nancy D. Polikoff, "Making Marriage Matter Less: The ALI Domestic Partner Principles Are One Step in the Right Direction," 2004 *U. Chi. Legal Forum* 353 (2004).

142. See, for example, Katherine M. Franke, "Longing for *Loving*," 76 *Fordham L. Rev.* 2685 (2008).

143. See chapter 7.

144. Nora Lauerman, "Nonmarital Sexual Conduct and Child Custody," 46 *U. Cin. L. Rev.* 647, 655–57 (1977). The question was "not one of abstract morals" but "rather whether the mother's indiscretions" had or would harm the "welfare of the children." Moore v. Moore, 150 A.2d 194 (Del. Sup. Ct. 1959) (quoting People ex rel. Geismar v. Geismar, 54 N.Y.S.2d 747, 755).

145. Jones v. Haraway, 537 So. 2d 946 (Ala. Civ. App. 1988) (Ingram, J., dissenting in part) (discussing Brown v. Brown, 218 Va. 196, 237 S.E.2d 89 [1977]).

146. Jarrett v. Jarrett, 78 Ill. 2d 337 (1979). For more on *Jarrett*, see Pleck, *Not Just Roommates*.

147. Lauerman, 658–59; Wildermuth v. Wildermuth, 542 P.2d 463 (Wash. Ct. App. 1975).

148. On custody and parentage cases involving gay and lesbian parents, see Carlos Ball, *The Right to Be Parents: LGBT Families and the Transformation of Parenthood* (NYU Press, 2012); George, *Family Matters*, chapters 2 and 4.

149. Nan D. Hunter and Nancy D. Polikoff, "Custody Rights of Lesbian Mothers: Legal Theory and Litigation Strategy," 25 *Buffalo L. Rev.* 691, 701 (1976).

150. Hunter and Polikoff, "Custody Rights," 707–8.

151. Hunter and Polikoff, "Custody Rights," 705.

152. See also Daniel Winuwe Rivers, *Radical Relations: Lesbian Mothers, Gay Fathers, and Their Children in the United States Since World War II* (University of North Carolina Press, 2013); Kimberly Richman, *Courting Change: Queer Parents, Judges, and the Transformation of American Family Law* (NYU Press, 2008).

153. Schuster v. Schuster, 585 P.2d 130 (1978); Ball, *Right to Be Parents*, 21–26, 38–39.

154. Irish v. Irish, 300 N.W.2d 739, 741 (Mich. 1980).

155. Rosalie Davies and Minna F. Weinstein, "Confronting the Courts," in *Lesbians and Child Custody: A Casebook*, ed. Delores J. Maggiore (Taylor-Francis, 1992), 34–35.

156. Ball, *Right to Be Parents*, 25–32; see also George, *Family Matters*, 62–63; Alison Lefkovitz, *Strange Bedfellows: Marriage in the Age of Women's Liberation* (University of Pennsylvania Press, 2018), 168.

157. Davies and Weinstein, "Confronting the Courts."

158. Rivers, *Radical Relations*, chapter 4; Ball, *Right to Be Parents*, 37; Geraldine Cole et al., "Lesbian Mothers' National Defense Fund: Lesbian Mothers Fight Back: Organizers' Dialogue," *Quest: A Feminist Quarterly* (1979): 62.

159. Hunter and Polikoff, "Custody Rights," 716–17. The Lesbian Mothers' National Defense Fund offered similar advice in 1979. Cole et al., "Lesbian Mothers," 66.

160. Sue Overstreet, "No Apology Offered," in *Politics of the Heart: A Lesbian Parenting Anthology*, ed. Sandra Pollack and Jeanne Vaughn (Firebrand Books, 1986), 38–39.

161. Minnie Bruce Pratt, "The Child Taken From the Mother," in Pollack and Vaughn, *Politics of the Heart*, 29. On Pratt, see Julie R. Enszer, "When We Say We Love Each Other: Loving the Life and Work of Minnie Bruce Pratt," *Lambda Literary Review*, July 3, 2023.

162. Stephanie Salter, "A Cruel Close to the Case of Mary Ward," *S.F. Examiner*, Jan. 28, 1997. Ward died of a heart attack at age forty-seven while her appeal was pending.

163. Maggiore, *Lesbians and Child Custody*; Rivers, *Radical Relations*, chapters 3–4. Litigation's primary value lay in "educational and consciousness-raising work on underlying issues," yet publicity could "destroy the chance of victory." Nan Hunter and Nancy Polikoff, "Lesbian Mothers Fight Back: An Organizers' Dialogue: Political and Legal Strategies," *Quest: A Feminist Quarterly* (1979), 56.

164. Ball, *Right to Be Parents*.

165. Nancy D. Polikoff, "Why Are Mothers Losing?: A Brief Analysis of Criteria Used in Child Custody Determinations," 7 *Women's Rights Law Reporter* 235 (1982).

166. Polikoff, "Why Are Mothers Losing?"

167. Ball, *Right to Be Parents*, 46–48.

168. Nancy Polikoff, "Lesbian Mothers, Lesbian Families: Legal Obstacles, Legal Challenges," 14 *NYU Rev. L. & Social Change* 907, 907–8 (1986).

169. AP, "Opposition Lifted on Adoption by Gays," *LAT*, Nov. 23, 1999.

170. See, for example, Maria Gil de Lamadrid, "Lesbians Choosing Motherhood: Legal Implications of Co-Parenting," in Maggiore, *Lesbians and Child Custody*, 195–200.

171. See cases cited in Nancy Polikoff, "This Child Does Have Two Mothers: Redefining Parenthood to Meet the Needs of Children in Lesbian-Mother and Other Nontraditional Families," 78 *Georgetown L. J.* 459 (1990); Paula Ettelbrick, "Who Is a Parent? The Need to Develop a Lesbian Conscious Family Law," 10 *N.Y. L. Sch. J. Hum. Rts.* 513, 522 (1993).
172. Ettelbrick wrote in 1993 of "hundreds, if not thousands, of cases in which courts have recognized the functional parental relationship and given it some legal effect." Ettelbrick, "Who Is a Parent?," 530.
173. Polikoff, "This Child Does Have Two Mothers"; Douglas NeJaime, "Marriage Equality and the New Parenthood," 129 *Harvard L. Rev.* 1185 (2016).
174. For a comprehensive review of functional parenthood cases between 1980 and 2016, see Courtney G. Joslin and Douglas NeJaime, "How Parenthood Functions," 123 *Columbia L. Rev.* 319, 329–45 (2023).
175. Katharine Bartlett, "Rethinking Exclusive Parenthood," 70 *Virginia L. Rev.* 879, 944 (1984).
176. Michael H. v. Gerald D., 491 U.S. 110 (1989). For more on *Michael H.*, see Serena Mayeri, "Foundling Fathers: (Non-)Marriage and Parental Rights in the Age of Equality," 125 *Yale L. J.* 2292, 2369–72 (2016).
177. See NeJaime, "Marriage Equality and the New Parenthood."
178. Ball, *Right to Be Parents*, 89–90.
179. Braschi v. Stahl Associates, 74 N.Y. 2d 201 (1989).
180. See Eskridge and Riano, *Marriage Equality*, 71–74.
181. Alison D. v. Virginia M., 77 N.Y.2d 651 (1991). "Similar functional indicia" comes from Ettelbrick, "Who Is a Parent?," 528. For more on *Alison D.*, see Ball, *Right to Be Parents*, 83–94; Suzanne B. Goldberg, "Litigating Law Reform: Unrecognized Parents and the Story of *Alison D. v. Virginia M.*," in *Family Law Stories*, ed. Carol Sanger (Foundation Press, 2007).
182. Nancy S. v. Michele G., 228 Cal. App.3d 831 (1991); Elaine Herscher, "For Nancy Springer, a 1991 Court Case Over Custody of Her Children Was a Victory, But . . .," *S.F. Chronicle*, Aug. 29, 1999.
183. Betty Levinson to Jane Doe and Jill Roe, Mar. 30, 1992, PE Papers, Box 1, Folder 14.
184. James Marks, Intake Checklist: Gay/Lesbian Second Parent Adoption, in PE Papers, Box 1, Folder 14 (quoting Section 115-d [5] of NY DRL).
185. ACLU committee draft report in PE papers, Box 1, Folder 14.
186. Memorandum of Points and Authorities in Support of Petitions for Adoption and Request for Hearing, In the Matter of the Petition of LS and VL For the Adoption of a Minor (M. & T.), Adoption No. 269–90, 270–90, D.C. Superior Court, Family Division, May 17, 1991, PE Papers, Box 1, Folder 1.
187. Memorandum, In the Matter of Petition of LS and VL, 3, PE Papers, Box 1, Folder 9. Memorandum, In the Matter of Petition of LS and VL, 4, PE Papers, Box 1, Folder 9; Ball, *Right to Be Parents*, 166.
188. By the end of 1993, Paula Ettelbrick estimated that between two hundred and three hundred second-parent adoptions had been granted around the

country, "mostly in major metropolitan areas." Paula Ettelbrick to Marjorie Fujiki, Re: Second-Parent Adoptions, Nov. 29, 1993, PE Papers, Box 1, Folder 9.

189. Polikoff, "This Child Does Have Two Mothers," 526.

190. Ball, *Right to Be Parents*, 115–29; Alexis Soloski, "In 'Nuclear Family,' A Filmmaker Frames Herself," *NYT Magazine*, Sept. 22, 2021. On gay fathers' custody disputes with ex-wives, see Ball, *Right to Be Parents*, chapter 2.

191. Polikoff, "Lesbian Mothers, Lesbian Families," 910.

192. Troxel v. Granville, 530 U.S. 57 (2000). See also Ariela R. Dubler, "Constructing the Modern American Family: The Stories of *Troxel v. Granville*," in *Family Law Stories*, ed. Carol Sanger (Foundation Press, 2007), 107.

193. Polikoff, "Lesbian Mothers, Lesbian Families," 910.

194. As they had in the stepfather adoption cases of the late 1970s; see chapter 7.

195. Joseph Goldstein, Anna Freud, and Albert J. Solnit, *Beyond the Best Interests of the Child* ([1973] Simon & Schuster, 1979), 98.

196. "Book Review," *Indian Family Defense*, cited in Laura Briggs, *Somebody's Children: A History of Transnational and Transracial Adoption* (Duke University Press, 2012), 87.

197. For a detailed account, see Chambers and Wald, part 3 (Smith v. OFFER), in *In the Interest of Children: Advocacy, Law Reform, and Public Policy*, ed. Robert H. Mnookin (W.H. Freeman, 1985).

198. Peggy C. Davis, "Use and Abuse of the Power to Sever Family Bonds," 12 *NYU Rev. L. & Social Change* 557 (1984).

199. See Joseph Goldstein, Anna Freud, and Albert J. Solnit, *Before the Best Interests of the Child* (Free Press, 1986), 4, 59–90; Peggy C. Davis, "'There Is a Book Out . . .': Judicial Absorption of Legislative Facts," 100 *Harvard L. Rev.* 1539, 1545 (1987).

200. Davis, "Use and Abuse," 557.

201. On how a modern version of psychological parenthood could transform family law for the better, see Anne L. Alstott, Anne C. Dailey, and Douglas NeJaime, "Psychological Parenthood," 106 *Minn. L. Rev.* 2363 (2022).

202. Davis, "Use and Abuse," 559, 569.

203. Polikoff, "Lesbian Mothers, Lesbian Families," 910.

204. Nan Hunter and Nancy Polikoff, "Lesbian Mothers Fight Back: An Organizers' Dialogue: Political and Legal Strategies," *Quest: A Feminist Quarterly* (1979), 55; see also Ellen Agger and Francie Wyland, "Lesbian Mothers Fight Back: Organizers' Dialogue: Wages Due Lesbians," *Quest: A Feminist Quarterly* (1979), 57–59; Cole et al., "Lesbian Mothers," 63. Grassroots lesbian feminist groups, too, viewed their custody activism as part of a broader challenge to capitalism and patriarchy. Rivers, *Radical Relations*, 81, 139.

205. Martha Minow, "Redefining Families: Who's In and Who's Out?," 62 *U. Colo. L. Rev.* 269 (1991).

206. See chapter 2; Linda Gordon, "The Perils of Innocence, or What's Wrong with Putting Children First," *Journal of the History of Childhood and Youth*, vol. 1, no. 3 (Fall 2008): 331–50.

207. Ettelbrick, "Who Is a Parent?," 548 n. 176.

208. Ettelbrick, "Who Is a Parent?," 548.

209. Polikoff, "This Child Does Have Two Mothers." Polikoff saw the "psychological parent" theory as "useful in assessing which of two parents with equal legal rights should get custody."

210. See Lynn Wardle to Marygold Melli, Nov. 12, 1992, ALI Records.

211. Section 7.215, Preliminary Draft No. 1: Rights and Responsibilities of Cohabitors in Parental Relationship with Child (1992?). When Katharine Bartlett became a reporter for ALI in 1995, the functional theory of parenthood gained ground in both custody and parentage provisions. See McClain and NeJaime, "ALI Principles," 353.

212. Robin Fretwell Wilson, "Undeserved Trust: Reflections on the ALI's Treatment of De Facto Parents," in Wilson, *Reconceiving the Family*. NeJaime and Joslin found in their empirical study of functional parenthood cases that such scenarios occurred rarely in their sample. Courtney Joslin and Douglas NeJaime, "Domestic Violence and Functional Parent Doctrines," 30 *Virginia J. Social Policy & L.* 67 (2023).

213. John DeWitt Gregory, "Blood Ties: A Rationale for Child Visitation by Legal Strangers," 55 *Wash. & Lee L. Rev.* 351, 400 (1998).

214. Lynn Wardle to Marygold Melli, Nov. 12, 1992.

215. Lynn Wardle, "The Potential Impact of Homosexual Parenting on Children," 1997 *U. of Illinois L. Rev.* 833. On the religious right and gay parenthood, see George, *Family Matters*, chapter 2.

216. Wardle to Melli, 1.

217. See NeJaime, "Marriage Equality and the New Parenthood."

218. Joslin and NeJaime's empirical study suggests that, at least in appellate cases, functional parenthood doctrines did not bear out skeptics' worst fears, instead preserving primary caregiving relationships—often between relatives. See Joslin and NeJaime, "How Parenthood Functions."

219. John J. Sampson, "Preface to the Amendments to the Uniform Parentage Act (2002)," 37 *Fam. L. Quarterly* 1, 1–4 (2003).

220. For more on the development of the ALI Principles' functional parenthood standards, see McClain and NeJaime, "The ALI Principles," 353–57. See also June Carbone and Naomi Cahn, "Marriage, Parentage, and Child Support," 45 *Fam. L. Q.* 219 (2011).

Chapter 9. Securing Marital Privilege

1. Personal Responsibility and Work Opportunity Reconciliation Act of 1996, Pub. L. 104–193, 110 Stat. 2110, 42 U.S.C. section 101 (Findings).

2. For a detailed account of states' sexual regulation of poor women under PRWORA, see Anna Marie Smith, "The Sexual Regulation Dimension of Contemporary Welfare Law: A Fifty State Overview," 8 *Mich. J. Gender & L.* 121 (2002). See also Khiara Bridges, *The Poverty of Privacy Rights* (Yale University Press, 2017); Anna Marie Smith, *Welfare Reform and Sexual Regulation* (Cambridge University Press, 2007); Marisa Chappell, *The War on Welfare: Family, Poverty, and Politics in Modern America* (University of Pennsylvania Press, 2010); Kaaryn Gustafson, *Cheating Welfare: Public Assistance and the Criminalization of Poverty* (NYU Press, 2011).

3. See, for example, Pew Research Center Report, "The Decline of Marriage and the Rise of New Families," Nov. 18, 2010; Richard D. Reeves and Christopher Pulliam, "Middle Class Marriage Is Declining, and Likely Deepening Inequality," Brookings Institution, Mar. 11, 2020; Pew Research Center, "The Reversal of the College Marriage Gap," Oct. 7, 2010.

4. Ellen Goodman, "Liberals: President Belies His Rhetoric," *Miami Herald*, Aug. 1, 1990.

5. On advocacy leading up to the passage of the FMLA, see Kirsten Swinth, *Feminism's Forgotten Fight: The Unfinished Struggle for Work and Family* (Harvard University Press, 2018); Ann O'Leary, "How Family Leave Laws Left Out Low-Income Workers," 28 *Berkeley J. Empl. & Labor L.* 1 (2007); Deborah Widiss, "Equalizing Parental Leave," 105 *Minn. L. Rev.* 2175 (2021); Megan Sholar, *Getting Paid While Taking Time: The Women's Movement and the Development of Paid Family Leave Policies in the United States* (Temple University Press, 2016).

6. See Widiss, "Equalizing Parental Leave."

7. Goodman, "Liberals." The FMLA also left out siblings. Jill Hasday, *Family Law Reimagined* (Harvard University Press, 2014), 163-65

8. Jill Quadagno, "Why the United States Has No National Health Insurance: Stakeholder Mobilization Against the Welfare State, 1945–1996," 45 *J. Health & Social Behavior* 25 (2004).

9. For an insider account by Paul Starr, see www.princeton.edu/~starr/20starr.html.

10. See Chai Feldblum, "The Federal Gay Civil Rights Bill: From Bella to ENDA," in *Creating Change: Sexuality, Public Policy, and Civil Rights*, ed. Urvashi Vaid et al. (St. Martin's Press, 2000).

11. Baehr v. Lewin, 852 P.2d 44 (Hawaii 1993); William Eskridge and Christopher Riano, *Marriage Equality: From Outlaws to In-Laws* (Yale University Press, 2020), chapters 4–5.

12. David L. Chambers, "Couples: Marriage, Civil Union, and Domestic Partnership," in Vaid et al., *Creating Change*, 293.

13. The General Accounting Office (GAO) estimated in 1997 that 1,049 federal laws incorporated marital status as a relevant factor. See GAO, Defense of Marriage Act: Update to Prior Report, Jan. 23, 2004.

14. On Kennedy's background and *Romer,* see Eskridge and Riano, *Marriage Equality,* 129–32.

15. Romer v. Evans, 517 U.S. 620 (1996).

16. For more on *Moreno,* see chapter 4.

17. Chambers, "Couples," 295; see also Eskridge and Riano, *Marriage Equality,* chapter 5.

18. DOMA garnered enough House votes to override a presidential veto.

19. For an account of internal machinations in the White House, see Sasha Issenberg, "Bill Clinton Tried to Avoid the DOMA Trap Republicans Set. Instead He Trapped Himself," *Politico,* Sept. 18, 2021.

20. According to Gallup: https://news.gallup.com/poll/1651/gay-lesbian-rights.aspx.

21. Sasha Issenberg, "Gay Rights Advanced Significantly in the Last 25 Years— No Thanks to Congress," *WP,* Sept. 17, 2021.

22. Lynn Fujiwara, "Asian Immigrant Communities and the Racial Politics of Welfare Reform," in *Whose Welfare?,* ed. Gwendolyn Mink (Cornell University Press, 1998), 105.

23. See Neeraj Kaushal and Robert Kaestner, "Welfare Reform and Health Insurance of Immigrants," *Health Services Research,* vol. 40, no. 3 (June 2005): 697–722.

24. Fujiwara, "Asian Immigrant Communities," 106.

25. Alison Lefkovitz, *Strange Bedfellows: Marriage in the Age of Women's Liberation* (University of Pennsylvania Press, 2018), 189.

26. Smith, "Sexual Regulation Dimension," 172–79.

27. Briggs, *Somebody's Children.*

28. Dorothy Roberts, *Torn Apart: How the Child Welfare System Destroys Black Families—And How Abolition Can Build a Safer World* (Basic Books, 2022), 121.

29. On the rise of mass incarceration, see, for example, Michelle Alexander, *The New Jim Crow: Mass Incarceration in the Age of Colorblindness* (New Press, 2d. ed., 2020); Naomi Murakawa, *The First Civil Right: How Liberals Built Prison America* (Oxford University Press, 2014); Elizabeth Hinton, *From the War on Poverty to the War on Crime: The Making of Mass Incarceration in America* (Harvard University Press, 2016).

30. Lily Geismer, *Left Behind: The Democrats' Failed Attempt to Solve Inequality* (Public Affairs, 2021).

31. On the roots of Clinton's welfare reform initiatives in 1980s Arkansas, see Geismer, *Left Behind.*

32. See Felicia Kornbluh and Gwendolyn Mink, *Ensuring Poverty: Welfare Reform in Feminist Perspective* (De Gruyter, 2019), 65–67.

33. Michael Wines, "Team in Place, Gingrich Comes Out Slugging," *NYT,* Dec. 7, 1994.

34. Smith, "Sexual Regulation Dimension," 145–47.

35. PRWORA's good cause exception for domestic violence marked a departure from detailed, non-discretionary pre-1996 federal regulations. See Smith, "Sexual Regulation Dimension," 156–58. Smith found "tremendous variation" among states' implementation strategies as of 2000, and she concluded that "only a very few states have adopted adequate policies." Smith, "Sexual Regulation Dimension," 158–59.

36. Smith, "Sexual Regulation Dimension," 144.

37. See generally Mink and Kornbluh, *Ensuring Poverty*, chapter 4. On the inability of progressives to unite in opposition to welfare reform after the 1994 elections, see Geismer, *Left Behind*.

38. See Mink and Kornbluh, *Ensuring Poverty*, 62–63. For more, see Judy Tzu-Chun Wu and Gwendolyn Mink, *Fierce and Fearless: Patsy Takemoto Mink: First Woman of Color in Congress* (NYU Press, 2022), chapters 8–9.

39. See Mink and Kornbluh, *Ensuring Poverty*, 67.

40. Mink and Kornbluh, *Ensuring Poverty*, 73.

41. Gwendolyn Mink, "Feminists, Welfare Reform, and Welfare Justice," *Social Justice*, vol. 25, no. 1 (1998), at 146.

42. Mink, "Feminists, Welfare Reform, and Welfare Justice," 148.

43. The feminist–fiscal conservative coalition to toughen child support enforcement stretched back to the 1970s. See Libby Adler and Janet Halley, "'You Play, You Pay': Feminists and Child Support Enforcement in the United States," in *Governance Feminism: Notes from the Field*, ed. Janet Halley, Prabha Kotiswaran, Rachel Rebouché, and Hila Shamir (University of Minnesota Press, 2019).

44. For a vivid description, see Adler and Halley, "'You Play, You Pay,'" 287–89. On the operation of child support enforcement vis-à-vis poor fathers, see Tonya Brito, "Fathers Behind Bars: Rethinking Child Support Policy Toward Low-Income Non-Custodial Fathers and Their Families," 15 *Iowa J. Gender, Race, & Justice* 217 (2012).

45. See Adler and Halley, "'You Play, You Pay,'" 309.

46. Marian Wright Edelman, "Say No to This Welfare 'Reform,'" *WP*, Nov. 3, 1995.

47. Alison Mitchell, "Two Clinton Aides Resign to Protest New Welfare Law," *NYT*, Sept. 12, 1996.

48. Harry Krause, "Child Support Reassessed: Limits of Private Responsibility and the Public Interest," 24 *Fam. L. Quarterly* 13, 15, 27–28 (1990).

49. Ian Fisher, "Moynihan Stands Alone in Welfare Debate," *NYT*, Sept. 27, 1995. Jeffrey O'Connell and Richard Bland write that Moynihan would not ally himself with critics of PRWORA on the left because they had harshly criticized his approach to family structure and poverty in the past. O'Connell and Bland, "Pats for Pat," Book Review, 2000 *Illinois L. Rev.* 1287 (2000). Robin Toner, "New Senate Push on Welfare Revives Tensions in Both Parties," *NYT*, Sept. 9, 1995.

50. Primus touted a statistic showing for the first time "more legal paternities established" than "out-of-wedlock births" in 2000 and declared welfare reform was "working better than I thought it would. . . . Whatever we have been doing over the last five years, we ought to keep going." Primus quoted in Blaine Harden, "2-Parent Families Rise After Changes in Welfare Laws," *NYT*, Aug. 12, 2001.

51. Theodora Ooms, "Marriage Plus," *American Prospect* (Mar. 28, 2002), https://prospect.org/features/marriage-plus/.

52. He continued: "If young men cannot find work, they are far less likely to marry." Peter Edelman, "The Worst Thing Bill Clinton Has Done," *Atlantic*, March 1997. See also Mink and Kornbluh, *Ensuring Poverty*, 79 (discussing Edelman's and other liberals' "patriarchal" assumptions). For more on the rise of the marriage movement, see Melanie Heath, *One Marriage Under God: The Campaign to Promote Marriage in America* (NYU Press, 2012); Rebecca L. Davis, *More Perfect Unions: The American Search for Marital Bliss* (Harvard University Press, 2010), chapters 6–7.

53. Prior to 1996, states had to seek federal waivers to implement a family cap. Smith, "Sexual Regulation Dimension," 168. According to some sources, twenty states had enacted a family cap by 1996. See Marie McCullough, "Effect of N.J. 'Family Cap' Is a Matter of Argument," *Philadelphia Inquirer*, June 2, 1996.

54. The numbers continued to fall precipitously, reaching 20 percent in 2020. Center for Budget and Policy Priorities, Policy Basics: Temporary Assistance for Needy Families, updated Mar. 1, 2022; Mink and Kornbluh, *Ensuring Poverty*.

55. Dylan Matthews, "How Bill Clinton's Welfare Reform Changed America," *Vox* (June 20, 2016); Center on Budget and Policy Priorities, TANF, 26.

56. Smith, "Sexual Regulation Dimension," 194.

57. Tamar Lewin, "Sexual-Abstinence Grants Put to Broad Use By States," *NYT*, Apr. 4, 1999.

58. Heath, *One Marriage Under God*, 3; Mink and Kornbluh, *Ensuring Poverty*, 96.

59. Martha Fineman, Gwendolyn Mink, and Anna Marie Smith, "No Promotion of Marriage in TANF!," *Social Justice*, vol. 30, no. 4 (2003). See also Dorothy Roberts, Killing the Black Body: Race, Reproduction, and the Meaning of Liberty (Pantheon, 1997), 222–25.

60. Martha Fineman, *The Neutered Mother, the Sexual Family, and Other Twentieth-Century Tragedies* (Routledge, 1995).

61. Mink and Kornbluh, *Ensuring Poverty*, 99–100.

62. Mink and Kornbluh, *Ensuring Poverty*, 101–2. On the positive valence of early welfare reform press coverage, see James M. Avery and Mark Peffley, "Race Matters: The Impact of News Coverage of Welfare Reform on Public Opinion," in *Race and the Politics of Welfare Reform*, ed. Sanford F. Schram, Joe Soss, and Richard C. Fording (University of Michigan Press, 2003).

63. Some welfare activists looked explicitly to those models. See, for example, Felicia Kornbluh, "The Goals of the National Welfare Rights Movement: Why We Need Them Thirty Years Later," *Feminist Studies*, vol. 24, no. 1 (Spring 1998): 65–78.

64. See chapter 2; King v. Smith, 392 U.S. 309 (1968). See also Mink and Kornbluh, *Ensuring Poverty*, 7–8.

65. See chapter 6.

66. On paternity cooperation requirements in the early to mid-1980s, see Stephen D. Sugarman, "*Roe v. Norton:* Coerced Maternal Cooperation," in *In the Interest of Children: Advocacy, Law Reform, and Public Policy*, ed. Robert H. Mnookin (W.H. Freeman, 1985).

67. Planned Parenthood v. Casey, 947 F.2d 682, 721 (3d Cir. 1991) (Alito, J., concurring in part and dissenting in part); Serena Mayeri, "Un-Dueing Roe: Constitutional Conflict and Political Polarization in *Planned Parenthood v. Casey*," *Reproductive Rights and Justice Stories*, ed. Melissa Murray, Katherine Shaw, and Reva B. Siegel (Foundation Press, 2019), 146–47.

68. Planned Parenthood v. Casey, 505 U.S. 833, 856, 887–98 (1992); Mayeri, "Un-Dueing Roe," 151–52.

69. See Loretta Ross and Rickie Solinger, *Reproductive Justice: An Introduction* (University of California Press, 2017).

70. Planned Parenthood v. Casey, 505 U.S. 833 (1992); Mayeri, "Un-Dueing *Roe*."

71. Frances Schwartzkopff, "Critics: Welfare Plan Defeats Purpose," *Atlanta Journal-Constitution*, Nov. 7, 1993.

72. See Dorothy Roberts, *Killing the Black Body: Race, Reproduction, and the Meaning of Liberty* (Penguin, 1997), chapter 5.

73. Brief of Women's Legal Defense Fund et al., *C.K. v. Shalala*, 24.

74. C.K. v. Shalala, 883 F. Supp. 991 (D.N.J. 1995), aff'd sub nom. C.K. v. New Jersey Dept of Health & Hum. Serv., 92 F.3d 171 (3d Cir. 1996).

75. Plaintiffs' Memorandum of Law, C.K. v. Shalala, D. N.J., Dec. 5, 1994, at 12–14, NOW LDEF Papers, Box 472, Folder 6. See also Memorandum of Law of Association for Children of New Jersey et al., C.K. v. Shalala, U.S. Court of Appeals for the Third Circuit, No. 95-5454, NOW LDEF Papers, Box 474, Folder 7.

76. Brief Amici Curiae on Behalf of Appellants C.K. et al. for Women's Legal Defense Fund et al., C.K. v. Shalala, No. 95-5454 (3d Cir.), 1, 16, NOW LDEF Papers, Box 475, Folder 2.

77. Brief of WLDF et al., *C.K. v. Shalala*, 2. The brief noted that many teenagers became pregnant from coerced sex with older men. Brief of WLDF et al., *C.K. v. Shalala*, 35.

78. See, for example, Brief of the Commonwealth of Virginia and the States of Alabama, Arizona, California, New York, South Carolina, and Wisconsin as Amici Curiae in Support of Defendants-Appellees, C.K. v. Shalala, No. 95-5454 (3d Cir.).

79. Natalie Pompilio, "N.J.'s Welfare Cap Can Fuel Two Sides of National Debate," *Philadelphia Inquirer*, Oct. 10, 1995, A1, A4. Bryant also sponsored New Jersey's "bridefare" legislation, which gave "mothers monetary rewards for marrying." Roberts, *Killing the Black Body*, 225.

80. Memorandum of Law of Amici Curiae American Legislative Exchange Council (ALEC) et al., in Support of Defendants' Motion for Summary Judgment, C.K. v. Shalala, Civ. Action No. 93–5354, Sept. 23, 1994, NOW LDEF Papers, Box 472, Folder 5; Editorial, "New Jersey Limited Benefits Report Finds Welfare Illegitimate Births Down," *Tyler Courier-Times* (Texas), Mar. 17, 1995.

81. Brief Amici Curiae on Behalf of Appellants C.K. et al. for Women's Legal Defense Fund et al., C.K. v. Shalala, No. 95–5454, Third Circuit, at 13, NOW LDEF Papers, Box 475, Folder 2.

82. Brief of Amici New Jersey Right to Life Committee, Inc., and Citizens Concerned for Life, Inc., in Support of Plaintiffs' Motion for Summary Judgment, C.K. v. Shalala, Docket No. 93–5354 (NHP), Sept. 23, 1994, D. N.J., NOW LDEF Papers, Box 472, Folder 5; Thomas Ginsberg, "Study of N.J. 'Family Cap' Law Says Welfare Rule Led to More Abortions," *Philadelphia Inquirer* (South Jersey edition), Nov. 3, 1998. See also Brief of Amici New Jersey Right to Life, *C.K. v. Shalala*, 19–20, 27–28.

83. Jeffrey Gold, "U.S. Won't Reveal Family Cap Reports," *Courier-Post* (Camden, N.J.), Sept. 4, 1998, 7B. Attorney Sherry Leiwant of NOW LDEF also warned of "women . . . under pressure from their caseworkers to have abortions." Thomas Ginsberg, "Study Finds N.J. Welfare Cap May Have Led to More Abortions," *Philadelphia Inquirer*, June 9, 1998.

84. Brief of WLDF et al., *C.K. v. Shalala*, 25–26.

85. AP, "Welfare Research Project Yields No Solid Results," *Herald-News* (Passaic, N.J.), Sept. 12, 1997.

86. AP, "Welfare Research Project Yields No Solid Results"; AP, "Groups Want to See State Report on Welfare-Abortion Link," *Asbury Park Press* (N.J.), July 23, 1998.

87. Ovetta Wiggins, "No Evidence Welfare Cap Reduces Births," *The Record* (Hackensack, N.J.), Sept. 12, 1997; Thomas Ginsberg, "Study Fails to Prove Link Between Birth Rates, Welfare Pay," *Baltimore Sun*, Feb. 1, 1998.

88. C.K. v. Shalala, 883 F. Supp. 991, 1012, 1014–15 (D. N.J. 1995).

89. Politan's opinion closely tracked the arguments made by the government. See [Brief of the United States], C.K. v. Shalala, Dec. 1995; *C.K.*, 883 F. Supp. at 1014–15. For more, see Roberts, *Killing the Black Body*, 236–43.

90. See, for example, "Law Fails to Curb Births to Welfare Mothers," *Baltimore Sun*, July 2, 1995.

91. C.K. v. New Jersey Dept. of Health & Hum. Serv., 92 F. 3d 171 (3d Cir. 1996).

92. Roe v. Wade, 410 U.S. 113 (1973); Goldberg v. Kelly, 397 U.S. 254 (1970); Dandridge v. Williams, 397 U.S. 471 (1970).

93. Maher v. Roe, 432 U.S. 464 (1977); Harris v. McRae, 448 U.S. 297 (1981).

94. See Washington v. Davis, 426 U.S. 229 (1976); Personnel Administrator v. Feeney, 442 U.S. 256 (1979); Geduldig v. Aiello, 417 U.S. 484 (1974).

95. Doe v. Maher, 515 A. 2d 134 (Ct. Super. Ct. 1986) (Berdon, J.). Similar arguments succeeded in New Mexico Right to Choose/NARAL v. Johnson, 126 N.M. 788 (1998).

96. See, for example, Doe v. Gomez, 542 N.W.2d 17 (Minn. 1995); Moe v. Sec'y of Admin., 417 N.E.2d 387 (Mass. 1981).

97. Right to Choose v. Byrne, 91 N.J. 287 (1982); Planned Parenthood of Central New Jersey v. Farmer, 165 N.J. 609 (2000). Further, C.K. v. Shalala had focused primarily on administrative law arguments about the validity of a waiver obtained from HHS, an issue mooted by PRWORA. See "Third Circuit Upholds 'Family Cap' for Welfare Recipients," *New Jersey L. J.*, Aug. 19, 1996, at 5–6.

98. Kathy Hennessey (AP), "Court Caps Welfare Payments," *Courier-News* (Bridgewater, N.J.), Aug. 5, 2003; Sojourner A. v. New Jersey Dept. of Human Services, 177 N.J. 318, 322 (2003).

99. Complaint, 10, Sojourner A. v. N.J. Dept. of Human Services, NOW LDEF Papers, Box 609, Folder 6.

100. Her fourth child resulted from an unplanned pregnancy and left her family with inadequate funds for housing, food, and clothing. Complaint, Sojourner A. v. N.J. Dept. of Human Services, NOW LDEF Papers, Box 609, Folder 6.

101. Complaint, 18, Sojourner A. v. N.J. Dept. of Human Services, NOW LDEF Papers, Box 609, Folder 6.

102. Thomas Ginsberg, "Study Fails to Prove Link Between Birth Rates, Welfare Pay," *Baltimore Sun*, Feb. 1, 1998.

103. Brief in Support of Plaintiffs' Motion for Summary Judgment, *Sojourner A.*

104. The case was filed in September 1997; an application for preliminary injunctive relief was denied in October. A class action was certified in 2000.

105. Brief in Support of Plaintiffs' Motion for Summary Judgment, *Sojourner A.*, 36, NOW LDEF Papers, Box 609, Folder 6.

106. Sojourner A. ex rel. Y.A. v. New Jersey Department of Human Services, 794 A.2d 822, 825 (N.J. App. Div. 2002) (quoting oral ruling by Iuliani).

107. *Sojourner A.*, 794 A.2d at 832 (citing *Califano v. Jobst* [1977]).

108. *Sojourner A.*, 350 N.J. Super. at 325.

109. See www.njcourts.gov/public/museum/meet-the-justices/chief-justice-deborah-t-poritz. For more, see Justice Virginia A. Long, "The Purple Thread: Social Justice as a Recurring Theme in the Decisions of the Poritz Court," 59 *Rutgers L. Rev.* 533 (2006–2007).

110. Sojourner A. v. New Jersey Dept. of Human Services, 177 N.J. 318, 335 (2003).

111. *Sojourner A.*, 177 N.J. at 335. See also Mitch Lipka, "Court Upholds Child Limit for Mothers on Welfare," *Philadelphia Inquirer*, Aug. 5, 2003. Hennessey, "Court Caps Welfare Payments."

112. See Risa E. Kaufman, "State ERAs in the New Era: Securing Poor Women's Equality by Eliminating Reproductive-Based Discrimination," 24 *Harvard Women's L. J.* 191 (2001).

113. See Berkeley Law Center on Reproductive Rights and Justice, "Bringing Families Out of 'Cap'tivity: The Path Toward Abolishing Welfare Family Caps," August 2016.

114. Eight months after her twenty-first birthday. See Miller v. Christopher, 96 F.3d 1467, 1467 (D.C. Cir. 1996).

115. Miller v. Christopher, 96 F.3d 1467, 1471 (D.C. Cir. 1996) (citations omitted).

116. On the racial and gender politics at the intersection of nationality, citizenship, and family and administrative law, see Kristin Collins, "Illegitimate Borders: Jus Sanguinis Citizenship and the Legal Construction of Family, Race, and Nation," 123 *Yale L. J.* 2134 (2014).

117. Oral Argument of Donald R. Patterson on Behalf of the Petitioner, Miller v. Albright, No. 96–1060, Nov. 4, 1997, 1997 WL 699809.

118. Brief of Appellant, Miller v. Christopher, U.S. Court of Appeals for the D.C. Circuit, 1995 WL 17907819, at *6-*7. The State Department did not agree, however. The D.C. federal district court judge Royce Lambert granted the government's motion to dismiss the Millers' constitutional challenge in 1994. Miller v. Christopher, 870 F. Supp. 1 (D. D.C. Apr. 29, 1994).

119. Charlie Miller's claims had been dismissed early in the litigation. See Miller v. Christopher, 96 F.3d 1467 (D.C. Cir. 1996) (finding that Mr. Miller's sex discrimination claim was not properly before the court).

120. LeBrun v. Thornburgh, 777 F. Supp. 1204 (D.N.J. 1991).

121. *LeBrun*, 777 F. Supp. at 1211–13.

122. The court also cited Parham v. Hughes, 441 U.S. 347 (1979) (see chapter 7). Miller v. Christopher, 96 F.3d 1467, 1472 (D.C. Cir. 1996).

123. Neil A. Lewis, "Patricia Wald, First Woman to Preside Over D.C. Appeals Court, Dies at 90," *NYT*, Jan. 12, 2019.

124. Miller v. Christopher, 96 F.3d at 1475–777 (Wald, J., concurring in the judgment).

125. See Caban v. Mohammed, 441 U.S. 380 (1979); Lehr v. Robertson, 463 U.S. 248 (1983); chapter 7.

126. United States v. Virginia, 518 U.S. 515 (1996).

127. Brief of Amici Curiae the American Civil Liberties Union and NOW Legal Defense and Education Fund, Miller v. Albright, 1997 WL 327565.

128. Miller v. Albright, 523 U.S. 420, 443–45 (1998) (Stevens, J.)

129. Some sources suggest that Hung Thi "abandoned [her son] at birth." See, for example, Geraldine Sealey, "High Court Considers Immigration Case," ABC News, Jan. 9, 2001; Linda K. Kerber, "Top Court Took a Step Backward on Gender Bias," *Boston Globe*, June 23, 2001.

130. Brief of Petitioners, Nguyen v. INS, 2000 WL 1706737.

131. Nguyen v. INS, 533 U.S. 53 (2001).

132. Miller v. Albright, 523 U.S. 420, 460 (1998) (Ginsburg, J., dissenting).

133. Kristin Collins, Note, "When Fathers' Rights Are Mothers' Duties: The Failure of Equal Protection in Miller v. Albright," 109 *Yale L. J.* 1669 (2000).

134. Brief of the National Women's Law Center et al. as Amici Curiae in Support of Petitioners, Nguyen v. INS, 533 U.S. 53 (2001) (No. 99–2071), 2000 WL 1702034; Nguyen v. INS, 533 U.S. 53, 92 (2001) (O'Connor, J., dissenting).

135. *Nguyen*, 533 U.S. at 70.

136. Patty Reinerti, "Father Loses Deportation Decision," *Atlanta Constitution*, June 12, 2001. By the time of the Supreme Court's ruling, Nguyen had completed his prison sentence and returned to Houston; Vietnam had refused to repatriate him, but he remained subject to indefinite INS detention.

137. Five years after Charlie Miller's death, his daughter's Facebook page featured a photo of him with her children. See also www.dignitymemorial. com/obituaries/canton-tx/charlie-miller-10149639.

138. "Father's Presence Is Daughter's Present," *Press-Enterprise*, May 30, 2015, https://www.pressenterprise.com/2015/05/31/menifee-father8217s-presence-is-daughter8217s-present/.

139. Worcester Housing Authority v. Massachusetts Comm'n Against Discrimination, 547 N.E.2d 43 (Mass 1989); Foreman v. Anchorage Equal Rights Commission, 779 P.2d 1199 (Alaska 1989).

140. County of Dane v. Norman, 497 N.W.2d 714, 716 (Wisc. 1993). For further discussion, see Deborah Widiss, "Intimate Liberties and Antidiscrimination Law," 97 *Boston Univ. L. Rev.* 2083 (2017); Elizabeth Pleck, *Not Just Roommates: Cohabitation After the Sexual Revolution* (University of Chicago Press, 2012).

141. Employment Division v. Smith, 494 U.S. 872 (1990).

142. Religious Freedom Restoration Act of 1993, Pub. L. No. 103–141, 107 Stat. 1488, codified at 42 U.S.C. section 2000bb through 42 U.S.C. section 2000bb-4.

143. In 1997, the Court held that Congress had exceeded its power under section 5 of the Fourteenth Amendment when it applied RFRA to state governments. City of Boerne v. Flores, 521 U.S. 507 (1997). States passed their own RFRAs before and after the enactment of the federal statute and the *Flores* decision.

144. On these organizations, see Amanda Hollis-Brusky and Joshua C. Wilson, *Separate But Faithful: The Christian Right's Radical Struggle to Transform Law and Legal Culture* (Oxford University Press, 2020).

145. Smith v. Fair Employment & Housing Comm., 913 P.2d 909, 912 (Cal. 1996).

146. Attorney General v. Desilets, 636 N.E.2d 233 (Mass. 1994).

147. Swanner v. Anchorage Equal Rights Commission, 874 P.2d 274 (Alaska 1994).

148. See Douglas NeJaime and Reva B. Siegel, "Conscience Wars: Complicity-Based Conscience Claims in Religion and Politics," 124 *Yale L. J.* 2516 (2015).

149. Brief Amici Curiae of Gay and Lesbian Advocates and Defenders and the Women's Bar Association, Attorney General v. Desilets, 1993 WL 13156919, at *33–34.

150. *Smith,* 913 P.2d at 925.

151. *Swanner,* 874 P.2d at 283.

152. *Desilets,* 636 N.E.2d at 239.

153. *Desilets,* 636 N.E.2d at 246 (O'Connor, J., dissenting).

154. *Swanner,* 513 U.S. 979 (1994) (Thomas, J., dissenting from denial of certiorari).

155. "Lawrence Yetka, Former Minnesota Supreme Court Justice, Dies at 93," *Pine Journal,* Nov. 22, 2017; "Lawrence Robert Yetka," *Minneapolis Star-Tribune,* Nov. 22, 2017; State v. French, 460 Nw. 2d 2, 11 (Minn. 1990).

156. Institute for American Values, *The Marriage Movement: A Statement of Principles* (2000).

157. Judith Stadtman Tucker, "The Mothers Movement Online: An Interview with Enola Aird," June 2003.

158. Mark Oppenheimer, "The Making of Gay Marriage's Top Foe," *Salon,* Feb. 8, 2012.

159. The marriage movement initially avoided the same-sex marriage issue, according to Oppenheimer. Gallagher left the IAV in 2003.

160. Nancy F. Cott, *Public Vows: A History of Marriage and the Nation* (Harvard University Press, 2000). See also George Chauncey, *Why Marriage? The History Shaping Today's Debate Over Gay Equality* (Basic Books, 2004); Rachel Hope Cleves, "History from the Witness Stand: An Interview with George Chauncey," *Notches,* June 23, 2016.

161. Many feminists and marriage equality proponents, Cott included, professed ambivalence about marriage. Gay conservatives such as Andrew Sullivan and Jonathan Rauch insisted that marriage would "civilize" gay men, disciplining their sexuality. Lawyers like Mary Bonauto hoped to boost a broader agenda of family equality. Andrew Sullivan, *Virtually Normal: An Argument About Homosexuality* (Basic Books, 1995); Jonathan Rauch, *Gay Marriage: Why It's Good for Gays, Good for Straights, and Good for America* (Times Books, 2004). On Bonauto, see, for example, Eskridge and Riano, *Marriage Equality.*

162. Nan D. Hunter, "Marriage, Law, and Gender: A Feminist Inquiry," 1 *Law & Sexuality* 9 (1991).

163. Nancy D. Polikoff, "We Will Get What We Ask For: Why Same-Sex Marriage Will Not 'Dismantle the Legal Structure of Gender in Every Marriage,'" 79 *Virginia L. Rev.* 1535 (1993).

164. Barbara Cox, "The Lesbian Wife: Same-Sex Marriage as an Expression of Radical and Plural Democracy," 33 *Calif. Western L. Rev.* 155, 158 (1997).
165. Federal defeats in the 1980s and 1990s pushed gay rights advocates, like feminists, into state constitutional litigation, where they enjoyed some success. See William C. Rubenstein, "The Myth of Superiority," 16 *Constitutional Commentary* 599 (1999).
166. Lawrence v. Texas, 539 U.S. 558 (2003); Goodridge v. Dept. of Public Health, 793 N.E.2d 941, 948 (Mass. 2003).
167. *Lawrence* cited, inter alia, *Griswold, Eisenstadt, Roe, Casey, Carey, Pierce*, and *Meyer. Lawrence v. Texas, 539 U.S. 562, 565 (2003). See also Goodridge*, 793 N.E.2d at 971 (Greaney, J., concurring); *Goodridge*, 793 N.E.2d at 948 (citing *Lawrence*).
168. Ariela R. Dubler, "Immoral Purposes: Marriage and the Genus of Illicit Sex," 115 *Yale L. J.* 756 (2006).
169. Lawrence v. Texas, 539 U.S. 558, 585 (2003) (O'Connor, J., concurring).
170. *Lawrence*, 539 U.S. at 590 (Scalia, J., dissenting).
171. Katherine M. Franke, "The Domesticated Liberty of Lawrence v. Texas," 104 *Columbia L. Rev.* 1399 (2004).
172. Melissa Murray, "The Space Between: The Cooperative Regulation of Criminal Law and Family Law," 44 *Fam. L. Quarterly* 227, 228 (2010). See also Katherine M. Franke, "The Politics of Same-Sex Marriage Politics," 15 *Columbia J. Gender & L.* 236, 244 (2006).
173. Franke, "Politics of Same-Sex Marriage Politics," 244.
174. *Goodridge*, 798 N.E.2d at 948.
175. *Goodridge*, 798 N.E. 2d at 955.
176. *Goodridge*, 798 N.E. 2d at 955–57.
177. *Goodridge*, 798 N.E. 2d at 956.
178. Nancy D. Polikoff, "For the Sake of All Children: Opponents and Supporters of Same-Sex Marriage Both Miss the Mark," 8 *NYC L. Rev.* 573 (2005).
179. Franke, "Politics of Same-Sex Marriage Politics."
180. Franke, "Politics of Same-Sex Marriage Politics," 244.
181. Franke, "Politics of Same-Sex Marriage Politics," 242. See also Melissa Murray, "What's So New About the New Illegitimacy?," 20 *American Univ. J. of Gender, Social Policy, & Law* 387 (2012).
182. "Is Gay Marriage Racist? A Conversation with Marlon M. Bailey, Priya Kandaswamy, and Mattie Udora Richardson," Spring 2004, https://www.scribd.com/doc/239502228/Is-Gay-Marriage-Racist.
183. "Is Gay Marriage Racist?," 91.
184. On the evolution of movements to abolish prisons and policing, see Keeanga-Yamahtta Taylor, "The Emerging Movement for Police and Prison Abolition," *New Yorker*, May 7, 2021.
185. Mattilda Bernstein Sycamore, introduction to Sycamore, ed., *That's Revolting: Queer Strategies for Resisting Assimilation* (Soft Skull, 2004), 7. Outside

of academic and activist circles, however, such views were as marginal in the early 2000s as they had been in the late 1960s.

186. Monthly Review, "Beyond Same-Sex Marriage: A New Strategic Vision for All Our Families and Relationships," July 2006 (available at MROnline.org, accessed June 14, 2023).

187. See, for example, the "Fragile Families and Child Well-Being Study" initiated by Sara McLanahan, Irwin Garfinkel, and Ronald B. Mincy.

188. Kathryn Edin and Maria Kefalas, *Promises I Can Keep* (University of California Press, 2005).

189. Andrew Cherlin, *The Marriage Go-Round: The State of Marriage and the Family in America Today* (Knopf, 2010).

Conclusion

1. Press release, "Norton Supports Marriage Accounts to Continue Her Long Struggle for Strong Black Families," Oct. 6, 2005.

2. See, for example, "Norton Praises Senate Appropriation with Budget Autonomy In and Guns and Vouchers Out," press release, July 21, 2005.

3. Eleanor Holmes Norton, "Restoring the Traditional Black Family," *NYT Magazine*, June 2, 1985.

4. See Serena Mayeri, "Historicizing the 'End of Men': The Politics of Reaction(s)," 93 *Boston Univ. L. Rev.* 729 (2013).

5. See chapter 3.

6. Norton, "Restoring the Traditional Black Family."

7. Norton called for robust affirmative action in employment, extensive job training programs, and "work for women on welfare at a standard wage rate with professionally provided day care, with Medicaid." Quoted in Joan Steinau Lester, *Fire in My Soul* (Atria, 2003), 226.

8. See, for example, Contract with America—Welfare Reform, Hearing before the Subcommittee on Human Resources of the Committee on Ways and Means, House of Representatives, 104th Congress, First Session, Jan.-Feb. 1995, vol. 104, issue 43, at 582. Norton endorsed employment as an organizing principle for welfare reform in 1994. See Eleanor Holmes Norton, "America's Welfare Wake-Up Call," *WP*, Apr. 3, 1994.

9. Cf. Reva B. Siegel, "The Modernization of Marital Status Law: Adjudicating Wives' Right to Earnings, 1860–1930," 82 *Georgetown L. J.* 2127 (1994).

10. On feminist divorce reformers' successful litigation on behalf of wealthy divorcing women, see Suzanne Kahn, *Divorce, American Style: Fighting for Women's Economic Citizenship in the Neoliberal Era* (University of Pennsylvania Press, 2021), chapter 8.

11. Simeone v. Simeone, 581 A.2d 162 (Pa. 1990).

12. Washington state had already incorporated a somewhat ascriptive regime that provided a model for the ALI.

13. See Jennifer Mittelstadt, *The Rise of the Military Welfare State* (Harvard University Press, 2015).

14. Dorothy Roberts, *Shattered Bonds: The Color of Child Welfare* (Civitas Books, 2002); Elizabeth Bartholet, *Nobody's Children: Abuse and Neglect, Foster Drift, and the Adoption Alternative* (Penguin Random House, 1999).

15. Cf. Reva Siegel, "Why Equal Protection No Longer Protects: The Evolving Forms of Status-Enforcing State Action," 49 *Stanford L. Rev.* 1111 (1997); Reva B. Siegel, "'The Rule of Love': Wife-Beating as Prerogative and Privacy," 105 *Yale L. J.* 2117 (1995).

16. See, for example, Monthly Review, "Beyond Same-Sex Marriage"; Suzanne A. Kim, "Skeptical Marriage Equality," 34 *Harvard J. L. & Gender* 37 (2010).

Epilogue

1. Oral Argument Transcript, *Obergefell v. Hodges*, 10–11. GLAD changed its name to GLBTQ Advocates and Defenders in 2016.

2. Obergefell v. Hodges, 576 U.S. 644, 675 (2015). On the marriage equality movement, see, for example, George Chauncey, *Why Marriage: The History Shaping Today's Debate Over Gay Equality* (Basic Books, 2004); William Eskridge and Christopher Riano, *Marriage Equality: From Outlaws to In-Laws* (Yale University Press, 2020); Kenji Yoshino, *Speak Now: Marriage Equality on Trial* (Yale University Press, 2015); Jo Becker, *Forcing the Spring: Inside the Fight for Marriage Equality* (Penguin Books, 2014); Sasha Isenberg, *The Engagement: America's Quarter-Century Struggle Over Same-Sex Marriage* (Penguin Books, 2022); Marie-Amélie George, *Family Matters: Queer Households and the Half-Century Struggle for Legal Recognition* (Cambridge University Press, 2024), introduction and chapter 7. On the justices' deliberations in *Obergefell*, see Eskridge and Riano, *Marriage Equality*, chapter 21.

3. *Obergefell*, 576 U.S. at 646.

4. See Nancy Polikoff, "Concord With Which Other Families? Marriage Equality, Family Demographics, and Race," 164 *U. Penn. L. Rev. Online* 99 (2016).

5. "Lawyer Mary Bonauto Remarks on the Supreme Court Ruling on Same-Sex Marriage," June 26, 2015, www.c-span.org/video/?c4542179/lawyer-mary-bonauto-remarks-supreme-court-ruling-marriage.

6. Barack Obama, "Speech About Same-Sex Marriage Ruling," *Time*, June 26, 2015.

7. David Blankenhorn, "How My View on Gay Marriage Changed," *NYT*, June 22, 2012.

8. Andrew Sullivan, "Here Comes the Groom: A (Conservative) Case for Gay Marriage," *New Republic*, Aug. 28, 1989; Jonathan Rauch, "For Better or Worse? The Case for Gay (and Straight) Marriage," *New Republic*, May 6, 1996.

9. Jonathan Rauch, "The Supreme Court Weds Gay Marriage to Family Values," *Brookings Institution*, June 26, 2015.

10. *Obergefell*, 576 U.S. at 742 (Alito, J., dissenting). Alito had replaced Justice O'Connor when she retired from the Court in 2006 to care for her husband.

11. Melissa Murray, "Obergefell v. Hodges and Nonmarriage Inequality," 104 *Calif. L. Rev.* 1207 (2016). See also Serena Mayeri, "Marriage (In)equality and the Historical Legacies of Feminism," 6 *Calif. L. Rev. Circuit* 126 (2015).

12. R. A. Lenhardt, "Race, Dignity, and the Right to Marry," 84 *Fordham L. Rev.* 53, 56 (2015).

13. Nan Hunter, "Interpreting Liberty and Equality Through the Lens of Marriage," 6 *Calif. L. Rev. Circuit* 107, 108 (2015).

14. Katherine Franke, *Wedlocked: The Perils of Marriage Equality* (NYU Press, 2015).

15. Polikoff, "Concord With Which Other Families?" See also Nancy D. Polikoff, *Beyond (Straight and Gay) Marriage: Valuing All Families Under the Law* (Beacon Press, 2008); Naomi Cahn and June Carbone, *Marriage Markets: How Inequality Is Remaking the American Family* (Oxford University Press, 2014), 14.

16. For a collection of writings critical of marriage equality, see "Against Equality: Queer Challenges to the Politics of Inclusion," www.againstequality. org/about/marriage/.

17. For survey data on LGBT Americans' attitudes toward marriage in the early 2010s, see Pew Research Center, *A Survey of LGBT Americans: Attitudes, Experiences, and Values in Changing Times*, June 13, 2013. That study found "nearly universal support" (93 percent of respondents) for the legalization of same-sex marriage. Fifty-eight percent thought marriage should be the top priority for the movement even if it detracted from other issues. Thirty-nine percent, however, agreed that marriage equality had "drawn too much attention away from other issues that are important to people who are LGBT."

18. Eskridge and Riano report that some states and employers have ceased to recognize domestic partnerships and other alternative statuses, while others continue to do so. See Eskridge and Riano, *Marriage Equality*, chapter 24.

19. Suzanne Goldberg, "Reflections on Obergefell and the Family-Recognition Framework's Continuing Value," 84 *UMKC L. Rev.* 707 (2016).

20. See, for example, Melissa Murray, "Rights and Regulation: The Evolution of Sexual Regulation," 116 *Columbia L. Rev.* 573 (2016).

21. Russell K. Robinson and David M. Frost, "Marriage Equality and Intersectionality," *Analyses of Social Issues and Public Policy*, vol. 23, no. 2 (August 2023): 20.

22. Courtney Joslin, "Marriage Equality and Its Relation to Family Law," 129 *Harvard L. Rev.* 197 (2016).

23. Douglas NeJaime, "Marriage Equality and the New Parenthood," 129 *Harvard L. Rev.* 1185 (2016).

24. NeJaime, "Marriage Equality and the New Parenthood."

25. Aimee Green, "Lesbian Partner Isn't 'Parent' of Baby Born Through Artificial Insemination, Appeals Court Rules," *OregonLive.com*, May 14, 2015.

26. In re Madrone, 350 Pd. 495 (Or. App. 2015) (emphasis added).

27. Pavan v. Smith, 137 S.Ct. 2075, 2077 (2017) (per curiam).

28. Dvash-Banks v. Pompeo, 2019 WL 911799 (9th Cir. 2019).

29. Sessions v. Morales-Santana, 582 U.S. 47, 59 (2017).

30. For more, see Kristin A. Collins, "Equality, Sovereignty, and the Family in *Morales-Santana*," 131 *Harvard L. Rev.* 170 (2017).

31. Courtney G. Joslin, "Federalism and Family Status," 90 *Indiana L. Rev.* 787 (2015).

32. Movement Advancement Project, "Parental Recognition Laws," www.lgbtmap.org/equality-maps/recognition/parenting (visited May, 16, 2024).

33. Sharon Yoo, "Logan's Law and What It Could Mean for Two Moms Expecting a Baby," KARE 11, May 8, 2019.

34. Uniform Parentage Act, Section 609 (2017). Some states that have adopted the 2017 UPA do not extend voluntary acknowledgment provisions to male same-sex couples.

35. To qualify, individuals must have lived with the child for a significant period, "engaged in consistent caretaking," taken on "full and permanent responsibilities of a parent" without compensation, "held out" the child as their own, and "established a bonded and dependent relationship . . . parental in nature" with the support of another recognized parent. UPA (2017), Section 613, Alternative B.

36. Blumenthal v. Brewer, 69 N.E.3d 834 (Ill. 2016).

37. Albertina Antognini, "Nonmarital Contracts," 73 *Stanford L. Rev.* 67 (2021); Albertina Antognini, "Nonmarital Coverture," 99 *Boston Univ. L. Rev.* 2139 (2019).

38. Uniform Law Commission, Uniform Cohabitants' Economic Remedies Act (2021).

39. See Courtney G. Joslin and Douglas NeJaime, "How Functional Parent Doctrines Function," 35 *J. of Amer. Acad. of Matrimonial L.* 589 (2023), citing Brian Bix, "Against Functional Approaches," *Jotwell*, Jan. 12, 2022; Katharine Baker, "Quacking Like a Duck? Functional Parenthood Doctrine and Same-Sex Parents," 92 *Chicago-Kent L. Rev.* 135 (2017); Katharine Baker, "Equality and Family Autonomy," 24 *U. Pa. J. Const. Law* 412 (2022); Greg Strauss, "What Role Remains for De Facto Parenthood?," 46 *Florida State Univ. L. Rev.* 909 (2019).

40. Joslin and NeJaime, "How Functional Parent Doctrines Function," 605–17; Courtney G. Joslin and Douglas NeJaime, "How Parenthood Functions," 123 *Columbia L. Rev.* 319 (2023). See also Courtney G. Joslin and Douglas NeJaime, "Domestic Violence and Functional Parent Doctrines," 30 *Virginia J. Social Policy & L.* 67 (2023); Courtney G. Joslin and Douglas NeJaime, "*Multiparenthood*," 99 *N.Y.U. L. Rev.* 1242 (2024).

41. Elisa B. v. Superior Court, 37 Cal. 4th 108 (2005).

42. Anna Marie Smith, "Reproductive Technology, Family Law, and the Post-Welfare State: The California Same-Sex Parents' Rights 'Victories' of 2005," *Signs*, vol. 34, no. 4 (Summer 2009): 827–50. On how functional family doctrines privatize dependency, see also Melissa Murray, "Family Law's Doctrines," 163 *U. Pa. L. Rev.* 1985 (2015).

43. See Deborah A. Widiss, "Legal Recognition of Same-Sex Relationships: New Possibilities for Research on the Role of Marriage in Household Labor Allocation," *Journal of Family Theory & Review*, vol. 8, issue 1 (March 2016); Suzanne A. Kim and Edward Stein, "The Role of Gender and Gender Dynamics in Same-Sex Divorce and Dissolution," in *LGBTQ Divorce and Relationship Dissolution*, ed. Abbie E. Goldberg and Adam P. Romero (Oxford University Press, 2019).

44. Melanie Zaber, "After 20 Years of Same-Sex Marriage, Research Finds No Harms to Different-Sex Couples; Growth for Overall Support of Marriage," Rand press release, May 13, 2024.

45. Melissa S. Kearney, *The Two-Parent Privilege: How Americans Stopped Getting Married and Started Falling Behind* (University of Chicago Press, 2023). On the ensuing debate, see, for example, Will Holub-Moorman, "What Are Families For?," *Boston Review*, Oct. 5, 2023; Rebecca Traister, "The Return of the Marriage Plot," *New York Magazine*, Sept. 27, 2023; Eleanor Brown, Naomi Cahn, and June Carbone, "Marriage Is Not As Effective an Antipoverty Strategy As You've Been Led to Believe," *The Conversation*, Feb. 21, 2024. See also Brad Wilcox, *Get Married: Why Americans Must Defy the Elites, Forge Strong Families, and Save Civilization* (Broadside Books, 2024).

46. Justin McCarthy, "Record-High 70% in U.S. Support Same-Sex Marriage," Gallup, June 8, 2021.

47. By 2019, the share of adults who had cohabited with a nonmarital romantic partner exceeded the proportion of Americans who had ever married. Juliana Menasce Horowitz, Nikki Graf, and Gretchen Livingston, "Marriage and Cohabitation in the U.S.," Pew Research, Nov. 6, 2019. The percentage of all U.S. births to unmarried women hovered around 40 percent between 2007 and 2022. Michelle J. K. Osterman et al., "Births: Final Data for 2022," National Vital Statistics Reports, vol. 73, no. 2, Apr. 4, 2024.

48. Gretchen Livingston, "The Changing Profile of Unmarried Parents," Pew Research Center, Apr. 25, 2018.

49. Courtney Joslin, "Marital Status Discrimination 2.0," 90 *Boston Univ. L. Rev.* 805 (2015).

50. Advocates connected family caps to past punitive policies of reproductive control, including coercive sterilization and suitable home laws, and called for their demise. See Ife Floyd, "States Should Follow New Jersey: Repeal Racist 'Family Cap,'" Center on Budget and Policy Priorities, Oct. 14, 2020; Berkeley Law Center on Reproductive Rights and Justice, "Bringing Families Out of 'Cap'tivity: The Path Toward Abolishing Welfare Family Caps" (2016).

51. Cindy Huddleston, "5 Reasons Why Florida Lawmakers Should Repeal the Outdated 'Family Cap' Law," Florida Policy Institute, Feb. 7, 2024.
52. For example, Massachusetts includes "domestic partners" regardless of whether they are formally registered with the state. Colorado permits covered workers to take leave to care for "any other individual with whom the covered individual has a significant personal bond that is or is like a family relationship, regardless of biological or legal relationship." Several states include individuals who have "the equivalent of a family relationship" with the covered employee. Deborah A. Widiss, "Chosen Family, Care, and the Workplace," 131 *Yale L. J. Forum* 215 (2021).
53. Meredith Goldstein, "Somerville Celebrates Another First for Polyamorous People," *Boston Globe*, Mar. 24, 2023.
54. Bostock v. Clayton County, 590 U.S. 644 (2020).
55. Jason DeParle, "In the Stimulus Bill, a Policy Revolution in Aid for Children," *NYT*, July 12, 2021.
56. See, for example, Carson v. Makin, 596 U.S. 767 (2022); Kennedy v. Bremerton School Dist., 597 U.S. 507 (2022); 303 Creative v. Elenis, 600 U.S. 570 (2023).
57. See, for example, W. Bradford Wilcox and Patrick T. Brown, "The Child Tax Credit Should Promote Work and Marriage," *First Things*, Dec. 19, 2022; Scott Winship, "The True Cost of Expanding the Child Tax Credit," *NYT*, Dec. 20, 2022; Scott Winship, "The Conservative Case Against Child Allowances," *American Enterprise Institute*, March 5, 2021.
58. Dobbs v. Jackson Women's Health Organization, 597 U.S. 215 (2022).
59. Though the majority opinion disclaimed wider consequences beyond abortion, Justice Thomas's concurrence called on the Court to reconsider its previous substantive due process jurisprudence.
60. Kimberly Mutcherson, "*Dobbs* as a Catalyst for Reproductive Justice," *Bill of Health*, May 18, 2023.
61. Elie Mystal, "The Supreme Court Just Took Its First Swipe at Marriage Equality," *The Nation*, June 25, 2024.
62. Department of State v. Muñoz, 144 S.Ct. 1812 (2024).
63. Muñoz, 144 S.Ct. at 1834 (Sotomayor, J., dissenting).

Acknowledgments

I BEGAN THIS PROJECT in a very different world. One constant throughout has been the generosity and support of friends, colleagues, and mentors without whom this book could not have come to fruition. The example, guidance, and friendship of Sally Gordon—along with her unparalleled service to the legal history community—has inspired and sustained this work. Since our first conversation about the topic in the summer of 2011, Sally's wisdom and judicious red pen have shaped its contours. Sophia Lee's insights enriched my thinking at every turn, and the legal history writing group she launched a decade ago has provided an invaluable forum for moral and intellectual support throughout. I miss her presence next door but am grateful beyond measure that she now occupies the dean's office. It is difficult to imagine a worthier person to carry the legal history torch at Penn than Karen Tani, who shares with Sally and Sophia a talent for institution-building and, more importantly, their rare confluence of brilliance and kindness.

My debts to colleagues at Penn alone are legion. I have learned more than I can say from Regina Austin and Dorothy Roberts, whose intellectual inspiration and guidance have enriched this book and my life more generally. Tobias Wolff, Tess Wilkinson-Ryan, and Jean Galbraith have been the best of comrades throughout this journey. Shaun Ossei-Owusu's encyclopedic knowledge and incisive questions improved every draft. Anita Allen, Tom Baker, Shyamkrishna Balganesh, Mitch Berman, Maggie Blackhawk, Steve Burbank, Cary Coglianese, Angus Corbett, Bill Ewald, Bridget Fahey, Kara Finck, Jill Fisch, Frank Goodman, Jasmine Harris, Allison Hoffman, Seth Kreimer, Howard Lesnick, Cara McClellan, Chuck Mooney, Sarah Paoletti, Gideon Parchomovsky, Wendell Pritchett, Kim Roosevelt, Jennifer Rothman, David Rudovsky, Amanda Shanor, Kate Shaw, Beth Simmons, and Cathie Struve are among those whose feedback benefited the project. Deans Michael Fitts, Wendell Pritchett, Ted Ruger, and Sophia Lee were unfailingly generous in their support.

I have benefited enormously from Penn's rich interdisciplinary community, especially colleagues in the history and political science departments, in the

Gender, Sexuality, and Women's Studies Program, and at the Andrea Mitchell Center for the Study of Democracy, including Mia Bay, Sigal Ben-Porath, Mary Frances Berry, Kathleen Brown, Brent Cebul, Marcia Chatelain, Hardeep Dhillon, Jeff Green, Sarah Gronningsater, Nancy Hirschmann, Amy Offner, Eric Orts, Kathy Peiss, Sophie Rosenfeld, and Rogers Smith. Zain Lakhani, my dear friend and incomparable co-instructor in seminars on feminist legal advocacy in the twentieth-century United States, and students in those courses and in seminars on law and the family over the past decade have helped me to develop and refine my ideas.

Special thanks are due to members of our legal history writing group, the Writers' Bloc(k), who read dozens of draft chapters, often more than once; in addition to colleagues named above, Greg Ablavsky, Jeanine Alvarez, Amber Armstrong, Alexis Broderick, Chelsea Chamberlain, Felipe Ford Cole, Brittany Farr, Nancy Gallman, Smita Ghosh, Rachel Guberman, Scott Heerman, Christen Hammock Jones, William Kuby, Ada Kuskowski, Jane Manners, Sara Mayeux, Mary X. Mitchell, Peter Pihos, Allison Kirkpatrick Powers, Lolo Serrano, Natalie Shibley, Justin Simard, Ronit Stahl, Evan Taparata, Sarah Winsberg, and Adnan Zulfiqar are among those whose feedback and camaraderie benefited this project. We cherish the memory of two treasured members, Anne Fleming and Laurie M. Wood.

At the Biddle Law Library, Alvin Dong, Ionelia Engel, Annmarie Geist, Paul George, Ed Greenlee, Andrew Lang, Sarah Oswald, Paul Riermaier, Amanda Runyon, Mary Shelly, Merle Slyhoff, Timothy Von Dulm, and Thomas Wheeler went above and beyond the call of duty. Magali Duque, Shachar Gannot, Smita Ghosh, Jarron McAllister, and Emily Prifogle lent their expertise in legal and historical research. Jacob Burnett, Emily Gabos, Elana Handelman, Carolyn Hartwick, Sennett Rockers, Tosh Scheps, David Strecker, Victoria Wang, Robert Blake Watson, Keiko Wolfe, and Yiyang Wu provided valuable assistance gathering, organizing, and analyzing sources. Careful reads by Will Holub-Moorman and Madeleine Morales improved the final product.

Friends, colleagues, and mentors beyond Penn, too, provided indispensable support and examples. Nancy Cott is an unparalleled scholarly model; this project owes an enormous debt not only to her foundational work on marriage but also to her encouragement and input at several critical junctures, including an invaluable read of the entire manuscript. I am grateful to Reva Siegel for intellectual and personal contributions too numerous to name, related and unrelated to this book. Barbara Welke's boundless generosity included transformational conversations and critical reads of multiple drafts. Margot Canaday's scholarship, feedback, and companionship on the long journey of book-writing was revelatory and sustaining. Melissa Murray fundamentally shaped my thinking about marriage and nonmarriage; every chapter benefited from her insights. Doug NeJaime gave generously of his time, expertise, and encouragement at several critical moments; his thoughtful comments on earlier drafts and on the full work improved the manuscript immensely. Kris Collins spent hours on Zoom and in person poring over chapter drafts, discussing conceptual and structural puzzles, and sharing her deep knowledge of family and citizenship law. Jill Hasday's incisive comments and questions buttressed each chapter. Deborah Dinner's careful read helped me address problems that had long evaded resolution; her wise counsel was a balm in the final stages of revision. Courtney Joslin's scholarship and advocacy in related fields enhanced my understanding throughout, and her comments on draft chapters were invaluable. Mary Ziegler always made time to read drafts and to offer astute advice and expertise. Rebecca Davis's guidance on substance and strategy, her expertise on marriage, sexuality, and religion, and her unstinting moral support were heroic. Since graduate school, she, along with Bethany Moreton, Julia Ott, and Rebecca Rix have been the very best of compatriots and friends on whom I can call in any emergency, academic or otherwise. Robin Meezan, Rachel Thompson, Jamie Z. Goodson, and Kristie Starr provided homes away from home and moral support along the way.

Commentators who helped me to think through earlier iterations of this book project include Felice Batlan, Ariela Gross, Suzanne Kahn, Laura Kalman, Linda Kerber, Michael Klarman, Felicia Kornbluh, Regina Kunzel, Rose Cuison Villazor, Laura Weinrib, and John Witt. Many others in the legal history community have nurtured this project over the years, including Constance Backhouse, Rabia Belt, Susanna Blumenthal, Tomiko Brown-Nagin, Jefferson Decker, Jane De Hart, Justin Driver, Ariela Dubler, Laura Edwards, Katie Eyer, Catherine Fisk, William Forbath, Cary Franklin, Marie-Amélie George, David Golove, Risa Goluboff, Linda Gordon, Robert W. Gordon, Joanna Grisinger, Michael Grossberg, Dirk Hartog, Daniel Hulsebosch, Martha Jones, Elizabeth Katz, Alice Kessler-Harris, Pnina Lahav, Alison Lefkovitz, Tim Lovelace, Anna Lvovsky, Kenneth Mack, Stephanie McCurry, Ajay Mehrotra, William Nelson, Farah Peterson, Gautham Rao, Kate Redburn, Noah Rosenblum, Christopher Schmidt, Mitra Sharafi, Daniel Sharfstein, Jed Handelsman Shugerman, Brad Snyder, Katherine Turk, Stephen Vider, and Leandra Zarnow.

The American Society for Legal History, the Legal History Consortium, the Organization of American Historians, the Law and Society Association, the Family Law Scholars and Teachers Conference, the New York Area Family Law Scholars Workshop, and the American Bar Foundation are among the organizations that provided opportunities to present work, along with law school faculty workshops too numerous to name. Generous workshop hosts and interlocutors also have contributed mightily; they include Kathryn Abrams, Elizabeth Anker, Albertina Antognini, Katharine Bartlett, Bethany Berger, Michael Boucai, Khiara Bridges, Tonya Brito, Naomi Cahn, June Carbone, David Cohen, Peggy Cooper Davis, William Eskridge, Katherine Franke, Jamal Greene, Linda Greenhouse, Joanna Grossman, Kaaryn Gustafson, Tabatha Abu El-Haj, Clare Huntington, Aziz Huq, Anil Kalhan, Amy Kapczynski, Anita Krishnakumar, Genevieve Lakier, Stephen Lee, Robin Lenhardt, Kevin Noble Maillard, Solangel Maldonado, Terry Maroney, Linda McClain, Kimberly Mutcherson, Mark Nevitt, Angela Onwuachi-Willig, Nancy Polikoff, Rachel Rebouché, Rebecca Roiphe, Shayak

Sarkar, Sarah Song, Edward Stein, Dara Strolovitch, Stephen Sugarman, Julie Suk, Judith Surkis, Deborah Widiss, and Noah Zatz. For sharing their recollections, I am grateful to Peggy Cooper Davis, Ann Freedman, Martin Guggenheim, Charles Victor McTeer, Nancy Polikoff, David Rudovsky, John Henry Schlegel, Jane Greengold Stevens, Louise Trubek, and Jim Weill. Twenty years after my clerkship with Judge Guido Calabresi, I continue to benefit from his shining example of brilliance and humanity.

In addition to the Writers' Bloc(k), I was fortunate to have the company and counsel of Rebecca Davis, Bethany Moreton, and Lila Corwin Berman, who eased the solitude of book-writing. It was a privilege to learn from and collaborate on amicus briefs and other law-related projects on subjects related to this book, from abortion to family separation to employment discrimination, with scholars and advocates including Kerry Abrams, Margot Canaday, Patricia Cline Cohen, Kristin Collins, Nancy Cott, Ann Estin, Clare Huntington, Robin Lenhardt, Anna Lvovsky, Melissa Murray, Hiroshi Motomura, Hillary Schneller, Reva Siegel, and Mary Ziegler.

Material related to this project has appeared in book chapters and journal articles whose editors helped to refine key ideas: Margot Canaday, Nancy Cott, and Robert Self, editors of *Intimate States: Gender, Sexuality, and Governance in Modern U.S. History* (University of Chicago Press, 2021); Rebecca L. Davis and Michele Mitchell, editors of *Heterosexual Histories* (New York University Press, 2021); Nancy Dowd and Robin Lenhardt, editors of a forthcoming volume on families of color and the law; Jill Hasday, editor of *Constitutional Commentary;* and the staffs of the *California Law Review* and the *Yale Law Journal.*

This project relied on the assistance of Patrick Kerwin of the Library of Congress; John Jacob of the Powell Archives at Washington and Lee School of Law; Sarah Hutcheon and Ellen Shea of the Arthur and Elizabeth Schlesinger Library on the History of Women in America; and dedicated staff at numerous institutions: the National Archives and Records Administration's College Park, Fort Worth, Kansas City, New York City, Philadelphia, and Seattle branches; the Human Sexuality Collection at Cornell University; Princeton University's Mudd Library; Yale University's Sterling Memorial Library; the ONE Archives at the University of Southern California; the Wisconsin Historical Society in Madison; the GLBT Historical Society in San Francisco; the Schomburg Center for Research in Black Culture at the New York Public Library; the Tamiment Library and Wagner Labor Archives at New York University's Bobst Library; the Sophia Smith Collection of Women's History at Smith College; the Barnard College Archives and Special Collections; the Court of Appeals of Maryland; and the Illinois Supreme Court. For assistance collecting and digitizing far-flung sources, I thank Uma Bhatia, Meagan Buckley, Breanna Forni, Zachary Frazier, David-James Gonzales, Elizabeth Hoveland, Patricia Jerjian, Sophie Chen Jin, Maya Mau, Andrew McDonnell, Luke Ohnmeis, Aye Thant, and Caitlin Verboon.

Pamela Haag, developmental editor extraordinaire, gave my manuscript draft a careful, critical read in the summer of 2022. I am grateful to Bill Frucht for seeing promise in this book; to Amanda Gerstenfeld and Mary Pasti for patiently shepherding it and me through the publication process; and to Liz Casey and Fred Kameny for superb copyediting and indexing.

This is a book about family, and it would not have been possible without the love and support of mine. Amelia and Bronwyn Glaser have been like sisters to me since childhood. Maame Ewusi-Mensah Frimpong's steadfast friendship and unswerving moral compass have guided and sustained me for more than three decades. I am grateful to count the Klenoffs and Brumbergs as well as the Kays and Mayeris among my extended family. My mother, Harriet Mayeri, has supported this book and me with unconditional love and limitless generosity; she and my father, Ray, have provided us with a second home. My son Alex delights in reminding me that this book is older than he is, and his brother, Sam, has grown from a toddler into a teenager since I began. They bring me indescribable joy, as does my husband of more than two decades, Jason Klenoff, to whom it is a privilege to be married.

Index